NO SIMPLE VICTORY

NORMAN DAVIES

NO SIMPLE VICTORY

World War II in Europe,

1939–1945

VIKING

VIKING
Published by the Penguin Group
Penguin Group (USA) Inc., 375 Hudson Street,
New York, New York 10014, U.S.A.
Penguin Group (Canada), 90 Eglinton Avenue East, Suite 700,
Toronto, Ontario, Canada M4P 2Y3
(a division of Pearson Penguin Canada Inc.)
Penguin Books Ltd, 80 Strand, London WC2R 0RL, England
Penguin Ireland, 25 St. Stephen's Green, Dublin 2, Ireland
(a division of Penguin Books Ltd)
Penguin Books Australia Ltd, 250 Camberwell Road, Camberwell,
Victoria 3124, Australia
(a division of Pearson Australia Group Pty Ltd)
Penguin Books India Pvt Ltd, 11 Community Centre, Panchsheel Park,
New Delhi – 110 017, India
Penguin Group (NZ), 67 Apollo Drive, Rosedale, North Shore 0632,
New Zealand (a division of Pearson New Zealand Ltd.)
Penguin Books (South Africa) (Pty) Ltd, 24 Sturdee Avenue,
Rosebank, Johannesburg 2196, South Africa

Penguin Books Ltd, Registered Offices:
80 Strand, London WC2R 0RL, England

First American edition
Published in 2007 by Viking Penguin,
a member of Penguin Group (USA) Inc.

1 3 5 7 9 10 8 6 4 2

Copyright © Norman Davies, 2006
All rights reserved

Published in Great Britain as *Europe at War 1939–1945: No Simple Victory* by Macmillan,
an imprint of Pan Macmillan Ltd.

Photograph credits appear on pages vii–ix.

LIBRARY OF CONGRESS CATALOGING IN PUBLICATION DATA
Davies, Norman, 1939–
No simple victory : World War II in Europe 1939–1945 / Norman Davies.
p. cm.
Includes bibliographical references and index.
ISBN 978-0-670-01832-1
1. World War, 1939–1945—Europe. 2. Europe—History—1918–1945. I. Title.
D743.D33 2007
940.53'4—dc22   2007012653

Printed in the United States of America
Set in Dante MT

Contents

List of Tables

List of Illustrations

Section One

1. The Free City of Danzig (akg-images)
2. Nazi demonstration in Danzig (akg-images)
3. The Nomanhan Incident at Khalkin River (Mainichi Newspapers, Tokyo)
4. Signing of the Nazi-Soviet Pact, Moscow
5. The Schleswig-Holstein at Westerplatte (akg-images/Ullstein)
6. Red Army tanks in Brześć (Imperial War Museum)
7. Adolf Hitler (akg-images)
8. Joseph Stalin (akg-images)
9. Heinrich Himmler (akg-images)
10. Lavrenty Beria (akg-images)
11. Benito Mussolini (akg-images)
12. Marshal Pétain (akg-images)
13. Field Marshal von Manstein (akg-images/Ullstein)
14. Marshal Kulik (public domain)
15. The Winter War in Finland (akg-images)
16. Narvik, Norway (akg-images)
17. The Fall of France, Paris (akg-images)
18. Battle of Britain (akg-images)
19. The Baltic States swallowed (akg-images)
20. Yugoslavia ravaged (akg-images)

Section Two

21. Operation Barbarossa (akg-images)
22. The Battle for Moscow (akg-images)
23. The Siege of Leningrad (akg-images)
24. A German campaign of encirclement (akg-images)
25. U-boat war (akg-images)

Section Three

Section Four

The German–Soviet attack on Poland, September 1939

Map legend:

Sweden

Denmark

BALTIC SEA

Free City of Danzig

Gdynia

Danzig

Elbing

Hamburg

Kolberg

Pomerania

Stettin

Bydgoszcz

Torun

Notec

Vistula

Hannover

Brandenburg

Berlin

Oder

Poznan

Warta

THIRD

Frankfurt an der Oder

Kalisz

P

Łódz

Elbe

Neisse

Saxony

Görlitz

Breslau

Oder

Częstochowa

Dresden

Silesia

Opole

REICH

Bohemia

Prague

Katowice

Cracc

100 miles

150 kilometres

&

Ostrava

Cieszyn

Moravia

Brno

Slovakia

German forces

Soviet forces

'Peace boundary' 28/9/39

Austria

Morava

Danube

Vienna

Operation Barbarossa, and the aftermath, 1941–2

200 miles

300 kilometres

Maximum extent of Axis control, 1942

December 1941 front

Axis advances to 1942

Major battles with dates

Neutral countries

R U S S I A

Moscow, *Dec 1941*

Tula

December 1941 front

Orel

Voronezh, *July 1942*

Kursk

Kharkov, *May 1942*

SOVIET

UNION

Stalingrad, *Nov 1942–Feb 1943*

August 1942 front

Rostov, *May 1942*

rivoy Rog

Mt Elbruz

Caspian
Sea

Crimea

Kerch

Georgia

Sebastopol, *Oct 1941–July 1942*

Baku

Tbilisi

Black Sea

Armenia

Turkey

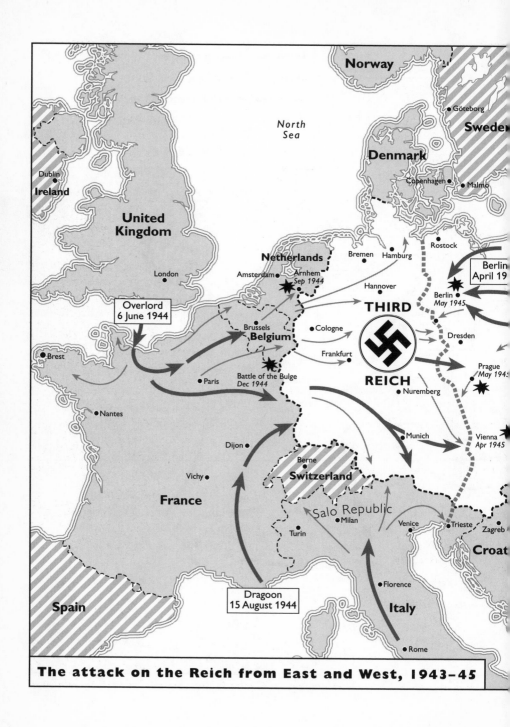

The attack on the Reich from East and West, 1943–45

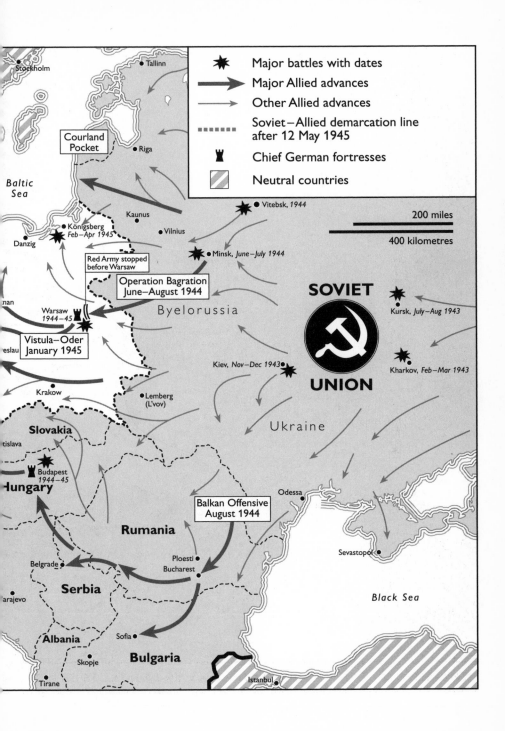

Stockholm

Tallinn

Major battles with dates

Major Allied advances

Other Allied advances

Soviet–Allied demarcation line
after 12 May 1945

Chief German fortresses

Neutral countries

Courland
Pocket

Riga

Baltic
Sea

Kaunus

Königsberg
Feb–Apr 1945

Danzig

Vilnius

Red Army stopped
before Warsaw

Operation Bagration
June–August 1944

Warsaw
1944–45

Vistula–Oder
January 1945

eslau

Krakow

Lemberg
(L'vov)

Slovakia

tislava

Budapest
1944–45

Hungary

Rumania

Serbia

Belgrade

Albania

Skopje

Tirane

Sofia

Bulgaria

Vitebsk, 1944

200 miles

400 kilometres

Minsk, June–July 1944

Byelorussia

SOVIET

Kursk, July–Aug 1943

UNION

Kharkov, Feb–Mar 1943

Kiev, Nov–Dec 1943

Ukraine

Balkan Offensive
August 1944

Odessa

Sevastopol

Ploesti
Bucharest

Black Sea

arajevo

Istanbul

nan

Introduction

OVER SIXTY YEARS HAVE passed since the end of the Second World War. And most people would assume that the broad outlines of that terrible conflict had been established long since. Innumerable books have been published on the subject. Thousands of films have been screened, portraying every aspect of military events and civilian ordeals. Countless memoirs of participants great and small have been collected. Hundreds of major monuments and scores of museums have been created to keep the memory of the war alive. One might think that there is nothing new to add. At least, one is tempted to think that way until one starts to examine what actually *is* said and what is *not* said.

The sixtieth anniversary of the end of the war was commemorated in 2005 in many different ways. In the United States, for example, a splendid new Memorial to World War Two was opened in Washington, DC, in advance of the anniversary. It takes the form of two linked oval concourses adorned with fountains, one representing the war in the Pacific theatre, and the other the war across the Atlantic. It stands in the pleasant parkland beside the obelisk of the Washington Monument, and opposite the National Holocaust Museum. And it invites visitors to stroll round the fountains and to contemplate the large numbers of inscriptions and high-minded quotations on the surrounding plinths. Over the gateway at one end one is the word 'PACIFIC', and over the gateway at the other end 'ATLANTIC'. And the main inscription reads, 'WORLD WAR TWO, 1941–45'.

At this point, if not earlier, one begins to suspect that the memorial is not dedicated to the Second World War as a whole, but rather to the USA's involvement in the war. Almost any European would be able to point out that the war did not begin in 1941. But millions of Americans are being taught to think otherwise. The unwritten message states that the USA fought the good fight and won. At no point is any mention made of the USA's allies or comrades-in-arms. The unsuspecting visitor could be forgiven for thinking that the USA had won the war on its own.

The sixtieth-anniversary year, 2005, opened with an impressive ceremony in Poland marking the liberation of Auschwitz on 27 January 1945. Since the notorious German concentration camp had been built on German-occupied Polish territory, the President of Poland, Aleksander Kwaśniewski, presided. And, since the camp had been liberated by the victorious Red Army, the President of the Russian Federation, Vladimir Putin, headed the list of foreign guests. Others present included the President of Israel, the President of Germany, President Chirac of France, and the chairman of the International Association of Roma. Most importantly, a diverse congregation of former prisoners attended, representing numerous nationalities, many of them wearing their pyjama-like prison uniforms. The assembled guests sat in the open, braving the freezing temperatures of a Central European winter. The speakers battled the snow flurries, and spoke many fine words such as 'Liberation', 'Triumph over Evil' and 'Never Again'. Many appropriate tributes were paid in memory of more than a million dead, the majority of them Jewish.

Yet at no point did anyone care to mention the realities of January 1945. No speaker mentioned the fact that, as Auschwitz was liberated, other ex-Nazi concentration camps were being used by the Soviet security forces to incarcerate a new wave of captives. Overwhelmed by the heart-warming concept of 'Liberation', almost all journalists present avoided the embarrassing topic of just how limited the liberations of 1945 really were. No one disturbed the peace by saying that the Nazi SS was not the only organization to run concentration camps during the Second World War. And no one cared to tackle the thorny question of defining what the universally condemned 'Evil' actually consisted of.

On 9 May 2005 major celebrations were staged in Moscow. President Putin played host to fifty heads of state, including President George W. Bush, and presided over a grand military parade. Leading the tributes to the immense achievements of the Soviet armies in their triumph over Fascism, he declared that Victory Day marked 'a sacred date', 'the day that had saved the world'. Then, standing in the same place where Joseph Stalin had led the victory parade in Red Square sixty years earlier, he gave the signal for the ceremonies to proceed. Thousands of troops dressed in the historic uniforms of the Red Army marched past, or rode past. Martial music of the war period blared out. And truckloads of bemedalled veterans from the 'Great Patriotic War', elderly men and women carrying flower-wreathed portraits of 'the Great Stalin', saluted the tribunes. It was all made to look as if time had stood still.

No one with a generous heart could object to that moment of

recognition for the veterans. They, after all, had made the greatest sacrifices of all the combatant armies. Yet few foreigners noticed the political sleight of hand that was being practised. President Bush had made a telling point on the eve of his trip to Moscow when he had briefly visited Latvia, one of the three Baltic States which had been attacked and annexed by Stalin in 1940 and whose present-day presidents now felt unable to participate in the Moscow festivities. But, generally speaking, few commentators questioned the dubious historical assumptions that framed the occasion. They accepted, quite incorrectly, that the 'Great Patriotic War' was just a Russian synonym for the Second World War, and, as a result, they were not prompted to ask what the Soviet Union was doing in the years before the Great Patriotic War started. They did not inquire too closely about Stalin's methods or Stalin's war aims. And, above all, they did not object to the quiet elision of the fifteen Soviet republics of 1945 with the Russian Federation of today.

President Yushchenko of Ukraine, the leader of the latest ex-Soviet republic to slip away from Moscow's control, attended Mr Putin's festivities. But Westerners were still so accustomed to mistaking Ukraine for part of 'Russia' that they saw no reason to interest themselves in the fate of Ukraine in 1939–45 as opposed to that of Russia or of the USSR as a whole. President Yushchenko, modestly, did not make a show of the fact that his own father, a village schoolteacher, had been a survivor of Auschwitz (prison number 11369).

Britain's celebrations to mark the sixtieth anniversary took place on 8–9 July 2005. On the 8th, Queen Elizabeth II unveiled a monument in Whitehall to 'The Women of World War II', and on the 9th she and the Prime Minister, Tony Blair, attended a 'memorial show' on Horse Guards Parade. This last nostalgic event betrayed a great deal about the narrowing of focus which has crept up in London no less than elsewhere. It took the form of a series of musical and comic items from the wartime repertoire linked by a historical narrative. The latter was read by the actor Simon Callow and was interspersed with a selection of Churchill's speeches in which Timothy West impeccably impersonated the wartime leader. Hence 'Bluebirds Over the White Cliffs of Dover' alternated with 'We shall fight on the beaches!', and Flanagan and Allen numbers were followed by the theme tune from *Schindler's List*, by 'A Nightingale Sang in Berkeley Square' and, in the grand finale, by 'We'll meet again, don't know where, don't know when'.

As entertainment, the 'memorial show' was well received. But as a history lesson it suffered from some obvious shortcomings. For it ignored the essential differences between 'then' and 'now'. Apart from very brief appearances by some Indian Army buglers and by a dance troupe dressed in American uniforms, it took no pains to recall Britain's wartime allies or to evoke the 'Grand Coalition' that headed the Allied cause. And it glossed over the fact that in 1939–45 the war effort was made not by Britain alone, but by the British Empire. There was no sign, alas, of the Canadians, Australians, New Zealanders, South Africans and many others whose participation had been paramount.

Britain's premier military museum, the Imperial War Museum, in Lambeth, organized a series of complementary events under the slogan of 'Sixty Years On'. These included a Veteran's Awareness Week, a 'Living Museum' in St James's Park, and an exhibition called 'Captive' about British POWs in the Far East. They ran alongside the museum's excellent collections of wartime weapons, artefacts, pictures and paintings, the permanent Holocaust Exhibition concerning 'the persecution of Jews and other peoples', and special exhibitions on the 'Children's War' and 'Great Escapes' – not forgetting the museum's subsidiaries such as the Cabinet War Rooms in Whitehall, the Duxford Air Museum in Cambridgeshire, and the new IWM North in Manchester. From the historian's point of view, many of these items invite both praise and comment. But by far the oddest thing to be encountered is the inscription on the memorial outside the IWM to '27 million Soviet citizens and servicemen' who supposedly died during the war in the cause of 'Allied victory'. It would be a good test of visitors' knowledge to ask what is wrong with that wording.

Of course, Britain, the USA and Russia were not the only countries to mark the sixtieth anniversary. And it would be wrong to judge the efficacy of memory entirely from events in London, Washington and Moscow. Yet the 'Big Three' of 1945 were undoubtedly the principal Allied powers. And if the depiction of the war in their capitals is built on misconceptions, it is unlikely to be more accurate or comprehensive elsewhere.

Similar objections can be raised about the state of historiography. Certainly, as far as the war in Europe is concerned, no historian to date has managed to reconcile the contradictory perspectives that exist. There is a 'Western view', inspired by experiences on the Western Front; and there is a 'Soviet view', inspired by the Eastern Front. Westerners who write in the wake of Churchill's *The Second World War* acknowledge the prowess of the Red Army. But they cannot bring themselves to compare the Red Army's performance with that of their own country's forces.

Similarly, the Soviet and post-Soviet apologists, while fully aware of the supreme military achievements of Stalin's regime, are loath to publicize its criminal record. As a result, no writer from the Soviet school has gained widespread recognition. Naturally, many excellent books have been written about the war, in the genres both of history and of literary fiction. But, with few exceptions, they all tend to deal with partial aspects or particular exploits. Attempts to present an overall synthesis are not overabundant; and they don't differ widely. The last major venture in that direction, written by an Americanized German, cannot be rated higher than an honest summary of the Western view. It was conceived in the conventional mode of anti-Fascism and, as such, avoids most of the weighty political and moral teasers involved.[1]

Germany's main contribution to the anniversary consisted of a controversial Memorial to the Murdered Jews of Europe, which was unveiled in the centre of Berlin in May 2005. The monument, designed by the American architect Peter Eisenman, proved controversial on various grounds, not all of them aesthetic. Its expansive labyrinth of dark, tomb-like granite blocks is very large and, in the eyes of its critics, invasive. At the same time it was bound to provoke strong reactions by making no reference to the millions of the Nazis' non-Jewish victims, or to war victims in general.

For many groups are now growing impatient to see that their own tragedies are recognized. One of them is the German League of Expellees, which has long been campaigning for a memorial centre of its own in Berlin. Its case does not fit the conventional image of Germany as an aggressor nation. But it is not without substance. Large nations can contain both warmongers and war victims. In 1944–5, well over 10 million civilians from Germany's eastern provinces either fled before the threat of the Red Army's advance or were forcibly expelled thereafter. And perhaps 2 million perished. Their permanent expulsion was an act of collective punishment authorized by the 'Big Three' at the Potsdam Conference, and was of dubious legality. Yet the main argument against the present campaign derives from the fact that its organizers think only of German expellees and not of wartime expellees in general. After all, the Potsdam decision was taken to facilitate the influx of several million Polish refugees who in that same period were being driven out of territories seized by the Soviet Union.

As a prelude to various talks and lectures on the Second World War, therefore, I have often chosen to raise some of these problems by presenting the audience with four or five simple questions:

- Can you name the five biggest battles of the war in Europe?
  Or, better still, the *ten* biggest battles?
- Can you name the main political ideologies that were
  contending for supremacy during the war in Europe?
- Can you name the largest concentration camp that was
  operating in Europe in the years 1939–45?
- Can you name the European nationality (or ethnic group)
  which lost the largest number of civilians during the war?
- Can you name the vessel that was sunk with record loss of
  life in the war's largest maritime disaster?

These have usually been followed by a deathly silence, and then by a
hubbub of guesses and queries. Quelling the hubbub, I then offer the
audience an opinion. 'Until we have established the correct answer to
basic factual matters,' I say, 'we are not properly equipped to pass
judgement on the wider issues.'

All of which points to the increasing fragmentation of memory, to the
use of wartime history for political purposes, and to the domination of
such history by national or particular interests. In my view, therefore,
there is a strong need for a review of the principles on which the
framework for a definitive and comprehensive history of the Second
World War may some day be based. This book aims to rehearse those
principles, and, at least in outline, to sketch out the resultant conceptual
framework.

A formative experience on my own intellectual journey took place
when I served as one of the consultants to the *Oxford Companion to the
Second World War*, which was published in 1995.[2] The general editors of
the volume were keen to give due recognition to the Eastern Front and
to the latest advances in scholarship in that sphere. And I was duly
appointed as advisory editor for Eastern and Central Europe. What I soon
realized, however, was that Soviet Studies formed a completely separate
compartment of knowledge in the minds both of the editors and of the
contributing scholars who dominated the field. I was able to obtain the
services of a first-rate German specialist, Professor Heinz-Dietrich Löwe,
who wrote the main entry on the USSR. But it remained very difficult to
integrate Soviet affairs into the main-line categories. For example, the
editors were happy enough to accept an entry on the GULag during the
war, but not to place it within the main heading of 'Concentration Camps'.
By the same token, an entry on the Katyn Massacres was accepted, but

not under the heading of 'War Crimes'. Entries on Soviet marshals, or on the battles of the Eastern Front, were always written by 'Soviet specialists', and never by the same people who wrote on Eisenhower or Montgomery. What is more, it soon became clear that matters could not be managed otherwise. The 'Western experts' possessed only the vaguest idea of events in Eastern Europe. Historical training is compartmentalized, no less than historical publications. A leading American authority on the Second World War, for instance, had never heard of the wartime losses of any East European nation other than 'the Russians'. This blinkered mindset underlies much of what a British historian has rightly dubbed 'the frozen perspective of winners' history'[3] that is perpetuated by Western commentators who were still writing in 2000 what they had been writing in 1950.

One of the principal aims of the present work, therefore, is not to present spectacularly new facts, but rather to rearrange, to juxtapose and to reintegrate well-established facts that have hitherto been strictly segregated.

To this end, there seems no point in footnoting every other sentence for the purposes of verification. As a rule, endnotes will be reserved for specific purposes. Facts and statements that appear in the regular sources of reference, especially in the *Oxford Companion*, will not be noted. Endnotes will be mainly employed for direct quotations, for lesser-known sources, and for assistance to further reading.

Finally, I should also explain that I have consciously minimized comment on secondary matters in order to keep the main argument clear and convincing. I am well aware that much more could have been written about the roles of countries like France, Poland or Yugoslavia, which were far from insignificant. On the other hand, I wished to draw attention to the nature and actions of the main participants in Europe, and in consequence to concentrate on the principals – the Third Reich, the Soviet Union, the USA and the British Empire. In the past, I have myself objected to the way that European history is often conceived with exclusive reference to the Great Powers. But this time I felt that the priority should lie with the task of redefining the structure of the conflict and the proportions of its main constituents.

As usual, a word of thanks is due to numerous co-workers and colleagues and to the family support team. My wife's selfless indulgence of the foibles of a writer–husband remains miraculously undimmed. And once again

Roger Moorhouse has been willing to act as principal assistant, although he is now an independent scholar. I am very grateful to my agent, David Godwin, for moral as well as professional support; to my publisher, Georgina Morley, for much-appreciated words of encouragement; and to Krzysztof Mościcki for help in logistical and administrative matters.

On this occasion, however, I would like to express my special sense of indebtedness to a select band of historians who in the last decade or so have succeeded in taming the Soviet enigma. Western views on the events of 1939–45 took shape in the early post-war years, when information about the largest combatant power, the Soviet Union, was sparse and frequently speculative. Throughout the decades of the Cold War, when bones of political contention proliferated, the admirable work of pioneers like Robert Conquest was often mired in partisan quarrels and combats. As a result, public opinion usually kept its distance, and historians of the war were often unwilling to reconsider their interpretations. Only since the collapse of the USSR has it become possible to put an end to the confusion. Today there is no longer any doubt that Stalin's regime was a mass-murdering monster and that the prominence of its role in the defeat of the Third Reich demands far-reaching adjustments to the conventional picture. Much of the new certainty can be ascribed to the work of historians who have recently supplied the hard evidence. And many passages in the present volume have been inspired by the pressing need to incorporate their findings with the better-established knowledge on other subjects. I feel, in fact, that my own long-standing convictions and instincts, which derive from the study of a neighbouring neck of the woods, have been greatly enriched and strengthened. Indeed, I would never have dared to attempt a new overview of the war without the knowledge that I was not entirely alone. My special thanks, therefore, go to colleagues who have put the reality of wartime Stalinism and its context beyond reasonable doubt. In this regard I would mention Anne Applebaum, Antony Beevor, Geoffrey Hosking, Simon Sebag-Montefiore and Robert Service.

NORMAN DAVIES
Kołobrzeg/Kolberg

CHAPTER ONE

INTERPRETATION

Five Factors

EVERY NATION THAT PARTICIPATED in the Second World War has its own version of events. Britons and Americans, Germans and Italians, French and Dutch, Russians and Poles, Jews and many others, all accentuate the experiences of their own people. Wittingly or unwittingly, they all diminish the diversity of experience and inhibit the presentation of a grand panorama. They obstruct an overall view. So much, given human nature, is inevitable. Nonetheless, the fact remains that the whole is more important than the particular. Every attempt to examine one part of the scene should be accompanied by or perhaps precede the wider framework into which the part can be placed. It is this framework that the present essay hopes to outline.

It is equally inevitable that a complex of conflicts as tangled as that subsumed by 'the Second World War' should have produced a mass of myths and legends. These myths form a necessary strand of the story. It is not the historian's job to banish them. It is the historian's duty to examine them, to explain their origins, and then to demonstrate the difference between events and the perception of events. For example, any impartial observer is bound to describe the campaign which ended on the beaches of Dunkirk in June 1940 as a marked German success and a catastrophic setback to the Allied cause. At the same time, the same historian is required to show how the 'Dunkirk Spirit' was born, how survival was snatched from defeat, how the setback was turned into an opportunity to recuperate and to rebuild. The disaster, and the reaction to the disaster (from the British point of view), just like the victory and the failure to exploit the victory (from the German point of view) are inseparable aspects of the same story.

It is unavoidable that historians come up with different interpretations, or at least with different points of emphasis. No narrative is ever going to win universal approval, however homogenized. Yet precautions can be taken against the grosser forms of inaccuaracy. Like must be compared with like; proportions must be observed; and standards of judgement that are applied to one party in the conflict must be applied even-handedly to all parties in the conflict. For example, the Battle of El Alamein and the Battle of Stalingrad were both Allied victories which contributed to the 'turning of the tide' in the dark days of 1942–3. Yet the two battles cannot be fully equated. One of them knocked out six Axis divisions in a peripheral theatre of action: the other knocked out twenty Axis divisions in the central sector of the principal front. By the same token, moral judgements cannot be based on the illusion that mass murder by the enemy was proof of despicable evil, whilst mass murder by one's own side was merely an unfortunate blemish.

Perhaps I should explain my own point of departure. I am British. I was born in 1939. I am a professional historian. And I have spent much of my career as a specialist in Eastern Europe, particularly in the history of Poland and Russia. From this, one may correctly gather that I grew up in wartime Britain and that my education proceeded at a time when the war loomed large. It is fair to say, I think, that for everyone of my generation, even though we were too young to participate directly, the Second World War was the biggest event in our lives – just as the 'Great War' of 1914–18 had been the biggest event in our parents' lives. My first school trip to the continent, at Easter 1955, took us to Vienna, and my photograph was taken standing next to a Soviet sentry in a fur cap. I now realize that the war in Europe had ended less than a decade earlier. One watched the *Dam Busters* and *The Cruel Sea*, or *Passport to Pimlico* and *Mrs Miniver*. As a result, one could not help but take an interest in the war years. Since then I have constantly garnered fresh information on the subject from books, films and research, while noticing how memories and the sense of personal involvement gradually fade.

As a historian, on the other hand, I watched as the more familiar aspects of the war in Western Europe were steadily overtaken by an ever-rising tide of information about the vast horrors on the Eastern Front. When I was a student at Oxford, Alan Bullock had published *Hitler: A Study in Tyranny* not long before, and my tutor, A. J. P. Taylor, was still busily engaged in writing *The Origins of the Second World War*.[1] The Faculty of History offered no undergraduate courses on 1939–45, believing it to be too recent for serious study. And the Holocaust had hardly been heard of. In the 1960s news of the '20 million Soviet war dead' filtered through, as did the realization, largely inspired by Khrushchev and Solzhenitsyn, that the Soviet GULag had constituted a mass crime on a scale previously unimagined. In the 1970s one learned of the unique character of the Holocaust, and began to wonder how it fitted into the wider context. In the 1980s historians like Bullock dared to examine Hitler and Stalin in parallel. And in the 1990s the collapse of the Soviet Union finally silenced the GULag-deniers, showing that Robert Conquest and other critics of the USSR had been much closer to the truth than many had wished to concede. It says much about long-standing inhibitions that Antony Beevor's brilliant books *Stalingrad* (1998) and *Berlin: The Downfall 1945* (2002),[2] that finally revealed the full savagery of the Eastern Front for Western readers, had few earlier counterparts or rivals.

My own research into Polish wartime history gave me a strong sense of the inbuilt bias. One quickly learned that the Soviet Union had invaded and occupied one half of Poland in September 1939, just as Germany had invaded and occupied the other half. Yet Western historians continued to write exclusively about 'the Nazi invasion of Poland'. The Soviet zone of occupation was simply not regarded as a zone of occupation. Nazi propaganda on such matters was dismissed out of hand. Soviet propaganda was not questioned. One knew that mass deportations and murders were carried out by the Soviet occupiers, alongside other atrocities perpetrated by the Germans. Yet, increasingly, Western awareness focused on the Holocaust alone. One read about thousands of villages razed to the ground, and of their massacred inhabitants. Yet the only one that Western commentators could ever name was Lidice, in Bohemia (see p. 313). One learned about colossal operations, like Barbarossa and Bagration, and of colossal tragedies like the Siege of Leningrad and the Warsaw Rising. And one saw how these events were always consigned to a separate emotional compartment. Somehow they did not form part of 'our war'.

Above all, there were the Katyn massacres – not the biggest atrocity by any means, but one that acted as a litmus test of historical honesty. By the time that I entered the fray, in the 1970s, the circumstantial evidence was overwhelming. Around 25,000 Allied officers had disappeared in Russia in 1940. But apart from 4,500 corpses uncovered by the Germans in the Katyn Forest, near Smolensk, in 1943, most of the missing men had never been found. There was no absolute proof, but the probability was high that the remaining 15,000 or 20,000 were lying in other mass graves, and that their deaths had been ordered by Stalin not Hitler. For once, Goebbels could have been telling the truth.[3] Yet for decades British officialdom refused to comment, unless to point a finger at the Nazis. British officers were forbidden to participate in Katyn memorial ceremonies. Plans for a monument in London were squashed. And the British public showed no signs of interest in recognizing either a major crime or a reprehensible cover-up. The stance seemed to be: what had the Eastern Front to do with us? Finally in 1990, on the eve of the fiftieth anniversary, President Gorbachev came clean and admitted that the massacres at Katyn and at two other sites had been the work of the Soviet security forces. President Yeltsin later produced a document bearing Stalin's signature and recording the execution order dated 5 March 1940. A British Foreign Office spokesman praised the Russians' candour. But the British War Crimes Act (1991) was carefully framed to exclude events like Katyn from its remit. And the Foreign Office, lacking all fortitude, did not release a selection of its documents on the subject until 2002.[4]

As late as 1984 or 1985, I can remember being invited with my wife to A. J. P. Taylor's house, where Katyn became a topic of dinner-table conversation. Taylor's wife, a former Hungarian Communist, was adamant that the Soviet Union was incapable of such misdeeds. My wife and I stuck to our guns, saying that the balance of probability lay with Stalin's guilt. A. J. P. had to act as mediator. Soviet guilt was not inconceivable, he said, but, in the absence of proof, historians had to keep an open mind and to refrain from anti-Soviet insinuations. There it was in a nutshell. A. J. P. was no middle-of-the-roader. He was a left-wing firebrand, fearlessly independent, and with no special brief for the Soviet Union. Yet even he, on such an issue, could not bring himself to be even-handed. One may be sure that no one would have called for restraint if someone had argued for a clear probability of guilt lying with Hitler and Himmler. The Nazis were known to be evil. They were capable of anything. They were our enemies. One is always free to cast insinuations on them; but not on one of the victorious Allied powers. Such, in my experience, is the ingrained prejudice not only of most historians, but also of most members of the British and American public.

Convinced of this bias, I then began to look more carefully at the particular forms of slant that Western books on the Second World War display. One could meet exceptions. Generally speaking, however, Western opinions became increasingly self-absorbed, and the same blinkered judgements were repeated over and over again. If historians commented on the Eastern Front, they tended to follow the example of the late John Erickson, to repeat Soviet interpretations without comment, or at most to quibble over details. In time, I came to believe that an 'Allied Scheme of History' had been established:

Contemporary views of Europe have been strongly influenced by the emotions and experiences of two World Wars and especially by the victory of the 'Grand Alliance' [of 1941–5]. Thanks to their victories in 1918, 1945, and at the end of the Cold War in 1989, the Western Powers have been able to export their interpretation of events worldwide . . . The priorities and assumptions which derive from Allied attitudes of the wartime vintage are very common in accounts of the twentieth century and are sometimes projected back into more remote periods. They may be tentatively summarized as follows:

- The belief in a unique, secular brand of Western Civilization in which the 'Atlantic Community' is presented as the pinnacle of human progress . . .
- The ideology of 'anti-Fascism' in which the Second World War of 1939–45 is perceived . . . as the defining event in the triumph of Good over Evil . . .
- A demonological fascination with Germany, the twice-defeated enemy [and] the prime source of [Europe's ills] . . . (N.B. German culture should never be confused with German politics.)
- An indulgent, romanticized view of the Tsarist Empire and the Soviet Union, the strategic ally in the East, commonly called 'Russia'. Russia's manifest faults should never be classed with those of the enemy . . .
- The unspoken acceptance of Europe into Western and Eastern spheres . . .
- The studied neglect of all facts which do not add credence to the above.[5]

Pursuing the same line of thought, I also began to categorize the manifold shortcomings that were encouraged by the Allied Scheme and could be observed in works on the Second World War. In due course, I came up with an article called 'Ten Forms of Selectivity', which identified the following sources of misunderstanding:

1. political propaganda,
2. personal prejudices,
3. parochial perspectives,
4. stereotypes,
5. statistics,
6. special-interest groups,

7. the procedures of professional historians,
8. Victors' History,
9. History of the Defeated,
10. moral selectivity.

On the last point, I demonstrated how narratives of the war have often fallen into the oversimplified schemes of 'Right' fighting 'Wrong'.[6]

This was all very well. The article was widely praised. But it left me with a feeling of unease. Not only was I out of step with the great majority of my professional colleagues. I had no coherent alternative to offer. It is all too easy to find fault with the prevailing interpretations without risking a clear vision of one's own. It is not difficult to criticize, or to deconstruct the schemes of others. It is a much more arduous task to be positive, and to produce a fresh and reasoned outline of a subject's parameters. But the exercise must be attempted. In my view, there are five main factors to be taken into consideration when examining the Second World War: geographical, military, ideological, political and moral.

Geographical limits

Once the Soviet Union had established a durable truce with the Japanese (on 15 September 1939), no further link remained between the European and Pacific theatres of the Second World War. It is this fact which permits historians to treat the war in Europe as a separate chain of conflicts from those in Asia. The Soviet–Japanese conflict – intense during the Battle of Khalkhin-Gol (see p. 149) – was not renewed until the summer of 1945, when the war in Europe had already finished. The truce of 1939 was consolidated by the Soviet–Japanese Neutrality Pact of 13 April 1941.[7]

With the sole exception of North Africa, the fighting in the European theatre did not spread beyond the geographical confines of Europe. But Britain in Palestine and Egypt, France in Syria, Lebanon and Algeria, and Italy in Tripoli all held territorial possessions in the Levant or in super-Saharan Africa, and the conflict between the Western Allies and the Axis eventually spilled over to all points from Morocco to the Nile.

From 1941 onward both the USA and, to a lesser extent, Britain and her Dominions, were engaged simultaneously in Europe and the Far East. Their dual involvement obviously affected logistical matters and strategic planning. But it never resulted in the close integration of the two theatres. Whilst millions of American, Canadian, Anzac, Indian and South African servicemen served in Europe, no European forces – with one possible, minor exception – ever set foot with hostile intent in the Americas. No Soviet troops fought outside Europe during the course of the European war.

The extreme boundaries of the European theatre were marked by Gibraltar, Greenland, Narvik, Leningrad, Stalingrad, Mount Elbrus, Bulgaria, Cairo and Casablanca. Yet one must not assume that all locations within the ring were brought into play. The basic configuration of the war in Europe consisted of an inner core held by the Axis powers and of a periphery dominated by the Axis's enemies. In the first phase the Axis core fortress expanded rapidly to include several neighbouring countries – Poland to the east, Denmark and Norway to the north, Benelux and France to the west. And territory to the east of Poland was controlled by the pro-Axis USSR. The Western Powers were expelled from the continental mainland, to their great disadvantage. Thereafter, although Soviet forces manned a front contiguous with German-occupied territory, Western forces could engage with Axis troops only if they first undertook complicated, costly and hazardous amphibious landings – as in North Africa, in Sicily and in Normandy. This was perhaps the main reason why the much-heralded 'Second Front' was so slow to materialize.

It is often said, somewhat rashly, that 'the war engulfed the whole of Europe.' This is clearly an exaggeration. The neutral countries did not become directly involved at all (see p. 286). Some countries, like Britain or Spain, which sent forces to fight abroad, did not themselves undergo foreign occupation. Britain, which endured severe bombing for a relatively short period in 1940–41, retaliated against Germany over a much longer period in 1941–5, and escaped with only sporadic retaliation from the V-1 and V-2 campaigns in 1944–5. Bulgaria, Romania and Hungary, which all joined the Axis Powers, were engaged in various ways in the earlier stages of the war, and did not join the list of occupied countries until the final phase. Even countries which suffered grievously from fighting and occupation could have large expanses of their territory virtually untouched. In France, for instance, the southern 'free zone' remained essentially inviolate for three of the war's six years. The eastern provinces of the Reich, which lay beyond the range of Allied bombing, spent still longer in relative tranquillity. Most surprisingly, unless one thinks of it, over 90 per cent of the USSR – the state which also contained by far the largest and most intensely fought over of the war zones – remained completely untouched throughout the war, providing a vast base for marshalling resources, for organizing resistance, and for training the armed services.

In reality, therefore, the main European war zones of 1939–45 were limited to a relatively small number of countries and/or regions. These were:

- Albania, 1939–45
- Poland, 1939–45
- Norway and Denmark, 1940–45
- Benelux, 1940–45
- northern France, 1940–44
- Baltic States, Byelorussia and Ukraine, 1940/41–4
- Yugoslavia, 1941–5
- Greece, 1941–5
- Italy, 1943–5

Germany and Austria were exposed to the mounting Allied bombing offensive from 1942 onward, but their frontiers were not breached until October 1944 or later. In addition, one notes several other locations which were visited by the more severe aspects of warfare for only relatively short periods:

- Finland, 1939–40, 1941–2
- southern England, 1940–41
- Leningrad, 1941–3
- western Russia, 1941–2
- southern Russia, 1942–3
- Romania, Bulgaria, Hungary, 1944–5

Precision is vital, therefore, when discussing the geography of the war in Europe. It is important to distinguish between pre-war and post-war frontiers. And it is essential to beware of misleading abbreviations. During the war, it was quite common for 'England' to be used in place of the clumsier 'United Kingdom of Great Britain and Northern Ireland'. Yet most commentators would understand the more complicated realities underlying the convenient shorthand label. Similarly, it was very common for 'Russia' or 'the Russians' to be used in place of 'the Union of Soviet

Socialist Republics'. In the latter case, however, one needs to realize that the shorthand is more than merely imprecise. It masks some of the central issues at stake in the largest theatre of operations. For Russians represented barely half of the USSR's population. And it was the western Soviet republics – not Russia – which were the scene of the heaviest fighting, and which bore the brunt of the German occupation. Nowadays, when Estonia, Latvia, Lithuania, Belarus and Ukraine have emerged as sovereign countries, one can see from a glance at the map where the borders of Russia lie. But for fifty years most Western historians wrote in blissful ignorance of those countries, or otherwise assumed – quite mistakenly – that the political, national and ethnic geography of the Eastern Front was unimportant.

The war at sea covered enormous distances. Although not on the same scale as operations in the Pacific, the Battle of the Atlantic (1939–45) involved thousands of ships of all shapes and sizes, from aircraft carriers to submarines and humble merchantmen. Its extreme points included Greenland and Murmansk, Montevideo and Cape Town. The Battle of the Mediterranean (1939–43) was fought over Britain's line of communication to the Suez Canal, and via Suez to India. Thanks to the control of the Straits by neutral Turkey, it did not extend into the Black Sea.

The war in the air was more confined. In the 1940s, aircraft could not fly as far as ships could sail. Bomber fleets based in Britain had a return range of about 1,600 km. Their counterparts based in southern Italy from 1943 could barely reach Warsaw. Their fighter escorts were still more restricted. All longer transport flights had to proceed by stages. Flying from the USA to Britain involved refuelling stops in Gander Bay (Newfoundland), Reykjavik (Iceland) and often Belfast, or later in Bermuda and the Azores. Flying from London to Moscow had to be effected via Gibraltar, Cairo, Teheran, and Kuibyshev (now Samara).

Finally, on the subject of geography, one wonders if the war in Europe can be said to have had a 'centre of gravity' – a place which reflects the relative weight of military action to the north, east, west and south. No precise calculations can be made. But, given the overwhelming weight of the Eastern Front, the gravitational pull in that direction can have been only partly counterbalanced by the influence of other directions. The focal point would *not* have been Central Europe – halfway between East and West – but somewhere well to the east or south-east. The answer therefore is almost certainly Byelorussia (now Belarus) and western Ukraine. These countries lack all sense of individual identity in conventional histories of Europe. Yet they saw both the most intense warfare and the worst civilian horrors: the deportations, the Soviet and German occupations, the scourging of the *Lebensraum* and the Holocaust. They were involved in the thick of the fighting from the very beginning in September 1939 (when they were still best known to the world as eastern Poland) right to the final phase in 1944–5, when they provided the Red Army's main point of re-entry into Central Europe. They provided the ground over which the war's two biggest campaigns – Barbarossa and Bagration – were fought. It is no accident that Belarus lost a higher proportion of its civilian population than any other country in Europe, and that Ukraine lost the highest absolute number. The history of these countries deserves to be better publicized.

Military parameters

The textbooks make a distinction between military potential and military capacity. The former is a purely theoretical estimate which tries to calculate the quantity and quality of the armed forces which, given time and preparation, a country might raise. In its simplest form, it involves multiplying the total number of young males available for service by a figure representing the maximum economic resources that could be provided for training, equipping, transporting, supplying and sustaining them. It is an important indicator, not least because the country with the greatest military potential, the USA, in 1939 was also the country with the lowest developed capacity. A well-known estimate was made in 1939 by the Royal Institute of International Affairs. It used a crude economic measure that omitted the demographic factor – presumably on the grounds that a large population was implicit in a large GNP (see Table below).

Of course, there can be many objections. For example, a poor country that is prepared to field badly trained, half-armed and underfed soldiers might appear to have a greater potential than a country of the same size which insists on training, arming, feeding and clothing its soldiers to the highest possible standards. One is then faced with the conundrum of what

	Production, 1938	Relative manufacturing strength (world output = 100%)		Military expenditure, 1933–8	Relative war potential, 1937
Military potential[8]					
	(1932 GNP = 100%)	*1929*	*1938*	(£ million)	(world = 100%)
France	108	6.6	4.5	1,088	4.2
Germany	211	11.0	13.2	3,540	14.4
UK	143	9.4	9.2	1,201	10.2
USA	153	48.3	28.7	1,175	41.7
USSR	258	5.0	17.6	2,808	14.0

happens when quality confronts quantity. Will the better trained and better armed troopers of an elite force, with good rations and warm overcoats, hold the hordes of a supposedly inferior enemy at bay? Or will they be overwhelmed by sheer numbers? This is exactly the sort of calculation that was regularly made on the Eastern Front.

Military capacity, in contrast, measures standing forces which already exist. In its simplest form, it is concerned only with numbers:

Military capacity in 1939[9]

	Military	Relative
France	900,000	41,600,000
Germany	3,180,000	76,800,000
Italy	1,899,600	44,200,000
Poland	1,200,000	35,000,000
UK	681,000	47,900,000
USA	175,000	132,100,000
USSR	9,000,000	190,000,000

Yet the nature of the forces is no less relevant than the numbers, and the balance between navy, air force and land army is crucial. In 1939, for instance, Britain was in possession of the second strongest navy in the world, a rapidly expanding air force and a minuscule army. This meant that its capacity for defending the British Isles was high, whilst its capacity for contesting a successful enemy landing or for conducting an independent continental campaign was virtually nil. The United States, which possessed the world's largest navy but a land army smaller than Poland's, found itself in a similar exposed position.

An examination of the distribution of capacity among the main combatants at different times during the war would suggest that Germany possessed the best balanced overall force and hence the highest capacity to challenge allcomers. As time wore on, however, the Kriegsmarine was decimated and confined to port; the Luftwaffe was hopelessly over-stretched, unable to replace its losses; and the beleaguered Wehrmacht, though fighting with wonderful resilience, was inexorably ground down.

Of course, innumerable objections arise once again. Crude statistics about men and equipment tell us nothing about other key factors, such as generalship, manoeuvrability, surprise and morale. The army with the highest capacity rating or with the finest equipment is not always bound to win the battle. The classic illustration of this comes from the French Campaign of May–June 1940. In total numbers, the tank park of the French army was roughly the same size as that of the Wehrmacht. The tanks, mainly Renault B1s, were technically competent. Yet the French planners dispersed their tanks in defensive mode among large numbers of infantry units, whilst the Germans concentrated theirs in offensive mode in dedicated spearhead units, thereby waging blitzkrieg. The result was astounding.

The historian's prime concern, therefore, is neither potential nor capacity, but active deployment. One needs to know what forces were deployed where, and when, and for how long, and in what strength. On the micro scale, an analysis of deployment goes a long way to explain the outcome of particular engagements, battles or campaigns. And on the macro level it enables one to see both the overall shape and size of the war and the relative importance of its component parts (see Table opposite). As a rough guide, the volume of commitment may be measured in man-months, assuming that 1 soldier fighting for 6 months is equivalent to 6 soldiers fighting for 1 month. If one takes the first campaign of the war, in Poland (1 September–5 October 1939), for example, one finds 800,000 Polish soldiers pitted against 1.25 million German soldiers for 5 weeks. This would work out as 800,000 × 1.25 or 1 million man-months for the Poles, 1.25 million × 1.25 or 1.56 million for the Germans, and a total of 2.56 million man-months for both sides. It compares with a much higher figure of 9 million man-months for the Finnish Campaign of 1939–40, when 300,000 Finns and 1.2 million Soviets fought each other for 6 months between November 1939 and March 1940.

The objections here would refer to the fact that bald calculations of time and troop numbers convey neither the dynamic nature of military

Military deployment[10]			
	Warships in service	Warplanes in service	Deployed troops
September 1939			
Britain	251	1,660	402,000
France	97	950	900,000
Poland	4	678	1,200,000
Germany	28	2,916	2,730,000
April 1945			
Britain (western Europe)	744	8,000	2,000,000
USA (western Europe)	1,172	21,572	3,467,000
USSR	–	17,000	12,000,000
Germany	–	2,175	6,100,000

operations nor the marked changes of fortune. In any case, troop numbers do not indicate the real strength of an army. In any standard *ordre de bataille* of Second World War vintage, infantry would be distinguished from cavalry, armoured, motorized and airborne units, while troop strengths would always be accompanied by numbers of tanks, aircraft and field guns.

Nonetheless, the active-deployment indicator, rough and ready though it is, does enable the historian to determine the relative weight of successive campaigns, and from that the overall dimensions of operations as a whole. Having quantified the fighting of the Finnish Campaign, for example, it is a straightforward matter to dismiss Soviet claims that this was some sort of border skirmish, or that the Soviet Union was a neutral observer of the war before June 1941. What is more, the full list of these calculations gives some surprising results:

Active deployment of forces in Europe	
Campaign	Man-months (millions)
Poland September 1939	2.56
Finland 1939–40	9.00
German invasion of Norway and Denmark 1940	0.04
German Western Offensive May–June 1940	9.00
German–Soviet War 1941–5	406.00
North Africa 1941–3	5.00
Italy 1943–5	4.40
Western Front June 1944–May 1945	16.50

From this, one may safely conclude that attempts to equate the war effort in the West with that in the East are manifestly misguided.[11]

Casualties – especially figures for 'killed in action' – are another useful indicator of levels of military activity. Statistics in this field are notoriously unreliable. There are almost as many estimates as there are investigators, and the results can differ wildly. Nonetheless, one can be fairly confident of the general order of magnitude of the main listings:

Military war dead in Europe 1939–45 (estimated)[12]	
USSR	11,000,000
Germany	3,500,000
Romania	519,000
Yugoslavia	300,000
Italy	226,000
UK	144,000
USA	143,000
Hungary	136,000
Poland	120,000
France	92,000
Finland	90,000

One must be honest. These estimates would be better described as 'rough guesses'. The slaughter on the Eastern Front was so intense that the distinction between 'killed in action' and 'missing in action' was often irrelevant. So too was the possibility of counting the dead and keeping records. Yet the most obvious conclusion stands out a mile: the war assumed a far grander scale in the East than in any of the fronts where the Western Allies were involved.

Similar conclusions can be drawn from the death statistics of individual campaigns or battles. There is simply no comparison between the order of magnitude of the struggles in the East and of those elsewhere (see Table opposite).

People in Britain or America who follow these things will be well aware that Leningrad, Stalingrad and Kursk were big battles. But they are less likely to have registered the huge margin of preponderance of the East over the West, or to have grasped that relatively 'minor' operations like the battle for Budapest or the Warsaw Rising involved fighting on a similar scale to Normandy or the Battle of the Bulge.

Deaths in individual battles and campaigns[13]

Operation 'Barbarossa': battles of Byelorussia I, Smolensk I + Moscow *1941*	1,582,000
Stalingrad *September 1942–31 January 1943*	973,000
Siege of Leningrad *September 1941–27 January 1944*	900,000
Kiev *July–September 1941*	657,000
Operation Bagration *1944*	450,000
Kursk *1943*	325,000
Berlin *1945*	250,000
French Campaign *May–June 1940*	185,000
Operation Overlord *6 June–21 July 1944*	132,000
Budapest *October 1944–February 1945*	130,000
Polish Campaign *September 1939*	80,000
Battle of the Bulge *December 1944*	38,000
Warsaw Rising *1 August–1 October 1944, excluding civilians*	30,000
Operation Market Garden *September 1944*	16,000
Battle of El Alamein II *October–November 1942*	4,650

All in all, the open-minded observer will be tempted to view the war effort of the Western powers as something of a sideshow. Certainly in the sphere of land warfare it was not of first-rate importance. British forces accounted for perhaps 5–10 per cent of German casualties, American forces for slightly more – perhaps 15 per cent. Yet it would be wrong to give exclusive prominence to the campaigns of armies and to the resultant 'blood price'. There were other spheres of action in which the Western Allies played a weightier role, and which must necessarily form a part of the ultimate reckoning.

The war at sea

The navies and merchant fleets of the Western Powers were of great importance. In 1939, there were five naval powers that really counted. (The Soviet and Polish fleets were both relatively small, and both were trapped in enclosed seas.)[14] The entry into the war of the USA, which possessed the largest fleet in the world, made a big difference. By 1943 the original five had been reduced to three, and shortly afterwards, with the Kriegsmarine unwilling to risk the open sea, they were down to two. The

British and the Americans achieved similar predominance on the oceans as the Soviets achieved on land:

Allied tonnage lost in the 'Battle of the Atlantic'[15]	
Year	Tonnage lost
1939	299,000
1940	1,861,000
1941	2,556,000
1942	5,934,000
1943	1,892,000
1944	226,000
1945	132,000

There were two main theatres of action – in the Mediterranean and in the North Atlantic. In the former, the British and the French initially faced the Italian navy and a small number of German vessels that managed to slip past the watch at Gibraltar. Within six months the Royal Navy was on its own, and felt itself obliged to take the drastic step of sinking the fleet of its erstwhile French ally to prevent the warships falling into Vichy hands (see p. 84). In 1941–2 the combination of Italian capital ships out of Naples, a German air corps in Sicily, and a large pack of German submarines not only succeeded in supplying Axis forces in North Africa, they also put the British lines of communication between Gibraltar, Malta and Alexandria in mortal danger. For a few months, marked by the heroic defence of Malta, British fortunes hung by a thread. They were not fully secured until September 1943, when Italy surrendered.

The Battle of the Atlantic raged from 1939 to mid-1943, and continued at lower levels of intensity thereafter. It was fought over Britain's watery lifeline to Canada and the USA. So long as the lifeline was kept open, Britain had a chance to survive. If it was broken, Britain would have been forced to surrender or to face siege and starvation. As in the Mediterranean, the outcome was touch and go. With 200 U-boats at his disposal in early 1943, Admiral Dönitz was confident of victory. He was defeated by a sharp increase in Britain's technical ability to counter the U-boats and, above all, by an astonishing rise in the rate of US ship construction, which rocketed from 1.18 million gross tonnes in 1941 to 13.7 million gross tonnes in 1943. From then on, the Western Allies were putting far more new vessels into their supply convoys than the Germans could hope to sink. On 18 May 1943 Dönitz ordered his subs to pull out of the North Atlantic 'temporarily'. They never gained the upper hand again.

However, contrary to some impressions, the naval war did not stop. U-boats continued to operate, and to restrict the convoys' freedom. In April 1945, with the Third Reich on its knees, they still sank 74,000 tonnes of Allied shipping. What is more, as the Baltic was cleared, the Soviet navy began to operate. The biggest naval disaster of the war was brought about on 30 January 1945, when a Soviet submarine sank a large German transport, the *Wilhelm Gustloff*, with some 10,000 passengers aboard.

The strategic importance of the Allied victory at sea is hard to guage. It was not a war-winning event. Yet, without it, Germany would have been free to assert its interests round the world, to escape the blockade, and to revive its trading lines. Britain would have been totally isolated or defeated, and its assets turned to Germany's benefit. The USA, denied its 'tethered British aircraft carrier', would have been unable to intervene in Europe in any major way. Amphibious warfare would have been ruled out. The Allied landings in Sicily and in Normandy would have been impossible. The Wehrmacht could have turned its undivided attention on to the Eastern Front. And the Allied Strategic Bombing Offensive, based in Britain – the preferred Western concept for winning the war outright – would never have taken off.[16]

The war in the air

The Western Powers came to be similarly preponderant in aerial forces, which they employed with ever greater levels of efficiency. In pre-war days, air power had still been conceived as a new form of tactical support for traditional land or sea forces. Warplanes were needed to observe the enemy, to bomb lines of communication, to disrupt troop concentrations, to attack fortified positions, to protect shipping, and, naturally, to neutral-ize the enemy's air forces. In most countries, aerial commands remained subject to either the army or the navy. The air forces of the USSR were divided into the Red Army's air force and the Red Navy's air force. It was the same in the USA. The USAAF, which grew into the most powerful force of its kind in the world, was throughout the war a subordinate

branch of the US Army, and its commander could sit with the Joint Chiefs
of Staff only by permission of his army superiors. In Britain and the Third
Reich, the Royal Air Force and the Luftwaffe enjoyed a greater degree of
autonomy, but both had to accept their status as a 'junior service'.

In 1939 there were six air forces in Europe that really counted. The
Soviet air force was by far the largest:

Air forces in 1939[17]	
	No. of aircraft
USSR	8,105
Germany	2,916
Italy	1,796
Britain	1,660
France	950
Poland	678

All these countries possessed the capacity for aircraft production. But
the scene was to shift. The Polish air force was knocked out in September
1939, even though a magnificent contingent of its pilots was to escape and
to participate in the Battle of Britain. The French air force was knocked
out in 1940. And the Soviet air force was so damaged in 1941, when it lost
3,000 aircraft in ten days, that it could not assume ambitions beyond the
original tactical role until the final phase of the war. The remnants of
the Italian air force were too small to have more than local significance
after 1943. Step by step, therefore, the scenario was created where only
Germany, Britain and the USA were left to compete for aerial supremacy.

As time went on, however, strategic planners were forced to realize
that fundamental advances were occurring in the nature and role of air
power. Firstly, air power was well on the way to superseding sea power.
A well-managed aircraft carrier, equipped with torpedo-carrying planes,
was now able to sink or to disable a battleship long before 'the king of the
seas' could bring its heavy guns to bear. The days of the capital ships were
numbered. Secondly, massed formations of long-range bombers could aim
to destroy the urban and industrial centres of an adversary, and hence to
end its ability to wage war. Thirdly, military transport was revolutionized.
As the size, range and lifting power of aircraft increased, an air force could
undertake to ferry large numbers of troops over large distances, even
across the Atlantic. (One must remember that the first non-stop flight

across the Atlantic had been achieved by Charles Lindbergh only in 1927.) Fourthly, warplanes could be used as a vehicle for mass terror against civilians. This possibility, first demonstrated by the RAF in Iraq in the 1920s, and then used by the Luftwaffe at Guernica in Spain in 1937, was openly exploited during the German invasion of Poland in 1939. Though not publicly approved, it was implicit in the Strategic Bombing Offensive of the RAF, which preferred the more gentlemanly vocabulary of 'area bombing' and of 'breaking the morale of enemy civilians'.

The impressive growth of Western air power took place in the context of a strangely unbalanced strategic landscape, where, in the years 1941–4, there was no major 'Second Front' to support. The British and American navies were fully occupied with the ongoing Battle of the Atlantic. The British and American armies were engaged in North Africa, and later in southern Italy, far beyond the range of aircraft based in Britain. As a result, the only major task that the British and American air forces could entertain was a sustained bombing offensive against Germany's heartland. They applied themselves to the task with mounting ferocity. The principal author of the strategy, the head of RAF Bomber Command, Sir Arthur Harris, seemed to believe that his scheme would render plans for a 'Second Front' redundant. He set out to reduce all of Germany's cities to ashes, one by one, till none was left to function (see pp. 69, 102–3). The first 'Thousand-Bomber Raid' took place on 30/31 May 1942. Cologne, Germany's most ancient city, was trashed in the space of two hours. In August 1942 the USAAF brought over its B-17 Flying Fortresses, and began a daily programme of escorted daylight raids to supplement the RAF's night-time activities. At the Casablanca Conference of January 1943 the Allied leaders ordered that priority be given to 'precision bombing' of submarine yards, aircraft factories, railway lines and oil refineries. But this was largely ignored. On 27/8 July 1943 Hamburg, Germany's premier port, was destroyed by a firestorm in which 43,000 people perished and a million were made homeless. Berlin was repeatedly attacked, so that it resembled a moonscape of rubble long before the Red Army arrived. On 3 February 1945 a USAAF raid on Berlin killed 25,000 people at one go. Less than two weeks later, a combined British and American raid on Dresden caused a second firestorm, as at Hamburg, in which perhaps 60,000 people died for no known military purpose. The simple fact is that the Strategic Bombing Offensive did *not* bring the German economy to a halt, and it did *not* break the morale of the German public. What it did do was to demonstrate that in the last year of the war the Western air forces enjoyed virtually total supremacy in the skies of Western Europe.[18]

Neither the Luftwaffe nor the Red Air Force could afford such luxuries. Both of them were committed to supporting the titanic ground war on the Eastern Front. The Luftwaffe was torn between the Wehrmacht's increasingly strident calls for help in the East and the equally desperate need for air defence in the West. It was never able to reassemble the sort of medium-sized bomber groups of 400–500 machines that had attacked Britain in 1940–41. It also lost the technological race. By 1944 the updated versions of pre-war designs proved unable to compete on equal terms with either the Soviet Yakovlev-3s or the American P-51 Mustangs.

For its part, the Red Air Force recovered steadily from the near-catastrophe of 1941. Soviet aircraft production outstripped Germany's by a widening margin, so that, with Western assistance, the loss of some 45,000 machines in battle was more than offset. By 1944 Soviet front-line superiority stood at 3:1 or more. A heavy-bomber force was built to attack industrial targets behind the front, particularly in Romania. And a fleet of 800 Soviet bombers accompanied Marshal Zhukov on his final march to Berlin. The USSR was entering the top league.

As always, adversity is the mother of invention, and Germany's vulnerability to strategic bombing led to the development of so-called *Vergeltungswaffen* or 'vengeance weapons'. The V-1, which was developed from 1942 onward, was a pilotless monoplane carrying a 1-tonne high-explosive warhead at 560 km/h. Over 15,000 such missiles were fired between June 1944 and May 1945, and perhaps 9,000 reached their targets, principally in London and Antwerp. Accuracy was not their forte. The V-2, in contrast, was a genuine liquid-fuelled rocket, flying at supersonic speeds. Its payload was no greater than that of the V-1, but the height of its trajectory at nearly 80 km made it virtually impregnable to air defences. Research on it had begun as early as 1938, and but for Hitler's uninterest might have produced better results quicker. About 5,000 V-2s were fired in late 1944 and early 1945. Neither Britain nor the USA possessed anything to match this ground-breaking programme.[19]

Armaments and industrial production

Wars cannot be fought without regard for 'the sinews of war'. And here is another sphere in which the Western Powers, and one Western power in particular, excelled. Though the USA was the last of the major combatant states to enter the fray and its delayed contribution to ground fighting was relatively limited, there can be no doubt that its contribution to the war's logistics was of primary significance.[20]

Military planners try to foresee future requirements. So it is important to understand that the Second World War did not proceed along predicted paths. In 1939 none of the combatants was properly prepared for the ensuing conflict. Hitler was not expecting German rearmament to peak before 1942–3. His attack on Poland was supposed to be a swift local affair that would not involve the Western Powers, except perhaps in a token protest. At the time, Stalin had just called off the Great Terror, the *Yezhovschina*, which had destroyed millions, and was engaged in a massive purge (i.e. cold-blooded killing) of the officer corps. Despite the success of the five-year plans, he would have been very conscious that the economic and industrial base of the USSR still lagged behind that of potential adversaries. France in 1939, obsessed with the 'Maginot Mentality', was conscious of a drastic decline of the birth rate and of its uncompleted fortifications. Britain was headed by a government which until recently had been intent on appeasement and disinclined to raise defence spending. At Churchill's insistence, a start had been made on the expansion and re-equipment of the RAF. But the chief assignment of the British Army was to defend the Empire, and the four meagre divisions earmarked for service on the continent represented less than 10 per cent of Poland's standing army and barely 5 per cent of France's.

Nor did preparations run even vaguely to plan. In 1940 France, which was counting on a war of three to four years, as in 1914–18, collapsed and surrendered in six weeks flat. And Britain, though totally isolated by the fall of France and barely intact after the Battle of Britain, was able to survive only through the improvised arrangements of the US Lend-Lease Act. In 1941 Hitler prepared an invasion of the USSR which was supposed to be finished in four to five months, and which made no allowance for widespread winter fighting. According to the prevailing interpretation, Stalin was completely taken by surprise (see p. 95). At all events, he failed to put the Red Army and Air Force into defensive mode, and consequently lost astronomic quantities of men and machines. In December 1941, with advance German troops peering through their binoculars at the Kremlin, the leaders of the Third Reich declared war on the USA, clearly believing that no time would be left for the USA to intervene. In 1942 the USSR surprised all the experts by holding out, while the Battle of the Atlantic

festered in stalemate. In 1943 the solemnly promised 'Second Front' failed
to materialize in the West (for the second year running), while the
resurgent Red Army unexpectedly carried everything before it in the East.
In 1944, the Red Army flabbergasted everyone, including its Anglo-
American allies, by halting its triumphal march before Warsaw and by
making a left turn into the Balkans. It was also Germany's turn to hold
out and to wrong-foot the experts. After the success of Operation Overlord – the invasion in Normandy – the over-optimistic generals who told
Churchill and Roosevelt that the war would be 'over by Christmas' were
proved, once again, to be wrong.

All of this is worth emphasizing if only to show that logistical planning
in the Second World War was a nightmare. No one had a clear view of
future requirements. And the only realistic policy for those left in the race
was to go for maximum production and to pray that performance would
somehow meet demand. In the event, all the major parties performed
much more efficiently than might have been foreseen.

Given that the Third Reich became embroiled in a series of long-
drawn-out conflicts, which its leaders had hoped to avoid, the German
economy reacted magnificently:

German GDP, 1939–45[21]							
1938	1939	1940	1941	1942	1943	1944	1945
100	109	110	117	118	121	124	88

It was greatly assisted, of course, by the human and industrial assets
of the conquered nations. Tanks built in the former Skoda factories at
Pilsen, for instance, played a prominent role in the invasion of France.
Two million French POWs toiled in the mines and the fields to release
German manpower for army service. Inmates of the Nazi camps and
ghettos in German-occupied Poland were forced to assist the war effort.
Taxes and tribute were extracted from all sides. Millions of slave labourers
were imported from the East. So too were trainloads of black earth from
Ukraine and oil from Romania.

Even so, it is remarkable that Germany's industrial output did not stop
rising until the last months of 1944 (see Table opposite).

Deliveries of equipment to the armed services also maintained a steady
increase until late in the day (see Table opposite).

German industrial output, 1941–4[22]

	1941	1942	1943	1944
Steel *(millions of tons)*	31.8	32.1	34.6	28.5
Coal *(millions of tons)*	248.3	264.2	266.9	249.0
Synthetic oil *(millions of tons)*	4.1	4.95	5.7	3.8
Synthetic rubber *(millions of tons)*	69	98	117	104
Aluminium *(thousands of tons)*	233.6	263.9	250.0	245.3

German military deliveries, 1939–45[23]

	Tanks	Aircraft	Heavy guns
1939	247	8,295	1,214
1940	1,643	10,826	6,730
1941	3,790	11,776	11,200
1942	6,180	15,556	23,200
1943	12,063	25,527	46,100
1944	19,002	39,807	70,700
1945	3,932	7,544	12,650

Germany's Achilles heel was oil. Since the Wehrmacht failed to reach Baku (the Soviet oil port on the Caspian Sea), since the Kriegsmarine failed to lift the blockade, since the badly damaged Romanian fields were lost in mid-1944, and since the ersatz, coal-based fuel system did not live up to expectations, the fuel tanks of Germany's armoured divisions, air squadrons and transport columns began to run dry. The scene in the film *Battle of the Bulge* where a German panzer commander accepts the inevitability of defeat when he finds a chocolate cake flown from Kansas in a captured US tank may have been invented. But it rings true.

Britain's wartime economy also performed surprisingly well. From 1940 onward Britain was essentially bankrupt, and relied on emergency loans from the USA to keep going. Even so, British industrial output survived the Blitz, survived the interruptions to supply, and continued to rise (see Table overleaf).

The USSR was the only combatant state to possess a centrally planned, militarized economy before the war started. The five-year plans, launched in 1929, were an undisguised bid to provide the Soviet Union with the heavy industry, and hence the sustained military capacity, that the Tsarist

British GDP, 1939–45[24]							
1938	*1939*	*1940*	*1941*	*1942*	*1943*	*1944*	*1945*
100	101	111	121	124	127	122	116

Empire had lacked. Stalin had set the target of achieving a viable, modern economy within ten years, 'lest all be not lost'. The wonder is that the planned economy continued to function even when the most industrialized regions of the state, in Ukraine, were overrun by the Germans. Heroic efforts and draconian methods were needed to evacuate whole factories with their machines and their workforce to the Urals and to Siberia. Treasured triumphs from the 1930s, like the dam at Dnepropetrovsk, were dynamited. People starved. Millions lingered in the camps of the GULag. Women took charge of the collective farms. Men were thrown into battle without the least regard for their welfare. But the rising flow of materiel to the Red Army never stopped:

Soviet military production[25]			
	Tanks	*Aircraft*	*Heavy guns*
1940	2,794	10,565	15,300
1941	6,590	15,735	42,300
1942	24,446	25,436	127,000
1943	24,089	34,845	130,000
1944	28,963	40,246	122,400
1945	15,419	20,052	62,000

Yet nothing could compare to the miracles achieved by the wartime economy of the USA. In 1939 the American war machine was but a fraction of its future self. Isolationism ruled. There were no thoughts of war, no plans for rearmament or expanded defences. Two years later, the giant still slept. A modest increase was instigated to meet the commitment to Lend-Lease. But it was not until the very end of 1941 that the order was given to put the peacetime economy on to a war footing. The response was spectacular. Automobile plants switched to tank production. Shipyards turned from merchantmen to warships. Aircraft factories dropped airliners for fighters and bombers. Everything changed gear as if

with effortless ease. Steelworks, coal mines and railways responded ener-
getically to the challenge. The tempo quickened. The numbers multiplied.
And the labour force, not long after the Depression, sweated willingly.
The results were truly staggering. By 1943 it was reputedly a tank every
five minutes, an aircraft every half-hour, and an aircraft carrier every week.
This was industrial expansion such as the world had never seen:

US military production[26]			
	Tanks	*Aircraft*	*Warships*
1940	331	12,804	–
1941	4,052	26,277	5
1942	24,997	47,836	146
1943	29,497	85,898	559
1944	17,565	96,318	410
1945	11,968	49,761	127

The consequences of the economic and industrial explosion in the
USA were manifold. Firstly, since the production of goods moved faster
than the training and deployment of troops, a vast surplus accumulated to
be shared with America's allies. Secondly, since concessions could be
exchanged for largesse, the USA quickly established a dominant political
position, particularly over Britain. Thirdly, since rocketing production
meant rocketing tax revenues, the US Treasury built up a vast holding of
tax dollars that could be used for post-war reconstruction. And finally,
since a war-ravaged Germany could not hope to compete for long with a
coalition transformed by American deliveries, the prospect of total, irredeemable defeat stared Hitler in the face.

The value of US war deliveries to the United Kingdom is well known.
They made all the difference between drowning and staying afloat. But
the benefits which they gave to the USSR were not publicized, and were
rarely acknowledged by Soviet historians. In reality, they were considerable. In this case, however, it is not possible to state that they made the
difference between defeat and victory. The Red Army had already gained
the upper hand on the Eastern Front at the turn of 1942–3, before the full
weight of Western assistance could be felt. The Arctic convoys that were
sent from Britain to Murmansk, beginning in 1941, were extremely perilous
and hardly defensible in terms of tonnage delivered against tonnage lost.

They were a bold gesture of solidarity. But the overland route from Iran – along which from late 1943 flowed an uninterrupted stream of military trucks, petrol tankers, jeeps, aircraft, ammunition, hard rations, canned food, boots and uniforms – ensured that the Red Army lacked for nothing during the final drive into Eastern Europe and the Reich. Soviet soldiers were told to tell the locals that equipment marked 'MADE IN THE USA' meant 'MADE IN [THE USSR FOR EXPORT TO] THE USA'. But few were fooled:

Lend-Lease deliveries to the USSR, 1943–5[27]	
Aircraft	14,795
Tanks	7,056
Jeeps	51,503
Trucks	375,883
Motorcycles	35,170
Tractors	8,071
Guns	8,218
Machine guns	131,633
Explosives	345,735 tonnes
Building equipment valued	$10,910,000
Railway freight cars	11,155
Locomotives	1,981
Cargo ships	90
Submarine hunters	105
Torpedo boats	197
Ship engines	7,784
Food supplies	4,478,000 tonnes
Machines and equipment	$1,078,965,000
Non-iron metals	802,000 tonnes
Petroleum products	2,670,000 tonnes
Chemicals	842,000 tonnes
Cotton	106,893,000 tonnes
Leather	49,860
Tyres	3,786,000
Army boots	15,417,000 pairs

For some reason, the US government never tried to use Soviet dependence on US supplies as a political lever.

Military Technology

Science, technology, industry and engineering constitute a vital aspect of modern 'total war'. All the major combatants of the Second World War constantly competed to improve the design and production of existing weapons. And the 1940s saw several pioneering projects to develop entirely new technologies. The first electronic computer, built at Bletchley Park for the Ultra programme, was one (see below). Jet engines, ballistic rockets and nuclear fission were others.

The RAF and the Luftwaffe both introduced jet fighters into squadron service in 1944. Both the Meteor and the Me-262 were twin-jet monoplanes. In the Me-163 the Germans also possessed a near-sonic, tailless, rocket-motored fighter that flew on liquid fuel for twelve minutes before returning to base as a glider. Its numbers were minuscule.

All combatants developed a variety of battlefield rocket weapons, including the Soviet Katyusha multiple rocket-launcher, the German *Panzerfaust* and the American bazooka. But the Germans alone developed long-range rockets.[28]

The economic and industrial prowess of the USA had many spin-offs in the field of science and technology. The most crucial of them lay in the ability to bear the astronomic costs and organizational burdens of creating the world's first atomic bomb. In 1941 work began in the UK on the large-scale separation of uranium isotopes. But, thanks to the colossal development costs, Anglo-American cooperation had to be the basis for the $2 billion 'Manhattan Project', which was inspired by the false belief in a German head start. Once the Germans' own nuclear programme was disrupted by Allied bombing and then scuppered by Norwegian saboteurs, it was only a matter of time before America possessed a unique military advantage. The Soviets contented themselves with the cheaper route of espionage. However, no atomic bomb had been tested anywhere by May 1945, and the bomb came too late to affect the war in Europe. Concessions made to the USSR at Yalta in early 1945 were motivated by the desire for Soviet assistance in the final onslaught on Japan and by the uncertainty that the bomb would actually work. Whether or not the USA would have launched a nuclear attack on Germany, if the European war had persisted until the bomb was available, is, of course, an unanswerable and unhistorical question.[29]

The Ultra secret

Code-breaking is one of the few activities that enable the weak to right the balance against the strong. So it was of special interest to the British in their 'dark days' in the early years of the war. With the help of a loyal ally, the genius of some very intelligent people, and the hard work of some 15,000 men and women sworn to absolute secrecy, they succeeded beyond their wildest dreams.

All sides in a major modern war use codes, break codes, and change codes. The Germans broke some British naval codes. The Soviets broke some German codes. But the Ultra operation was different for two reasons. It broke the 'Enigma' code of Germany's central military command. And Enigma stayed broken, from 1940 to the very end of the war. Britain's ability to read the enemy's intentions was of inestimable worth.

The story began in Poland. Pre-war Polish intelligence learned that the German military were developing an automated, perpetually changing code based on a commercially available machine called 'Enigma'. Polish agents penetrated the factory where the enhanced machine was being built, and learned the exact details of its design. Three young mathematicians from Warsaw University, led by Marian Rejewski, then worked out a set of formulas whereby the code could be read. At the outbreak of war in 1939, Britain and France were both presented with a reproduction of an Enigma machine together with instructions on how it worked. (It is said that when a Polish agent showed up at the British Embassy in Bucharest, carrying what appeared to be a typewriter, he was told, 'Please come back on Monday morning.')

The Germans had good reason to believe that Enigma was unbreakable. A fresh setting was adopted every day at midnight. After that, the code changed every single time that a letter key was pressed. The possible permutations for each letter of a transmitted text ran into billions. What is more, the machine was regularly upgraded. Extra notched wheels were added, and each new wheel increased the permutations by a factor of 100. In 1944 an especially sophisticated variant called the *B-schreiber* was introduced. No wonder the operators never suspected that they had been rumbled.

The Ultra Project was established at Bletchley Park in the English Midlands in late 1939. It attracted an extraordinary company of eccentrics, scientists, linguists and mathematicians, most notably a gay loner from

Cambridge called Alan Turing. Thanks to the Poles, they knew exactly what they were up against, without finding a quick way in. But they had some lucky breaks. They found that a number of German radio operators, especially a man called Walter, were ignoring instructions and were starting their machines with the same setting every day. They rightly guessed that German units all over Europe would be transmitting almost identical messages on the Führer's birthday in April 1940. And they eventually got their hands on an updated Enigma machine which the Royal Navy had obtained from a German weather ship captured off Greenland. After that, 'Turing's Bomb', an electro-mechanical calculator, was able to sort out the permutations and to produce the answers. By the second year of the war, the 'Bletchley Parkers' were reading all Enigma transmissions within three hours from the start of every day. They kept up with all the German updates. And in 1944, to counter the *B-schreiber*, they invented the world's first electronic computer, the Colossus.

The British government could never admit to the source or the extent of its detailed knowledge of German activities. Indeed, the secret remained hidden from the public for thirty years after the war. Hitler remained puzzled and irritated by British attitudes. He said that 'the British did not know when they were beaten'. The British, in contrast, knew exactly what Hitler was doing. Almost every day Churchill received verbatim copies of all the Führer's directives to his generals and of most of the generals' signals to their troops. The British chiefs of staff, who were otherwise pushed against the ropes, had this one priceless advantage. They knew of Göring's intentions during the Battle of Britain. Since every U-boat received instructions via an Enigma machine, they were able to plot the positions of the German submarine fleet and to dumbfound Admiral Dönitz during the Battle of the Atlantic. They tipped off Montgomery about Rommel's dispositions before El Alamein. They heard of movements to strengthen Germany's air defences. And they knew before the Normandy landings that their schemes of deception had worked. Through leaks engineered by the traitor John Cairncross, the Ultra group even assisted the Soviets. From mid-1940 to late 1943, Britain's position was dire. Without Ultra, it would have been much worse. But one needs to remember that the Second World War was not decided by Germany's struggle with Britain.

One has to conclude, therefore, that Ultra was not so much a war-winning operation as a vital element in Britain's long struggle for survival. With the possible exception of the Battle of Kursk (see pp. 110–12), it did not play any part in the key conflicts on the Eastern Front. There is no evidence that Soviet cryptographers broke Enigma independently. The Red Army had to cope without Ultra.[30]

Partisans

Nazi rule fostered resistance movements like rain encourages mushrooms. Some of them, especially those run by Communist agencies, loved the word 'partisans'. Others, like the Polish Home Army, avoided it because of its Communist associations.

The earliest, and the largest, underground army began to operate in Poland before the end of the September Campaign in 1939. Drawn from disparate elements loyal to the exiled government in London, it was supplied and in part trained by the Polish Section of Britain's Special Operations Executive (SOE), and acted as the military arm of a fully fledged underground state. From 1942 it assumed the name of the Armia Krajowa (the Home Army), and recruited 300,000–400,000 men and women. It engaged in widespread sabotage, in the assassination of SS and Gestapo personnel, and in brilliant intelligence work. (The AK captured an intact V-2 rocket, which it dispatched to London.) But it postponed large-scale military action until the Warsaw Rising (see pp. 119–20).[31] The Communist underground was negligible in Poland, since Stalin (not Hitler) had wiped out virtually the whole Polish Communist movement in 1938–9.

Norway's Milorg came into being in 1940, and it too was helped by SOE. Small isolated groups conducted sabotage and information services, but regarded themselves more as 'a clandestine force in being' than as a secret army preparing for action. They played a role with SOE in the destruction of the Germans' heavy-water plant at Ryukan in February 1943.

Serbia, like Poland, had a long insurrectionary tradition. The Chetniks, formed after the fall of Yugoslavia in 1941, were led by Major 'Draza' Mikhailovič, who, like the Poles, set about forming a 'Home Army'. Yet the infernal complexities of wartime Yugoslavia, with its four occupation zones and five rival ethnic groups, led to endless conflicts. And in 1942–3 the initiative passed to the Communist formation of Josip Broz, aka 'Tito'. A vicious civil war between Tito and the Chetniks took precedence over the fight against occupation. In 1944, when the Allies chose to support Tito, the scene was set for a post-war Communist takeover.[32]

In Ukraine, an independence movement surfaced in 1941 – as in the

First World War – only to find its leaders cast into German concentration camps. From then on, the Ukrainian Insurrectionary Army (UPA) attempted the impossible by fighting under the slogan 'Neither Hitler nor Stalin'. It soon became entangled in multi-sided conflicts with Poles and Soviet partisans as well as with the Germans.

In Byelorussia the Soviet partisans dominated. They formed a regular branch of the Red Army, operating behind enemy lines, receiving airborne supplies, and supporting politically sympathetic groups, especially Jewish ones, but not the local Polish Underground. The main sufferers were the civilians who were thrown to the mercy of the Wehrmacht's murderous 'anti-partisan' campaigns.

In Italy and France, significant resistance movements did not develop until 1943–4, when the Germans were in retreat. In both cases, Communist elements were prominent.

Such was the violence, destruction and unpredictability of the Second World War that most of the combatant states lost all sense of war aims beyond mere survival. The Nazi leaders did not abandon their plans for a New Order in Europe. But, faced with demands for unconditional surrender (see p. 129), they knew that defeat would leave them with no place at the conference table. The Soviets, having lost 27 million citizens, were mainly interested in reconstruction and in extracting reparations from Germany. The French, like all occupied nations, were wondering when and how they would get their republic back. The British, politically dependent and economically destitute, were looking to hold on to their empire, especially in India, and to avoid social unrest.

Of all the combatant states, therefore, the USA alone possessed the space and time to make systematic plans for a future world order. Untouched by the fighting, and daily growing in confidence, power, wealth and prestige, the Americans must have sensed that the era of their supremacy was fast approaching. Their armies were victorious in the Pacific, as in Western Europe. Their navy and air force could hardly be challenged. Their nuclear project would soon make them the world's sole atomic power. Their economic clout was in a league of its own. Above all, their only possible rivals were contending with varying degrees of disruption, debilitude and devastation. So there was no reason to hesitate. In 1944, before the war was won, and before Roosevelt was re-elected as president for a third term, the foundations were laid for the United Nations Organization, for the World Bank, for the International Monetary Fund and, by extension, for the reconstruction of Europe. No one else could have drawn up such proposals. No one else could have financed them. The USA was gearing up for world leadership. It had not made the largest military contribution to the war – at least not in Europe. But it would be the chief beneficiary.

A number of intangibles were also important. War is not fought by guns and logistics alone. Psychological factors need to be taken into account too. Here, Britain's superb gamble in defying the Third Reich in 1940–41, when discretion might have favoured accommodation, had significant consequences. Not only did it give heart to all opponents of Nazism, including the oppressed populations of German-occupied countries. It also did much to undermine American isolationism, and thereby to prepare the way for the entry of the USA into the war. It did little in practical terms to weaken Hitler's grip on Europe. But it was crucial in facilitating what was to follow. Without it, the USA would have no base from which to intervene; German industry would have been free from bombing; the USSR could have been attacked in isolation; and the final outcome could have been very different.

The ideological framework

Ideology, supposedly, provides the theory. Politics describes the practice. Ideology tells us about the mindset of the players in the game. Politics tells us how the game was actually played. Politics deals with decisions, policies, initiatives, mistakes, successes; ideology with ideas.

From the start, one must state that three main ideological camps were competing with each other during the Second World War. There were no other serious contenders to Fascism, Communism and liberal democracy. The Fascist camp, founded by Mussolini in Italy, was headed from the mid-1930s onward by the Nazi regime in Germany. It had a fellow spirit in General Franco's non-combatant Spain, some imitators, like the Iron Guard in Romania, and a few marginal admirers in democratic countries where they were allowed to function. The Communist camp was based in the Soviet Union, 'the world's first socialist state'. (For socialist, read 'the Communist version of socialist'.) As yet, it had not inspired any ruling fraternal regimes; but it was the motor of a worldwide revolutionary movement with strong support in France and Italy, still stronger support in Germany until suppressed by the Nazis, a presence in most East European countries, and a fashionable following among left-wing intellectuals in the West. The democratic camp had come together among the victorious Western Powers of the First World War – France, Italy, Britain and the USA. Though Italy had dropped out and the USA was an isolationist absentee, it was the patron of the Versailles Settlement, of the League of Nations, and of the states of 'New Europe' that were formed after 1918. Its standing had taken a beating in the 1930s through the emergence of numerous dictatorships, through the failure of the League of Nations to exert its authority, and from the policy of appeasement which in 1938 had thrown a democratic country, Czechoslovakia, to the wolves. The advocates of democracy were defending the status quo (not very successfully). The Fascists and the Communists were challenging.

Czechoslovakia holds a special place in the story. Not only was it the democratic country that held out most doggedly against the rise of the dictators. It was a country which had broken free from Austria–Hungary at the end of the First World War, and whose national ethos was anchored in the struggle against German domination. For historical reasons, it had aways looked to Russia as a counterweight to Germany. This combination of circumstances had turned the Czechs into the favourites of the West (and of Western history books) and of the wartime coalition. Their pre-war fate switched the spotlight of world attention on to the threat of Fascism in general and of Germany in particular.[33]

Fascism, which started out as the name for Mussolini's movement in Italy, soon became a generic label for all the political groups which Mussolini's example inspired: the National Socialists in Germany, the Falange of General Franco in Spain, the ONR in Poland, the *Ustashe* in Croatia, the Iron Guard in Romania, the Arrow Cross in Hungary, the Rexists in Belgium, the Action Française in France, and Sir Oswald Mosley's 'Black Shirts' in Britain. Thanks to its rivalry with Communism, it is often classed as 'ultra right wing' or 'the extreme Right'. In reality it drew on a strange mixture of right-wing and left-wing features, and frequently attracted disillusioned socialists or, like Mussolini himself, ex-Marxists. It was radical-revolutionary, aiming to supersede the vested interests of court, aristocracy, clergy and business; and it talked of mobilizing and liberating the masses. It was highly nationalistic and militarist, aiming to achieve its goals by coercion. It believed in the dictatorship of a one-party state, in repressive police methods, in bombastic propaganda, and in the cult of the *Duce/Führer/Caudillo* or 'Leader'. Together with Communism, which in many respects it resembled, it was the founding exemplar of totalitarianism.

Nazism, which grew quickly in the 1930s to be the leading member of the Fascist family, is the name given to the movement headed by Hitler's NSDAP: the National Socialist German Workers Party. The socialist part of its make-up, like that of Mussolini, was revolutionary, populist and militant, and brought it into a head-on clash with other socialist and workers' organizations, especially with the Communists and the trade unions. Running battles disturbed the peace of the German streets for over a decade until the Nazi 'storm squads' gained the upper hand in 1933.

The nationalist part of the Nazi make-up was unusual, even in Fascist circles. The Nazis believed, against all the evidence, that the Germans belonged not just to a nation, but to an exclusive and superior biological breed, a 'master race'. They followed their racist star implicitly, in both foreign and domestic policy. They had no special quarrel with fellow Germanics, like the English. They tolerated the somewhat inferior Latins, like the Italians and the French, who via the Lombards and the 'Franks' were thought to possess a suitable admixture of 'Germanic blood'. But they despised the Slavs, like the Poles, Ukrainians and Russians, whom they classed as *Untermenschen* – 'subhumans'. Above all, they hated the Jews, to whose (non-existent) conspiracies they attributed all the ills of Germany and the world. Without revealing any specifics, and before the war began, Hitler quite openly declared his intention of 'removing' the Jews. His special hatred for Communism was partly driven by the battles of the German streets, but mainly by the conviction that the Communist parties were run by Jews and that he was defending Europe from 'Jewish Bolshevism'.

Mixed with old-fashioned German nationalism, Nazi racism made a potent cocktail that fuelled all the long-term visions of the Third Reich. Once in control, the Nazis knew that they could field the best army in Europe. They were going to use it to rectify the wrongs of the Versailles Settlement, and to banish all of Germany's recent humiliations. After that, they aimed to expand the German state to the east, to move into their *Lebensraum* or 'living space', to deal with 'the filthy mixture' of Slavs and Jews now living there, and to construct a racially pure 'blood base' for the Thousand-Year Reich. To foreigners, this scheme – well publicized from 1925 in Hitler's *Mein Kampf* – sounded too fantastic for

words. But the Nazi leaders were deadly serious. They pursued their plan
with accelerating devotion. In September 1944, when the Reich stood
on the brink of defeat, Himmler contemplated the total levelling of Warsaw, once the largest of the Slav–Jewish cities, which his SS forces were
about to complete, and he rejoiced. 'This city', he told Hitler, 'has
blocked our path to the East for 700 years ... [it will] cease to be a
problem for our children and for all who will follow us.'[34] To the Nazi
mindset, defeat in the military war was less significant than victory in the
'racial war'.

Nonetheless, Nazi policies against the Jews did not appear to be given
any special priority for a number of years. The abhorrent Nuremberg
Laws were issued in 1935, forbidding sexual intercourse between Jews and
Aryans, breaking up families, and encouraging all manner of harassment.
But they did not usher in a season of pogroms, and many German Jews
were able to emigrate. The first act of major anti-Semitic violence occurred
on Kristallnacht, the night of 9/10 November 1938, when around 100 Jews
were killed. But the death toll was not enormous, and it was the Nazis'
euthanasia campaign of 1938–9 – which was not specifically directed at
Jews – that has to be counted as Hitler's opening act of genocide. Even
when Poland was invaded, and 3 million Jews came under Nazi control,
there was no hurry to kill them. The Nazis' first campaign of mass murder in Poland was aimed at Polish intellectuals. The Jews were corralled
into Nazi-built ghettos, and treated very cruelly, but the SS policymakers
seemed to be hesitating. This strengthened the impression that the
objective really might, after all, be resettlement. Even when the 'Final
Solution' began, in 1941–2, it was effectively concealed, (see p. 168).[35]

Communism, like Fascism, spawned a worldwide movement with
many variants: among them Leninism, Stalinism, Trotskyism, Titoism and
Maoism. Thanks to its self-definition as 'the only true form of socialism',
it regarded itself as the avant-garde of the Left. In many political-science
classifications it is presented as 'the extreme Left', to match the Fascists on
the 'extreme Right'. In reality, like Fascism, it drew on its own mixture of
leftist and rightist features. It was revolutionary-radical, and, having
overthrown the revolutionary regime that had overthrown the Tsar, it
gained possession of the largest state on the surface of the globe and
turned it into the biggest political laboratory of the early twentieth century.
Its official name was Marxism–Leninism, i.e. Lenin's improvement on
Marxism. Yet its guiding ethos remained that of a politico-religious sect, a
tiny band of embattled 'comrades', totally fanatical, totally self-absorbed,

totally intolerant of dissent, and totally ruthless. What is more, since Lenin's Bolsheviks had seized the reins of mighty Russia, the world took them seriously, not simply as successful political practitioners but as sophisticated political thinkers. Power brought mindless adulation. Failed experiment followed failed experiment. But bone-headed professors wrote massive admiring tomes. Fellow-travellers among the Western intelligentsia queued up to adulate. Colossal abuses passed unnoticed. In practice, the Communists proved to be incompetent at almost everything except espionage, deception and war. It was to take seventy-four years, and tens of millions of wasted lives, for the system to collapse of its own accord and for the world to realize that the sum total of the Bolshevik experiment was 'a People's Tragedy'.[36]

The Marxist part of Marxism–Leninism provided the bulk of the theory. Dialectical materialism, i.e. the clash of opposing forces driven by socio-economic contradictions, supplied a flexible philosophical tool for interpreting all aspects of human life. (Since it was used to explain the whole of history, it was also known as historical materialism.) Politics was defined as conflict between the forces of progress (now led by the Bolsheviks) and the forces of 'reaction' (led by the Bolsheviks' enemies.) Society was seen as a seething mass of group antagonisms which could never calm down until the 'Bolshevik-led' working class emerged triumphant. Economics was a sphere where public and private interests contended for control of the 'means of production': power resources, transport, industry and agriculture. International relations were reduced to a conflict between the socialist camp (the USSR and its allies) and the capitalist camp (led by an assortment of 'anti-Soviet' imperialists, bankers, and businessmen). Dialectical materialism was the motor of Marxist history. It offered a guide to the future as well as an explanation of the past. In accordance with the 'spiral of progress', mankind was bound to pass through five successive stages of development. The most advanced countries – meaning Britain and Germany – had already reached the penultimate stage, dominated by capitalism, after which a revolution launched by representatives of the working class would herald the classless era of socialism.

Marx, who died in 1883, never lived to see the revolution. But his disciples in Soviet Russia were quick to claim that in October 1917 they had carried out his bidding. In fact, as a German exile living in London, Marx had naturally assumed that the revolution would occur spontaneously in one of the countries of Western Europe where a strong proletariat already existed. A backward peasant country, like Russia, where the proletariat was tiny, did not fit the bill. For Marx was not planning change through massive violence. On the contrary, as he worked away in the Reading Room of the British Museum, financed by his friend Friedrich Engels, who was a factory-owner in Manchester, Marx was thinking of socio-political processes that were maturing of their own accord and that would some day deliver the revolution 'like an apple falling from the branch'. In this light, it is not unreasonable to speculate that he would have turned in his grave if he could have seen what the Bolsheviks had actually made of his theories.[37]

The Leninist part of Marxism–Leninism supplied the guidelines for practical political action. It told how a group of highly disciplined activists could manipulate their opponents and seize power; how they could transform their revolutionary opposition group into a dictatorial state executive; and how the organs of a one-party state could control all elements of society and all their activities. Leninists used the language of Marxism and democracy, but twisted its meaning to their own purposes. Hence 'the dictatorship of the proletariat' envisaged the dictatorship of the ruling party over the proletariat; 'socialism' meant Lenin's personal variant of socialism, i.e. Communism; 'the party' did not mean just a political party, but an all-embracing organization with monopoly powers; and 'democracy' meant the coercive subordination of the people to the state, i.e. tyranny. The soviets, or state councils, which formed the basic building blocks of the Leninist state, were mere pawns in the controlling hands of the ruling party. The Leninist concept of 'democratic centralism' sounds fine to the unsuspecting. In fact it referred to the dual mechanism of the party state whereby the party organs gave the orders and the officials of the centralized state – the presidents, ministers, and chairmen of soviets – simply obeyed. The CEO of any such Soviet-style system was not the president (although such a cipher existed), but the general secretary of the party – unless, as sometimes happened, the general secretary chose to appoint himself president as well. Stalin was never Soviet president.

In Lenin's time, all these intellectual gymnastics were given institutional form. The Bolsheviks' party, the RSDP(b) (Russian Social Democratic Party (Bolshevik)), assumed dictatorial control of Soviet Russia, the Russian Federation of Soviet Socialist Republics. The feared security police of the tsarist empire, the Okhrana, was replaced by a still more fearsome force, Felix Dzerzhinsky's Cheka. The GULag network of state

concentration camps was established. The 'Red Terror' was unleashed to
outperform the White Terror and to eliminate all active 'enemies of the
people' – aristocrats, clergy, capitalists, non-Marxist socialists, non-Leninist
Marxists (the Mensheviks), independent trade unionists (the 'Workers'
Opposition') and free peasants. Leon Trotsky's Red Army conducted a
series of victorious campaigns to win the Civil War in Russia, and then to
reconquer most of the non-Russian provinces of the former empire which
in the meantime had opted for independence.

Yet two things the Bolsheviks could not fix. One was a competent
economy. The other was a firm institutional link with Western Europe.
They were internationalists. They believed they had a universal remedy
for all nations; and they knew that their revolution in backward Russia
could not survive in recognizable form unless they linked up with an
advanced, industrial country like Germany. So they repeatedly attempted
to forge a link. In the summer of 1920 they sent the Red Army westward
in the most serious such attempt. Unfortunately, to march from Russia to
Germany, their forces had to cross Poland; and the Poles were not
disposed to see their own new republic trampled on. At the Battle of
Warsaw, the Red Army was badly beaten. Lenin's big experiment in
international expansionism collapsed. The network of Communist states
stretching from Moscow to Berlin, which Lenin had briefly hoped for,
never came into being. Instead, a more limited Soviet Union had to be
formed from just three republics: Russia, Byelorussia and Ukraine. It
opened for business on 1 January 1924. But the long-term goals were
never abandoned.

The region of Europe that lies between Moscow and Berlin, sometimes called East Central Europe, has never been well known to Westerners.[38] But the observant reader may have noticed that the area of the
Bolsheviks' dashed internationalist hopes, to which they would some day
return, coincided very closely with the area of Hitler's projected *Lebensraum*. Even in the 1920s or '30s, a prescient analyst might well have
spotted where the next great European clash of arms might be
concentrated.

After Lenin died, in 1924, the Leader's mantle fell to Joseph Vissarion-
ovich Dzhugashvili, alias Stalin ('Man of Steel'), sometime commissar for
nationalities; and the ideology changed as the mantle passed. Stalin did not
give priority to Lenin's internationalism. Indeed, he had suffered personally
from the catastrophe in Poland, after Trotsky had accused him of disobeying orders. And he wouldn't let the disaster happen again. He sought an

ideological accent that supported his vision of a new Russia that was stronger and more modern than the old. He first coined a slogan, 'Socialism in One Country', which indicated that all resources should now be concentrated on building up the USSR. For the time being, foreign adventures were over. Then, in 1929, after disposing of the opposition, he set out on the grandiose scheme to transform the Soviet economy into a modern, industrial and military giant in the shortest time possible. The team of philosophers and historians who had been preparing textbooks in the internationalist mode were shot, and Stalin let it be known that a bit of old-fashioned Russian chauvinism would not be out of order. Henceforth the Russians were to be officially championed as the 'elder brother' of all other Soviet peoples. And Russia's imperial traditions were to be respected – no more poking fun at Ivan the Terrible or Peter the Great. In this way the Stalinists arrived at the recipe for mixing their own brand of nationalism with their own brand of socialism.

In the 1930s the USSR was turned into a grotesque, gargantuan laboratory of social engineering and human misery. Tens of millions toiled in indescribable deprivation to build the dams, canals, factories and new towns that the five-year plans demanded. Millions died from exhaustion, maltreatment or executions. Whole classes like the kulaks, or small landowners, were slated for elimination when agricultural land was collectivized. Whole generations were uprooted and sent for slave labour. And whole countries, like Ukraine, which had resisted, were laid waste. Never in human history has such a gigantic spectacle of applied ideology been staged. Yet few outsiders saw it. Great care was taken to ensure that Western visitors could report only the most positive images. The chief luminaries of the British Labour Party wrote a glowing survey of the 'New Civilization'.[39] The chief reporter of the *New York Times*, Walter Duranty, probably a victim of blackmail, was awarded a Pulitzer Prize for his enthusiastic descriptions, which have since been found to be completely and knowingly false.[40]

To add to the misery, Stalin mounted a campaign of state terror that makes all other forms of terrorism pale into insignificance. The scale and the audacity of the killings were unprecedented, breathtaking. Lenin had killed off most of the regime's active opponents and undesirables. The collectivization campaign had accounted for the peasants, the largest class of non-sympathizers. But from 1934 to 1939 Stalin conceived a programme for killing a large part of the regime's most devoted servants. He aimed to sow such fear and trembling, such mental paralysis, that no one, least of all his close associates, could even imagine dissent. He killed every single surviving member of Lenin's original Bolshevik government. Through endless false accusations, he created a climate of collective paranoia which cast everyone and anyone into the role of suspected spy or traitor or 'enemy'. Through orchestrated show trials, he forced distinguished Communists to confess to absurd, indecent charges. Through the so-called 'purges', he would thin the ranks of the Communist Party, and then, having put the comrades into a mood of zombie-like deference, he would order the exercise to be repeated again and again. Everyone accused would be cajoled or tortured into naming ten or twenty supposed associates in crime. By 1938 he reached the point where he was ordering the shooting of citizens by random quota: 50,000 this month from this province, 30,000 next month from the next province. The OGPU (the latest incarnation of the Cheka) sweated overtime. (They too were regularly purged.) The death pits filled up. The GULag became the biggest employer of labour in the land. State officials, artists and writers, academics and soldiers were all put through the grinder. Then, in March 1939, it stopped, or at least slowed down. The Census Bureau had just enough time to put an announcement in *Izvestia* saying that 17 million people were missing, before the census-takers themselves were shot.[41]

No society in history has ever been subjected to such traumatic self-immolation. And one wonders what effect Stalin's mass murders might have had on the Soviet Union's ability to fight the war that was coming. One suspects that a foreign war, against a genuine enemy, came as a great psychological relief. It can be no accident that the Red Army would produce both the greatest number of deserters and the greatest number of men who threw themselves into certain death with cheers on their lips. (See Chapter Four.)

The Western Powers had long believed that Soviet Communism and Soviet-inspired subversion presented the most dangerous threat to the international order. Churchill himself was an unashamed anti-Communist, and had talked of the 'baboonery' of Bolshevism. The Bolsheviks had deprived the West of its major Russian ally at a critical moment of the Great War, and had expressed nothing but contempt for the 'decadent', 'bourgeois' and 'imperialist' governments that had won the fight against the Central Powers. Western leaders were specially concerned for the fate of the fledgling states of the 'New Europe', all of which had been designed on Western models. One group of the fledglings – Poland, Czechoslovakia, Finland and the Baltics – had adopted republican constitutions based on the French Third Republic. Another group – Yugoslavia, Romania, Bulgaria and Greece – were constitutional monarchies of the quasi-British type. All of them, without exception, were firm believers in President Woodrow Wilson's theory of 'national self-determination'. All were fearful of Communism. All were squeezed into that most uncomfortable of zones with Hitler on one side and Stalin on the other.

Thanks to the victory of 1918, the prestige of Western democracy had never stood higher. Yet the 'New Europe' lay beyond the reach of immediate Western influence, and one by one the West's client states ran into trouble. Governing countries with little experience, wrestling with poverty and illiteracy, reeling from the demands of leftists and rightists, and surrounded by hostile claims from restive neighbours, the democratic rulers of East Central Europe gradually succumbed. They gave way to the temptation to demand emergency powers, and stepped onto the slippery slope of authoritarian rule. It is important to be precise. None of these 'little dictators' succumbed to Fascist or to Communist ideology. None of them introduced a one-party state. None of them resorted to the mass bloodletting that characterized Fascist and Communist mores. Instead, they restricted the powers of parliament, subjected the opposition to political chicanery, or increased the role of the army. In the process, they weakened the reputation of democracy, and undermined the trust of their original Western sponsors.

Western democracy of the interwar period, however, was beset with a much deeper problem. All the leading democratic states of Europe ran overseas empires, which they had no intention of relinquishing. By a strange sleight of hand, not always noticed, their statesmen managed to act as democrats or as imperialists as the moment required. They did so by pretending that the political rules which they enjoyed at home could not and should not be enjoyed by their subjects abroad. As a result, they were also allergic to the concept of 'national self-determination'. They were happy enough to see it applied in distant parts, like East Central Europe, where they had few vested interests, but not, God forbid, in the British Isles or the French Empire. Some of the world's leading political thinkers were well aware of the contradiction. When Mahatma Gandhi visited Europe for the first time, in 1925, he left ship at Marseilles and was immediately asked by an American reporter, 'What do you think of Western civilization?' The reply was, 'It would be a nice idea.'[42]

One has only to look at the career of Winston Churchill. A famous parliamentarian, and the author of the finest rhetoric about freedom in the

English language, he was a totally committed imperialist. He had ridden in the charge of the imperial cavalry at Omdurman, and he had served with distinction as Colonial Secretary. By the time of the Second World War, in late middle age, he had lost none of the fervour of his Victorian childhood. 'I have not become the King's First Minister,' he declared in May 1940, 'in order to preside over the demise of the British Empire.'[43] But he did.

Hypocrisy on this topic was rife. And the USA was no better than its European partners. American ideology did not stop at the Constitution. It also had a very large dose of 'anti-imperialism', dating from the War of Independence. Yet the history of US expansion across North America, and the plantation of white settlers on native-American land, is barely distinguishable from the history of expansion of European powers across Asia, Africa, South America and Australia. What is more, the USA had acquired a considerable bag of overseas colonies, from the Philippines and Hawaii to Puerto Rico and Cuba, which it showed no inclination to relinquish. Franklin D. Roosevelt, like Winston Churchill, saw no contradiction in this strange amalgam of democracy-with-imperialism.

The Soviet Union was a similar case in point. Having overthrown the Russian empire, and butchered the Tsar, the Bolsheviks were loud in their denunciation of imperialism. Yet they had not hesitated to invade and re-annexe fourteen independent countries, from Ukraine to Uzbekistan, and to incorporate them as union republics. Whenever the Soviets absorbed a new territory, a delegation would be formed to tell the Supreme Soviet that the nation concerned was begging for admission to the USSR of its own free will. All this meant is that hand-picked delegates with no independent standing had been rounded up at gunpoint to do what they were told. The dual-party state, which controlled the affairs of fraternal parties abroad, was an ideal vehicle for expanding the Soviet Empire and for giving it a semblance of spontaneity.

At first sight, apart from the Italians, the Fascists were not specially interested in imperialism. Germany had been stripped of all its colonies in 1918, and Hitler showed little enthusiasm for claiming them back. The Nazis' priorities clearly lay in Europe, and their basic assumption seems to have been that if the Axis were given a free hand there, the Western Powers would be free to hold on to their empires. (One of the house journals of the SS was called *Europa*.) The Western appeasers of 1938 saw this quite clearly. They knew that to fight simultaneously on the European continent and in distant parts of the Empire would be well-nigh impossible.

So they made a choice. Chamberlain and Halifax, both old imperialists, thought that ceding the Sudetenland was a small price to pay for saving the British Empire.

Most historians would agree that the Munich Conference revealed some very short-sighted calculations (see p. 143). Hitler swallowed the Sudetenland, and within a few months was back demanding concessions from Poland. But another, more global, mechanism was already at work. Imperial Japan was at war with China, and was looking for a European partner. After lengthy preliminaries, the Tripartite Pact of 1940 brought Germany and Italy together with Japan. It is sometimes thought to have been a somewhat vacuous treaty, signed more for the symbolism than for the substance. Yet a rarely discussed scenario was lurking in the shadows. If the Axis were able to knock out or to neutralize the Western Powers, they would automatically cut Europe's links with its overseas empires. From the viewpoint of Tokyo the prospect was irresistible. Hong Kong, Indochina, the Straits Settlements, and the Dutch East Indies (i.e. Indonesia) would all grace the list of hors d'oeuvres. For the main course, the Empire of the Sun would be thinking of Fiji, Tahiti, the Solomon Islands and Australia in one direction, and Burma, Ceylon, Madagascar and possibly India in the other.

Tokyo, however, had some further calculations to make. Japanese troops had been in China since 1931, and had set up the sham state of Manchukuo. In 1937 they had invaded the Chinese Republic, and had thereby offended the USA. Their moves had also brought them into direct contact with the eastern provinces of the USSR. The strategic implications were immense. The Red Army could not easily fight in Europe if it was also trying to defend the Far East. And the Japanese Imperial Army could not march in strength against the Russians to the north if its main resources were to be thrown against British, French and Dutch colonies to the south. Above all, the USA was not revealing its hand. Before 1941, none of the prospective participants knew which of the alternatives would materialize.[44]

In the second half of the 1930s, the rapid rise of Fascism – and in particular of Nazism – made everyone redo their sums. Everyone needed to know where the main threat was coming from. Stalin moved first. In the middle of the Second Five-Year Plan and on the eve of the purges, he was far from ready to commit the USSR to war. So he ordered Maxim Litvinov, his foreign commissar, to don a black top hat, to join the League of Nations, and to proclaim the policy of 'collective security'. All the European Communist parties, who had been striving for nearly twenty years to subvert their democratic rivals, were ordered to switch tack and to engage in leftish coalitions or 'popular fronts'. At the same time, all Soviet propaganda organs began to disseminate a new ideological construct. 'Anti-Fascism' proved quite attractive. The Italian and German regimes were identified as the threat. All right-thinking people, whatever their particular views, should stand shoulder to shoulder against the mounting menace. Western intellectuals fell for the ploy en masse. They felt little affinity with Germany, though some believed the Germans had been harshly treated at Versailles. But they regretted the alienation of Russia, and welcomed the rehabilitation of the Soviet Union as a normal, 'peace-loving' country. They were also aware of a selfish, geopolitical angle. Russia was far away. Even if the Bolsheviks were going to cut loose, it was Eastern Europe that would be ravaged. But the Germans and the Italians were close at hand. If the Fascists went on the rampage, they would try to settle accounts in Western Europe. Better by far, therefore, to strengthen the fences against Fascism.

Needless to say, 'anti-Fascism' did not offer a coherent political ideology. In terms of ideas, it was an empty vessel, a mere political dance. It showed its adherents what to oppose, not what to believe in. It gave the false impression that principled democrats believing in the rule of law and freedom of speech could rub along fine with the dictators of the proletariat, or that democratic socialists had only minor differences with Communism. What is more, it opened up a wonderful arena for the activities of disciplined activists, whose training in the Leninist techniques of splitting and dividing adversaries would run rings round woolly intellectuals. But no matter! If you were a French trade unionist, tired of the wrangles of the Left, or a British Empire loyalist baffled by the complexities of modern politics or a Christian peace worker hoping to avoid another war, anti-Fascism was for you! Only in the background was the unspoken dialectic that, if Fascism was to be Bad, the Good had to lie with the originator of anti-Fascism – Joseph Stalin's USSR.

In 1936–9, many thinking Westerners still sat on the fence. They disliked Fascism, but they were uneasy about Communism. However, they felt that war might be coming, and that they could not fence-sit indefinitely. They were dismayed when, despite much rhetoric, their governments failed to deter Mussolini in Abyssinia. They were disgusted by the fall of Czechoslovakia. But they were thoroughly scared by developments in Spain. It was the Spanish Civil War that finally pushed them into making up their minds. It is difficult to know what might have transpired if Franco had lost. Western public opinion might have woken up to the fact that the republican cause had been usurped by Stalinists, and that in Barcelona the Stalinists had been mass-murdering their fellow leftists. But in the spring of 1939 Franco won, and, with the support of Italian troops and German warplanes, Fascism triumphed. Franco could be blamed for everything. Spain was uncomfortably close. Western Europe needed to fight Fascism to survive.

Within six months of Franco's victory, Hitler had invaded Poland and the war began. The anti-Fascist movement would have been universally acclaimed, but for the awkward surprise of Stalin joining up with Hitler. For almost two years the anti-Fascists were in total disarray. In 1940, following Stalin's refusal to withdraw from Finland, Britain and France came within an ace of finding themselves at war with the Soviet Union as well as the Third Reich. Then the world came to rights. Hitler invaded the USSR, and declared war on the USA. The Grand Coalition was formed. The 'Big Three', consisting of the world's chief capitalist, the world's most eloquent democrat-imperialist and the leader of world Communism, joined forces. And anti-Fascism came back into fashion with a vengeance. It proved particularly well suited to the American outlook, which badly needed a moral crusade against Evil, which warmed to Soviet denunciations of imperialism, and which reacted well to pragmatic appeals for all to pull together. Roosevelt's entourage was riddled with fellow-travellers, who were incapable of grasping the nature of Stalin's regime. Churchill's ministries were penetrated by Soviet agents, who blocked many attempts at more realistic thinking. And Stalin posed unruffled as the benevolent 'Uncle Joe'. Such was the reigning political climate of the wartime coalition. Such was the spirit in which the pioneering accounts of the war were written. And such are sources of the misconception which have bedevilled any proper understanding ever since.

The political context

It is a tautology to say that the Second World War was first and foremost a power struggle. Of course it was. All wars are struggles for power. Both Hitler and Stalin were minded to overthrow the interwar settlement, which had been framed without the active participation of either Germany or Soviet Russia. Mussolini was of similar mind. The Western Powers – which by 1939 meant Britain, France and Poland – were determined not to relinquish the established European order without a fight. They had the sympathy, if not yet the active support, of the US administration. So a clash of political wills had self-evidently arisen.

However, if politics may be likened to a game, it is not a sport with fixed rules of play, with two balanced sides, or with a referee. One of the manifest complications of the international situation in 1939 was that the recognized referee appointed after the preceding world war – the League of Nations – had already been sidelined. Chamberlain and Daladier, the prime ministers of Britain and France, who should have been its protectors, had addressed the Czechoslovak crisis in 1938 without reference to the League. The Third Reich had left the League, just as the Soviet Union was to be expelled in 1940.

Personalities provide an important factor in politics. They determine how the leading players will react when the ball comes in their direction. Adolf Hitler was impetuous, reckless, boiling with resentments, disinclined to seek advice. Joseph Stalin was paranoically mistrustful, cold, calculating, patient and, when the time came to strike, deadly. Both had the traits of gangsters: hardened to killing, fond of humiliating others, allergic to opposition. Churchill, in contrast, had practised democratic politics for nearly forty years. He had the constitution of a horse, a head for hard liquor, and a fearless disregard for the quirks of fortune. Psychologically, he was a fighter, a man who could not be bullied, who freely chose his ever more dominant partner. Roosevelt was far more devious, an adept at political marketing, a smooth-talking operator who, by the time of his third term, was confident of his historic mission to bring the USA from Depression to world dominance. All made mistakes. All survived to the last month of the European war. None was effectively challenged.

Above all, politics is a chaotic, unscrupulous and dynamic game, in which the players are not equal, the goalposts are frequently shifted, and any of the parties can take the lead and drive the action according to their own whim or judgement. On this latter point, almost all observers are agreed that in the late 1930s and early 1940s it was Adolf Hitler's Germany which was driving the action. Whereas the Western leaders were essentially conservative, aiming only to keep what they held, and whereas Stalin was as cautious as he was cunning, Hitler was a gambler, a bluffer and a shameless poseur. He was prepared to chance his arm, to risk bringing the world down in flames. He was a Hun in a hurry. And his haste was not completely reckless. Huge industrial capacity meant that Germany could probably rearm faster than any rival. The Western Powers were led by indecisive mediocrities. The USSR was embroiled in the most appalling craze of internal bloodletting. Like the Kaiser before him, Hitler must have been forcibly impressed by the argument that Germany must strike before its rivals were fully on their feet.

So Hitler struck – time after time. In 1938 he struck against Austria – with impunity. Later that year he threatened to strike against Czechoslovakia, and the appeasers came running. In 1939 he struck against Czechoslovakia in March, and he struck against Poland in September, at minimal cost, and the Soviets joined him. In 1940 he struck at France and Britain, winning a famous victory. In 1941 he struck at Yugoslavia in April and at the USSR in June. After each strike his forces grew stronger. He could have been forgiven for thinking that his modus operandi was based on hard experience and a sound record.

In the first phase of the war, the configuration of combatants took a shape that few had foreseen. The Third Reich and Fascist Italy faced the Western Powers (Britain, France and Poland), but, thanks to the Nazi–Soviet Pact of 1939, Hitler and Mussolini were joined by Stalin's USSR, which emerged as a political partner of the Axis, if not a formal ally. A proposal to bring the USSR into the Tripartite Pact was made, but the terms were never agreed (see Diagram below).

Having participated in the invasion of Poland, Stalin put the USSR into a state of war with the Polish Republic, but not with France or Britain. Soviet oil flowed to Germany to strengthen Hitler's war machine, and Soviet propaganda attacked the 'decadent', 'reactionary' 'capitalists' of the West with venom. In this setting, the dictators could attack their neighbours with impunity. With the Reich's eastern border secure, Hitler was free to turn against the West. Stalin was free to invade Finland, then

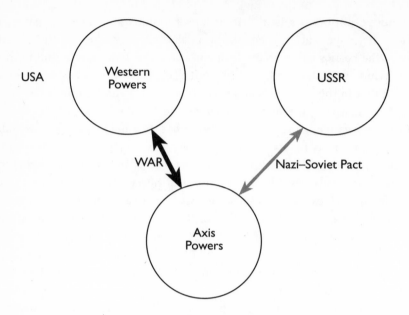

Estonia, Latvia and Lithuania, and to threaten Romania. This was the season for international gangsterism.

The politics of the Axis Pact were at best perfunctory. The leaders of the eight member states never met together. No serious attempt was made to give greater substance to the Tripartite Pact with Japan, signed in September 1940. After 1941, the only big issue was the coordination of support for the Wehrmacht on the Eastern Front. The Nazis proposed and the underlings disposed. Friction arose between Berlin and Rome when the Italians refused to hand over their Jews. But Hitler never lost his affection for Mussolini, who 'showed that everything was possible'. When Mussolini was deposed and arrested, in July 1943, he was rescued by German parachutists and set up for the rest of the war in the puppet 'Republic of Salò' in northern Italy. (See p. 180.)

Throughout those years, the world merely reacted to the events which Hitler had set in motion. As often as not, it reacted by choosing to do nothing. The USA, in particular, chose not to intervene. It did not move even when Nazi Germany invaded the USSR and brought the Allied cause to the brink of disaster. But then the Americans were attacked themselves. The US Pacific Fleet was dive-bombed without warning at Pearl Harbor in Hawaii on 7 December 1941, the 'day of infamy'. Three days later, to please his Japanese allies, Hitler declared war on the USA. With German

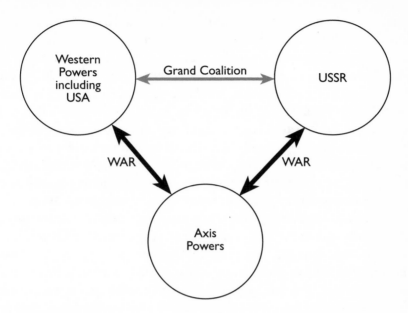

panzers at the gates of Moscow, he calculated that the war would be over before his act of bravado could be punished.

In the middle phase of the war, therefore, the configuration of powers changed diametrically. The Soviet Union, the largest combatant state, ceased to be Hitler's partner and became his mortal enemy overnight. The USA, the world's leading economic power, joined Britain at the head of the remaining Western Allies. The Third Reich found itself in the uncomfortable position of facing a war on two fronts – Germany's historic nightmare. Although the 'Second Front' was very slow to emerge, it was always going to happen if the Wehrmacht was unable to deal a knockout blow to one or other of its main opponents (see diagram above).

After a long period of near paralysis, the Western Powers began to make some important plans of their own. In 1941–2 Churchill took the lead in forming what he called the 'Grand Coalition'. He had won the goodwill of President Roosevelt long before the USA formally entered the war. As early as January 1941, arrangements were made for British and US staffs to discuss military logistics; and the Lend-Lease scheme was operating as from March 1941. The Atlantic Charter of August 1941, signed aboard USS *Augusta*, was a disappointment to Churchill, since it was a poor substitute for his desire to draw the USA into the war immediately. And, in any case, some of its clauses were never observed. But it was a public declaration of intent which bore fruit in January 1942 when it was endorsed by the twenty-six signatories to the Joint Declaration of the United Nations. It was Churchill who also decided to formalize the common cause between the Western Powers and the Soviet Union, even though, as he freely admitted, he was 'supping with the Devil'. The Anglo-Soviet Treaty of 26 May 1942, signed by Eden and Molotov, stated the principles of 'no territorial aggrandisement' and of 'non-interference' in foreign countries – both totally ignored. But it also included a vital clause that was honoured, forbidding either party to declare a unilateral truce with Nazi Germany. A further clause about mutual military assistance led to Stalin's well-grounded demands for a 'Second Front' in the West.

Apart from Lend-Lease, which was extended to the USSR, Roosevelt's main contribution to these arrangements was the concept of 'unconditional surrender', first unveiled at a press conference following the Casablanca Conference of January 1943. At the time, he tried to pretend that it was a spontaneous idea. But historians would later establish that it was the fruit of a well-considered policy. It angered people who wished for an early end to the war and who wanted to enjoy flexibility when negotiating with Italy and Germany. Yet there can be little doubt that it was inspired by the realization in Washington's ruling circles that the USA was emerging as a superpower. Whilst all the European combatants were damaged and increasingly exhausted, America was feeling its rapidly growing strength, and was concerned lest the war be ended before its strength could be used to reap a wide range of strategic benefits. So Roosevelt was merciless. At a slightly later stage he was to agree a proposal that Germany be reduced to a primarily agricultural economy. In other words, the European continent would cease to be a serious competitor for US firms.[45]

The politics of the Grand Coalition have spawned many books and many interpretations. They provide a prime example of 'the long night of incompatible bedfellows'. A short description might show how the Western leaders talked intensively on their side of the bed, while largely leaving their Soviet bedfellow to his own devices. Their relations possessed two main characteristics. Firstly, and from the start, the 'Big Three' rejected any form of democratic management and kept all major decisions under their personal control. The great majority of coalition members were rarely consulted, even on matters that affected their vital interests. Secondly, business was conducted at periodic international conferences, and between conferences by telegram and less frequently by radio telephone. (There was no transcontinental telephone cable available for secure conversations.) The 'Big Three' managed to get together on only two occasions: at the Eureka Conference in Teheran (November–December 1943) and at the Argonaut Conference in Yalta (February 1945). At Yalta, Roosevelt secured Stalin's promise to join the war against Japan, and in return accepted a face-saving formula over the future of Eastern Europe. The cracks were cleverly papered over. By the time of Potsdam, in July 1945, Roosevelt was dead and the European war was over. (See Chapter Three, pp. 131–203)

It was obviously a triumph of international diplomacy to keep the Grand Coalition in being throughout three momentous years. It should also be obvious that mistakes were made. But some of the mistakes were not mended, and some of the splits were not healed. Chiang Kai-shek, the Chinese ally, was excluded from senior counsels, despite being a major combatant. So too were the Poles. In April 1943 the USSR broke off diplomatic relations with the government of Poland on a trumped-up pretext, thereby fulfilling the Nazis' hopes of creating a rift in the Allied camp. Enormous pressure was put on the Poles to admit what they knew to be untrue about the Katyn massacres. But no pressure was put on the Soviets to drop the feud for which they were almost solely responsible. Similarly, the Allied Yugoslav government and its exiled king, Peter, were callously dropped in 1944, when the Western Powers decided to switch support to Tito's partisans. All these decisions were to have catastrophic consequences in the post-war period.

In the last phase of the war, the political clout of the USA was growing by leaps and bounds. Churchill had to cede much to Roosevelt. Washington was the place where the most important plans were being laid. The USA was the only power to be fully engaged both in the Pacific and in Europe. It was the quartermaster of the coalition, and the paymaster of many struggling allied states, including Britain. And its home territory was completely unscarred. What is more, its ruling circles were motivated by a cheerful political philosophy of extreme naivety. They ensured that Roosevelt's goal of unconditional surrender against Germany and Japan would be achieved, and that the British Empire would disintegrate. But also, by feeding Soviet ambitions, they ensured that the world would be brought to the brink of destruction as soon as the Soviet Union achieved nuclear parity.

In this context, therefore, one needs to consider some of the matters that were not decided. The most important of these was the issue of spheres of influence. In 1942–3 the Western Allies, who had no significant troops on the continent, had been obliged to give priority to the task of keeping the Red Army fighting. So they assumed that the USSR should enjoy a sphere of influence on the Eastern Front, just as they would have their own sphere in liberated West European countries. They were pretty disturbed when Stalin took an interest in the future of Italy – where there was a strong Communist movement – and they were inhibited at the prospect of 'interfering' in Eastern Europe. As a result, nothing was done to define what a sphere of influence actually implied. Was it just a theatre of military action, for example, where the dominant Power or Powers were entitled to a free hand in all military decisions? Or was it supposed to be a sphere of total political control, where the dominant Power could install puppet governments at will, shoot political opponents, deport civilians by the million, and suppress the anti-Nazi underground? No one ever said. None of the Western leaders could bring themselves to ask whether the Atlantic Charter was supposed to apply to all its signatories. In the short run a possible source of friction was avoided. But in the long term the consequences were fatal. In the first instance, the price would be paid by the Baltic States and by Poland, a Western ally whose territory lay in the (undefined) Soviet sphere. But eventually the price would be paid by the Western Powers themselves. For their failure to address this key wartime issue sowed the seeds of the Cold War. From the historical point of view, the interesting question concerns the reasons why the Allies persisted with their non-dialogue to the very end of the war. It may have been politic to let a sleeping dog lie when the coalition was fragile. But in 1944–5, when the Western Powers were gaining in strength and when Stalin would not have offended them lightly, it was in everyone's interests to clarify matters. One cannot say how Stalin might have reacted. The point is: the Western leaders never even tried.[46]

As the European war approached its denouement, no shift occurred in the configuration of major powers. The Grand Coalition stood firm. But, as Germany proved ever more incapable of protecting its clients, the clients switched sides. Italy switched in 1943. Romania followed Italy's example in August 1944, France in the same month, Bulgaria in September 1944, Belgium in October 1944, and Hungary in January 1945. Elsewhere, liberation came too late for pro-coalition regimes to be formed. Several extra-European states, notably Mexico and Brazil, had declared war on the Axis earlier. But the ultimate act of political daring was committed by Chile, which declared war on Germany on 11 April 1945. By that time, as the Reich was being crushed, only two significant political groupings were

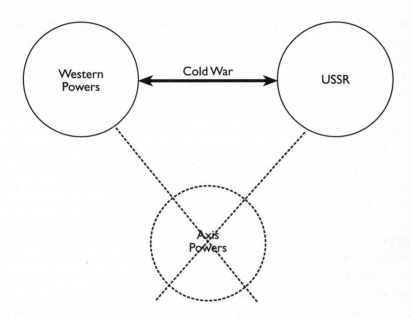

left: the Western Powers and their clients on one side, and the Soviet Union and its satellites on the other. Stalin suspected to the very end that the German leadership might jump into the Western camp and that a grand capitalist crusade would be launched against the USSR. It never materialized. Instead, having destroyed the Axis completely, the two parts of the victorious Grand Coalition were left chin to chin, eyeballing each other in a stand-off that would soon be called 'the Cold War'.[47]

The moral landscape

All sound moral judgements operate on the basis that the standards applied to one side of a relationship must be applied to all sides. It is not acceptable that certain acts by an ill-favoured party be condemned as 'foul murder' if similar acts by a more favoured party be somehow excused or overlooked. Double standards are abhorrent.

Secondly, as Nurse Edith Cavell commented before her execution in 1915, 'Patriotism is not enough.' 'My country, right or wrong!' is an amoral slogan. We cannot hold that bad behaviour by our own side is automatically beyond reproach, or that it is necessarily ennobled by association with a good cause. By the same token, we cannot deny that particular sorts of conduct by the enemy may be judged good, even if the enemy is rightly associated with an evil cause.

Lastly, it is essential that all moral judgements, all attempts to assess whether something be 'Good' or 'Evil', be made by reference to universal principles and not to partisan feelings of hatred or contempt. In this regard, it is useful to recall the categories of conduct that were established by the Nuremberg Tribunal in order to define wartime criminality. The three categories were (1) waging war against international peace, aka wars of aggression; (2) war crimes; and (3) crimes against humanity. Of course, the tribunal was dealing with conduct that could be judged criminal in the light of international law, and not just with conduct that might be judged morally reprehensible. Nonetheless, one may assume that anything that is criminal and illegal will probably be reprehensible as well.

Waging war is not in itself either illegal or reprehensible. All moral systems recognize the right of self-defence, both for individuals and for states. Countries which are attacked, and whose troops observe the highest standards of minimum force, may thus wage war with a clear conscience. But wars of aggression are a different matter. They may be defined as conflicts that are launched as a deliberate act of policy, without provocation, and without regard for the injured party's rights to security and sovereignty. Fascist Italy's attack on Abyssinia in 1936 and the Third Reich's attacks on Poland, Norway, Denmark, Holland, Belgium, Yugoslavia and the USSR would be clear examples of aggression. Germany's attack on France and Britain in 1940 presents a more complicated case, at least technically, since France and Britain had both declared war on Germany – not vice versa.

War crimes may be defined as breaches of the Geneva and Hague conventions regarding prohibited practices in warfare. They cover a host of categories, including the maltreatment of POWs, refugees and non-combatants, the use of unreasonable force and of prohibited weapons (such as poison gas); the violation of hospitals and of medical staff, the taking of hostages, the bombing or shelling of civilian targets; the prevalence of looting, rape, beatings and murder by undisciplined soldiery. Generally speaking, German forces were thought to have behaved with much greater restraint in the West than on the Eastern Front. They may have been influenced by the fact that their British and American adversaries had signed the relevant conventions, whilst the USSR had not. Nonetheless, there were numerous instances of war crimes in the West. One may mention the shooting of American POWs at Malmédy, or the massacre of civilians at Oradour-sur-Glane near Limoges in June 1944, or the indiscriminate bombardment of London by V-1 and V-2 rockets.

The category of crimes against humanity was entirely new and untried in 1945. It concerned campaigns of mass terror, mass repression, mass deportation and genocide. The concept of genocide gained currency from 1944 onward only thanks to the efforts of a Polish lawyer, Rafał Lemkin, who was employed by the United Nations. The modern term of 'ethnic cleansing' had not been invented. But the type of atrocity with which it is now associated was common enough in 1939–45, especially in Yugoslavia, in the Baltic States, and in eastern Poland. The perpetration by the Nazis of the 'Final Solution of the Jewish Question', subsequently known as the Holocaust, is almost universally recognized as the prime example of a crime against humanity.

Few analysts would argue with this categorization. The trouble arises when an attempt is made to apply these categories in an even-handed manner to all the combatant states. For many war crimes that were revealed or documented only twenty or thirty years after the war were simply not known about in the immediately post-war period. And citizens of the victorious Powers grew accustomed to the idea that the war record of their own nations was immaculate. The censorship of the Soviet Bloc ensured that all war crimes were exclusively attributed to the defeated Fascist enemy. Owing to the indisputably atrocious record of the Axis Powers in general, and of the Nazis in particular as revealed at Nuremberg, no conflict has ever aroused such strong convictions in Britain and America of being a just war, fairly contested by the Allies, and rightly won by the champions of freedom and democracy.

Yet a cursory glance at the full list of horrors as subsequently established will suffice to show that the record is not so simple. On many counts, the anti-Fascist coalition was responsible for unnatural death on no less vast a scale than the Fascist enemy. From what is now known about the forced-collectivization campaign, the Ukrainian terror famine, the purges and the GULag, it is manifestly evident that the Stalinist party state in the USSR must be classed as a criminal regime before the war began, and it continued to commit mass crimes both during and after the war. It can be charged with wars of aggression – against Poland, Finland and the Baltic States – with war crimes of every sort – from the murder and maltreatment of POWs (including its own) to the sinking of refugee ships and the mass raping of German women – and with crimes against humanity. On this last point, the *Black Book of Communism*, which was inspired by a group of ex-Communists after the fall of the USSR, argues with some force that the crime of 'classocide', i.e. the killing of human beings simply because of their social class, is no less pernicious than the crime of genocide.[48] Other deplorable episodes in which wholesale mortality was the norm would include the mass deportations to Siberia and the Arctic of millions of innocent civilians from Soviet-occupied countries, and the mass expulsion to Central Asia on trumped-up charges of collaboration of entire nationalities, such as the Chechens, the Crimean Tatars and the Volga Germans. These massive offences left a deep stain.

The tremendous scale of Soviet transgressions was kept hidden for decades. The world had watched the show trials of the 1930s and had vaguely heard of the GULag, but a devoted band of Moscow-inspired 'specialists' insisted for years that victims were to be numbered in only hundreds, or perhaps thousands. Even after Khrushchev's speech in 1956, which limited its criticism to crimes against the Communist Party, interested Westerners were constantly told that the writings of Alexander Solzhenitsyn, or the research work of Robert Conquest, were vicious 'anti-Communist fantasies'. Another tack was to say that bad things might have happened in the 1930s, when Stalin's social omelette-making broke some eggs, but that the Soviet war record was unblemished. Eventually, when the USSR finally collapsed, it turned out that nothing much had improved during the war, that Conquest had been pretty close to the truth all along, and that the victims of Stalin's rule were to be counted not in hundreds or thousands, or even millions, but in tens of millions.

The most frequent reaction in the West was to say that, whilst the crimes of Nazism were proven and officially condemned, the crimes of Stalinism were still under investigation. Some people recoil from condemning Bolshevism, knowing that the Nazis saw Bolshevism as their chief foe and fearing to share a platform with Hitler. They should have a bit more faith in their own principles. Anyone genuinely committed to freedom, justice and democracy is duty-bound to condemn both of the great totalitarian systems without fear or favour. If one finds two gangsters fighting each other, it is no valid approach at all to round on one and to lay off the other. The only valid test is whether or not they deserve the label of gangsters. If they do, it may be politically inconvenient but the only moral response is to declare 'a plague on both your houses'.

Historians of the Second World War, therefore, cannot indefinitely ignore the implications of the catastrophic collapse of Stalin's reputation since the good old days of 'Uncle Joe'. Hard evidence now exists that he was a habitual mass-murderer throughout his career, and the idea that his crimes were somehow less obscene because he fought on the right side is worse than dubious. After decades of hesitation, commentators are at last beginning to express the unthinkable, namely that 'the contest of the evil dictators was really too close to call.'[49] In response to the latest damning study of 'The Court of the Red Tsar', a British socialist and historian gave vent to feelings that most would now share:

> Because I want to retain my faith in human nature, I would like to believe that Stalin and his henchmen were all clinically insane. Surely, people who wallow in blood – metaphorically when they order the slaughter of seven million kulaks and literally when they beat old friends to death – must have lost the ability to distinguish between right and wrong . . . Stalin and those who served him continued the policy of mass murder for almost 30 years, liquidating all who were thought to stand in their way. And for good measure they liquidated their enemies' wives and children, too. The blood ran so thick and deep that it presents historians with a problem . . . Contempt mixed with disbelief is the only decent reaction to the discovery of what Stalin did. It was beyond any sort of justification . . .
>
> Yet Stalin retained the admiration of some Western democrats right to the end of his life. Of course, they did not know how vile he was, but they should at least have suspected. [Nowadays] there is no longer the slightest justification for thinking that Joseph Stalin was anything other than a monster.'[50]

Nor should the Western Powers feel too smug about numerous accusations against themselves. The Strategic Bombing Offensive, which killed perhaps half a million civilians, has long been the subject for charges of 'excessive force', and if the German raid on Coventry, which killed 380 persons, is judged a crime, it is hard to see why the British raids on Cologne, Hamburg, Kassel, Berlin and Dresden should not be classed in the same way. In morality, two wrongs do not make a right, and pleas of justified response do not wash. If a criminal kills another man's brother, the injured party is not entitled, even in the middle of a just war, to go off and kill all the criminal's neighbours and relatives. And there are further matters to be examined. One of them would be the forcible and large-scale repatriation of Soviet citizens in 1945 to near-certain death at the hands of Stalin's security organs. Another would be the joint Allied decision that was reached at Potsdam to expel by force several million German civilians from lands newly allotted to Poland, Czechoslovakia and Hungary. To contemporary sensitivities, the Potsdam decision put into motion a campaign that looks suspiciously like 'ethnic cleansing'.

The fact is: British and American officialdom does not have a track record of impartiality. Like Soviet officialdom, it has upheld the fiction that all war crimes were committed by the enemy. The British War Crimes Act (1991), for example, confines its scope to acts 'committed by the Germans or on German-occupied territory'. Anything more self-evidently biased it would be hard to find. Yet it is not an isolated example. US immigration law, which once (unjustly) discriminated against Communists, now excludes only individuals who in some way were connected with the repressive organs of the Third Reich. In other words, former executioners from the NKVD – the wartime Soviet Security Service – are still welcome. The Office of Special Investigations only pursues wretched persons like John Demjanjuk, who have been charged and punished, often unjustly, with Nazi connections real or imagined.[51] The notion of regarding all war criminals as equally abhorrent is absent. Official prejudice of this sort inevitably strengthens the impression that the Grand Coalition of 1941–5 was not whiter than snow.

Even so, a moral reckoning can still be drawn up. In this regard, the balance sheet between Hitler's Third Reich and Stalin's Soviet Union is worth outlining. Examples abound in all categories. Morally, the German invasion of the USSR in 1941 was no more blatant than the Soviet invasion of Finland in 1939. A war crime such as the murder of eighty-six American POWs at Malmédy is dwarfed by the Katyn massacre, where up to 25,000 POWs were murdered. The Nazis' 'Final Solution' had no parallel. But there were any number of Soviet atrocities, including mass deportations and repressions and man-made famines, that fit the criteria for crimes against humanity.

One should perhaps add a rider to insist that no exact 'equivalence of evil' is implied. Moral reckoning is not a mathematical exercise. Whilst the total volume of Soviet criminality clearly outstripped that of the Third Reich – partly because the USSR was operating for much longer – it is not evident that the Soviet machine of repression replicated all the worst categories of inhumanity. For example, the biggest installations of the GULag, at Kolyma or Vorkuta, easily outsized the largest SS concentration camps at Auschwitz or Majdanek.[52] Yet the Soviet system seems to have had no equivalent to the dedicated Nazi death factories such as Treblinka, Sobibór or Bełżec (see p. 168). In this respect it is only to be regretted that Auschwitz, and not Treblinka, has been chosen as the emblematic site of remembrance for the Jewish Holocaust. It is no less paradoxical that the liberators of Auschwitz were servants of a regime that ran still larger concentration camps than the one which they liberated. Unless one grasps this paradox, one can never really face the issues at stake.

Much ink has flowed on the subject of the Strategic Bombing Offensive, and it would be rash to offer a final judgement. Two questions have to be answered, however. One asks whether the policy of 'area bombing' was consciously designed as 'terror bombing' from the outset. The other would ask why the RAF persisted with the policy even when it became manifest that vast numbers of innocent men, women and children were being slaughtered to no purpose. Anyone seeking the truth in this conundrum has to wrestle with the quotation from Bomber Harris himself: 'We shall take out one German city after another,' he boasted, 'like pulling teeth.'[53]

The issue of people forcibly repatriated to the Soviet Union in 1945 has attracted less attention, though it involved huge numbers. Those concerned were a diverse collection of people whom the Soviet authorities claimed as their own, even though many had never set foot in the USSR and most of the others expressed the strongest disinclination to return. Mass suicides were common. And mass shootings on the dockside were reported by British observers who escorted the repatriation ships to Odessa or Murmansk. The first contingent was collected by British forces in 1944 from the slave labourers used by the Nazis to build the Atlantic Wall in Normandy. The biggest single contingent came from the Cossack Brigade and its dependants, who eagerly gave themselves up to the British Army in Austria in May 1945.[54]

The expulsion of all ethnic Germans from the former German provinces to the east of the River Oder provoked little comment in the years between 1945 and 1948 when it was put into effect. British and American opinion looked aside, believing the transfers to be the natural fate of members of a defeated and guilty nation. Certainly the government of Czechoslovakia, which formulated the harshest 'Beneš Decrees', was not yet dominated by Communists and made no effort to hide its belief in the justice of collective punishment. In Poland, whence the largest contingent of Germans was removed, the transfers were deemed essential to make room for the millions of Poles then being expelled by the Soviets from

Poland's lost eastern provinces. (Few people in Allied circles doubted the right of the victorious Soviets to do as they thought fit.)[55] In Slovakia, a large contingent of Hungarians suffered the same fate. The German expellees were received and sheltered in West Germany, but were widely seen as a vociferous community of right-wing troublemakers. It was only after German unification in 1990 that the issue resurfaced. The median estimate of the total expelled stands at 8 million. Many were children who could not by any stretch of the imagination be held responsible for the sins of the Nazi regime. Innocent and guilty were punished indiscriminately. Though the original proposal came from Moscow (which revived a similar plan dating from 1914), the final decision was the work of Truman and Attlee, as well as Stalin. Anyone who cannot see that deep moral problems were involved must be morally astigmatic.

Taken overall, therefore, the landscape of war crimes is rather more complicated than many Westerners might like to admit. Any discussion of wartime morality does not end with war crimes, however. Most crimes may be immoral, but all forms of immorality are not necessarily criminal. The absence of criminal charges is not the same thing as a clean moral sheet. This conundrum was to raise its head in 1945 at the Nuremberg Tribunal, which the historian A. J. P. Taylor chose to characterize as a 'macabre farce' (see p. 198).

Two conclusions spring to mind. Firstly, no side in the Second World War possesses a monopoly either of virtue or of immorality. Even when fully justified, war is a dirty business which can foul those who set out with pure hearts and noble intentions. It is a collective activity governed by severe discipline, where individuals can be caught up in activities which they personally may abhor. And, since it is a branch of politics that shuns compromises so long as the fighting lasts, it turns victory into an absolute desideratum and drives combatants into desperate alliances, sometimes with indecent company. In the case of the Soviet Union, it drove Stalin to combine first with the hated Nazis and then with the despised Western democracies. Both of these steps were contrary to the conventions of Communist morality. In the case of the Western Powers, the exigencies of war drove them to ally with a totalitarian state whose commitment to freedom, justice and democracy was no greater than Hitler's. Victory was achieved. Moral and political principles were deserted.

Secondly, the standard dialectical model of 'Good' fighting 'Evil' is demonstrably inappropriate. A dialectical or 'bipolar' view of the world was shared both by Soviet Communists and by some Anglo-Saxons. A single-minded crusade against Fascism suited the predispositions of the Soviet elite for reasons of political philosophy and of many Anglo-Americans for reasons connected with their puritanical traditions. Both of them had a Fascist devil before their eyes, and both were too preoccupied to worry very much about the implications.

Yet, sixty years on, it is high time to weigh the moral implications more carefully. No proper definition of 'Evil' can rest on the simple assertion that Evil is the Enemy. Before deciding that a particular political leader or a particular regime can be fairly classified as evil, the moralist must make a cold calculation based on the candidate's stated intentions and proven practices. Here the historian stands on firmer ground than was possible half a century ago. If one sits back and forgets one's ingrained reactions, one should be able to see that the war in Europe was dominated by two evil monsters, not by one. Each of the monsters consumed the best people in its territory before embarking on a fight to the death for supremacy. The third force in the struggle – the Western Powers – was all but eliminated in the opening stage, and took much of the war to reassert its influence. Its essentially conservative stance, its devotion to democracy and the rule of law, its respect for the rights of individuals, and its attachment to traditional Christian teachings (still apparent in the 1940s) were all completely alien to both Communists and Fascists alike. Everyone who values the concept of liberty as it developed in Europe and America must give thanks that the 'third force' helped prevent both Hitler and Stalin from attaining hegemony. At the same time, they must also admit that the outcome was at best ambiguous, that the victory of the West was only partial, and that the moral reputation of the Allied Coalition was severely tarnished. If, after considering all this they can still bring themselves to identify the West with the 'Good', they are entitled to do so. But they can surely do it only with extensive reservations. At least they can rest assured that there was no other candidate among the combatants to lay claim to moral admiration.

All in all, the moral landscape emerges as a bumpy terrain, with many deep canyons and few commanding heights. Yet, having sketched its contours, one can now proceed to consider the priorities for an outline narrative of the war in Europe. Geographically, the emphasis must unquestionably lie in Eastern Europe – the object of Nazi ambitions, the base of Soviet power, the scene of the Holocaust and other major atrocities, and the region where perhaps three-quarters of the fighting took place. It cannot possibly be in Western Europe. Militarily, the focus must centre on German–Soviet hostilities, though sufficient space must also be found for the Battle of the Atlantic, for the war in the air and, in the final months, for the Western Front. Ideologically, priority must be given to the three-sided arena in which Fascism, Communism and liberal democracy confronted each other. It cannot possibly be given to the jaded and inadequate concept of anti-Fascism. And it cannot avoid the reality that the democratic camp was inextricably bound up with imperialism. Politically, the priority must be to stress how the war passed through successive stages: the first, where the Third Reich and the USSR were acting in concert; the second, where the Grand Coalition came into being; and the last one, where the military dominance of the Red Army was joined by the fast-growing political and economic dominance of the USA. All other events must somehow be related to this central scenario. To make sense, the wartime narrative must be preceded by a summary of how the pre-war order was steadily subverted, especially in Eastern Europe. And it must be followed by a short postscript showing how the unfinished business of 1939–45 set the agenda of the Cold War. Finally, in the moral sphere, the essential aim must be to demonstrate that the conflict of 1939–45 was largely concerned with the clash of two great evils, and that the third force – sometimes identified by Westerners with the Good – was fortunate to survive and to figure among the victors.

CHAPTER TWO

WARFARE

Military Action in Europe, 1939–1945

Phase 1, September 1939–June 1941:
the pre-war order overturned

THE SECOND WORLD WAR did *not* start in 1941, in 1940, or even on 3 September 1939. It began at 4.45 a.m. on 1 September 1939. At that exact minute the German cruiser *Schleswig-Holstein*, moored in the port of Danzig (Gdańsk) on a friendship visit, opened fire at point-blank range on the Polish fort of Westerplatte. Simultaneously, as dawn broke, the German Wehrmacht poured across the frontier of Poland in a score of locations – from the west, from the north and from the south. It was an act of undeclared war: but of war undisputedly.

Taken by surprise, many thought that Hitler might have launched a limited, local conflict. In reality, much more was in play. For one thing, since appeasement had clearly failed, the Western Powers were not going to take this latest provocation sitting down. For another, the Soviet Union was already actively involved. Hitler had invaded Poland only on the unpublished understanding that Stalin would follow suit. Unknown to the outside world, the secret protocols of the Nazi–Soviet Pact, and the secret talks in Moscow that surrounded them, had provided for the joint partition of Eastern Europe. German officials would soon begin to scream when the Red Army did not appear quite as quickly as they had expected.

The declaration of war by Britain and France on 3 September had serious military implications. Despite the failure to come to the aid of their Polish ally, the planners in London and Paris were not going to fall into the trap of 1914, when a supposedly short war turned out to be a long one. This time they were set to prepare methodically for a long war from the start. Their disposition had very definite consequences. It meant not only that Poland could be sacrificed, but also, even if Poland fell, that the state of war in Europe would continue.

The Western Powers were in a quandary, and much of the confusion of September 1939 has remained unchallenged in the history books. They had been told during the Munich Crisis of the previous autumn that the cession of the Sudetenland was 'Herr Hitler's final demand'. They had been outmanoeuvred into accepting a self-evident lie. They were now being told by Soviet diplomats that the USSR was 'neutral'. They accepted it, at least in public, not because they necessarily believed it, but because the prospect of fighting simultaneousy against both Germany and the Soviet Union was less than convenient. Even so, the time would soon come when preparations for such a double war would have to be made.

Many historians, wise after the event, continue to argue that the Nazi–Soviet Pact was just 'a temporary arrangement', a convenient holding manoeuvre between reluctant partners who were simply 'gaining time' before the inevitable conflict between them erupted. This is reading history backwards. Obviously, the Pact was not designed to provide a lasting peace. Hitler and Stalin were both political rivals and ideological enemies, and a major conflict between them was always a possibility. Yet in 1939 it was not the only possibility. Neither of the dictators was really ready to fight. Neither German nor Soviet planners had hopes of reaching maximum military capacity before 1942–3 at the earliest. And Berlin and Moscow agreed that the first task was to bring down the political order created and supervised by the Western Powers. Everything depended, therefore, on the outcome of that first move. And after that several outcomes were on the cards. If the Western Powers repeated the victory of 1918 over Germany, for example, Hitler would no longer be in place to trouble the peace, and a Nazi–Soviet war would be avoided. After their victory, the Western allies would either keep their distance from the USSR or else, as Leninist ideology suggested, mount a combined attack of the capitalist world against 'the home of socialism'. More likely, though, the capitalists would fight each other to a standstill, and at the end of it would be far too exhausted to challenge the growing strength of the Soviet homeland. Once again the USSR would be able to avoid a major war in the foreseeable future. Or else, if it chose, it would be free to take the military or political initiative itself. This would appear to have been the scenario on which Stalin was banking (see p. 148).

The 'September Campaign': Poland, 1939

The Wehrmacht possessed a marked supremacy, especially in tanks and modern aircraft: 55 German divisions and 1,500 warplanes lined up against 39 Polish divisions and 400 aircraft. Both sides deployed large contingents of cavalry, of horse artillery and of horse-drawn transport. The result was not the hopeless walkover that is often portrayed. Indeed, the Poles performed rather better than the British and the French were to do when Hitler turned west in the following year.[1]

Both sides were taken by surprise. The Polish High Command had planned to defend the frontiers in strength. But they were caught out by an Allied request to delay mobilization so as not to provoke Hitler. As a result, many Polish units did not reach their positions before the invasion began, and an armoured German spearhead that had set out from the vicinity of Breslau was approaching Warsaw by the end of the first week. Much worse, however, was the gut-wrenching realization at Polish HQ that the Western Allies were not going to honour their stated obligations. Poland's leaders had gone to war on the understanding that their task was to hold the Wehrmacht at bay for fifteen days before the French delivered a devastating attack on western Germany. General Gamelin, who was the supreme allied commander, had talked in Warsaw of deploying *le gros de nos forces*, 'the bulk of our forces'. In the event, no serious operation was mounted. Indeed, many historians believe that Gamelin 'had no intention' of keeping his promise.[2] The British, whose army in 1939 was far smaller than Poland's, had little to contribute. (They dropped some pamphlets over Berlin.) The French, whose army was larger than Germany's, were paralysed. Their difficulties seemed to lie in an elaborate restructuring exercise, which temporarily stripped all the elite French formations of an offensive capacity. So the good intentions, if they had ever existed, were abandoned. An Anglo-French staff meeting held on 12 September decided that Poland would receive no support.

The Germans, too, had difficulties. They were surprised both by the strength of Polish rearguard actions, which kept the German spearheads isolated from the infantry, and by the resistance of Warsaw. The German High Command announced on 15 September that Warsaw had fallen, only to find that it held out for a total of four weeks.

One incident in the campaign gained worldwide publicity. A Polish cavalry regiment, holed up in a forest, learned that it was being surrounded by panzers. Instead of surrendering, the commander ordered his troopers to race for safety through the last narrowing gap. They were cut to pieces by tankfire. Goebbels then announced that the Polish army had been reduced to charging tanks with sabres. He had created a brilliant myth. The Poles rather liked it, because it confirmed their age-old reputation for reckless bravery. And it has been endlessly repeated ever since.

Like many aspects of Soviet conduct in this period, Stalin's inaction in early September 1939 was, to quote Churchill's remark, 'a riddle wrapped in a mystery inside an enigma'. It cannot have escaped the Great Stalin's attention that it would be much to his advantage in the international field if he posed as a tardy, and hence reluctant, aggressor. Yet the real reason for the delay would seem to have lain far to the east. Stalin was waiting for news that the Japanese had definitely signed a truce on the Manchurian frontier (see p. 154). He could not afford two wars at the same time. News of the truce reached Moscow on the 15th. On the 16th, Stalin gave orders to Soviet forces to invade Poland. And on the 17th, at dawn, the Red Army rumbled out of the morning mist without warning. Soviet officers told the astonished Polish frontier guards that the USSR was coming to rescue them from the Fascists, then opened fire. Soviet diplomats told the world that, since the Polish state had collapsed, they had been obliged to 'rescue our Byelorussian and Ukrainian brothers'.[3] Many Western historians do not question these specious statements.

From then on, the die was cast. The last Polish counteroffensive, on the River Bzura, was repulsed. The siege of Warsaw was brought to a close on the 28th. The Red Army, exceeding German expectations, crossed the Vistula into central Poland. At Lwów it met the Wehrmacht, which generously gave way. In several locations joint Nazi–Soviet victory parades were held. A German–Soviet Treaty of Friendship, Cooperation and Demarcation was signed. In Moscow and Berlin the press praised the virtues of the great leaders, the *Führer* and the *Vozhd*. The last Polish unit in the field was forced to capitulate on 5 October.

The war at sea began alongside the war on land. Germany ordered its merchant vessels to return home, and Poland ordered both military and commercial ships to make for British or French ports. The result was a series of hunts and chases, and a number of daring escapes. The German liner SS *Bremen*, for example, which had sailed from New York on 30 August, managed to outrun the Royal Navy across the Atlantic and to take refuge in the Russian port of Murmansk (a useful benefit of the Nazi–Soviet Pact). Still more astonishing was the escape of the Polish submarine

Orzeł, which had been interned, disarmed and holed up in the Estonian port of Tallinn but which, nonetheless, succeeded in completing a perilous and chartless month-long voyage down the Baltic, through the Skaggerak and across the North Sea to Rosyth in Scotland.

The consequences of the September Campaign were far-reaching. Two of Europe's largest armies were left guarding contiguous territory along a long, new frontier, the 'Peace Boundary', that ran through the middle of occupied Poland. Thanks to the feeble passivity of the Western Powers, both dictators were given the impression that they could pursue their expansive designs with impunity. Hitler, in particular, was as pleased as Punch. His panzers and dive-bombers had given him the first, heady taste of triumphant blitzkrieg. Despite the Wehrmacht's 60,000 casualties, he had proved his point against doubting generals that risks were worth taking. He was ready for the next adventure. He must have sensed that criticism was subsiding.

The Poles paid the price. Hitler had called them 'animals' deserving 'the harshest cruelty'.[4] They were the first victims of 'total war'. Refugees were strafed on the roads. Cities were bombed indiscriminately. Fifty thousand died in Warsaw alone. Elsewhere, 20,000 died in German reprisals. Europe had never seen anything like it. 'There was little to choose between the savage cruelty of the German and the Soviet occupations.'[5]

On 9 October – the day before his victory parade in conquered Warsaw – Hitler directed his generals to prepare plans for the invasion of Western Europe.[6] Stalin must have been doing something similar, because his plans to invade Finland came to a head in the course of the following month.

The 'Winter War': Finland, November 1939–March 1940

The Soviet Union's invasion of Finland clearly provided an instance of Goliath attacking David. Just like Hitler's dealing with Poland, Stalin had demanded a number of unacceptable concessions, played for a few weeks with fruitless negotiations, then ordered his army to march.

Soviet apologists justified the aggression by claiming that the USSR was merely 'strengthening the defences of Leningrad'. In reality the action was designed to remove a problem that had existed ever since Peter the Great had built his capital city on captured foreign land over two centuries before. Historic Finnish settlements reached still right up to the suburbs of

Leningrad, and Stalin was aiming to deport the entire Finnish population of the area. Finland, proudly independent, was to be tamed.

Yet the disproportion in military forces was less than is often described. By calling on all reservists, the Finns put around 140,000 well-trained men into the field, leaving the Soviet 7th Army with a numerical superiority of only 3:2. The real discrepancy lay in armour. The Soviets fielded 3,000 tanks. The Finns had none. But they made up with skill and daring for what they lacked in heavy metal. When the Soviet columns moved ponderously forward on 30 November, they were picked off by fast-moving Finnish ski troops and snipers operating amid the snowy forests and ice-bound marshes in front of the defensive Mannerheim Line. Soviet casualties were ten times higher than those of the defenders. Tens of thousands of Soviet soldiers surrendered. And hundreds of tanks were ambushed before firing a shot. Despite the bombing of Helsinki, the Finns were not inclined to submit. From the Soviet point of view this 'December Miracle' represented a humiliating catastrophe.[7]

Finland's gallant stand provoked a string of reactions. The USSR was expelled from the League of Nations, condemned as a manifest aggressor state (p. 155). More practically, the Western Powers woke up to the fact that they were facing a concerted attempt by Moscow and Berlin to redraw the map of Europe. Since the Red Army had also invaded northern Finland – 2,400 km from Leningrad, near the frontiers of Norway and Sweden – Scandinavia's valuable iron and nickel deposits were equally entering the equation. In these circumstances, the British and French decided to prepare an expeditionary force to intervene via northern Norway. A force of 100,000 men was assembled. A race against time developed. Would the Finnish army hold out for long enough to permit Western intervention to take place? The French government dreamed up a far-fetched plan to bring Moscow to its senses by bombing Baku. The idea did not win British approval.

The fighting in January and February 1940 saw no spectacular Soviet recovery. But Finnish resources were gradually stretched to breaking point. The Red Army had limitless reserves of cannon fodder, and was moving into Finnish territory by land and by sea on a dozen fronts. What is more, the Finns suspected that the West was mainly interested in iron mines. So they sued for peace, while they were still capable of avoiding total defeat. The campaign ended on 16 March. The Anglo-French expeditionary force never sailed. War between the Western Allies and the Soviet Union was averted at 'one minute to midnight'.

From Hitler's point of view, the lessons of the Finnish campaign were obvious. Firstly, despite its enormous size, the Red Army was *not* fighting fit. 'We only have to kick in the door,' the Führer remarked, 'and the whole rotten structure will come crashing down.' Secondly, Scandinavia was becoming an absolute priority. The Reich's supplies of iron and nickel ore, particularly from Sweden, were threatened. If the Wehrmacht did not strike, the British and the French might beat them to the draw. German preparations took less than three weeks. Fortunately for Hitler, the Royal Navy had already infringed Norway's territorial waters. He had a plausible pretext.

Denmark and Norway, April–May 1940

On 9 April 1940 the Danes and Norwegians woke up to find that the Germans had already taken control of their countries. Nine divisions, supported by a powerful Luftwaffe presence, were sufficient to knock out Denmark in a single day, and at the same time to seize all the ports and airfields of southern Norway. The British navy was powerless to prevent it. According to Berlin Radio, the Reich was offering Denmark and Norway 'protection'.

This lightning operation was achieved without interrupting the Wehrmacht's principal preparations for a major offensive on the Western Front. Britain and France were caught flat-footed, and their response was ineffectual. Two brief landings at Andalsnes and Namsos were followed by a more serious operation at Narvik, where a seaborne brigade of British, French and Polish troops was put ashore on 28 May. By that time, seven weeks after the initial attack, the German defences were much too strong. Narvik would have to be evacuated simultaneously with Dunkirk.[8]

Failure in Norway brought down the British government. Chamberlain stepped aside. Halifax declined the highest office. And Churchill accepted with alacrity. His policy was 'Victory: victory at all costs.' It was the evening of 10 May. In the morning, action of a far greater magnitude had been unleashed.

The Western Front, May–June 1940

Throughout the winter of 1939–40, Britain and France had experienced an eerie period without combat that was dubbed *la drôle de guerre* or, in

English, the Phoney War. The assumption was that, if Britain and France were not engaged, no one was fighting. Nothing could be more redolent of the blinkered attitudes of the period. Lord Halifax remarked, 'The pause suits us well.' A rude awakening beckoned.

In reality, the Phoney War was disastrous for the Allied cause. The Germans and the Soviets had seized the initiative in all spheres. The French waited stolidly behind the Maginot Line. Some 800,000 tonnes of British shipping was sunk, almost without reply. A German U-boat penetrated the Royal Navy's main base at Scapa Flow, and sank a battleship, the *Royal Oak*. In December 1939 the RAF's first daylight raids on Germany suffered over 50 per cent losses.

Allied complacency was born of the fact that Britain and France had been the victors of 1918 and that, on paper at least, they enjoyed numerical supremacy. They possessed 3,500 tanks, for example, against Germany's 2,500. In theory, British and French strengths were complementary. The French army was huge. The British navy was unsurpassed. And Allied air power was expanding. In practice, the Allies were poorly coordinated, and led by men without imagination. In April 1940 Chamberlain made the priceless observation, 'Hitler has missed the bus.'[9]

Germany's plans had changed over the winter. The original Case Yellow (*Fall Gelb*), which foresaw a massive 1914-style 'push' across the plains of the Low Countries, was dropped after secret papers fell by accident into Allied hands. It was replaced by General von Manstein's *Sichelschnitt* plan – a 'Sweep of the Sickle'. The plan envisaged a surprise armoured assault through the ill-defended Ardennes. Army Group B, with 28 divisions, was to advance in the north, Army Group C, with only 17 divisions, was to take over the southern sector; and Army Group A, with 44 divisions (including no less than 10 mighty panzer divisions), was to deliver the devastating knockout blow in the centre. No less than 47 divisions were held in reserve in case of problems.

There were no problems. Operation Sichelschnitt worked to perfection. Army Group B invaded the Netherlands on 10 May. Rotterdam was bombed (and the scale of bombing was grossly exaggerated). Dutch resistance folded on the fifth day. Thirty-five Allied divisions, including France's mobile reserve and the tiny British Expeditionary Force, moved up into Belgium, expecting to receive the weight of the main German thrust. Instead, Army Group A moved stealthily into the hilly and supposedly impassable terrain separating the Belgian fort of Namur from the western terminus of the Maginot Line. For three or four days, 'the biggest traffic jam in history' went unobserved by Allied reconnaissance, until Guderian's panzers descended out of the hills, crossed the Meuse, captured Sedan, and accelerated into the open countryside. As A. J. P. Taylor put it, 'When they ran out of petrol, they filled up at the local pump without paying. They occasionally stopped to milk a French cow.'[10] On 16 May they covered 95 km to reach the Channel coast near Abbeville. The lines of communication between the Allied front lines in Belgium and their rear areas had been completely severed.

The terminal phase of the campaign lasted barely a month. In the north, the Allied armies were corralled into a large pocket in the hinterland of Calais and Dunkirk. Their fate appeared to be sealed, until, to the astonishment of his generals, Hitler ordered the panzers to halt. It was a largely political decision, probably inspired by the mistaken belief that Britain would wish to sue for peace. It provided the chance for the survivors of the BEF to escape, without their equipment, from the Dunkirk beaches. Despite the later myth, it was not a British victory. In the east, the Wehrmacht toured the rear areas of the Maginot Line, capturing the helpless fortresses one by one by the 'back gate'. In the centre, the French fell back in confusion. Paris was declared an open city, to save it from aerial bombardment. And the French government retreated to Bordeaux. The agony ended at Compiègne on 22 June. France's capitulation was signed in the same railway carriage that had been used for the signing of the armistice of November 1918.[11]

Immediately before the capitulation, Britain suffered its worst ever maritime catastrophe. On 17 June the Cunard liner SS *Lancastria* was sunk off Saint-Nazaire by German aircraft. It was carrying between 6,000 and 9,000 evacuees, a mixture of troops and civilians. Only 2,500 were saved. The loss of life was at least twice and possibly four times as great as that among the passengers of the *Titanic*. But Churchill imposed a news blackout, and the event has largely escaped notice.[12]

Enter Italy, June 1940

Mussolini entered the war like a vulture. On 10 June, the day that Paris was abandoned, he stood on the Piazza Venezia in Rome and declared war on the Allies. Italian troops occupied Menton and several alpine valleys, but made little attempt to go further.

Italy's démarche, however, had much broader implications. For

Mussolini harboured far-reaching ambitions. Italy already controlled Albania (see p. 154), and was casting ominous glances at some of the Greek islands. It possessed Tripoli in North Africa, adjacent to British Egypt, and had a large army in Abyssinia. Most importantly, following the demise of France, it was now the principal naval power in the Mediterranean, which would soon become a theatre of action. Britain, in particular, could not afford to permit a break in its empire's maritime lifeline from Gibraltar to Malta and Suez.

Such was the background to one of the most ruthless actions of the war. After the fall of France, the fate of the French Navy was undecided. General de Gaulle (see p. 173) ordered it to sail out of harm's way to French West Africa. The British expected it to pass under British command. At all events, they were absolutely determined to prevent it falling into German or Italian hands. Hence, when a French admiral in the Algerian naval base of Mers el-Kébir refused to cooperate, his fleet was pitilessly shelled at its moorings on 3 July 1940, and sunk with all hands. Both the death toll and the moral outrage were tremendous. 'Britain meant business.'[13]

Equally significant was something that didn't happen. General Franco, who had joined the Anti-Comintern Pact and had signed a friendship treaty with the Reich, did *not* follow Mussolini's lead. On 23 October 1940 the Führer travelled by train to the Spanish frontier at Hendaye, and talked to the Caudillo in person. He understood that Spain was exhausted by the recent Civil War. But he had reason to hope that Germany would be granted military bases from which the Bay of Biscay and the western Mediterranean could be dominated. He even revealed a plan called Isabella-Felix, which foresaw the capture of Gibraltar by German troops who were to march through Spain. To his great annoyance, he was rebuffed. To his credit, Franco said 'No'.[14]

The Baltic States, June 1940

At the other end of Europe, Stalin was not sleeping. With the world's attention focused on France, he was presented with a golden opportunity for overturning one of the most irritating aspects of the Versailles Settlement. The Stalinists, like their tsarist predecessors, were unashamed imperialists. Their slogan of 'Socialism in One Country', which had appeared in parallel with the USSR in 1924, was fundamentally incompatible with the Wilsonian doctrine of 'national self-determination' that had appealed so strongly to Central and East Europeans after 1918. When Stalin had served as Lenin's commissar for nationalities, therefore, the Red Army, having won the Civil War in Russia, had been sent on a systematic orgy of reconquest in all the former tsarist provinces that had dared to reject Russian rule. Starting in Ukraine and Byelorussia, it extinguished all traces of independence in the Caucasus, Central Asia, Siberia and even Outer Mongolia. Yet five former provinces had escaped, and Stalin had never forgiven them. Like all his disciples, he thought of them not as foreign countries, but as the 'near abroad', part of Russia's sacred and indivisible patrimony. By the spring of 1940, Poland and Finland had been brought into line. Estonia, Latvia and Lithuania – all sovereign members of the League of Nations – remained obdurate.

None of the three Baltic States was Russian by history, culture, religion or language. They had been swallowed by the Tsarist Empire as a result of Russia's wars against Poland and Sweden, and of long-forgotten treaties that paid no regard to the wishes of the population. During the First World War they were among the first to demand independence. Estonia was closely associated with Finland. Together with Latvia, it had formed part of the Swedish realms for centuries, and was predominantly Prot-estant. Lithuania, in contrast, was historically associated with Poland, and the Lithuanians were predominantly Catholic. All three countries, which jointly covered an area considerably larger than England and Wales, possessed significant German and Jewish minorities. The 'Baltic Germans' had played a prominent role in tsarist history, but, like the rest of their neighbours, had no desire whatsoever to join the Soviet Union.[15]

The situation in Lithuania was particularly interesting. During the September Campaign of 1939, the Red Army had seized the city of Wilno (Vilnius) from Poland, and Stalin had handed it as a gift to the Lithuanian Republic. The Lithuanian nationalists were cock-a-hoop. It was the perfect way of disarming their vigilance.

Given the fiasco of the 'Winter War', however, Stalin continued to act more by guile than by overt aggression. First, the Soviet government surrounded the frontiers of the three Baltic States with overwhelming forces. Then, as with Finland, it demanded 'concessions', including military bases and territorial adjustments. Finally, it ordered subservient elements within the Communist parties of each of the countries to beg Moscow for 'protection against foreign aggression'. The ruling Baltic authorities col-lapsed, and the Red Army marched in to restore order. The NKVD set to work without delay. Soviet 'protection' was to cost the Baltic States up to a quarter of their population. Most Western history books don't even mention it: or if they do, they employ the blandest of tones.[16]

The Battle for Britain, 1940–41

In the West, Britain alone hung on, rashly defiant. The defiance emanated from one person, Winston Churchill, who became prime minister on the day that Hitler launched his Western offensive. On a visit to the BEF in France, Churchill was to exclaim, 'Never in my life have I seen such mismanagement.'[17] Churchill's greatness was that he roared defiance at a time when all rational men would have judged the predicament hopeless.

Churchill was war leader not merely of the United Kingdom, but of the British Empire. Despite later myths, this was not 'England' playing against Germany. And, from the military point of view, Britain's sole aim was survival. The bigger question, already present in Churchill's mind, was the integrity of the Empire. Both the Mediterranean and the Atlantic would have to be cleared of Axis forces before Britain's pre-war position could be re-established.

Within three weeks of Churchill's elevation, Britain lost the greater part of its army, together with all capacity for participating in continental warfare. The Royal Navy had traded the *Hood* and the *Glorious* for the *Graf Spee* and the *Bismarck*, but had found no answer to the magnetic mines or the U-boats. The merchant navy was delivering less food than was being consumed. The RAF still awaited its heavy bombers, and its fighter squadrons were only just receiving delivery of Hurricanes and Spitfires. Prospects were bleak. If Britain were somehow to avoid a German invasion, the chances were that she would be rapidly starved into submission.

From Germany's point of view, Britain was a matter of secondary importance. Britain was a nuisance, but not a serious challenger. What is more, the Führer still harboured hopes of an arrangement. For him, 'the English' were racial brothers who could be sensibly accommodated if assured of their empire in return for Germany's control of Eurasia. He had not sought conflict, and was deeply stung by Britain's hostile declaration of war. Apart from the Royal Navy and the RAF, the British Isles were virtually defenceless. Air power was overtaking naval power, and, with the defeat of France, the issue of land warfare had been settled. Once the

Wehrmacht landed on British soil, it would face less opposition than in Holland or Belgium. One is reminded of the threat once issued by the Persian king to the Spartans. 'If I enter your land,' he opined, 'I will annihilate you.' The Spartans replied with one laconic word: 'If.'

The snag lay in the realm of aerial supremacy. The Luftwaffe possessed a marked numerical advantage. But it was mainly designed for tactical ground support, and it had not yet confronted an adversary armed with modern warplanes. So it had to test its strength. The German General Staff was unwilling to risk a sea crossing without full cover from the air. Such was the origin of the Luftwaffe's twin-engined plan of campaign: the daylight 'Battle of Britain' and the night-time 'Blitz'.

The Battle of Britain consisted of a long series of daily massed bombing raids over southern England. The Luftwaffe was trying to drive the RAF from the sky as a prelude to Operation Sealion: the invasion of Britain. It did not succeed. There was no clear start or finish, though the conventional dates are 10 July and 31 October 1940. At first, Air Marshal Göring's *Luft-flotten* operating from France concentrated on hitting RAF airfields. They later added urban and communication targets. But, with mounting losses, they gradually lost their resolve. RAF Fighter Command triumphed through the excellence of its Hurricanes and Spitfires, through its mastery of radar, through a superior rate of aircraft production, and through the availability of foreign, especially Commonwealth, pilots.[18] The highest-scoring fighter ace was a Czech flying with the Polish 303 (Kościuszko) Squadron.[19]

The night Blitz opened on 7 September 1940 and tailed off in June 1941. The targets were economic: docks, railways, factories and ships. No precaution was taken to safeguard civilians. Two thousand Londoners died on the first night during the attack on Docklands. Britain was to be 'brought to its knees', economically and psychologically. On 14 November 1940 Coventry and its cathedral were devastated. In the last mass raid, on 10 May 1941, 5,000 houses were razed in London's East End. It was an efficient form of slum clearance, but not of waging war.[20] RAF Bomber Command was to make the same mistake on a far grander scale. Göring's bombers were soon to be transferred to fresh pastures in the East.

Britain's survival proved as important as it was improbable. In German eyes, it was a mere detail that could be rectified whenever convenient. The point is: it never became convenient, and within a couple of years it was becoming impossible.

The key factor here was the USA. President Roosevelt had watched Britain's ordeal with sympathy, and determined to give all possible assistance short of declaring war. It was not in America's long-term interest for Britain to go under. But the aid had to be surreptitious. The USA had no substantial standing army. And Congress was still gripped by isolationism. In a re-election address in the autumn of 1940, Roosevelt assured the voters, 'Your boys are not going to be sent to any foreign wars.'[21] Nonetheless, the US Navy began to provide partial cover for the Atlantic convoys. And in March 1941 the President instituted the Lend-Lease scheme. Britain was saved by the USA from financial insolvency, thereby ceasing to be an independent Great Power. Few people recognized the historical shift when it happened. But the shift proved irreversible. Thereafter, Britain served as a floating platform for America's unseen interests: 'an island aircraft carrier' to which US military assets could be transferred as the need arose. Without Britain's unlikely survival, it is hard to see how the USA could ever have been directly involved in the European war.

Romania, August 1940

Romania was one of those 'small states' in Europe whose significance was not in reality quite so small. Its army was three times bigger than Britain's. Its oilfields were of great interest, especially to Germany. And its strategic location, trapped between the German and Soviet spheres, was ultra-sensitive.

In August 1940 Stalin decided to move in. Once again he sought to repossess territory whose population had opted to reject Russian rule. Bessarabia (now Moldova) was largely inhabited by Romanians who twenty years before had freely chosen to join Romania. To Stalin's way of thinking, this was an insult. So he called in the Romanian ambassador and demanded the appropriate 'concessions'. Bucharest contacted Berlin, seeking help. Berlin refused it, and the Romanians reluctantly conceded. They were furious, not because they were 'anti-Soviet' or 'nationalistic', but because they had been robbed in broad daylight. Stalin took Bessarabia and Bukovina to boot. Hungary and Bulgaria joined in the robbery, too. Not a single Westerner protested.[22]

★

About this time, Hitler first mooted the idea of attacking the Soviet Union. The attack on Romania was getting rather too close for comfort: before 1918 Bukovina had belonged to Austria, and Stalin had acted without prior consultation. The Western Powers were virtually prostrate. And the 'great gambler' needed no reminders about striking while the iron was hot. For the time being, however, he put the idea to one side for political negotiations that took place in November).

Once the negotiations had failed, however, the idea returned. On 12 December 1940 Hitler ordered the German General Staff to draw up a plan in great secrecy. Its code name was Barbarossa, after the medieval German emperor. The Wehrmacht was to be ready for action by May.[23] Of course, this did *not* mean that the Führer had decided irrevocably on a decisive campaign in the East. It meant that he wanted to put Germany into a position to act swiftly if circumstances in the coming year warranted it. Germany's huge victories in 1939–40 had presented its leaders with the great luxury of choosing the time and place of their next step. Germany's adversaries had no such luxury.

Systematic German planning had no equivalent in the USSR. It is hard to exaggerate the confusion in military thinking that reigned in Moscow at this stage and at the highest level. Policy was in maximum disarray. On 13 January 1941, when Meretskov was dismissed as Chief of Staff and replaced by Zhukov, Stalin's innermost circle had been discussing the mechanization of the army. Marshal Grigory Kulik (1890–1950), who had commanded the operations both in Poland and in Finland, argued that tanks were overrated. He preferred horse-drawn guns. 'It's as if he preferred the wooden plough to the tractor,' Stalin joked. A couple of months later Kulik successfully championed production of 107-mm howitzers of First World War vintage, delaying the advent both of the T-34 tank and of Katyusha rocket-launchers, and he was deeply implicated in the intrigues that accompanied the purge of senior Soviet aviators. The Red Air Force had lost numerous aircraft to unexplained crashes, and someone had to be blamed.[24]

All these disastrous technical debacles were conducted in a paralytic climate of suspicion and bloodletting. Kulik's promotion to marshal had occurred in May 1940, in the same week that Beria kidnapped and murdered his noble-born wife, Kira. Kulik's main opponent, Boris Vanni-kov, the commissar of armaments, was arrested, and under torture denounced the Commissar for Aircraft Production, Mikhail Kaganovich – brother to one of Stalin's closest cronies. Pavel Rychagov, chief of the Air

Force directorate, dared to tell Stalin, 'You're making us fly in coffins.' He was shot, but not before heaping more odium on Kaganovich. Stalin and Beria dreamed up the allegation that aircraft production had been located near the western frontier to help Berlin, and that the Commissar was the secret head of a pro-German government-in-waiting.[25] Rational military preparations were impossible in such circumstances.

The Mediterranean theatre, 1940–41

Fighting in North Africa, which began in September 1940, opened up a theatre that was of vital import to Italy, of major concern to the British Empire, of peripheral interest to Germany, and of minimal significance in the final outcome of the war in Europe. It is, however, too much a part of the story to be left out.

General Graziani, commanding a force of fourteen divisions, edged into the western fringes of British-occupied Egypt. At the time, Egypt was officially neutral, but no one had noticed. Outnumbered by 5:1, the British thought of abandoning Egypt. But they stayed, and by staying they prompted a series of romantic, fast-moving campaigns, from wadi to wadi, that were to last for three years.

The naval war hotted up on 11 November, when Royal Navy aircraft sank three capital ships in Taranto. The purpose was to deny the Italians control of the narrow Sicilian Channel through which the main north–south and west–east sea routes passed. Malta lay in the centre of the Sicilian Channel. For the British it was a crucial staging post between Gibraltar and Suez. For the Axis it was an insolent obstruction to the supply line to Tripoli. It fast became the scene of constant bombardments, privations and heroics.

The British Army's response to Graziani was launched on 7 December. General O'Connor's counter-offensive raced westward for 800 km all the way to Benghazi. At Beda Fromm he gained a victory that a British historian has dubbed 'one of the most important of the whole war'.[26]

The Axis response was to dispatch an experienced German tank general, Erwin Rommel, 'the Desert Fox'. His Afrikakorps counted just two divisions. He had soon counter-attacked, captured General O'Connor, and set off on the long chase back to Egypt. He carried all before him except for the tiny enclave of Tobruk, held by an obstinate garrison of Australians and Poles.

The British response to Rommel's response took the form of two successive operations on the Egyptian frontier – 'Brevity' and 'Battleaxe'. They both failed. The Commander-in-Chief Middle East, General Wavell, was replaced. It was 21 June 1941.

The Balkans, 1940–41

Romania was not the only Balkan country to be assaulted. In October 1940 Mussolini attacked northern Greece from his base in Albania. He opened up yet another can of very persistent worms. The Greeks fought manfully, and pushed the Italians back across the border. Before long, the Duce was calling on the Führer for a rescue.

In those same months, Germany was applying the familiar 'protective' methods to consolidate its influence in several Balkan countries. The Wehrmacht was invited into Romania, then into Hungary, and in March 1941 into Bulgaria. But Yugoslavia declined such protection. And so too did Greece, which had received a British guarantee. So the Führer decided to resolve the impasse by force. He was not prepared to embark on any other venture before this troublesome region was pacified. Two simultaneous operations were prepared: one called 'Punishment' against Yugoslavia, the other called 'Marita' against Greece. As in Poland, but not in Western Europe, the Wehrmacht was ordered to apply 'the harshest cruelty'. The issue was forced by a *coup d'état* in Belgrade on 27 March 1941, when the regent was overthrown by a group of anti-German Serb officers. In this way, a vicious civil war in Yugoslavia was provoked even before the Germans invaded.

Three weeks sufficed for the Wehrmacht to subdue the two countries. Belgrade was bombed with the loss of 17,000 civilians in one week. 'Punishment' sent armoured spearheads crashing into Yugoslavia from four directions – from Austria, Hungary, Romania and Bulgaria. Coherent defence was impossible. 'Marita' drowned Greece in an irresistible wave of panzers, Stukas and fast-moving columns. By the end of April, German troops were crowding to be photographed round the Temple of Sounion at the tip of the Peloponnese.[27]

A coda to the chapter was provided in May by the battle for the island of Crete – a textbook lesson in modern warfare. The British garrison, mainly Anzacs, possessing huge naval support, felt safe. They were rapidly overwhelmed by German airborne forces. The Royal Navy then suffered

grave losses through organizing an evacuation without air cover. The
Germans thought that the casualty level among their own parachutists
was unacceptable, and dropped the concept of major airborne attacks. The
British drew the opposite conclusion, believing paratroops to be the perfect
answer to the waning of sea power.[28]

Strategic overview

In twenty-one months of warfare, the armed forces of the Third Reich had
outperformed their wildest dreams. (One might say they had been too
successful for their own good.) With the sole exception of Britain, they
had soundly beaten all their enemies. With the sole exception of Sweden,
which was compliant to their wishes, they completely controlled Northern
Europe. With the exception of Portugal and Spain, which were in neutral
Fascist hands, they controlled all of Southern Europe. With the sole
exception of neutral Switzerland, they controlled the whole of Western
and Central Europe, and of Central Europe's eastern approaches from the
Baltic to the Black Sea. They possessed the finest military machine ever
devised. It takes no strategic genius to see that there were only three
directions left in which their power could be further projected.

What is more, all of this had been achieved without provoking the
two major powers which might have attempted to stop it. The USA had
no intention of involving itself in Europe's bloody quarrels. Apart from
shoring up Britain, the most that President Roosevelt would say – and
only in private – was, 'If we are attacked, we will have no choice.' The
Soviet Union was similarly disinclined to engage fully. As we now know,
Stalin's policies in the 1930s had cost millions of lives. His priorities in the
early 1940s were to recover internal stability, to press on with the Third
Five-Year Plan, to nurse the Red Army back to health, to re-arm, and to
absorb the countries that he had recently annexed. Or so it seemed.

One possibility was that the Wehrmacht would be sent into the
Middle East. Britain's hold on Palestine, Egypt, Iraq and Iraq's priceless oil
reserves was tenuous. Once in Crete, the Germans established an air
bridge to Vichy-held Syria, and from Syria to Iraq. (In a little-known
incident, on 18 May 1941 a German bomber killed the commander of the
Zionist Irgun terrorist organization, whom the British had released from
jail in Tel Aviv in order to help them against rebels in Baghdad.) Air

power increasingly held the key to the battlefield. And it would be much easier for the Luftwaffe to dislodge the British from Suez than for the British to defend it. Turkey would be a problem, though it was generally well disposed towards Germany. And the Afrikakorps, now rampant in the Western Desert, could be massively reinforced. Some historians say that Hitler was 'uninterested'. It is probably more accurate to say that he thought that the Middle East could wait.[29]

Another possibility was that the full weight of Germany's armed might be sent into the Soviet Union. Indeed, by the spring of 1941 the possibility was rising to a probability. The plans were approaching completion. The prospect of London and Moscow joining forces, as in 1914–17, was marginal. And, for many reasons, the Nazi leaders were faced with the promise of a lifetime. 'Jewish Bolshevism' was their ideological bogey. The rich lands of the 'Baltikum', Byelorussia and Ukraine, provided the body of the long-proclaimed *Lebensraum*. They were also the very lands which the Kaiser's undefeated army had been forced to relinquish by the 'Stab in the Back' only twenty-two years before. Seen this way, and given that German forces had been massing on the Soviet frontier, many observers rated the probability a near certainty.

The third possibility, of course, was that Hitler would return to the attack on Britain. And the German disinformation machine was pulling out all the stops to persuade Moscow that Britain was the real target. For months, the Abwehr, German intelligence, let it be known that Operation Sealion Mark II had top priority. And Soviet agents round Europe reported home accordingly. The poor performance of German airborne units in Crete in May 1941 was used as an argument for dismissing the likelihood of an airborne attack on Britain. It was all a bluff. The disinformation worked.

Assembling the strike force for 'Barbarossa' caused some headaches. Roughly 10 per cent of the best German divisions were diverted for six weeks to the Balkan campaign, and about 40 per cent had to be supplied with captured French materiel. The Romanian and Hungarian contingents were of untried quality. And the Italian contingent, which Mussolini insisted on sending, had not even been requested. German transport vehicles had no tracks. Horse-drawn vehicles were in the majority. Three million men were expected to live off local food supplies. And most of the quartermasters were making no provision for winter living. But why should they? British intelligence gave the Red Army ten days. Roosevelt's military experts forecast a campaign of one month 'and a possible maximum of three'. This time round, no member of the German General Staff was openly expressing doubts.

Nonetheless, the question of timing was crucial. In 1941 the Reich could comfortably sustain the planned short war on the Eastern Front. And if, as anticipated, the British capitulated on the defeat of the USSR, the whole competition for supremacy would be over. By 1942 or 1943, drawing on the reserves of all Europe, the Reich could build up a war chest, an arsenal and a pool of manpower to sustain a longer war. On the other hand, if granted respite, the Soviet Union would also be better armed, better organized and better prepared. The Führer was not one to funk such a challenge. Ever since the re-occupation of the Rhineland in 1936, he had repeatedly demonstrated that boldness and accelerated timetables paid dividends. On 20 June, he issued the order for Operation Barbarossa to be unleashed before dawn two days later.

Phase 2, June 1941–June 1944: the Reich rampant, then checked

If justice were done, all books on the Second World War in Europe would devote perhaps three-quarters of their contents to the Eastern Front. Some historians actually apologize for not doing so.[30] The step is not taken, partly because historians are tempted to exaggerate the actions of their own countries, partly because they have numerous other bits and pieces to cover, and partly because very few of them comprehend the sheer scale, or the full implications, of the German–Soviet conflict. A grasp of proportions, however, is essential to a proper understanding.

Estimates vary. But, in round terms 410 divisions were engaged at the start of Barbarossa, and the campaign continued without a break for 46 months – a total of 226 million man-months. In comparison, the Western Campaign of 1940 had involved 285 divisions for 6 weeks or 1½ months. The Italian Campaign would involve 40 divisions for 21 months. And the Western Campaign of 1944–5, from D-Day to Lüneburg Heath, involved 120 divisions for nearly 10 months. The method of measurement is imprecise. The colossal preponderance of the Eastern Front is indisputable.

Operation Barbarossa, June–December 1941

At 3.00 a.m. on 22 June 1941, the shortest night of the year, German troops raced across the bridge on the River Bug, in the middle of occupied Poland, and stormed the fortress of Brześć (Brest-Litovsk). The Soviet garrison fought to the last man. Thus opened the colossal onslaught of Barbarossa. In the words of A. J. P. Taylor, it was 'the greatest event of the Second World War'.[31] Shortly afterwards, vast columns of men and machines moved off to the north and the south. Their hopes were high. They had been told they were fighting an inferior enemy.

The 'Battle of the Frontiers', which lasted for almost six weeks, contained two discrete operations of major importance – which appear under various labels, but which are perhaps best described as the Minsk Pocket and the Smolensk Pocket. The Germans swamped all opposition. Despite immense confusion, and desperate resistance, the armoured spearheads surged forward into Lithuania, Byelorussia and Ukraine. Some 1,500 Soviet aircraft were destroyed on the ground in the opening days. Thousands of Soviet tanks were knocked out. Almost 2 million Soviet soldiers were taken prisoner. Army Group North was heading for Leningrad. Army Group South was approaching Kiev, the capital of Ukraine. Field Marshal von Bock's Army Group Centre, having pushed forward 650 km, was standing before Smolensk – Russia's most westerly city.

Nonetheless, as the Germans quickly realized, there was something distinctly odd about Soviet dispositions. For reasons that have never been explained, the Soviet High Command had not availed itself of the defence positions that were available. On the contrary, it had abandoned the defensive 'Stalin Line' built in the 1930s, putting a large part of its forces into vulnerable forward locations, in the direct path of the German attacks. Despite having the largest country in the world, it had not put its air force out of harm's way in the depths of Russia. The Luftwaffe was able to cause so much damage only because its opponents were conveniently stationed on the most westerly airfields. German tanks rolled at speed over newly rebuilt roads and bridges. And the colossal hordes of Soviet soldiers that were surrounded and captured in the frontier zone were in the worst possible deployment for defending themselves.

Many years later an ex-Soviet officer was to claim that Stalin had been on the point of attacking Germany, and that the Red Army was caught out at the very last minute by the amazing speed of the Wehrmacht's final preparations. The thesis has been as vehemently denied as supported, but no conclusive evidence has been produced one way or the other about Stalin's real intentions.[32] One possibility is that Soviet military doctrine viewed attack as the best means of defence, and hence that the unorthodox deployment was inspired by faulty military calculations, not by plans of aggression. Certainly, last-minute requests by front-line officers to assume a more orthodox defensive stance were turned down. And Stalin's first reaction on 22 June was to order them to advance.[33] At all events, Hitler's gamble came perilously close to success at the very outset.

The Minsk Pocket, which developed in late June 320 km to the east of the start line, was the result of the opening drive by the central panzer groups to encircle the four armies of General D. G. Pavlov's West Front. In order to escape a pincer movement round Białystok, Pavlov ignored his orders and pulled back, only to find that he was being overtaken on both flanks, by Hoth's 2 Panzer Group and Guderian's 3 Panzer. By the 29th he had lost contact with his army commanders, and on the 30th he and his staff were recalled to Moscow, where they were unceremoniously shot. The panzers pressed on to close the pocket at Minsk, while the German infantry mopped up all the trapped Soviet armies. In all, 338,000 prisoners were captured, and 3,300 tanks destroyed. On 3 July, speaking on Moscow Radio in his heavy Georgian accent, Stalin declared the 'Great Patriotic War' and called for the defence of 'Holy Russia'. The German High Command was already discussing the prospect of a victory parade on Red Square before the end of August.

The Smolensk Pocket developed less than a week later and over 240 km further east. Hoth and Guderian had reached the strategic gap between the Dvina and upper Dnieper rivers that forms the historic gateway to Moscow. They were faced by Stalin's old comrade Marshal Timoshenko, who had improvised a new West Front from five armies previously destined to march on Germany. This time the haul of prisoners numbered 348,000. But Timoshenko's front managed to keep fighting for more than a month, and the gap was not properly closed until 5 August. Resistance was stiffening. The Wehrmacht was falling behind schedule.

More vital weeks were lost in mid-August while the Führer pondered the next step. His initial concept was to advance in maximum strength on the northern and southern wings, before linking up for the final knockout blow against Moscow. Field Marshal von Leeb's twenty-eight divisions in the north, and Field Marshal von Rundstedt's thirty-three divisions in the south restarted in late August. But overconfidence produced unnecessary delay. The panzer strike force was inexplicably diverted to the south. And Bock in the centre did not really move, with Operation Typhoon, until 2 October. Nonetheless, spectacular successes were achieved. Siege was laid to Leningrad. Huge 'cauldrons', or pockets of encircled Soviet troops, were created at Vyazma, Bryansk and Kiev. Once again, hundreds of thousands of prisoners were taken. Soviet losses in tanks, aircraft and heavy guns were incalculable. In the far south, the Romanians took Odessa, and added 'Transnistria' to their country.

For three weeks in late October/early November, however, the German offensive ground to a halt. Heavy rain turned the unpaved rural roads into impassable mud traps, and the High Command was forced to decide whether to give priority to the capture of Moscow or to other aims such as the securing of industrial areas or the continued destruction of Soviet forces. This second delay was crucial. Stalin, who seems to have briefly entertained capitulation, returned to the fray. General Georgiy Zhukov was appointed to restore discipline at the front and to plan the 'Battle for Moscow'. No less than nine new Soviet armies were put into the field, even if they consisted of press-ganged, over-age veterans, a trawl of Moscow's jails, and conscripted zeks from the GULag. Astonishingly, the Red Army kept on fighting.

Operation Typhoon resumed on 15 November, after the weather cleared. The panzers rolled across crisp snow and frozen tracks. They reached the Moscow–Volga Canal in the north and the Oka River to the south. By the first week of December, Bock's scouts captured a terminus of the Moscow tramway system. German binoculars caught sight of the gleaming towers of the Kremlin. But a huge snowfall was followed by the thermometer falling to − 30°C. Progress had slowed to a crawl. The Germans were now taking huge casualties themselves. Bock reported to Hitler, 'It is hard to see what sense there is in continuing the offensive.'

Then the counter-blow fell. Zhukov had been holding back a strong force of twenty-five divisions freshly transferred from Siberia. They were heavily armed, warmly clad and, like the Finns in 1939, equipped with skis. On 5 December, as the temperature hit − 40°C, they glided across the snows and pushed back a German strike force that was no longer capable of waging blitzkrieg. Their rescue of the Russian capital coincided exactly with news of the Japanese attack on Pearl Harbor.

Zhukov's victory before Moscow is usually attributed to the winter, to Hitler's inconstancy of purpose, and to the successive delays in implementing Barbarossa's later stages. Yet other factors were at work.

One was logistics. The Red Army was able to draw on unseen reserves of manpower, and had six railway lines along which to deploy them. The Germans had few reserves, and the use of only one line to supply the key central sector. Another factor lay with intelligence. Earlier in the year Stalin had refused to believe the reports of his master spy Richard Sorge in Tokyo about German preparations for Barbarossa. He now paid attention when Sorge reported that the Japanese High Command had definitely rejected proposals for an attack on the USSR.[34] Soviet forces in Siberia and the Far East were no longer needed to confront Japan. Their transfer to European Russia, unspotted by the Germans, tipped the balance during the defence of Moscow. By January 1942 the Wehrmacht had been pushed back to the line from which Typhoon had started two months before. Hopes of a short campaign were dead.

The Battle of the Atlantic, 1941–3

During Operation Barbarossa no effective land or air warfare was waged in the West, and Grand Admiral Raeder, the Commander-in-Chief, was hopeful for victory of the Kriegsmarine in the Atlantic. He calculated that, if the combined efforts of German aircraft and U-boats could sink an average of 700,000 tonnes of shipping per month for a year, Britain would be starved into submission. The war of attrition which developed was to be decided as much by the competition in shipbuilding as by the exchanges of torpedoes and depth charges at sea.

The Allied navies had a bad year in 1941. U-boats based in Brittany concentrated their attacks on 'the Gap' in mid-Atlantic where the slow-moving convoys were not protected by air patrols operating from Canada, Greenland or Oban in Scotland. And for a time it looked as if they might reach the desired sinking rate.

1942 was no better. In the months following US entry to the war, the U-boats feasted hungrily off the eastern seaboard. Only slowly did improved technology, like ASDIC (underwater directional sound detection), 'Hedgehog' mortars and surface radar, and increased numbers of escorts begin to have effect. Even so, 1,667 merchantmen were lost as against 87 U-boats.

The turning point came in 1943. Although March of that year was one of the blackest months, April brought considerable relief, and in May more U-boats were lost than Allied ships. Raeder wrote in his diary, 'We have lost the Battle of the Atlantic.' This was the point when the Western Allies could begin to think with confidence about transporting a major American army to Britain.

Of course, the sea war never stopped. It continued to 1945. But German attacks became ever less painful pinpricks. Massive air patrols over the Western Approaches kept the U-boats in their pens, while US shipyards were building three or four 'Liberty ships' every single day. Overall, well over 100,000 British and German sailors perished. But the ratio of merchant ships sunk to merchant ships that safely made the crossing was only 1:131.[35]

The Eastern Front, 1942

Only after Barbarossa did the Germans begin to comprehend the enormity of their task. Their victories in Western Europe had given them a false sense of reality about warfare in the East, where conditions were far harsher and distances far greater. Nor was it just that their troops were dressed in unsuitable clothing. Their guns had not been tested in low temperatures. Their engines had the wrong sort of antifreeze. Their tanks had to use oil with the wrong degree of viscosity. Motorized transport was in short supply and could not move through the mud and snow of near-trackless wastes. Worst of all, the Red Army could not be dealt a decisive blow. It reeled from vast losses that no other army in the world could contemplate, yet it fought on. It enjoyed seemingly infinite reserves of men (and women). It was held together by discipline of unimaginable ferocity (198,000 were shot by the NKVD in 1941–2 alone – *pour encourager les autres*). It was receiving increasing supplies of tanks, planes and guns from the 1,500 factories that had been spirited away to the Urals and beyond. And it had endless open spaces in which to retreat and manoeuvre. Hitler had embarked on the biggest campaign of territorial expansion in European history and yet had barely brushed against the outer fringes of Russia: 97 per cent of the Soviet Union remained unoccupied. Worst of all, having savagely maltreated the 'subhuman' enemy, which had long been savagely maltreated by the Stalinist regime, it was facing opponents who scorned the grisly prospect of dying and killing.

In March, General Halder, the German Chief of Staff, took a rueful look at the logistics. One-third of the invasion force assembled for Barbarossa had been either destroyed or withdrawn. Replacements for a million casualties were forthcoming, since no other demands were in the offing. But only 873 out of 3,500 tanks could be replaced. In 1941 Hitler had actually reduced military-industrial production, believing it surplus to needs. And there was a desperate shortage of oil.

There was a further significant shift. In December, Hitler had dismissed General von Brauchitsch, the C.-in-C., as a scapegoat for Barbarossa, and had taken personal control of the High Command. Yet he was now faced by an array of previously unheard-of Soviet generals – Zhukov, Rokossovsky, Vatutin, Chuikov – who were proving supremely competent. Unlike the amateur ex-corporal, they knew all about the management of space, the exploitation of natural conditions, the use of numbers, and the virtue of patience. By a process of natural selection, most of the inefficient Soviet commanders had been eliminated.

The Wehrmacht's summer offensive of 1942, while holding on to positions in the north and centre, was designed to capture the grainfields of the southern steppes and the oilfields of the Caucasus. Another mighty strike force of sixty-eight divisions had been assembled. It was divided into two army groups – Group A, including the 6th Army, to strike due east to the rivers Don and Volga; Group B, headed by the 1st Panzer Army, to strike south-east to the Caucasus.

Before the offensive could move, however, the Red Army had first to be dislodged from the Crimean Peninsula. The operations and counter-operations designed to control the Crimea deserve a volume in themselves. On one side was Manstein, author of Sichelschnitt; and on the other was General I. Petrov's Independent Maritime Army, working in conjunction with the Soviet Black Sea Fleet. In September 1941 Petrov had made a daring landing behind the Romanian forces besieging Odessa. But he then was obliged to be evacuated by the fleet in Dunkirk style. In December 1941 twenty-five separate landings on the Kerch Peninsula were aimed at German control of Sevastopol, and succeeded in clearing the Crimea completely. But Manstein was back in the spring; and he returned the compliment with a vengeance and won his marshal's baton. Sevastopol held out until July, long after the main German offensive on the southern sector was under way.

As in 1941, the German push of 1942 made enormous gains, equivalent to those of the French and Polish campaigns combined. A panzer corps under Hyazinth Graf Strachwitz from Army Group B reached the banks of the Volga, and gazed into the shimmering steppe beyond. One German army from Group A took the first oilfield at Maikop in the Kuban, and another reached the outskirts of Grozny in Chechnya. A party of German and Austrian alpinists planted the banner of the swastika on the summit of Mount Elbrus, the highest peak in Europe.

Yet the gains were insecure. The spearheads drew ever further apart and were incapable of supporting each other. The tempo of their advance decreased with every kilometre conquered, and they were left wide open to counter-attacks. There was no hope, as in Central or Western Europe, of introducing a systematic occupation for exploiting the territory. The ultimate destination of Baku, capital of the Caspian oil industry, remained tantalizingly out of reach.

The most critical situation, however, began to develop in the autumn at Stalingrad. In origin, the operation had been intended to provide a buffer for protecting the main advance, further south, to the Caucasus. And this objective was satisfactorily accomplished. Five armies – the 6th under General von Paulus, the 4th Panzer under General Hoth, two Romanian armies and one Italian – edged forward until 'the City of Stalin' came into bombing range. The Luftwaffe then razed the right-bank suburbs of the city to rubble. The surrender of Stalingrad seemed imminent.

Unfortunately for the Germans, the Soviet High Command had other ideas. As Chuikov's infantrymen fought stubbornly in the ruins, Rokossovsky, commander of the Don Front, painstakingly drew a ring round the overstretched German positions. He struck on 19 November, and four days later the ring was sealed. Paulus, his 6th Army and a large panzer force were trapped.

Contrary to many accounts, however, their predicament was far from hopeless. True, Hitler had forbidden retreat. But retreat would not necessarily have been the best course of action. It would have released Rokossovsky for a determined drive to the south to cut off the German Army Group strung out on the Caucasus Front. So Paulus favoured sitting tight. So did his superior, Manstein, who was told 'Sixth Army will still be here at Easter'. The key to the strategy was supply. Reichsmarschall Göring had assured the Führer that the Stalingrad pocket could be satisfactorily supplied from the air. And Manstein believed strongly in a plan called 'Winter Storm' whereby Paulus and Hoth would pierce the encircling ring from either side and would set up a regular supply corridor. Their colleague, Field Marshal von Kluge, had held on to his exposed outpost before Moscow throughout the previous winter. They expected to do the same. Their expectations were not unreasonable

One should remember that the Soviet High Command had ordered its generals to launch 'pre-emptive blows' on all possible occasions, and that many of these ill-judged operations had come to grief. In May 1942, for example, Marshal Timoshenko led five Soviet armies across the River Donets in a bid to encircle and to recover the city of Kharkov. In the ensuing contest with the 6th and 1st panzer armies he ended up by being totally encircled himself. He lost over a quarter of a million men, and 1,200 tanks. He was lucky that Stalin merely relieved him of his command.

At the time when Paulus was approaching Stalingrad, the Western Allies mounted their only military operation on the continent that year. On 19 August 1942 a small force of 6,000 Canadian, British and US troops was landed at Dieppe in Normandy to test the German defences. Their bravery contrasted with the scandalously poor planning of their superiors. Air cover was woefully inadequate. The navy accidentally gave advance notice of its approach. And intelligence had failed to locate German gun positions. The result was slaughter. The Canadians suffered over 60 per cent casualties.[36] It was the sort of event that on the Eastern Front was a daily occurrence.

The Western air offensive, 1942–5

Air Vice-Marshal Sir Arthur Harris (1910–84) was appointed C.-in-C. of the RAF's Bomber Command in February 1942. He was the prime advocate of 'area bombing': that is, of a strategy whereby huge fleets of massed bombers concentrated their night-time attacks on the enemy's urban areas. He owed his position to the fact that the RAF's previous programme of precision bombing had failed. An experiment conducted in August 1941 showed that only 1 in 3 bombers had come within 8 km of its designated target, and that in a raid over the Ruhr only 1 in 10 claims of successful target hits was true. In effect, the RAF was obliged either to move over to indiscriminate area bombing or to abandon the bombing offensive altogether. One could not attack Germany with the Royal Navy. The British Army, eighteen months after Dunkirk, was convalescent. So area bombing was, without exaggeration, the only way that Britain had of 'hitting back'. So, with Churchill's support, Harris got his way.

Harris was a pitiless character. He had developed his theories fighting insurgents in pre-war Iraq, where whole villages were levelled, and where he had seen with his own eyes the death and mutilation inflicted by his warplanes on innocent civilians. 'The only thing the Arab understands', he said, 'is the heavy hand.'[37] The Arabs were now German. The philosophy also appealed to the USAAF.

George Bell, Bishop of Chichester (1883–1958), expressed moral outrage from the start. It was no sound argument, he maintained, that the Nazis had used similar methods during the Blitz. And attacks where civilians could not be distinguished from legitimate military or industrial targets breached the Geneva conventions. In a speech to the House of Lords, he described the bombing of non-combatants as 'a degradation of the spirit of all who take part in it'.[38] Area bombing is also known under the names of 'blanket bombing' and, in Germany, of 'terror bombing'.

In the course of 1942 the bombing offensive gathered pace. It absorbed one-third of Britain's military expenditure. Production lines of the Lancasters and Halifaxes came on stream. The 'Pathfinder Force', using 'Oboe' radar navigation and dropping marker flares and target-illuminators, went into action.

Thereafter, area bombing rose inexorably in a ceaseless crescendo. The RAF concentrated on night raids. The Americans, whose 8th Army Air Force had been sent to Britain, concentrated on daylight raids. Their P-51 Mustang escorts were capable of flying with the B-17 bombers all the way to Berlin and back. Day after day the skies over Germany were saturated. The Luftwaffe, overstretched in its main role of ground support on the Eastern Front, was overwhelmed by sheer numbers.

Officially, the aim was to destroy legitimate targets. In practice, no secret was made of the intention of causing uncontrollable conflagrations and thereby 'breaking civilian morale'. One of the early targets, Lübeck, was chosen for its wooden houses, and for the hope that the fires ignited by the first wave of bombers would lead the second wave to their destination. On 22 August 1943 a mass raid on Hamburg triggered a firestorm – the incendiary equivalent of a hurricane – and 43,000 people were incinerated in one night. This was regarded as 'success'.

Nonetheless, one cannot argue that area bombing was merely a criminal diversion. One million German soldiers were tied down in anti-aircraft defence, and an increasing sector of Germany's inadequate aircraft production had to be turned over to night fighters. Moreover, the magnificent exploits of Squadron Leader Guy Gibson's 617 Squadron (the 'Dambusters'), who attacked the Möhne, Eder and Sorpe dams on 16/17 May 1943, proved that the honourable tradition of precision bombing had not been forgotten. It was 617 Squadron that would eventually sink Germany's last remaining battleship, the *Tirpitz*, in a Norwegian fjord.

North Africa, 1941–2

In October 1941 Churchill wrote to General Auchinleck, 'It is impossible to explain to Parliament . . . how our forces . . . have to stand for months without engaging the enemy, while . . . Russia is being battered to pieces.' Auchinleck was ponderously consolidating the six divisions of his Eighth Army for 'Operation Crusader', which in November–December pushed the Italians and the Afrikakorps back through Cyrenaica, relieving Tobruk on 'Pearl Harbor Day'. Rommel promptly launched a counter-attack, and in May a second one that took him all the way to the Egyptian border. Some 38,000 British troops were captured at the third battle for Tobruk. Just as the Germans found in Russia, the British were learning that the mere conquest of desert expanses was meaningless. Rommel was only one victory away from the seizure of the Canal Zone. He could be defeated only if he was drawn into a major engagement in which the substance of his army could be broken. For this purpose, Churchill removed Auchinleck and put the Eighth Army in the hands of General Bernard Montgomery.

'Monty' was cocky in his bearing but cautious in tactics, and considerate of his men. Knowing that the Afrikakorps was bound to press eastward, he decided to maximize his advantage in numbers, in guns, in short supply lines and in the information from Ultra. He now commanded 195,000 mainly Commonwealth troops, over 1,000 tanks, an imposing artillery park, and, critically, copious reserves of petrol and ammunition. In fact he outmatched Rommel in all departments. He struck at El Alamein on 23 October 1942, when Rommel was on leave. The opening barrage obliterated the Axis front lines. The ensuing 'dogfight' gave the edge to the weight of British numbers. And the breakout gave unstoppable impetus to Monty's tank force. The Afrikakorps conducted a brilliant retreat, which in 1943 was to lead to Rommel's departure from North Africa for good.

In British history books, the victory at El Alamein marks, in Churchill's words, 'the turning of the tide'. He was referring to the tide of Britain's survival. In the broader perspective, El Alamein barely registers as a major event. It did not compare with the recent battle of Midway, where the Americans put an end to Japan's naval supremacy, still less to the forthcoming battle of Stalingrad. After Alamein, the crushing supremacy of the Third Reich in Europe was still intact.[39]

Stalingrad, November 1942–February 1943

It is often said that the fate of Stalingrad was sealed by Hitler's obstinate refusal to retreat. This is only partly true, for Stalin had the same obsession. He absolutely refused to order a withdrawal from the city that bore his name. It might have been prudent to extract Chuikov's beleaguered 62nd Army from the ruins, and to concentrate on the defence of the Volga's eastern bank. Instead, huge reinforcements were ferried across the river to keep the defenders going and to tighten Rokossovsky's encirclement. Stalin, like Hitler, well understood the power of a symbol.

What followed has been described as the biggest meat-grinder on earth. It could also be compared to a giant contest of arm-wrestling, with neither side willing to concede a centimetre. It was not conventional urban warfare. It was a super-intensive slugging match between two professional armies, each using heavy artillery, tanks, dive-bombers, and – in the case of the Red Army – frontal infantry assaults at close quarters. It lasted for eleven weeks.

In mid-December 1942 Hoth's 4 Panzer attempted to punch a hole in Rokossovsky's ring from the west. Considerable progress was made, and the tip of Hoth's spearhead came within 32 km of Paulus's outer lines. Yet slow-moving tanks, floundering in the slush and snow of early winter, offered easy targets for the massed Soviet guns – and, in any case, Paulus did not have the strength to come out and meet them. The counter-attack crumbled. The supply corridor was never opened.

Then the Luftwaffe faltered. Improvised runways had been constructed inside the ring; and dozens of planes landed and took off every day. But the type of heavy transports that was needed to lift large quantities of food, ammunition, petrol and spares did not materialize. And, as the ring closed, the number of serviceable airstrips decreased. The Red Army piled on the pressure. The Germans, Italians, Hungarians and Romanians froze, starved and despaired. Their guns jammed. Their vehicles stalled. Their wounded were not evacuated. Those who did not die from the shells and the bullets began to lose heart.

The full horrors of life on the Soviet side of the Stalingrad ring were long concealed from a Western audience. But they were not just the horrors of massive battle deaths.

The Soviet authorities were pitiless. 'In the blazing city,' wrote Chuikov, 'we did not suffer cowards, we had no room for them.' Soldiers and civilians alike were warned with Stalin's quotation from Lenin: 'Those who do not assist the Red Army in every way . . . are traitors and must be killed withut pity.' All 'sentimentalism' was rejected. . .

Establishing a ferocious discipline was hard at first. Not until 8 October did the political department of the Stalingrad Front feel able to report to Moscow the 'defeatist mood is almost eliminated, and the number of treasonous incidents is getting lower'. That the Soviet regime was almost as unforgiving towards its own soldiers as towards the enemy is demonstrated by the total figure of 13,500 executions, both summary and judicial, during the battle of Stalingrad. . .

Chuikov's weakest units were the militia Special Brigades made up mainly of workers from factories in the northern part of Stalingrad. Blocking groups of well-armed Komsomol volunteers or NKVD detachments were placed behind them to prevent retreat . . . In the case of the 124th Special Brigade facing the 16th Panzer Division at Rynok, the blocking groups forced those who were cracking under the strain to escape to the enemy. . .

Sometimes deserters were shot in front of an audience of a couple of hundred fellow soldiers from their division. More usually, however, the condemned man was led off by (an NKVD) squad to a convenient spot behind the lines. There, he was told to strip so that his uniform and boots could be re-used. . .

The Special Department of the 45th Rifle Division must have contained unusually inaccurate marksmen . . . encouraged in their work with an extra ration of vodka. On [one] occasion, they were ordered to execute a soldier for a self-inflicted wound. He was stripped as usual, shot and thrown into a shell hole . . . Two hours later, his underclothes caked in blood and mud, [he] staggered back to his battalion. The same execution squad had to be called out to shoot him again . . . Self-inflicted wounds were regarded as desertion by dishonesty. . .

The ultimate self-inflicted wound was suicide. Like the Wehrmacht, the Soviet authorities defined it as 'a sign of cowardice' or the product of 'unhealthy moods'. . .

The NVKD and the political department of Stalingrad Front worked extremely closely on any hint of 'anti-Soviet activity' . . . Most of the cases took place behind the lines. Newly arrived conscripts were more likely to be denounced by fellow conscripts. A Stalingrad civilian in Training Battalion 178, who ventured to say that they would freeze and starve when winter came, was quickly arrested 'thanks to the political consciousness of Trainee K and I'. . .

Even day-to-day administrative policy confirmed the impression of soldiers as discardable items . . . For front-line soldiers at Stalingrad replacement [boots and uniforms] did not come from the quartermaster's store; they came off the bodies of dead comrades. Men were sent forward at night into no-man's land to strip corpses to their underclothes. The sight of fallen comrades, left semi-naked in the open revolted many. . .

The many thousands of women and children left behind in the city sought shelter in the cellars of ruins, in sewers and caves . . . [They] faced the virtual impossibility of finding food and water. Each time there was a lull in the bombardments, [they] appeared out of holes in the ground to cut slabs of meat off dead horses. . . The chief foragers were children . . . German soldiers made use of Stalingrad orphans. Daily tasks, such as filling water-bottles were dangerous when Russian snipers lay in wait for any movement. So, for the promise of a crust of bread, they would get Russian boys and girls to take their water-bottles down to the Volga's edge to fill them. When the Soviet side realised what was happening, Red Army soldiers shot children on such missions. . .[40]

The ring inexorably shrank. To begin with, its diameter had measured about 65 km. In January 1943 it was reduced by a succession of sudden collapses. On the 8th, Rokossovsky called for surrender. On the 10th, he initiated a general offensive. On the 14th, active German soldiers received only 200 grams of bread. On the 22nd, the last substantial German airfield was lost. The temperature had dropped to −20°C. The Red Army radio mocked, 'The cruel Russian winter has only just begun.' Paulus also had his radio link. The Führer refused to countenance capitulation. German troops, he said, were to make 'an unforgettable contribution to the salvation of the Western world'. Their contribution was certainly unforgettable.

At the end of the month, German soldiers in the front line began to wave white flags from their icy foxholes without permission to do so. Others wrote notes about their undying love for the Führer before shooting themselves. On 31 January, Paulus himself accepted the inevitable. He was followed into captivity by 90,000 survivors of the quarter of a million with whom he had set out three months before. Half of the survivors perished within a week or two of capture. Only 5 per cent would outlast the Soviet camps and return home to Germany and Austria to tell the tale.

The final scene was immortalized by a Soviet photographer for the next day's issue of *Izvestia*. The handsome Rokossovsky, commander of the Don Front, is sitting at his desk in his austere command post. Paulus, balding and dejected, is signing the act of capitulation. Next to Rokossovsky sits the NKVD colonel Konstantin Telegin, the party watchdog and political commissar, and in practice Rokossovsky's superior. For reasons best known to the Soviet censorship, Telegin's face was erased.[41]

Contrary to later accounts, Stalingrad was not the decisive event of the Second World War. It was far from being the largest battle on the Eastern Front. The 90,000 troops who were captured numbered only half as many as the British were to take at the end of the North African campaigns. And on the scale of military disasters it was no more significant than Timoshenko's recent disaster before Kharkov. Yet Stalingrad, in psychological terms, was immensely significant. It showed, for the first time, that Hitler's Wehrmacht was fallible. It showed that Stalin's Red Army was not the shambolic giant with feet of clay that many experts had predicted. It sent shivers through Berlin, and gladdened the hearts of all Hitler's enemies. One cannot exaggerate its impact on the minds of Britons and Americans, who at the time had no single soldier fighting on European soil.

With the 6th Army eliminated, the Germans were forced to retreat along the length of their southern lines. Army Group B raced back from the Caucasus to avoid being cut off. The Wehrmacht's brief incursion into the expanses of Russia proper came to an end as it withdrew once again into Ukraine. Germany's second grand offensive on the Eastern Front had failed ignominiously. And there was no end in sight.

Operation Torch, November 1942–May 1943

At the time that the Battle of Stalingrad was joined, in November 1942, an Allied expeditionary force sailed over the western horizon and landed troops both in Morocco and in Algeria. The ships were mainly British, the troops mainly American. And their landing grounds were French, subject to Vichy control. On the advice of General de Gaulle, the leaders of the expedition were hoping that the 25,000 men who came ashore near Casablanca, and the 35,000 near Oran and Algiers, would soon be joined by most of the 150,000 strong French garrison in North Africa. This was 'Operation Torch' – the first serious initiative by the Western Powers for over two years.

Calculations about French cooperation were ill-judged. Over 1,000 US soldiers died from French fire on the beaches near Casablanca. And it was many weeks before the French general could be persuaded to change sides and the Allies could advance on German and Italian bases in Tunisia.

At first, the Axis positions in Tunis looked set for a long defence. Heavily reinforced, and supported from Sicily with extra air power, they were confident of holding their own against the American First Army advancing from the west and the British Eighth Army advancing from the east. Indeed, Rommel struck a few sharp blows. At the Kasserine Pass, he taught the 1st US Armored Division a very painful lesson. But then he was ordered home. For once, the Axis chose to cut its losses. The Allies were left holding the full length of the African shore.

Axis strategists were surprised and puzzled by Operation Torch. It consumed a large portion of the Allies' available resources for the sake of a fairly remote foothold. In fact it resulted from an awkward compromise between the Americans' insistence on immediate action and Churchill's determination to avoid a risky landing in Europe. The Allies could not afford another Dunkirk. Yet Torch brought some definite benefits. It delivered a large bag of POWs – mainly Italians who had no wish to fight. It forced Hitler to order the occupation of southern France, thereby eating into the Wehrmacht's reserves. It gave the Allied armies some much needed experience in a large-scale seaborne offensive. And it left them with a springboard for the next jump.[42]

Kursk, July 1943

In the wake of Stalingrad, the Red Army pressed steadily forward. It had discovered a technique ideally suited to its superiority in men and guns: constantly probing the German lines with hundreds of local attacks, prising open the weak spots, and denying the enemy time for effective recovery. In four months it drove the southern sector of the front back for nearly 500 km, until a huge salient had developed that threatened to split the Germans' Army Group Centre from their Army Group South. In the centre of the salient lay the small Russian town of Kursk, due south of Moscow and adjacent to the Ukrainian border. It is the one name which all historians of the Second World War should remember, even if they forget the others.

The essence of 'Kursk' lay in the fact that both sides knew that it was going to happen. As a result, both sides amassed unheard-of quantities of men and machines in the hope of gaining a decisive advantage. The German High Command had been planning its third summer offensive for some time. And it knew that the Kursk salient had to be lanced. So it decided to use a grand attack on the salient as the starting point. For its part, the Soviet High Command realized in very good time that the salient would not be left undisturbed. Indeed, it was warned both via Ultra and via its own spies in Germany that Kursk was going to be the target.

The German plan for 'Operation Citadel' foresaw a classic pincer movement that would slice through the neck of the salient, isolate the bulk of the Soviet forces from their supply lines, and facilitate a grand encirclement. It was to be the revenge match for Stalingrad, but conducted in the burning summer heat. Kluge in the north, facing Rokossovsky in the centre, had seventeen armoured divisions at his disposal. Manstein in the south, facing Vatutin, was given an equally lavish array. The faith of the panzer commanders lay in their new Tiger – the most powerful tank of the war. The start was fixed for 3 July 1943.

The Soviet plan, devised by Zhukov and Stalin, foresaw a scenario in which a massed panzer attack – indeed a double mass panzer assault – would be stopped in its tracks for the very first time in the war. Already, in April, Zhukov had calculated that if sufficient defences could be put in place to soak up the initial attacks, the Red Army possessed more than sufficient reserves, especially of tanks, to deliver a devastating armoured counterpunch of its own. For the first phase, he put his faith – and an

incalculable amount of hard labour – into concentric rings of minefields
and of batteries packed with traps, anti-tank guns, long-range howitzers
and Katyusha rocket-launchers. For every single German tank, he lined up
3 anti-tank weapons, 9 assault guns, 50 rockets per hour, and 150 mines.
For the second phase he put his faith in 3,500 T-34s, a much smaller and
less powerful tank than the Tiger, but amazingly speedy and manoeuvra-
ble, and designed to hunt in packs. Crucially, he had breathing space to
put his dispositions into place before 'Citadel' began.

Phase 1 of the battle lasted for a week. Time and again, day after day,
the panzers roared forward, tracks screeching and guns blazing, rushing to
navigate the obstacles and to penetrate the clouds of metal that were
hurled at them. Led by the Tigers, they picked off their frontal adversaries
with ease. Some of them passed through the first lines of defence. Yet
time and again they ran into barriers, fell to flank fire, or were broken up
from a distance by saturation rocket salvoes. After a week, they had
advanced a maximum of 6.5 km in the north and 15 km in the south.
None of them was anywhere near Kursk.

Phase 2 began on 12 July. Three panzer divisions aiming for the village
of Prokhorovka, on the southern perimeter, suddenly found their advance
blocked by the 5th Guards Tank Army, with three times as many tanks as
they had. It is estimated that a total of 1,200 armoured vehicles were
engaged in the biggest and most intense tank battle of all time. Packs of
steel monsters blasted each other from point-blank range. Hundreds of
stricken aircraft fell from the skies. Blazing wrecks and carbonized corpses
littered the steppe. But it was the panzers that finally yielded. On the third
day the swarms of T-34s broke into the weakly defended German lines
and wreaked still greater havoc. The Germans lost 70,000 men and 3,000
tanks. Numerically, the Soviets probably lost more. But they won the field
without exhausting their reserves. As Zhukov knew well, the Red Army
could sustain the greater losses, and still fight on.

Kursk, like Waterloo, was a set battle, which both combatants had
sought to fight in expectation of victory. The Red Army defenders on the
perimeters were a modern equivalent of 'the thin red line' that withstood
all the charges of the Imperial Guard. The T-34s played the role of the
Prussian cavalry which arrived with perfect timing to sweep Napoleon
from the field. The difference between Zhukov and Wellington is that
Zhukov always knew when the cavalry would arrive.[43]

The significance of Kursk cannot be overrated. This was the decisive
battle. The Wehrmacht's prime strike force was destroyed so completely

that a major offensive could never be launched again. In 1939, 1940, 1941, 1942 and 1943 Hitler had repeatedly waged an annual season of blitzkrieg. And each of those five seasons had depended on the ability to assemble huge concentrations of armoured forces together with all their support services. The season of 1943 was to be the last one. The Red Army, in contrast, though sorely mauled, had emerged psychologically strengthened and logistically equipped for pursuing all branches of warfare with great energy. On the day that Zhukov unleashed his counter-attack at Kursk, the Western Powers had not yet landed a single soldier on the European mainland. And from Kursk Zhukov was heading relentlessly for the *Führerbunker* in Berlin.

The Italian Campaign, 1943–4

Before the battle of Kursk was finished, a modest Allied amphibious force crossed from North Africa to Sicily. Once again the Western Powers had decided to err on the side of caution. Once again it would be Soviet soldiers who would have to die in large numbers if the momentum of the war against Hitler was to be maintained. Southern Sicily is further from Berlin than Kursk is.

'Operation Husky', the conquest of Sicily, took seven weeks. Patton's Seventh Army shot round the west coast and captured Palermo. Montgomery's Eighth Army drove round the east coast under the shadow of Mount Etna. The Italian divisions facing them folded. Then Field Marshal Kesselring, C.-in-C. South-West, stepped in, strengthened the approaches to the Messina Strait, and managed an orderly retreat. Delaying tactics were to provide the essence of German conduct.

The conquest of southern Italy, from Calabria to Rome, took no less than nine months. The terrain was very mountainous. The rains were heavy. Any number of natural defensive positions blocked progress. What is more, as a result of the Italian political crisis, the number of German divisions was increased from four to eighteen. If it weren't for Allied air power, it is doubtful if the advance could have kept going. Each of the Allied amphibious landings – at Salerno in September 1943 and at Anzio in January 1944 – was accomplished with the greatest difficulty. And the German defences of the Gothic Line held out for four months. The storming of Monte Cassino by two Polish divisions, after the Indians and New Zealanders had both been rebuffed, and the conquest of the Hitler

Flashpoint 1939: The Free City of Danzig

Claimed both by Germany and Poland, Danzig (now Gdańsk) had been established by the League of Nations as a self-governing city state.

Above. The old Hanseatic port.

Below. A Nazi demonstration, August 1939: 'Danzig is a German city, and wants to join Germany.'

Prelude to war

Above. The Nomanhan Incident, August 1939. Japanese troops march towards defeat at the Khalkin River on the frontier of Soviet-held Outer Mongolia. The Red Army's victory freed the USSR for action in Europe.

Below. The Nazi-Soviet Pact, 23 August 1939, the diplomatic licence for war. Ribbentrop signs; Stalin beams. 'I know', said Stalin, 'that the German nation loves its Fuhrer.' Hitler remarked, 'I have the world in my pocket.'

Joint operations

Above. The first salvo, 1 September 1939. The German cruiser, Schleswig-Holstein, starts the conflict by opening fire on the Polish fort of Westerplatte.

Below. Red Army tanks join the Wehrmacht in the victory parade at Brześć (formerly Brest-Litovsk), 23 September 1939, before dividing Poland into German and Soviet spheres of occupation.

Accomplices in crime

Above. Adolf Hitler, *Führer*, and Joseph Stalin, *Vodz*: partners 1939–41, enemies, 1941–5.

Below. Reichsführer-SS Heinrich Himmler and NKVD Chief Lavrenty Beria. At Yalta, President Roosevelt pointed across the table and asked Stalin, 'Who's the man with the pince-nez?' Stalin replied, 'That's Beria; he's our Himmler.'

Falling stars

Above. Benito Mussolini, *Duce*: dismissed 1943, murdered 1945, and Philippe Pétain, Marshal: hero of 1918, Vichy leader, 1940–5.

Below. Field Marshal Erich von Manstein: author of victory in the West in 1940, dismissed 1944, and Soviet Marshal Grigoriy Kulik: commander in Poland and Finland, 1939–40, and an unlikely survivor.

Scandinavia under attack, 1939–40

Finland invaded, Norway and Denmark occupied, Sweden forced into pseudo-neutral neutrality.

Above. The Winter War. Skilful Finnish troops bravely resist the Soviet invasion.

Right. Narvik. The British–French–Polish Expeditionary Force comes to grief in a vain attempt to interrupt the German invasion of Norway.

The fall of the West, May–June 1940

Above. Arc de Triomphe. The victorious Wehrmacht parades through Paris before turning France into a disarmed, client state.

Below. The Battle of Britain. Thanks to the RAF, Britain lives to fight another day, despite the defeat of its land forces. Hitler postpones Operation Sealion, giving priority to the Soviet Union instead.

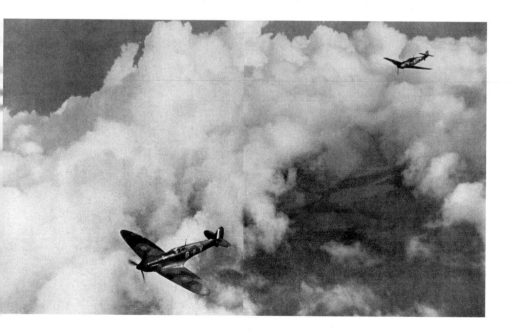

The spoils of the East, 1940–1

Stalin and Hitler continue to carve up Eastern Europe.

Above. The Baltic States swallowed. Hand-picked Communist delegations beg the USSR to accept the incorporation of Estonia, Latvia, Lithuania and Moldavia.

Right. The Balkans ravaged. Heading for Athens, German forces pause in front of the Yugoslav parliament in Belgrade.

Line by the French Expeditionary Corps finally opened the road to Rome in May. The 'Eternal City' was captured on 4 June, but only after US General Mark Clark's vanity had thrown away a golden opportunity to block the German retreat.

In effect, the German plan of campaign – to use a minimum of forces to cause the maximum delay – was highly successful. The same rate of progress would not bring the Allies to the alpine foothills before the spring of 1945. Before the Alps were reached, the Germans would feel no special threat to the safety of their homeland from the south. And the Alps formed the best defence line in Europe.

Nonetheless, like Torch, the Italian Campaign cannot be dismissed as a token affair. It put an end to the senior Fascist experiment; it deprived the Reich of its most important ally; and it tied down a German army that was badly needed elsewhere. Above all, it gave the Western Powers the satisfaction of active participation, and a valid answer to the accusation that they were not pulling their weight.[44]

Operation Bagration, June–August 1944

After Kursk, the conduct of war on the Eastern Front underwent a marked change. But the change cannot be attributed solely to Zhukov's great victory. For the Red Army not only had the spirit and the confidence to go over to a general offensive: it now possessed the means to do so on a colossal scale. Its logistical advantage derived from two complementary sources. One was American Lend-Lease aid, which was now pouring in vast quantities of trucks, petrol, rations, boots and ammunition via Iran as well as Murmansk. The other was the unexpectedly dynamic performance of relocated Soviet industries, whose greatly increased production of tanks, guns and warplanes was now on stream. American aid kept the Red Army on the move. Soviet industry armed it with first-class weapons of modern warfare. The delivery of vehicles and aircraft in large numbers was particularly significant. The Red Air Force could now provide air cover for the advancing tank armies, much as the Luftwaffe had protected the panzers in earlier phases. All but the most blockheaded Nazis could see the writing on the wall.

In the second half of 1943, German forces in the USSR were still grouped, as in 1941, in the three concentrations of North, Centre and South. And communication between the three army groups was still intact.

Henceforth, Soviet priorities were also threefold. They were to raise the Siege of Leningrad in the north; to exploit the confusion caused in the south by the victory of Kursk; and to build up an overwhelming concentration of forces in the centre in preparation for the spring offensive of 1944. At this stage, Soviet planners were already aiming at the expulsion of all German units from all Soviet territory (as defined by them).

The 'Hero City' of Leningrad, blockaded since December 1941, was relieved in gradual stages. For most of the first year it had been supplied only across the winter ice and summer waters of Lake Ladoga. But in February 1943, after an intense battle, a corridor 10 km wide was opened to the east, and trains steamed through. In October 1943 Army Group North was building the top section of its 'East Wall' when the Soviets attacked in force. The Germans, now themselves beleaguered, held on for three months. Hitler ordered no retreat. The 900-days ordeal, which had cost perhaps a million lives, ended on 27 January 1944.[45]

The southern theatre, where the winter set in later and the spring began sooner, offered numerous opportunities. The Donbass industrial region was recovered in August 1943. Kharkov fell in September, Kiev in early November. All the major German salients had been eliminated, and no less than eighteen 'Soviet fronts' (or army groups) were rolling forward along a 1,000-km front line adjacent to the Dnieper.

Hitler was certainly shaken by the fall of Mussolini. And he became increasingly anxious about the prospect of Allied landings in France. For the first time, he openly admitted that territory would have to be yielded in the East in order to meet the Wehrmacht's obligations in the West. For the first time, panzer divisions were pulled out for transfer westward. Inspired by General Model, the 'lion of defence', the Germans thereafter adopted a policy of phased withdrawal combined with the barbaric policy of 'scorched earth', which the Red Army itself had not hesitated to use in 1941–2. All buildings were torched, all bridges were blown, all food and livestock was killed or removed from vast areas. Yet the sheer weight of Soviet attackers prevailed, especially in the south. The pull-out to the line of the Dnieper turned into a race. Soviet bridgeheads west of Kiev turned into another burgeoning salient. Field Marshal von Kleist's Army Group A, which a year before had been heading for the Caucasus, barely scrambled across the Kerch Strait into Crimea, where it faced yet another evacuation. By the time that the pre-war Polish frontier in Volhynia was reached, in January 1944, a chunk of territory larger than France (or Texas) had been cleared.

In spring 1944 two further actions consolidated previous Soviet gains. One at Korsun, where Vatutin won his marshal's star, encircled the last remaining German pocket on the Dnieper. The other drove the Germans from the Crimean Peninsula. The scene in May on the beaches of Sevastopol, whence the remnants of a 150,000-strong German force were ferried to safety, were reminiscent yet again of Dunkirk.

The critical operation was brewing in the centre, however, where the Soviet High Command had determined to expel the Wehrmacht's main force for good. Planned by Zhukov and Stalin, it was entrusted to Rokossovsky – half-Pole, half-Russian – who had shone both at Stalingrad and at Kursk (after being released from the GULag). It provided him with 2.4 million troops, 5,200 tanks, 5,300 aircraft, and a numerical advantage of nearly 4:1. His opponent, General von Busch, a fervent Nazi, could be counted on to implement the Führer's orders implicitly. Though lacking in anti-tank guns and artillery, and notwithstanding transfers to the sagging southern sector, the German defenders adopted a strategy of fixed 'fortresses' – at Vitebsk, Orsha, Bobruisk and Mogilev. Vitebsk alone was filled with five divisions. The garrisons were ordered to fight to the last man.

By this time Rokossovsky could afford to finalize the build-up without risk of interruption. Stalin approved his dispositions on 30 May, although he did not unleash 'Operation Bagration' until 23 June. But when he did, the effect was shattering. All the German fortresses were surrounded within four days. Two decimated German armies were struggling to retreat. And the 9th Army had disintegrated. On the 28th, Hitler dismissed Busch, and brought in Model.

In Bagration's second phase, starting at Minsk in Byelorussia, Model skilfully extracted the remnants of Army Group Centre, committing the final reserves. His only hope was to create a new defence line on the River Vistula, 400 km to the west. Meanwhile, Rokossovsky's juggernaut thundered on, offering not a moment's respite. He was rewarded with his marshal's star when he crossed the River Bug – on the so-called Curzon Line – on 19 July. He was now in central Poland, and heading for Warsaw. At the same time, two fronts on his right wing were freed to peel off northward in the direction of East Prussia and thereby to cut off Army Group North from its rear. Two of the Ukrainian fronts moved up parallel to his left wing, doubling the force that was heading for the Vistula.

Rokossovsky's orders at this point were to capture Warsaw on 2 August. On that day he actually scanned the city from an observation post across the river. The Polish capital was in flames. Soviet radio had called on the citizens to rise against the German oppressors. Yet on that same fateful day Model had also launched a powerful counter-attack with four panzer divisions, including the elite Hermann Göring division brought in from Italy. The liberation of Warsaw would have to wait.[46]

Nonetheless, in the view of the Soviet commanders, the setback was only a temporary and a local one. Two Red Army spearheads had already crossed the Vistula, and were holding their ground on the west bank. Operation Bagration may have been running out of steam. But the overall balance of forces still stood crushingly in the Red Army's favour. And it was not in the Soviet handbook to give the enemy leisure to recover. In this spirit, on 8 August Zhukov and Rokossovsky drew up a plan for a fresh offensive. They proposed that within a fortnight, having contained Model's counter-attack, they would mount an attack to liberate Warsaw. The city would be surrounded by thrusts delivered from north and south. After that, the stage would be set for a general westward assault across the great European plain. German defences had not been organized. Berlin beckoned. The plan was presented to Stalin, and his response was awaited.[47]

The dynamic tempo of the Soviet advance merits notice. From Stalingrad in February 1943, the central front had surged forward by leaps and bounds. The average rate of progress was 5.3 km a day. At that rate, with 592 km to go, and not allowing for the shrinking of the front, Rokossovsky was due to enter Berlin on 11 December.

Phase 3, June 1944–May 1945: the fall of the Third Reich

In the short interval preceding the launch of Bagration in June 1944, the Western Allies succeeded in landing a large force in Normandy. Operation Overlord was smaller than Bagration, but it radically changed the strategic framework of the war. Henceforth the Reich was going to be pincered from two sides.

From the Western viewpoint, the task facing the British and American armies was tough, but straightforward. The policy was unconditional surrender (see p. 60). After securing their bridgehead in northern France, they aimed to drive hell for leather for the Reich, to join up at some point with Soviet forces coming from the east, and then jointly to strangle the hydra in its nest.

From Stalin's point of view, however, the asymmetry of the situation called for some tricky decisions. The Western armies were three times further from Berlin than Rokossovsky was, and it was unlikely that they would ever field a force more than a fraction of the size of the Red Army. (The Wehrmacht was deploying only a quarter of its total resources – roughly sixty divisions – in the West.) The prospect loomed, therefore, not only of the Soviets taking Berlin singlehanded, but also of them overrunning most of Germany before the expected link-up. Surely, in that situation, the Nazi regime would be overthrown, and, as Communist ideology suggested, the danger would arise of a post-Nazi Germany joining the 'capitalist camp' in an anti-Soviet crusade. Stranger twists of fortune had already occurred.

Unfortunately, historians have never gained access to the archives which may still contain the details of Stalin's thinking as he watched Overlord develop in parallel to Bagration. Yet it is not too difficult to divine his main anxieties. One, undoubtedly, was Poland, where the Warsaw Rising inexplicably continued (see pp. 119–20). Stalin of all people, whose own career had come close to disaster during the Polish War of 1920, was not going to repeat Lenin's mistake of taking the Poles for granted. The last thing he wanted was to advance into Germany and then find that Red Army lines were threatened from the rear.

Another anxiety emanated from the Balkans, where Hitler's allies in Romania, Bulgaria and Hungary were daily growing more restless. Which way would they jump, especially if the Western Allies landed a force in their region? Perhaps Overlord was a feint, designed to secure France while leaving the way open for Churchill's lifelong obsession: a second landing in 'the soft under-belly of Europe'.

The third anxiety was Germany. Stalin no doubt relished the idea of the Red Army's conquest of Berlin. At the same time, he could have had no wish to carry all the costs and risks of occupying and administering Germany, while the Western Allies busied themselves with other matters. In this way, a major strategic decision hung both on military and on non-military calculations.

Stalin's course of action was faciliated by the Red Army's considerable time advantage. The Soviets were about to enjoy at least three or four spare months before the Western armies could begin to threaten western

Germany. The prime question was: how should these months be best employed? Stalin's answer became clear in the course of August 1944, when the Red Army was put into defensive mode on the central Vistula sector, whilst launching a crushing onslaught on Romania. The plan submitted by Zhukov and Rokossovsky had evidently been rejected. The main advance into Germany had been postponed. Instead, the Soviets set out to secure as much as possible of South-Eastern and Central Europe before the final reckoning came. In this way, at one stroke, they would forestall any chance of an Allied Balkan operation; they would give themselves the choice of entering the Reich either through Vienna or through Berlin; they would exploit the resources of several conquered countries to aid the USSR's post-war recovery; and they would put themselves into the strongest of positions for inter-Allied negotiations. And they could wait to see what happened in Poland. Stalin was playing the longer game.

Operation Overlord, June–July 1944

Most British and American historians rate D-Day as the decisive military event of the Second World War. It was certainly a very risky operation, magnificently executed, and of prime importance to Western interests. Had it failed, the chances of a second attempt in the foreseeable future were slim. And the fate of Europe would have been exclusively decided by the terminal trial of strength between the Wehrmacht and the Red Army.

Debarkation Day, D-Day was fixed for 5 June 1944, but postponed for 24 hours through stormy weather. The steady nerve shown on that occasion by General Eisenhower, the supreme Allied commander, can almost be described as 'true British grit'. Everything could easily have ended, like the Spanish Armada, on the bed of the English Channel. But it didn't. The Allied armada of 1,200 ships crossed in safety. The Germans had been effectively deceived as to its destination. Rommel was on leave. Allied air cover, with 260 planes per infantry division, was ten times greater than that of the Luftwaffe at the start of Barbarossa. The initial glider landing at Pegasus Bridge, near Ouistreham, was performed with brilliant precision, the parachute drop at Sainte-Mère-Eglise less so. None-theless, 156,000 troops were landed in one day on the five beaches code-named 'Sword', 'Juno', 'Gold', 'Omaha' and 'Utah'. Casualties – which included 2,500 dead, or 1.6 per cent – were historically light. The technical support, including the artificial 'Mulberry' harbours and PLUTO – the 'Pipe-Line [for petrol] Under The Ocean' – was a triumphant success. Two years late, but with great elan, the 'Second Front' had finally been opened.

A cardinal problem emerged within days, however. The British and American troops did not possess the weapons, training or leadership to overcome equivalent numbers of the better-performing Germans. Once established, they possessed 'an effective superiority of twenty to one in tanks and twenty-five to one in aircraft. Yet they could not bring their superiority to bear. Time and again they had to call up air support: rocket-firing Typhoons to dislodge panzers, and heavy bombers to bust German defences. As a result, progress on the ground was painfully slow. Mont-gomery was supposed to take Caen on the first evening. He reached the totally ruined town on the thirtieth day. The Americans were due to 'break out' within a fortnight. They did so after seven weeks.[48]

The campaign in Normandy closed with the bloody battle of the Falaise Gap on 19–21 August. The German Army Group B was trying to pull out eastward, but was forced to run the gauntlet between the 2nd Canadian Army to the north and American columns sweeping round from the south. The 1st Polish Armoured Division, fighting with the Canadians, heroically held 'the cork in the bottleneck'. Some Germans escaped, but most were trapped. They were rocketed from the air, or pulverized by heavy artillery. Some 10,000 died, and 50,000 surrendered. It was a mini-Stalingrad.

The Warsaw Rising, 1 August–5 October 1944

Not to be confused with the uprising in the Warsaw Ghetto in 1943, the Warsaw Rising was the biggest military action undertaken by any of the wartime resistance movements. It pitted 50,000 lightly armed Home Army fighters against a similar number of SS and auxiliary troops, including the renegade Russian RONA brigade armed with tanks, heavy artillery and warplanes. It was supposed to last five or six days, and went on for nearly ten weeks. None of the experienced observers, including Stalin, could understand it. The explanation was raw courage.

The Home Army, having seized much of the city, expected to receive assistance both from the Western Allies and from the Red Army. It received very little. The RAF was refused landing rights on Soviet-held territory. And the Red Army, though in sight of Warsaw, failed to react. One division of Polish soldiers from one of the Communist-run armies crossed the river, only to be slaughtered. Altogether, some 20,000 soldiers were killed on each side.

The civilian population bore the brunt of the tragedy. About 50,000 were massacred by the SS, at least 100,000 perished from German bombardments, and some 500,000 were sent to the camps, or to slave labour. After the compulsory evacuation, the ruined and empty city was razed to the ground on Hitler's personal orders. The losses – human and material – were sixty times as great as those in New York on 11 September 2001. They resembled a World Trade Center disaster every day for two months.

In military terms, Warsaw provides a textbook example of urban guerrilla warfare. An amateur force, with high motivation, held a ruthless and professional army at bay for weeks, defying tanks, heavy guns and dive-bombers. In political terms, the rising is often seen as a cynical betrayal by the Western leaders, who dismally failed to intervene with Stalin on behalf of their Polish allies. Confusion, poor preparations and faulty intelligence provide an alternative explanation.[49]

The Red Army's Balkan Campaign, 1944–5

Western historians rarely pay much attention to the Red Army's activities in the autumn of 1944. They are dismissed as a lull before the concluding operations of 1945. Yet in those few months Marshal Tolbukhin's armies occupied four countries, conquered an area twice the size of France, and substantially weakened the Wehrmacht's ability to defend the Reich.

Romania, which had participated in the German invasion of the USSR, was knocked out in a fortnight. The government of General Antonescu was overthrown, and harsh surrender conditions were imposed. The Romanian armed services were then obliged to fight their erstwhile German allies.

Tolbukhin moved into Bulgaria on 9 September. The local Communists put an end to the existing political order, and a Bulgarian army of 350,000 men was added to the Soviet reserves.

Romania and Bulgaria are both adjacent to Yugoslavia, whence Tito had appealed for Soviet aid. Belgrade was liberated on 20 October. And a joint Soviet–Titoist campaign finished off the original Chetnik resistance movement.

Like other countries before it, Hungary was in the middle of negotiating a settlement when disaster struck. The Wehrmacht moved forward to occupy Budapest, to remove the Regent, Admiral Horthy, and to install a Fascist regime run by the Arrow Cross – the Hungarian counterpart of the Romanian Iron Guard. The Germans' coup forestalled the Soviet advance, and precipitated an apocalyptic struggle for Hungary's capital.

The siege of Budapest lasted from November 1944 to 13 February 1945. Apart from Leningrad, Stalingrad and Warsaw, there was no urban battle to match its intensity. The German garrison possessed a specially strong panzer contingent, excellent fortifications on Buda Hill, and orders to fight to the death. Over 150,000 strong, they held off twice their number. On one occasion, tanks of the 4th Panzer Corps reached the perimeter, and could have broken out. But Hitler ordered them back. A force of 16,000 Germans was killed after the formal capitulation. Over 100,000 POWs were taken. The civilian death toll was of the same order.[50]

As the Soviet steamroller trundled through the Balkans, and the Vistula sector remained quiescent, Moscow's intentions in the Baltic region were clarified. Finland successfully negotiated an armistice in September. The three Baltic States – whose independence was still recognized in the West – were reincorporated into the USSR for a second time. Yet the occupying German army was not so much destroyed as corralled. Once Soviet forces had established a corridor from Byelorussia to the Baltic shore in Lithuania, German Army Group North was cut off. From then on it was gradually pushed from all sides into the Courland Pocket, whence the only exit was by sea. Further south, the Soviets could begin the demolition of East Prussia, which they intended to annex. One temporary incursion into the village of Nemmersdorf in September yielded pictures of German women stripped and crucified on barn doors. Goebbels hoped to use the pictures to stiffen resistance. They caused panic. And the *Ostflucht*, the great 'Flight from the East', began. The Courland Pocket looked like a side issue. It did not involve much spectacular fighting and some of the units were in poor condition. Yet its dimensions deserve comment. For no less than thirty-one undefeated German divisions were trapped on the Courland Peninsula in western Latvia, and they were denied any significant role in the last months of the war. Their numbers represented roughly 10 per cent of the Wehrmacht's establishment in early 1945, and were greater than those of the entire British Army. Indeed, they were equivalent to half the total German deployment on the Western Front. The exact consequences of their loss cannot be calculated. But if they had been available to plug the gaps in German defences as the Wehrmacht retreated into the Reich, the task of the Allied armies must necessarily have been so much harder.

The Liberation of France, July–December 1944

The breakout from Normandy was combined with a second series of landings on the Riviera, where 'Operation Dragoon' was launched on 15 August 1944. The British armies pushed eastwards through northern France; Patton's US Third Army drove at twice the pace in a wide arc through central France; and units from Dragoon pushed north up the Rhône valley. The Wehrmacht conducted a dogged retreat, until a continuous defence line could be established along the approaches to Germany's frontier.

Eisenhower had no plans to seize Paris, but a spontaneous rising by the French resistance forced his hand. A week's fighting with a demoralized German garrison sufficed. The German governor refused orders to dynamite the city monuments, and the armoured division of General Leclerc, who was serving under American command, was detached from the US Third Army to complete the action. This was exactly the scenario that was supposed to unfold in Warsaw. The Varsovians, still fighting their lonely battle, radioed congratulations to Paris.[51]

In the autumn of 1944 the Allied advance lost its impetus, giving the Wehrmacht an opportunity to reconsolidate. Brussels, for example, was liberated amid scenes of popular excitement on 3 September. But the Channel ports, including Antwerp, were not secured quickly, thereby causing a shortage of supplies. Field Marshal Model – now dubbed 'the Führer's Fireman' – had arrived to stiffen opposition.

Montgomery, increasingly criticized for his snail's-pace progress, reacted with a rash plan for an airborne assault on the bridges at Eindhoven, Nijmegen and Arnhem, 160 km ahead. 'Operation Market Garden', executed in late September, proved a glorious failure – a 'bridge too far'. But it was not an act of responsible generalship. The British 1st Airborne Division suffered cruel casualties. And the Polish Parachute

Brigade, which had trained for two years to liberate Warsaw, was sacrificed.[52]

The Americans subsequently ran into still greater trouble in the central sector. Drawn into the mountainous Ardennes, the scene of the panzers' triumph in 1940, they walked straight into the Wehrmacht's last major counter-offensive in the West. Veiled by bad December weather, two German armies containing nine panzer divisions attacked without warning, rapidly creating a deep and dangerous 'Bulge' in the Allied lines. Their aim was to repeat the success of 1940, to capture the Allied supply hub of Antwerp, and to free the Wehrmacht for the defence of the East. For two weeks the issue hung in the balance. Deprived of air cover, the Allied armies could not cope. The US 101st Airborne Division was encircled in Bastogne. When called on to surrender, its commander delivered the untranslatable reply of 'Nuts'. Then the weather cleared. The panzers could be blasted from the skies. The German advance quickly ran out of fuel and will. The Americans had lost 19,000 dead. The Germans lost up to 100,000 killed, wounded or captured, together with 800 tanks and 1,000 aircraft. General von Manteuffel's verdict was, 'It spelled bankruptcy: we could not afford such losses.'[53]

Even so, from the Western point of view the campaign was not going well. At the time of D-Day, the Combined Chiefs of Staff had estimated, like their forebears in 1914, that the war would be over by Christmas. The New Year now passed, and the Western armies had still not entered German territory. They had not even liberated the Netherlands. They still stood further from Berlin than the Red Army had been since July.

The Vistula to the Oder, January 1945

While the Western armies were edging cautiously forward in the direction of Germany, the Soviet High Command was planning an offensive to surpass all previous offensives. A total of 3.8 million troops were put at Zhukov's disposal to advance from the Vistula to the Oder in fifteen days, and from the Oder to the Elbe beyond Berlin in a further thirty days. In critical sectors, the Red Army was to enjoy a superiority of 10:1. Nothing to compare had ever been seen before. Military might on this scale could not be matched by any other power.

Not surprisingly, therefore, despite many advance warnings, German countermeasures were woefully inadequate. German industry had not fallen too far behind with arms production, except for aircraft. But the Reich was now suffering an acute shortage both of recruits and of fuel. Desperate efforts had been made to draft in *Hitlerjugend*, untrained youths and over-age veterans, but the pool was drying up. All the exploited resources of foreign-occupied countries – manpower, industrial production, food, soldiers, and, in the case of Romania, oil – were now flowing into the Soviet war chest. This, no doubt, is one of the reasons why Stalin had been in no hurry to provoke the final confrontation. Time was on his side.

The blow fell with explosive fury on 13 January 1945. (At Churchill's request, it had been put forward a week to take pressure off the Americans after the Ardennes offensive.) Twelve parallel thrusts smashed through enemy lines, particularly from the Vistula bridgeheads. And long columns of Soviet tanks were soon careering across the snowbound Polish plains. The ruins of Warsaw were taken on the 17th. Kraków fell on the 18th. The infamous camp at Auschwitz, largely evacuated, was discovered on the 27th. The German Army Group A in central Poland disintegrated. And a new 'Army Group Vistula' had to be improvised under the unlikely command of Heinrich Himmler. By the end of the month, Soviet forces had lined up along 100 km of the Oder facing Berlin, and the great city of Breslau was encircled, starting a titanic four-month siege. Progress had been slower in East Prussia, in front of the Pomeranian Wall on the Baltic coast, and in Hungary – whither, in a terminal throw of the dice, Hitler had dispatched the 6th Panzer Army.

The fate of Breslau illustrates the unparalleled ferocity employed by all sides. On 19 January 1945, when the city was designated a fortress, the Nazi authorities summarily ordered all women, children and non-combatants to leave. Some 600,000 civilians were forcibly expelled in a couple of days, and thousands perished as they trudged through the snow to distant collection centres. Many of the surviving refugees made it to Dresden, where they were duly incinerated by RAF Bomber Command. The Red Army then pulverized the city by weeks of incessant bombardment, which gradually reduced it to the same state as Dresden. The defenders, who consisted of a desperate cocktail of SS, reserve soldiers and slave workers, were decimated. They did not surrender until 6 May – a week after Berlin. Shortly before the surrender, the Nazi gauleiter bid farewell to his comrades, climbed into a light plane parked on an improvised airstrip among the ruins, took off, and disappeared forever.[54]

Following the Yalta Conference in February, Stalin seems to have put off the second stage of the winter offensive. The Red Army did not press on from the Oder to the Elbe as originally planned. Konev drove on at one point, in the direction of Dresden, then stopped. The only serious further advance was made in the south after Budapest fell and Soviet troops pressed up the Danube valley towards Vienna and 'the Reich's back door'. Stalin appeared to be waiting to see what the Western Allies intended.

Dresden, February 1945

Given that the Strategic Bombing Offensive was spreading eastward, and that the Red Army was rolling westward, it was clear that the two were going to meet. Indeed, at Yalta, Stalin specifically asked the Western leaders to bomb the cities of eastern Germany to assist the Red Army's advance. The result was 'Operation Thunderclap'. The targets were Magdeburg, Berlin, Chemnitz and Dresden.

On the night of 13/14 February 1945, RAF Bomber Command sent 796 Lancasters over Dresden in two waves, releasing 1,500 tonnes of high explosive and 1,200 tonnes of incendiaries. A firestorm ensued of still more fearsome proportions than that at Hamburg. Then a fleet of US B-17s struck in broad daylight to compound the damage. Estimates of civilian deaths vary from 30,000 to 120,000.

Dresden was virtually undefended. It was a historic city full of architectural treasures and terrified refugees. No war industries were located in the city centre, where the Pathfinders had dropped their flares. No major disruption of transport was caused. Trains started running again within a couple of days. As if to underscore the pointless savagery of the episode, the Red Army did not bother to attack.[55]

The endgame takes shape

By the spring of 1945 the Nazi regime had no way out. Hitler had taken to his bunker, from which he would never emerge. The Red Terror was raging in the East. The Soviets were not taking prisoners in combat. Male German civilians were murdered. German women were being gang-raped to order. Any German soldier who had the chance of surrendering to the British or the Americans was doing so.

In consequence of the Arnhem disaster, the Netherlands was subjected to a 'Hunger Winter'. It had been a luxury to eat tulip bulbs. Allied planes were now dropping potatoes instead of bombs. Amsterdam was not liberated until early May, eight whole months after Brussels. When the Canadians and Poles of the First Army marched into towns like Breda or Utrecht, the welcome was more ecstatic than anywhere in Europe.

The British Second Army moved further east towards Hamburg, and eventually to Schleswig-Holstein (where Himmler was bagged) and Lübeck. Denmark fell into the hands of the resistance movement – except for Bornholm, which was stormed in May by a Soviet force reputedly consisting largely of women.

Model had concentrated his defences in the Ruhrland. But he was outflanked when the US First Army found that the Rhine bridge at Remagen was still intact. Montgomery crossed the Rhine downstream at Wesel on 24 March, setting the stage for the isolation of the Ruhr Pocket, which Hitler had declared to be an invincible fortress. Model shot himself on 17 April, unable to carry out the Führer's orders.

The junction of US armies advancing from the Rhône valley and from Lorraine created a powerful group straddling the Saarland and Alsace. They were joined by General de Lattre's 1st French Army, the swallow of France's resuscitation. Wrongly convinced that the Nazis were about to stage a last stand in the so-called Alpine Redoubt, a Franco-American army group poured through Bavaria to the Swiss and Austrian borders.

In 1944–5 Allied armies in Italy moved up the peninsula from the Gustav Line near Rome to the Gothic Line near Florence, and eventually to the Venetian Line near Padua. Despite Churchill's obsession with the so-called 'Ljubljana Gap', which was going to give them entry to the Reich, they never drew close enough to see whether the gap really existed. And they never even considered an assault on the alpine passes. On 2 May they finally entered Italy's most easterly city, Trieste, only to find it full of Tito's partisans. A long stand-off ensued.

All in all, given a marked superiority in logistics and air power, the Allied advance was far less muscular than expected. The commanders were cautious, the tempo was slow. The men were disinclined to lose their lives needlessly on the point of victory.

The one exception could be found with the flamboyant General George Patton – 'Old Blood 'n' Guts' – and his US Third Army. Patton, like Rommel and Rokossovsky, knew all about speed and surprise. He had made the British in Sicily look like plodders, and he had saved his comrades at the Battle of the Bulge with a remarkable dash through the snow. Crossing the Rhine at Mainz on 22 March, he now crashed into central Germany at breakneck pace. His tanks outran the war correspondents driving captured Mercedes who were trying to find where he'd gone. Night and day they pushed through the thick Thuringian Forest – shades again of the Ardennes – until they emerged in Saxony, approaching Leipzig. They then crossed the Böhmerwald to Pilsen in Czechoslovakia, heading for Prague.

Almost everyone, especially Churchill and Montgomery, had assumed that a joint Western and Soviet assault on Berlin was in the offing. Yet in the last week of March Eisenhower called a halt, informing both Churchill and Stalin of his shocking decision. Churchill protested to Washington, grumbling about soldiers overreaching their authority, but to no avail. By now the Americans were in the Western driving seat, and they had their own interests to protect. They were most concerned to ensure that the US armies in Germany would not be decimated by the coming showdown in Berlin, and that most of their soldiers would soon be available for transfer to the war in Japan. Eisenhower informed the Soviets accordingly that their armies could meet on the Erfurt–Leipzig–Dresden axis, and that the Western offensive would be going no further. Stalin's reaction was inimitable. He told Eisenhower that Berlin had 'lost its strategic significance'. He told Roosevelt that the West had done a dirty deal with the Germans in order to pile pressure on the Red Army. And he told Zhukov to prepare the attack on Berlin without a moment's delay.

Götterdämmerung: Berlin, April 1945

Zhukov, receiving his orders on 31 March, fixed dawn on 16 April as the start of the culminating Battle for Berlin. Some 2.5 million troops were available – equivalent to all the Western armies then present in Germany. They were supported by 6,250 tanks and 7,500 aircraft. A saturation attack was coming, regardless of human lives and material destruction. Three Soviet fronts were lined up. Zhukov, with the 1st Byelorussian Front, was to lead the assault in the centre. His HQ was at Küstrin on the Oder, where the young Frederick the Great had once been incarcerated by his father. Marshal Konev's 1st Ukrainian Front took up position on the left wing to the south, and Marshal Rokossovsky's 2nd Byelorussian Front was to move out of Stettin on the right wing in the north. Fifty-seven kilometres separated Küstrin from the *Führerbunker*. The three Soviet marshals had been set up by Stalin to compete for the victor's laurels.[56]

Thanks to the delay of the two preceding months, Berlin's defences were much stronger that they might otherwise have been. Four concentric rings of fortifications had been built, the first at a radius of 32 km, the second at 16 km. The third ring followed the suburban *S-bahn* railway, and the fourth enclosed 'Zone Z', in the vicinity of the Reichstag and the Brandenburg Gate. (It was all rather reminiscent of the successful Soviet defences inside the Kursk salient.) Every able-bodied man was mobilized to swell the depleted ranks of 3 Panzer Group, the 9th Army and Army Group Vistula. Heavily armed squads of German military police, the 'chained dogs', roamed the city, shooting any Berliner who appeared to be 'neglecting his duty to the Fatherland'. They learned on 12 April that President Roosevelt was dead.

Amazingly, when Zhukov's massed hordes swarmed across the Oder on 16 April, using searchlights to blind the defenders, the outer line of fortifications held firm. On the 17th, no less than six armies, including two tank armies – N.B., not divisions – failed to capture the nearby Seelow Heights. On the 18th, a third frontal tsunami made a couple of deep inroads, but did not drown the defenders. The scenario would not be the same as that on the Vistula three months earlier. So Zhukov changed tack, and began a slow encircling movement to the north, calling on Rokossovsky for support. Hitler obliged him by ordering the 9th Army, which had performed so well, to stand still facing the Oder instead of wheeling to face the new threat. The most significant advance, however, was made by Konev on the southern flank, who captured the Wehrmacht's largest arsenal at Jüterbog and paralysed its central communications centre at Zossen. On the 20th, Hitler received officers who visited the *Führerbunker* to present congratulations on his birthday; they were rewarded by permission to escape the city by the few roads still open. Outside the bunker a human life was lost, on average, every five seconds.

Zhukov finally closed the ring on 25 April, to the west of Berlin. On the same day, Konev's men and women swept round in a wide arc and ran into American troops waiting at Torgau in Saxony. The Reich had been cleanly sliced into two parts. The 12th German Army of Lieutenant-General Wenck was in the vicinity, and tried to break the ring – without success. (Wenck was also put in nominal control of the Nazi 'Werewolves', who were supposed to wage a guerrilla war against the invaders.)

From then on, nothing but dire news reached the bunker. On the 29th, the commander of Berlin reported that ammunition would run out at any hour. The Führer married his mistress, Eva Braun. On the 30th, Field Marshal Keitel reported from beyond Berlin that no further rescue was possible. Soviet soldiers were climbing onto the Reichstag, and Polish soldiers had clambered onto the Brandenburg Gate. Adolf Hitler wrote his testament, blaming 'Jewish Bolshevism' for everything and claiming innocence of the war with Britain and the USA. Having appointed Admiral Dönitz his successor, he retired with Eva Braun to the bedroom, where poison capsules and a revolver were waiting. The wife swallowed the poison. The husband shot himself. Their fate remained unknown to the world above ground until the city commandant surrendered three days later. Units of the Waffen SS Charlemagne Division were the last formation to lay down their arms. Berlin had fallen. The Führer was dead. And the Third Reich was dying.

Fighting continued sporadically throughout Germany for the next week. The Strategic Bombing Offensive had been suspended two weeks earlier. Wherever possible, German soldiers rushed to submit to the Western armies. On 4 May, Montgomery received an official delegation on Lüneburg Heath, after which all German forces in northern Germany laid down their arms. On 5 May, Eisenhower at Rheims received a group of emissaries from Dönitz, who wished to surrender to the Americans. They were told that it was general and unconditional surrender or nothing. So on 7 May, at 0241 hours, they signed the necessary document, which required all German forces to cease fighting by 11 p.m. the following day. Churchill and Truman, Roosevelt's successor, thereon announced 8 May to be VE Day.

Stalin, however, was having none of it. He judged the Rheims document to be invalid or 'preliminary'. He wanted the act of unconditional surrender to be made to his own representatives. So another German delegation was obliged to repeat the performance at Karlshorst in Berlin at 2330 hours on the 8th. Due to the difference in time zones, Moscow had already entered the 9th. And Victory Day is celebrated in Russia on 9 May.

Even then the war was not completely over. There had been three surrenders, but no formal armistice and no legal peace. The ceasefire did not hold in all places. Germans and Soviets carried on fighting in Prague.

And in all Soviet-occupied countries the NKVD was hunting down a variety of political opponents and freedom fighters. Admiral Dönitz, who was technically a POW at large, continued to rule the non-existent Reich until he was arrested in Flensburg on 22 May. In these circumstances, it is difficult to say exactly where and when the Second World War in Europe ended.

CHAPTER THREE

POLITICS

Before, During and After the War

IF, AS CLAUSEWITZ OBSERVED, WAR is a continuation of politics 'by other means', it is important to stress that political activities do not stop when war begins. On the contrary, they intensify. In this regard, the political action of 1939–45 forms but one part of an unbroken continuum that operated before, during and after the war.

It is also quite proper to see the Second World War as the final stage in a broader chain of conflicts that began in 1914. Europe's second 'Thirty Years War' – an opera in two acts with a long interval – is a perfectly viable concept. For in large measure (though not completely) the Second World War arose through the unfinished business of the First.[1]

In the sphere of geopolitics, for example, two of Europe's major powers had been forced by the post-war settlement into subordinate positions that aroused much resentment. Both tsarist Russia and imperial Germany had been destroyed in the final phase of the First World War, and the representatives of their successor states were excluded from the counsels of the victors. The Bolsheviks, who had seized power in the second Russian Revolution of October 1917, were not even invited to the Peace Conference. The republican government of Germany was invited only in order to sign the Treaty of Versailles without comment, to accept sole guilt for the preceding war, and to pay astronomic reparations. It should have caused no surprise, therefore, that the resurgence of the two excluded powers provoked accute tensions.

In the ideological sphere, the First World War spawned two radical movements, Communism and Fascism, which both appealed to violence and which manifestly spelled trouble for the democratic order. It was no accident that each of the excluded powers was drawn to one of these 'totalitarian' alternatives, rather than to liberal democracy. Indeed, in Germany, the Nazi Party was able to gain a hold on the country by acting as a counterweight to the German Communist movement, which in the early interwar years had seemed markedly more dangerous. The German Communists were threatening to join forces with the Soviet Communists to launch a Europe-wide revolution, and in 1920 they had come within an ace of doing so. Unfortunately, most analysts have emphasized the incompatibilities of the Fascists and Communists. Few at the time saw the totalitarian similarities. And few had the imagination to predict a scenario where the totalitarians would postpone their differences in order to engineer the overthrow of the hated 'Versailles Settlement'. Yet it was to be the unexpected junction of the German Fascists (the Nazis) and the Soviet Communists which precipitated the Second World War.

Talk of continuities, however, equally prompts discussion about post-war events. If 1918 can be viewed as the start of a hiatus in the middle of a longer conflict, so, too, can 1945. There are very good reasons to regard the Cold War as a continuation of the unfinished business of the Second World War. In that case, one has to envisage Europe's 'Seventy-Five Years War' (1914–89), and to think in terms of an opera in three acts with two intervals, 1918–39 and 1945–48. This could well be the framework which historians of the future will adopt.

The interwar years, 1918-39

It is a very 'Occidentocentric' mindset which lays down that fighting stopped in Europe in November 1918. The idea holds good for some parts of Europe, but not for others. Quiet may have broken out on the Western Front in November. But the Eastern Front had fallen quiet in March, whilst local conflicts raged on in many other parts of Europe after the Armistice. Major campaigns were fought in Hungary and Romania (1919), between Poland and its sovietized neighbours (1919–20), between Greece and Turkey (1920–21), and above all in most parts of the former tsarist empire (1918–21).

The concept of a 'Russian Civil War', in particular, is highly mislead-ing. It conveys the impression of an internal conflict among Russians that did not affect other peoples. In reality, the Bolshevik Revolution of October 1917 provoked both a civil war in Russia and a series of international wars between Soviet Russia and the tsarist empire's other successor states. For the revolution fragmented the empire into a score of independent countries. As a result, the Bolsheviks' own actions forced them to wage war first internally against 'the Whites' and then externally against all their neighbours who had dared to declare independence. They could not think of forming a 'Soviet Union' until all their victories were complete; and the USSR was brought into being only on 1 January 1924.

In this light, historians risk serious criticism if they try to draw a clear line between a state of war before November 1918 and a state of peace afterwards. They have to make allowance for a transitional period of three to four years when a general settlement was reached either by diplomacy at the Peace Conference or by armed conflict elsewhere. Similarly, they cannot pretend that the war of 1939 fell without warning from a clear blue sky. Everyone would agree that dark clouds were gathering for several years beforehand, and that many tensions simmered in parts of Europe beyond the influence of the Western Powers. The net result is a threefold periodization of the interwar years: (a) the disorderly settlement, 1918–21: (b) the uneasy peace, 1921–34; and (c) the rising storm, 1934–9.

The disorderly settlement, 1918–21

The Peace Conference which assembled in Paris in January 1919 was conceived by the victors, organized by the victors, and implemented by the victors. Although the theory was dominated by talk of 'Western democracy' and of 'national self-determination', the practice was characterized by the near-incontestable will of the Great Powers: France, Britain, Italy and the USA. The representatives of states and nations whose future was being determined came to the conference as petitioners and clients, and their arguments were accepted or rejected in large measure in accordance with their status as friend or foe. The Czechs, for example, who were seen to be stoutly anti-German, were considered very reasonable. The Poles, who were seen to be anti-Russian as well as anti-German, were thought to be troublesome. And the Ukrainians, whose independence had been recognized only by Germany, were thought unreasonable. The Irish, who at the time were claiming independence from one of the Great Powers, had no place at all.

The outcome of the Peace Conference was a series of treaties signed between the Allied Powers and each of the defeated states. No formal instrument was drawn up to deal with matters that were not of direct relevance to one of the treaties, which were:

- the Treaty of Versailles (28 June 1919) with Germany,
- the Treaty of Saint-Germain (10 September 1919) with Austria,
- the Treaty of Trianon (4 June 1920) with Hungary,
- the Treaty of Neuilly (27 November 1919) with Bulgaria,
- the Treaty of Sèvres (10 August 1920) with Turkey.

For example, the Treaty of Versailles delineated Poland's frontier with Germany, and the Treaty of Saint-Germain delineated Czechoslovakia's frontier with Austria. But no treaty delineated Poland's frontier with Czechoslovakia. Czechoslovakia then used force to overthrow a local agreement and seize a slice of territory in the former Austrian Silesia. The resultant dispute over Těšin/Cieszyn simmered angrily for the next twenty years.

The Western leaders were frequently baffled by the torrent of unfamiliar places, unpronounceable names, quarrels among experts, and irreconcilable differences. When Silesia came up for discussion, Lloyd George thought that they were discussing Cilicia. Not surprisingly, as soon as the main treaty with Germany was fixed the leaders went home, leaving the rest of a very long agenda to their officials.

The foundation of the League of Nations, however, must be counted as a promising achievement. The brainchild of the US President, Woodrow Wilson, it sought to bring a measure of orderly conduct to Europe's international affairs. The outbreak of the 'Great War' in 1914 had convinced most people that the age of unbridled national sovereignty was failing, and that an international body operating within a framework of law, arbitration and goodwill was badly needed. The League's charter was signed by most European countries – though not by Germany or Soviet Russia – and its headquarters in Geneva opened for business on the same day, 1 January 1920, as the Treaty of Versailles. Its first task was to administer the free city of Danzig, which neither Germany nor Poland had been able to claim for themselves.

Despite the hopes surrounding its foundation, the League contained several inbuilt flaws. Firstly, since it possessed no independent instruments of enforcement, it depended very largely on the armed forces of its founding Western patrons. Secondly, thanks to the very limited range of those armed services – no French or British plane could fly non-stop to Danzig and back in 1920 – it had no means of exerting pressure on large expanses of Europe. And thirdly, thanks to the unexpected hostility of the US Congress, it never received the support of its original American patrons.

Nonetheless, by far the most obvious flaw in the so-called Versailles Settlement lay in the fact that the most turbulent parts of Europe lay in the East, far beyond its reach. Throughout the period of the Peace Conference, the Bolsheviks launched any number of military campaigns against the neighbours of Soviet Russia. The Red Army had to be expelled from Finland. It meddled unsuccessfully in the complicated politics of the nascent Baltic States. It suppressed the brief independence of Byelorussia and Ukraine, before joining with those countries in a concerted attack on Poland. It then turned on the federation of independent republics of the Caucasus – Azerbaijan, Georgia and Armenia – while projecting Soviet power into the deepest recesses of Central Asia, from Uzbekistan to Outer Mongolia. Curiously enough, since all Westerners of that generation had been brought up to regard the tsarist empire as a permanent and natural fixture on the map of Europe, and since 'Russia' until very recently had been an Allied Power, nobody really cared or noticed what was happening. The Bolsheviks' seizure of power in Petrograd, and their penchant for atrocities during the Civil War, were widely condemned. But their brutal reconquest of a dozen countries which had clearly expressed the will to separate was *not* the subject of widespread protest. The Western leaders at the Peace Conference, bewailing their inability to influence the Bolsheviks, nonetheless declared themselves to be 'trustees for Russia'. In other words, they wanted the Bolshevik regime to disappear. But they also wanted the Russian Empire to be restored. In this, they showed themselves to be convinced imperialists, and less than half-hearted democrats.

Of all those conflicts in the immediate aftermath of the Great War one in particular possessed more than regional significance. The 'Polish–Soviet War', which lasted from February 1919 to March 1921, is something of a misnomer, for in essence it was not caused by a territorial or political dispute between the Republic of Poland and the three neighbouring Soviet republics (although such a dispute existed). In essence, it was inspired by the Bolsheviks' desire to spread revolution from Lenin's homeland in Russia to Marx's homeland in Germany. According to Marxist theory, the proletarian revolution should not have been engineered in backward Russia, but should have been spontaneously launched by the class-conscious proletariat of industrialized Western Europe. Hence the Bolsheviks' eagerness to rectify their mistake as quickly as possible, and to send the Red Army westward without delay. For them, Poland was of marginal importance. It was a troublesome country, run by arrogant noblemen and Catholic priests. They called it their 'Red Bridge', across which the triumphant revolutionaries would march with banners waving.

Lenin attempted to dispatch the Red Army across the Red Bridge on three separate occasions – in December 1918, in the spring of 1919, and again in the spring of 1920. On each occasion he failed, although on the third occasion he came preciously close to success. Fortunately for the Versailles Settlement the Polish forces of Marshal Piłsudski destroyed the invading columns at the Battle of Warsaw in August 1920, 'the Miracle on the Vistula'. And in March 1921, at the Treaty of Riga, the Poles and the Soviets settled the differences which the Peace Conference in Paris had been unable to address.[2]

The uneasy peace, 1921–34

Once the fighting died down, in the early 1920s, Europe moved through a dozen years or so when the prospects for a lasting peace appeared to improve. The most pressing problems were social and economic. An enormous pandemic of 'Spanish flu' had wiped out more human beings than the Great War. The Russian Civil War was followed by the devastating Volga Famine; and relief agencies were at work in many parts of the continent. Millions still toiled from infancy to the grave for a pittance. Post-war unemployment caused cruel hardship. And the plague of hyperinflation wiped out the savings of the middle classes in much of Central Europe. The ground was being prepared for the rise of the political extremes. Communism came first, with its unlikely victory in Russia. But Fascism was not slow to follow, gaining a foothold with Mussolini's 'March on Rome' in 1922.

Generally speaking, though, the political scene did not arouse fears of massive instability. A trend towards dictatorship became apparent. But the dictators came in various colours, and showed no sign of uniting. In Germany, the danger of a Communist uprising passed after 1923, and the Weimar Republic survived its teething troubles. In the Soviet Union, the new general secretary of the Communist Party, Joseph Stalin, put international revolution on to the back burner while launching the slogan of 'Socialism in One Country'. The New Economic Policy, which had replaced War Communism in 1921, had stepped back from radical solutions and was bringing a modicum of prosperity to Russia's peasant masses. The world sighed a breath of relief.

None of the crises of the period proved too disruptive, though in retrospect one can see that confidence in the existing order was successively undermined:

- In 1922 German and Soviet delegates left a reparations conference at Genoa and signed a German–Soviet economic agreement at Rapallo. It was an act of defiance which showed that Europe's two pariahs could join forces and outwit the Powers.
- In 1923–5 French troops occupied the Ruhr in a vain attempt to enforce reparation payments. It was a resort to force that failed to achieve its goal, but sparked an international financial crisis and destroyed France's willingness to take preventive measures again.
- In 1925, at Lausanne, Germany's foreign minister, Gustav Stresemann, brought his country back into the diplomatic fold by guaranteeing the inviolability of its western frontiers. Stresemann pointedly did *not* undertake to refrain from changes of Germany's eastern frontiers. Western opinion judged him a jolly good chap.
- In 1926 Marshal Piłsudski led a military *coup d'état* in Poland to forestall a right-wing takeover. The resultant Sanacja regime did not abolish the parliamentary system, but entered the dubious realms of 'guided democracy'.
- In 1929 Stalin abandoned the New Economic Policy and initiated a command economy characterized by 'five-year plans' and the forcible collectivization of agriculture. Henceforth, the USSR was laying the foundations of a modern industrial state and of massive militarization. Stalin commented, 'If we don't succeed in ten years, we'll be annihilated.' Western Europe was unconcerned
- Also in 1929, the Wall Street Crash ruined the US economy, and provoked the onset of a deep and worldwide slump. All of Europe's industrial economies were hard hit: unemployment, public soup kitchens and protest marches were the order of the day in countries with no welfare net.

The free-market economies favoured by the Western democracies lost much of their appeal.

- In 1931 Japanese armed forces invaded Manchuria, detaching it from China and establishing the puppet state of 'Manchukuo'. This was the most blatant instance of international aggression since the Great War. Yet neither the League of Nations nor the individual Powers could prevent it.
- In 1932 the king of Yugoslavia was assassinated during a visit to Marseilles. People remembered Sarajevo, and fears of Eastern Europe being a source of incendiary politics were strengthened.
- In 1933 Adolf Hitler's right-radical National Socialist Party gained a leading position in the German *Reichstag* after three years of electoral see-saws and of street battles with the Communists. His rise to power was entirely legal. But his gangsterish methods on reaching high office, particularly the declaration of emergency powers after the Reichstag fire, revealed him to be an outright enemy of the democratic republic which he headed.
- In 1934, having removed all the surviving Bolshevik leaders, Stalin began the first of several purges of his subservient Communist Party. Rumours were circulating that his 'war against the kulaks' and the state-sponsored famine in Ukraine could have killed millions. But Western opinion was divided about the truth of the reports, and once again did not feel directly threatened.

In the 1920s much thought was given to strengthening Europe's security by multilateral military alliances. Britain and France were still linked by the Entente Cordiale; and Germany was officially disarmed. So, after Lausanne, East Central Europe was inevitably the focus of attention. Poland, the largest country in the region, was allied to France, but not yet to Britain. The 'Little Entente' was organized by France to neutralize Hungary, still viewed with suspicion. Even so, the USSR was not covered by the system, nor was the prospect of Germany picking a quarrel with its eastern neighbours.

New vistas opened up when Aristide Briand became French foreign minister in 1925. France was still Europe's principal military power, and Briand was a visionary: a pan-European and an anti-militarist. The Kellogg-

Briand Pact of 1928, signed with US Secretary of State Frank Kellogg, introduced a new concept of official declarations of peaceful intent. 'Non-aggression pacts' – fifty-four in all – were signed all over Europe. Poland, which was attached to a very realistic 'doctrine of two enemies', took the precaution of signing one pact of non-aggression with the USSR (1932) and another with Germany (1934). Before the Polish–German Pact, Marshal Piłsudski was the only European statesman to sound out his Western partners on the subject of a preventive war against Germany. In the era of non-aggression, such soundings got nowhere.

The difference between perceptions and realities presents a fascinating topic. In the mid-1930s, the 'Versailles Settlement' was increasingly challenged by two potentially rogue states. Of the two, the USSR, had gained a head start over Germany in constructing the instruments of internal repression and external war. Long before Hitler came to power, it already possessed a secret police, a well-oiled machine for state terror, concentration camps, slave labour, a militarized economy, and a massive programme of military–industrial expansion. What is more, it organized a secret series of joint military manoeuvres with German forces on Soviet territory. Yet with few exceptions, Western observers did not feel disturbed by Stalin. Russia was far away from Western Europe. Hitler, in contrast, sent shivers down the spine from the start. The German threat was seen to grow by leaps and bounds:

- In 1934, having carried out a purge of their own ranks in the 'Night of the Long Knives', the Nazis overthrew the institutions of the Weimar Republic and set up a dictatorial party state with Hitler as Führer.
- In 1935 the Nazis subjected German society to the racist Nuremberg Laws, directed principally against the Jews, but equally serving notice of their far-reaching radicalism.
- In 1936 Hitler ordered the reoccupation of the Rhineland, thereby breaching one of the clauses of the Treaty of Versailles. Western opinion was divided. Some people thought it perfectly reasonable for Germany to take full control of its national territory. Others thought that an act of successful insubordination, if unpunished, would feed Hitler's ambitions.

In those same years, the Nazis began to fan grievances among Germans in neighbouring countries, and thereby to disturb the peace. In

Austria, which was Hitler's homeland, they gained many recruits in a drive to suppress the democratic republic. In Czechoslovakia they egged on the German separatists of the so-called Sudetenland. And in the Free City of Danzig, which had once been a stronghold of Social democracy, they promoted a campaign for reunion with the Reich.

The rising storm, 1936–9

One should not imagine, however, that the antics of the Nazi regime were a sure-fire recipe for international war at the earliest opportunity. On the contrary, Hitler among other things was a master of bluff, and it was impossible to tell from the outside how much substance his blood-curdling boasting contained. Historians now know for certain what some politicians suspected: that his rearmament statistics were exaggerated. They can also read in the much discussed *Hossbach Memorandum* of 1937, which records one of Hitler's pep talks to his generals, that the Führer foresaw war in 1942–3, not in 1939. Hitler's intentions were from from clear.

Moreover, in 1935 the Western powers initiated the policy of 'collective security'. As the German Reich walked out of the League of Nations, the USSR was invited in; and the Communist parties in the West were ordered to follow a strategy of 'popular fronts' or coalitions. Germany was not yet strong enough to challenge the West directly. And it was unlikely to go on the rampage in the East, so long as the USSR was keeping Western company.

In the late 1930s, therefore, the essential framework of international affairs in Europe saw Britain and France striving with increasing anxiety to preserve the status quo that had been created by their victory twenty years earlier. Their dominance began to crumble thanks to the impotence of the League of Nations, the threat of unilateral action by malcontent countries, and the growing realization of justified grievances. Their inability to impose restraints on the Spanish Civil War (1936–9), in which Hitler and Mussolini openly assisted the Fascists and Stalin aided the overthrow of the Republic, boded ill for the future.

For many years after the Russian Revolution of 1917, Soviet Communism had been widely viewed as the principal subverter of international stability. But perceptions shifted with the rise of the Third Reich. Though Soviet military capacity was rising the USSR was thought to be preoccupied by its colossal internal transformations. And, since the realities of

Stalinism were long concealed, it was widely assumed that the Soviets would seek to avoid a major international war. The Third Reich, in contrast, was rattling its sabres, and its public statements were brazenly aggressive. After the definitive victory of General Franco in Spain (March 1939), few people in Europe doubted that rampant Fascism provided the more credible danger.

In the late 1930s Nazi sabre-rattling reached a level of intensity at which the European order started to disintegrate without recourse to open war. In 1938 Austria fell into the Nazis' lap as the result of internal Nazi-led subversion. The *Anschluss*, or 'Merger', was announced: Hitler and his Wehrmacht marched triumphantly into Vienna without firing a shot. And Austria joined Germany in the Reich.

After Austria the spotlight turned on Czechoslovakia. Hitler whipped up fears by announcing that the lot of the Sudeten Germans was intolerable, and by hinting at a military solution. At the time, it is doubtful if the well-equipped Czechoslovak army would have been easily dislodged from its well-fortified mountain frontiers. But it was given no chance. On the initiative of the British prime minister, Neville Chamberlain, two conferences were held in Munich to meet Hitler's demands by diplomatic agreement. The Czechoslovak government was told to accept the arrangement. And the Soviet Union was pointedly excluded. Chamberlain flew back to London flaunting a piece of paper and claiming 'Peace in Our Time'.

Of course the rot did not stop with the annexation of the Sudetenland. In the winter of 1938–9, the Slovaks demanded separation from the Czechs; and the German Danzigers, together with the German minority in western Poland, began screaming about their own intolerable predicament. In March 1939 Czechoslovakia collapsed: Hitler marched into Prague as he had marched into Vienna. Bohemia and Moravia joined the Reich as a German 'protectorate'. And Slovakia was set up as an independent client state. Non-military aggression was changing the map of Europe.

The descent into war

By the spring of 1939, therefore, Hitler had pulled off his third stunt in a row, and no one had managed to stop him. Given his success, and his gambler's nature, it was next to certain that he would try a further throw of the dice. A cursory glance at the map indicated that, after the Rhineland, Austria and Czechoslovakia, he would next pick on Poland. Yet he had no clear strategy, let alone a detailed plan. Recent experience had taught him that if he stirred up a crisis and threatened to disturb the peace, somehow he would get his way.

In retrospect, one can see that Poland was a step too far in the gambler's game, and for several good reasons. Firstly, any German move against Poland would directly affect Russia, and would thereby bring the Great Powers into play. Second, the Poles, unlike the Czechs or the Austrians, were not disposed to be bullied. If attacked, they would fight, and would fight bravely, thereby reducing the chances of a 'short, clean campaign'. Thirdly, the Western Powers were losing patience. The Munich agreement was their test of appeasement's validity. If Hitler were to embark on another adventure, London and Paris would not take him at his word again. Even Chamberlain could not be deceived indefinitely.

Hitler's first move in late 1938 had been to call in the Polish ambassador in Berlin and to propose a joint German–Polish campaign against the Soviet Union. He may or may not have been serious in this proposal, but it is very doubtful whether he would ever have delivered on the various benefits promised. In essence, he was testing the water to see what the attitudes of the Polish government really were. He was infuriated to find that they were almost completely negative. Despite several attempts, he elicited no response. The Polish colonels who held the reins in Warsaw considered the jumped-up Austrian corporal rather vulgar. Though they had no love for the Soviet Union, they had no love for the Third Reich either.

Hitler's next tack took him in the opposite direction. If the ungrateful Poles were unwilling to dance to his tune, he would make them sweat. Early in 1939 the Nazi propaganda machine switched on a flood of revindications and recriminations. The Poles were persecuting the Danzigers. Their possession of the so-called 'Polish Corridor' was insufferable. Their repression of decent Germans in Upper Silesia and Pomerania was intolerable . . . Once again, significant segments of opinion in France and Britain were induced to believe this poppycock – or even, since their knowledge of Polish affairs was close to nil, to suspect Polish troublemaking. Very few people in Paris or London were prepared to think of the defence of Poland as a worthy cause to fight for. 'Mourir pour Danzig?' a French deputy was to ask rhetorically in the National Assembly. Are we supposed to die for Danzig?

Nonetheless, the March events had inexorable consequences. The demise of Czechoslovakia left a vacuum which Hitler readily filled. In the space of a few days, Bohemia and Moravia had been swallowed by the Reich. Not a shot had been fired. Hitler's methods of threat and bluster were again bringing results, at no apparent cost. Yet Hitler's easiest triumph set the international alarm bells ringing. At Munich, the Führer had solemnly assured Chamberlain and Daladier that after the Sudetenland he had 'no more territorial demands'. He was now shown beyond doubt to be an unashamed expansionist and a barefaced liar. On 31 March 1939 Great Britain issued a formal guarantee of the independence of Poland.

The British guarantee was intended as a declaration of intent, a shot across Germany's bows. But it was also a piece of bluff, since Britain in 1939 had no means either of restraining Germany or of defending Poland. Nonetheless, when the French followed suit, the Polish crisis was becoming the object of far-reaching international concern. What is more, everyone saw that the key to further developments lay with Poland's eastern neighbour, the USSR. If Moscow were openly to side with the Western Powers, a unilateral German attack on Poland would be too risky to contemplate. If Moscow were to adopt an ambiguous position, the world would be kept guessing. And if Moscow were to throw its weight behind Berlin, Hitler would be given the green light. In 1938 Stalin had been shut out of negotiations. He was still smarting. Next time round, he was not going to allow himself to be treated so shabbily. In the summer of 1939, therefore, the Soviets would be courted both by the Western Powers and by Germany.

The outlines of the coming contest were now taking shape:

Europe in 1939 was, in Stalin's own words, a 'poker game' with three players, in which each hoped to persuade the other two to destroy one another and leave the third to take the winnings. The three players were the Fascists of Adolf Hitler's Nazi Germany, the Capitalists of Neville Chamberlain's Britain allied with Daladier's France – and the Bolsheviks. Though the Georgian admired the flamboyant brutality of the Austrian, he appreciated the danger of a resurgent Germany . . . [And he] regarded the western democracies as at least as dangerous as Germany.[3]

The Führer, however, was not to be deterred, especially as he felt himself to have been slighted by the non-cooperation of Poland and Britain. On 3 April 1939 he issued a formal directive for war preparations. In a covering letter to Field Marshal Keitel, chief of the High Command, he explained that he still wished 'to maintain peaceful relations with

Poland', but also said, if things changed for the worse, that 'it may be necessary to settle the account for good'. In that case he was resolved 'to annihilate' the Polish armed forces, and 'to create a situation in the East corresponding with the needs of Germany's defence.' Attached was a detailed document outlining the requirements for *Fall Weiss* ('Case White'), the projected attack on Poland.[4]

Some historians have wrongly assumed that these contingency plans may be taken as proof that Hitler was already hell-bent on war. In reality the delicate balance between war and peace hung on several unforeseeable factors – in particular on the uncertain prospect of the Nazis' ability to strike a deal with the Soviets. Ever since the 1920s Nazi propaganda had made no secret of the main aim of absorbing Germany's so-called *Lebensraum* in the East – which in the first instance meant the conquest of Poland. Yet Hitler knew very well that he could not safely launch an early invasion of Eastern Europe without prior agreement with the region's largest military power, which had its own ideas about 'living space'.

In the USSR also, the decks were cleared for change. The policy of collective security was losing its attractions. The hardliners were losing patience:

> When Stalin concentrated on diplomacy, he first aimed his guns at his own diplomats. On the night of 3 May 1939, NKVD troops surrounded the Foreign Commissariat, bringing home the urgency of the countdown to war and the coming revolution of alliances. Molotov, Beria and Malenkov arrived to inform Maxim 'Papasha' Litvinov, . . . the champion of 'collective security', that he was sacked . . . The Foreign Commissariat was almost next door to the Lubianka, and the two ministries were nick-named 'the Neighbours'. Molotov's deputy . . . supervised the purge of diplomats . . . The Press Officer of the Foreign Commissariat . . . was taken to Beria's office where he was ordered to confess to spying . . . Beria ordered him to lie on the floor while the Caucasian 'giant', Kobulov, beat him on the skull with blackjacks. . . . Stalin's diplomatic Terror was designed to appeal to Hitler: 'Purge the Ministry of Jews,' [Stalin] said, 'Clean out "the synagogue".'[5]

Molotov was the new Foreign Commissar.

Britain and France, meanwhile, were greatly underestimating the tempo of developments. Having urged the Poles to stand firm (without organizing a system of practical cooperation), they sent a joint military mission to Russia by sea. The progress of negotiations was as slow as the form of travel. Admiral Sir Reginald Aylmer Ranfurly Plunkett-Ernle-Erle-Drax failed to bring the correct credential papers. Stalin and Molotov felt insulted.

During those same weeks in the summer of 1939, the Soviets opened so-called trade talks with Germany. They created an atmosphere in which the talks could stray far beyond trade. But their demands were steep. If Berlin were to be given the go-ahead for an attack on Poland, it would have to agree to the creation of a Soviet zone of influence in Eastern Europe, and also to the inclusion of eastern Poland and the Baltic States into that zone. To the Nazis, it must have seemed that they were being invited to do the fighting, while Stalin took half of the spoils. It was hardly fair, but the Nazis knew that the Soviets were making an offer that the West could not match.

As the summer wore on, the Soviets were increasingly drawn towards the deal with Germany. As a well-rehearsed paranoic, Stalin would have guessed that Hitler's proffered friendship could easily revert to hostility. At the same time, as a lifelong Communist, he was troubled less by the threat of Germany alone than by the possibility of the Fascists and capitalists joining forces for a combined assault on the USSR. In this light, it would be advantageous if the Polish crisis could be manoeuvred so that the Western Powers and Germany could be pitted against each other. Like many military analysts still impressed by the outcome of the First World War, he calculated that the winner would be exhausted whoever came out on top. From the standpoint of 1939, it was clearly in the Soviet interest to watch the opposition tire itself out whilst Soviet resources grew and the Red Army recuperated.

Moscow, however, had a further problem, which most Western commentators did not appreciate. For eight years previously Japanese forces had been consolidating their hold on Manchuria; and they were fanning out into the confines of Outer Mongolia (which was a Soviet protectorate) and of the Soviet Far East. In other words, the USSR was feeling the pressure on two fronts: both in Europe and in Asia. The Kremlin needed to stabilize its relations with Germany, in order to guard against developments on the front with Japan. After all, the Japanese were already on the march, whilst for the time being the Nazis were only growling. By the same token, Stalin was unlikely to react definitively to the German proposals so long as the alert in the Far East persisted.

Nor should one assume that war between Germany and the USSR, if avoided in the short term, would inevitably follow later. It is all too easy for historians to be wise after the event. In 1939 it was not yet known what the future held. As mentioned above, Hitler had been thinking of reaching Germany's maximum war potential in 1942–3. Stalin may well have had a similar timetable in mind. Yet both leaders gave ample proof of opportunism, and of breathtaking changes of direction. In the summer of 1939 everything in Eastern Europe was still to be played for. Stalin could not have ruled out the possibility of a future war with Germany. But, equally, he would have been weighing the possibility either of German defeat in the West or of a stalemate which a strengthened USSR could exploit to its advantage.

Everything fell into place in the third week of August, including the removal of the Japanese danger. Stalin had already taken steps to eliminate the military threat in the Far East; and he decided in principle both to terminate discussions with the British and French and to accept the German feelers. On 19 August he addressed the Politburo at a meeting where foreign members of the Comintern recorded his remarks. 'We must accept the proposals of Germany,' he said, 'and diplomatically discard the British and French delegation. The destruction of Poland and the annexation of Ukrainian Galicia will be our first gain.' 'Nonetheless,' he continued, 'we must foresee the consequences both of Germany's defeat and of Germany's victory. In the event of a defeat the formation of a Communist government in Germany will be essential . . .' 'Above all,' he concluded, 'our task is to ensure that Germany be engaged in war for as long as possible and that Britain and France be so exhausted that they could not suppress a German Communist government.'[6] Despite his low profile, Stalin was preparing for revolutionary change. He was not the innocent or passive observer that later legend would try to portray.

So far the two dictators had been circling each other at a distance. But the essence of the game was for the German Führer, who was the more eager for a quick result, to get a grip on his slippery Soviet partner. On 20 August, Hitler dispatched a personal telegram addressed to 'Dear Mr Stalin'. He was sent a reply addressed to 'Chancellor of Germany A. Hitler'. It agreed that Ribbentrop should pay Stalin a visit. It reached Berlin at 8.30 p.m. that same evening. 'Marvellous!' Hitler exclaimed. 'I have the world in my pocket.'[7]

Also on the 20th, having assembled a massive strike force of tanks and warplanes, General Zhukov attacked the Japanese intruders on the Halka River in Mongolia and drove them back to Manchukuo. His victory was so crushing that the battle – variously known as Khalkhin-Gol or 'the Nomonhan Incident' – persuaded the Japanese High Command to drop the Northern Option, i.e. war against the USSR, in favour of the Southern Option, i.e. expansion into Indochina, the Philippines and Indonesia.[8] On the 21st, Ribbentrop set off for Moscow.

The negotiations of the Nazi–Soviet Pact, held in Stalin's 'little corner' in the Kremlin, were concluded rapidly. Ribbentrop, who had arrived at 1 p.m. in Hitler's personal Condor plane wearing a leather coat and striped trousers, was falling over himself to please. He found the airport bedecked with swastikas, and the band played 'Deutschland, Deutschland über Alles'. He told Stalin and Molotov that Germany demanded nothing from Russia – only 'peace and trade' – before promptly contradicting himself as they discussed the division of Poland. Then, as he launched into extravagant praise of German–Soviet friendship, he earned a reprimand. 'Don't you think', Stalin remarked acidly, 'we have to pay a little more attention to public opinion? We have been pouring buckets of shit over each other's heads for years now ... Are we to make our peoples believe all is forgotten and forgiven?' But the moment passed. The secret protocols were hammered out on the 22nd. Hitler accepted the terms by telegraph. At 10 p.m. the celebration party started. Stalin raised a toast. 'I know how much the German nation loves its Führer,' he said. 'He's a good chap.' At 3 a.m., as the party broke up, Stalin again addressed Ribbentrop. 'I can assure you on my word of honour,' he told him, 'that the Soviet Union will not betray its partner.'[9]

On the surface, the Nazi–Soviet Pact appeared to be no more than an agreement for closer ties of friendship, trade and political cooperation. Thanks to the secret protocol, however, it amounted to much more. It foresaw the division of North Eastern Europe into German and Soviet spheres of influence; and it gave free rein to both signatories to devour their inconvenient neighbours (in the interests of self-defence).

MOSCOW, 23 AUGUST 1939

On the occasion of the Non-Aggression Pact between the German Reich and the USSR, the undersigned plenipotentiaries ... discussed ... their respective spheres of influence in Eastern Europe, [and reached] the following conclusions:

1. In the event of a territorial and political rearrangement in the Baltic States (Finland, Estonia, Latvia, Lithuania), the northern boundary of Lithuania will form the boundary of the spheres of

influence of Germany and the USSR . . . The interest of Lithuania in the Vilna area is recognized by each party.

2. In the event of a territorial and political rearrangement of the areas belonging to the Polish state, the spheres of influence of Germany and the USSR shall be bounded approximately by the line of the rivers Vistula, Narev and San. The question of whether the interests of both parties make the maintenance of an independent Polish state desirable . . . can be definitely determined . . . by means of a friendly agreement.

3. With regard to Southeastern Europe, attention is called by the Soviet side to its interest in Bessarabia. The German side declares its disinterest in that area.

4. This protocol shall be treated by both parties as strictly secret . . .

For the Gov't of the German Reich   Plenipotentiary, Gov't of the USSR

   J. von Ribbentrop   V. Molotov[10]

Hitler and Stalin were in business. Poland's fate was sealed.

Not surprisingly, although the secret protocols remained secret, news of the pact aroused the deepest suspicions. The British and Polish governments were not slow to envisage the harm which the harmless-sounding Nazi–Soviet Pact might unleash. On 25 August 1939 they concluded an Anglo-Polish treaty which formalized Britain's guarantee of Poland's independence and, foreseeing war, made provision for mutual cooperation against an unnamed 'European power'. A secret protocol named that power as Germany. France, too, was allied with Poland. And Britain was still linked to France by the Entente Cordiale. So an anti-German coalition was now in place.

There is no evidence to suggest that Hitler was planning anything beyond a quick local war. Indeed, he may still have been hoping for a repeat of the last-minute appearance of appeasers. At all events, he was fairly confident that he was not leading Germany into a general debacle. Poland would be quickly crushed. The Soviet Union would not obstruct. Britain and France might declare war, but they weren't likely to *do* much. Britain possessed no significant armed forces with which to intervene. France's forces were holding to their defensive position. So Poland would fall before any assistance could be given. After that, the Western Powers, humiliated, could somehow be pacified or bought off.

Some such reasoning is clearly indicated by Germany's military dispositions. Virtually every battle-ready German division had moved to the borders with Poland – in East Prussia, in Pomerania, in Silesia – or, in the south, to Slovakia. No significant reserve was left behind to guard Germany's borders with France. Even a modest French offensive could have rolled into the heart of Germany unopposed. But, as Hitler had correctly guessed, the French were not thinking of crossing the Rhine. Instead, they were sitting comfortably behind the Maginot Line, assessing developments from a purely static standpoint.

As usual, Soviet intentions as seen from the outside were extremely opaque. Winston Churchill would soon be calling them 'a riddle wrapped in a mystery inside an enigma'. Moscow, unlike Berlin, was not issuing threats. It was not deploying battle-ready divisions. And it was not betraying any outward sign of war preparations. There were good grounds for this caution. Stalin had only recently called off the Great Terror, which had destroyed millions of Soviet citizens and which had culminated in a massive purge of military officers. In 1938–9 almost half of all senior ranks had either been killed or dumped into the GULag. The Red Army was in no condition for major operations. What is more, despite Khalkhin-Gol, a definitive and formal truce with the Japanese was still awaited.

Anxieties about Soviet intentions may well have contributed to Hitler's unexplained decision on 25 August to freeze the launch of the Polish campaign. There would undoubtedly have been sceptics saying that Stalin had laid a trap. Some historians maintain that the Führer panicked; others that he was checking to ensure that the Soviets had not double-crossed him. Tensions during the last week of waiting rose to fever pitch.

Throughout those critical days, the Western Powers and their Polish client were impotent observers of events that were being driven by the ambitions of Hitler and Stalin. The Americans were absent. The French were supine. The British, having abandoned appeasement, could not initiate warfare. The Poles, who were determined to defend themselves, were advised by their allies to postpone mobilization so as to avoid provoking Germany. They significantly weakened their chances of survival.

After a week's delay, Hitler approached the point where he would be obliged either to unleash the attack on Poland or to call it off. His generals were straining at the leash, advising that the glorious late summer heatwave would not last forever. Chamberlain was obviously not showing up. So the choice had become one between war or an abject climbdown. Hitler chose war, not certain whether he could contain the conflict or not. He issued the order on 31 July. The Wehrmacht, the Luftwaffe and the Kriegsmarine would all move against Poland at dawn.

One final detail was put in place. An SS officer, Alfred Naujocks, was given the task of staging an incident that could be made to look like a Polish attack on Germany. He took a band of convicts to a German radio station at Gleiwitz (Gliwice) on the border of Silesia, and dressed them up in Polish uniforms. In due course the convicts were mowed down by their SS guards, who thereafter identified the corpses to the police as the bodies of Polish raiders. A few hours later, as German forces invaded Poland, the world woke up to the surprising news from Berlin that Germany was responding to an unprovoked Polish attack.

Adolf Hitler had received the news of the Nazi–Soviet Pact during dinner at the Berghof in Berchtesgaden. He led his guests on to the balcony to watch the dying moments of a blood-red alpine sunset. 'Looks like a great deal of blood,' he remarked. 'This time we won't bring it off without violence.'[11]

The war years, 1939–45

Once the fighting began, the distinctions between domestic policy, diplomacy, military affairs and grand strategy became blurred. All combatant governments controlled the activities of their armed services, and to a lesser or greater extent all political leaders became *ipso facto* 'war leaders'. Some of them, like Hitler and Stalin, gradually took everyday control of their country's supreme military command, handling military and political business as an indivisible whole. Others, like Churchill and Roosevelt, kept a greater distance from the military hierarchy, but in all important matters the ultimate decisions were theirs.

For obvious reasons, the wartime agenda differed markedly from the peacetime one. Priority was given to campaign planning, to inter-Allied relations, to industrial production and supply, to civil defence, and in the case of countries occupying foreign countries, to the administration of occupied territories. Even in democratic states, the remit of government departments grew enormously.

One topic, however, did not develop. Unlike in the First World War,

no significant political contacts were established between the opposing
warring parties, and no diplomatic overtures were made to encourage a
separate peace. Hitler may have expected Britain to come to terms in
1940–41, but the expectations were never even discussed, as indicated by
the forlorn mission of Rudolf Hess. The Italians certainly hoped to
negotiate with the Western Allies in 1943, but were forced to surrender
without doing so. Stalin constantly feared that his western partners in the
Grand Coalition (1941–5) might cut a deal with the Germans and turn
against him. But the fears were unfounded. Once the Allies adopted the
policy of unconditional surrender (see p. 60), it was adhered to. The
Second Word War was a conflict *à l'outrance*.

Phase 1, 1939–41: the era of the Nazi–Soviet Pact

The Nazi–Soviet Pact operated on the basis of clearly defined spheres of
influence, and of limited cooperation in matters of common concern. In
the autumn of 1939, for example, each of the contracting parties took its
allotted shares of conquered Poland, and dealt with its own share as it
thought fit. In the Nazi zone, the Gestapo secret police began filtering and
segregating the population according to racial criteria, whilst in the Soviet
zone the NKVD began filtering and deporting people according to social
and political criteria. Yet in matters of security the Gestapo/SS and the
NKVD worked closely together. The SS handed over Ukrainian nationalists, in return for the NKVD handing over German Communists. And
both partners acted in unison against the Polish resistance.

In redrawing the map of Europe, the Soviets annexed all their
conquered territories directly to the USSR. Finnish Karelia was added to
Russia. The three Baltic States became the three Soviet Baltic Republics.
Eastern Poland and Bukovina were added to the Byelorussian and Ukrainian SSRs. And eastern Romania became the Moldovan SSR.

The Germans made somewhat more calibrated dispositions. Western
Poland, Alsace-Lorraine and Slovenia were incorporated directly into the
Reich, whilst the General Government of Poland became a subdivision of
the Greater Reich. Most of the other occupied countries – Belgium,
Holland, Denmark, Norway, France and Greece – were allowed to keep
their separate identities, though they were subjected to servile pro-German
regimes, like that of Norway's Vidkun Quisling. Vichy-ruled France was
forced to sign a humiliating treaty of submission, thanks to which the

southern half of the country was left temporarily free of military occupation. Yugoslavia was broken up. Croatia (like Slovakia) became a client state ruled by the Fascist Ustashe. Macedonia was given to Bulgaria, and Kosovo to Italian-run Albania. Serbia, Bosnia and Montenegro became German military occupation zones.

The Axis Powers, being dictatorships, were not given to a culture of cooperation. Mussolini, for example, loved to spring surprises, thereby repaying the fait accomplis which the Führer had sprung on him. In the autumn of 1940, however, an effort was made to coordinate their activities with those of Japan. A high-ranking Japanese official visited Rome and Berlin, and the Tripartite Pact was signed on 27 September. An offer was even made to include the USSR in the pact, in a step that Stalin seemed ready to bargain over. Nonetheless, in a separate negotiation, Moscow succeeded in upgrading its ceasefire with Japan in the Far East into a formal armistice. The Japanese were covering their rear whilst definitely embarking on the Southern Option, which in the following year would lead to Pearl Harbor. The Soviets were clearing the decks in Asia to give themselves a free hand in Europe.

In this first year of the war, Britain and France were acutely aware that they had declared war on Germany without having secured the participation of all members of the winning coalition of the First World War. Tsarist Russia, though defeated in 1917–18, had taken enormous weight off the Western Front. Yet now, only twenty-one years later, Stalin was consorting with Hitler and the Soviet media were roundly condemning the iniquities of the 'capitalist–imperialist oppressors'. It made little difference whether London and Paris were already cognizant of the secret protocols of the Nazi–Soviet Pact: the Soviets were making no secret of the clear shift in Moscow from an anti-Nazi to a pro-Nazi stance. As for the USA, which was widely believed to have tipped the scales in the West's favour in 1917–18, it now appeared to have turned its back for good on Europe's quarrels. Under Roosevelt's New Deal it was recovering from the Great Depression. Except for the US Navy, it was comprehensively disarmed. And Congress was comprehensively isolationist.

Western relations with the USSR went from bad to worse in 1939–40. To begin with, London and Paris held out some hope that the Soviets might somehow see sense and revert to the shared aims of 'collective security'. With this in mind, they behaved abysmally towards their Polish ally. They either pretended that the Soviet invasion of eastern Poland had not taken place or else they tried to justify it. (David Lloyd George, the former premier, was one of the more crass performers on this occasion.) When asked by the Polish ambassador to invoke the terms of Britain's guarantee of Poland, the British Foreign Office produced a wonderful piece of sophistry which argued that the guarantee of an ally's independence could not be interpreted as a guarantee of the ally's frontiers. Later, when some 25,000 Polish officers went missing in Soviet captivity, the British and French made no effort to press enquiries.

After the Soviet Union's gratuitous invasion of Finland, however, the Western Powers could hardly continue giving Stalin the benefit of the doubt. The French, in particular, were incensed. The USSR was expelled from the League of Nations, and an inter-allied force was readied to intervene in Scandinavia, on Finland's behalf (see p. 80). In retrospect, one can only describe the delusions of the Western governments at this juncture as *folie de grandeur*. While gearing up for a major campaign against Nazi Germany, they were also reckoning to fight a secondary campaign against the Red Army. They had learned nothing from the September blitzkrieg. They presumably thought that Poland's defeat was due to Poland's third-rate army. They presumably thought that France was safe behind the Maginot Line, that the Wehrmacht did not possess the numbers to press an attack though the Low Countries, and that in consequence the first-rate Western armies enjoyed a comfortable margin. They were riding for a fall.

The politics of the fall of France produced high drama. The Führer insisted on the ritual submission at Compiègne, which he attended in person, and on the triumphal march of the Wehrmacht through Napoleon's Arc de Triomphe. The choice of Marshal Pétain, the victor of 1918, as the collaborating leader of 1940 was poignant in the extreme. Winston Churchill, Britain's new premier, made the equally dramatic, but necessarily abortive, counter-offer of a formal union of Britain and France.

The project of bringing the USA back on board fell to Churchill, and it involved eighteen months of painstaking diplomacy. The US President, Franklin D. Roosevelt, was favourably disposed. And, thanks to the reporting of the Battle of Britain and the London Blitz by Ed Murrow and others, the American public warmed to the stand of the British underdog. But the US Congress remained stubbornly aloof. The President and the Prime Minister could only work together to achieve the maximum possible within the constraining circumstances that persisted until December 1941.

The Anglo-US Lend-Lease Agreement of March 1941 kept Britain financially and logistically afloat, whilst surrendering an important degree of British independence. Britain was given interest-free loans and payment-deferred supplies – in the first instance fifty outdated destroyers – while the USA took as collateral a number of British Caribbean colonies, which it leased as naval bases. In essence, Britain was buying short-term benefits to ensure her survival, in return for long-term dependence on the USA. The President described it as 'lending one's hose to a neighbour so he can put out the fire'.[12]

All the while, the USA maintained diplomatic relations both with the Third Reich and with the USSR. American correspondents were free to report the first two years of the war from Berlin and from Moscow.

The Reich, meanwhile, was cruising from success to success. Hitler had surpassed his wildest dreams – so much so that the opportunity loomed for a campaign in the USSR far sooner than anyone had imagined. The war was less than two years old, and he had already overrun all of Germany's immediate neighbours, destroyed Europe's most powerful army, and (as he thought) mortally wounded the obstinate British. Strange to say, he was running out of options. The central choice lay between refraining from the eastern venture in order to finish off Britain in 1941 or postponing Operation Sealion Mark II in order to finish off the USSR. The first alternative was easy; the second was difficult, but infinitely more exciting. In any case, as the Führer said more than once, the British would come begging on their knees as soon as 'Russia' was knocked out.

To begin with, however, Hitler had first to examine what might be gained by prolonging the Nazi–Soviet Pact. After all, the Soviets could not have failed to notice Germany's greatly enhanced position, and Stalin might be persuaded to make some interesting concessions or to enter into some grand plan for dividing up the world. To this end, Molotov was invited to Berlin in November 1940. He was peculiarly unforthcoming. He either said 'No' or said nothing. He did not react when a test plan was dangled in front of him suggesting that the USSR take over the Middle East, starting with Iran. He made no proposals of his own, and when told that the British were defeated he pointedly asked why the meeting was taking place in an air raid shelter. The Germans would probably not have known that Molotov's wife had been locked up in the GULag as a hostage. But they must have guessed that he had not come on a charm offensive.

Two issues brought negotiations to an impasse. One was Romania, which both Germany and the USSR wished to dominate. The other concerned the conditions on which Stalin might agree to join the Tripartite Pact. Contrary to the opinion of historians who are wise after the event, there really was a moment in the autumn of 1940 when the Soviet Union could have joined the Eurasian configuration made up of Germany, Italy and Japan. Ribbentrop sent a proposal to that effect via Molotov, and in a note of 25 November Stalin provisionally agreed. The devil lay in the details. The Nazis sought to use the Tripartite Pact as an instrument for keeping Stalin out of Europe and for giving him a new sphere of interest in the Persian Gulf. Stalin, in contrast, sought to use it as a means of reviving historic Russian claims in the Balkans. Apart from demanding the withdrawal of all German troops from Finland, his note of 25 November envisaged not only a Russo-Bulgarian treaty, but also a Soviet naval base on the Bosporus. This last demand was a demand too far. It would have revived the spectre of conflict over 'the Straits' that had so exercised Bismarck, and in the longer run of Russian expansion into the Mediterranean. Neither Germany nor Italy could tolerate such a prospect. Indeed, Berlin and Rome must have woken up to the fact – which the West did not realize until ten years later – that the Soviet Union, once internally stabilized, would prove no less imperialist and aggressive than its tsarist predecessor. No reply was ever sent to Stalin's note of 25 November. Instead, on 18 December 1940, Hitler drew up Directive 21, 'Case Barbarossa':

> The German Armed Forces must be prepared, even before the conclusion of war against England, to crush Soviet Russia in a rapid campaign . . . Preparations . . . will be concluded by 15 May 1941. It is of decisive importance that our intention to attack should not be known.[13]

The implications are obvious. Hitler had *not* been following a long-standing plan or timetable. Although his dreams of winning *Lebensraum* in the East were always present, he had been prepared to postpone those dreams and to consider an alternative scenario. Stalin's attitudes, no less than Hitler's, determined the shift towards German–Soviet conflict. The decision to prepare plans for 'Case Barbarossa' was driven by 'the combination of Britain's refusal to make peace and the expansionist aims of the Soviet Union'.[14]

For his part, Stalin must have been sorely torn by doubts over the wisdom of prolonging the pact. He seems to have weighed the implications of conflict with the USA, which could materialize if his German partner persisted with the anti-Western tack. On the other hand, like all Russian imperialists, his heart would begin to bleed when the German influence began to spread into the Balkans – a traditional Russian hunting ground. However, in January 1941 he certainly went out of his way to strengthen economic ties with the Reich and to keep the Nazis happy with regular deliveries.

Nonetheless, one of the greatest puzzles of the war still surrounds Stalin's actions and non-actions in those months. Historians, deprived of adequate sources, simply do not know the full truth, though some offer dogmatic opinions about it. It is known for certain, for example, that Stalin received many warnings about the growing imminence of Barbarossa. It is also known for certain, from German sources, that the Red Army and the Red Air Force did not assume a suitably defensive stance. And it can fairly be deduced that Stalin's diplomats were not instructed to take steps in mitigation of the impending conflict. Rumours abound about the nervous breakdown which Stalin reputedly suffered on hearing of the German attack. However, since one speculation is no worse than another, it is more likely that Stalin's nerves were most severely strained at some point just before the attack, when he was most likely to have realized the scale of his miscalculations.

The complexity of the situation is not always appreciated. Stalin was certainly given due warning of Barbarossa by frontier and railway intelligence, by the military-intelligence representative in Berlin, by the NKVD's agent in Warsaw, by Churchill, whose Ultra operation was reading German directives, and most notably by his own master spy, Richard Sorge, in Tokyo. Yet he was also given much advice to the contrary. The new head of Soviet Military Intelligence in 1940–41, General Filip Golikov, was an inexperienced incompetent, who fed Stalin only what he judged innocuous. He was determined to avoid the fate of his predecessor, Lieutenant General Proskurov, who had long warned of Germany's hostile intentions, but who had been removed for speaking his mind over the fiasco of the Winter War in Finland. Golikov was a prime sucker: he swallowed German disinformation concerning Operation Sealion, and on 20 March 1941 he assured Stalin that the Germans would renew their attack on Britain before turning on the USSR. The argument was that the growing concentration of German forces in the East was a feint designed to put the British off their guard.[15]

Another factor was at work. In April 1941 Stalin launched a further purge against senior military officers. The group that had aroused suspicion consisted of men who had served in the Spanish Civil War and who had retained the devious habit of addressing each other with 'Salud, compañero!' The chief suspect was Lieutenant General Yakov Smushkievitch, deputy chief of the Air Staff of the Red Army, and his immediate associate generals: Sztem, Proskurov and Volodin. Throughout the spring and summer of 1941 the NKVD tortured these men, and in several cases their wives, extracting false confessions and through cruel 'confrontations' forcing them to denounce each other. The victims were eventually shot in the 'October Massacre' at Kuibyshev. Stalin was in no mood to trust his closest military advisers. And his entourage was paralysed by fear.[16] No rational discussions were possible.

The core question, however, is why Stalin believed one scenario rather than the other. Here the answer would seem to lie with a series of personal assurances which Hitler sent to Moscow in 1940–41 and whose very existence was not discovered until 1997. Only two of a possible six missives have been identified. One, dated 3 December 1940 – two weeks before Directive 21 was signed – informed Stalin that German forces were going to be stationed in the East in order to reorganize beyond the range of British bombers. The other, dated 14 May 1941, was written one day before plans for Barbarossa were supposed to be completed. It was delivered on a highly unusual courier flight by a Junkers JU-52 that entered and left Soviet airspace without regular clearance. It gave Hitler's 'word of honour as head of state' that all talk of 'differences between us' was 'gossip'. It also informed Stalin that German troops would be moving off from their present stations in the near future.[17] Stalin either believed it or pretended to believe it in order to pursue some devious manoeuvre of his own.

The last few hours of the Nazi–Soviet Pact witnessed no outward signs of the impending explosion:

> Saturday the 21st was a warm and uneasy day in Moscow. The schools had broken up for the holidays. Dynamo Moscow, the football team, lost their game. The theatres were showing *Rigoletto*, *La Traviata* and Chekhov's *Three Sisters*. Stalin and the Politburo sat all day, coming and going. By early evening Stalin was deeply disturbed by the persistently ominous reports that even his Terror could not disperse.[18]

In Berlin, Hitler, who knew what was brewing, spent the evening in his office with Goebbels, drawing up the next day's proclamation. 'This cancerous growth has to be cut out,' they opined. And 'Stalin will fall.'

Stalin, however, was taking no advice from anyone. The Commissariat of Defence drew up a 'Full Alert' order, but it was already after midnight before Stalin agreed to release a modified version. At 12.30 a.m. Zhukov phoned to say that a third German deserter had swum across the River Prut on the border of Romania and Ukraine. The man, a Communist worker from Berlin called Alfred Liskow, informed the Soviet border guards that his unit had been issued with the invasion order. Stalin commanded him to be shot 'for disinformation'.[19]

Sometime later, Stalin's cavalcade of limousines drove through the Kremlin gates and out along the darkened street towards the dacha at Kuntsevo. When he retired to bed at around 4 a.m., Hitler, who was running an hour ahead on German Summer Time, was probably already asleep. The dawn was breaking. There wasn't even time to have Liskow shot.

One fact cannot be doubted. The onset of Barbarossa completely transformed the configuration of the war, widened the conflict and ushering in an entirely new round of political activity.

Phase 2, 1941–4: the rise of the Grand Coalition

The central phase of the war saw all the major combatants aligned in a pattern that would hold good for the rest of the conflict. Yet it was overshadowed by the fact that almost all the fighting was to take place on the Eastern Front, between Germany and the USSR. Politics had to adapt itself to this asymmetry, which greatly inhibited the attempts of the Western Powers to exert an equal influence within the Allied coalition. All the peripheral campaigns in which the British and/or the Americans were involved – in the Western Desert, in the Atlantic, in Morocco/Algeria, and from July 1943 in Italy – were essentially defensive in character. They were primarily designed to secure and protect existing Allied positions: namely, the sea route to India, the convoy routes between Britain and the USA, and the Mediterranean theatre threatened by Fascist Italy. The Strategic Bombing Offensive (see above) was the only major Western operation which may be described as 'taking the war to the enemy'. On the Eastern Front, in contrast, the armed services of the USSR were engaged with the principal war machine of the Axis Powers throughout this period. And the Soviets passed from the defensive to the offensive much earlier, and on a much grander scale. This imbalance between East and West was not specially felt at the beginning, but it was to have serious consequences in the long run.

Constructing the 'Grand Coalition', 1941

Ever since the fall of France, the Allies of 1939 had been reduced from three to two. France dropped out. Britain and Poland remained. And various others combatants, with very limited military potential – including the Free French, the Dutch, the Belgians, the Norwegians, the Czechs and the Yugoslavs – set up base in London. Such was the situation which British textbooks insist on calling 'Britain standing alone'.

Yet the onset of the German–Soviet War created possibilities which Churchill, in particular, was quick to exploit. Churchill had been a leading politician and strategist during the First World War, and it was natural for him to re-create the victorious combination of those years. France, for the time being, was prostrate. But 'Russia' and 'America' were there to be recruited. The task went on for six months. Churchill called the result the 'Grand Coalition', after the diplomatic formation of Marlborough's time, about which he had written in the 1930s.

In the summer of 1941 Churchill was pressing Roosevelt for a much closer partnership. The Germans were rapidly eating into the USSR, and the USA looked to be the sole source of long-term salvation. Churchill was disappointed. All he got, as the two leaders cruised round Placentia Bay in Newfoundland, was the Atlantic Charter and a promise to invite Stalin to a three-power conference.

The Atlantic Charter, signed on 14 August 1941, was a vacuous document of high-sounding principles that could not be put into practice:

- no country seeks any kind of aggrandisement;
- no territorial changes are to take place without the express agreement of the people concerned;
- all peoples have the right to choose their own government;
- all countries, victors and vanquished, shall have equal access to world trade;
- international economic cooperation is essential to secure improved labour standards, economic advancement and social security;

- a lasting peace is to be established to give all nations the means of dwelling safely within their own borders;
- all men should be free to sail the high seas unhindered;
- all nations must abandon force.

It is important only because it subsequently became the basis for membership of the United Nations.[20]

The three-power conference was held in Moscow in September 1941 and was attended by Lord Beaverbrook, Averell Harriman and Soviet representatives. It was not a happy occasion, since it coincided with the Wehrmacht's second round of crushing victories, and Stalin complained of being badly treated. Nonetheless, it extended the system of Lend-Lease to the USSR, raised the profile of Soviet–American cooperation, and regulated the arrangements for the Arctic convoys from Britain.

As an old anti-Bolshevik, Churchill had no illusions about the betrayal of democratic principles that was involved by doing business with Stalin. He was required, as he told the House of Commons, to 'sup with the Devil'. Yet, driven by dire necessity, he was not deterred. (Stalin, who had been Hitler's closest partner for the previous two years, was required to make a still more dramatic volte-face.) The two of them realized that an Anglo-Soviet rapprochement would be hobbled by the lack of a Soviet–Polish rapprochement. Such was the agenda of the winter of 1941–2.

During the currency of the Nazi–Soviet Pact, British relations with the USSR had reached the brink of war. Tensions had been so strained that their relaxation generated the feeling of a return to normality, a breath of fresh air. Ideological differences were thrown to the winds. Recent quarrels were forgotten. All attention was focused on the common enemy. And 'anti-Fascism' provided the slogans. Both the extreme Left and the extreme Right of British opinion were exhilarated. The Communist Party of Great Britain was released from the purgatory of the Nazi partnership. And the empire loyalists of Lord Beaverbrook, who was doing a grand job as minister of aircraft production, rejoiced mightily. Misgivings were confined to the moderate socialists. No one openly protested. At the government level, however, relations were extremely difficult. Soviet officials were notoriously suspicious and obstructive.

A formal Anglo-Soviet treaty, therefore, was very slow to materialize. The main sticking point lay in the Soviet demand that Britain recognize the western frontier of the USSR, which had been agreed with the Nazis in 1939 and which ran through the middle of Poland. Soviet intransigence on this issue, which thanks to the German advance was a pure abstraction at the time, was wonderful to behold. It meant that the treaty would be largely reduced to a series of generalities, including acceptance of principles of 'non-interference in internal affairs' and of 'territorial non-aggrandisement'. More practical were the mutual undertakings to seek the other's approval before a separate truce or treaty with Germany, and to render each other military assistance. On this last score, Churchill decided to show goodwill without standing on ceremony. The first Arctic convoy sailed from Scapa Flow to Murmansk on 21 August 1941. The treaty was not signed until 26 May 1942.

The phraseology of the agreement sounds harmless enough. But it conceals an ugly reality. 'Non-interference' meant that a supposedly democratic state had resigned its right to protest against its partner's inhuman practices of slave labour, concentration camps and mass murder. For his part, Stalin suspended the usual practice of using foreign Communist parties as instruments of subversion. 'Territorial non-aggrandisement', which had already featured in the Atlantic Charter, here meant that the USSR would not extend its territory beyond the aggrandisement already achieved before 1941. No one mentioned non-territorial aggrandisement.

The Soviet–Polish Treaty of 30 July 1941 was attended by still more painful negotiations. Less than two years earlier Stalin had helped Hitler to dismember Poland. His dreaded security forces had carried off huge numbers of Polish citizens. And his only explanation for the *c*.25,000 missing officers – that they might have 'escaped to Manchuria' – was preposterous. Yet General Sikorski, Poland's prime minister, was obliged to bear it all with fortitude, knowing that his government was dependent on Churchill, and that Churchill wanted a result. He was mortified to find that all attempts to discuss the frontier issue were met with a stony refusal. In essence, he agreed to cooperate with the USSR in the war against Germany on condition that Stalin released the surviving deportees, and to raise a Polish army in Russia from the resultant pool of manpower. The deal was struck. Stalin duly approved a so-called 'amnesty' for hundreds of thousands of innocent people. And General Władysław Anders was let out of the Lubyanka jail to take command of the army. It was the start of a famous odyssey.[21]

The road to war taken by the USA was extremely tortuous. In November 1940 Roosevelt had been re-elected president on the strength of a pledge that the USA would *not* go to war. He was bowing to isolationist public opinion which nearly prevented him from amending the Neutrality

Act and which had come within two votes of Congress rejecting an extension of the Selective Service Act. He could not fail to notice that, at 265,000 men, the US Army, though growing, was smaller than Poland's had been in 1939, and that the prospects of early involvement in the war were nil. US military expenditure in the late 1930s was half that of Germany or the USSR, and little more than Italy's.[22] His strategy at the start of his third term, therefore, was to rearm, to turn the USA into 'the great arsenal of democracy', to support the Allies, but to stop 'short of war'.

Throughout 1941 the strategy was energetically developed and refined. In twelve months the trained force of the US Army nearly tripled; the vessels of the US Navy more than doubled; the President promised to build 50,000 aircraft; and US industry geared itself up for one of the miracles of the twentieth century. American strategists adopted 'Plan Dog' (otherwise known as Rainbow 5), which in the event of war was to give precedence to the European theatre and which in the spring of 1941 was the subject of secret talks with the British and the Canadians. The Lend-Lease Bill was passed in March, and extended to the USSR by the three-power conference. The sinking of the US destroyer *Kearny* by German U-boats in the same month led to further modifications of the Neutrality Act. But the pretence of non-involvement was upheld.

The USA's predicament in the last quarter of 1941 was extraordinary. The navy was engaged in hostilities against German warships. Active support was being given to three combatant states: to the UK, to the USSR, and to China. All Japanese assets in the USA were frozen; and thanks to the 'Magic' cryptographic intercepts, Washington knew very well that the Japanese government was moving towards war. Yet the American government categorically refused to take the first step. Even the vicious Japanese attack on the Pacific Fleet at Pearl Harbor on 7 December 1941 did not provoke a general declaration of war. It led the following day to Congress voting for war against Japan, and to a crushing silence about American intentions towards Japan's Axis partners. The silence was broken by Adolf Hitler. On 11 December in the Reichstag he declared war on the USA. Mussolini followed suit. They reckoned that their dramatic gestures would cost them little.

Even then the USA did not react in the conventional way. Despite its best efforts, it found itself in a state of war with Japan, Germany and Italy. In consequence, it was prepared to give unstinting assistance to its friends and to the enemies of its enemies. But it made few formal commitments. There was to be no treaty with the British Empire, no treaty with the

USSR, no binding engagements with British or Soviet allies. The only European countries on which the USA bothered to declare war – on 5 June 1942 – were Bulgaria, Hungary and Romania.[23]

The Axis at its height

One is always tempted to think of the Second World War exclusively in terms of battles, bombings, broadsides and bloodshed. One forgets that the duration of the fighting in any particular location tended to be short, and that the intervals of relative calm, if not of peace, were long. Poland, for example, saw five weeks of fighting in 1939 followed by five years of occupation. France saw six weeks of fighting in 1940 followed by four 'quiet' years. Even in the East, in Lithuania or western Ukraine, the front rolled though in the summer of 1941 and did not return until the spring of 1944. For the occupiers, this was a time of intensive administrative, diplomatic and political work.

The assault on the USSR created several new areas of Axis occupation. The so-called *Distrikt Galizien*, centred on the city of Lemberg (Lwów), was added to the General Government and hence to the Greater Reich. Further east, the *Reichskommisariat Oberost* in the north and the *Reichskommisariat Ukraine* in the south were zones of military occupation. On the Black Sea coast the city of Odessa became the centre of the province of Transnistria that was added to Romania.

Unlike their predecessors during the First World War, the Nazis did not seek to foster the national independence movements in any part of the territory taken from the USSR. Surprisingly, they did not restore the Baltic States, where they were initially welcomed as liberators, and they arrested the leaders of the Ukrainian national movement, many of whom had lived in exile in Berlin in the 1920s and '30s. By such acts they showed that they were not in the least interested in winning the hearts and minds of the population; and they deliberately turned their backs on the chances of fruitful cooperation. Ukraine in particular, where Stalin had killed several million people during the collectivization campaign and terror famine of the previous decade, was seething with anti-Russian and anti-Soviet sentiment. Yet it was spurned. Many historians would see this as one of the Nazis' most costly mistakes.

Nazi policy in the East was purely exploitative. It exploited and abused the people by introducing racial selection, killing unwanted categories, and forcing millions into various forms of slave labour. And it exploited the land, not simply by seizing vast quantities of grain, livestock and timber without payment, but also by attempting to transport to Germany the fertile 'black earth' itself. Not surprisingly, it generated fierce resistance, and it revived pro-Soviet sentiment.

Diplomacy among the Axis powers followed a special set of priorities and proprieties. There were those who were wont to command, and those who were wont to obey. Nonetheless, Berlin had to observe a modicum of restraint, especially towards countries which were not fully occupied by the German army. Each of the Reich's main allies – Hungary, Romania and Italy – followed internal policies of its own devising. In Romania, for example, General Antonescu suppressed the Fascist Iron Guard in 1941 and, with Hitler's approval, instituted a purely military dictatorship. In Hungary the actively pro-German government of László Bárdossi gave way to the 'see-saw' stance of Miklós Kállay, who in 1942–4 endeavoured to balance Hungarian interests with German demands. In Italy, both the royal court and the army had begun to lose faith in Mussolini before the Allied landings; and even in Vichy France Pierre Laval constantly pressed the Germans for concessions. The Vichy government, which was formed by French politicians and by French choices, was not a puppet regime; and it saw itself as the guardian of the broad middle ground between the outright collaborationists, like Jacques Doriot's PPF, and the pro-resistance circles including the PCF and de Gaulle's Free French. Bulgaria, however, was the only Axis country to deflect insistent German demands for the deportation of its Jews.

News of Stalingrad and Kursk caused deep consternation in the Axis camp. From 1943 onward, all the Reich's satellites were thinking of separate peace feelers with the Allied Powers. Their aim was to preserve a modicum of independence both from Germany and from the USSR. None of them succeeded.

Nonetheless, in the eyes of Germany's Nazi elite, the Reich's military expansion into Eastern Europe provided a historic opportunity that was not to be missed. It opened the way not just to the 'Final Solution of the Jewish Question' (later called the Holocaust), but to the wholesale racial reconstruction of all the inhabitants of Germany's eastern 'living space'. To the Nazi mind, this was the most important of all tasks. No sacrifice was to be spared: no mercy shown.

Nazi ideology divided Europeans into a hierarchy of desirables, undesirables, and disposables; and its advocates held that practical action must be taken to 'purify' the community's blood pool. (One should stress that these pseudo-scientific ideas were propagated before the advent of modern genetics.) At the top stood the so-called 'Aryan Master Race', which was identified with Germans and other Germanic peoples including the Dutch, the Scandinavians and the English. At the bottom lay Jews, Roma – 'Gypsies' – the mentally handicapped and the congenitally deformed. In between there were a variety of categories, of which people in the higher ones were judged capable of Germanization and those in the lower ones, including the Slavs, were classed as *untermenschen*, or 'subhumans'. In reality the Slavs are nothing more than a linguistic group. But the fact that the various Slavonic nations – such as the Russians, Poles, Ukrainians, Czechs and Serbs – make up the majority of Eastern Europe's population, heralded a revolution in the region's ethnic and national patterns. According to the Generalplan Ost, which the SS drew up in 1940, the racial reconstruction scheme was designed to stretch as far as the Urals, with millions of undesirables being expelled to Asia and Siberia. But for practical purposes, the key question was: how much time would be given for the plan to be implemented?

The General Government of Poland was chosen as the experimental laboratory for the scheme. It was administratively separate from the Reich, and was not subject to German law; it was the nearest part of the new *Lebensraum* contiguous to Germany; and it was the area in which the SS and the Gestapo had been consolidating their control for the longest time. Above all, it contained the largest concentration of Jews in Europe. Some small-scale measures were taken in 1939–40. They included complicated processes of filtration, segregation, deportation, concentration and extermination.

The Nazis did not hesitate to perpetrate mass murder from the start. Having just completed their euthanasia programme in Germany, their officials toured the General Government's hospitals, mental institutions and homes for the aged in the autumn of 1939 to make selections for killing. In the so-called AB Aktion, they shot some 18,000 academics, priests, professionals and politicians. In October 1939, for example, they rounded up the entire faculty of the Jagiellonian University in Kraków on the first day of the academic year. The Poles, as an inferior nation, were judged not to require universities, secondary schools or educated leaders. Racial-testing centres were set up to determine suitability for Germanization, especially of children. And concentration camps, including Auschwitz I, were established to repress unreliable elements. Poles and Jews were expelled en masse from several western districts annexed to the Reich, and several thousand Catholic priests were shipped off to Dachau. Some 100,000 people were removed from the port of Gdynia, which was renamed Gotenhafen. German settlers removed from the Baltic States by agreement with Stalin were shipped in. The entire population was processed by the Gestapo, racially categorized, and issued with *Kennkarte*, or identity cards, and ration cards. Food was rationed by racial categories.

At that stage the Nazis were content to segregate Jews and to herd them into ghettos, the largest of which were opened in Warsaw, Lublin and Łódź. By Nazi definitions, Jewishness was determined by 'blood', not by religion or by self-identification, and thousands of individuals who did not regard themselves as Jewish, but who happened to have one or more Jewish ancestors, were refused Aryan papers. They would perish like the rest.

The Führer's decision to launch the 'Final Solution' has not been traced by documentary evidence, but it had self-evidently been taken some time before January 1942, when the Wannsee Conference assembled in Berlin to implement it. Indeed, since *Einsatzkommandos*, or special death squads, had been organized to kill Jews in the rear areas of Operation Barbarossa, it appears that the military decision to attack the USSR was accompanied by a series of other decisions designed to promote 'racial reconstruction' in the East. For instance, the merciless policy towards Soviet POWs had no previous counterpart, and, incredibly, an estimated 2.8 million prisoners were done to death in the winter of 1941–2 alone.[24]

With regard to 'the Final Solution', a key development was a new logistical plan to build fixed exterminatory installations in the General Government. Henceforth the majority of victims were to be transported to their deaths, instead of waiting for death to reach them. A large shipment of German Jews began on 15 October 1941, and the first shipment of Jews from France on 27 March 1942. From then on, the grisly routine continued for nearly three years.

Here it is important to distinguish the existing network of SS concentration camps (Konzentrationslager, or KL), including Auschwitz, Majdanek and Mauthausen, from the new generation of 'death factories' at Treblinka, Sobibór and Bełżec. The former, like their Soviet counterparts in the GULag system, were designed as slave-labour centres where a fair proportion of the inmates would inevitably die from institutionalized maltreatment. The latter were designed for the sole purpose of killing human beings as quickly and efficiently as possible. KL-Auschwitz II–Birkenau (see pp. 327, 362) straddled the two categories.[25]

It is also important to stress the complicity of numerous organs of the German state. The driving force undoubtedly emanated from the Nazi Party in general and from the SS in particular. But many other institutions, from the Wehrmacht to the Foreign Ministry, both knew what was afoot and participated. One historian has attempted to implicate German society in general and not just the German party state.[26]

Nor is it idle speculation to consider what the Nazis had in mind for the period following the intended conquest of the USSR. The SS were certainly thinking about it, and their experiments with sterilization obviously formed part of the answer. So too did their policy of mass starvation, which would seriously diminish the Slavic population over huge regions. After that, their existing policies of German resettlement would have been given free rein. Limited exercises in resettlement were concluded in occupied Poland, first in the so-called Warthegau and later in the district of Zamość. There can be little doubt that similar policies were due to be implemented elsewhere on a much greater scale. Loyal German soldiers would have been rewarded with broad acres. Victorious generals would have entered into vast fiefdoms. And the *Lebensraum* would have been transformed into new German provinces.

As the war progressed, however, plans for the future were abandoned, and the Nazi principles of 'racial reconstruction' were compromised beyond repair. One of the most acute pressures came from military recruitment. Despite the influx of slave labourers, which released German men for army service, the Reich's pool of manpower was drying up, and extraordinary measures had to be taken. In 1941 the Führer forbade the recruitment of ex-Soviet *Hiwis* or 'auxiliaries'. But the ban was soon reversed. And the turncoat General Andrei Vlasov gradually overcame opposition to the formation of a near million-strong auxiliary army under German command. Even the SS relaxed its rules. In its origins, the Waffen SS had seen itself as the praetorian guard of the Aryan race. Recruits to its earliest divisions like the Leibstandarte or the Totenkopf had to present impeccable proof of their Aryan descent. But the practice did not long outlast the onset of war.[27] Most surprisingly, it did not protest when the Führer's office issued 'certificates of German blood' to Jews.[28]

Management of the Grand Coalition

Given that the coalition of the three leading Allied Powers gelled only slowly over a period of six months, it is perhaps surprising that no plans had been drawn up concerning its organization or procedures. Yet in December 1941 nothing was ready. As yet there was no Anglo-Soviet treaty, and no understanding between the British and the Americans about how they might run the war effort. Churchill sailed for the USA within a week of Pearl Harbor. He spent Christmas and the New Year in Washington, and in a series of conferences code-named 'Arcadia' he and Roosevelt and their officials forged the basic structures of future cooperation. Their most important achievement was undoubtedly the creation of the Combined Chiefs of Staff committee (CCS), which was given a permanent office and secretariat in Washington, and which was to hold weekly meetings under the chairmanship of the President's personal representative. The CCS formed the essential link between the American Joint Chiefs of Staff and the British Joint Staff Mission. It was assisted by a battery of contributing combined committees for planning, intelligence, transportation, munitions, communications, meteorology and civil affairs. Its dominant personalities were Admiral William D. Leahy (1875–1959), chairman from April 1942, and Churchill's representative, Field Marshal Sir John Dill (1881–1944). Its 200 meetings between January 1942 and the end of the war witnessed many heated arguments, but also gave rise to all the major strategic, logistical and political decisions of the western alliance. When Dill died in November 1944, he was buried in Arlington National Cemetery – the only foreigner to be so honoured.

It is important to note, however, that the CCS was a somewhat unbalanced structure, and it was not designed to manage the affairs of the coalition as a whole. Its being based in Washington put the British at a disadvantage from the start, and American influence gradually rose from the preponderant to the near-absolute. What is more, it contained no inbuilt mechanism for involving the USSR. After Stalin declined to attend the Arcadia meetings, which took place at the height of the Battle for Moscow, the British and Americans went ahead on their own, creating structures from which the Soviets were excluded. This development was unavoidable, partly because in early 1942 the Western Powers feared for the USSR's survival and partly because Stalin never betrayed any desire for an integrated, inter-Allied organization. But it had consequences. It meant that the war against the German Reich had to be run from two separated centres, and that tensions would almost inevitably arise between the two. The Grand Coalition was never to be blessed with a unified system of coordination and command.

Furthermore, no steps were ever taken to integrate Soviet representatives into the CCS. The Soviet Union was represented both in Washington and in London by very active embassies and by large military missions. And the arrangement was reciprocated in Moscow. But that is as far as arrangements went. The Western Powers and the Soviet Union were to fight Germany in parallel, but not as a unified force.

Churchill and Roosevelt continued their practice of intermittent personal meetings. In all, they met on nine occasions:

Placentia Bay (Newfoundland), 9–12 August 1941
Arcadia (Washington), 22 December 1941–14 January 1942
Symbol (Casablanca), 14–23 January 1943
Trident (Washington), 11–25 May 1943
Quadrant (Quebec), 17–24 August 1943
Sextant (Cairo), 23–26 November and 3–7 December 1943
Eureka (Teheran), 28 November–1 December 1943
Octagon (Quebec), 12–16 September 1944
Argonaut (Yalta), 4–11 February 1945

Stalin attended two of the nine 'summits', at Teheran and Yalta. The tenth inter-Allied conference, Terminal, held at Potsdam in 1945, took place after Roosevelt's death and after the end of the war in Europe.

Apart from launching the CCS, the Arcadia conference laid the groundwork in several other fields. It confirmed the strategy of 'Europe First' – that is, of giving priority to the war in Europe over the war against Japan – but did not appoint a command for the European theatre. There was no military action there to be commanded. Its attempt to form an international American–British–Dutch–Australian Command (ABDA) for the Pacific proved abortive. But its decision, at Lord Beaverbrook's insistence, to increase US industrial targets and, on Roosevelt's initiative, to issue a United Nations Declaration of Allied war aims proved eminently successful. The community of the 'United Nations', which was brought into being by the twenty-seven signatories of the declaration, was to provide the framework not just of the Allied war effort but also of the post-war order.

Throughout 1942, sharp differences arose between the British and the Americans on strategic issues. The Americans urgently demanded action on the European mainland. The British urged caution. Churchill wanted to focus on the Mediterranean. The intended build-up of forces in the UK – code-named 'Bolero' – was frustrated by the Battle of the Atlantic. The lack of results was embarrassing. In the USSR it looked like betrayal.

The Symbol conference at Casablanca set out priorities for the rest of 1943. Roosevelt pulled the policy of 'unconditional surrender' out of his hat, without discussion. It was all the more ironic because the intended landing in France, code-named 'Round-Up', was again judged impractical. The decision to expand Allied bombing of Germany into a systematic day-and-night combined bombing offensive was the sole available substitute. The absence of a Second Front had become doubly embarrassing.

The Trident conference in May 1943, which definitively postponed Round-Up to the following year, gave the green light to the Italian Campaign. Churchill argued forcibly that the Axis Powers should be attacked at their weakest point, and that German reserves would be drawn away from the Eastern Front.

The Quadrant conference in August finally made provision for Round-Up, now renamed Overlord, to take place in May 1944. Churchill and Roosevelt signed a secret agreement concerning common control of the Manhattan Project, which by now was promising practical results.

A major conference was planned for November 1943, but had to be divided into two parts because Stalin, who was not at war with Japan, refused to allow Soviet delegates to attend alongside Chiang Kai-shek. The solution was to hold two meetings – one in Cairo to discuss the Pacific theatre and another in Teheran to discuss Europe.

In the meantime, the outlines of the endgame in Europe were already coming into focus. Barring accidents, the Red Army was going to overrun Eastern Europe. The Western armies were going to drive through France and the Low Countries, and possibly over the Alps from Italy. And they were all going to meet in Germany, where the final showdown would occur, and where the leading members of the coalition would be left in charge of a damaged and defeated country. This scenario carried certain obvious implications. And, if there is a fundamental criticism of Allied political strategy, it is that a long list of foreseeable problems was not addressed before the problems became crises.

The most pressing of these problems concerned spheres of influence. Ever since 1941, the coalition had operated on the unwritten but oft-repeated assumption that the Western Powers and the Soviet Union each had a sphere of influence within which they could act without restraint. This assumption caused few ripples so long as the Western Front was non-existent and the Eastern Front lay deep inside Soviet territory. But it called for much greater precision once the Allied armies were preparing to enter foreign countries. For instance, it was not beyond the wit of political planners to ask whether 'a sphere of influence' was equivalent to a theatre of military action or whether, in addition to military decisions, the dominant Allied power was entitled to take unilateral political, social and economic decisions, on the formation of post-liberation governments or the management of foreign industry. Were members of the United Nations expected to observe the Geneva conventions and other minimum standards of conduct, or did they, as victors, possess a completely free hand? At its starkest, did the Allied Powers possess the right to apply the same methods in the treatment of foreign populations that the Fascist enemy had done?

All the evidence suggests that the Soviet authorities had been giving more thought to these questions than the Western governments. One only need look at the case of France which the Western Powers had been preparing to invade for at least two years. Since 1940, the British and Americans had supported a French client in the figure of Brigadier General Charles de Gaulle and his Free French Movement (FFL), which had a tenuous hold in some of France's overseas colonies and in parts of the resistance. Yet they signally failed to consult him about their invasion of the French Levant in 1941 or about Operation Torch in 1942. In preparation for the occupation of French North Africa, without informing de Gaulle they reached an agreement with Admiral Darlan, a Vichy minister; at Casablanca they attempted to subordinate de Gaulle to an organization to be headed by General Giraud, who was an escapee from occupied France; and in the fighting in Algeria and Tunisia they employed a former Vichy commander, General Juin. At every stage they were keen to engage French soldiers, notably the 110,000 men of the French Expeditionary Corps (CEF) that fought with distinction in Italy. Of course, all the Allied leaders thought de Gaulle was a pain in the neck or worse. Roosevelt tried unsuccessfully to have him removed; and he doggedly refused to recognize de Gaulle's Committee for National Liberation (CFLN) long after Giraud had dropped out of sight. As Overlord loomed, no agreement of any sort had been reached about the administration of liberated French territory. Eisenhower presumed that he would head a system of military government. De Gaulle intended to replace the Vichy *préfets* with commissionaires of his own choosing. But then de Gaulle wasn't even told about D-Day.

The mindset underpinning this debacle can be partly explained by the widespread belief that politics could be held over until a post-war peace conference, which, as in 1919, was going to settle all disputes. But it must also be attributed in part to an old-fashioned and highly undemocratic culture of political hierarchy according to which 'Great Powers' took decisions and lesser breeds fell into line.

The same mindset can also be observed in the semi-dysfunctional relationship between the Western Allies and the Soviet Union. 'Russia' was undoubtedly a great power, and many Westerners, brought up in an imperial world, would have felt it no more appropriate for Moscow to be grilled about the future of Finland or Poland than for London to be asked about India, or Washington about the Philippines. But other factors were at work. One was related to the widespread euphoria generated by the Red Army's stunning victories. Another must be linked to highly successful campaigns of misinformation and manipulation.

Soviet propaganda had worked wonders in concealing the true horrors of Soviet history and of current Soviet conditions. Wide sections of British and American opinion had been convinced that Soviet Communism was a force for good. Whilst Fascist sympathizers were locked up, Communist Party members operated freely in the civil service, and even in the armed forces. Fellow-travellers abounded in academe and in the press. And a large number of professional Soviet spies had penetrated all levels of the political, economic and scientific establishments. The Manhattan Project was penetrated. So too were the State Department, the Foreign Office, the OSS and MI6, and Roosevelt's immediate entourage. The work of 'the Cambridge Five' – Blunt, Burgess, Cairncross, Maclean and Philby – was not discovered until after the war, and the continuing closure of British intelligence files obstructs any accurate estimate of the enormous damage they might have inflicted. Soviet spies scored more hits against their allies than against their enemies. But their successes were made possible only by the highly indulgent climate in which they operated. In London, the information officer at the Soviet Embassy doubled up as lecturer in Russian history at London University.[29]

Soviet wartime realities

Two essential points need to be made at once. Firstly, barely 5 per cent of Soviet territory was occupied by the German invasion, leaving well over 90 per cent unoccupied. Secondly, the Stalinist party-state dictatorship, which had killed millions of its citizens before the war, remained in place.

It modified some of its practices to meet the demands of the war; but nothing fundamental was changed. Soviet wartime realities were very different, and generally much worse, than most people in the outside world could imagine.

Furthermore, in the absence of solid information, Western attitudes to the Soviet Union have often been distorted by memories of the wartime alliance. We were fighting Nazism, people say – and the USSR was fighting the Nazis harder than anyone. So, if Hitler was a monster, Stalin can't have been so bad, can he? This is a non-sequitur of the first magnitude. Regimes have to be judged on their merits. Westerners need to step back from the partisanship of the war years and ask themselves if there weren't *two* monsters fighting on the Eastern Front.

Stalinism revolved round the personal dictatorship and the personality cult of the Great Leader, the *Vozhd*. And the prestige of Stalin's leadership hit rock bottom in the last week of June 1941. On the 26th, General Voroshilov was sent to the front to locate the commanders. He found Marshals Kulik and Shaposhnikov and General Pavlov sitting in the rain in a sort of 'Gypsy encampment', totally inactive. On the 28th, Stalin and his entourage descended in person on the Commissariat of Defence and demanded an explanation. A flaming row ensued. Zhukov asked pointedly, 'Comrade Stalin, do we have permission to get on with our work?' Beria shouted back, 'We, too, can give orders.' Zhukov reportedly burst into tears. Molotov comforted him. On the way back, Stalin said, 'Everything's lost. I give up. Lenin founded our state. And we've fucked it up.' Stalin retreated to his dacha, and disappeared from view. He may have suffered a relapse or a breakdown. But he was also testing his comrades' nerves, as Ivan the Terrible used to do. When the Politburo eventually raised the courage to drive out to Kuntsevo and beg him to return to work, he thought they had come to arrest him. Instead, they told him: 'There's no-one more worthy than you.'[30] And the Stalinist regime resumed. Yet it did not fully resume before Stalin apparently took steps to contact the Germans and to explore the possibility of a truce. For this purpose, he tried to use a Bulgarian intermediary, who failed to deliver the message. And the episode, if it ever took place, was virtually forgotten.[31]

The Stalinist terror permeated every sphere of Soviet life. And, now that the facts are better known, one cannot deny that it was in the same league of infamy as the practices of the Third Reich. It lasted longer; it certainly killed more human beings; and in the destructive irrationality which we call Evil it plumbed the depths. For, having killed all his rivals from the original Bolshevik circle, Stalin moved from the killing of 'social enemies' and political opponents to the killing of his own supporters. During the Great Terror of 1936–9 he practised mass killing for mass killing's sake. On the eve of the Second World War he had been ordering the OGPU to kill by random quotas. Thousands upon thousands of totally innocent citizens were shot after being forced to denounce others who would then be shot in their turn. And the cycle of false denunciations and murders snowballed until it threatened to paralyse the whole country. Stalin then denounced his chief murderer, the chief of the OGPU, Nikolai Yezhov (1895–1940), who had killed his predecessor, Genrikh Yagoda (1891–1938), and who was now promptly killed by Lavrentii Beria, a wild pervert, the commander of wartime Soviet security services and the ringmaster of the next wave of Stalin's killers. A climate of fear was created in which literally no one, including Beria, could feel safe.[32]

Suffice it to say that paralytic fear and savage coercion drove all the policies whereby the Stalinist state was mobilized to fight the war. Indeed, for all Soviet citizens who weren't in the front-line regions the difference between peacetime and wartime was barely noticeable. The death toll was not much lower in the 1930s than it was to be in the 1940s. Ever since 1929 the command economy had depended on a captive workforce and on the iron discipline of state planning. The food supply depended on collectivized agriculture whose workers, robbed of their land, lived as state serfs. The GULag (the State Board of Concentration Camps) was the largest employer in the land. And in the army it was a great relief to fight a foreign enemy instead of cowering at home for fear of the purges. All state institutions, including the Red Army, were subject to the absolute control of corresponding organs of the Communist Party. All party cadres owed absolute obedience to the higher party echelons, which were headed by the Central Committee and, at the very top, the Politburo. The Politburo, the Central Committee, all party organs and all state institutions were at the mercy of the Security Service (the OGPU or, from 1944, the NKVD). And the Security Service was the creature of Joseph Stalin. If Stalin had not been a slave to his own paranoia, he would have been the sole free man in the whole system.

Soviet industry had already been fully militarized with the creation of a Military–Industry Commission in 1938, and strategic commodities had been stockpiled from that date. Yet plans were far from complete when Barbarossa erupted and the Wehrmacht bore down on regions, especially in the north-west and in Ukraine, where 60 per cent of Soviet armament factories were then located. Wholesale evacuation was, therefore, ordered. On 29 June 1941 a decree was signed for the removal of eleven aircraft factories. Thereafter, a torrent of evacuations began. Entire factories were dismantled and, together with their stock and their workforce, were loaded on to flatcars and sent eastward. A total of 450 train convoys moved 197 factories and 350,000 labourers from Kiev alone. The most usual destinations were the metallurgical centres in the Urals, like Magnitogorsk, or the Kuzbass coal basin in western Siberia. Here was a grand triumph in true Soviet style. Huge quantities of dismantled equipment fell into German hands. Huge quantities were lost en route. But enough was saved to justify the operation. A tractor factory removed from Kharkov in August was converted to tank production 2,414 km away at Chelyabińsk in the Urals, and sent its first consignment of T-34s to the front in December.

As a result, almost miraculously, Soviet industry kept abreast of demands:

Soviet military production, 1941–5[33]				
1941	*1942*	*1943*	*1944*	*1945*
Aircraft	15,735	25,436	34,845	40,246	20,102
Tanks	6,590	24,446	24,089	28,963	15,419
Artillery	67,800	356,900	199,500	129,500	64,600

To these totals, one must add weapons imported via Lend-Lease and subtract the losses incurred at the front. In the vital period from November 1942 to July 1943, one can see how the impressive results were obtained:

Soviet military build-up, 1942–3[34]		
	Combat aircraft	*Tanks and self-propelled guns*	*Artillery and mortars*
Initial force	3,088	6,014	72,500
Domestic supply	18,537	15,708	175,067
External supply	4,355	2,413	–
Estimated losses	17,690	12,142	148,777
Margin	8,290	11,993	98,790

Of course, the German, the British and especially the American war industries also worked wonders. The Soviet case was exceptional because its starting point was so low and because no one expected such a formidable performance. Soviet people lived in abject poverty. But they passed the test of extreme wartime stresses. The five-year plans had served their purpose.

Yet the Soviet authorities were not content to relocate just the war economy. They relocated national groups, uprooting millions in the process. In the immediate pre-war period they had forcibly removed some 500,000 Poles from the western borders and resettled them in closed districts on the Chinese frontier in Kazakhstan. In 1939–41 massive deportations took place from all the lands annexed by the USSR (see pp. 84–6); and, once the Great Patriotic War started, strategic deportations began with an order to remove all Finns from the vicinity of Leningrad. Later in 1941 a long-standing plan (first mooted in 1915) was activated to deport the entire population of the Autonomous German Republic of the Volga. Some 2.5 million Germans were sent either to the labour armies or to Kazakhstan to join the exiled Poles. Within a decade over half of them were dead. The forced deportation and resettlement of seven Muslim nations in 1943–4 was specially brutal (see p. 349).

It stands to reason that the continuing series of repressions would continue to blight Soviet life for decades, even though the 'excess, non-military deaths' were lower than in the 1930s. Robert Conquest gives figures of 18 million for the decade before 1939 (or 1.8 million p.a.), and an estimate of 6 million (or 1 million p.a.) for 1939–45. Nonetheless, the death rate among a reduced population in the GULag doubled during the war, due to irregular food supplies. And the massive demands of the NKVD on railways and rolling stock can only have contributed to the transport crisis of 1943–4.

Yet one needs to look at the other side of the coin and to ask how the Soviet war machine managed to keep turning in the face of such colossal losses, both military and civilian. One answer to this must surely lie in the peculiar rhythms of Soviet demography. In the first years of Soviet rule, millions had been lost due to war, revolution and famine. But in the post-Civil War period population levels were restored by an astronomic birth rate which rivalled India's and which by 1928 had brought the population of the USSR back to that of the tsarist empire in 1913. The natural boom of the 1920s was then followed by the unnatural trough of the 1930s. But it gave rise to a spectacularly large surplus of young adults in the 1940s.

One could argue that this unplanned human bonus enabled the USSR to survive the inhuman policies of its rulers. Certainly the Red Army's recruitment offices must have noticed that numbers were rising rapidly in the classes of 1922–7 and that the supply of eighteen-year-old conscripts in 1940–45 was unusually copious. Red Army commanders prepared tactics and strategy accordingly.

From 1943 onward, Soviet political activity returned to a theme that had been neglected since 1939: namely, the propagation of Communism in the outside world. The organization devoted to this purpose, the Comintern, had been severely hit both by the purges, which decimated its ranks, and by the Nazi–Soviet Pact, which crippled its ideological tenets, and its activities virtually ceased. In May 1943, therefore, Stalin dissolved the Comintern, while reviving many of its functions under the auspices of the International Department of the Communist Party of the Soviet Union. Contacts were to be revived with the underground communist movements in Western Europe, and the pre-war policy of popular fronts was to be reactivated in anticipation of post-war politics. At the same time, new organizations were set up and new political manifestos were drafted in Moscow, and prospective leaders were groomed, to make the Communist presence felt in all the countries of Eastern Europe where it had been effectively suppressed. Walter Ulbricht (1893–1973) was Moscow's candidate for Germany, Bolesław Bierut (1892–1956) for Poland, and Klement Gottwald (1896–1953) for Czechoslovakia (see p. 380).

Nonetheless, it is wrong to assume that Moscow produced a blueprint for Soviet-backed Communist takeovers throughout Eastern Europe. For one thing, until the terminal phase of the war the Soviets did not know how far their sphere of direct control would reach. For another, they were very conscious of the major differences between individual countries. In the case of Czechoslovakia, for example, they recognized the exiled government of President Beneš, with whom in December 1943 they signed a treaty of friendship, mutual assistance and post-war cooperation. In Bulgaria, a multi-party Fatherland Front was operating in the underground. And in Poland a particularly awkward problem prevailed, given that in 1938–9 Stalin had himself liquidated the entire leadership of the Polish Communist Party (KPP), thereby eliminating the badly needed cadres.

In many ways, however, Moscow faced the trickiest situation in Yugoslavia. Tito (1892–1980), a Comintern agent, was gaining the upper hand in the Yugoslav underground. But to achieve this his partisan movement had changed its colours from revolutionary to patriotic, and was busy fighting a vicious civil war against the Serb-based Chetniks. What is more, Tito was rather too wayward for Moscow's liking. He had conducted secret talks with the Germans, had flown to Italy to meet Churchill, was receiving military assistance from Britain, was entertaining a British military mission, and was posing as president of an anti-Fascist council that was doing business with the exiled government. It was anyone's guess what the final outcome of these unfathomable complexities might be.

Problem countries: Italy and Poland

Italy was widely seen as the weakest link in the Axis chain. And it was for this reason, on Churchill's insistence, that the Allied landings of July 1943 were directed to Sicily. The reasoning proved sound. Within a fortnight, dissatisfaction with Mussolini's regime grew to a fever pitch. And, after a meeting of the Fascist General Council on 24 July, Mussolini was deposed. By agreement with King Victor Emmanuel, the Duce was arrested as he left a royal audience, and was spirited away to internment in the mountains of Gran Sasso. He was replaced as head of government by Marshal Pietro Badoglio (1871–1956).

For some time Badoglio's circle hoped that they had room for manoeuvre. After all, Italy had changed sides in the First World War, and might do so again. This time proved different. The Western Allies insisted on the Casablanca principle of unconditional surrender or nothing. And the Germans pressed on with their own plans, ignoring Badoglio's people almost completely. In the summer of 1943 they increased the number of Wehrmacht divisions in Italy from seven to eighteen, and they treated their half of the country as occupied territory. In September they occupied Rome, sending Badoglio scuttling south to Brindisi, where his government sought refuge under Allied protection. Politically, he had reached the end of the road. After signing the terms of a 'short armistice' on 3 September, he flew to Malta to sign 'the long armistice' on the 29th. Italy was now divided into two zones of military occupation: the Allied zone in the south, and the German zone in the north.

A major surprise awaited, however. On 8 September, in a daring glider raid, the Germans freed Mussolini from internment on the Gran Sasso and set him up in northern Italy as the figurehead of a puppet regime for their zone of occupation. The so-called Italian Social Republic (RSI), first formed at Salò, was a liability from the start. Entirely dependent on the German military, it achieved nothing except for waves of strikes and the launch of the determined resistance movement. Its only consolation lay in the fact that Badoglio's government in the south was equally powerless.

The Italian people paid a huge price for the messy collapse of the Fascist order. When Badoglio fled south, he left over a million troops at the mercy of the Germans. Some, like the Granatieri Division in Rome and the Acqui Division on Cephalonia, fought back and were massacred. Others laid down their arms, joined the partisans, or simply went home. No fewer than 650,000 Italian soldiers were sent to the Reich for hard labour, whilst half that number on the Eastern Front were rounded up and treated as POWs deprived of all rights.

In the winter of 1943/4 the Italian resistance movement blossomed. Memories of the Risorgimento were revived; and in the cities of the north clandestine organizations sprang up, crossing all social barriers. In the mountains, more politicized bands of partisans went into action, while vast tracts of land in Liguria, Emilia and Piedmont were taken over by local 'republics'. In June 1944 a united command was established under General Cadorna, who thereby forged a link between north and south.

The Allied Powers must take their share of responsibility for the prevailing chaos. Some developments could not have been foreseen. But the insistence on unconditional surrender had far-reaching consequences. So, too, did the distaste of Allied commanders for political matters. When the British commander General Alexander publicly announced on the radio that that he was not planning an offensive for the winter of 1944/5, he opened the floodgates for a second wave of German revenge in the north.[35]

Within the Allied camp, Poland was seen to be the most vulnerable member. This was not because the Poles were dispirited, like the Italians, or were divided among themselves, like the Yugoslavs. On the contrary, they were continuing to fight with great resolve, both under British command and in the underground. The problem, in fact, was not of their making. It derived from the rising status of the Soviet Union within the Grand Coalition and from the unresolved issues caused by Soviet misconduct towards Poland during the currency of the Nazi–Soviet Pact. Nothing had been done, for instance, to clarify the fate of the 25,000 Polish officers missing since 1940 in Soviet captivity. The Western Powers, increasingly beholden to the USSR, were apt to let such matters lie – or even, by permitting the rising tide of Soviet propaganda, to allow their loyal Polish ally to be slandered.[36]

In April 1943 Goebbels struck. On the eve of the final SS clearance of the Warsaw Ghetto – which was effectively veiled – he revealed to the world that the corpses of 4,500 murdered Polish officers had been uncovered in mass graves in the Katyn Forest near Smolensk, and that the atrocity was the work of the NKVD. The revelation was well documented. Grisly photographs were circulated. International observers had been present at the exhumation, and they confirmed the German version of events. The implication was that another 20,000 such murdered victims were waiting to be found elsewhere in Russia. Western opinion assumed that the story was a piece of deliberate enemy disinformation. With few exceptions, British and American commentators followed the line of the Soviet response, which was to say that Katyn was obviously a Nazi crime and that anyone repeating the fabrications of Goebbels's ministry was guilty of 'anti-Sovietism'. When the exiled Polish government referred the matter to the International Red Cross for mediation, the Kremlin reacted angrily. The Polish leaders were publicly denounced, and diplomatic relations between the Polish and Soviet governments were severed. Goebbels rejoiced. A wedge had been successfully driven into the heart of the Allied coalition.[37]

One should stress that in 1943, in the heat of wartime, no one outside the Kremlin and the NKVD could know the truth about Katyn for certain. For this reason, Stalin could expect to brazen it out, and in the process to weaken the Polish position. British experts, especially in the Foreign Office, were divided, although an official report (prepared by Sir Owen O'Malley) put the balance of probability firmly on Soviet guilt. Nonetheless, the weight of public opinion was overwhelmingly pro-Soviet, and the British authorities actively encouraged the notion of Katyn being a Nazi crime. British soldiers were threatened with court martial for 'loose talk' suggesting otherwise. British Communists and Soviet sympathizers wrote relays of letters to the press condemning the Poles as 'Fascists', 'anti-Semites' and 'irresponsibles': ungrateful allies who weren't pulling their weight. The brilliant cartoonist David Low produced a series of devastating images of Poles portrayed as 'troublemakers', 'irresponsibles' and 'disturbers of the peace'. George Orwell, a socialist, was one of the very few to see through the fog of bewilderment.

In July 1943 Poland suffered another disaster when its prime minister and commander-in-chief, General Sikorski, was killed in an air crash at Gibraltar. Sikorski had been close to Churchill, and had pursued the policy of rapprochement with the USSR. His removal left a gaping void. After his death the Polish government splintered into quarrelling factions; and the new PM, Stanisław Mikołajczyk, lacked the stature to continue Sikorski's policies effectively. A split opened up between the Polish government and the Polish military leadership. Worse still, rumours spread widely, hinting that the Gibraltar crash had been a deliberate assassination. The Soviets were blamed. The Germans were blamed. Dissident Polish officers were blamed. Even Churchill was blamed. The atmosphere round the future of Poland was turning sour.

Also in 1943, a third source of bad feeling emerged. The Polish army in Russia decided to leave the USSR, preferring to join the British in the Middle East rather than to fight under Soviet command. General Anders claimed that his men had not been adequately fed or armed by the Soviets and that they were incessantly harassed by the NKVD. He ordered them to make for Iran, and from Iran to Iraq, Palestine and the British Eighth Army in Egypt. More than 100,000 Polish women and children, including 40,000 orphans, were evacuated to British India. These refugees were the only substantial group ever to leave the Soviet Union for the outside world, and their stories of death, deportation, hunger and misery troubled all who heard them.[38]

Nonetheless, the Polish issue had not yet come to a head. In the summer of 1943 the Red Army was still a long way from Poland. There would be several months, if not a year, when the coalition could address the Polish–Soviet issue and attempt to heal the breach in its ranks. The Polish government could do little on its own. But the Western Powers did have levers of influence in Moscow. If they chose to mediate, it might not be impossible for a solution to be found. Time was of the essence. The Soviets had recently created a Union of Polish Patriots (ZPP) in Moscow, which was to be the focus for pro-Soviet activities. And a tiny refounded Polish Communist movement was already operating in the underground alongside forces loyal to London. The significance of these bodies would grow with every westward step that the Red Army took. Every cause of delay would lessen the chances of a viable settlement.

Eureka

The Teheran Conference, code-named 'Eureka', which took place in late
November 1943, was from the strategic and political point of view the
most crucial of all the wartime conferences. Not only was it the first time
that the 'Big Three' had met. It was the first and last time that Churchill,
Roosevelt and Stalin had an opportunity to thrash out the main purposes
of the coalition before the conclusive military campaigns were joined.
Historians, therefore, have to weigh both the achievements and the sins of
omission.

The relative standings of the Big Three did not present a clear-cut
picture. The Soviets had gained the upper hand on the Eastern Front, and
they played their diplomatic hand astutely. On the other hand, they had
been liberally supplied with Lend-Lease aid; and they had no doubt that
Roosevelt was the paymaster. The two Western leaders, in contrast, were
both embarrassed and hesitant. They could only apologize tamely for the
absence of a 'Second Front'. And they had arrived without an agreed
position on key issues such as Eastern Europe. Unlike Churchill, Roosevelt
was inclined to humour Stalin so as to secure his support for the final
phase of the Pacific war. Agreement was quickly reached on the main
strategic decision, which was to coordinate the spring offensive of the Red
Army in the East with the launch of Overlord in the West.

Nonetheless, much in the war remained to be played for. The Red
Army, though riding the wave of success, was still confined to Soviet
territory: it had not yet entered the East European countries which it
would eventually overrun. And the outcome of Overlord was a great
unknown. Fascist Italy had been knocked out. Strategic bombing was
pulverizing German cities; and vast quantities of Lend-Lease materiel were
being shipped to the USSR. Even so, Churchill and Roosevelt performed
poorly, and left things unsaid that would come to haunt them. Two
unspoken factors also played a role. They were China and the shifting
balance among the Big Three.

Before 1943 the USA had always assumed that Chiang Kai-shek was
the principal ally in the Pacific war, and that Chinese troops would supply
much of the manpower for the final assault on Japan. By Teheran,
however, Roosevelt was seriously concerned about Chiang's limitations
and was increasingly looking to the Red Army as the only suitable
substitute. This preoccupation made him specially solicitous of Stalin's
good humour.[39]

Churchill had passed the apogee of his influence. In previous times he had provided the guiding vision and the driving force of the coalition. But he was now losing out to the two partners who commanded the biggest battalions and the biggest purse. He could not contest the points where Roosevelt and Stalin agreed – for example, on the projected Anvil landings in southern France – and within the Western camp it was US interests that were moving into overdrive.

The outcomes of Eureka, therefore, were rather mixed. There was general agreement on the main issue, the Normandy landings, and there was a clear decision to support Tito in Yugoslavia. (The British and Americans were motivated here less by a desire to humour Stalin than by a wish to cover their flank in the Italian campaign.) But on several points disarray was allowed to prevail. On the troublesome matter of Poland, for instance, real differences of opinion were papered over and little sense of urgency was evident. Churchill, knowing the sensitivities, took the initiative, and in a private talk with Stalin proposed that Soviet demands (for the so-called Curzon Line) could provide the 'basis for discussion' on the post-war Soviet–Polish frontier. He did not set out a timetable for discussion, and he did not clear his initiative with Roosevelt in advance. When Roosevelt met Stalin in a private chat of his own, and casually let slip that the Polish frontier 'should not cause any problem', one can see that Stalin was given the distinct impression that he had nothing more to worry about on that score.[40] (Anyone wondering about the origins of the Cold War can start here.)

For the time being, however, smiles were the order of the day. The 'Great Dictator' had been confronted, and had caused no trouble. The big issue – the common assault on the Reich – had been agreed. Stalin had offered to match the Western attack with a grand offensive of his own, though no one pressed him on the offensive's objectives. The Allies had started to talk about the future administration of a defeated Germany, and there had been no blazing row.

Stalin, too, must have been content. He had ventured abroad for the first time in his career, had confronted the captains of world capitalism, and had come through unscathed. It really looked as if the capitalists were intending to attack the Reich after all. And, when it came to the Eastern Front, no one had posed difficult questions about spheres of influence, or standards of political conduct, or division of the spoils. On Germany, it looked as if the USSR was going to get its share and would be able to extract reparations. In the eyes of a hard-line, paranoic Leninist, things could have been much worse. So, what was wrong with these capitalists? Were they just dimwitted, or what?

For six months after Teheran, all attention in the Western camp was focused on the forthcoming landings in Normandy. The task of assembling the combined operation force was unparalleled. The logistics of flying and shipping vast quantities of men and weapons from the USA were immensely complicated. Politics took a back seat.

But not completely. In 1944 there would be an election in the USA. President Roosevelt was standing for an unprecedented fourth term. So he and his advisers would be increasingly drawn to issues that played well with the great American public. Good news from the front acquired prime importance. So too did good relations with the Soviet Union, whose victories had raised its popularity to unprecedented heights.

Britain, meanwhile, together with the political issues under Britain's control, slipped down the list of priorities. With regard to Western Europe, much time and energy was expended on the continuing argument over the relative weight to be given to Overlord as opposed to the Mediterranean theatre, which was Churchill's passion. Although everyone took it for granted that a liberated France would resume its rightful place among the Allies, no clear programme was prepared for establishing a post-Vichy regime. With regard to Eastern Europe, the watchword was 'Friendship with Russia', and the Czechoslovak–Soviet Treaty, signed by Beneš in December 1943, was held up as the model for others to follow. A military mission was dispatched to Yugoslavia to facilitate support for Tito. But when in February 1944 the Polish premier begged Churchill in person to authorize a similar mission to the underground Home Army in Poland repeated delays occurred. In line with Churchill's proposal at Teheran, the British Foreign Office spent months preparing at least four versions of a draft Polish–Soviet frontier, and on every occasion the experts agreed that as an absolute minimum the city of Lwów (Lemberg) must stay on the Polish side. Beyond that, anything resembling agreement escaped them. The Soviet authorities ignored the Polish government, and the realization slowly dawned among Western leaders that intervention at the highest level was required. To this end a Polish military and political delegation was invited to Washington to meet both the Combined Chiefs of Staff and President Roosevelt. The delegation was sailing across the Atlantic at the very time that the D-Day force sailed across the Channel.[41]

Phase 3, June 1944–May 1945: the Allied Triumph

Once the troops were safely ashore in Normandy, the Americans in particular returned to politics in a big way. The prospects for a quick end to the European war were good, not to say over-optimistic, and planning for the post-war order had to be put in place before peace arrived. Three matters were pressing: the projected United Nations Organization, the creation of global financial institutions, and the expansion of the existing coalition to finish off Japan. On top of those tasks, the presidential election loomed ever closer.

Mid-1944, in fact, was the moment when the USA came into its own as the world's leading power. Having treated the British as partners, if not quite as equals, it now surged effortlessly ahead, leaving the British and everyone else trailing in its wake. Virtually untouched by the war, riding an unprecedented economic boom, and now fully armed, it called all the shots over the battered Europeans. The effect was that Washington occupied itself with its long-term global vision, and the European Powers were left scrambling to sort out their parochial matters as best they could.

In November 1943, for example, at the same time as Eureka, a conference was taking place in Atlantic City, New Jersey, for the founding of the United Nations Relief and Rehabilitation Administration (UNRRA). This body was dedicated to the welfare of refugees and of the distressed population of liberated countries. Its work began in North Africa, in the wake of Operation Torch. In the next four years, 1943–7, it was to dispense $44 billion of largesse to seventeen countries.

The United Nations Organization (UNO), which was intended as an improved successor to the defunct League of Nations, took longer to take shape. Its history began on 1 January 1942 with the launching of the UN Declaration, which was little more than a commitment by Allied countries to observe the Atlantic Charter and to avoid a separate peace with the Axis. Yet by August 1944 a conference had convened at the Dumbarton Oaks estate near Washington to discuss proposals concerning the organization's aims, charter and organs. Final arrangements did not materialize until April 1945, when delegates of the now fifty-strong United Nations met in San Francisco. The opening ceremony of the organization would take place on 24 October 1945, following the ratification of the charter by the five permanent members of the Security Council – China, France, the USSR, the UK and the USA.[42]

Before the meeting at Dumbarton Oaks, a large UN Monetary and Financial Conference had started work at the Mount Washington Hotel at the Bretton Woods resort in New Hampshire, where 730 delegates from 45 allied countries pondered the problems of post-war finance and decided on the establishment of the World Bank and of the International Monetary Fund. The system of exchange rate management which was set up at Bretton Woods was to last to the 1970s.

Roosevelt had always kept his distance from the minutiae of European commitments. With such initiatives he now glided into higher realms, holding London at arm's length, and repeatedly ignoring British advice. Such was the peculiar prejudice of the Americans that they could be on their guard against the cunning old imperialist Churchill, yet could be completely disarmed by a cunning new imperialist – Stalin. Indeed, though Stalin commanded a vast and growing empire, few people in Washington viewed the USSR in those terms.

Though the European war did not progress as fast as expected, the Pacific war was moving even more slowly. US forces had clearly gained the initiative, but they were still thousands of watery kilometres from the Japanese mainland. At the time of the Normandy landings, Tokyo had only just come within range of US bombers, after the capture of the Marianas; the main fighting was located on Papua and New Guinea. The reconquest of the Philippines did not begin until October 1944, and was incomplete by the end of the war in Europe. The first attacks on the smaller Japanese islands – Iwo Jima in February 1945, and Okinawa in April 1945 – produced fanatical resistance, protracted battles and severe American casualties. US planners inevitably turned their minds to the Pacific, while leaving the final act of the European theatre to the Red Army.

Meanwhile the coalition was running into difficulties in Europe through poor political coordination. In France, the first country to be liberated, Eisenhower's armies approached Paris without any concept of how political change should be managed. Indeed, Eisenhower had no intention of liberating Paris until a spontaneous rising in the capital forced his hand. The Armoured Division of General Leclerc arrived in the nick of time before a Communist-dominated resistance group took charge. It was no thanks to the Allies that events in Paris did not take a turn for the worse. It was the German governor who saved the city from physical destruction by defying the Führer's orders to destroy it. And it was the dramatic, and totally unheralded, arrival of General de Gaulle that presented the opportunity for compromise and unity among the competing post-Vichy factions. De Gaulle conducted himself magnificently. On 26 August he walked serenely down the Champs-Elysées, braving snipers' bullets. And when urged to announce the re-establishment of the Republic he simply said, 'The Republic has never ceased to exist.' At the time, he had no official standing. His movement, the FFL, was not recognized by the Western Allies as the provisional government of France until October 1944.[43]

In Poland, the Grand Coalition presented itself in the worst possible light. An ally of the Western Powers was about to be liberated by another ally, the Soviet Union, and a rising against the Germans in Poland's capital, Warsaw, was about to be triggered as the Red Army approached at the end of July. Moscow Radio had urged the Varsovians to rise. And the Western Powers had been informed.

The decision to launch the rising was taken by the Polish government in London, though it had left the timing to the underground commanders. The premier, Mikołajczyk, faced down critics who opposed his twin policy of fighting the Germans and seeking an agreement with Moscow. In June he had talked on three occasions with Roosevelt, who granted a huge subsidy for the Home Army while urging face-to-face talks with 'my friend', Stalin. Mikołajczyk left for Moscow on the day that he issued orders for the rising to be prepared.

From then on, confusion was followed by treachery and tragedy. The Polish premier was given no support in Moscow by British or American diplomats. Urged by Churchill and Roosevelt to negotiate, he faced Stalin alone and found him intransigent. The insurgents in Warsaw seized the city on 1 August, expecting the Red Army to arrive within days. Instead, the Germans brought in a strike force of savage SS troops and started to reduce the capital to rubble and to slaughter its inhabitants. There was no sign of the Red Army. Delayed for a time by a German counter-attack, it could have advanced at any point after mid-August. But its plans for advance were rejected by Moscow. Worse still, when Churchill ordered the RAF to organize relief flights to Warsaw from Italy, Moscow refused landing rights to the British planes on Soviet-held territory. Worst of all, when Churchill begged Roosevelt to join him in a joint plea and to challenge Stalin, Roosevelt refused.

So the Home Army fought on – spurned by the Soviets and abandoned by its Western allies. The coalition proved incapable of pulling itself together, and of saving one of its members in distress. The rising lasted for nine weeks. Some 18,000 soldiers were killed on each side, and 200,000 civilians perished, many of them massacred in cold blood by the SS. Capitulation was followed by forced evacuation. And on Hitler's orders the ruins of the rebel city were burned and bulldozed. *Varsovia delenda est.* The causes of the catastrophe were more political than military.[44]

In Italy a different sort of catastrophe ensued. After the declaration of Mussolini's 'Republic of Salò', tens of thousands of partisans took to the field, and in the winter of 1944/5 over fifty districts were cleared of German occupiers. Local officials set up free zones of their own. The largest of these partisan republics were located in the mountainous Langhe, Cunese and Ossola in the north-west, at Ottrepó and Bobbio in the northern Appenines, at Bolzano and Belluno in the north, and round Trieste in the north-east. Since the Allied front had stood since August 1944 on a line running from Florence to Ancona, the assumption was that a major Allied offensive into northern Italy would be launched to complement the Allied drive across northern France. Instead, the Italian Campaign ground to a halt. The Gothic Line, north of Florence, held fast throughout the winter. A serious difference of opinion divided British and American strategists, and General Alexander was ordered to concentrate on pinning down German forces in their current position. Churchill's dream of advancing through the Ljubljana Gap to Vienna was never realized. As a result, German commanders were given a free hand to take ruthless action against the partisans. Scores of expeditions were mounted from each of the German bases. Villages were burned. Civilians were slaughtered. Reprisals and counter-reprisals took on murderous overtones. Northern Italy began to look like Byelorussia.[45]

Churchill's improvised visit to Moscow in October 1944 was a symptom of the coalition's disarray. He was forced to go because the Red Army was swallowing the eastern half of Europe without reference to Western interests; and no prior arrangements had been made about the spoils. His main concern was to secure British control of Greece – for which he was ready to relinquish a stake in most of the other countries involved. The notorious percentages agreement, which was sketched out on the back of an old brown envelope pulled from Churchill's pocket, was an example both of rank amateurism and of arbitrary exploitation. The ratios of Western:Soviet influence proposed by Churchill and apparently accepted by Stalin were: Greece 90:10, Bulgaria 10:90, Yugoslavia 50:50, Hungary 25:75, Romania 25:75.[46]

The percentages agreement did not affect Poland, however, and Churchill sent for Prime Minister Mikołajczyk to participate in nego-tiations. But negotiations were there none. Molotov angrily produced a map of the so-called Curzon Line frontier, and challenged Churchill to admit that the matter had been settled at Teheran. Churchill 'hung his head in shame', not caring to clarify what exactly had transpired a year earlier. Afterwards he flew into a rage, blaming the Poles for their unreasonable, obstructive refusal to relinquish half their country. After the Warsaw Rising Stalin held all the cards. The Polish government could be effectively sidelined.[47]

By February 1945, when the Big Three met again at Yalta, Stalin's position had been further strengthened. The Red Army, having overrun half a dozen countries, stood on the River Oder – within walking distance of Berlin. The Western armies had not yet taken the Netherlands, and were firmly stuck in Italy. They had not achieved what their leaders foresaw in the summer of 1944; and they inspired no great will to bargain. Roosevelt was tired, nearing death, and was eager to clinch the deal with Stalin over the war against Japan. He was in no mood to haggle over Eastern Europe. All three leaders wanted to fix the guidelines for adminis-tering post-war Germany, and Churchill's belated attempt to salvage something from the Polish fiasco ended in the face-saving formula of a so-called Government of National Unity.[48]

At Yalta, Stalin stood on the pinnacle of power in Europe and on the brink of victory. His position vis-à-vis the Americans would never be higher, and he received his Western guests as a tsar received petitioners. His mood fluctuated between the truculent, the benign and the grimly humorous. He took offence when Roosevelt revealed that the Americans' nickname for him was 'Uncle Joe'. FDR had to apologize. Then, when talk turned to the Vatican, Stalin asked his famous question, 'How many divisions has the Pope?' Beria was not officially introduced. So when FDR enquired, 'Who's that in the pince-nez sitting opposite Ambassador Gro-myko?' Stalin obliged. 'That's Beria,' he said. 'He's our Himmler.'[49]

The Western guests could not have imagined the symbolism of the occasion, nor the precautions that were taken. Stalin was lodged in the Yusupov Palace, the residence of Rasputin's assassin. Roosevelt was put into the Livadia Palace, home of the last tsar, Churchill in the Moorishbaronial Vorontsov Palace. Five districts, inhabited by 74,000 people, had been combed by the NKVD for 'suspicious elements'. Three circles of guards surrounded the conference by night, and two by day. Dog-handlers roamed the grounds. Churchill called it 'the Riviera of Hades'. Stalin arrived with a security cordon of 620 men, plus his personal bodyguard of twelve tommy-gun-toting Georgians. Everyone was bugged, with Beria's son, Sergo, acting as chief eavesdropper. FDR was followed round the garden by directional microphones. If he knew, he didn't care.

Indeed, Roosevelt's circle did not care much about many of the issues that worried Churchill. Within a couple of weeks of the conference, Churchill would be lamenting to Roosevelt that they had 'signed up to a phoney prospectus' over Poland.[50] The Americans had no such qualms. Roosevelt's closest adviser, Harry Hopkins, talked of 'a new dawn':

> We really believed in our hearts that this was the dawn of the new day we had all been praying for ... The Russians had proved that they could be reasonable and far-seeing, and there wasn't any doubt in the mind of the President or any of us that we could ... get along with them peacefully for as far into the future as any of us could imagine.[51]

The Yalta Agreement did not possess the force of international law. It was intended only as a temporary inter-Allied understanding; and it contained no binding treaties. At least on the Western side, its authors assumed that it would be soon superseded by the deliberations of a peace conference. It was typical of a phase when Stalin had made real progress on the ground, and the Western Allies made improvised solutions on paper. The peace conference never met.

In the dying months of the war, the Soviets made all the running. They controlled all the territories which they intended to remodel, including East Prussia, whence most of the German population had already fled. They were busy installing puppet administrations in all the countries which had not made alternative arrangements by prior consent with Moscow, like Czechoslovakia. The Red Army, standing on the Oder from the end of January, could afford to watch as the British and Americans struggled to cross the Rhine and to establish a foothold in western Germany. The NKVD risked Western wrath by tricking the democratic leadership of the Polish underground into talks, then arresting them and flying them in secret to Moscow. But there was no reaction. Anthony Eden found out that his allies were in a Russian jail only when he asked Molotov about them at the San Francisco Conference. The British were out of the picture, Churchill being denied information about the true terms on which the USSR would declare war on Japan. Roosevelt was embroiled with Congress over domestic affairs. Stalin had held up the assault on Berlin, and was clearly waiting for reassurances about stalled Allied intentions in Europe. He had still had no answer when Roosevelt died on 12 April. But shortly afterwards he was informed by Eisenhower that the western offensive was about to halt and that no one would interfere in the Soviet triumph at Berlin. The mood among Western politicians was summed up by the US Chief of Staff, George Marshall. 'Personally,' he said, 'I would be loath to hazard American lives for purely political purposes.'[52]

News of Hitler's suicide reached Moscow on the morning of May Day, the Communist holiday. Zhukov put through a personal call to Stalin's dacha, telling the guards to wake him. After some delay, the dictator picked up the phone. His comment was: 'So that's the end of the bastard.'[53]

Post-war, 1945–8: from peace to Cold War

When the guns fell silent in early May 1945, peace officially arrived. It was the moment which Germans called *Stunde Null*, or 'Zero Hour'. There was a brief pause after the wartime order had died and before the pain of post-war problems was fully felt. And the problems were daunting. Europe contained an estimated 30 million refugees, who would now try to find their way home. Railway and road links were fractured. Numerous cities from Leningrad and Kiev to Warsaw and Budapest and most major urban centres in Germany lay in ruins. Food supplies were short. Millions of displaced persons (DPs) and POWs were living in makeshift camps. In many parts of Soviet-occupied Europe, fighting continued between Communist security forces and local resisters. Civil war was to break out for a second time in Greece, after Churchill had attempted to mediate in person in December 1944. Trieste was the scene of an ugly stand-off between the British and the Yugoslavs. And spontaneous reprisals were being inflicted on collaborators in many places. Soldiers in all armies were longing to pack up and leave.

Exhaustion apart, there were several reasons why the victorious Allies were prevented from quarrelling immediately. They were all aware, for example, that they needed to cooperate in the administration of Germany, whose government and economy had collapsed. (In the case of the Soviet Union, the interval provided the opportunity for so-called 'reparation squads' to dismantle surviving German industrial plant and to carry it off.) They were also eager to give flesh and bones to the United Nations Organization, which was finalized at the San Francisco Conference of April–June 1945, and which was due to open for business in October. But a further factor was perhaps critical. American officials made no secret of their intention of withdrawing all US forces from Europe at the earliest opportunity. They were giving notice of a situation where the Red Army would soon become the unchallenged arbiter of Europe. Indeed, at Yalta, Roosevelt had told Stalin in person that the US Army would have gone within two years. From Stalin's point of view, it made no sense to provoke anything that might make the Americans change their mind.

One issue that raised suspicions, however, was that of Soviet re-patriates. From autumn 1944 the British and Americans came across large groups of Soviet citizens who had been taken by the Nazis to Western Europe for slave labour, and who, it was assumed, would now welcome the chance of repatriation. To their surprise, however, the prospective repatriates actively resisted, to the point of absconding and even commit-ting suicide. There had been disturbances in the port of Liverpool when the first repatriation ships docked on their way from Normandy to Murmansk. And there was constant trouble in the DP camps whenever Soviet representatives visited. A British officer who sailed with the first repatriation ship from Italy to Odessa reported his suspicions on return that the passengers were being shot on arrival. Yet the policy remained in place – firstly to cooperate with Soviet demands and secondly to keep quiet about it. The British argued that the Soviets might otherwise detain ex-British POWs held in Eastern Europe. To their credit, they refused to hand over prisoners from the Waffen SS 15th Division, who were not suspected of war crimes and who were not Soviet citizens. But in April 1945 the British Army used force in Austria to remove soldiers and dependants of the Cossack Brigade, which had been raised among White Russian exiles and had fought under German command. The result, at the border bridge at Lienz in Austria, was scenes of mass suicide.[54]

More happily, UNRRA moved into most parts of Europe, bringing much-needed food, medical supplies and comfort. It was one of the few instances of successful planning for the post-war crisis. It helped victors and vanquished alike, and was a great healer.

Apart from the UK, the USSR was the only combatant country in Europe where the pre-war political order had survived. Stalin and Stalinism were still in place – unregenerate, as murderous as ever, and victorious. Yet, behind the bullish façade, huge wounds needed to be tended. The loss of life ran into tens of millions. The western Soviet republics were shattered. And the task of reconstructing the 'fraternal' satellites in the Soviet image would absorb all surplus resources for years. The USSR needed a breathing space. And the idea that began to emerge in right-wing American circles that Stalin was preparing to seize Western Europe at any moment was not based on hard evidence. In any case, by the summer of 1945 the war against Japan was not over; and Stalin intended to participate.

Nonetheless, the gulf of misunderstanding between the Western Powers and their Soviet partners was all but unbridgeable. 'The Allies' armed forces and their states of mind operated in disconnected spheres,' wrote one astute observer, 'and at the war's end they confronted each other across a divided continent, and with largely mythical ideas about one another's capabilities, intentions and ambitions.'[55] The mutual mis-comprehension was well illustrated by the Moscow Trial of June 1945, when sixteen leaders of the wartime resistance movement were accused of various forms of 'illegal activity'. The defendants were Poles – British allies, and subjects of the exiled government, which at the time was still recognized both by Britain and by the USA. All were survivors of the Warsaw Rising. Among them were leaders of the democratic parties, who in the normal way would have formed their country's governing elite. The soldiers, including the last commanding officer of the Home Army, General Okulicki, had originally been flown into Eastern Europe by the RAF. Their trial, by Western standards, was obscene. Yet it provoked no official protests. The Western press was largely exercised by the leniency of the verdicts, which, unlike the pre-war Soviet show trials, had included no death sentences.[56]

The inter-Allied conference held at Potsdam from 17 July to 2 August 1945 was aptly code-named 'Terminal'. It was the last meeting of the wartime Big Three, although Truman had succeeded Roosevelt and Clement Attlee replaced Churchill halfway through. The principal item on the agenda was the future surrender terms for Japan. But much time was given to other matters, including the future government and western frontiers of Poland. Here, the discussions descended into near-farce. The

Polish Communist representative, Bolesław Bierut, no doubt well rehearsed, managed to keep a straight face when telling Churchill that he and his comrades intended to follow 'the Westminster model'. (He forgot to mention the dictatorship of the proletariat.) And, when studying the map of the Oder–Neisse Line, which marked Poland's western frontier, the British delegation learned that there were two Neisse rivers and that Stalin was pressing for the more westerly one. Churchill had said that Breslau – where he had attended imperial manoeuvres in 1906 – would be given to Poland 'over my dead body'. But, after he left, the Americans and the Soviets settled the matter on their own. Finally it was decided that the German minorities in Poland, Hungary and Czechoslovakia were to be deported wholesale.

On 16 July, one day before the Potsdam Conference opened, the first atomic-bomb test was successfully completed near Alamogordo in New Mexico; and the USA became the world's first atomic power. Truman casually told Stalin that he was in possession of a weapon of 'unusual power'. Stalin, forewarned by his spies, didn't even blink. Even so, the world had changed. The atomic age had begun. The Potsdam Declaration called on Japan to surrender.

By the time of Postdam, Stalin was styling himself 'Generalissimo', and behaved with an air of impervious superiority. When Churchill, presaging his 'Iron Curtain' speech a year later, tried to complain about the 'iron fence' that was cutting off Eastern Europe, Stalin replied, 'Fairy tales.' When Truman told him about the A-bomb test, stressing a new weapon 'of extraordinary destructive power', Stalin's low-key response had been pre-rehearsed with Beria. What he said was, 'A new bomb! Of extraordinary power! Probably decisive on the Japanese. What a bit of luck!' But two weeks later, when Stalin heard about Hiroshima in his dacha at Kuntsevo, his daughter Svetlana reported a sharper reaction. 'War is barbaric,' Stalin said, 'but using the A-bomb is a super-barbarity.' He obviously felt that American power was turning against him. 'A-bomb blackmail is American policy.'[57]

The end of the war was finally in sight. On 6 August 1945 Hiroshima suffered a devastating atomic attack. On the 8th the USSR declared war on Japan, invading both Manchukuo and southern Sakhalin. On the 9th a second atomic bomb was dropped, on Nagasaki. The response came on the 15th, when Emperor Hirohito broadcast to his subjects, instructing them to 'endure the unendurable' and to prepare for capitulation. Whether this decision was more inspired by the atomic bombs or by the impending

Soviet invasion is a matter of dispute. At all events, the Red Army had already landed on Japan's most northerly island, Hokkaido, before the general surrender was enacted aboard the USS *Missouri* in Tokyo Bay on 2 September. Six years and one day had passed since the opening shots of the war had been fired in the port of Danzig. By the official reckoning, both Asia and Europe were now at peace.

As peace arrived, Europe's imperial powers raced to recover their lost empires, only to find that they were lost beyond repair. The Japanese and the Americans had vied with each other in denouncing imperialism, and both had given encouragement to national liberation movements. As a result, the end of the war saw a rash of declarations of independence. In Indonesia, for example, Achmad Sukarno announced the end of the Dutch East Indies on 2 September 1945, the day of Japan's surrender. In French Indochina, Ho Chi Minh declared the formation of the Republic of Vietnam. And in Algeria, in May, a demonstration against French rule at Séfir had led to the slaughter of 8,000 people by panicky French soldiery. All these developments preceded lengthy conflicts which the imperialists could hardly win. The cause of anti-imperialism was greatly strengthened by Article III of the Atlantic Charter, which, on Roosevelt's insistence, asserted 'the right of all peoples to choose the form of government under which they will live'. Churchill stated lamely that the article applied only to Europe.

The British, whose empire had surpassed all others, had the most to lose. They recovered a few smaller possessions, like Singapore and Hong Kong; they hung on to what they could; and in some instances, like Ceylon, they entered independence negotiations without delay. But the test case was India, and Britain's hold on India was slipping. In 1939 the Viceroy had committed the Raj to war without consulting a single Indian; the nationalist Congress Party withdrew cooperation, and numerous Indian politicians, including Mahatma Gandhi, spent most of the war in British jails. 'Quit India' campaigns multiplied, and heavy-handed actions, such as the sequestrations of food supplies in the Punjab, alienated large groups and regions on which British rule relied. By 1945 the arch-imperialist Churchill reluctantly admitted that the game was up. All that remained, he told a collegue, was to pull out the army and the administration in one piece and to leave the locals to 'a good civil war'. In essence, that was what happened. India and Pakistan gained their independence in 1947 amid horrendous communal killings.

The Levant witnessed similar troubles. French rule in Syria and

Lebanon was compromised by repressions in 1944–5, while the British mandate in Palestine was abandoned in 1947, following Zionist terrorism and Arab–Jewish hostility. In Egypt, growing Arab nationalism undermined the puppet monarchy of King Farouk, who finally abdicated in 1952. Europe's domination of the world was slipping away.

In Europe itself, meanwhile, the victorious Allies were intent on bringing German war criminals to justice. The British had initially opposed this move, but on 8 August 1945 American pressure brought an agreement to create an International Military Tribunal, which was to be held, symbolically, in Nuremberg. There were twenty-two individual defendants, and four counts of indictment: 'conspiracy', 'crimes against peace' (war of aggression), 'war crimes' and 'crimes against humanity'. The fourth count broke new legal ground. But in the event, through the abundant evidence of Nazi genocide and atrocities, it proved far less controversial than expected.

The authors of the tribunal were reasonably aware of its shortcomings from the start. It was always open to the charge of imposing 'victor's justice', which Göring was quick to voice. And the participation of Soviet prosecutors, representing a country which would have had difficulty defending itself against all four counts, was a glaring embarrassment. On the other hand, it was widely accepted that the opportunity should not be missed to lay the foundations of a system of international criminal justice; and the good sense of the chief prosecutor, Lord Justice Geoffrey Lawrence QC, created a climate in which the defence could not claim to have been denied a fair hearing. The verdicts, announced on 1 October 1946, included twelve sentences of death by hanging, three life sentences, four sentences of lengthy imprisonment, and three acquittals. Martin Bormann, Hitler's deputy, had been tried *in absentia*. And Göring would cheat the hangman by swallowing cyanide.[58]

A determination to make war between sovereign states impossible underlay the European Movement, whose founding congress took place at Zurich on 19 September. Its chief patron was Winston Churchill, now out of office, who saw Europe, the British Empire and the USA as three benevolent and interlocking spheres. The British, in fact, could well have taken the lead were it not for the uninterest of Attlee's Labour government, and the initiative fell very largely into continental hands. Equally, in those early post-war days, the intention was to include all parts of Europe, not just the West. At the Hague Conference of May 1948, the Spanish delegate, Salvador de Madariaga, declared,

This Europe must be born. And she will, when Spaniards say 'Our Chartres,' Englishmen 'Our Cracow', Italians 'Our Copenhagen,' and Germans 'Our Bruges' . . . Then Europe will live. For then it will be that the Spirit which leads Europe will have uttered the creative words: FIAT EUROPA.[59]

However, high-minded ideals of that sort were already impractical. Europe was beginning to split into two distinct spheres. Stalin had predicted that the political systems of post-war Europe would coincide with the final locations of the respective armies, and, in the absence of any alternative arrangement, that predicted divide was becoming a reality. On 5 March 1946, at Fulton, Missouri, Churchill made a prophetic speech, which contained those famous words:

From Stettin in the Baltic to Trieste in the Adriatic, an iron curtain has descended across the continent. Behind that line lie all the capitals of the ancient states of Central and Eastern Europe. Warsaw, Berlin, Prague, Vienna, Budapest, Belgrade, Bucharest and Sofia, all these famous cities and the populations around them lie in what I must call the Soviet sphere, and all are subject in one form or another, not only to Soviet influence, but to a very high and, in some cases, an increasing measure of control from Moscow. From what I have seen of our Russian friends and allies during the war I am convinced that there is nothing they admire so much as strength and nothing for which they have less respect than military weakness.[60]

The 'iron curtain' phrase had been used before, but it now became the standard way of describing the dominant feature on the map of Europe. In all the countries of the East, which were occupied by the Soviets, the basic freedoms of movement, speech, assembly and conscience were suppressed; and the contrast between East and West was growing with every day that passed.

In 1945–8 one could also observe a process whereby the differences between the regimes of the various East European countries were reduced as Stalinist norms were everywhere imposed. To begin with, the USSR had been content to exercise overall control, and had tolerated particularities. But the 'Soviet Bloc' was visibly solidifying. Moscow urged the Communist Party in each country to assert its grip and to eliminate its rivals. In 1946, for example, Romania saw the Communists assume a dominant role in parliament and provoke a crisis which would end with the abdication of the King and the abolition of the monarchy. In 1947 Poland experienced rigged elections which put an end to hopes for a genuine compromise between the Soviet-controlled government and the democratic opposition. In February 1948 Czechoslovakia lost its democratic government when President Beneš was overthrown by a Communist coup. Where manipulation had failed, violence was used with impunity. The Communists were getting their way by hook or by crook.

The one exception was Yugoslavia – the one country where a Communist dictator had held power since the end of the war. Tito resisted Moscow's efforts to enforce standardized Stalinism, and, defying prospects of Soviet intervention, built his own 'Yugoslav Road to Socialism'. Under Yugoslav influence, neighbouring Albania took a similar route.

Europe's most pressing problems, however, were economic. And in the Marshall Plan of 1947 the USA took steps to address them. No American could forget the Great Depression of the 1930s, which had been caused by the backwash of Europe's financial and economic dysfunctions after the First World War. And the administration of President Truman was not going to allow anything similar to develop again. The plan developed by his Secretary of State, General George Marshall, was there-fore a quintessential piece of enlightened self-interest. In the simplest terms, it aimed to pump capital into Europe's spluttering economies, and thereby to restore industrial production and the creation of wealth from which everyone concerned, including the USA, would benefit. Its official name was the European Recovery Program, and it was designed to cover the fiscal years of 1947–51. It put $13 billion (equivalent to $100 billion in 2005) at the disposal of all countries which joined the Organization of European Economic Cooperation (OEEC).

General Marshall unveiled the plan during a speech at Harvard on 5 June 1947, which was then broadcast in full by the BBC. At the time, he and his supporters – who included both Dean Acheson and George Kennan – were battling a number of alternative proposals which would have repeated the mistakes of the previous generation. The Morgenthau Plan, backed by the US Treasury, would have imposed punitive reparations on Germany, as in 1919, and contained the novel suggestion of the 'pastorali-zation' of the German economy. The Monnet Plan, preferred by France, would have put most of Germany's heavy industry under French control. Kennan's interest was strategic. Convinced of the USSR's designs for expansion, he saw the Marshall Plan as an essential element of his policy of containment.

Marshall's original speech contained a specific invitation to the USSR to participate. As Kennan predicted, however, Stalin declined – though not before sending Molotov to make detailed enquiries. He also prevented Poland and Czechoslovakia from attending the Paris conference at which the workings of the plan were agreed. The USSR would compensate itself by exacting compulsory deliveries at minimal prices from all the satellite states. Nonetheless, one should add that the British Foreign Secretary, Ernest Bevin, took a hand in ensuring the absence of the Soviets. He told Molotov that the economic performance of all participating countries would have to be scrutinized. He well knew that Moscow would never wear such a condition. In this way, by early 1948 the European divide was taking on economic as well as political and military dimensions. The countries which benefited most from Marshall Aid were Britain, France and the Netherlands. Germany's share, less than half Britain's, was relatively modest. Franco's Spain was the only Western country to be excluded.[61]

Throughout these years, no decision was taken on the future of Germany. For their different reasons, both the Western Allies and the USSR wished to keep the country as one entity. But all the pressures were moving in the opposite direction. Soviet-style restrictions were introduced into each of the Soviet occupation zones – in eastern Germany, in East Berlin and in eastern Austria. In the British, French and American occupation zones, in contrast, efforts were made to uphold Western-style freedoms, notably in local government and in economic management. Konrad Adenauer, sometime mayor of Cologne, for example, had been organizing his Christian Democratic Party in the British zone long before there was a central parliament in which it could operate. On 23 June 1948 the occupation currency was withdrawn from the three Western zones, and the Deutschmark was introduced. The Soviets responded with the Berlin Blockade. But they could not halt the wider developments. A constitutional commission began work on drafting the Basic Law, and the Federal Republic of Germany came into being in May 1949. Its capital was Bonn. Adenauer was its first chancellor. In practice, if not in theory, Germany was divided.

The term 'Cold War' had been coined by the British writer George Orwell in an article for the socialist journal *Tribune* in October 1945. And it is perfectly respectable to argue that an incipient 'Cold War' between the West and the Soviet Union was already in progress long before the accompanying institutions and terminology were in place. Certainly, important steps toward the conflict were taken in 1946, when the USSR refused to join the Baruch Plan for the peaceful uses of atomic energy under UN auspices, and in 1947, when the Truman Line curtailed Soviet/ Communist expansion into Greece and Turkey. George Kennan's anonymous 'X Article' on 'The Sources of Soviet Conduct', which provided the rationale for the policy of 'containment', was published in *Foreign Affairs* in October 1947. 'To avoid destruction,' he concluded, 'the United States need only measure up to its own best traditions and prove itself worthy of presentation as a great union.'[62]

Yet conventional wisdom holds that the Cold War started with the Berlin Blockade, when all the preceding incipient causes culminated in open confrontation. The US military in Germany were indeed faced with a very tricky challenge. The Soviets had closed all road and rail links between Berlin and western Germany, and they would have had a marked advantage in any shooting incident that might have ensued. The immediate American proposal was to send an armoured column down the Autobahn towards Berlin, and to blame the Soviets for the consequences if it was fired on. This was withdrawn in favour of a proposal made by the US officer who had organized the airlift to China over the Burma 'Hump' five years earlier, and who now advised beating the blockade by flying in supplies by air. The result was outstanding. Over the next nine months, 278,228 sorties were flown. Berlin was fed and supplied. And pro-Western attitudes among Berliners became unshakeable.[63]

Unfortunately, when the blockade was called off, the Cold War continued. NATO had been formed. Western Europe was becoming an armed camp to match the armed camp already created in Eastern Europe. The 'War without Bullets' was all set to last for four long decades. And the US Army never went home.

History is full of examples of states and warriors who 'won the battle but lost the peace'. And one is tempted to apply the dictum to the events of 1945–8. The victorious Allies had defeated the Third Reich; but they quarrelled over the spoils, and they failed to forge the lasting peace which their noble victory merited.

This scenario is attractive, but unconvincing. It takes no cognizance of the manner in which the war in Europe was won, nor of the unequal contributions of the victors, nor of their differing aims. The Western Powers did not possess a dominant position in 1945 which they could subsequently have squandered. The principal victor was undoubtedly the Soviet Union, which had entered the war in 1939 in the hope, among other things, of seeing the Western powers eliminated. Indeed, from the Soviet perspective, the conflict with German Fascism in 1941–5 was an intensive but very short interval in the much longer struggle against capitalism as a whole.

As for the Western Allies, one should be careful not to exaggerate either the scale of their contribution or the speed of their recovery. The chances of Stalin entering a lasting post-war partnership with the USA were always very slim. In the first phase of the war, when the USA had not been a combatant, France had been eliminated and Britain was all but floored. Almost half the European war had passed before the USA even began to compete. And it was only in the final phase that American wealth and might began to tell. Indeed, one could argue that the USA did not start to exert its power and influence fully until after the European war was complete. The crucial date was self-evidently 16 July 1945. Such was the political and territorial lead that the USSR had gained in the war years that the West was desperately scrambling in the immediate post-war period to achieve some degree of parity.

The period between Yalta and the Berlin Blockade was a time when the West grew in wisdom. Roosevelt's term of office had been marked both by idealism and by grave delusions, especially about the nature of the USSR. Truman's term, in contrast, was brought down to earth by a severe dose of realism. By 1948, though much had been achieved, it was clear that the defeat of the Third Reich had been but one episode in a much longer struggle. The continuum of politics never stopped.

CHAPTER FOUR

SOLDIERS

From Enlistment to War Grave

Identity

ALL ARMIES HAVE SHORT forms and nicknames for referring to the enemy. When the Wehrmacht fought the British Army, it habitually called its adversaries *die Engländer*, 'the English', or more popularly 'the Tommies'. When it faced the Red Army, it called its opponents *die Russen* or 'the Russians', or more popularly 'the Ivans'. For their part, the British were convinced that they were fighting 'the Germans', whom they often called 'the Krauts', i.e. 'cabbage-eaters', or, as in the Great War, 'the Hun'. Red Army men referred to *Germantsy*, 'the Germans', though their favourite nickname for them was *Fritsy*, 'the Fritzes'. Needless to say, all these labels concealed a mass of complexities.

'The English', for example, were not always, or even predominantly, English. The British Army of 1939–45 contained a large number of Scottish, Welsh and Irish regiments, who would have been mortified to be confused with the English, and the British Empire supplied a huge variety of troops from every continent on earth. The Dominions were particularly prominent, and Canadians, Australians, South Africans and New Zealanders fought in all the major campaigns and in all the services. The much-feared Gurkhas were from India, though not from the Indian Army, which contained a huge variety of men from assorted races, regions and religions. All answered to English as the language of command, but all swore their oath of allegiance to a British, not an English, monarch.

In addition, a number of foreign contingents fought under British command. The largest of these came from Poland, though soldiers of the Polish Army were by no means exclusively ethnic Poles. They included Jews, Ukrainians and Germans. The last of these hailed mainly from the western regions of Pomerania, Posnania and Silesia, where conscription into the Polish Army was in force before 1939, as was conscription into the Wehrmacht after 1939. In these circumstances it was not uncommon for an elder brother to serve 'with the Poles' and a younger brother to

serve 'with the Germans'. By the same token, conscripts from the eastern
borders could be drafted into the Polish army in the 1930s and into the
Red Army following the Soviet occupation of 1939.

The Free French, who numbered nearly a quarter of a million after
the fall of North Africa, formed the second largest contingent. They
divided themselves into the *hadjis*, who had made 'the pilgrimage' round
one or other of the French colonies, and the *moustachis*, who were
professionals raised in one of the Vichy-controlled territories. Yet the most
visible distinction lay between the Frenchmen from France and the
colonials from North or West Africa.

The racial factor was less prominent in forces under British command,
however, than in the US Army, where in the 1940s separate black units
were raised in many of the southern states. Yet, generally speaking, the
Americanization of US Army recruits from the most diverse backgrounds
was well advanced. The officer corps contained a high proportion of
WASPs, whilst the typical 'GI Joe' was often of Italian-American or Polish-
American descent. The German-Americans were equally numerous,
though many of their families had changed their surnames during the First
World War. The Eisenhowers, from Pennsylvania, were one family that
had bucked the trend.

'The Germans' were far more of a mixed bunch than either the Western
Allies or their Nazi leaders cared to ponder. Official policy in the early
years of the war was to maximize the 'Germanity' of the Reich's armed
services by bringing foreign manpower into the farms and the factories
and thereby releasing German boys for the military. The influx of 3–4
million Poles, Frenchmen and Soviets in 1939–42 served the purpose very
well. Yet the results were never as desired, and over time the policy broke
down completely. The Reich spread steadily from its original base to
Austria, Bohemia, western Poland, Alsace and Slovenia, and conscripts
from these areas inevitably watered down the whole. By the middle years
of the war the Wehrmacht would take almost anyone who was available.

In any case, the Nazis were obsessed with 'blood', not nationality.
From their viewpoint, a Dutchman or a Dane was as good as a German,
while the Slavs were spurned. The most interesting phenomenon, though,
lay in the readiness of the Führer's Chancellery to grant certificates of
Deutschblutigkeit or 'German bloodline' to German Jewish men who wished

Operation Barbarossa, 1941

The full weight of the German war machine was thrown against the Soviet Union, which reeled before the onslaught for six months before stemming the tide.

Above. Panzer forces prepare to cross the 'Peace Boundary' in June.

Below. Soviet reserves fighting in -40° C of December cold ensure the survival of Moscow.

War of attrition, 1941–2

Along 1,500 miles of the Eastern Front, scores of battles raged as the Germans continually pressed on and the Soviets stubbornly resisted.

Right. Soviet infantry storm a trench during the long Siege of Leningrad.

Below. German officers on the open steppe observe one of the campaigns of encirclement that netted over 2 million prisoners.

Preserving Western lines of communication, 1941–2

The Battle of the Atlantic saved Britain's lifeline with North America, while the desert campaigns in North Africa kept Axis hands off the Suez Canal.

Above. View from a U-boat's deck as a torpedo sinks a merchantman.

Below. The desert provided a vast open arena for the chivalrous duel of Rommel's Afrikakorps with Montgomery's Eighth Army. Axis ambitions ended at El Alamein.

War in the air and the ether

Unable to launch a 'Second Front' in Europe, the Western powers concentrated on strategic Bombing and on radio intelligence.

Right. B-24 Liberator bombers drop a payload over Germany.

Below. Colossus, the world's first electronic computer, was developed by Britain's Ultra Project to break advanced versions of German Enigma codes.

Germany's last glories, 1942

The Wehrmacht's second summer offensive on the Eastern Front aimed to capture the oilfields of the Caucasus, but fell short.

Above. Austrian mountain troops symbolically scale Europe's highest peak, Mount Elbruz (5,633m).

Below. Soviet defenders engage the VI Army of General Paulus on the banks of the Volga at Stalingrad.

Kursk: the decisive battle, July 1943

Stalingrad had proved that the Nazi Wehrmacht was not invincible, but it was Kursk that broke its capacity for large-scale offensive warfare.

Above. A Panzer VI Tiger, the war's strongest tank, seeks a path through Soviet defences.

Below. A T-34, the war's most versatile tank, leads the Red Army's counter-attack that swarms victorious over the battlefield.

Partisan warfare

The activities of partisans in the occupied countries depended on the support of local sympathizers, and they provoked savage reprisals.

Above. In the marshes of Byelorussia (eastern Poland), supplies are delivered by boat.

Below. In the islands and highlands of Greece, royal and communist factions competed for post-war control.

Distinguished generals

None of the generals who had established top reputations by the end of the war had been prominent in the early stages.

Above. Georgiy Zhukov, Stalin's deputy, and Konstanty Rokossovskiy, released from the Gulag.

Below. George Patton, 'Old Blood'n'Guts, and Walter Model, 'the Führer's Fireman', extrication specialist.

to serve. The practice had started before the war for the benefit of men who had distinguished service records from the First World War; and it was extended after 1939. It was applied most frequently to so-called *mischlings*, that is, to men whose family was only partially Jewish. Notwithstanding the Holocaust, up to 150,000 Jews were granted such status.[1]

The composition of the Waffen SS – the Waffen Schutzstaffel, or Armed Protection Echelon – provides an object lesson in these matters. Designed as the elite military wing of the Nazi Party's shield, the earliest divisions were formed in the 1930s from recruits whose German and Aryan credentials had been carefully screened. After 1940, however, fresh divisions like Wiking and Nordland began to draw on Germanic foreigners, especially on Scandinavian volunteers. And from 1942, when the man-power shortage became very apparent, systematic efforts were made to raise volunteers from every occupied country except Poland and Greece. Frenchmen, Walloons, Italians and Hungarians were all made welcome. In the last years of the war, all pretence of racial exclusivity was abandoned. No less than six of the Waffen SS's thirty-eight divisions were composed of Slavs – Russians, Ukrainians, Czechs, Serbs, Bosnians and Croats – even though Nazi science had classed Slavs as 'subhuman'. This development put the Nazi leaders in a quandary. During a pep talk to Waffen SS officers in September 1944, Himmler described the task of the organization as a struggle against 'the yellow peril', the oriental troops who were making up an ever-higher proportion of the Red Army (see below).[2]

A similar progression occurred in Nazi policy towards military auxiliaries, or *Hiwis*. To begin with, the Nazis were reluctant to arm non-Germans, consigning them most often to work battalions. Indeed, in the winter of 1941/2 they allowed over 2 million Soviet POWs to die in custody, making little attempt to use them either as forced labour or as military auxiliaries. From then on, however, they realized their mistake, and permitted a variety of formations to be raised. There were militarized police battalions from Ukraine and the Baltic States. There were numerous infantry regiments formed from the various nationalities of the USSR. And there were quite large entities, such as the SS Russian Liberation Brigade (RONA) or the Vlasov Army, which had distinct political programmes. General Andrei Vlasov was a successful Russian officer who had distinguished himself during the Battle for Moscow but who was persuaded by his German captors to lead an anti-Stalinist movement among Soviet

POWs. His army, which ended the war defending Prague, did not have the time to reach its potential, but it had a pool of a million men on which to draw.[3]

These paradoxes became very apparent during the Warsaw Rising of 1944. The Polish Home Army had assumed that it was fighting 'the Germans', and the appalling massacres of civilians that took place are generally denounced as 'German atrocities'. Yet the picture looks rather different if examined in detail. The Wehrmacht was loath to release units from the front, and the SS was obliged to assemble an improvised 'strike force' from the most motley elements. The Dirlewanger Brigade was made up of paroled convicts and 'ex-Soviet' citizens; the RONA Brigade consisted mainly of Russians and Byelorussians (not Ukrainians, as many Poles believed); and the largest infantry group was made up of Azeris. Two divisions of Hungarians had to be withdrawn because of their ill-concealed sympathy for the insurgents.

'The Russians', as the Red Army was almost universally known outside the USSR, subsumed people from seventy official nationalities. According to Soviet statistics, Russians made up between 55 and 60 per cent of the Soviet population. This meant that 40–45 per cent were non-Russians. According to Red Army practice, however, Russians were given precedence in the officer corps, and, according to Russian custom, Byelorussians and Ukrainians were counted as Russians. The most one can say, therefore, is that the Red Army was a Russian-led army, and that Russian was the language of command. (It changed its name to 'the Soviet Army' in 1944.)

A terminological digression may do no harm. The full name of the people whose native tongue is Russian and who have formed the dominant element both of the tsarist empire and of the USSR is 'Great Russian'. It distinguishes them from the inhabitants of 'Little Russia' (which is the old tsarist name for Ukraine). In the popular parlance of almost all their neighbours they are known as 'Muscovites', since Moscow was the historical centre of their expansion-prone state. From early times they had ambitions to absorb all the East Slavs into their ranks, and to impose the rule of the Muscovite tsar and patriarch on one and all. But their empire spread far beyond the East Slav lands, taking in Finns, Balts, Poles, Georgians, Armenians and a score of Asiatic peoples. And the population expanded at a rate that far outpaced the imperial policy of assimilation.[4]

Western commentators have been particularly slow to grasp the difference between Soviet theory and practice. It's true that the Bolshevik leaders dreamed of creating a new nation of *Homo sovieticus* – Communist by loyalty and Russian by culture. Yet the dream never came near to realization. The Soviet population never took on the characteristics of the American melting pot, in which all previous cultures and ethnic differences could be broken down. Instead, throughout the USSR, coherent blocks of non-Russian, and frequently anti-Russian, national groups held their ground in their own homelands and republics. Under Stalin, they were coerced into participating in all the regime's ventures, including the Second World War. But whenever the chance came, in 1918–21 or later, under Gorbachev, they broke away in droves, and created a dozen sovereign nation states. To call them all 'Russians', instead of Soviets, is simply to miss the point. This fact, which has become common knowledge since the collapse of the Soviet Union, was not widely appreciated in 1939–45.

Within this overall kaleidoscope, the position of the Ukrainians was particularly complicated. They were the largest Soviet minority (around 18 per cent), and they spoke a language that is as close to Russian as Dutch is to German (*Deutsch*). Indeed, they had always been treated by the tsarist and Soviet authorities as the Russians' 'younger brothers', who would lead the way towards Russification and Sovietization. Ukrainian nationalism therefore was of necessity anti-Russian. And the fact that a separate Ukrainian state had been set up with German help in 1918–21 made it specially suspect. As a result, Stalin's persecutions in Ukraine were merciless. Well over 10 million Ukrainians were killed in the 1930s, if not by the policy of forced collectivization, then by the terror-famine of 1932–3 and the Great Terror. If only the Nazis could have thought to accept the Kaiser's policies of twenty-five years earlier the course of history would have been very different. As it was, betrayed by the Germans and humiliated by the Russians, the Ukrainians had little option but to suffer the next wave of war and occupation with stoicism. The surprising thing is not how many Ukrainians volunteered to join the Wehrmacht, but how few.[5]

The Central Asians should also be treated as a special case. Their homelands in Kazakhstan, Uzbekistan or Tajikistan were far removed from the conflict in Europe, and they had little immediate interest in sending their young men to be slaughtered in the German war. Yet, though racially similar, they were deeply divided among themselves by languages and traditions, and they could form no common front against the Moscow-led

Soviet juggernaut. What is more, Soviet rule had broken the bonds of traditional societies and of Islamic solidarity, and a huge demographic boom was putting the first sons of the modernizing Central Asian republics at the disposal of the Red Army. When fighting the Soviets, ordinary Germans imagined that they were fighting 'Russland', whilst Nazi racists boasted that they were stemming the tide of the 'hordes of Asia' or of 'the successors of Genghis Khan'. Ironically, as the war wore on, the Nazi nightmare came ever closer to reality. Columns of olive-skinned, narrow-eyed oriental youths increasingly refilled the depleted Soviet ranks, and the composition of the Red Army visibly shifted. What enemies and allies alike continued to call 'the Russians' was, if truth be told, Eurasia on the march.

Finally, there were groups that cut across all the boundaries of combatant armies. In 1939–45 there was no state of Israel. But in later times Israeli leaders would take pride in the large numbers of Jewish soldiers who reportedly took part in the struggle against Nazism. In his very last Independence Day speech, in 2005, Prime Minister Ariel Sharon paid homage to an estimated 1.5 million Jewish soldiers of the Second World War, 250,000 of whom, he claimed, were killed. He mentioned by name: Captain Paulina Gelman, a Soviet pilot; Lieutenant Tommy Gould, RN, a British submarine commander; and Lieutenant Raymond Zussman, a US tank commander. He talked of 200,000 Jews in the ranks of the Red Army – but not of those who served in the German Wehrmacht.[6]

Enlistment

The processes whereby men and women were taken out of civilian life in order to serve in the armed forces were not a simple matter. In all the combatant states, they involved volunteering, recruitment of professionals and, above all, conscription. Together, they formed the first stage on the road to training, placement, mobilization and active service, along which every recruit would travel.

Conscription – meaning the compulsory enlistment of citizens for military service – was the norm in the age of total war. In the USA it was known as 'the draft'. Every country took steps to put the maximum number of young able-bodied people into uniform. But each followed its own rules and practices, thereby affecting the ethos and performance of the armies that were raised.

It is often said that democratic countries are worse prepared for war than their totalitarian rivals are. In 1939–45 this was generally true. But this does *not* mean that all the democracies were equally unprepared, or that all the dictatorships had mobilized their forces with equal efficiency.

In 1939, two of the three combatant democracies possessed large standing armies. Both France and Poland had lived through the 1930s in the immediate shadow of the Third Reich, and both had introduced peacetime conscription. Given the conventional wisdom that an aggressor would need a supremacy in numbers of 3:1, both were reasonably prepared to fight a defensive war at short notice. Britain, in contrast, possessed no standing army. It did not introduce even partial conscription before 1939, and in consequence it was not ready to play anything but a very marginal role when war broke out. Despite a lull of eight months before fighting came to the Western Front, the British Army was able to contribute only ten divisions to the French Campaign of 1940. Its contribution was approximately one-tenth of the French army's.

Britain and the USA followed a very different policy from the French, guided by their very different traditions and priorities. Confident in their reliance on naval defence, they did not need a massive land army to guarantee their basic security, and they had worked on the assumption that 'the draft' was not a socially acceptable peacetime measure. As a result, neither of them was in position to enter the fray in a major continental campaign before the second or third year of hostilities. Neither of them had made provision for the possibility that the war might last for less than two or three years.

The German General Staff would have been well aware of this situation. And it is not hard to see what calculations would have been made. If Germany could knock out Poland, France and the USSR within two years of the outbreak of war, there would be no significant rivals left. Germany would be in sole control of the entire continent. And the Anglo-Americans, whatever their initial intentions, would have no option but to desist. The disaster of Dunkirk probably gave the Wehrmacht an extra year's leeway. In this light, Hitler's decision to give priority in 1941 to the rapid conquest of the USSR, and to leave Britain to its own devices, made perfect sense.

As it was, the Soviet Union was not conquered; Britain was not brought to book; and, not withstanding its very late entry, the USA was unexpectedly given time to make itself felt in Europe. For this, the Red Army and the Red Army alone was responsible.

Even so, one cannot stress too strongly that the build-up of British and American forces was painfully slow. In Britain's case, the reasons included the late start, the dispersal of professional cadres round imperial garrisons, the pre-eminence of the Royal Navy and the Royal Air Force, and the very low ratio of 1:9 between combat troops and service troops. In numerical terms, the results were modest. The one and only pre-war conscription act was undertaken for the limited purpose of forming five Territorial Army divisions for anti-aircraft service. Full-scale conscription was not pursued until the winter of 1939/40, and the British Army never overcame the glaring discrepancy between the large pool of potential soldiers available and the very small number of military units sent into action. By May 1940, for example, when the British Expeditionary Force saw action in France, the British Army had been supplied with over 1.5 million personnel. But only 13 divisions had been formed – only one of them armoured, and lacking the requisite complement of tanks – and only 10 of the 13 actually ever saw action in France. Overall, between 1939 and 1945 some 3–5 million men and women enlisted, and the strength of the British Army rose steadily from 1.88 million in September 1940 to 2.69 million in September 1943 and a peak of 2.92 million in June 1945. From this sizeable pool of manpower, however, only 9 armoured divisions, 25 infantry divisions, and 2 airborne divisions were actually put into the field.[7]

There should be no difficulty, therefore, in explaining the extreme caution, not to say timidly, of the British High Command throughout the war. All the other major combatant states were dealing not with tens but with hundreds of divisions.

American problems centred on time and priorities more than on numbers. The USA possessed unrivalled economic resources, splendid transport facilities, and a large population second only to the Soviet Union. But it came into the war as the back runner, and it faced very different demands for the war in the Pacific – which was largely naval – from those required in Europe. Fortunately, basic moves were taken in advance. The call-up of the National Guard and the introduction of selective conscription in 1940 brought troop levels from a puny 175,000 to 1.4 million by mid-1941. And the creation in June 1941 of the US Army Air Force, which was to remain under army control, laid the basis for an up-to-date combined military force. From then on, the aim was to assemble an establishment consisting of 105 divisions (8.25 million men) plus almost 300 air groups (2.30 million). In the event, only 100 divisions were raised: 76 infantry, 16 armoured, 5 airborne, 2 cavalry and 1 alpine. A total of 10.42 million men and women served in the US Army during 1941–5. This relatively low figure reflects the high priority given to air power and to technical branches, especially high-class artillery. In the winter of 1944–5, when large-scale operations against the main Japanese island were in prospect, critics of the US Chief of Staff, General Marshall, complained bitterly of undermanning. And Eisenhower's posture in Europe inevitably came under severe strain.

According to the Treaty of Versailles, the German army was limited to an establishment of 100,000. The treaty was ignored by Hitler, who in 1939 was able to deploy 58 divisions, including 9 panzer divisions, against Poland. A further 40 reserve divisions, though ill-equipped and incomplete, were still forming. By the time of the Western offensive, only seven months later, the Wehrmacht could field 128 divisions, and in June 1941 during Operation Barbarossa it had no fewer than 142 divisions, including 17 panzer divisions. Thereafter the German military establishment climbed to a peak of 304 divisions, including 176 standard infantry and 32 panzers. Of these, 58 divisions – the same number that was sent into Poland in 1939 – including 7 panzers, were allocated to the Western Front (see Table overleaf).

In purely numerical terms, therefore, the German performance was phenomenal. The Third Reich managed to mobilize many more bodies than the British and the Americans put together, from a smaller population. Conscription held up, especially when applied to the occupied countries. Casualties were largely offset by foreign volunteers (like the Vlasov Army). And an absolute shortage of manpower did not make itself felt until the last year of the war.

However, the numbers concealed severe deficiencies. Nazi plans were predicated on a short war. Each major offensive in 1939, 1940 and 1941 achieved its manpower targets by drafting training, service and reserve

Wartime fighting strength of the Third Reich (thousands)[8]				
	Army	Navy	Air force	Waffen SS	Total
1939	3,740	122	677	23	4,562
1941	5,200	404	1,545	160	7,309
1943	6,550	780	1,700	450	9,480
1945	5,300	700	1,000	830	7,830

units into the front line, thereby undermining the capacity for long-term sustainability. The recruitment age was gradually reduced from twenty-one to eighteen, and in 1945 to sixteen. Veterans had to be called up. And, in the last throes of the Reich, schoolboys – raw recruits without training – had to serve alongside middle-aged men who had already served in the First World War. The Nazi planners had banked on quick victory, and led their country to total collapse.

There is an old Russian proverb which says, 'U nas mnogo' – meaning 'We have lots [of men]' or 'There are lots of us.' This knowledge had always encouraged the fatalistic conviction that human life was expendable. Added to the unparalleled coerciveness of Stalin's regime, and the wholesale militarization of Soviet society since 1929, it led to a set of attitudes and practices that had no counterpart elsewhere.

Soviet commanders knew, for example, that they could afford to sustain two or three times the number of casualties as the enemy, and still win the day. They were not encouraged either to care for their men or to emphasize training, and they were constantly ordered to overwhelm the opposition by sheer numbers. In June 1941 the Red Army supposedly held 5.37 million men under arms. Yet within ten days of the start of Barbarossa a further 5 million were mobilized. There was no way that these crowds of recruits could be properly trained and equipped. As a result, one of the Red Army's characteristics was to maintain a minority of first-class units accompanied by a vast array of half-fed, half-clothed, half-trained troops in second- and third-line formations.

Conscription in the USSR was applied not just to military service, but to all branches of industry and to all adult citizens. (This was the land of the GULag, where up to 10 per cent of the population were slave labourers.) Everyone was directed to a place of work according to their qualifications and the will of the state. As likely as not, healthy young men and women would be put by their local soviet at the disposal of one of the fourteen military districts, where training and political education took place.

In districts close to the front, conscription resembled press-ganging. Armed conscription squads simply rounded up all the youths they could find, and marched them off. 'In a report to Stalin, a high-ranking official complained that in the Orel *Okrug* (district) only 45,000 out of 110,000 men could be mobilized, and that on the way to the front large numbers of men were often "lost". He called for increased political education, and commented that there were too few executions.'[9]

The Soviet obsession with quantity as opposed to quality could also lie behind the unusual size of Soviet military formations and the amount of their equipment. A Soviet tank division, for example, was designed to have 375 tanks, whereas a German panzer division had up to 209. A Soviet rifle division had 1,204 machine guns; a Wehrmacht infantry division only 486.[10] In effect, when Soviet officers complained that their units were under strength, they were usually on a par with their adversaries.

In the early part of the war the Red Army's principal problem lay with the supply of trained officers. Stalin's peacetime purge (see p. 151) had killed more senior officers than perished in the wartime fighting. And the shortage was not satisfactorily made good until 1943–4 (see 'Officers', p. 225).

Soviet statistics were notoriously wayward – perhaps deliberately so. And German estimates of opposing forces invariably exceeded Soviet declarations. Historians have to resort to complicated balancing acts:

The balance of personnel on the German–Soviet front, 1941–5 (thousands)[11]

	June 1941	July 1943	Jan. 1945
Soviet forces	2,900	6,442	6,000
German estimates thereof	4,700	13,200	12,400
German forces	5,500	5,325	3,100
German sources	3,200	3,100	1,800

Neither the Wehrmacht nor the Red Army recognized the right to conscientious objection to military service. Nor, incidentally, did the

French Army. But Britain and America had both recognized conscientious objectors during the First World War, and in 1939–45 they extended their provisions. In Britain, where civilian labour tribunals decided the issue, roughly 6 per cent of applicants were given exemption; 10 per cent were imprisoned for absolute refusal; and the rest were permitted to work in the mines, in hospitals, in agriculture or as medical auxiliaries. In the USA, exemption was generally granted to religious objectors but not to politicals or to principled pacifists. The rest were drafted into 'Civilian Public Service', which was a polite name for harsh, penal-style work camps. Britain produced about 60,000 objectors, or 1.2 per cent of conscripts, and the USA about 100,000. Famous conscientious objectors included Michael Tippett, then a rising British composer, and, in the USA, Lew Ayres, star of the 1930 film *All Quiet on the Western Front*.

Not everyone who wanted to enlist, however, was able to do so smoothly. In 1941, for example, William Patrick H. (1911–87) wrote personally to President Roosevelt to allow him to serve in the US forces. He was a British citizen born in Liverpool, fit, and of military age. But he had lived in Germany, and he was kept waiting for nearly three years. He was eventually admitted to the US Navy, in whose service he was wounded in action. The trouble was this volunteer was Hitler's nephew, the son of Adolf's half-brother, Alois. His family still live in a small town on Long Island, New York, where he settled down after the war.[12]

Women

If the First World War introduced women to 'war work' – mainly to industrial labour in munition works or shipyards – the Second World War brought them into military units, and, in the Soviet forces, into active combat.[13]

In Britain, all single women aged twenty to thirty became liable for national service as from 1941, and 3 million extra women entered paid employment over the pre-war level. All three services organized auxiliary services, and young women in the uniform of the Wrens (navy), the WRACs (army), the WAAFs (air force) or the Land Army became a common sight. The movement was publicized by Princess Elizabeth, who served as a trainee military truck driver and mechanic. Almost half a million served in the traditional profession of military nurses.

In theory, British women were not entitled to fire a gun or to enter combat. In practice, the rule was breached when large numbers of women in the Auxiliary Territorial Service (ATS) staffed anti-aircraft units. Some 56,000 served in the London district alone, and 389 were killed. Mary Churchill, the PM's daughter, showed the way. Searchlight units were also frequently womanned by female volunteers. The RAF accepted women for pilot training, and many were used for ferrying new aircraft from the USA.

In the USA, where labour shortages were less severe, women were kept at bay for longer. But the Women's Auxiliary Corps (WAC) was formed in 1943, and the poster of 'Rosie the Riveter' became one of the great successes of wartime recruiting.

In Germany, Nazi ideology sought to keep women in the home. But pressures built up, and nearly half a million *Blitzmädchen* were recruited into female air-defence units. The rules were similiar to those in Britain: women could join the military, but could not fire a gun.

The Soviet Union ignored all such inhibitions. Women were subject to conscription as men were, and some 8 million, or 8 per cent, were directed to military training, where they were prepared for a number of specialized tasks including truck-driving, sniping and machine-gunning. Women became common in the Soviet transport system, and female traffic-controllers were ubiquitous. All-women combat units were also formed, especially in the air force. The 585th Fighter Wing, the 587th Dive-Bomber Wing and the 588th Night-Bomber Wing were all staffed exclusively by female flyers.

One woman came to symbolize the role of the Soviet amazon. Lyudmila Pavlichenko had been a history student at Kiev University in 1941, when she volunteered to join the 25th Division of Infantry as a sniper. She fought in the defence of Odessa, and had 309 'kills' to her credit before being invalided out. In August 1942 she became the first Soviet citizen to visit the White House, at the invitation of Eleanor Roosevelt.

Training

All soldiers have to be trained. And some branches of the armed services demand more training than others. The authorities could expect to turn out an infantryman in three to four months, for example, whilst a fighter pilot might reach a squadron only after eighteen months. And all countries were under great pressure of time. The British and Americans had to start almost from scratch. The Germans had been restricted by the limitations of disarmament. And the Red Army was in the throes of the purges and of reorganization.

What is more, all the combatant armies followed their own training methods. The British Army was wedded to 'battle drill': that is, to instilling pre-set reactions to a list of given challenges. The US Army, like the French army, was inspired by 'Taylorism': that is, to the analytical methods advocated by Frederick Taylor, the pioneer of time-and-motion studies. Taylor's 1911 textbook on scientific management had promoted techniques for reducing complex tasks to a set of simple actions. The Wehrmacht, in contrast, made wide use of war games, designed to develop enterprise and flexibility. The Red Army's manuals were imbued with theories about mobilizing the class enthusiasm of the masses.

The British Expeditionary Force of 1940 was well trained and – unlike the greater part of the German infantry – fully motorized. Yet the stately tempo set by the authorities put minimal numbers of trained men into the field before Dunkirk. Thereafter, the biggest problem for the British and American training programmes lay in the challenge of amphibious warfare, of which no one had much experience. Raw recruits had to be brought up to high standards of preparedness while officer and staff training schemes had to instil familiarity with the most complicated tasks of combined operations – that is, of land, naval and air forces operating in unison. One could say that the Western armies had to pass from the kindergarten to university study with little in between. And precious few trial runs were possible. The Dieppe raid of 1942 showed how much had still to be learned, and Operation Torch, which served as the only major practical exercise for the Americans, revealed glaring flaws. The success of Husky, and later of Anzio, Salerno and Overlord, depended on ironing out the creases beforehand, for which time and patience were essential. None of the other major armies faced the same sort of problem. And in this context one can see why the original idea of opening up the 'Second Front' in 1942 or 1943 was thought unrealistic. Armies embarking on amphibious warfare get only one chance.

Such was the background to the little-known tragedy of Slapton Sands on the Devon coast, where in April 1944 nearly a thousand American soldiers were killed or drowned after a German E-boat patrol penetrated an offshore training exercise and sank many ships. The disaster was hushed up. The victims' families were sent misleading death certificates. But once again, as at Dieppe, the dangers of an amphibious operation were brutally underlined.[14]

By general consent, the German Wehrmacht was the best-trained army of 1939–45. Its prowess was due partly to long-standing German traditions and partly to the head start provided by Hitler's pre-war orders. Even so, there were serious problems created by an accelerating timetable, and the German military was repeatedly required to do its learning 'on the job'. As revealed by the Hossbach Memorandum, the top brass was told in 1937 that five to six years would be available to prepare the Wehrmacht for a major conflict. In the event, war broke out within two years; the campaign in France, which everyone expected to present the severest test, was fought only eight months after the Polish Campaign; and the attack on the Soviet Union was ordered within a year of the fall of France. Hitler's generals were aghast at the Führer's haste, which did not allow for methodical training schedules. But the war machine responded with great professional competence, and the policy of springing surprises on the enemy brought its rewards.

Standard German procedures foresaw an initial eight-week training course in which recruits would receive basic instruction in weapons use and maintenance, tactics, parade ground discipline and physical training. In addition, Wehrmacht conscripts would receive further training in a number of further sectors, including reconnaissance, infantry combat or armoured warfare. Lastly, additional training would be given in one specialist area, such as motor transport, artillery or radio operation.

For officer candidates a further programme of training was required. First they would attend an eight-week course at a *Kriegsschule* which aimed at giving them a good knowledge of the basics of command. Thereafter, they would proceed to a *Truppenschule* or branch of service school, where the specifics of their chosen area of expertise would be taught. An example of the latter is the *Panzertruppenschule* in Münster, where a sixteen-week course of tactics and leadership would be taught. On graduation, the recruit was promoted to *Oberfähnrich* and sent on field probation.[15] But the process was speeded up in the late 1930s by recalling trained men to the colours, and the German divisions that invaded Poland had more than the usual proportion of middle-aged troops. Experience, however, is a useful leaven to any army. And from 1939 the Wehrmacht possessed the priceless advantage of an expanding core of battle-hardened formations. Many units that fought in France had already fought in Poland, and had learned their lessons the hard way. Many units that drove into the Soviet Union were boosted by the skills and confidence gained in France. When the British and Americans came on to the scene, they quickly recognized the huge difference between second-line enemy divisions and elite formations that had learned their trade in the hard school on the Eastern Front.

As in many other aspects of its performance the Red Army was extremely uneven in its training record. Some branches of the Soviet service, like the artillery, were first-rate. Others, like the second-line infantry, would frequently send men into battle with virtually no training at all. In 1941 the Red Air Force was markedly inferior to the Luftwaffe both in tactical skills and in equipment. But within a couple of years it enjoyed something like parity in training as well as superiority in numbers. Much of the initial disarray was due to chaos caused by Operation Barbarossa, which necessitated desperate improvisation and emergency measures of all sorts. Yet it is also true to say that the Red Army was long disadvantaged by the straitjacket of 'proletarian military doctrine', which was based on the experiences of the Civil War and which in many respects did not withstand the trial by fire of 1941. For example, modern blitzkrieg theory had been denounced as a 'bourgeois deviation', and, as in the French army, the enormous size of the tank park did not necessarily encourage provision in training either for the pursuit of tank warfare or for defence against it. The emphasis on political education – which by all accounts took the form of endless, dreary and jargon-laden pep talks – greatly reduced the time available for honing practical skills. Soviet soldiers spent three hours per day less on military training than did their tsarist predecessors. What is more, whilst Stalin's purges destroyed a large part of the pre-war 'corps of commanders', Operation Barbarossa destroyed a large proportion of the well-trained professional elements within the army of 1941 – all of which had to be replaced and, of course, trained. Training always rests to a large extent on the ability to pass on the skills of previously trained cadres. So, when the trained cadres themselves are destroyed, an army's ability to regenerate and to expand is inevitably weakened. It is truly extraordinary, therefore, that the Red Army not only survived the massive losses of 1941, but also succeeded in training successive waves of fresh troops, who duly won the war on the Eastern Front. Equally, it should cause no surprise that 'over much of the war, experimentation was one of the features of the Soviet military system'.[16]

Weapons

It is said that the bravest soldier can be nothing but rash unless he is provided with a good weapon. And much effort, both before and during the Second World War, was expended on providing the troops with up-to-date, efficient weapons.

Moreover, in the age of total war, when soldiers were counted in millions and tens of millions, the definition of a good weapon had to be tailored to the needs of mass production. A gun or an aircraft which performed brilliantly but which was difficult to produce did not match requirements. The best example of this truth was the German 'King Tiger' (PZKpfw VI Ausf B) tank, which in good conditions outperformed all its rivals on the battlefield, but which cost so much time and money to manufacture and maintain that only hundreds were ever produced.

Among the infantry weapons, the prize would go either to the MP 38/40 machine pistol, commonly known as the Schmeisser, or to the more advanced MP 43/44 Sturmgewehr, which was the model for the post-war Soviet Kalashnikov AK-47. The British Sten gun was also popular, despite its alarming tendency to jam. (Germany manufactured its own Sten copies.) In sheer numbers, however, nothing equalled either the US M-1 carbine or the Soviet 'pepesha', the PPSh-41 – known as the 'burp gun' – of which 6 million were produced.

Among transport vehicles, the laurels probably go to the Willys Jeep (1942), the small sturdy staff car, pioneer of four-wheel drive, which could drive up the steps of the Capitol, cruise along a railway track, or pull a field gun from a quagmire.

Artillery had much improved in precision, range and mobility – especially with the introduction of self-propelled guns and observation of targets by spotters who could guide the gunners by radio. The star could well have been the German 88-mm anti-aircraft gun, which could also double up as a tank-buster. The Soviet Katyusha multiple rocket-launcher, also known as 'Stalin's organ', was another extraordinary piece of equipment.

Tanks were the offensive weapon par excellence of 1939–45. British Churchills and American Shermans were notably uncompetitive compared to the German panzers. But nothing rivalled the Soviet T-34 for all-round ability. Fast, sturdy, punchy, reliable, well armoured and relatively simple to manufacture, it was a major factor in the Soviet victory on the Eastern Front.

Warplanes, which had been in their infancy in 1914–18, came into their own twenty years later. The RAF's Hurricanes and Spitfires, designed before the war, proved their quality during the Battle of Britain, while the massive Halifax, Lancaster and Wellington bombers turned out to be Britain's only offensive arm. The Luftwaffe, which was mainly geared to a ground-support role, presented numerous excellent aircraft, which enjoyed unchallenged superiority for a long time. The Focke-Wulf FW-190, Messerschmitt Bf-109 and Heinkel He-111 and no doubt many others, deserve mention. Yet the really momentous developments were connected with the surprising recovery of the Red Air Force, which began to dominate the skies over the Eastern Front from mid-1943 onward, and the fantastic explosion of American aviation. The Soviet MiG-3, Ilyushin Il-2 Shturmovik and Yak-3 were all very successful aircraft, while the long list of fine American machines would have to include the P-38 Lightning, P-47 Thunderbolt, P-51 Mustang, B-17 Flying Fortress and B-24 Liberator. Western air power compensated for the shortcomings of ground forces, and set the standards for defence activities in the post-war world.

By 1941, when the *Hood* and the *Bismarck* were lost, the age of the battleship was evidently passing. But the aircraft carrier was not much used outside the Pacific theatre, and the Battle of the Atlantic was mainly fought between U-boats and small convoy escorts. In nominating the key vessels of the war, therefore, one is tempted to name either the LCT landing craft which made Allied amphibious warfare possible, or the mass-produced Liberty ships, which were 'produced by the mile' in the Kaiser Shipyards in Los Angeles, and 'chopped off by the yard' to keep the Atlantic sea lanes open. Neither Germany nor the Soviet Union, as land-based powers, gave similar priority to naval affairs.

Nothing better symbolized Germany's distress in the naval war than the fate of the aircraft carrier *Graf Zeppelin*. Launched at Kiel in December 1938, it displaced 33,550 tonnes and was to be one of four such vessels. Yet it was never completed nor commissioned for service. A vicious inter-service feud between Admiral Raeder and Air Marshal Göring, who insisted on keeping all aircraft under his control, prevented progress. Work on the sister ship, 'Carrier B', stopped in 1940. Work on the *Graf Zeppelin* stopped in 1943, when it was 95 per cent complete. In 1944, it was moved from Kiel to Stettin to avoid Allied bombs. On 25 April 1945, it was scuttled in Stettin harbour to save it from the Red Army. Refloated by Soviet engineers, it was towed to Leningrad only to be brought back to the western Baltic in August 1947 and sunk for target practice.[17]

The pressures of the Second World War drove weapons technology forward at a tremendous pace. The war started in the age of the horse and the machine gun; it ended in the age of rockets, jet engines, atomic power and the computer. In human terms, it was a terrible step backwards; in terms of science and technology, a great leap forward.

Officers

European armies had been led by officers for centuries, and all European countries possessed a traditional officer class – drawn mainly from the landed nobility – and a well-established system of military academies and officer training. Yet the First World War had pushed many of the old traditions aside. In 1939–45 all the major armies were adapting in different ways to new conditions.

In Britain, the Royal Navy was still regarded as the 'Senior Service', and its officers had long been less socially exclusive than those in the army. The Empire still offered an outlet for professional military careers, and the rise of the Royal Air Force, as a prestigious service free of former prejudices, attracted many of the best talents. Nonetheless, as the army expanded rapidly after 1939, no attempt was made to limit the officer corps to the sons of county families or to public schoolboys. Montgomery, though arrogant to his peers and allies, had a genuine rapport with his troops. And many men who would make their mark in post-war British life, like Edward Heath or Denis Healey, first found their feet as army officers of a new type.

In the USA, European-style military families still existed in the south. But, generally speaking, the officer corps was more open and democratic. West Point chose its cadets more by competitive entry and promise of leadership than by social origin, although a colour bar functioned in practice, if not in theory. All the top US officers of the Second World War had made their way on their merits (see 'Generals', p. 239).

Resentments against the officer class were much stronger in Germany. In the interwar period, both Communists and Fascists included the army leaders among the 'traitors' of 1918, who had permitted the 'Stab in the Back'. It was no accident that the Nazi Party developed its own party-based army, the SS, with separate ranks, separate recruits and separate training, which was to form the new elite of the New Order. Tensions between the SS and the Wehrmacht therefore had social and political as well as purely professional overtones. Claus von Stauffenberg, who planted the bomb in Hitler's HQ in July 1944, came from a traditional military family. His colleague Henning von Tresckow, who had been plotting against Hitler on the Eastern Front since 1941, regarded the removal of the Führer as 'a matter of honour'.[18]

The Soviet Union was still more radical in these matters. Bolshevik doctrine viewed the Red Army not as a national force, but as 'the bulwark of the workers and peasants'. An officer class was judged inappropriate, and was twice abolished, only to be restored in face of a war crisis: firstly in 1920, during the Polish War, and secondly, for good, in 1936. On the second occasion its restoration was followed by the most vicious of purges, in which Stalin killed a large proportion of its senior cadres, including the brilliant Marshal Mikhail Tukhachevsky. After 1939, when the purge was called off, the ravages were still being made good, and the Red Army was capable of only limited operations such as those in Poland and Finland. Indeed, the Wehrmacht struck before the new officer corps was fully functional, thereby compounding the chaos of 1941–2. Even then, pro-found suspicions remained. Unsuccessful generals, like Pavlov, were shot; and every Soviet officer had to bear the indignity of a dual system of command, in which a political controller (commissar) had to approve all orders and in many cases was physically billeted in the officer's personal quarters. Soviet officers were left in no doubt that they were no more than subordinate professionals, whose authority could be overturned by the NKVD, at any moment. One has to wonder if Wehrmacht officers would ever have tolerated such detailed and suffocating supervision by the SS (see 'Political control', p. 234).

All the leading Soviet marshals were self-made men from within the service. Zhukov had started as an NCO in one of the imperial cavalry regiments. Rokossovsky, another cavalryman, was the son of a Polish train driver and a Russian mother. Too successful for Stalin's liking, he had endured four years in the GULag in the late 1930s, and in 1944–5 was sidelined after his astonishing triumph during Bagration. These men had to withstand pressures that officers in any other army would have found unimaginable. They were living in the shoes of comrades who had been unjustly killed not by the enemy, but by their own 'Great Leader'. Inured to the fragility of their own fate, they could not afford to be sentimental about the unparalleled levels of slaughter imposed on their men.[19]

Discipline

The armies of all countries, including democratic ones, are subject to the severest forms of discipline. Soldiers must be conditioned to kill and to face being killed, and indiscipline is the greatest threat to the coherence of their actions. So all modern armies follow a military code; all operate a system of military justice; and all possess the sanction of summary execution for serious offences such as insubordination, desertion or mutiny during combat.

Nonetheless, it is also true that each army develops its own ethos, which in turn encourages a harsher or a milder approach to discipline. There was a marked difference, for example, between the British Army of 1914–18 and the British Army of 1939–45. The former, not recognizing shell shock or battlefield fatigue, shot hundreds of its own men for so-called cowardice. The latter abandoned such practices. Similarly, a marked contrast could be observed between armies like the British and the American, in which tradition and respect for the individual found a place, and others, like those of Nazi Germany or the USSR, which prided themselves on their uncompromisingly harsh attitudes.

Every army maintains a corps gendarmerie or military policemen (MPs), whose role is to enforce discipline among the ranks. In garrison towns they keep the soldiery and civilians apart if necessary, breaking up fights, dragging lads out of brothels, arresting military drunks. In army camps they are at the call of NCOs and officers, who put soldiers on minor charges, and they run the 'glasshouse', i.e. the army jail. In battle they stop would-be deserters or other suspicious characters at gunpoint. But they are hardly more threatening than civilian police are for civilians.

In the Second World War British MPs wore red hats like continental stationmasters. American MPs – known as 'snowdrops' – wore white helmets. These formations should not be compared to the ferocious outfits maintained by totalitarian states. The *Feldgendarmerie*, for example, wore a metal gorget round their necks, which gave them the sobriquet of 'chained dogs'. They had powers to shoot on sight, and in all but routine matters they answered to the SS. The British and American armies were not subject to any organization similar to the SS or the NKVD.

In Britain, the King's Regulations, which governed military conduct, had been somewhat modified since 1918. They envisaged a long list of minor offences, such as late return from leave or verbal insubordination, for which soldiers paid fixed fines, and four types of court martial which tried more serious offences. All soldiers convicted by court martial were automatically 'reduced to the ranks', i.e. deprived of all former status, and could be sentenced to long periods of penal servitude. In addition to imprisonment, officers could be 'cashiered': that is, stripped of their commission and dismissed from the service. Following the Army Act of 1930, court martials were no longer empowered to pass death sentences for desertion or cowardice.

US Army regulations followed a similar evolution, every change being overseen by acts of Congress. One peculiarity which persisted, however, related to prohibition. Even when Congress had ruled prohibition to be unconstitutional, in 1933, the military services refused to conform. 'Intoxication at military posts', which was a serious offence, had been defined as having 1.8 per cent alcohol in the blood. Though the definition was raised to 3.4 per cent in 1944, prohibition remained in force until the 1950s.

In practice, therefore, the US forces imposed strict discipline on their men, and were not slow to execute the more recalcitrant. Over 100 American soldiers were hanged in Europe in 1941–5 for serious offences against civilians, whilst only two or three were shot for purely military contraventions. By far the best known of these was Eddie Slovik (1920–45), an infantryman from Detroit, about whom a film would be made in later years. Slovik left his regiment in France for several weeks in the summer of 1944, and survived by working as a cook for the Canadians. When he returned, he told his superiors quite openly and in writing that he would desert again if put into a combat unit; and he applied for transfer to one of the support services. He even wrote to General Eisenhower for clemency, but all to no avail. He was shot on 31 January 1945 after all procedures had been exhausted, and buried in the Allied cemetery of Fère-en-Tardoise.[20]

The German armed forces of 1939–45 contained a rich mixture of social elements and competing institutions: senior professionals of imperial vintage, a younger middle-ranking generation schooled by the Weimar Republic's Reichswehr, and the recent, upstart injections connected with the Nazi Party. Generally speaking, the older conservative-minded men – whether staff officers or NCOs – were respected so long as they kept off politics, and there were no purges in Germany parallel to those which afflicted the Soviet Union. Even so, whenever a difference of opinion arose, the SS, quoting the authority of the Führer, would invariably win the argument. What is more, the SS was known to be vengeful. Any mere soldier who crossed it, whatever his rank, could expect retribution.

Among other things, the Nazis introduced the principle of collective guilt, and in particular of *Sippenhaft* or 'family liability'. In their own minds, they were restoring one of the features of ancient Germanic tribal law, which meant in practice that large groups of people could be held responsible for offences committed by any of their individual members. In the military, whole units could be punished for the shortcomings of individual soldiers. Thus anyone who contemplated breaking regulations had to reckon with the prospect that a heavy price would be paid not only by the offender but also by the offender's family and comrades. The Wehrmacht felt the full weight of the system after the unsuccessful Bomb Plot of July 1944. And Field Marshal Rommel was one of many who sacrificed himself in order to save his family.[21]

An important geographical distinction also operated. When Poland was attacked, in 1939, the Führer made a point of ordering his generals to act with 'the harshest cruelty'. In effect he was inviting the Wehrmacht to ignore the conventions of civilized warfare when fighting in the East. He repeated the injunction in 1941 before the attacks on Yugoslavia and the Soviet Union. But he never did so in relation to the campaigns in Western Europe. It was no accident, therefore, that German soldiers assumed that the normal rules of conduct concerning civilians and combatants did not apply on the Eastern Front, whilst in the West (with a few exceptions) they did.

Many years later, a debate was sparked in post-war Germany over the 'barbarization' of soldiers on the Eastern Front.[22] It was widely believed that the Wehrmacht, unlike the SS, had generally upheld the standards of good soldiering, and that ordinary German soldiers had not been guilty of serious atrocities. This myth was easily shown to be false. Evidence abounds to prove that men from the Wehrmacht were involved in all manner of excesses with or without encouragement from the SS, and that their barbarities were directed against enemy civilians and combatants as well as against Jews. Nazi ideology held that the non-German population of the *Lebensraum* had no rights. And the Wehrmacht made no significant effort to insist otherwise.

Nowhere was this Nazi attitude towards the Eastern Front more evident than in the Warsaw Rising of August 1944. An Allied capital containing nearly a million people had risen against German misrule, and a German 'storm group' under SS command was sent to suppress it. In the ensuing weeks, over 50,000 civilians were massacred in cold blood – hospitals were burned; sick and wounded were slaughtered in their beds; no prisoners were taken – and random shelling and bombing killed perhaps 100,000 more. According to his testimony at Nuremberg, SS General von dem Bach called off the needless killing of civilians in Warsaw at the end of the first week, because it was interfering with the battle against the insurgents. His statement is not specially credible, because he had used exactly the same barbarous methods in his previous job as chief of anti-partisan warfare in Byelorussia. What is true is that SS Brigadeführer Bronislav Kaminsky, a former Soviet soldier and head of the RONA Brigade in Warsaw, was executed by his own side, following a fake car accident. The charge, apparently, was the use of excess violence. If so, it must be unique.[23]

All of which shows how ruthless the SS leadership could be. They were ready to kill all and sundry to bolster their power, and indisciplined soldiery was a dangerous category. The Wehrmacht was the only institution which in certain circumstances would have had the means to overthrow the Nazi regime, and, as the prospect of victory faded, the SS exercised the greatest vigilance. The least sign of discontent in the army was stamped on. In 1944–5, amid the gathering gloom, the discipline of the SS held, and the army men, whether officers or pitiful schoolboys, were mercilessly bullied. All in all, the total numbers of German soldiers shot for indiscipline reached 212,000.

Soviet attitudes were no less inhuman, and they were fired by the fanatical sectarian spirit of the political department which enforced them. Unlike the Wehrmacht, the Red Army no longer possessed a leaven of old imperial professionals who might have tempered the fanaticism. As a result, life in the ranks of the Red Army was so unbearably harsh that death before the guns of the enemy was often embraced as a welcome relief.

Whereas Western armies set great store on building a bond of trust between officers and men, the Soviet style was to create such a climate of suspicion and fear that men would compete to please their political masters. Informers and denunciations were rife, and officers could not bond with their men against the ubiquitous spies of the NKVD. The model Soviet soldier – thoroughly disliked by his comrades – was a dutiful, politicized zealot, who aimed not simply to follow orders, but to foresee the correct behaviour enjoined by party manuals. Western observers could comprehend the ethos of such an organization only if they imagined an army taken over by an extreme sect of religious fundamentalists who were absolutely certain of their truths. When political exhortations did not work, physical brutality was resorted to.

Penal battalions were not unknown in other armies, including the Wehrmacht. But the reputation of the Soviet variant, the *shtrafbat*, as a quick way to instant death, was not without foundation. It is not true that enemy minefields were always cleared by human feet. But penal battalions were put at the disposal of every Soviet front, and they were regularly used for all the most life-threatening operations. Comprising 800 men, with a guard company at the rear, they contained a mixture of petty offenders, recidivists, would-be deserters, convicts and officers stripped of their rank, and they were provided with weapons only a few moments before being ordered to advance. If they halted or hesitated, they were shot from behind; if they escaped injury, they would be held ready for the next penal attack. Hence, like Roman gladiators, they had no hope of release – only the hope of being seriously wounded, or of living to be killed another day.[24]

To Western sensitivities these practices may seem simply barbaric. But in the eyes of the fanatical politicos who insisted on applying them they possessed a semi-religious aura. The Soviet state was both right and benevolent by definition. Men who transgressed its rules were degenerate ingrates who had forfeited their rights. By sacrificing their miserable lives they were saving themselves from the disgrace of their wrongdoing.

The USSR published a Military Code for the first time in 1939. Yet many of the amendments introduced during the war to stem the tide of retreat and desertion were truly vicious. Order 227, signed by Stalin on 28 July 1942, was known as 'Not One Step Back'. In theory at least, it deprived officers of all tactical flexibility. Order 270 from the previous August introduced the principle of family responsibility:

(1) Anyone who removes his insignia during battle and surrenders should be regarded as a malicious deserter whose family is to be arrested as the family of an oath-breaker and betrayer of the Motherland. Such deserters are to be shot on the spot.

(2) Those falling into encirclement are to fight to the last and try to reach their own lines. And those who prefer to surrender are to be destroyed by any available means, while their families are to be deprived of all state allowances and assistance.[25]

Mothers and fathers were to be punished for the shortcomings, real or imagined, of their sons. Here was the Soviet version of *Sippenhaft*.

It is not known with any certainty how many innocent lives were lost as a result of these orders. But one report from the critical period of 1941–2 mentions 790,000 death sentences, of which nearly 200,000 were carried out. Another report from Stalingrad states that 15,000 Red Army men were shot by the NKVD in that one battle. It appears to be possible, therefore, that the Red Army's self-inflicted losses exceeded the total number of battle deaths of the British and US armies combined (see pp. 106–7).[26]

Not surprisingly, soldiers of the Red Army developed a hearty dislike for the NKVD and for the humiliating slavery prevailing in the rear areas. Oddly enough, the front-line zone of maximum physical danger, under fire from the enemy, became a zone of psychological liberation, even of gay abandon, which no doubt contributed to the willingness of the 'Ivans' to rush to their deaths with a hurrah on their lips. The phenomenon was frequently observed by the Germans. But it was also noted by outsiders who, having encountered the advancing Red Army, were forcibly struck by the friendliness of the front-line troops and the hostile, predatory character of the NKVD men in the cordon behind them.[27]

The reality of the inhuman conditions prevailing inside the Red Army was successfully concealed for decades. Soviet propaganda painted a uniformly uplifting picture of patriotism and heroism. And Soviet veterans were themselves unwilling to talk openly, especially to foreigners. Pride in the victory of the 'Great Patriotic War' was one of the few sources of self-respect left to men of Stalin's generation; and 'love of the Motherland' or 'the defence of Russian soil' (even when it wasn't Russian) were the standard explanations for the Red Army's performance. Only when the USSR collapsed in the 1990s did it become possible for the remaining survivors to talk more freely about all aspects of the war – about the amazing feats of fortitude and self-sacrifice for sure, but also about the contempt for human life, the misconduct of Soviet troops against enemy civilians, and, above all, the horrendous maltreatment of Red Army soldiers by their own side.[28]

Yet the overall picture continues to escape notice. The public of Western countries in particular are habituated to the idea that barbarity is supposed to be associated with Nazi Germany, and with Nazi Germany alone. Serious gaffes can occur in consequence. A well-meaning photographic exhibition which was touring Germany in the 1990s with the aim of publicizing the misdeeds of the Wehrmacht had to be temporarily withdrawn when many of the the gruesome incidents depicted were identified as the work of the Soviet NKVD.[29]

Discipline tended to disintegrate in the last weeks of fighting in 1945. On the Soviet side of the front, all semblance of law and order between the Red Army and the Germans broke down. But many arbitrary acts were committed by Allied soldiers as well. A Frenchman who had joined the Légion Volontaire Française in 1944, and saw service in the SS Charlemagne Division, witnessed the wrath of his compatriots. The main body of the division surrendered to the 1st Polish Army at Colberg (Kołobrzeg); but some elements fell back to Berlin, where they defended the *Führerbunker*, whilst others struggled across the Reich to reach France. It was the misfortune of this latter group in Alsace to run into the troops of General Leclerc. He ordered them to be shot on the spot as traitors.[30]

All of which puts 'the biggest mutiny in British military history', for which no single soldier was shot, into some sort of perspective. In October 1943, 192 men of the British Eighth Army sat down in a field near the beach at Salerno, and steadfastly refused to budge, even when the army regulations were formally read out to them. They were Tynesiders and Highlanders of the 50th and 51st Divisions; veterans of the Desert War;

and their spokesmen maintained that certain officers had lied to them. At a transit camp at Tripoli in North Africa, they had been told that they were rejoining their units in Sicily. Instead, when already at sea, they had been informed that they were being sent as reinforcements to the Salerno beachhead. None of them were allowed to speak in their own defence at the court martial which took place at Constantine in Algeria. Three sergeants were sentenced to death. All the others were sentenced to seven or ten years' penal servitude. A month later, following an official inquiry, the sentences were suspended. The men were sent back to their units. And the major responsible for the inquiry reported 'a series of officers' blunders'.[31]

The very last British soldier to be put to death for indiscipline was a man of Anglo-Swiss origin, Theodore Schurch (1918–46), who served in the Western Desert as a truck driver of the Royal Army Service Corps. Captured in Tobruk in 1942, Schurch subsequently acted as an informant for German and Italian intelligence. He was retaken by the Eighth Army in Rome in 1945, and was put on trial on nine counts of treachery and one of desertion. He appears to have had a connection before the war with Mosley's Blackshirts, and at his trial he objected to one of the prosecuting officers being Jewish. The objection was upheld. The defendant was hanged.

Political control

None of the major armies of the Second World War was put into the field by a military dictatorship in which generals or a junta exercised ultimate control. All were servants of civilian regimes – some democratic and some very undemocratic, but all with mechanisms whereby the civilian authorities kept the military in check.

Since time immemorial, soldiers have been restrained by the swearing of an oath of allegiance. Of course, the political authorities determine to whom the allegiance is to be rendered. In the British Army it was to 'His Majesty, King George VI, his heirs and successors'. In the US Army it was to 'the Constitution of the United States', according to which the elected president is commander-in-chief. Germany's armed forces, like all branches of government, were subjected to the so-called 'Führer Oath': 'To you, my Führer, and to all superiors whom you may appoint, I swear obedience unto death.'

The Soviet military oath as operative in 1941–5 needs some explanation. 'I, a citizen of the USSR,' it read, 'swear to observe the Soviet constitution and to defend my homeland, the USSR and its government, without sparing blood or life. If I fail, may I be punished by the severity of Soviet Laws and by the hatred and contempt of the people.' It lacked the religious sanctions of earlier times, and, unlike some earlier (and later) versions, it contained little that was overtly political. There was no mention, for instance, of a 'Socialist [meaning Communist] Homeland'. The *rodina*, the land of one's birth, was simply the USSR. One should point out, however, that the most important article of the Soviet constitution of 1936 was the one affirming the 'leading role' of the Communist Party, which was thereby empowered to override all other articles. Whether the Soviet recruit knew it or not, he was swearing allegiance to the Party, and to the Party's *Vozhd* or 'Leader' – Joseph Stalin.

Political control did not stop at oaths, however. It came in many forms. In the Western armies it was largely informal. In the Wehrmacht it was formal, but unpredictable. In the Red Army, it was near-absolute.

As well as being subject to laws of the land, British and American soldiers were bound by the Military Code, which contained an ominous injunction against 'helping the enemy'. They were formally forbidden, for example, to belong to a Fascist group. On the other hand, they were not banned from activities on behalf of the Communist Party. Numbers of British officers were card-carrying Communists, and after 1941, when the performance of the Red Army created great enthusiasm, they helped to set the tone. Speaking well of the Nazis – even of their Autobahns and Volkswagens – was taboo, while speaking well of 'Uncle Joe' was near-obligatory. British soldiers were threatened with court martial for opining (quite truthfully) that the Katyn massacres were a Soviet atrocity. And factual statements about the USSR possessing concentration camps, or having been expelled from the League of Nations for international aggression, were beyond the pale.

The British and US authorities censored soldiers' mail. They did so quite openly, reading the soldiers' letters and stamping the envelopes 'PASSED'. Praising Stalin was not on the list of offences for which letters would not be passed.

In accordance with Fascist principles, the Third Reich was not just a 'one-party state'. It was a state in which the ruling party exercised dictatorial powers over all government institutions, including the army, and where the party itself was a one-man dictatorship. Adolf Hitler was party chief, commander-in-chief and 'Leader of the Nation' all rolled into one. His portrait hung in a place of honour in every school, shop and barracks, and his baleful influence filtered down to the lowliest levels of German life.

Nazi control over the armed services was exercised partly by the oath, partly by a short-term experiment in Soviet-style commissars, but largely by the supervisory role of the SS, whose armed wing was supplied with all the best weapons, and whose superior status implied the promise of instant revenge for insubordination. Any officer or soldier who thought of revolt could be sure not only of his own barbaric punishment but of savage reprisals against his comrades and family. After the Bomb Plot of July 1944, the Gestapo arrested and tortured some 7,000 suspects, while the chief conspirators were hung on meat hooks and filmed in their agonies.

Yet one has to ponder some deeper, psychological, mechanisms when asking why the Wehrmacht never successfully revolted against the Nazi grip. One explanation may lie in the knowledge of complicity. Most German soldiers cheered when Hitler's early gambles paid off. They tramped through Poland, they drove through France, and they marched into Byelorussia and Ukraine, singing. All too many of them allowed themselves to participate, or at least to revel in the mass atrocities organized by the SS. When it came to the reckoning, they were compromised. Like a prisoner who has drained a bottle with his tormentor, they were paralysed by guilt and remorse.

One forgets how short a time the *Hitlerzeit* lasted: only six years passed between the Nazis' assumption of power in 1933 and the outbreak of war. Within twelve years from start to finish it was all over. Stalin, who rose to the top in 1922, had much longer to perfect his system.

It is highly instructive to examine what happened on the few occasions when the Wehrmacht dared to defy the SS. Such incidents were possible since the chains of command in the Wehrmacht and the SS were separate; and close coordination was not always achieved. In July 1942, for instance, the SS decided to deport some 18,000 Jews from the town of Przemysl in the General Government to the death camp of Bełżec. They ordered the local Security Police or Sipo to make preparations; but they failed to inform the town's military commander, Major Max Liedtke. The omission led to an armed stand-off. Liedtke, who had recently been transferred from Piraeus in Greece, had formed a Jewish work brigade, some 4,500 strong, and had issued each of them with a special red military *Ausweis* or pass. In his view, the brigade performed vital services in the Wehrmacht's supply operations. What is more, his adjutant, Lieutenant Albert Battel, a member of the Abwehr, was known to be friendly to Jews. As a lawyer in pre-war Breslau, he had lent money to Jews in distress and had openly ridiculed the Gestapo in court. In his previous posting, at Lemberg, he ended up under house arrest for obstructing the deportation of Jews. Liedtke and Battel took decisive action. On Sunday 26 July, they closed the bridge over the River San and sent a heavy machine-gun company to guard it; and informed the SS that all police movements were forbidden. Even more surprisingly, they sent a column of trucks to the Ghetto, and brought out a hundred Jewish families under armed guard, and offered them protection in the *Orts-kommandatur*. In the evening, the SS Hauptsturmführer Martin Fellenz arrived, screaming blue murder. 'We will not allow it,' he fumed. 'Jews cannot act as officers' shoeblacks and servants under the pretext of doing war work for the Wehrmacht!' His rant fell on deaf ears. A compromise was only reached after a meeting between the highest military officer in the General Government, General Freiherr Curt von Gienanth, and the highest police officer, SS Obergruppenführer and Head of Police-*Ost*, Wilhelm Kruger. The San Bridge was to be reopened. The deportation of Jews was to proceed. But all Jewish Wehrmacht workers either under 35 or possessing special passes were to be exempted. Most of the exemptees survived. In due course, Liedtke was disciplined and posted to 1 Panzer Army in the Caucasus, where he was killed. Battel was protected by membership of the Nazi Party. He was sent back to Breslau, dismissed on health grounds, remobilized into the *Volkssturm*; and captured by the Red Army. Both Liedtke and Battel were posthumously awarded the title of 'Righteous among Nations' by the Yad Vashem Institute in Israel.[32] Their defiant gesture was barely conceivable on the Soviet side of the front.

Western observers often failed to see how the Soviet system actually worked. They found it hard to imagine that the Red Army, which became the most formidable military machine in the world, was itself a captive, a slave of its political masters. Since it was so strong, it had to be shackled not only from the outside, but from the inside as well. On the one hand there was the Political Administration of the Red Army (PURKKA), which masterminded the military's subservience to the Communist Party.

Nominally it answered to the Party's Central Committee, but from 1937 it was headed by Lev Mehlis, one of Stalin's more obnoxious creatures, who personally oversaw the military purges. On the other hand there was the NKVD, the State Security Commission, under Lavrentii Beria, who, like Himmler, had a large private army at his disposal. The NKVD was like the SS, the Gestapo, the Border Guards, the Prison Board, the Concentration Camp Directorate, and the Intelligence Service rolled into one. It also controlled PURKKA. Without its prior approval the Red Army could not fire a single shot.

Apart from political education, PURKKA ran the network of *politruki* or 'political directors' (commonly known abroad as 'commissars'), who were spread throughout the Red Army at every level. Each of the *politruks* wore army uniform and looked like a normal Red Army man. But each of them possessed two ranks – one military, the other in the security service – and they served two masters: one, nominally, the commander of their military unit, and the other their superior within the NKVD hierarchy. They functioned as counsellors and instructors of the soldiers in non-military matters, and more importantly as Party informers in matters of loyalty and morale. They shared the hardships of the men in the training camp or at the front. But they were virtually untouchable by standard military discipline, and they inevitably spread the suspicion that they were simply spying on their comrades – which of course they were. But to criticize their activities in such a crude way would have been to challenge the Party's absolute right to its leading role, and could be promptly denounced as a 'bourgeois deviation' deserving the harshest consequences. And the consequences really were harsh. As Alexander Solzhenitsyn found to his cost, one unguarded word against Stalin could trigger transfer to the GULag or to a penal battalion. Political considerations held absolute priority. Solzhenitsyn was an experienced artillery officer, and a valuable military asset. But a minor political transgression ensured instant arrest.

Such a system can be called diabolical. But it only reflected the social climate of terror that had been created in the USSR during the trials and purges of the 1930s. It would have been unworkable among the products of a free society who were taught to tell the truth and to speak their mind. They would have ducked their commissar in the nearest river, or have put an accidental bullet in his back. But – among a generation of youths who had been taught at school that it was patriotic to inform on one's parents – it worked.

Political invigilation of the military was nowhere more systematic than in the higher commands. Every general was shadowed night and day by his guardian angel, who had to countersign all orders. And political generals, like Nikita Khrushchev or Leonid Brezhnev, who wore a general's uniform with a general's stars but who were essentially party minders, dominated all the command staffs of the various armies and fronts. In the Soviet system, therefore, it was not Zhukov or Rokossovsky who would rise to the top after Stalin's demise – as Eisenhower rose to the top in the USA. It was the politicos like Beria, Khrushchev and Brezhnev. In the post-war showdown, Khrushchev would have to shoot Beria to reach his goal.

The NKVD performed duties in all spheres of Soviet life, but in wartime the military sphere took on special importance. Like the SS in Germany, the NKVD possessed its own private army, equipped with tanks, artillery and aircraft, and its prime function was to keep the Red Army in check. It terms of size, if one counts all available formations, it numbered several hundred thousands, and was hence the third largest army on the continent before the Normandy landings. In emergencies – which meant most of 1941–2 – it could be sent to the front line. But its natural role was securing the rear, locking the Red Army into a sealed capsule, and subduing the local population. For this purpose it held ready a large number of so-called 'blocking regiments', which rode behind the back-markers of the front as it advanced – in Willys Jeeps once Lend-Lease deliveries began – firing forwards. Nothing of its size or style existed in other armies.[33]

Generals

Armies are organized hierarchically. There is a chain of command with marshals/field marshals/generals of the army at the top and privates/general infantrymen/*Gefreiten* at the bottom. The commanders give the orders, and all the lower ranks obey.

In the Second World War there were hundreds of generals and scores of marshals. Each army used its own nomenclature (see Table overleaf).

People eternally ask, 'Which of these generals was the best?' There is no clear answer, because there are no clear criteria. One can say with

		Equivalent army ranks		
British Army	**US Army**	**Wehrmacht**	**SS**	**Red Army**
Field Marshal	General of the army	General-feldmarschal	–	Marshal of the USSR
General	General	Generaloberst	SS-Oberst-gruppenführer	Army general
Lieutenant general	Lieutenant general	General	SS-Ober-gruppenführer	Colonel general
Major general	Major general	Generalleutnant	SS-Gruppenführer	Lieutenant general
Brigadier	Brigadier general	Generalmajor	SS-Brigadeführer	Major general

Airforces and navies had their own ranks.

some confidence, however, that each nation is reluctant to slate its own generals, and is eager to overrate the enemy generals who fought well against them. The British, for instance, greatly overrate Montgomery, while boosting the claims of Rommel and Rundstedt, who fought against the British Army. German historians put none of them into the top bracket.

The British Army produced no first-rate generals during 1939–45. This was partly because it always acted as a junior partner – first to the French in 1939–40, and then to the Americans after 1942 – and partly because it was condemned by its political superiors to ultra caution. The Desert Campaign of 1940–43 was the only one in which the British exercised undivided control; and the victory at El Alamein – where Montgomery possessed markedly superior resources – was the fruit of competent rather than brilliant generalship. Air Vice-Marshal Hugh Dowding of Fighter Command and Air Vice-Marshal Arthur Harris of Bomber Command both faced severe criticism within their own services. And the Royal Navy, despite many gallant actions, was never called on to fight a Trafalgar.

The USA, too, possessed few outstanding field commanders, since practical experience was severely lacking. But in George Marshall and Dwight D. Eisenhower it produced two excellent military administrators who successfully led the Anglo-American military machine.[34]

General George Marshall (1880–1959), once the chief aide to General

Pershing, served as US chief of staff throughout the war. Having served in the War Plans Division, he reached his top post, symbolically, on 1 September 1939. It was long assumed that he would command the Allied Expeditionary Force in Europe during the Normandy landings, but Roosevelt said that he wouldn't get a night's sleep if Marshall left Washington. So Eisenhower was appointed instead.

Dwight D. Eisenhower (1890–1969), the son of poor Mennonites, was a staff officer par excellence. He never commanded a military unit in action, and was chosen for his political and man-management skills. From June 1942 he was the highest-ranking US officer in Europe, first as Commander of the Mediterranean Theatre, then as commander of the Allied Expeditionary Force from Overlord to war's end. He held the Anglo-American effort together brilliantly. 'I don't mind someone being called a son-of-a-bitch,' he once remarked, 'but I'll be damned if I let someone be called a "British SOB" or an "American SOB".'

General George Patton (1895–1945) was the only Western general to show real flair. He was twice suspended from duty – once for slapping a shell-shocked soldier, and once, at the end of the war, for permitting Nazi officials to work in administrative jobs. Significantly, he was one of the few senior US commanders to have seen action at the front in the First World War, when he had headed a tank brigade. He was fearless, flamboyant and loud-mouthed, but, out of sight, a perfectionist planner and a reader of poetry. From November 1942 to May 1945 Patton held a succession of commands – at Casablanca, in Sicily and with the US Third Army in France and Germany – but his service totalled a mere thirteen months. It was enough to earn him the reputation of the best American general of the war. He was killed in Germany in a car accident.[35]

Germany put a score of field marshals into the stakes – several of outstanding quality. Their performance was frequently blighted by Hitler's interference, and some of their greatest exploits were undertaken by extricating German forces from impending disaster. Their reputation has inevitably suffered through fighting on the losing side. But in terms of professional skill and brilliance several of them were unsurpassed.

General Heinz Guderian (1888–1954) was the true author of blitzkrieg as propounded in his book *Achtung Panzer* (1937). He put his theory into brilliant practice in Poland, in the Netherlands and France and in Operation Barbarossa. In December 1941, however, he was dismissed for criticizing Hitler's inconsistencies and for withdrawing his units from an exposed position. He languished without a command for nearly eighteen months before being reinstated, first as Inspector General of Panzer Forces, and then as chief of the Army General Staff. His mounting exasperation with Hitler led to an outburst in March 1945 that preceded his official 'sick leave'.[36]

Field Marshal Erich von Manstein (originally Lewiński, 1887–1973) was the war's finest exponent of offensive warfare. He was the author of the Sichelschnitt, the campaign-winning war plan of 1940, and as commander of 38 Corps was first to cross the Seine. In 1941–3 he conducted a succession of superb operations, most notably his conquest of Crimea. It is significant that Manstein's fortunes declined as the Wehrmacht lost its capacity for offence. He was dismissed in March 1944.[37]

The career of Field Marshal Walther Model (1891–1945) followed the opposite trajectory from Manstein's. Model's star rose in parallel to the Wehrmacht's need for skilful defence. He won his general's rank by extracting the encircled 9th Army from the Rzhev Pocket in March 1942, and he repeated the performance south of Moscow in 1943. He did not lose the Führer's confidence, despite responsibility for the delay to Manstein's plan for Kursk, and thereafter as 'the Führer's Fireman' he rushed from desperate assignment to desperate assignment. His ingenious policy of *Schild und Schwert* ('Shield and Sword'), which masked a general withdrawal with a brief preceding counter-offensive, overcame the Führer's reluctance to sanction retreat, and worked successfully on numerous occasions – with Army Group South (March 1944), Army Group Centre (June 1944), in East Prussia (August 1944), and on the Western Front (August 1944–March 1945). Model's defence of the Scheldt estuary robbed the Western Allies of victory in 1944. He committed suicide when his forces finally found no means of escape from the Ruhr Pocket.[38]

Wilhelm Keitel (1883–1946), Hitler's closest military adviser, has a place at the other end of the scale. Lacking talent and backbone, he followed his Nazi masters slavishly and was hanged at Nuremberg.

The Soviet marshals worked in Stalin's shadow, just as their German counterparts suffered from Hitler's. Yet their ordeals of fire arrived at the start of the German–Soviet War. And the fruits of their tenacity came in the later phases. The Red Army had its share of failed generals, notably Voroshilov and Timoshenko, both of whom had gained prominence through familiarity with Stalin. And its war-winning stars were relatively slow to emerge.

Marshal Alexander Vasilevsky (1895–1977) was lucky to have survived long enough to rise to the upper ranks. Trained as an Orthodox priest, he had belonged to the tsarist officer caste and did not join the Communist Party until the height of the purges in 1938. Nonetheless, he showed great ability as a staff officer, and in May 1942 he became chief of the Supreme Planning Command, the Stavka. Together with Zhukov, he was responsible for the successful preparations that were rewarded by Stalingrad, Kursk and Bagration. As a field commander, he took charge of the Baltic fronts in the winter of 1944–5, and in August 1945 he was chosen to head the Soviet forces in the Far East fighting Japan.

Marshal Konstanty Rokossovsky (1896–1968) was only saved from Stalin's suspicions by his undoubted brilliance and by his friendship with Zhukov. Brought up in Warsaw, he had been a classmate of Zhukov's at the Soviet cavalry academy in the 1920s, and his chances of surviving the Terror must have been much reduced by the fact that, as Soviet military attaché to Chiang Kai-shek, he had seen the outside world. Nonetheless, he came through his years in the GULag, and at Zhukov's request he was reinstated during the crisis of 1941. From then on he rose inexorably as commander of the key Don Front at Stalingrad, of the Central Front in the Kursk salient, and of Operation Bagration. As the Red Army's leading battlefield commander, he might have expected to lead the final march on Berlin. But in October 1944, after the Warsaw Rising, he was sent to play on the extreme right wing along the Baltic coast. After the war, he was sent back to Poland as the Soviet-imposed minister of defence.[39]

The greatness of Marshal Georgiy Zhukov (1896–1974) lay in the variety of his accomplishments. He managed to combine a distinguished career as an active front-line commander with parallel successes both in military planning and in high-level staff work. At various points he worked closely with Stalin and with Vasilevsky, and despite an abrasive temperament he never fell foul of the dictator's ruling elite. Altogether, he was the most prominent marshal of the Red Army, and, since the Red Army must be counted the ultimate victor in Europe, the most prominent general of the war.

Nonetheless, Zhukov's career prospered through more than one moment of good fortune. Ordered in the autumn of 1941 to the Leningrad front, which appeared to be collapsing, he appeared to work a miracle when German Army Group North was stopped in its tracks. Stalin was delighted, but unaware that Hitler had chosen not to attack Leningrad but to besiege it. Similarly, in early December 1941, when the Wehrmacht seemed certain to capture Moscow, the front was suddenly paralysed by a record frost, and Zhukov was given the vital respite to launch the counter-attack whereby the city was saved. Before Berlin, in April 1945, Zhukov did not perform at his best, and the decisive manoeuvres were made by Konev to the south and Rokossovsky to the north. But Zhukov was the C.-in-C., and the victory made him a world figure.

The final touch to Zhukov's image was added during the victory parade of May 1945. As originally planned, Stalin himself was due to ride into Red Square on a pure-white stallion. However, the Great Leader fell off his spirited mount during practice, and resigned. The old tsarist cavalryman rose to the challenge. Zhukov did not merely ride the Arab charger: he cantered across the cobbles of the square in grand Cossack style, and stole the limelight. Stalin never forgave him.[40]

Soldiers, sailors, airmen and others

Such is the power of popular stereotypes – of RAF fighter pilots 'scrambling' into their Spitfires, of American GIs wading ashore on Omaha Beach, or of Soviet infantry attacking through the ruins of Stalingrad – that one is apt to forget that all the major combatant forces were highly complex organizations consisting of many different arms; also, that the balance between those arms was different in every case.

The British and the Americans, for instance, necessarily put much greater emphasis on sea power and air power. In Britain's case, three services gained special importance: Bomber Command, the merchant navy, and the Fleet Air Arm.

Germany started the war with the best-balanced forces. But in the middle years of war the Kriegsmarine was effectively neutralized by Western navies, the Luftwaffe ceded dominance of the skies in Western Europe, and the Wehrmacht lost the initiative in the East. All these developments interacted. In the final showdown the Luftwaffe was too weak to remedy the shortcomings of the German land forces, whilst Western air power compensated for Western armies, which in any case were by then facing a much weakened Wehrmacht.

All branches of the Soviet services were decimated in 1941–2. The Red Air Force was all but eliminated on the ground, whilst the Red fleets in the Baltic and the Black Sea had no escape routes. In the years of recovery, therefore, the greatest burden fell on the Red Army and its extraordinary powers of resilience. Nonetheless, in 1943–5 the Soviet Union staged a remarkable comeback by air and by sea, as well as by land. It was producing aircraft and trained pilots to outperform the Luftwaffe, whilst Soviet submarines were wreaking havoc on German shipping in the Baltic.

Hence all the stereotypes need to be supplemented. It is not sufficient to recall the most prominent or the most glamorous servicemen. There were many sorts of soldier, many sorts of sailor, and many sorts of airman – and in modern warfare a huge array of technical and support staff. One of the aces of the Battle of Britain, when he returned from a sortie, would always kiss the hands of his chief mechanic. 'These are the hands', he would say, 'which keep me alive'.[41]

Artillery, cavalry, engineers and the special services

Until the Great War of 1914–18, all armies had consisted of four main services: infantry, cavalry, artillery and engineers. But in 1939–45 the scene changed rapidly. The role of cavalry was diminishing, and that of artillery was combining with the newfound capacity of ground-support aircraft. Even so, misconceptions abound.

All armies in 1939 fielded cavalry regiments. It was well understood from the First World War that the prowess of the machine gun had put an end to frontal cavalry charges. But, at a stage when the greater part of the infantry, specially in the Wehrmacht, was still unmotorized, horse-mounted soldiers still possessed great advantages in reconnaissance, in flanking manoeuvres and in communication. The Red Army, which relied increasingly on the sheer weight of its tank force, also maintained traditional Cossack formations. And horse-drawn transport was the norm in the East both for the Germans and, until the arrival of Lend-Lease American trucks in 1943–4, for the Soviets.

The much broadcast incident of September 1939 when Polish lancers encountered German panzers was simply a sign of the times. It was not evidence of Polish foolishness. If the Poles had ignored the advice of their Western allies and had followed the German example of putting their tanks into a dedicated armoured force, it would have been perfectly possible for a regiment of German uhlans to have encountered a column of Polish panzers.

What is more, one can easily find other instances where cavalry met catastrophe. In October 1941, a Mongolian cavalry division in the Red Army lost 2,000 men without inflicting a single casualty on the opposing Germans.[42] Few would conclude that the Mongolian national character was flawed by foolish bravery.

Everyone tends to think of massed artillery as the dominant weapon of the trench warfare of an earlier age. Yet devotees of artillery also claim that the Second War was an 'artillery war' on the grounds that heavy guns caused over half of the battle casualties.[43] What is undeniable is that all armies deployed huge numbers of field guns and howitzers; that an artillery barrage continued to precede all pre-planned infantry attacks; and that artillery duels – bombardments and counter-bombardments – formed a regular feature on both the Eastern Front and the Western Front.

British and especially American artillery was judged to be state of the art, particularly in the techniques of so-called 'predicted fire'. 'Creeping' or 'rolling' barrages could be exactly calibrated to the progress of the infantry, while 'Time on Target' (or TOT) adjustments could ensure that all the shells of a barrage would explode in unison to devastating effect. The US 105-mm howitzer was designed to fire thirteen different types of shell, with contents from high explosive to propaganda leaflets.

German artillery had pioneered both airborne target-spotting and radio-controlled observation. This gave the Wehrmacht a clear advantage during Operation Barbarossa, as did the introduction of StuG self-propelled guns, which could keep pace with a panzer attack. The Wehrmacht also possessed an unparalleled collection of gargantuan railway guns, which were used to attack fortresses and fixed positions. The 80-cm Gustav, for instance, which was used in Warsaw, fired a shell weighing 4,800 kg over a range of 47 km.

The Red Army's artillery is often said to have relied more on numbers than on sophistication. But the judgement may be unfair, especially in the later phases of the war, when communication systems were greatly improved. One feature, however, was unusual in that the Soviet High Command built up huge dedicated artillery divisions and held them in reserve under separate control. These artillery divisions were designed either for offence, with a preponderance of mine-throwers, howitzers and rocket-launchers, or for defence, with a preponderance of field guns. And they were distributed to the various fronts (army groups) according to requirements. After 1943 the system was expanded to include 10 dedicated artillery corps, each with 700 guns. These units were more than three times more powerful than their counterparts in the US Army (whose concentrated barrages were known, inimitably, as 'serenade').

Military engineers also faced the challenge of new techniques. But their ancient tasks of building bridges, of laying or clearing mines, of erecting or dismantling fortifications, and of placing or removing obstacles remained exactly the same. Their new equipment included Bailey bridges, tank-dozers, mechanized mine-flails, floating 'Mulberry' harbours and plastic explosives. Apart from the fighting, the Italian Campaign took the form of a two-year engineering duel. The Gustav Line was particularly effective. On the Eastern Front, where many broad rivers impeded progress, bridge-building skills were paramount. In September 1943, for example, the Germans built seven bridges to withdraw across the Dnieper in a sector of 650 km. In the same month, Soviet engineers built fifty-two bridges in a small sector of 400 km.[44] Yet nothing compared to the task facing Allied engineers in Normandy. As was said at the time, it was the equivalent of moving the city of Chicago under fire to the opposite shore of Lake Michigan. The Germans had spent nearly four years building the concrete defences of the Atlantic Wall, with the muscle power of hundreds of thousands of slave labourers. The Allies had to smash it, and then rebuild the infrastructure, including fifty airfields, in as many weeks. The job was done.

Great play is made in British war mythology of the numerous special-service units – the Special Operations Executive, Royal Marines Commandos, parachutists, the Long Range Desert Group, the Special Air Service and the Special Boat Service – whose exploits have created the background to Ian Fleming's novels. The exploits – like the raid on the docks at Saint-Nazaire in March 1942 – were real enough, and their leaders, like Lieutenant David Stirling, were dashing, debonair heroes. Yet in the overall wartime scene their activities were extremely marginal – outward evidence of the basic fact that the British Army was incapable of challenging the enemy on an equal footing. Nor were they unique. The Germans had its own special units, including Otto Skorzeny's *Friedenthaler Jagdverbände*, which rescued Mussolini, the Brandenburg Commandos and the airborne KG 200.

In terms of sheer daredevilry, however, nothing excelled the Italians' Tenth Light Flotilla, which pioneered 'frogmen', the explosive motor boat and the midget submarine. The flotilla's successful attack on Alexandria Harbour in December 1941 put two British battleships out of action and significantly upset the balance of sea power in the Mediterranean.

Before the war, parachutists had been thought to be the decisive arm of the future; and already in 1931 joint Soviet–German manoeuvres in Ukraine had pioneered the basic techniques. Yet the promise was never fulfilled. Suitable aircraft were long unavailable, and, until it proved possible to drop a Willys Jeep from a C-47 Dakota, parachutists had no transport. The unopposed landing of German paratroopers in Norway and Holland in 1940 was well executed, and raised expectations. But the opposed landings on Crete proved so costly that the German High Command grounded its parachute units for the rest of the war. The British and Americans persisted, however, landing airborne forces during both Torch and Overlord, and forming an Allied Airborne Army in August 1944. This army prepared sixteen operations which never took place, through pressures of timing and coordination, and a seventeenth, code-named 'Market Garden', which met disaster at Arnhem. Finally, in March 1945, two divisions of a joint British–American Airborne Corps were successfully dropped beyond the Rhine, thereby restoring some of the confidence which the advocates of airborne warfare had long lacked.[45]

Elite formations

No army can claim that all its units reach the highest standards. And in the pursuit of excellence it has long been the practice to single out the best regiments for superior weapons, superior pay and superior prestige. In the British Army, tradition counted for much, and it was the royal 'Guards' regiments – the Coldstream, Grenadier, Scots, Welsh and Irish Guards, together with the 'Blues and Royals' of the Household Cavalry – which were judged to hold the highest status. Whether deservedly or not, they basked in the kudos of their professionalism and in the popular belief that they were somehow more grand and more invincible than the more numerous county regiments and the lowly Territorials. New formations of special forces such as the Royal Marines Commandos and the Parachute

Regiment were also added to the elite by virtue of their special training and exciting roles.

In the US Army, whose spirit was more democratic, tradition counted for less. Yet the distinction between professionals and conscripts or National Guards was not missed. And the US Marine Corps, which had a long tradition, was highly regarded. The marines raised special-duty battalions called 'Raiders' (not seen in Europe) while the US Army counterparts were called 'Rangers', which were modelled on the British commandos. Ranger battalions landed at Salerno, suffered badly in the aftermath of Anzio, and distinguished themselves in Normandy. Nothing gives a military unit more prestige, however, than a proud battle record. And in this regard none surpassed the 101st Airborne Division, which found itself in the heart of the hardest fighting both in Normandy and in the 'Bulge'.

In the German army, the traditional primacy of the old Wehrmacht regiments was overshadowed by new official preferences given to the Waffen SS. The latter wore special uniforms, carried the latest weapons, and were given the most generous support services. Yet the thirty-eight divisions of the Waffen SS by no means enjoyed equality. The 'true German' SS-Panzerdivisions, 1, 2 and 3 – the Leibstandarte Adolf Hitler, Das Reich and Totenkopf – were in a class of their own, while in the eyes of the more fanatical Nazis the numerous divisions of foreign volunteers were little more then fancy impostors. German parachutists, or *Fallschirm-jäger*, who were grounded after 1941, did not enjoy the same prestige as their Western counterparts. But the Wehrmacht's Grossdeutschland Division and the Hermann Göring Panzer Division, which belonged to the ground forces of the Luftwaffe, undoubtedly belonged to the elite of the elite.

Soviet ideology was opposed to all forms of elitism. The Red Army was 'the sword of the masses'. But practices changed. As from 1942, regiments or divisions that had performed well were given the designation of 'guards' as a form of recognition (with tsarist overtones), and in due course tank divisions received the same plaudit. Eventually 'guards armies' appeared, and would be brought from the Stavka's reserve to stiffen the line and to boost morale.

Elitism, in fact, has much to do with morale. Soldiers assigned to an ancient regiment or to a special formation could be expected to feel a sense of elevation over their less favoured comrades, and hence to fight more stubbornly. By the same token, troops were very sensitive to the reputation of their adversaries. In the British and US armies, the approach of a panzer division instilled a special thrill of fear and excitement. To the German army on the Eastern Front the deployment of a guards army, or still more of a guards tank army, was a sure sign that the Ivans meant business.

Intelligence

Intelligence-gathering has always been an essential branch of warfare. And military intelligence officers are soldiers like the rest of them. Indeed, wartime unites all branches of the security services, despite their rivalries. In 1939–45 signals intelligence (SIGINT) gained importance, but all the traditional activities of reconnaissance, espionage, counter-espionage, propaganda, deception, field security and political warfare were practised.

Britain's reputedly brilliant intelligence services, led by MI6, which answered to the Foreign Office, greatly helped to save the country from its military weaknesses. They were ably assisted by agents of allied governments-in-exile, notably by Poles, Czechs and Norwegians. The Ultra secret, resulting from the breaking of the Enigma codes, was only one of their successes. Others included the exposure of German radar defences and advance knowledge of the V-1 and V-2 rocket programmes. Notable failures included what the Germans called the *Englandspiel* operation to embed SOE agents in the Netherlands. Within the armed services, Naval Intelligence traditionally enjoyed senior status, though the growth of air reconnaissance inevitably raised the profile of the RAF. The Special Operations Executive (SOE), which grew out of the intelligence services, specialized in clandestine actions and support for European resistance movements. It was Churchill's near-private agency for 'setting Europe ablaze'. Its results were, at best, mixed.[46]

In the USA, competent intelligence services were slow to develop. The Office of Strategic Services (OSS), the ancestor of the post-war CIA, was not formed until June 1942, under William J. 'Big Bill' Donovan (1883–1959), a much decorated US officer, who had persuaded Roosevelt to ignore the pessimistic reports of Ambassador Joseph Kennedy and to believe in Britain's survival. Donovan worked closely with the Canadian-born William Stephenson (1896–1989), a former boxer, who headed British Security Coordination. OSS agents operated in all the theatres where US forces were engaged, frequently in close conjunction with MI6 and SOE. 'Force 266' was sent to Yugoslavia; 'Jedburgh teams' were parachuted into France; and Operation Sunrise, under the future head of the CIA, Allen Dulles, worked through the US Embassy in Berne to establish contacts with the German resistance. In the last phase of the war, a string of German refugees and anti-Nazi POWs was trained to penetrate the Reich and to report on its innermost workings.[47]

Deception is as old as warfare, and it is usually a speciality of the weaker party. The British, therefore, were acutely aware of the powers of deception. Indeed, when they captured a copy of the plan for the invasion of France from the wreck of a crashed aircraft on 10 January 1940, they firmly refused to believe that the plans were genuine. Yet they had their successes. In autumn 1942 Brigadier Dudley Clarke's 'A Force' laid dummy pipelines across the Western Desert, and persuaded Rommel that the battle of El Alamein would not begin before November. Rommel was absent on leave when Montgomery struck. In 1944 Operation Fortitude succeeded in persuading Hitler that a non-existent US First Army Group based in Kent was going to land on the beaches south of Boulogne. No major German units were moved from the Pas de Calais to Normandy, and the path for Overlord was greatly eased.[48]

Germany's wartime intelligence was characterized, and to some extent damaged by the intense rivalry of the Abwehr (the military intelligence department of the High Command) and the *Reichssicherheitshauptamt* (RSHA), the SS security office. The Abwehr had been implicated in a pre-war plot to remove Hitler, and its chief, Admiral Wilhelm Canaris (1887–1945), was anything but a Nazi enthusiast. Its most effective work was done in counter-intelligence. Teams from the Abwehr had successfully prepared the ground for the German annexations of Austria and Czecho-slovakia, and another group seized the strategic railway tunnel at Jablun-ków in Polish Silesia (Zaolzie) in the last week of August 1939. Contacts with the IRA brought no results, and the Abwehr never suspected the Ultra secret. The Abwehr's operations were taken over bit by bit by the RSHA. Canaris was temporarily suspended in 1942, banned from Berlin in 1943, arrested in 1944 following the Bomb Plot, and hanged in April 1945.[49]

Soviet intelligence has had a formidable reputation, though its achievements against unsuspecting allies were probably rather greater than against a vigilant German enemy. Like all branches of the Red Army, the military intelligence service (GRU) under General Golikov was subject to an all-powerful Military–Political Department and ultimately to the NKVD. In its foreign operations it relied heavily on Communists who supplied information in all European countries. Its main organization in Germany, the Rote Kapelle ('Red Orchestra') did not escape the attention of the Abwehr, though one section based in Switzerland, known as the Lucy Ring, kept going until June 1944. 'Lucy' was run by a Lucerne publisher called Rössler, who may have been controlled by Swiss intelligence. But it certainly had strong contacts both with German resistance and with high circles in the Wehrmacht. One of its agents, identified only as 'Werther', may well have been Canaris, or more probably Canaris's deputy, Major General Hans Oster. It has even been suggested that 'Lucy' was established to serve as a plausible conduit through which British Ultra intelligence could be passed to the Soviets. At all events, it provided Moscow with advance warning of several (though not all) German offensives in the East.

The Red Army's field intelligence had been virtually blind in 1941, owing to German air superiority. But it improved greatly as photographic reconnaissance gradually became feasible. And the Soviets were the undisputed champions of *maskirovka*, or 'deception'. Troop movements were made at night, dummy base camps were built, and phoney radio traffic filled the airwaves. Time and again, they spirited up huge reserves and whole tank armies from nowhere. They attacked at times and places where they were least expected – as at Moscow in December 1941 – and they sometimes stood still when the whole world waited on attack – as on the Vistula in August 1944.

Of course the climate of suspicion which pervaded every cranny of Stalin's regime could paralyse the workings of intelligence. A study of Stalin's manifold sources of information in 1941 – using diplomatic, military, NKVD, Party, radio and frontierguard channels – shows that paralysis grew in proportion to the conflicting advice.[50] Richard Sorge (1895–1944), a dedicated Communist who had joined the Nazi Party, worked in Tokyo as a German correspondent. He formed a ring, code-named 'Ramsay', with the best possible sources from inside the Japanese government. Yet when he correctly predicted Operation Barbarossa he was not believed. Indeed, he was long dead before his services were appreciated.[51]

Espionage, in fact, was an essential adjunct to warfare. Major 'Rygor' Słowikowski, an agent of the Polish government, set up an unlikely porridge business in Algeria, through which he organized the highly efficient Franco-Polish 'Agence Afrique' to prepare the ground for Operation Torch. Paul Thümmel, an employee of the Abwehr, was, in the words of the MI6 chief, 'an agent at whose word armies march'. Codenamed 'A-54', he had grown disillusioned by the German annexation of Czechoslovakia, and thereafter he systematically supplied information to Czech contacts. Elyeza Bazna, the Turkish valet of the British ambassador in Ankara, in 1943–4 sent copies of the contents of his master's safe to the German Embassy. Marie-Madaleine Fourcade was a determined Frenchwoman who coordinated a massive ring of 3,000 agents, called 'Noah's Ark', that collected details of German military activity in France. The Noah's Ark reports were flown out to England by light aircraft sent by MI6. Anton Turkul worked for the Abwehr's Max Organization in Sofia, Bulgaria, apparently providing details of the Red Army's activities for German consumption. In fact he was a Soviet double agent preparing to sabotage the movements of the Vlasov Army. Alan Nunn was a British atom scientist who passed samples of processed uranium to the GRU. And by 1944 Kim Philby, a Cambridge-educated recruit of the NKVD, was head of MI6's IX (anti-Communist) Section.[52] The sum total of these dealings, double-dealings and double double-dealings is impossible to calculate.

Communications

War has always accelerated technological advance, and 1939–45 was no exception. The era of motorcycle couriers carrying orders was not yet over, but most communications from command to front line, from admiralty to ships at sea, from ground to air, and later from soldier to soldier were now made by wireless telephony, otherwise known as 'radio'.

General Guderian had commanded a radio unit during the First World War, and he was instrumental in fitting reliable radio-telephone networks in his new panzer divisions. Radio was crucial, therefore, both to the development of blitzkrieg and to the 'combined-arms' doctrine that accompanied it. Tanks had to talk to HQ, HQ to aircraft, and aircraft to artillery. Mastery of radio was a major factor in the stunning German victories of 1939, 1940 and 1941.

Radio *en clair*, however, can easily be overheard. So advanced mechanical forms of encoding and decoding were introduced to all command structures. The German Enigma machine and the US SIGABA machine served the same purpose.

Owing to patchy reception, naval vessels still transmitted in Morse code. Radio messages, however, betrayed a vessel's location, and strict rules applied to transmission times and obligatory silences.

In 1917 Air Vice-Marshal Hugh Dowding had been perhaps the first man in the world to speak over a ground–air radio link. He now ensured that his Battle of Britain fighters were fitted with the latest equipment. Improved very-high-frequency systems had been fitted to only sixteen RAF squadrons by 1940.

Bomber fleets, like tank brigades, relied on closed radio networks. But, like naval fleets, they could easily betray their position. German bombers were guided by directional radio beams, while the British led the field in radio detection and ranging (radar).

From 1943 American technology made numerous advances. The 'walkie-talkie' (or 'handie-talkie') transformed the possibility for battlefield conversations. The 'Gibson Girl' transmitter revolutionized air–sea rescue, and portable VHF SCR-522 two-way sets made air-guided targeting a reality for ground artillery.

Nor should one underestimate the significance of radio for Europe's resistance movements. BBC broadcasts – starting with the unmistakable chimes of Big Ben, or the thrilling opening notes of Beethoven's Fifth Symphony – were listened to across the continent. The sturdy Pipstock transmitter-receivers, which could fit into a small suitcase, came as a godsend to underground fighters in Poland, France, Norway, Italy and Yugoslavia, who could now speak not only with themselves but equally with London.

Facsimile machines, IBM punch-card indexers and teleprinters all facilitated military administration. Only television, which had become operational before the war, does not seem to have been exploited. BBC TV broadcasting, which had began in 1937, closed down in 1939 and didn't recommence until 1945.

The importance of communications inevitably led to the development of countermeasures. (The term 'electronic warfare' had not yet been invented.) For example, each of the three German aerial navigation systems used during the Battle of Britain – 'Knickebein', 'X-Gerät' and 'Y-Gerät' – inspired a British system to counter it. In 1943 the RAF's 'Window' technique of dropping clouds of metal foil to confuse German radar was introduced in conjunction with the Hamburg raid, and the loss of only 12 out of 746 bombers, or 1.6 per cent, was a record low. A year later Allied countermeasures effectively discounted the German ability to recognize the approaching invasion fleet of Overlord. German radar stations in France were massively bombed in advance, and on the invasion night droves of aircraft carrying jamming devices prevented the surviving stations from calling up fighters from inland bases. Two 'ghost fleets' code-named 'Taxable' and 'Glimmer', loaded with jammers, headed for Le Havre and Boulogne, thereby complementing the deception measures that were already in place.[53]

Combat – the battlefield

War is concerned, above all, with fighting and killing. And in this regard the Second World War reached new heights of mechanized intensity. Yet it was also a war of movement, which, from the soldiers' point of view, made the fighting more bearable than the trenches of the Western Front a generation earlier.

Much thought was given in the interwar period to the impasse between offensive and defensive warfare that had brought the trenches into being. Time and again, in 1914–18, colossal efforts were made to break through the opposing line; and time and again those efforts failed, with the loss of millions of lives. Every great 'push' was preceded by an artillery barrage that dumped tonnes of metal on every square metre of the enemy's front. Wave after wave of infantrymen would then be sent 'over the top' towards 'the gap', only to find that enemy machine-gun posts had survived, or that enemy reinforcements had had time to re-form and to bar the way forward. Only once, at Cambrai in 1917, was a defensive line pierced, when the British brought up their newfangled contraption the tank, and successfully punched a hole in the German line. (Unsupported by infantry, and unsupplied with spare fuel, those first tanks duly returned to base.)

Between the wars, several military theorists identified the tank as the vehicle of the future. Charles de Gaulle in France, Władysław Sikorski in Poland and Major J. D. C. Fuller in Britain all wrote studies advocating mechanized warfare. All were ignored in their own countries. But 'Boney' Fuller (1878–1966), who was a member of Oswald Mosley's Fascists, was carefully read in Germany, where rising professionals like Erwin Rommel and Heinz Guderian were developing the concept of blitzkrieg. British battlefield tactics in 1939–45 were characterized by extreme restraint, however. British commanders were influenced by the memory of 1940 and by the lack of a dominant tank. Their stance was geared less to winning than to avoiding defeat and, as befitted a citizen army, to protecting their men. The British had good artillery, good discipline and excellent air cover. When they mounted a 17-pounder gun turret on the speedy M-1 Sherman, in 1944, they finally had a good tank – sarcastically known to its crews as the 'Ronson' (which 'lights up every time'). But the tanks were deployed as cover for advancing infantry, not as an independent spearhead, and bravado duels with panzers were not encouraged. The task of knocking out opposing armour was left either to specialized units of M10 Wolverine tank-destroyers or to the fearsome, rocket-firing Hawker Typhoon aircraft.

General Montgomery was the embodiment of such caution. His victory at El Alamein was the product of methodical preparation. And his progress in Normandy, and later in the Low Countries, was so slow as to provoke adverse comment. His disastrous insistence on Operation Market Garden can be construed as an overreaction to the criticism, and came close to costing him his job.

The US Army believed in 'victory through firepower'. Like the British, the Americans possessed neither a battle-winning tank nor a body of battle-hardened veterans. But they had no memory of recent defeat, no fear of limited reinforcements, and great faith in their lavish supplies of materiel. Their artillery was abundant and first class; the sheer number of their warplanes was staggering; and, unlike the Germans, they had no notion of conserving fuel. They did not care to modify standard Sherman tanks, and relied on summoning air support even more readily than the British did. As a result, the US Army's performance was erratic. Especially under General Patton, it was capable of sensational sustained surges – Patton's drive through France following the breakout from Normandy in 1944 and his drive through central Germany in 1945 were epic feats. At the same time, the Americans were frequently held up by stubborn German defence, or nonplussed by unexpected counter-attacks. The beachhead at Anzio, for example, where attacking US forces were pinned down for three months, does not belong to the most glorious of episodes. And the Battle of the Bulge in the Ardennes went very badly for many days, until the winter skies cleared and air power could be brought to bear.

In the early years of the war, in Poland and France, the German forces all but perfected the art of 'combined arms', and in Operation Barbarossa they came within a whisker of winning the war outright. Since they were ultimately defeated, and since they were fighting in the cause of a repellent regime, the scale and brilliance of their military achievements are often dismissed. Neither Western nor Russian opinion is willing to concede that man for man, or division for division, the Wehrmacht was superior to all its adversaries. In the end, Germany was defeated by overwhelming numbers, by logistics, by incontestable air power, by the inflexibility of its leading amateur strategist, and by sheer exhaustion. Even so, in purely military terms, its ability to keep fighting in the final phase against impossible odds was, frankly, remarkable.

The excellence of German battlefield tactics depended partly on first-rate equipment, partly on good training, and above all on commanding officers with a clear vision of their ambitious objectives. The high quality of standard German equipment goes without saying. From the Bf-109 in the air to the Panzer Mark IV, the 88-mm anti-aircraft gun and the Schmeisser machine pistol, German equipment set new standards for reliability and effectiveness. The Wehrmacht's training was thorough – not least because the supreme test of 1941–2 was preceded by campaigns of graduated difficulty in Poland and France, where important lessons were learned. And the high professionalism of the officer class was limited only by the failings of the Commander-in-Chief and his entourage.

Nor should one imagine that the Wehrmacht's performance went steadily downhill after the great defeats of Stalingrad and Kursk. On more than one occasion, German armies inflicted setbacks on the enemy that in any other context might have been counted as major victories. The counter-attack on the Vistula in early August 1944 was one of many examples.

Nonetheless, though Hitler was primarily responsible for the decision to attack the USSR in June 1941, the Wehrmacht and its generals cannot be entirely absolved from a share of responsibility. Above all, they should have paid heed to the teaching of Clausewitz, who had written so long ago about the 'fog of war' and the perversity of 'natural conditions'. Like most Germans, they allowed themselves to be psychologically disarmed by the Führer's early successes, and they made little provision for adverse developments. They invaded the largest country in the world with a daring Plan A, but with no Plan B. They showed the same arrogance as Napoleon; made very similar blunders, and suffered the same fate. It should have been no surprise that the endless open spaces of the steppe and the tundra offered the Red Army endless opportunities to retreat and to recuperate. It should have been no surprise that the roads of Byelorussia and Ukraine were turned into mud swamps by autumn rain, or that winter temperatures in Moscow were far lower than in Berlin. Even if they had captured Moscow, as Napoleon did, they would still have needed the fur coats, snowshoes and antifreeze that the German quartermasters had not thought of providing. Above all, if they were to have successfully occupied such a large country, they needed to emulate the Kaiser's army and to treat the aspirations of the local non-Russian population with sympathy. This last step was ruled out by Nazi ideology. In the last analysis, therefore, the German invasion of the Soviet Union failed because the Wehrmacht, like the German nation as a whole, had been enslaved by the Nazi way of thinking.

The Red Army, in contrast, was the principal victor of the war in Europe. Its performance exceeded the most optimistic dreams of its most fanatical advocates. Yet the big question remains: how was the victory achieved? The conventional answer mentions two factors – patriotism and numbers. 'The Russians were defending their motherland in the "Great Patriotic War", and their willingness to sacrifice their lives in unprecedented numbers overcame the barbarity and the technical superiority of the invaders.' Or words to that effect.

This explanation may satisfy unsuspecting foreigners, but it does not stand up to close examination. The German–Soviet War of 1941–5 was not fought in the main on Russian territory. It was largely fought on the territory of nations who had opted for independence only twenty years before and who would opt again for independence as soon as the USSR collapsed. Patriotism obviously played a part, especially among Russians, who had a different view of where there motherland lay than did Balts or Ukrainians. Indeed, Stalin broke all the rules of internationalist Communism to appeal for the protection of 'Holy Russia'. Yet the Red Army produced unprecedented levels of desertion as well as of heroism. And, despite Soviet propaganda, undiluted patriotism was far from ubiquitous. Some of the most nationalistic of Russians, like the Cossacks, were fundamentally opposed to the Soviet regime and joined the Germans in droves. Nor was barbarity the preserve of the Soviet Union's enemies. Stalin yielded nothing to Hitler in his appetite for mass murder. And terror in the ranks, no less than patriotism, must be viewed as a factor in the Red Army's motivation. The notion that Soviet soldiers charged to their deaths with 'Stalin' on their lips, is largely a fabrication of propaganda[54]

Which leaves the puzzle of numbers. There can be no doubt that the Red Army counted on vast supplies of equipment and on vast reserves of troops. Soviet generals were used to handling guns, planes, tanks and soldiers in quantities that no other army on earth could begin to match. The Germans were well aware of this, but had assumed that the equipment was outdated, that the men were half-trained, and that competent commanders were non-existent. So the factor of quality cannot be ignored – and it was the quality of the Red Army, above all, which the Germans would underestimate.

Numbers, however, were not unimportant. To some extent they offset the shortcomings of poor equipment, especially in the initial phase. They compensated for colossal losses, which would otherwise have been unsustainable; and in certain circumstances they could be used to good effect. There is evidence from German sources, for instance, that Wehrmacht gunners faced with 'human waves' of infantry could only keep firing until the piles of corpses blocked their view or their gun barrels overheated. One is tempted to conclude that the Soviet advantage in numbers may have helped the Red Army avoid losing, but it does not by any means explain the Soviet achievement in winning.

The strengths of the Red Army became evident only gradually. One was logistical, as revealed in the ability to manufacture and to distribute copious supplies of all the basic weapons of modern warfare. The second was technical, in that many of the improved weapons in the later phases were equal to the best of any army. And the third was organizational. Having survived the onslaught of 1941–2, and having built up a position of superiority in 1943, the Red Army never let its grip be relaxed.

Though Soviet commanders were forced to abandon some of their revolutionary military doctrines, their battlefield practices remained distinct. Many of these related to the use of infantry, of which there was a plentiful supply. For instance, during the first stage of an attack, the infantry was expected to move forward behind the artillery barrage and to effect a breach in the enemy's defences before tanks were called up to exploit it. To all appearances they were reverting to the pattern of First

World War battles, when tanks had not been available and when the casualty rate had been horrendously high. Unlike other armies, the Soviets did not flinch at sending unprotected massed infantry to assault fortified positions, and they paid a terrible price in dead and wounded. Similarly, when under attack themselves, Soviet soldiers were taught to let the first line of panzers pass, in order to engage the German infantrymen following behind. The aim was to separate the enemy tanks from their supporting units. But the cost, deliberately calculated, of helpless soldiers mown down by tank fire, could only be justified by Stalin's constant orders to his staff not to spare lives.[55]

The Red Army was slow to form dedicated armoured formations. The first tank corps was created in March 1942 from two armoured brigades. And in May of the same year, the 3rd and 5th Tank Armies were assembled for offensive action. Each tank army consisted of two tank corps, one independent tank brigade, one rifle division, one artillery regiment, one Katyusha regiment, and one anti-aircraft group. Each had its own HQ and war council. In 1943, elite guards tank armies were held in a special Stavka reserve. Hence, just as the Wehrmacht was losing a capacity for full-scale offensive action, the Red Army was gaining it.

Medical services

Military medicine had been well established in all European armies since the days of Henri Dunant and the founding of the Red Cross in 1863. It was concerned both with the prevention of disease and with the treatment of battle casualties.

In 1939–45 venereal disease was the most serious affliction among troops in the European theatre. Its prevalence caused all military staffs to stress hygiene and to monitor prostitution, and in the case of the Wehrmacht even to maintain a system of registered brothels. Tuberculosis was common among POWs, and typhus – which took 10,000 German lives on the Eastern Front in 1941–2 – threatened to reach epidemic proportions.

Penicillin, which was discovered in Britain in 1940, was available in the West within three years, and greatly reduced the incidence of death from wounds. Important advances were also made in blood transfusions, field surgery, anaesthetics, burns treatment, aviation medicine and military psychiatry.

In Britain, the Royal Army Medical Corps (RAMC) stood in the forefront not only of medical practice but also of medical research, especially into tropical diseases. Supported by the Royal Army Nursing Corps, it operated a system of regimental aid posts (RAPs) and advanced dressing stations (ADSs), motorized casualty evacuation, and an efficient network of field hospitals. Casualties from the Normandy beaches were often treated in southern England within twenty-four hours. Venereal disease was another constant danger. Indeed, in 1939–40 the predilection of the soldiers of the BEF for French prostitutes would become legendary. Montgomery, though the son of a bishop, took a pragmatic view – suggesting that the men take the necessary precautions when seeking what he called 'horizontal refreshment', and that the brothels be registered and inspected. Though sensible to modern ears, his suggestions caused no little controversy, and he was forced to withdraw them.

The US Army maintained similar standards. General Eisenhower attempted to enforce a policy of 'non-fraternization'. At home, there was a public outcry in 1941–2 over prostitution, but overseas the US Army continued to register prostitutes and to offer them prophylactic treatment. The US Army Medical Corps and the Army Nurses Corps ran segregated services for white troops and for black troops. The USAAF pioneered the use of air ambulances and specialized hospital ships.

In the German forces, a huge contrast developed between the medical services available at home and on the Western fronts and those in the East. Each Wehrmacht division was provided with two medical companies, each with its own field hospital. Frostbite caused unmanageable problems every winter for four years on the Eastern Front, and transport services often broke down in the first stages of evacuation. Field surgeons were increasingly overwhelmed. Even so, in 1942–3 planes continued to fly out casualties from the Stalingrad pocket so long as airstrips were operating. And in 1945 a patient on the last hospital train from Breslau to Berlin commented on the smartness of the nurses, the cleanliness of the sheets, and the nourishing bean soup. German techniques of blood transfusion were much improved following the capture of dried blood serum from a British army hospital in Tobruk in 1942.[56] During the final collapse of the Reich, battle fatigue and neurosis triggered at least 10,000 suicides.

Official descriptions of Soviet medical services differ markedly from eyewitness accounts of prevailing conditions. The Red Army possessed a Military–Sanitary Department, with trained surgeons and nurses, and from 1942 each front was supplied with mobile medical teams. All the evidence indicates, however, that medical provisions were grossly inadequate. Standard Red Army battle tactics (see pp. 259–60) generated such an overwhelming torrent of casualties that most wounded men could not expect to receive timely treatment. Evacuation procedures often broke down completely. And heroic army surgeons were forced to work in unbelievably primitive conditions. Descriptions of the Battle of Stalingrad, for example, record thousands of casualties ferried across the river to safety, only to be left to die on the riverbank for lack of attention.[57]

Eyewitness accounts can never paint the full picture, but they, too, point in the same horrifying direction. Forewarned of what awaited them, Red Army men put no reliance on the official services. They would form themselves into pairs or into informal teams before the battle, so that survivors could assist their wounded comrades afterwards. People who observed the scenes behind the front have described how roadways would be cleared by the NKVD for the columns of reinforcements moving forward, while the roadside ditches were filled with wounded men staggering in pairs or crawling on hands and knees towards the rear.

Descriptions of field hospitals on the Soviet side of the Eastern Front make for similarly grisly reading. Piles of mutilated bodies would be carried in on open trucks or carts, dumped on the ground in a heap, then doused with cold water to sort the living from the dead. Having no time to spare for lengthy operations, surgeons had a few seconds in which to assess each case. Their decision whether to operate or not depended on an instant estimate of the patient's chances of survival. Men with multiple or internal injuries were laid out to die in agony. Those with damaged limbs went straight onto the operating table for a shot of morphine and immediate amputation. A small boy, now a famous writer, who once stood in view of such a hospital tent remembers severed arms and legs flying through the open tent door into a bin, while commandeered peasants dragged corpses into a mass grave in the nearby forest.[58] This was the mid-twentieth century.

Aces and heroes

Human beings subjected to life-and-death combat conditions react in
different ways. Most have no aim but to stay alive. A few break down and
lose the will to defend themselves. A few conduct themselves with
extraordinary self-sacrificial courage. These are the ones we are urged to
remember.

Soldiers of the Second World War had many opportunities to show
daring and courage. Lieutenant Patrick Dalzel-Job, RN (1913–2003), for
example, served under Ian Fleming in Naval Intelligence and is often said
to have been the model for Fleming's James Bond. His memoir *From Arctic
Snow to Dust of Normandy* (1991) relates his exploits in the clandestine 30
Assault Unit.[59]

Lieutenant Audie Murphy (1924–71), a Texan, was the most decorated
US soldier of the war. He received a total of thirty-three medals, including
the Congressional Medal of Honor for a one-man stand at Holzwihr, in
Alsace, where he held off a regiment of white-clad German *Gebirgsjäger* by
firing his machine gun from a burning tank-destroyer. His autobiography,
To Hell and Back (1949), was made into a popular film of the same name.
He himself starred in forty films, including *Red Badge of Courage*, many of
them with James Cagney. Tellingly, he suffered from post-traumatic stress
disorder (PTSD), and became addicted to placydil sleeping tablets; by
going public about this he helped break the social taboos against medical
psychiatry. He died in a plane crash.[60]

Graf Hyacinth von Strachwitz (1893–1968), a Silesian nobleman, gave
distinguished service in both world wars. In September 1914, in advance
of the Battle of the Marne, his cavalry troop broke through French lines
and reputedly caught sight of Paris. In October 1942 his panzer group was
the first to reach Stalingrad and to gaze across the Volga 'at the steppes of
Asia'. He was one of 160 recipients of the Ritterkreuz with Oakleaves and
Swords.[61]

Alexander Matrosov (1924–43) was the archetypal Soviet hero, and his
story was widely publicized by official propaganda. He served in a
volunteer unit in the Pskov sector, and died an exemplary death – shielding
his comrades by blocking the barrel of a German machine gun with his
own body.[62] (According to some reports, he was a Bashkir boy who

changed his name of Shakiryan Muhamedyanov during a stay in a Russian orphanage.)

For obvious reasons, fighter pilots supplied a disproportionate number of wartime heroes. Their trade demanded great speed, skill and elan, and they were by nature individualists, daredevils, riding the skies in clouds of glory – or at least that is how they were seen.

Douglas Bader (1910–82) was perhaps Britain's leading fighter ace. His twenty-three 'kills' did not put him at the top of the league, but he was remarkable for having two amputated legs following a pre-war plane crash. His struggle to regain flying rights demanded exactly the same qualities which put him at the head of 242 Squadron flying Hurricanes in the Battle of Britain, and of the 'Tangmere Wing' commanding three squadrons of Spitfires. In August 1941, he survived a mid-air collision near Le Touquet and, despite his disability, parachuted safely to the ground. He spent the rest of the war in Colditz. His story featured prominently in the book and film *Reach for the Sky* (1956).[63]

All the top US fighter aces served in the Pacific theatre. This may reflect on the difference between the German and the Japanese opposition, but more probably on the length of time that US fighter wings were engaged against a dominant adversary. US fighter pilots reached Europe only at a stage when the Luftwaffe had been pressed on to the defensive.

Hans-Ulrich Rudel (1916–82) has been described as Germany's greatest war hero. Flying a Junkers JU-87 Panzerjäger, or 'Tank-Hunter', he completed 2,530 combat missions, survived 32 forced landings, and heard of a 100,000-rouble bounty put on his head. His confirmed 'hits' included 518 Soviet tanks, 700 trucks, 150 artillery batteries, 9 enemy aircraft, 70 landing craft, the Soviet cruiser *Marat*, the battleship *October Revolution*, and countless bridges, railway lines and bunkers. The German authorities ran out of medals to award him. In 1944 he was given the highest possible decoration, the Ritterkreuz with Oakleaves, Swords and Diamonds, after he landed behind enemy lines, swam the near-freezing Dniester, and made a 50-km barefoot trek through enemy-held territory to safety. But his exploits continued unabated. Following partial amputation of his right leg, he flew, like Bader, with a prosthesis, and in 1945 a new award, the Ritterkreuz 'with Golden Oakleaves, Swords and Diamonds', was invented to match his unprecented tally of doughty feats.

Rudel – an Austrian – was never a member of any Nazi organization, and was never suspected of a war crime. After the war he spent several years in Argentina, where he developed techniques of mountaineering for the disabled. He returned to Europe for a final career as a ski instructor – but not before conquering Aconcagua, the highest peak in the Americas. One can fairly say that if Rudel had been British or American he would have become the darling of Hollywood and the best-known aviator in the world.[64]

The story of Mikhail Petrovich Devyataev (1917–2002) presents a similar lesson in the ways that knowledge about the war can be manipulated. A Mordovian and a Soviet fighter pilot, he lost out in a dogfight with two FW-190s in July 1944 over Lwów, bailed out, and broke his leg on landing. Promptly arrested, he was placed in an Oflag, helped to recover by British prisoners, then transferred first to Sachsenhausen and after that to another camp near Königsberg. There he managed to swap identities by adopting the papers of a dead Russian, thereby escaping the opprobrium of being a Soviet officer. Next he was shipped with a slave-labour gang to the German rocket-testing centre on the island of Peene-münde. Underfed and maltreated, he worked on bomb disposal until he weighed only 41 kg and decided that escape gave him the only chance of survival. It was February 1945. Successfully stealing a twin-engined Heinkel with a group of companions, he soared out over the Baltic from Peene-münde, flew through Soviet flak, and crash-landed the plane safely into a snowdrift among friendly lines.

A happy end one might think. Not a bit of it. Devyataev's companions were promptly dispatched to penal battalions by the NKVD. And Devyataev himself was held in solitary confinement in between endless interrogations. He was told nothing of VE Day, and only learned of it after the NKVD took him back to Germany, to revisit Peenemünde and Sachsenhausen. His ordeal continued even when released in 1947. His papers, stamped as those of a former POW, marked him out as a social pariah. He was unable to work in a land that boasted of having no unemployment. An Allied war hero and a survivor of the Nazi camps, he was extremely lucky to be alive. Needless to say, his story was not revealed until after Stalin's death, when his exploits happened to be praised by the head of Soviet rocket research.[65]

The true tales of Rudel and Devyataev should prompt some troublesome reflections. Courage and virtue, it seems, were not the preserve of Allied fighters. People fighting heroically against Nazism were not necessarily decent. And warriors who fulfilled their patriotic duty without fear or reproach could be found on every side. This is not the moral framework which most Britons and Americans have been taught to believe in. But it is true. It is historical. It was hinted at by Marshal Zhukov when in 1945 General Eisenhower asked him about reports of men being shot for cowardice among Zhukov's troops. 'In the Red Army,' the Marshal replied, 'it takes a very brave man to become a coward.'[66]

After the fall of the Soviet Union, the removal of censorship raised a further problem: namely the spectre of falsification. In Stalin's times officialdom had been able to invent or embellish stories of Soviet heroism as the occasion demanded, and its inventions could not be publicly challenged for fifty years. In the 1990s, therefore, a series of questions surfaced that had been waiting for an answer. One of them, which caused a storm of controversy in the columns of *Izvestia* in 1994, concerned the aviator Nikolai Gastello (1908–41), whose heroism had been widely celebrated in Soviet children's books, in films, and on postage stamps. A popular song called 'Captain Gastello' was composed. According to the official version, as broadcast on Moscow Radio on 5 July 1941, Gastello had executed a kamikaze-style attack on a panzer column, destroying numerous enemy tanks in a *taran* or firestorm. According to the sceptics, the attack never took place or was performed by someone else or occurred by accident. The upshot, in 1996, was that President Yeltsin awarded a medal to a different aviator.[67]

Decorations

War is nothing if not competitive. And all armies give medals and awards to soldiers who have competed well.[68]

Britain's highest award for 'valour in the presence of the enemy' is the Victoria Cross, which can be won by any service personnel. In 1939–45 it was awarded 181 times, often posthumously. One soldier, Captain Charles Upham, a New Zealander, exceptionally won it twice, in Crete and in the North Africa campaign. The system for lesser awards such as the Distinguished Service Order (DSO), the Military Cross (MC) and the Distinguished Conduct Medal (DCM) was marred by the intrusion of the British class system, which used to insist on giving different medals for the same sort of distinguished conduct to officers, to NCOs and to other ranks. The George Cross (GC) and the George Medal (GM) were introduced to reward bravery in civilian life. Naval and air-force personnel were eligible for their own orders of recognition.

The USA's highest award was the Congressional Medal of Honor. It was followed by the Distinguished Service Cross, the Navy Cross and the Distinguished Flying Cross. The Silver Star and Bronze Star were awarded for gallantry, whilst the famous 'Purple Hearts' were awarded to service-men who were killed or wounded in battle. The Soldier's Medal was roughly equivalent to Britain's George Cross, whilst the Legion of Merit was a new order in four degrees.

In Germany, Hitler reinstated the Iron Cross on 1 September 1939, after a twenty-year interval. It was awarded in four grades: Grand Cross, Knight's Cross (Ritterkreuz), 1st Class and 2nd Class. The Ritterkreuz was awarded in three grades: with Oakleaves, with Oakleaves and Swords, and with Oakleaves, Swords and Diamonds. Only one man, Herman Göring, received the Grand Cross, and twenty-seven awards of the Ritterkreuz with Oakleaves, Swords and Diamonds were made. Only Hans-Ulrich Rudel was awarded the supplementary Ritterkreuz with Golden Oakleaves, Swords and Diamonds. Further new orders included the War Merit Cross (KVK), awarded in five grades, and the German Cross (DK), awarded in two grades for military leadership. Interestingly, no distinction was made between decorations given to the Wehrmacht and to the SS.

The USSR had abolished all military awards and decorations before the war, but it returned to the custom with gusto, often awarding two separate medals to every recipient. All people given the title of 'Hero of the Soviet Union', for instance, also received the Gold Star Medal. In 1941–5, there were 11,365 recipients. The highest-ranking award, the Order of Lenin, was not confined to military service. Other distinctions included the Order of the Red Banner, for outstanding courage; the Order of the Red Star; the Order of Victory, for successful generalship; the Order of Glory, for junior ranks, in three classes; the Order of Suvorov, for commanders; the Order of Kutuzov; the Order of Khmyelnitsky, for partisans; the Medal for Valour; and the Medal for Battle Merit. The USSR had started the war not recognizing military ranks. But it ended, like the British Army, by making clear distinctions for awards to generals, to officers and to other ranks. The average Soviet marshal wore so much metal on his dress uniform that standing up straight caused problems.

The most obvious blemish on Soviet military decorations lies in the fact that they were awarded with equal aplomb both to politicians, who might never have been near the front, and to genuine heroes. The list of 12,500 'Heroes of the USSR', therefore, contains a disreputable mixture of men and women who laid down their lives and names such as those of Brezhnev, Khrushchev and Stalin. Several of Stalin's old cronies, like Budyonny or Voroshilov, who did not perform well in 1941–5, were nonetheless received into the pantheon.[69]

Most combatant countries also awarded campaign medals to all military personnel who completed a successful tour of duty. These modest circles of metal, hung on a cheap ribbon, often look tawdry, unworthy tokens of nominal recognition. But they were much valued by men who had not chosen to serve and whose sacrifices were rarely noticed.

The British campaign awards were issued primarily on the basis of the theatre in which the soldier had served. Hence the main awards were as follows: Atlantic Star, Air Crew Europe Star, Africa Star, Pacific Star, Burma Star, Italy Star and France and Germany Star. In addition, all those who served in any capacity were awarded the 1939–45 Star, the Defence Medal and the 1939–45 War Medal.

American campaign awards followed similar lines, with a European–African–Middle Eastern Campaign Medal and an Asiatic–Pacific Campaign Medal for specific theatres, a Prisoner of War Medal and a Women's Army Corps Service Medal, and two general-service awards – the World War Two Victory Medal and the American Campaign Medal.

The campaign awards issued by the Soviet Union followed a very different model, being issued primarily on a city-by-city basis. From the first phase of the Nazi–Soviet War, they were mostly for the defence of Soviet cities: Defence of Leningrad, Defence of Moscow, Defence of Odessa, Defence of the Caucasus, Defence of Stalingrad, Defence of Sevastopol, Defence of Kiev, and the Defence of the Soviet Polar Region. As the Red Army then advanced into Central Europe, cities would be 'liberated' or 'captured' according to their role in the war against Moscow. Thus medals would be issued for the Liberation of Belgrade, the Liberation of Warsaw and the Liberation of Prague, while Königsberg, Vienna, Budapest and Berlin would all be 'captured'. In addition, and in line with most Allied forces, two general awards were issued, commemorating service in the Victory over Germany and the Victory over Japan.

The German system of campaign awards was perhaps the most

peculiar. With the exception of the Eastern Front Medal – the so-called 'Order of the Frozen Flesh', issued for service in the German–Soviet War in 1941–2 – campaign awards were made as a small metal shield which would be worn on the upper left sleeve. The campaign at Narvik, the encirclement battles at Cholm and Demjansk, the conquest of the Crimea and the defence of the Kuban bridgehead would all be commemorated in this way. Veterans of the North Africa campaign, the attack on Crete or the defence of Kurland were permitted to wear a fabric cuffband. Interestingly, no German campaign awards were issued for the conquest of France in 1940, the defence of Italy in 1943–5 or the western campaign of 1944–5.

Prisoners of war

International rules governing the humane treatment of prisoners had been agreed at the Hague conventions of 1899 and 1907. Among the combatant states of 1939–45, Britain, France, Poland, Germany and the USA had signed the conventions, but the USSR had not. As a result, the treatment of POWs between signatories followed civilized standards, while German prisoners in Soviet hands and Soviet prisoners in German hands were subjected to the most appalling savagery. The German authorities appeared to take the view that, since the Soviets did not observe the conventions, they would ignore them also. Their complacency matched ideological requirements.

According to the conventions, POWs were to be decently housed, properly fed, and allowed the privileges of religious worship, medical treatment and correspondence with their families. They were not to be beaten, interrogated, tortured or severely punished, even for attempts to escape. The rank and file could be put to work, and officers were to be held in separate quarters. All were to be accessible for inspection by the international Red Cross.

By and large, therefore, Western POWs in Axis hands and Axis POWs in Western hands survived the war in tolerable conditions. Even the prison camp for recalcitrant Allied officers at Colditz Castle in Saxony practised the mildest of regimes. Over 60,000 British POWs were held in German Oflags and Stalags, mainly veterans of the Dunkirk beaches, or bailed-out bomber crews. Some 100,000 Italians worked on British farms, whilst 2 million Frenchmen were sent to work in mines, farms and factories in the Reich. Serious atrocities or incidents of manifest maltreatment were rare. A group of soldiers from the Norfolk Regiment were shot on capture by the SS in May 1940, while ninety men of the Warwickshire Regiment suffered a similar fate at Wormhout. Eighty-four US captives were shot at Malmédy during the Battle of the Bulge. And up to 5,000 Italian prisoners, who had earlier fought their erstwhile German allies, were massacred on the island of Cephalonia in 1943. The only serious accusations of maltreatment of German POWs by the Western allies arose at the end of the war, in 1945, when vast numbers were held in the open after the fall of the Ruhr Pocket (see below).

The experiences of Polish POWs were unusual on several counts. In October 1939 more than a million Polish troops had surrendered either to the Germans or, in the east of the country, to the Soviets. According to Nazi ideology, and Hitler's express instructions, they should have been treated as Slavs with 'the harshest cruelty'. Instead, the Wehrmacht sent the officers to standard Oflags, such as Murnau or Woldenburg, where they spent the whole of the war in relative safety and comfort. The rank and file were released and sent home. The reasons for their good fortune are not entirely clear. But their fate compares very favourably with that of their comrades in Soviet captivity. The NKVD shot almost all the 25,000 Polish officers in their care (see Katyn, p. 182); and sent tens of thousands rank-and-file prisoners to face death in the Arctic camps.

Early in the war the British formed a secret organization code-named 'MI9', which specialized in helping escapees and evaders. (Its American counterpart was MIS-X.) It established an underground 'railway' – that is, a line of safe houses – stretching from Belgium to the Pyrenees, along which some 33,000 Allied servicemen passed. Most of its clients did not know who was helping them.[70]

German POWs under British control had little hope of escape. Only one man is known to have shown a clean pair of heels, by finding his way in 1941 from a work camp in Canada to the still neutral USA. At the end of the war, rumours circulated that important prisoners were being held in the so-called 'London Cage' for investigation under torture.[71]

German prisoners in the USSR numbered about 4.5 million. They were lucky to have been captured alive, since the Red Army had no compunction in killing wounded men or stragglers. But they were left in no doubt that they bore the collective guilt of 'the Fascists', and that they would come to wish they had been killed. They were usually taken to remote labour camps in the far north, separate from the GULag, where half would slowly die from overwork and underfeeding. Nor were they released in 1945. Most of the survivors were allowed home only after Stalin's death in 1953.

Important German prisoners were held in the Lubyanka prison in Moscow for endless interrogation by the NKVD. One such group consisted of the entire personnel of the *Führerbunker*, captured in 1945. They were held for a year, and systematically tortured to reveal everything they knew about Hitler's habits and opinions. Since the Führer's skull had been lost during the original storming of the bunker, they were all returned to Berlin in 1946 to re-enact the disinterment. On this occasion the skull was found, but the Führer's skeleton was stolen by Beria's deputy.[72]

Soviet prisoners who fell into German captivity fared worst of all. They numbered an estimated 5.2 million, of whom the great majority died within a few months of capture. Indeed, of the astonishing total of 3.2 million captured in 1941–2, 2.8 million did not live to see the summer. The reasons were simple. Hitler had given orders for all political commissars and most officers to be shot out of hand. Some 500,000 Soviet POWs were handed over to the SS to be sent to concentration camps, including Auschwitz. And the rest were held in open compounds in conditions that were worse than Auschwitz, if such can be imagined. In various locations behind the Eastern Front, the men were crowded into barbed-wire enclosures with no shelter from the elements. They were given no food, no drink, no barracks, no furniture; they just stood in the snow, or in the rain-sodden grass, until they dropped. And when they died they were cut up and eaten by their comrades. Cannibalism had not been unknown in the Soviet famines and terror campaigns of the 1930s. It now re-emerged in response to the belief of the SS that their captives were 'subhuman'. It also served as a prod to encourage the captives to volunteer for work as SS 'auxiliaries'. Unbeknown to the 'volunteers', the work would often turn out to involve guarding death camps.

After 1942, Nazi policy towards Soviet POWs began to change. A large pool of potential manpower was being wasted. And Field Marshal von Kleist, commander of Army Group A, and other German generals, argued that anti-Stalinist sentiments among the Soviet population should be exploited. 'If we don't win them over,' he once remarked, 'we are lost.'[73] Prisoners were put to work. Death rates dropped. And recruits were drafted into numerous formations of *Osttruppen* (Eastern troops) and of non-Russian *Ostlegionen* (Eastern Legions), consisting of Armenians, Balts, Georgians, Azeris, Kalmyks, Tatars and Turkmens. General Andrei Vlasov (1900–46), who was captured near Leningrad in July 1942, was chosen to lead a Committee for the Liberation of the Peoples of Russia (KONRR). He was allowed to tour cities behind the front, like Pskov and Riga, where he was warmly welcomed. His activities were then banned on Hitler's personal intervention, but were reinstated in 1944, when the manpower shortage became acute. The 'Vlasov Army', of two divisions, saw action in 1944–5 in Czechoslovakia.[74]

However, the ordeal of Soviet POWs did not end when the war ended. Stalin ordered their repatriation, then charged them with treason for disobeying Order 270 (see p. 232). Over a million were sent back to the USSR. The officers were promptly shot. The rank and file were dispatched to a slower death in the GULag.

Similarly impossible dilemmas were faced by Poland's underground resistance movement, the Home Army (AK), whose members were treated as 'bandits' both by the Nazi SS and by the Soviet NKVD. (The AK, one might recall, was the clandestine branch of a regular Allied military force.) During the Warsaw Rising, for example, the SS took no prisoners, shooting all AK captives on sight. They only recognized the Home Army as a legitimate combatant force at the very end of the Rising, so as to ensure its capitulation. They then agreed, exceptionally, that all AK fighters who surrendered should be sent to regular Wehrmacht POW camps. Yet the Soviets never made such a concession. In 1944–5, when the Red Army moved through Poland, the Communist press continued to call the Home Army 'bandits'. The NKVD redoubled their efforts to arrest its members, to shoot the officers, and to imprison the rank and file or to impress them into front-line service. After the war, the Communist authorities persisted in hunting down survivors of the wartime resistance, putting them on trial absurdly as 'collaborators', and sentencing their finest heroes to death.

Westerners who imagine the war to have been a simple conflict between good and evil may not follow the logic of these events. They should contemplate the fate of Field Marshal von Kleist, the good German who advocated treating Soviet people well. He was extradited to the USSR in 1948, and charged with 'alienating the Soviet population through mildness and kindness'. He died a prisoner in a Soviet jail.[75]

★

Talk of 10 million POWs leaves nothing more than a faceless blur. Yet every single one of the 10 million was an individual person.

Slavomir Rawicz (1915–2004) was a Polish cavalry officer who fought the Germans in 1939 but was captured by the Soviets and sentenced to twenty-five years' hard labour in a camp in eastern Siberia. He escaped with a small group of fellow inmates, and over twelve months in 1941–2, he walked the 6,500 km to Calcutta – crossing the Gobi Desert, Tibet and the Himalayas on the way. He later served with the British Eighth Army in Palestine. Several reviewers denounced his autobiographical book *The Long Walk* (1956) as a work of fiction, not to say fraud. But it wasn't, despite obvious embellishments. British officials in India and Afghanistan reported other similar Polish arrivals.[76]

Airey Neave (1916–79) was wounded near Calais in May 1940 and sent to a German Oflag near Toruń in occupied Poland. From there he was transferred to Colditz, whence, at the second attempt, he completed a 'home run' via Switzerland. Having worked for MI9, and served as a lawyer at the Nuremberg Tribunal, Neave became a prominent MP, and was eventually murdered by an Irish terrorist bomb in the House of Commons car park.[77]

Domenico 'Dommechino' Chiochetti (1910–99), an Italian from the Dolomites, was captured in North Africa and was interned in the Orkney Islands. Together with colleagues, he designed and built the Italian Chapel on Lambholm, using junk materials, which is now a thriving tourist attraction.[78]

Oberleutnant Franz von Werra (1914–41), born in Switzerland, a Luftwaffe fighter ace with twenty-one 'kills' to his credit, was shot down over southern England and sent to a POW camp in Canada. He escaped to the USA before returning to Germany via Mexico and South America, He and his plane were lost in a routine patrol over the Dutch coast.[79]

Yakov Dzugashvili (1907–43), a Soviet fighter pilot who crashed, was imprisoned in Sachsenhausen concentration camp. The Germans offered to exchange him for General Paulus. But he died in unclarified circumstances, apparently by throwing himself on to the camp's electrified fence. He was Stalin's elder son, estranged from his father.[80]

General S. A. Tikachenko had fought on the southern sector during Operation Barbarossa, and was also sent to Sachsenhausen. In February 1945 he was one of a group of prisoners who seized their guards' weapons, and died at the end of a lengthy gunfight.[81]

General Walther von Seydlitz-Kurzbach (1888–1976), an artillery commander, surrendered at Stalingrad. He was the last of the former officers of the German 6th Army to be released – in January 1956.[82]

Kurt Vonnegut (born 1922), a scout of the US 106th Infantry Division, was captured in December 1944 during the Battle of the Bulge, and as a POW witnessed the fire-bombing of Dresden. A well-known writer, he is the author of the semi-autobiographical *Slaughterhouse-Five* (1969). He succeeded Isaac Asimov as president of the American Humanist Association.[83]

Witold Pilecki (1901–48), like Rawicz, fought in 1939 as a Polish cavalry officer; at the end of the September Campaign he went underground. He spent 945 days in Auschwitz, having arranged to get himself arrested in order to produce the first detailed report of conditions there. Having escaped, he fought in the Home Army during the Warsaw Rising, and spent six months in a German Oflag before joining the British Army in Italy. Returning to Poland in 1945, he was seized by the Communist authorities, tried on false charges, and hanged. It was a prime case of judicial murder.[84]

No summary of wartime POWs would be complete without mention of the controversy surrounding the alleged maltreatment of German prisoners by the US military in 1945. The men had surrendered in droves during the final weeks of fighting, and they were held in the open for many months in a vast, half-tented city in the vicinity of Düsseldorf. No one contests the fact that mortality among them was unusually high, mainly from disease, and that the attendant administrative delays were indefensible. Yet the allegations, which have been supported by evidence, focus not only on culpable neglect, which left hundreds of thousands of helpless prisoners without elementary shelter or hygiene, but also on legal chicanery. The charge is: the prisoners were deliberately classified not as POWs but as 'disarmed enemy personnel', so as to avoid the attentions of the International Red Cross.[85]

Military casualties

Soldiering is a profession whose participants have always risked death, wounds and mutilation. But, to quote an authority, the level of casualties in the German–Soviet War, the 'epicentre of military action' in the Second World War, had 'never before been registered in the history of armed conflict'.[86] Furthermore, historians cannot agree with any precision about the exact totals of casualties. For instance, three separate entries by different scholars in the *Oxford Companion to the Second World War* (1995) give figures for Soviet military deaths that differ by no less than 1.232 million.[87] This discrepancy is more than twice the total quoted for the number of British and US deaths put together. And still greater discrepancies exist. The reasons are straightforward. The USSR, which by general consent suffered the greatest losses, was in no position during the war to count them. After the war, Soviet statements about losses see-sawed wildly according to the needs of official propaganda, and all estimates were merely demographic deductions. No credible studies of the subject were made for nearly fifty years.

There are further difficulties. For example, the round totals for British and American casualties do not always distinguish between losses in Europe and losses in the Pacific theatre, or between UK losses and British Empire/Commonwealth losses. Most post-war calculations have been made on the basis of post-war territories and post-war populations. Austria, for example, is said to have suffered 230,000 military deaths and 144,000 civilian deaths. Yet Austria formed an integral part of the Reich during the war, and one might expect that the losses of the Reich would be counted as a whole.

Another example might help elucidate the complications. At the Battle of Monte Cassino in May 1944 1,150 men of General Anders's II Corps were killed. They were Poles, nearly all of them serving in two border divisions from eastern Poland, i.e. from Wilno and Lwów. By international law, as then recognized by Great Britain, they were citizens of Poland. Yet, since eastern Poland had been annexed to the USSR in 1939, by Soviet law and practice they were citizens of the USSR. And at the time of their deaths, they were members of the British Eighth Army, and were fighting under British command. So under what heading does one place their deaths: Polish, Soviet or British? But that is not the end of it. Nowadays Wilno (Vilnius) is in Lithuania and Lwów (L'viv) is in Ukraine. When Lithuanians and Ukrainians try to estimate their wartime losses, both of them will be tempted to co-opt the Polish dead of Monte Cassino.

Nonetheless, in full awareness of the complexities, every historian must attempt to draw up an estimate, even a rough estimate. Without estimates, not even the broad outlines can be discerned. Hence:

Approximate totals of military deaths in Europe, 1939–45[88]

USSR	8,868,000	a
Third Reich	4,212,000	b
Italy	400,000	c
Romania	300,000	c
Poland	300,000	d
Yugoslavia	300,000	e
France	250,000	f
Czechoslovakia	250,000	g
United Kingdom	200,000	h
Hungary	160,000	i
USA	150,000	j
Finland	84,000	k
Others	103,000	l
Total	*15,577,000*	

Notes: (a) *Oxford Companion to the Second World War* (*OCSWW*), p. 1232; (b) ibid., p. 469; (c) ibid., p. 290; (d) including Home Army and Polish armies under Soviet command; (e) *OCSWW*, p. 290 – inexplicably, this figure far exceeds the total figure for soldiers under arms under 'Yugoslavia', pp. 1297–8; (f) ibid., p. 290; (g) as for Yugoslavia: see 'Czechoslovakia', p. 280; (h) includes 50,000 RN deaths and 60,000 RAF deaths, but not losses outside Europe; (i) *OCSWW*, p. 290; (j) includes naval and air-force losses, but not losses outside Europe; (k) *OCSWW*, p. 290; (l) not including British Empire/Commonwealth losses.

One may endlessly debate the details. But, given that estimates for military deaths during the Second World War in all theatres reach around 21–22 million, two conclusions seem incontrovertible. Firstly, military deaths in Europe were approximately twice as great as in the Pacific theatre. Secondly, since German losses on the Eastern Front accounted for about 80 per cent of the total, military deaths during the German–Soviet campaigns were approximately five times higher than those of all the other European campaigns put together.

War cemeteries

Soldiers are sometimes buried where they fall. Sometimes their bodies are moved by local villagers or by the victors of the battlefield to a nearby enclosure or churchyard. Sometimes they are taken to vast formal cemeteries, where they lie in neat rows, thousands upon thousands, as if on posthumous parade. Europe is covered with such burial grounds, formal or informal. In many places, especially in Western Europe, military cemeteries dating from the First World War were extended to store the harvest of the Second. War memorials were frequently reinscribed. Lists of names under the heading '1914–18' were joined by new lists headed '1939–45'.

As always, these things in the East were different. The numbers of dead on the battlefields of the Eastern Front were so enormous that peremptory burial in a mass grave became the norm. After the numerous winter battles, the corpses of men who had perished in the ice and snow could not be recovered until the spring. So long as the war lasted, neither the Germans nor the Soviets could do more than improvise temporary sites. And, when the war ended, all those sites had passed under Soviet control. The Soviet Union did not honour the war dead of the enemy. It deliberately sought to erase their memory, just as it erased the memory of its own domestic victims. However, it raised grandiose monuments to the glorious victories of the Red Army and to its Great Leader, Joseph Stalin. It decreed that every town and village in Eastern Europe through which the Red Army had passed should erect a memorial to the heroes of its liberation in its central square.

The cult of the war dead in Britain and the USA exudes a very different tone. It too is predicated on the assumption of total victory. But overt triumphalism is shunned. The preferred mood is quiet and restrained, and the war cemeteries are set out as soothing gardens of rest, with flowers and lawns. Official war-grave commissions perpetuate the care of these places. Gardeners trim the grass. Headstones are carefully inscribed with a name, a rank, a badge, a motto and an appropriate cross or star. Rolls of honour are kept in brass cases in the porches of the cemetery chapels. National flags fly from flagpoles. And regular visits are paid by unforgetting relatives and by regimental veterans. Nothing could be more soothing. Nothing could be more misleading about the nature and the overall outcome of the war.

Observant visitors, however, can sometimes spot when all is not as it seems. In the Allied cemetery at Fère-en-Tardoise, ninety-four American graves are marked by numbers, not by individual names. These are the anonymous resting-places of men who were executed by their own side for disciplinary offences. Shepton Mallet in Wiltshire was the site of the US headquarters prison in England, where parallel cases were dealt with in like manner.[89]

The war cemeteries which surround the sites of the bigger battles in the West are equally instructive, as at Monte Cassino. There the Polish cemetery on the hillside beside the abbey, which the Poles captured, contains neat rows of Catholic, Orthodox and Jewish graves. The British and American cemeteries lie on the plain below. There is also a French cemetery, an Italian cemetery and a German cemetery. One cannot help noticing that they are all separate. Europeans still tend to remember the war in separate national compartments.[90]

German war cemeteries necessarily exude an air of apology. They contain the graves of 'the defeated' – even if their occupants happened to win the campaign in which they fell. The designs are minimalist, and hence rather dignified. Apart from the names on the headstones, inscriptions are virtually non-existent. No sign here announces 'Dying to be Free' or 'Giving Our Today to Save Your Tomorrow'. The silence promotes reflection.

Forty years after the war, one of the many military cemeteries in Germany, at Bitburg, near Trier in the Rhineland-Palatinate, reached the world headlines. US president Ronald Reagan had agreed not only to go there during his European tour in 1985 but also to lay a wreath in memory of the fallen warriors. Uproar ensued, not least because forty-three of the graves in the cemetery belonged to members of the SS or Waffen SS. President Reagan, together with his host, Chancellor Helmut Kohl, intended to use the occasion as an act of reconciliation. He wanted to 'look to the future', he said. And he raised many eyebrows when he opined that the dead German soldiers were 'as much the victims of Nazism as were the victims of the concentration camps'. Who is to judge such matters? One of the forty-three offending gravestones reads simply:

SS-SCHTZ   *(SS GUARDSMAN*

PETER MEIO   *PETER MEIO*

5.5.25–15.9.44   *5 May 1925–15 September 1944)*

Guardsman Meio had died aged nineteen. Had he lived, he would have celebrated his sixtieth birthday on the day that President Reagan visited.

As befits the realities of the war, Soviet war cemeteries are the largest and the most ostentatious. One of the most moving Soviet memorials stands in the Piskarskoe Park in St Petersburg. It is dedicated to 'the Heroic Defenders of Leningrad', as the city was then called, and marks the 900-day siege of 1941–5. It is surrounded by 86 mass graves containing the remains of 420,000 inhabitants who perished. Its central feature is a gigantic maternal figure cradling a child and symbolizing 'The Motherland'. It is overpowering, and is meant to be.[91]

Soviet war monuments, however, often conceal a hidden story. The terrible realities of the wartime USSR could not be freely expressed even on war graves. In the cemetery beside the Gagarin Air Force Academy at Monino in the suburbs of Moscow stands the tomb of Lieutenant General Ivan Yozifovitch Proskurov (1907–41), Hero of the Soviet Union, and of his wife, Alexandra Ignatievna, who died in 1990. The tomb was donated by 'the Ministry of Defence of the USSR'. Yet Proskurov's body does not lie there. Indeed, no one in his family knows where the body lies. For Proskurov, who had served both as commander of Soviet Bomber Command and as head of Soviet Military Intelligence, fell victim to one of Stalin's recurring purges. He was arrested on 27 June 1941, the fourth day of the Great Patriotic War, and accused of fomenting a non-existent plot. Beaten and tortured, and unrepentant to the end, he was transferred to Kuibyshev, driven out of town by the NKVD on the morning of 28 October with eighteen others, and, in accordance with Beria's order no. 2756B, was shot without trial. Many decades later his mindful colleagues could only reward his memory with an empty grave and a misleading inscription.[92] He was one of very many.

The soldier's fate

Despite the horrendous losses, especially on the Eastern Front, the great majority of soldiers who served in the Second World War survived. The state of mind and body and the social predicament in which they survived is a different matter.

Soldiering in the Western armed forces was not particularly hazardous. It affected some families more than others, but the chances of becoming a casualty were low. In the present author's family, one cousin was lost in action with Bomber Command. A second served in the Royal Navy without mishap. A third lost her fiancé, who was serving with Fighter Command. A fourth cousin, then a student at London University, was nearly killed by a V-1 rocket. Her brother, who served throughout the war in RAF air–sea rescue, spent the whole time sunbathing and driving a motor launch up and down the coast of West Africa, and never saw the enemy once. In terms of a 'good war', this was approaching the top of the bill.

Military service gave many people the chance of educational and social advancement. Young men who were selected for officer training could rise from obscurity to prominent positions which gave them prospects of post-war success. One thinks of Edward Heath (1916–2005), the future British prime minister. But he was not alone. The war could even provide unorthodox business opportunities. Ludwig Koch (1923–91) started the war as a refugee from Sub-Carpathian Ruthenia. He finished it as a captain in the British Army, who ran a thriving cigarette business on the German black market, and who, as Robert Maxwell, had reinvented himself in the image of a popular tobacco brand.[93]

Military psychiatry made great advances over First World War practice. Shell shock, battle fatigue and mental disorders brought on by prolonged stress were all recognized. An interesting case is that of Spike Milligan (1918–2002), a popular British comic, who served in the Eighth Army and worked with the Entertainments National Service Association (ENSA).[94]

The rule of thumb said that two to three soldiers could expect to be wounded for every one killed. This rule generally held good – except in the Warsaw Rising, where the Home Army, critically short of ammunition, issued the order of 'One bullet, one German'. The Polish snipers were so good that the Germans suffered two men killed for every man wounded.

Few casualties were killed outright. Most deaths occurred among the badly wounded who failed to recover. Some casualties were able to return to service after treatment. Others were 'invalided out'. In aerial combat and tank warfare, burns could be as lethal as bombs and bullets.

Spacious war cemeteries, with green lawns and individual headstones, had been cultivated by the victorious Allies after the First World War, and the same respectful practice was continued on the Western Front for the dead of 1939–45. British and American families rarely realize what a luxury this is. For on the Eastern Front improvised mass graves were the order of the day. A high proportion of the dead, both German and Soviet, were in the category of 'missing in action'. The Soviet victors, who eventually took control of all the battlefields, were not well disposed towards German cemeteries, and frequently made no provision for their own. As often as not, therefore, the dutiful soldier who perished ended up as a nameless corpse with no known resting place. The Western experience was not typical.

Even in the Soviet Union, however, the proportion of service personnel who survived was greater than that of their comrades who perished. In all countries, the veterans became a potent social and cultural force. It is their memories which in large part mould the public's attitudes to wartime events.

CHAPTER FIVE

CIVILIANS

Life and Death in Wartime

A CONTINENT OF 500 MILLION people afflicted by total war presents a picture of immense, indescribable distress. And it was the civilian non-combatants who bore the brunt of the stress and the suffering. For every European who was involved in the fighting of the Second World War, there were at least ten civilians who were not directly involved but who nonetheless were forced to suffer the painful consequences of international conflict.

In times past, the impact of war was mainly felt on the battlefield, and by the people who were concerned with the preparation and prosecution of battles. Even in 1914–18, when vast conscript armies took the field and when the war provoked political cataclysms like the Russian Revolution, the effects on civilian life, though great, were relatively limited. Yet in 1939–45 civilians found themselves in the forefront.

Wartime civilian life, however, cannot be easily characterized. Firstly, it was extremely complex. The war affected people in different regions, in different countries, in different ethnic groups, in different social classes and occupations in very different ways. Secondly, civilian hardships need to be graded on a very broad scale. Some men and women felt hard done by if they were obliged to eat powdered eggs or to receive an uninvited lodger in their spare room. Others starved to death, lost their homes or their families completely, or were among the murdered millions. Thirdly, the horrors of war were not distributed evenly in time. In some instances they could last for years, and did not cease when the war officially ended. In other cases they brought pain in the first stage of the war but not later, or in the last stage but not earlier. One always thinks of the citizens of Dresden, who lived for six years in a haven of relative peace and normality, only to meet Armageddon on the eve of the Reich's collapse. The Grim Reaper harvested his crop with many swings of the scythe, and in no regular pattern.

Lastly, war does not simply bring misery and despair in its wake. It heightens human emotions in general. When death and destruction were all around, the depth of relief and guilt of those who survived, and the

raptures of joy of those who found their lost loved ones, were unimagin-
ably intense. Such extremes do not occur in peacetime.

The five spheres of wartime Europe

Many books on the Second World War in Europe are illustrated by a map
dividing the continent into two spheres: the one controlled by the Axis
Powers, the other *not* controlled by the Axis. This twofold division is too
simplistic. At any time between 1939 and 1945, Europe's political landscape
needs to be presented in terms of five separate spheres at least – each with
its own characteristic experiences.

The neutral sphere

People who belong to one of the many states which were drawn into
military conflict in 1939–45 tend to forget that a substantial body of
European nations steered clear of the conflict completely. There were
seven of them which remained neutral: Portugal, Spain, Eire, Sweden,
Switzerland, Turkey and the Vatican City.

Portugal was ruled throughout the war by António de Oliveira Salazar
(1889–1970), a dictator with Fascist sympathies, who nonetheless detested
the Nazis. His policies were not so much neutral as even-handed. Despite
Allied protests, he exercised the right to supply Germany as well as Britain
with tungsten – a valuable component of steel-making – and he only
desisted in the final months of the war. At the same time, he agreed to
lease bases in the Portuguese Atlantic islands to the Western Allies,
knowing that refusal would not have made much practical difference. The
Azores in particular became an important staging post for American
supplies. Lisbon, Portugal's capital, became a centre for Red Cross operations, for postal contacts between the combatants, and for espionage.

Franco's Spain, having signed the 'Pacto Ibérico' with Portugal,
followed a very similar path. Franco was officially a Fascist, formally a
member of the Anti-Comintern Pact, and a political debtor to Hitler and
Mussolini. Yet his ideology owed more to conservative Catholic national-

ism than to the rabble-rousing radicalism current in Berlin and Rome. And, like Salazar, he did not like Hitler. So he remained a committed non-belligerent. Spain sent its volunteer 'Blue Division' to the Eastern Front, in a gesture of support for anti-Communism, and, opposed to continuing British control of Gibraltar, made some port facilities available to the Italian navy. Otherwise it avoided hostilities.

Eire, ruled by Eamon de Valera (1882–1975), was the only British Dominion to refuse to support Britain. To Britons like Churchill, who did not take Irish independence seriously, it was little better than a traitor. Indeed, in 1939–40 the extreme republicans of the IRA conducted a terrorist bombing campaign in Britain. In consequence, Ireland lived in constant fear of a British invasion, and de Valera was obliged to declare a permanent state of emergency. Churchill, in particular, hoped to recover Ireland's Atlantic ports for the Royal Navy's use. Yet de Valera resisted temptations to draw closer to Germany, made no issue of British violations of Irish air space and Irish territorial waters, and in the end was left alone.[1]

Sweden, like Portugal, possessed valuable mineral deposits but no desire to wage a war. Swedish social democracy was inimical both to Fascism and to Soviet Communism. Yet from June 1940 the country was totally surrounded by German-controlled or pro-German neighbours: the link to the outside world via northern Norway was cut, and there was little room for manoeuvre. As a result, Stockholm bought its neutrality at the cost of selling its iron ore exclusively to Germany.

Switzerland faced the same problems in more acute form. From the fall of France it was completely surrounded by German-controlled territory, and could have been attacked at any time. It had little option, therefore, but to submit to Berlin's demands for free commercial transit and for access to Swiss financial services. Stalin, offended by the Swiss ban on the Communist Party, regarded Switzerland as a pigsty of capitalism, but Churchill was more sympathetic. He must have noted that the Swiss army had created a 'national redoubt' in the Alps, and was making serious plans to resist a German attack. Switzerland sheltered the HQ of several international organizations, including the League of Nations and the Red Cross, and with certain limitations acted in support of refugees.

Turkey had played a prominent role as a member of the Central Powers in the First World War, and had no wish to repeat the experience. After the death of Kemal Atatürk in 1938, his successor as president, Ismet Inönü, headed a cautious authoritarian state that balanced precariously between competing pressures. Fear of Russian expansion had always

provided the main spur of Turkish foreign policy. So the Nazi–Soviet Pact
came as a great shock to Ankara, as did Mussolini's encroachments into
Albania and Greece. Tensions relaxed after Hitler's attack on the USSR,
and Turkey signed a pact of territorial integrity with Germany. However,
all further blandishments were resisted. When the Soviet Union revived,
Stalin renewed demands for a Soviet naval base at the Straits, and Turkey
was pushed ever closer to the Western Allies.

Despite its tiny size, the Vatican City maintained its neutral and
sovereign status throughout the war. Pope Pius XII had denounced both
Nazism and Communism, but he was pusillanimous in avoiding any
practical application of his views. However, in 1943–4, during the German
occupation of Rome, the Vatican offered refuge to a number of Jews and
Allied POWs, and in 1944–5, a number of anti-Communist priests organized an unofficial escape route to South America for fugitive Fascists and
Nazis.

One should also spare a thought for those countries which declared
their neutrality but which were then gratuitously invaded. In September
1939 Queen Wilhelmina of the Netherlands joined King Leopold III of
Belgium in appealing to Britain, France and Germany to avoid conflict.
Hitler replied to Queen Wilhelmina assuring her that Dutch neutrality
would be respected. In May it was violently breached.

The neutral states of Europe never formed a coherent, political block,
but their presence was not insignificant. It limited the freedom of action
both of the Axis and of the Allies, and it guaranteed the continuity of a
number of havens of calm and moderation.

The Axis sphere

As established before the outbreak of war, the Axis sphere stretched from
the Baltic to the Mediterranean and from the Rhine to the Balkans.
Although Germany and Italy were partners, and although they were
supported by a number of associates, it is easy to exaggerate the coherence
of the group or to assume that they comprised a uniform block of like-
minded villains. Reality was more complex. The arrogance of the Nazis,
whose dominance was self-evident, could offend supporters as well as
enemies, and relations within the Axis camp did not always run smoothly.
Berlin found Mussolini an embarrassment long before he collapsed. In
Hungary the Nazis were eventually forced to remove Admiral Horthy by

force. In Romania they discovered that the promotion of their policies could be thwarted by a military dictatorship. And in Bulgaria they received something far short of full cooperation. Bulgaria's devious attempts to protect its small Jewish community, for instance, were crowned with at least partial success. All these Balkan countries were genuinely threatened both by Communist subversion and by Soviet invasion. And one must seriously consider the proposition that their stance can better be described as anti-Soviet than pro-German.

In the course of the war, in response to the fortunes of battle, the Axis sphere was first inflated and then deflated. In 1939–43 it reached from the Atlantic coast of France to the Volga, and from the North Cape to parts of North Africa. It included a total of seventeen occupied or partially occupied countries. From 1943 to 1945 it gradually shrank, losing the occupied Soviet republics by mid-1944, France, the Low Countries over half of Italy and most of the Balkans by the beginning of 1945, and Poland, Greece, Hungary, most of Yugoslavia and the greater part of Germany and Austria by the time of Hitler's death. Oddly enough, Norway, Denmark, Bohemia, northern Italy and various other pieces of territory remained in German control right up to VE Day. Prague and the island of Bornholm had both to be stormed after peace was officially declared.

Finland fits uneasily into the concept of an Axis block. Having been gratuitously invaded by the USSR in 1939–40, it willingly joined the German campaign against the Soviet Union in 1941–4. Yet it acted not as a formal German ally or client state, but as a voluntary co-belligerent, fighting, as the Finns put it, 'in parallel'. In 1944–5, Finnish forces were turned against German troops who had spilled over into northern Finland from Norway.[2]

Wartime experiences in the Axis sphere, therefore, were very variegated. They certainly included the pits of hell. But in some places they embraced quiet oases of relative calm, where the horrors of Fascism and the din of battle must for long periods have seemed far, far away.

Nor should one assume that life in Germany was necessarily worse than in Italy. One always has to answer the questions 'life exactly where?' and 'life for whom?' There were parts of the Reich that were spared the worst even in the final cataclysmic phase. And there were parts of Italy that suffered atrociously.

The Soviet sphere

The Soviet Union was the largest state of the world throughout the seven decades of its existence. In 1939 it consisted of eleven republics, of which the Russian Federation (RSFSR) was the largest both in territory and in population. Moscow was the capital both of the Union and of the RSFSR, and the seat of the Central Committee and Politburo of the All-Union Communist Party (Bolsheviks), which exercised a dictatorial hold over everything. Joseph Stalin had been the general secretary of the party, and hence the dictator of party and state since 1922.

In the course of the Second World War, the sphere controlled by the USSR first expanded, then, under pressure of the German invasion, contracted, before finally, as a result of the Red Army's victories, expanding again mightily. The important thing to stress is that the unoccupied area, which remained under Soviet control throughout, was many, many times larger than the occupied western republics.

The initial period of expansion during the Nazi–Soviet Pact saw significant developments: the western extension of the Byelorussian SSR and the Ukrainian SSR; the incorporation of Finnish Karelia as an autonomous republic of the Russian Federation; the creation of four new Soviet republics in Estonia, Latvia, Lithuania and Moldavia; and the delineation in September 1939 of a new western frontier. Stalin never dropped his claim to this frontier, which was the result of negotiations with the Nazis, and which he reinstated as soon as he could in 1944.

The period of contraction in 1941–3 involved the loss of Byelorussia and Ukraine and of the four new Soviet republics of Estonia, Latvia, Lithuania and Moldavia. Except for the districts adjacent to Leningrad and Moscow, it did not involve much of the territory of the Russian Federation, which remained largely inviolate. By the standards of Western Europe, the German-occupied area was vast. (Ukraine alone is bigger than France). Yet by Soviet standards it was really quite small, representing less than 5 per cent of the whole. In terms of population, the occupied area was more significant representing between a quarter and a third of the total.

These realities may perhaps be best imagined if one makes a hypothetical analogy with the USA. In this game, the German invaders land on the east coast of North America and overrun a number of states on the eastern seaboard. They lay siege to New York, but do not capture it. They are driven back from the gates of Washington. And, having rolled across the country as far as the Mississippi, they meet their first crushing defeat at Louisgrad. In the following year they drive south in an attempt to reach the Texas oilfields. But the spearhead becomes isolated, and they are forced to retreat. This time they never stop retreating. The biggest tank battle in world history takes place on the open prairie near a little place called Hazard (Kentucky). And from then on the invaders are steadily pushed back to their starting lines. The invaders cause untold disaster in the states and cities which they attack. Yet the greater part of North America in Canada, the Midwest, the South, the West and the Pacific remains completely untouched. And it is in those regions that recovery is organized. The ports of Houston, Los Angeles and Montreal remain open to receive the foreign aid that supplies the sinews of recovery.

The fact that most of the USSR remained unoccupied had numerous consequences. The Soviet government stayed in control of vast expanses of Eurasia in which to reorganize its industry and its armed forces. And it never lost access to the outside world. Via Vladivostok, it kept its outlet to the Pacific. Along its immense southern frontier it stayed in touch with the parts of China unaffected by Japanese occupation, and across the Caspian Sea it stayed connected with Iran and with the Middle East. The Germans did not even succeed in cutting the link between northern Russia and Western Europe. Despite German airbases in northern Norway, the sea route across the White Sea from Murmansk remained open throughout.

The resurgence of the Soviet sphere in 1943–5 started slowly, but turned from a creeping tide into a flood. By mid-1944 the USSR had recovered all the lands taken from it by Operation Barbarossa, and in the next nine or ten months its forces surged through a dozen European countries. As a result, the zone of German occupation in Eastern Europe was turned into a zone of permanent Soviet occupation, and the post-war world came into existence. For some time, many East Europeans feared that their countries, like the Baltic States, would be annexed by an enlarged Soviet Union as a new set of Soviet republics. Instead, they found that Stalin had taken a different option. Finland was left as an independent country, limited only by the Finno-Soviet Treaty of 1944. Greece was left in the throes of civil war. But Soviet-run governments were imposed on all the other East European countries, and the Soviet sphere was steadily transformed into a centrally controlled Soviet Bloc.

Zones of occupation

According to Western wisdom, the concept of 'occupied Europe' relates
almost exclusively to the large area subjected to German occupation. In
reality the list of occupied areas and of occupying powers is rather longer.
It is also fair to say that people, like the British and the Americans, who
have never suffered foreign occupation in their own countries are slow to
comprehend the implications. Even well-meaning occupants can easily
cause resentments that snowball into conflict, and occupying powers that
are intent from the start on domination and exploitation unavoidably raise
hell on earth.

In 1939–45 Europe witnessed a long series of foreign occupations –
some relatively benign, but most extremely hostile. The series actually
began before the accepted date of the outbreak of hostilities, and it
continued after the war's end: (see Table opposite).

Each of these occupations deserves consideration, and is the subject of
historical study. However, in terms of extent, intensity and duration, and
hence in terms of human misery, no one could seriously oppose the
contention that the Third Reich and the USSR rivalled each other for the
laurels of the top occupying power. Like all occupying powers throughout
history, they both claimed to be liberators.

Yet other considerations apply. For example, on several occasions
during the war, a country that had occupied its neighbours was itself
occupied when the pendulum of conflict swung in the opposite direction.
The phenomenon is important because it raised the ugly prospect of
revenge, and hence of protracted human suffering. Romania, which
occupied and annexed Transnistria from the USSR in 1941–3, and which
was then occupied by the Red Army in 1944–5, is an obvious case in
point. But there are others. Indeed, Germany itself is high on the list. The
merciless punishment of the German population by Soviet forces at the
end of the war can be explained to some extent by the merciless
occupation of several Soviet republics by German forces at an earlier stage.
Caution on this point is advisable, however. Few of the young Red Army
men who went on the rampage in 1944–5 – many from deepest Russia or
Central Asia – would have seen the effect of the German occupation with
their own eyes. Their anger and revenge, like the licence which they
displayed, were to a large extent the product of the official Soviet media.

Multiple occupation is another phenomenon whose destructive potential

Foreign occupations in Europe

Date	Occupying power	Occupied country or district	End date
March 1939	Germany	Memel (Klaipėda), from Lithuania	1945
April 1939	Italy	Albania	1945
September 1939	Germany	Western Poland	1945
September 1939	USSR	Eastern Poland	1941
October 1939	Lithuania	Wilno (Vilnius), from Poland	1940
1939–40	USSR	Karelia, from Finland	–
April 1940	Germany	Denmark, Norway	1945
May–June 1940	Germany	Netherlands, Belgium, northern France and the British Channel Isles	1944–5
June 1940	Italy	French Riviera, French Alps (in part)	1944
June 1940	USSR	Estonia, Latvia, Lithuania	1941
September 1940	USSR	Bessarabia, Bukovina	1941
October 1940	Italy	Northern Greece, Dodecanese	1941–3
April–May 1941	Germany	Serbia, Greece	1945
April 1941	Italy	Kosovo, Dalmatia, Fiume	1944–5
June 1941	Germany	Baltic States, Byelorussia, Ukraine	1944
June 1941	Romania	Transnistria	1944
June 1941	Great Britain	French Syria and Lebanon	1945
July 1942	Germany	Southern Russia, Crimea	1942–3
October 1942	USA, UK	French North Africa	1944
November 1942	Germany	Southern France	1944
July 1943	USA, UK	Sicily → mainland Italy	1945
January 1944	USSR	Eastern Poland	1991
May 1944	Germany	Northern Italy	1945
June 1944	USA, UK	Normandy → France, Low Countries	1944–5
July 1944	USSR	Poland (as recognized by the USSR)	1993
August 1944	USSR	Romania → Bulgaria, Yugoslavia, Hungary, Austria	1955–91
August–October 1944	USA, UK	Southern France	1944
September 1944	USSR	Slovakia → Czechoslovakia	1991
October 1944	USSR	East Prussia → eastern Germany	1990
March 1945	USA, UK	Rhineland → western Germany	–
April 1945	USA, UK	Northern Italy → Austria	1955
May 1945	USSR	Bornholm (Denmark)	1946
May 1945	Yugoslavia	Trieste	1946

is often disregarded. In Western Europe, most occupied countries suffered from only a single enemy occupation, which was then followed by liberation by friendly forces. France is the prime example. The Italian case is more complicated, since neither the German nor the Allied forces that fought over Italy were engaged in a straightforward campaign of liberation. In Eastern Europe, however, conditions were markedly more intense. There, two totalitarian powers dropped all restraints when fighting each other over the lands and the living bodies of states and populations which neither of them respected. In consequence, all the countries lying between Germany and Russia experienced two successive occupations, and some of them experienced three or even four. Bohemia, Hungary and Slovenia, for example, were occupied first by Germany and then by the Soviet Union. They were subjected to double occupation. In contrast, the three Baltic States, which were sovereign and independent until 1940, were occupied by the USSR in 1940–41, by Germany in 1941–4, and by the USSR for a second time in 1944–5. They exemplify triple occupation. As for Poland, in 1939 it was divided into two zones of occupation – one German and the other Soviet. In 1941 the Soviet zone was overrun by the Germans marching eastward, and in 1944–5 the whole of Poland was overrun by the Soviets marching westward. Here was a case of quadruple occupation.

Each of these multiple occupations compounded the pain and suffering. At each stage the occupying power would look for likely collaborators and would select its own categories of political, social or ethnic victims. At each subsequent stage the new occupying power would punish collaborators of the previous stage, the victims of the oppression would be tempted to wreak revenge on their erstwhile tormentors, and a new round of victimization and revenge would begin. A frequent outcome was civil war.

The length of foreign occupation is not without significance. The longer the occupation, the more protracted the torments became. The shortest period of occupation was probably that of the Kuban, in southern Russia, which lasted for barely two weeks. The longest was that of the city of Gdynia in Poland, which lasted for 5 years, 6 months, and 28 days.

Foreign occupation gave totalitarian powers a ghastly opportunity for extreme experiments and oppressions. The sheer weight of Nazi or Soviet power would destroy existing administrations and social structures, and the entire population would be left at the mercy of the SS or the NKVD for the purposes of racial or social engineering. There can be no doubt, for example, that the onset of the Jewish Holocaust in 1941 was closely connected to the 'historic opportunity' – as the Nazis would have put it – that was triggered by Operation Barbarossa.

Lastly, one needs to ponder the contention that one man's occupation is another man's liberation. There were people in the Baltic States, for instance, who warmly welcomed the German advance of 1941, thinking it to be a prelude to national independence, as had happened at the end of the First World War. Similarly, in 1944 there were lots of people in France or Belgium who were connected with the German-backed regime and did not welcome the advance of the Allied armies. Occupation affects a country deeply, and its impact is felt far beyond the immediate sphere of the stationing of foreign troops. As a result, the consequences of its removal can be no less painful than the consequences of its imposition.

The United Kingdom: an exception

In the extraordinary cut and thrust of the Second World War in Europe, no combatant state could hope to escape being hurt. Indeed, Britain started the war amid widespread forecasts of an airborne gas attack that never materialized. (Gas masks were distributed to the entire population, and a night-time 'blackout' was imposed in the winter of 1939/40.) What is more, as from 25 August 1940, British cities were systematically bombed, and the dangers of modern warfare were brought to the attention of the British public in the most alarming fashion.

Yet in one vital respect Britain defied the norms of all other combatant countries in Europe. It was never occupied. Though German planners drew up plans for Operation Sealion in May 1940, including the *Sonderfahndungliste GB*, which contained the names of 2,820 persons to be arrested, the intended invasion of the UK never took place, and Britons never experienced the ordeals and the emotions which foreign occupation invariably brings. Their good fortune was unprecedented. It probably explains the very special nature of British post-war perceptions of the war.

After the crisis of the Blitz had passed, Britain's unviolated status created conditions that no other European country enjoyed and which can only be compared – *toutes proportions gardées* – with those in the USA. Of course, by American standards, Britain had been in the thick of it; and admiration for Britain's performance under pressure acted as a powerful spur to the American public's support. Yet the American public was even more distanced from the war, both geographically and psychologically, than the British public was. As a result, it has been even more susceptible to post-war myth-making than anyone else. Nonetheless, the gap between the British and the Americans was much less than the gulf between the 'Anglos' and the continental Europeans. This gulf of experience must be taken into account when post-war attitudes and post-war historiography are assessed.

For several decades after the war, British people were kept in the dark concerning the realities in the Channel Islands of Jersey and Guernsey – the only British Crown possessions in Europe to have been subject to German occupation. When the truth finally emerged, it turned out that the record of resistance was not distinguished and that the record of collaboration was nothing to be proud of. The fact that the Channel Islands do not, and did not in 1939–45, form part of the UK is neither here nor there.[3]

Wartime experiences

If quizzed about the ordeals of civilians during the Second World War, most Westerners would be able to say something about the Holocaust, and perhaps the London Blitz. Germans might also add a word about the bombing of Hamburg and Dresden or about the expellees from the East. People from Central or Eastern Europe, depending on their nationality, would come up with the partisans, the Siege of Leningrad or the Warsaw Rising. Almost everyone can remember something. Very few are conscious of the whole.

In fact the greatest surprise, and indeed the greatest moral revulsion, arises from the sheer cumulative scale and variety of human suffering. The Holocaust, which has rightly been well publicized, was unique in concept and execution, and accounted for the death of nearly 6 million innocents. Yet it was not exceptional, either in scale or in pain. It occurred in a context where three or four times that number of other innocents perished. The historian's duty is to remember them all.

Bombing

The war began for many Europeans when a few tonnes of high explosive fell out of the sky, destroyed a railway station or a street of houses, buried a score of people alive, and maimed a few hundred others. Since 1918 the art of aerial bombing had made great strides. The planes flew faster. The bomb loads were heavier. The blast was bigger. The precision was somewhat improved. The range was longer. And far more people could be killed with far greater ease.

When the first bomb fell – on the morning of 1 September 1939, on the city of Kraków – the sensation of the day was the German dive-bomber, the Junkers JU-87B-2 or 'Stuka', which terrified its victims by screaming in vertical fall before killing them. But technology and method-ology moved on. 'Strategic bombing' overtook local or precision bombing, and new aircraft were developed to service the new needs. In 1940, in the first mass bombing raids, the Luftwaffe attacked British cities, using hundreds of Dornier DO-17s and Junkers JU-88s. They did not achieve all their aims, although they did inflict a lot of death and damage. On 14 November, for example, they used the X-Gerät electronic-beam system to find their target city of Coventry, where they levelled twelve armaments factories, gutted the medieval cathedral, and killed 380 people on the ground. Coventry was to become a symbol.[4]

The Luftwaffe's bombing techniques were developed not only by careful planning, but also by controlled experimentation. The outbreak of war had created opportunities that would have been unthinkable in peacetime. On 13 September 1939, for example, 4 Luftflotte systematically attacked a small country town near Lublin in Poland in conditions that permitted airborne observers to measure and to photograph the exact results. Frampol was chosen partly because it was completely defenceless, and partly because its baroque street plan presented a perfect geometric grid for calculations and measurements. Its eighteenth-century town hall, which stood at the centre of a broad, regular square, appeared to the bomb-aimers as an ideal 'bull's-eye' target. For several hours, 125 planes dropped 700 tonnes of bombs, obliterating 90 per cent of Frampol's buildings and killing almost half of its 3,000 inhabitants. For good measure, German fighters practised their strafing techniques as would-be escapees attempted to flee the inferno. All the world has heard of Coventry. Hardly anyone has heard of Frampol. Goebbels invented a new German verb –

Koventrieren – meaning 'to devastate by aerial bombing'; *Frampolieren* should be another one.[5]

Yet within a year the British had opted for a policy that meant that indiscriminate damage was bound to be inflicted on a far vaster scale. The Butt Report of August 1941 had concluded that only one RAF night bomber in three was coming within 8 km of its designated target, and that 'whole towns' presented the smallest feasible target. Fighter escorts did not possess the range to protect daylight bomber fleets all the way from Britain to Germany and back. So, to get results, 'area bombing' was adopted. By the spring of 1942 Bomber Harris had instituted the barbaric practice of fire raids, and 'Thousand-Bomber' fleets were going into action daily. The Avro Lancaster, with four Rolls-Royce Merlin engines, a payload of 10,000 kg, a range of 2,700 km, a sky ceiling of 7,470 m and a top speed of 460 km/h, came into service in March 1942. Nearly eight thousand were built. At the same time, the USA began turning out the North American B-24 Liberator and the Boeing B-17 Flying Fortress, both with smaller payloads and longer ranges. Eighteen thousand of the former and thirteen thousand of the latter were built. Every one spelled disaster for someone.

Second World War bombing, therefore, was principally an urban phenomenon which was prevalent mainly in Western Europe. But the targets were by no means confined to Britain or Germany. The Germans often combined terror bombing with local ground attacks, inflicting huge distress on cities like Warsaw or Belgrade, whilst the Allies turned their attentions to targets in Italy, France, Belgium, Holland, Romania, Hungary, Bohemia and Bulgaria. In the final year of the war, Axis Europe was ringed with bomber bases, systematically reducing Hitler's empire (and much more besides), to ruins. The 8th USAAF, based in Britain, was sending out fleets of 1,500 machines to cripple German land operations in France, while the 15th USAAF had deployed to bases in North Africa, Calabria (Foggia) and Ukraine (Poltava) from which to pound targets in southern Europe. The Strategic Bombing Offensive identified 30 key targets from Böhlen to Zeitz connected with the oil industry; 44 key railway facilities from Altenbecken to Würzburg; and 65 key industrial targets from Amsterdam and Augsburg to Wizernes (near Calais) and Wuppertal.[6]

The official insistence on the fiction that all bombing was directed exclusively at military targets did much to conceal the impact on civilians and, indeed, to lower the moral scruples of the bomber crews. The total

Principal bombing targets		
City	*Date*	*Estimated deaths*
Warsaw	1939–44	90,000
Berlin	1940–5	49,000
London	1940–1	43,000
Hamburg	July 1943	42,000
Dresden	February 1945	40,000
Cologne	1942–5	21,000
Pforzheim	February 1945	19,000
Belgrade	April 1941	17,000
Magdeburg	January 1944	15,000
Ruhr District	1942–5	15,000
Kassel	October 1943	13,000
Darmstadt	September 1944	12,300
Heilbronn	December 1944	7,500
Essen	1942–5	6,500
Munich	1942–5	6,300
Nuremburg	1942–5	6,000
Würzburg	March 1945	5,000
Bremen	1942–5	3,500
Caen	July 1944	3,000
Liverpool	1940–41	2,400
Rotterdam	May 1940	900
Coventry	November 1940	568

number of victims can be only roughly estimated: the executors of bombing counted their own losses, but not those of regrettable collaterals (see Table above).

The estimated total for civilian deaths from bombing undoubtedly tops a million. It includes 650,000 in Germany, 100,000 in Poland, 60,000 in the UK, 50,000 in France, 20,000 in Italy, 15,000 in Belgium and Holland, and 250,000 in the USSR.

Death from bombing can be particularly gruesome, not least because the life-stopping injury is often preceded by a period of sustained terror. Those who are close to the point of impact and who die instantly are the lucky ones. Most are burned or buried alive, crushed by falling masonry, asphyxiated, choked, pierced by flying glass or splinters, blinded or deafened, or otherwise struck down by insurmountable multiple injuries.

Front-line action

If well-laid military plans go well, the army marches, the enemy is pushed back, and the front line moves steadily forward. In this case civilians can be forewarned: local people can lock themselves in their cellars or take to the woods, and their anguish is cut to a minimum. Civilian casualties from stray bullets, misguided shells or careless air strikes are kept to a minimum. Such, generally speaking, were the German campaign in France in 1940 and the Allied campaign in Sicily in 1943. They were *not* usual.

More often than not, campaigns of movement would run into bottlenecks, would meet unexpected resistance, and would grind to a halt. The front line would move erratically, sitting for weeks or months in a fixed location, before lurching forward or back according to the balance of forces in the sector. Civilians caught up in a static front line became specially vulnerable. Their houses would be commandeered as defensive positions or lookout posts, and would draw enemy fire. Their streets would become the scene of hand-to-hand fighting. Their fields and woods would be saturated with nervous soldiers. Locals could be rounded up to dig ditches under fire. Peasants could be shot for defending their cows or their daughters. Casualties inevitably mounted. Such were the conditions in many sectors of the Eastern Front, in Italy, and in Normandy, where deaths of French civilians ran at levels similar to those of the Allied liberators.

Worst of all were urban centres that became locked into protracted front-line battles. Quite apart from cities that were formally declared 'fortresses' (see below), retreating armies would seek to hold on to railway junctions and river crossings, and wherever possible to build improvised fortifications. In its long retreat from the Volga to the Vistula in 1943–4, the Wehrmacht used these tactics repeatedly, as it did in Italy and in the long retreat through northern France and the Low Countries in 1944–5. Yet the decision by an army commander to dig in round a fortified town could mean a death sentence for many of its inhabitants. The town would then by shelled by artillery, bombed by planes, and assaulted by tanks and infantry.

The death of civilians at the front line was often put down to bad luck. Men and women caught in contending crossfire, picked off by mistake by snipers, or trapped in their shell-shattered homes were written off for being in the wrong place at the wrong time. They were not. It was the armies that were in the wrong place at the wrong time.

It is also worth asking where exactly in Europe the front lines most frequently passed. In every part of the Italian peninsula south of Bologna the front line moved through once. In northern France and the Low Countries, and in most parts of the western USSR, it passed through twice. And in Poland, Byelorussia and western Ukraine it visited the unhappy population on three separate occasions: in 1939, in 1941 and in 1944–5. It should come as no surprise that these were the countries where wartime mortality was highest.[7]

Liberation

Despite dictionary definitions, 'liberation' is a term which in the context of war is usually employed selectively and subjectively – i.e. for military operations that are approved. Hence in Allied literature the successful outcome of operations undertaken by the Western Allies or by the USSR is described as 'liberation', while the outcome of similar operations conducted by Axis forces is invariably classified as an 'invasion' or an 'occupation'. In Axis language, the roles of 'liberator' and 'occupier' were exactly reversed. And in some instances it is hard to deny that local populations, especially in the USSR, had much from which to be liberated.

In practice, the only true touchstone of liberation has to be sought in the feelings and attitudes of those who supposedly are liberated. Yet in 1939–45 those attitudes were often ambiguous. In many parts of Eastern Europe, for example, where the Soviet and Nazi regimes were equally resented, the arrival of the Red Army or of the Wehrmacht could be felt as a longed-for liberation and as a hated occupation at one and the same time. The German advance into Ukraine in 1941 was undoubtedly welcome to the extent that it put an end to the murderous Soviet occupation of the preceding decades. (Under Soviet rule, Ukraine had lost perhaps 10 million people before the war began.) At the same time, it brought terrible repressions and murderous policies of its own. By the same token, the western advance of the Soviet armies in 1944 was welcome to the extent that it put an end to the murderous German occupation. Yet it heralded reprisals and totalitarian practices that were hardly less vicious than those it removed. Liberations that do not liberate are not worthy of the name.

Nor should one be under any illusion about the human cost of liberation. In Normandy, for instance, more civilians were killed in the town of Caen, especially from the bombardment of 7 July 1944, than died during the D-Day landings. In France as a whole, military operations during the Liberation were often accompanied by acts of revenge perpetrated either by individual score-settlers or by members of the resistance. The number of deaths, which is sometimes put as high as 40,000, certainly exceeded those caused by occupying German forces in 1940–44.[8] Elsewhere, in Poland, Yugoslavia and Greece, official 'Liberation' was accompanied by civil war between pro-Communist and non-Communist elements. People who died during these episodes cannot be counted among Europe's liberated populations.

Sieges and fortresses

Unlike the Western armies, German and Soviet forces were regularly forbidden to retreat, and were ordered to defend a position to the death. German and Soviet generals, as well as ordinary soldiers, were faced with the direst penalties for ignoring such orders. As a result, set-piece battles repeatedly developed where defenders of a position failed to pull back as prudence dictated and found themselves cut off, condemned to hold out indefinitely or to perish. The Battle of Stalingrad developed in this way. Chuikov's 52nd Soviet Army, defending the city, refused to pull out to safety across the Volga when attacked. The German 6th Army of General Paulus was thereby tempted to press on with the attack, even when dangerously exposed. Rokossovsky duly came to Chuikov's assistance, and the German besiegers were themselves besieged. In this case the inhabitants of Stalingrad escaped the worst, having largely been evacuated.

The Siege of Leningrad, which lasted from August 1941 to January 1944, illustrates this type of tragedy on a gargantuan scale. It developed because the Soviet side refused to withdraw from the city to more defensible lines, and because Hitler refused to permit an all-out onslaught. The result was military stalemate. The population was gradually reduced by bombing, starvation, cold and disease. Estimates of the dead vary from half a million to a million. Quiet heroism and self-sacrifice were demonstrated abundantly. But the dominant fact is that the war leaders of both sides showed no mercy whatsoever for Leningrad's innocent civilians.[9]

The siege of 'Fortress Breslau' matched Leningrad in intensity if not in duration. It started in January 1945, when Hitler ordered a number of Silesian cities, including Oppeln, Glogau and Breslau, to be officially declared fortresses. The last gauleiter of Breslau then ordered all women, children, elderly and sick to leave immediately, but, despite a temperature of −20°C, failed to provide any transport. Tens of thousands perished in the trek through nocturnal blizzards to the nearest railhead. (The gauleiter flew out safely on the last plane, and was never seen again.) The garrison, however, was increased, especially by the Volkssturm and the Hitlerju-gend; a main boulevard was bulldozed to make a landing strip; and hundreds of thousands of slave workers – many of them survivors of the Warsaw Rising – were held back by the SS to strengthen the fortifications. The Red Army closed the circle round the city, blocking all supplies and reinforcements. But it made few strenuous attempts to storm it. Instead, it shelled Breslau incessantly, and killed the defenders slowly by a thousand cuts. Only a tenth or so remained when capitulation finally occurred on 8 May. By then Hitler had committed suicide, Berlin itself had fallen, and the Reich was only a few hours from extinction.[10]

Sieges are more usually conceived of as part of medieval as opposed to modern warfare. They cause extreme deprivation, outbreaks of plague, painful deaths from hunger and dehydration. They force people to eat grass, or cats and dogs, or their own dead children. Yet they happened in their most atrocious form in the mid-twentieth century.

Police states

No conventional definition of a 'police state' exists. But the term refers to a category of political regime in which the police, the security services and the special forces are authorized to bypass the normal procedures of the law. The Third Reich had moved into this category in 1934, when 'emergency powers' were introduced on the pretext of the Reichstag fire. The Soviet Union had been in the category from the start. The police and security apparatus – the NKVD – answered directly to the Politburo of the ruling Communist Party, whose 'leading role' was protected by the constitution to override all state institutions, including state law.

Nonetheless, several gradations of police state functioned in wartime Europe. Some operated in the Axis sphere, some in the Soviet sphere, and others in the slender ground for manoeuvre between them. What they had in common was the acceptance that the police, at the behest of the ruling circles, could exercise the power of life and death over the citizens. In addition to the Third Reich and the Soviet Union, three main types may be distinguished – client states, military Commissariats and the General Government.

Client states

Both the Third Reich and the USSR installed client regimes in countries which they conquered but which they did not wish either to annex or to destroy. The country remained technically independent, maintaining its own government and even its own diplomatic representation. However, the independence was a facade, rendered impotent by a limiting treaty, by continued occupation, by puppet rulers answering to the foreign master, or by all these things. Norway was a good example. Overrun by German forces in April 1940, it was subjected to a *Reichskommissar*, Josef Terboven, who first drove King Haakon into exile and then, after some delay, installed Vidkun Quisling (1887–1945) as *Ministerpresident*. Quisling was founder of the Fascist National Union Party, and had cultivated close relations with the Nazis since the early 1930s. A genuine admirer of Adolf Hitler, he was entirely dependent on German support behind the scenes. His name has passed into common usage as a term for a traitorous foreign puppet.[11]

Vichy France must be seen in the same light. Disarmed, bound by the terms of the armistice, and occupied by the German army – up to the Loire in 1940–42, and *in toto* thereafter – it had minimal room for manoeuvre. Its leader, Marshal Pétain, was a shadow of his former self, and the object of a phoney nationalist cult that was both laughable and shameful. Its paramilitary police force, the Milice Française, was organized under the leadership of the Gestapo by the Service d'Ordre Legionnaire, whose oath of allegiance ran, 'I swear to struggle against democracy, against de Gaulle and the Free French, and against the Jewish plague.' The Milice helped the Germans to combat the resistance, and to deport Jews. Their leader, Joseph Darnand (1897–1945) – a war hero of 1914–18 – was recruited as a POW, rose to be an officer of the Waffen SS, and died on the scaffold.[12]

Slovakia, Serbia and Croatia were Nazi client states from the start. Romania and Hungary were turned into such in 1944, when the preceding governments were overturned. Denmark had to believe Hitler's assurance not to interfere in its internal affairs, until in 1943 the Germans took over the country's administration wholesale.

In the first stage of the war, Stalin did not create client states. All the countries which he overran in 1939–41 were directly absorbed by the USSR. But in the political endgame of the war, in 1944–5, he was more circumspect. He did not install Soviet-style party states, preferring instead to rule through Committees of National Liberation, whose members were chosen not by their political biographies but by their willingness to obey Moscow's orders. The impression was created abroad that Poland or Hungary or Romania had been taken over by pro-Soviet patriots but not by Moscow's appointees. It was all very deceptive. All the armies of the post-war East European countries were run by Soviet officers. All the security services worked for the NKVD. And all the governments were bound by 'friendship treaties' that ensured Moscow's control. Full-blown Communist regimes were kept off the scene until 1948. Yet the reality did not change very much once the Red Army and the NKVD were in place. In Poland, for example, the unknown Bolesław Bierut, who appeared in 1944 in the baggage of the Red Army, and who played a prominent role as a 'non-party figure' in the Lublin Committee, turned out to be a Soviet employee formerly working for the Comintern. In 1948 he would be transformed overnight into the first secretary of the (Communist) United Polish Workers Party.[13]

Military commissariats

In various parts both of Western and Eastern Europe, the Nazis declined to rely on local clients, preferring to rule directly through German commissioners. The Netherlands was a case in point. Although a Dutch Nazi Party existed, and its leader, Anton Mussert (1894–1946), was eager to take control, he was passed over in favour of SS-Obergruppenführer Arthur Seyss-Inquart, who served as *Reichskommissar Nederlanden* throughout the war. The Nazis did not treat the Dutch with the same severity applied elsewhere, but they could not fail to notice their unpopularity. Their long-term aims of Germanizing the Dutch and of merging their country with Germany enjoyed virtually no support.[14]

In Belgium, a straightforward military regime was installed. The nominal head was General von Falkenhausen, but the chief administrator, Eggert Reeder, proved to be a wily operator. Reeder shared the interest of his Belgian subordinates, the *secrétaires-généraux* or 'prefects', to keep the SS at bay, and he kept his post until 1944. Fascist-style parties such as the Flemish Front (VNV), or Leon Degrelle's Rexist movement among the Walloons, inevitably gained prominence, but they were not permitted to govern.[15]

The Reichskommissariat Ostland was set up under Alfred Rosenberg in 1941. It consisted of the Baltic States and parts of occupied Russia, Byelorussia and Poland. It reflected the temporary nature of affairs pending the complete conquest of the USSR, which never happened. Although the Nazis viewed the Baltic peoples more favourably than the Slavs, they were unwilling to restore their independence or to grant them client status.

The Reichskommissariat Ukraine, established in 1941, was a very poor substitute for what most Ukrainians had wanted and expected. Its gauleiter, Erich Koch, was a particularly brutal Nazi, who once said, 'If I find a Ukrainian worthy of sitting at my table, I must have him shot.' The leaders of the Ukrainian national movement, who had lived in exile in Berlin since 1921, when the Bolsheviks had extinguished the independent Republic of Ukraine, hoped to be reinstated, but to no avail. Western Ukraine, with the city of L'viv (Lwów), was handed to the General Government of Poland (see below). The eastern districts, immediately adjacent to the Eastern Front, were left under the direct rule of the Wehrmacht. And Koch's *Kommissariat*, with its seat at Rivne (Równe), ran a regime that was probably the most exploitative in the whole of Europe.[16]

The General Government of Poland

The General Government in occupied Poland, with its mini-capital at Krakau (Kraków), fitted into the category neither of client state nor of military commissariat. It was part of the Greater Reich, but did not enjoy the blessings, even in theory, of German law. And, lying far to the west of the Eastern Front, it did not benefit from the moderating influence of a large Wehrmacht garrison (if such moderation can be imagined). Its governor general, Hans Frank (1900–1946), Hitler's former lawyer, was unusually clever and unusually unscrupulous. He declared that he was creating a colony, and that its people were to be 'slaves of the Reich'. What he meant, it transpired, was that an illiterate rump of Poles was to be kept alive as a pool of slave labour, whilst the educated Polish classes and the large Jewish community were to be liquidated. The General Government, in fact, was the racial laboratory of Nazidom. Known to the

helpless population as 'Gestapoland', or the kingdom of the SS, it was
ruled with unparalleled ferocity by fanatical Nazis, who felt they had a
limited time in which to put their fantasies into practice. It was the site of
the largest SS concentration and death camps, the main scene of the Jewish
Holocaust, and the repository of human misery on a scale unmatched
elsewhere in the Nazi or Soviet realms. Similar numbers of Jews and of
non-Jews were killed in the five and a half years of its existence. If ever a
method were discovered of calculating the quantities of innocent blood
spilled per hectare, this unhappy stretch of earth would hold the record.[17]

Not all police states use the same methods of policing or the same levels
of repression. But it is fair to say that the Nazi Gestapo/SS and the Soviet
NKVD were close rivals for the crown of repressiveness. And they had a
number of things in common. For a start, they regarded their own powers
as absolute, and the rights of individual citizens as negligible. They
conducted elaborate police screenings of the subject population, weeding
out undesirables, and issuing documents and passes that could be instantly
revoked. They had a passion for intensive interrogations, and a propensity
for torture. They filled the regular prisons so quickly that they were
obliged to build expanding networks of detention facilities where they
could hold and maltreat their clientele indefinitely. They could resort to
legal procedures or not, as they pleased, and they possessed powers of
summary execution. The Nazi police were given to public shows of
brutality: shooting suspects on the street, rounding up groups of hostages
for all to see, or beating out the brains of fugitive Jewish boys by swinging
them by the legs against a brick wall. The NKVD cultivated a more low-
key and more hypocritical style. They were specialists in silent arrests, in
the knock on the door before dawn, in forest massacres, and in the art of
sending their victims to places whence no one returned. The overall results
were much the same.

Illegitimate legality

The 'rule of law' is one of those great benefits of Western civilization for
which in 1939–45 many Britons and Americans thought that they were
fighting. Together with 'freedom' and 'democracy', it was supposedly one
of the things that we possessed and that the enemy didn't.

Reality, unfortunately, was rather different. Both Nazis and Stalinists were rather keen on laws and legality. Many top Nazis, like Hans Frank, were lawyers. Westerners forget that the 'rule of law' in itself means nothing. Laws passed by gangsters are likely to favour gangsterism. Laws passed by cannibals will punish vegetarianism. All laws depend on the underlying culture, and on the political system that controls them.

The Nazi approach to legality was to impose new layers of legal and judicial procedures on top of existing ones, and then to drive the whole system in their own interest. In democratic countries the police are subject to constitutional control and the judiciary is expected to be independent. But in Nazi Germany, with Himmler appointed as Reich commissar for state security, the police ran the courts and gave orders to the judiciary. After the introduction of emergency powers, summary military justice could be applied to the non-military sphere, and the so-called Volks-gerichtshof (VGH), or 'People's Court', was set up in April 1934 to try so-called political crimes. The VGH had no jury and allowed no appeal. It was presided over by Nazi Party judges, and passed 12,891 death sentences. Defendants who were released could simply be rearrested and, if the Gestapo so wished, sent to a concentration camp. In 1944 it tried the conspirators involved in the Bomb Plot against Hitler, after they had been released from military jurisdiction by a Court of Honour headed by Field Marshal von Rundstedt. In February 1945 the president of the VGH, Roland Freisler, was sitting in judgement over two women when a British bomb came through the ceiling and killed him. That, too, was a sort of justice – especially since the two women survived.[18]

In the USSR the concept of 'socialist justice' prevailed. As the saying went, it bore the same relationship to real justice as a chair does to an electric chair. For, like Nazi justice, it was totally politicized. The judges were appointed at all levels by the soviets or 'state councils', which in turn were run by the Communist Party. At the lowest level, the judges of the 'people's courts' (sic) were directly elected by popular suffrage, but, as in all Soviet elections, no one could register as a candidate without the Party's prior approval.

The NKVD was surprisingly keen to act through the legal system instead of by arbitrary whim. It knew that the law could be manipulated to obtain the desired effect. Stories abound of prisoners being tortured into signing their own death warrant, since the NKVD was reluctant to kill them without proof of the condemned person's consent. Judicial murder was a Soviet speciality. As the show trials of the 1930s had shown, defendants could be made to confess to almost anything, while state prosecutors could accuse them of fantastical crimes without fear of being gainsaid. (The Moscow Trial of June 1945, which put its seal on the Soviet conquest of Eastern Europe, used exactly the same methods).[19]

In that broad zone of Europe which for six years saw nothing publicly but Nazi law or Soviet law, the underground resistance had to choose whether to fight its oppressors by arbitrary violence or by legal sanctions of its own making. In many instances it chose the latter. The Polish Underground State, for example, possessed a secret but functioning judicial system. According to the rules of the Home Army, Gestapo agents or SS men could only be assassinated by warrant, whilst alleged collaborators were hauled before a secret three-man court that listened to testimony before passing judgement.

In other words, almost every system operates through laws and legal procedures. The eternal question turns on the issue of the system's legitimacy. At one time, laws were sanctioned by the Divine Right of Kings. In democracies they are justified by the will of the people as expressed through a constitution or through democratic institutions. Under the Nazi system they were dependent on the will of the Master Race, as embodied by its Führer. Under Soviet rule they derived from the iron rules of History as discovered by Marx and Lenin and as interpreted by Joseph Stalin.

Deportation

The forcible removal of individuals or of groups of people from their usual domicile – otherwise 'deportation' – was a very common feature of wartime Europe. It was mainly practised by the totalitarian regimes, but on rare occasions by the democracies. At least two instances arose in Great Britain – once to a village on the Dorsetshire coast, whose beaches were required for amphibious training, and once to a village on Salisbury Plain, which was used for tank exercises.[20]

The Nazi regime used deportation not merely for practical purposes such as clearing land destined for military training, but also for racist ideological purposes. Already in October 1939, for example, it cleared the port of Gdynia of its 100,000 Polish inhabitants and renamed it Goten-hafen.[21] Even before the war they had deported a similar number of Polish citizens from Germany, and in 1939–40, when the westernmost provinces of Poland were directly annexed to the Reich, they repeated the exercise. All the deportees in that wave were sent to the General Government, the Jews among them to the ghettos in Warsaw or Łódź. The Nazis did not like non-Germans living in Germany. French people were removed from Alsace, often to Algeria. Belgians were moved from Eupen and Malmédy. And Italians – German allies – were removed from the south Tyrol.

The Soviets, however, practised deportation on a far grander scale. For 'social engineering' was one of Stalin's specialities. In every country which the Red Army occupied, the NKVD would arrive with pre-prepared lists of 'undesirables', would screen the entire population, and would then deport the crowds of unwanted en masse. Their lists contained both individual names and categories of people to be removed. One such list which has survived from Lithuania mentions twenty-three categories. It starts with gamekeepers (who could protect fugitives in the forest) and ends with philatelists and Esperantists (who were notorious for sending secret communications abroad).[22] The deportees were removed either in accordance with a summary legal judgement or by administrative decree. The usual practice was to hand a formal judgement to known 'enemies of the people' – i.e. lawyers, teachers, priests, state employees and bourgeois politicians – and then to deport the person's entire family by decree. Deportees who had passed through a court and had been given a penal sentence – such as twenty-five years of hard labour for possessing a university degree – would be sent to the arctic camps of the GULag. Their dependants would be sent into 'free exile' in the wastes of Kazakhstan or the deserts of Central Asia. These measures, which were widely practised in 1939–41 and again in 1944–5, affected millions.[23]

Both Nazis and Soviets used deportation against specific ethnic groups. In November 1939, for instance, all Jews in the General Government were ordered to leave their homes and to take up residence in one of the designated 'ghettos'. There was relatively little coercion at that stage, and most Jewish families – and non-Jewish families with Jewish ancestors – simply acquiesced. The Gestapo registered all Jews individually, adding the moniker 'Israel' to men's names and 'Sarah' to those of the women. Not a few of those who simply stayed put avoided the subsequent oppression. In Warsaw alone, some 30,000 Jews survived outside the ghetto. The Soviets picked on other groups: Volga Germans, Tatars, Chechens and Ingush (see pp. 348–9).

By far the biggest waves of deportation occurred at the end of the war, in connection with the defeat of Germany. At the Potsdam Conference, by joint Allied decree, it was decided to expel all Germans living to the east of the Oder in Poland, in Czechoslovakia, Hungary and Romania. A total population of some 16 million was involved, though a considerable proportion had already fled before the decree was implemented. The source of the decision lay in the blank refusal of the USSR to hand back Polish, Czechoslovak, Hungarian and Romanian territory taken in 1939–40. Thanks to this refusal, millions of Poles and others had to be deported from their homes that were now in the USSR, and the Germans were deported to make room for the incomers.[24] The incoming Poles were cleverly named 'repatriants', whilst the outgoing Germans took the label of 'expellees'. But both groups were made to suffer for the same international problem. No doubt other factors were at play in the decision of 1945 to enforce the policy of German land and population transfers. But Soviet intransigence lay at the heart of it.

The concepts of deportation and expulsion are almost identical. Both imply compulsion and physical displacement. Both overlap with the concept of resettlement, in that all people being resettled have first to be deported from their homes. Deportation/expulsion focuses on experiences at the start of the journey. Resettlement focuses on the experiences which await at the destination. (See pp. 346–50)

Deportations were rarely associated with death sentences in the minds of their authors. But death was a frequent outcome. Little care was taken to provide for the welfare of deportees. Scores of men and women would be packed into closed cattle wagons without food, water or hygienic facilities. The sick and elderly would die even on the short journey from Germany to Poland, or from Poland or Czechoslovakia to Germany. And on the longer journeys between Europe and Central Asia or the Far East every Soviet deportation train carried hundreds of corpses – rock-hard frozen corpses in the winter; purulent, foul-smelling, disintegrating corpses in the summer. Deportees died slowly and agonizingly from hunger, thirst, disease or despair.[25]

Executions

Public sensitivity to executions was less refined during the war than during the post-war period. In a country like Britain, criminals were still executed for capital offences. And wartime traitors like William Joyce or John Amery were unceremoniously hanged. As is now known, Winston

Churchill proposed shooting the Nazi leaders as bandits, instead of putting them on trial. And King George, having objected to a winner of the Victoria Cross being stripped of his medal for a subsequent offence, ruled that the war hero/murderer should face the firing squad wearing his medal.[26] In the USA, some states have now abolished the death penalty, whilst others have not.

Nonetheless, executions of the sort that multiplied in occupied Europe make all such niceties pale into insignificance. The Nazis executed civilians as a matter of routine, and they did so without compunction, without restraint, and often with bestial cruelty. Firing squads were a luxury. In the war against partisans, they would execute villagers in reprisal wherever a German unit was attacked. In their struggle against the Polish resistance, they shot a hundred civilians in retaliation for every German killed. Indeed, German units would hold a hundred hostages in advance, publish their names on wall posters, then execute them in public 'as a lesson'. In Warsaw, in desperation, they took to capturing and shooting all the passers-by in a given street, or all the passengers in a train or tram. In Kraków in July 1943, in reprisal against suspected resistance activity, they buried all the menfolk of the parish of Wola Justowska in a pit and forced all the womenfolk to watch them die from suffocation.[27] In Yugoslavia, Nazi conduct was no better than in Poland or Byelorussia.

The Soviet NKVD, having shot up to a million people in the Great Terror of the 1930s, cannot be described as squeamish. In the Katyn massacres of 1940 they shot their 25,000 captives in cold blood, in daily batches. But shootings and public executions did not match their house style. Unlike the Nazis, they didn't like to appear cruel or oppressive. On the contrary, they pretended to be concerned about human progress and civilization. Generally speaking, they preferred to do their dirty work on the quiet, out of sight. But, when pressed, they rivalled the SS in brutality. They fought the non-Communist resistance movements with fury; they conducted reprisals; and they shot civilians. At the onset of Operation Barbarossa, when German forces stormed across the Soviet frontier, the NKVD executed all the inmates of all their prisons in the western regions.[28]

The difference between the SS and the NKVD in these matters may possibly have been the fruit of their ideological training. The SS were taught that the fault of their enemies lay in the blood, and was therefore irredeemable. Irredeemable enemies may as well be disposed of without delay. The NKVD, in contrast, were taught that enemies were obdurate because of social and economic conditioning. The fault lay in the mind, and if the counter-conditioning were strong enough, the fault might be reversed. So the duty of the guards of socialist truth was to educate, to reform, and to interrogate endlessly. Shooting people outright was a waste of salvageable lives.

Death by execution could be quick and virtually painless. Hanging was riskier than shooting, but neither was so aptly demonstrative as the guillotine, which was used in the Reich for civilian criminals. The condemned tended to cooperate, knowing that causing trouble could cause indescribable agonies.

Even so, executions sometimes went wrong. The firing squad could be drunk, having overdone the pre-duty tot, and could miss; or principled soldiers could fire high; or the officer be slow with the *coup de grâce*.

Of course, most of the war criminals who most deserved to be executed escaped scot-free. Of the Nazi leaders, a mere eleven were hanged following the Nuremberg Tribunal, and a further twenty-four were executed following US military tribunals. No war criminals other than Nazis were even considered for prosecution.

Nor should one assume that the British or American record was completely spotless. The biography of Robert Maxwell, for example, reveals that as a captain of the British Army, which entered German territory in the winter of 1944–5, he did not hesitate to shoot unarmed civilians. On 2 April 1945 he approached a German town, and proceeded to shell it with mortars. As related in a letter to his wife, to whom he had earlier admitted to 'taking no prisoners', he ordered the locals 'to fetch the mayor'. 'He turned up and I told him that the Germans had to surrender . . . or the town would be destroyed. One hour later he was back saying that the soldiers would surrender . . . but as soon as we marched off a German tank opened fire on us. Luckily he missed. So I shot the mayor and withdrew.'[29] Forty-six years later this incident led to a complaint from the public and to a police investigation under the War Crimes Act.[30]

Nonetheless, the village of Lidice near Prague in Bohemia remains the emblematic site of cold-blooded murder. Lidice was very obliquely implicated in harbouring a group of Czech resistance fighters sent from London to assassinate SS-Obergruppenführer Reinhard Heydrich. On 10 June the SS took their revenge. Sixty women were sent to the concentration camp at Ravensbrück. Eighty-eight children were sent for racial assessment – a few were deemed suitable for 'Aryanization'; the remainder were gassed. And 192 male villagers were executed by firing squad.[31]

Risings

One man's 'rising' is another man's uprising, rebellion, revolt or mutiny. Impartial commentators prefer to talk about an 'insurrection', although the modish term has become 'insurgency'. At all events, language is usually determined by a point of view. One may be sure that sympathizers with an insurrection will think of its authors as 'patriots' or 'freedom-fighters'. Their opponents, and those given the unpleasant task of suppressing an insurrection, automatically condemn the self-same people as 'bandits' or 'terrorists'.

In the Second World War, at least four major insurrections were recorded. All of them occurred in the later stages of the war, for time was needed for resentments to reach explosive proportions. And all of them were directed against German rule. If someone asks why no insurrections broke out against Soviet rule before the events in East Berlin in 1953 and in Budapest in 1956, one answer lies in the fact that the NKVD took elaborate precautions. The purpose of the mass deportations was political as well as social. They were designed, among other things, to render the idea of insurrection impossible.

The insurrection in the Warsaw Ghetto was launched in April 1943 as an act of defiance by those about to die. It had no chances of military success, but it destroyed forever the stereotype of Jews as a people unwilling to fight. Since the overwhelming consensus of post-war opinion admires the Jewish fighters, it is now called the Ghetto Uprising.[32]

The second insurrection in Warsaw broke out on 1 August 1944, and was the biggest act of resistance in the war (see pp. 119–20). Since it revealed Soviet conduct at its worst – in essence it was a belated example of de facto Nazi–Soviet cooperation – it was long condemned to oblivion by the post-war Communist regime. But it is now almost universally referred to as the Warsaw Rising (see also pp. 315, 316).

The insurrection in Paris in mid-August 1944 was a success, achieving exactly what the Warsaw Rising aimed at (see p. 315).

The insurrection in Slovakia in August–September 1944 was a complicated affair. It was started as a mutiny by Slovak officers serving under German command, then spread until it became a more generalized popular revolt. The Red Army heroically lost 70,000 men trying to cross the Dukla Pass into Slovakia in the kind of operation which it signally failed to undertake in an adjacent sector of the front before Warsaw. The insurrection was suppressed before help arrived.[33]

Risings/insurrections invariably wreak terrible damage on civilians. They can only hold out if the ill-armed fighters enjoy covert support from the general population. As a result, they invite reprisals, and the forces attempting to 'restore order' feel justified in attacking armed and unarmed insurgents alike. In the Ghetto Uprising, some 40,000 civilians were either killed on the spot or deported to the death camps. During and after the subsequent Warsaw Rising, up to 200,000 civilians were killed and up to 500,000 deported. In the Paris Rising, where the German commander was persuaded not to fight to a finish, civilian losses were kept to a minimum, i.e. to 1,500. In Slovakia they reached 5,000. Critics of the risings/insurrections use these figures, and the atrocious nature of civilian suffering, as ammunition for their criticism.

Random slaughter

Soldiers running amok have been known since time immemorial. Men whose trade is to kill each other can sometimes turn their weapons on passers-by through drunkenness, desperation or sheer depravity. The war of 1939–45 has its examples, like all the others.

The strange case of Oradour-sur-Glane has to be considered under this heading, for the atrocity had no clear motive. On 10 June 1944, when the SS panzer division 'Das Reich' was trying to make its way from southwest France to Normandy, one company of the 'Der Führer' regiment made a detour to the village of Oradour, rounded up the villagers, and then burned them alive. In all, 642 corpses were left, together with a string of charred, looted houses. The captain of the company was killed shortly afterwards in Normandy, so could never be interrogated. His men, mainly Alsatian conscripts, were prosecuted to no effect. So what was behind it? The division was massively frustrated, making slow progress through France owing to the constant sabotage and ambushes of the Maquis. A popular officer had been abducted the previous day. And arguments had been taking place about the division's looted gold holdings. It is quite possible that the men felt that they might soon be facing disciplinary hearings. But these facts by no means explain why one company and not others went briefly berserk.[34]

The killings that took place in August 1944 in the first week of the Warsaw Rising in the suburbs of Wola and Ochota are equally hard to understand, especially since they were nearly a hundred times more extensive than Oradour. The suburbs in question, on the western side of the city, had no military importance. They were filled with a mixture of factories, public buildings, hospitals and low-cost housing. But they happened to lie in the path of the SS Storm Group as it made its first drive from the German-controlled outskirts towards the insurgent-controlled centre. The two SS brigades concerned, those of Dirlewanger and Kaminsky, can hardly have been surprised to be fired on. But their reaction *was* surprising. Instead of engaging the Home Army units that were harassing them, they turned in fury on civilian non-combatants. In an orgy lasting five or six days, every manner of atrocity was perpetrated. A large crowd of men and women was driven into a churchyard and machine-gunned. Householders were dragged into the street to be butchered with sabres and bayonets. Pregnant women were drawn and quartered. Hospitals were invaded, and patients were mown down in their beds. Doctors and nurses who pleaded for relief were mutilated. Children were chopped to pieces. Streets and houses flowing with blood were then set alight. The number of victims is put at a figure between 40,000 and 50,000. A crazed mêlée of German convicts and Russian turncoats had joined forces to murder the largest number of Poles in as many ways as possible. Dante's *Inferno* contains no such scenes, and there is no convincing explanation for them.[35]

On the Soviet side of Europe, historians have to ponder the atrocious incident at Nemmersdorf. In October 1944 the advance guard of the Red Army's Baltic Front reached the frontier of East Prussia, and was poised to make the first incursion into German territory. On 21 October, however, a Soviet raiding party crept across the ill-guarded frontier, entered the nearest village, massacred the inhabitants, and withdrew. Two days later the German authorities discovered the remains of the victims, and photographs were taken. When news of the massacre reached Berlin, Goebbels's propaganda ministry decided to use the pictures as proof of Bolshevik savagery. The Nazi press seems to have thought that images of German women stripped and crucified on barn doors would strengthen the will of East Prussia to defend itself. They were mistaken. The population began to pack up and leave. And rumours arose that the massacre was the work not of the Bolsheviks but of the Nazis themselves.[36]

Partisans

Guerrilla warfare is as old as the hills. Its modern name derives from Spanish resistance to Napoleon's invading armies. But the tactics of hiding in the woods, of springing ambushes, of knifing sleeping soldiers in the night, of poisoning their supplies and of picking off stragglers were timeless. What is more, the marshes of Byelorussia, the forests of Poland and Ukraine, and the mountains of Greece and Yugoslavia were ideal settings in which to practise them. And there were lots of locals who were prepared to provide invaluable clandestine support.

The term 'partisan' derives from the Spanish Civil War of the 1930s. But it passed via the International Brigades into Russian usage, and it quickly gained a Communist colouring. It was adopted by the Soviet-supported resistance groups, and by Tito's movement in Yugoslavia. But neither the French Maquis, nor the Polish *Akowcy*, nor the Yugoslavian Chetniks would have dreamed of using it. The Germans used it only to denounce partisans as an obnoxious species of bandit.

Guerrilla-style fighting made little showing in the first phase of the war. But it gathered strength in 1942–3, not least because the Red Army made elaborate provisions to support it behind German lines. It became specially prevalent in Byelorussia, i.e. in eastern Poland, and, following Tito's long march to safety, in the mountains of western Bosnia.

Professional armies always stand at a disadvantage vis-à-vis guerrillas, if time cannot be spared to root them out thoroughly. Large numbers of soldiers must be employed if the necessary trawling operations through the countryside are to be effective. Increasingly stretched both on the Eastern Front and in lightly garrisoned Yugoslavia, the Germans could afford neither the men nor the resources. So they increasingly tried to make frightfulness compensate for military inefficiency. The main aim was so to decimate the local population that the partisan bands would be starved of food and cover. Villages were burned. Gallows lined the highways. And bloody reprisals became the order of the day.

Life in the woods, however, was far from idyllic. Communist partisans refused to cooperate with rival bands that were not controlled by Moscow, and different ethnic groups spawned conflicting movements. In Byelorussia, for instance, there were Soviet partisans, there were Jewish bands, there were representatives of the Polish underground, and there were common bandits. All of them preyed on the Germans, and most of them preyed on each other.

In Yugoslavia the picture was still more complicated. The initial anti-partisan campaigns had been launched by the Croat Ustashe, who fought both Tito and the Chetniks. But the Croats resented the Italian occupation forces, who had taken over Dalmatia. And the Germans increasingly mistrusted the Italians. 'Free-for-all' is an inadequate term for the resultant murderous chaos.

In Italy, partisan activity developed only after Mussolini's collapse in 1943. But it assumed impressive proportions in the north of the country. Unfortunately, it developed at a time and place where the Germans were well positioned to contest its growth. It involved 100,000 fighters, and its political fragmentation between Communists, democrats and Catholics was prevented from becoming total disintegration by General Cadorna and his coordinating committee. Even so, in the winter of 1944–5 the Germans were short neither of resources nor of the will to use them. In October 1944, when the SS panzer division 'Reichsführer-SS' moved into the Bologna district, it stopped at the village of Marzabotto and perpetrated a massacre three times the size of Oradour and ten times the size of Lidice. It was a warning of more to come. In the months when the British and Americans had halted for the winter, the Germans were free to employ three whole divisions, including the Cossack Brigade, in harrying the partisans and persecuting their infrastructure. Forty thousand were killed. The Communists, and others, said that British and American passivity was deliberate.[37]

SS-General von dem Bach-Zelewski was the Germans' chief specialist in anti-partisan warfare. His record in Byelorussia in 1943–4 was atrocious, and in the Warsaw Rising in 1944 no better. After volunteering to advise the US Army in 1945, he escaped prosecution.

Zoya Kosmodemyanskaya (1923–41), a partisan, was the first woman to gain the title of Hero of the Soviet Union. Only eighteen years old, she was still a student in Moscow when she volunteered for service. Crossing enemy lines not far from Moscow, she was captured by the Germans in the village of Petrischevo, interrogated, tortured and, on 29 November 1941, hanged. She is supposed to have said, 'There are 200 million of us. You can't hang us all.' Countless Soviet schools and collective farms, and two asteroids, were named after her.[38]

Civil war

Civil wars are not always called civil wars. But when people from the same state or nation engage each other in armed conflict, one may assume that something of the sort is in progress. Such was the case in 1939–45. Ethnic and political conflicts broke out in many places. Collaborating groups fought their rivals. Communists fought non-Communists.

Yugoslavia was undoubtedly the country where civil war became the most bitter and the most prolonged. Serbs fought Croats. Chetniks battled Tito. Separatists struggled with those who wished to restore a unified state. And the occupying powers stirred the pot by supplying arms to one side or the other. From 1943 onward, the main lines were drawn between the Serb-dominated Chetniks and Tito's partisans, who had toned down their Communist rhetoric and appealed to all Yugoslavia's nations. Tito twice evaded imminent capture by the Germans before setting up his HQ on the Dalmatian island of Vis, where he could receive supplies from the British in Italy. The Western Allies supported him because they believed that he was fighting hardest against Germany. They might have thought twice had they known that 60 per cent of the 1.7 million deaths were caused by Yugoslav fighting Yugoslav. In reality they didn't much care, so long as thirty-five German divisions stayed in Yugoslavia and made no sign of moving to Italy. Tito's revenge against his opponents at the end of the war can only be described as sadistic.[39]

The ending of occupation caused the violent settling of many wartime scores. In France, for example, the Milice had been fighting the Resistance throughout 1943–4, and the retreat of the Germans opened the way for a campaign of revenge. Special courts of justice condoned 10,800 executions, but the spontaneous *épuration* or purging of collaborators claimed many more victims, including women shaved and paraded through the streets. Marshal Pétain had to take refuge in Germany, before he returned for trial in July 1945.

Greece was another country where civil war flared as the German occupation ended. Greece's exiled government was royalist, and remained loyal to King George II. The Greek resistance movement, despite political differences, was overwhelmingly republican in sentiment. Fighting had broken out in the winter of 1943–4 between the two main branches of the resistance – EDES (the Greek League of National Republicans) and ELAS (the Greek People's Liberation Army). Yet a far more serious outbreak awaited, following the return of the government (but not the King) to Athens in October 1944. Unbeknown to the Greeks, Churchill had struck a deal with Stalin whereby Greece would remain in the British sphere of influence in return for Romania and Bulgaria remaining under Soviet control (see pp. 190–1). As a result, when the Communist-led political wing of ELAS called a general strike in December, British troops joined with the government and with EDES to suppress it. British air power proved critical in the trial of strength which continued for nearly two months. A flying visit to Athens by Churchill over Christmas brought no result. But a truce in January was followed by the Varkiza Agreement of 12 February 1945. The Prime Minister, Papandreou, was ousted. The King was obliged to appoint a regent. Police and administrators who had collaborated with the Germans were removed. ELAS was disarmed. A plebiscite was to be held on the future of the monarchy. And the Communist Party (KKE) was legalized.

Like all fraternal conflicts, the brief civil strife of 1944–5 was vicious. The British brought in Greek units from Italy, such as the Rimini Brigade and the commando-style Sacred Regiment, and, while Athens was secured, much of the countryside remained restless. Not surprisingly, the civil war reignited in 1946, and Greece was to remain bitterly divided until 1949. The only good news was that Stalin kept his distance.[40]

One must also recognize that the advance of the Red Army into Eastern Europe provoked a series of undeclared civil wars. In Poland, where the Communist resistance movement had been negligible, a Soviet-backed 'Liberation Committee' appeared in Lublin in July 1944 and prepared to assume power without reference to the legitimate government-in-exile in London. Its opponents declined at first to fight, and the wartime Home Army was disbanded in January 1945. Yet when the NKVD and its associates began to persecute anyone and everyone connected with the pre-war regime, serious fighting broke out. Some 40,000 men were killed in pitched campaigns between the Communist security forces (the KBW) and patriotic organizations such as Freedom and Independence (WiN). And an uneasy peace was not restored until the summer of 1947.[41]

Slave labour

All combatant countries in the Second World War took steps to control human resources, and industrial labour, like military conscription, was widely seen as a vital element of the war effort. Even democratic governments felt entitled to use compulsion. So one must be careful in defining the overused term 'slave labour'. One must also take account of the fact that the USSR had militarized its workforce in pre-war peacetime, and that the established Soviet conditions in spheres such as collectivized agriculture resembled a return to serfdom.

Compulsion in itself, therefore, does not provide an adequate basis for describing what slave labour involved. It was only one factor among many, including draconian discipline, poor diet and housing, lack of elementary hygiene, beatings, death sentences, minimal pay, restricted movement, life-threatening tasks, and, as often as not, deportation from the worker's home country. Concentration-camp inmates were but one category of slave labour. 'Forced labour' is a term that implies a lower level of maltreatment.

In Nazi Germany, the phenomenon developed slowly. Its first manifestation was the pre-war Todt Organization (OT), named after the constructor of the Autobahns, Fritz Todt (1892–1942), who was commissioned by Hitler in 1938 to build the fortifications of Germany's West Wall and whose name, by an appropriate coincidence, meant 'Mr Death'. Members of OT wore Nazi-style uniforms with swastika armbands, though they were neither soldiers nor employees of the Nazi Party. They were subsequently employed in the rear of all the Wehrmacht's campaigns, building fortifications, repairing roads and bridges, and clearing air-raid rubble. They also supplied the 'slave-drivers' who supervised a variety of lower categories such as ghetto work gangs, concentration-camp inmates and Soviet POWs. After Todt's accidental death, the organization was taken over by Albert Speer, under whom its complement of foreign workers expanded greatly. Its labour force was counted in millions, and its output of concrete in billions of cubic metres.[42]

The Reich's second major experience of forced labour grew out of the Poleneinsatz or 'Polish Employment Scheme' of 1939–40. Some 300,000 men from the pool of POWs captured in the September Campaign were sent to Germany to work in agriculture, and their number grew to at least a million within a year. Nazi authorities in the General Government also conducted regular manhunts, in which men, women and children were rounded up en masse in cinemas or even in churches and sent west as labourers. However, the influx worried the SS, who insisted that the Poles be separated from the German population and be housed in collective huts in special *Ostarbeiter* camps. The rules were strict. Like Jews in the ghettos, the workers had to wear an armband – in this case bearing the letter 'P'. They worked longer hours for lower pay, and were forbidden to enter German parks or public transport. Sexual intercourse between an 'East-worker' and a German citizen was punishable by death.

The absorption both of the Polish *Ostarbeiter* and of French prisoners was still in progress in 1941, when Germany attacked the USSR, and it may be that the very success of the scheme (from the Nazis' viewpoint) underlay the decision not to use the next big wave of potential workers – from among the Soviet POWs caught during Barbarossa. At all events, it was 1942 before the Reich returned to the recruitment of forced workers, Hitler appointing the ghastly Fritz Sauckel (1894–1946) as 'Plenipotentiary for Employment'. In the next three years Sauckel extracted 5.3 million workers from the occupied countries, raising the level of foreigners in the Reich's labour pool to 20 per cent.

Not surprisingly, as the Reich's predicament worsened, the treatment of its slave labourers deteriorated, too. The SS dreamed up a brilliant scheme for leasing concentration-camp inmates to private firms. But German employers complained that their underfed employees were neither strong nor skilled. Amazingly, the SS also complained that its valuable workforce was shrinking. Some 25,000 workers had died in the construction of the IG Farben factory at Auschwitz alone. In desperation, the SS Wirtschaft und Verwaltungshauptamt dropped earlier plans to kill all Jews outright, and began releasing Jewish work gangs alongside others. The construction of underground rocket sites was particularly labour-intensive – and, for the workers, lethal.

Forced labour in the Reich was directed mainly to farming, mining, metallurgy, chemicals, building and transport, and seven nationalities bore the brunt of the system:

Forced labour in the Reich			
Soviets	2,406,895	Czechs	177,679
Poles	1,440,254	Belgians	177,451
French	954,966	Dutch	174,358
Italians	486,326	*Total*	*5,817,929*

Of these, 4,375,882 – or 75 per cent – were civilians.[43]

Of the 600,000 workers loaned out by the SS, some 140,000 were assigned in 1944 to underground projects, 130,000 to the Todt Organization, and 230,000 to private industry. The very precision of these figures is curious.[44] So, too, is the fact that historians make little attempt to estimate the death rate amongst these workers, other than to say that it was 'enormous',[45] or that for many 'work was synonymous with extermination'. One is left wondering how much is 'enormous'. One-quarter of 5.8 million would come to 1.45 million; one-third to 1.93 million; one-half to 2.9 million. Most instructive of all is the fact that no historian to date has thought of comparing the conditions and statistics for forced labour in the Reich with those for forced labour in the USSR. Given that the USSR was considerably larger than the Reich, one can be fairly confident of a 'general but very guarded statement' to the effect that the relevant Soviet figures would be 'more enormous' than 'enormous'.

Child-stealing

As racialist fundamentalists, the Nazis were deeply interested in children, in what they called 'the blood pool' and in human reproduction. The most important aspect of their mission was to 'purify' the blood pool by eliminating poisoned elements and multiplying healthy ones.

In October 1939, when Himmler toured conquered Poland in his special train *Heinrich*, he noticed that the local children in the northern districts contained a high proportion of the tall, blond, blue-eyed 'Aryan' types which the Nazis so admired. He concluded that they were Polonized Germans, and he set his mind on stealing them. Historians have written much about Nazi attitudes to groups whom the Nazis hated. Much less is known about the fate of human beings to whom the Nazis took a liking and whose 'blood' they coveted.

The scheme was activated in 1940, and continued for at least three years. It was run by women auxiliaries of the Nazi Party, and consisted of three successive operations – capture, testing and delivery. To begin with, the child-snatchers toured orphanages and took the desired individuals away. Later they would simply kidnap them on the streets or in the villages. After that, the children were taken to racial testing stations, where they were stripped, examined and measured by Nazi scientists. In the final stages the children judged unsuitable for Germanization were discarded. The others were sent to one of several *Kinderlager* or 'child camps', such as the one at Brockau near Breslau, then delivered to the SS Lebensborn organization in Germany.

Lebensborn, meaning 'Fountain of Life', specialized in the theory and practice of human reproduction. It is often thought to have been a hedonistic organization that ran brothels and pleasure homes for SS men. In fact it was planning in all seriousness the improved human bloodstock of the future, and sexual intercourse between racially approved men and carefully selected young women was an essential part of the programme. Mature girls from among the kidnapped children were put at Lebensborn's disposal. All the other boys and girls were assigned to German adoption agencies, disappearing into the mass of Germany's population.[46]

The workings of the operation were discovered after the war from the testimonies of those few victims who had been old enough to remember a Polish childhood, for they had all been given new names and false biographies. What is more, the Allied administration in post-war Germany ruled that, in the children's interest, their cases should not normally be reopened. Only a small percentage ever returned. Numbers are also hard to determine. Tens of thousands, at the very least, were delivered to Germany. How many were kidnapped in the first place cannot be established.[47]

The worst horror in this horrendous story concerns the fate of the discarded children. Some, it seems, were sent back to their orphanages. Some were summarily killed. And some were packed off to concentration camps. The episode is mind-numbing. But one thought occurs. If the Nazis could go in for child-stealing in one occupied country, they could equally have done it elsewhere. Perhaps they didn't have time.

Concentration camps

No term conjures up more horror in the modern imagination than 'concentration camp'. Such are the negative emotions surrounding it that few people realize either that such camps were not a Nazi invention or that the Second World War witnessed only one stage in a long chain of development.

The early origins are easily dealt with. The concept of *campos de reconcentración* was first put into practice by the Spanish administration of Cuba in the 1890s. It was designed to separate rebellious peasants from their lands, and hence from their source of livelihood. It was then taken up by the British during the Boer War in South Africa, with similar purposes in mind. The British used the term 'concentration camp' for the detention centres of interned Boer civilians.

The German language received the calque of *Konzentrationslager* in 1905. It was first used in the colony of German South-West Africa, where a hostile tribe of Hereros were forced into work camps and where Dr Heinrich Göring was the commissioner. Dr Göring's colleagues carried out medical experiments on the Herero in the interests of racial research. His son Hermann was to introduce similar practices into Germany thirty years later. 'It can be argued, therefore, that the corrupting experiences of some European colonists helped pave the way for the European totalitarianism of the 20th century.'[48]

In 1914, when all 'enemy aliens' in Britain were temporarily interned, another 'concentration camp' was opened at Douglas on the Isle of Man. It was located in the buildings of a holiday camp.

Totalitarian regimes were certainly attracted to the concept, and introduced a more distinctly punitive element. Soviet Russia was the first, having the precedent of the tsarist empire's penal system to stimulate thought. Trotsky, who was familiar with the Boer War, used the term *kontslager* in June 1918 in relation to some unruly Czech POWs. Lenin used it in August 1918 in relation to the suppression of an anti-Bolshevik rising. And it was formally included in the decree of 5 September 1918, which launched the Red Terror against the Bolsheviks' enemies and which specifically called for their 'isolation in concentration camps'.[49] The implementation of the Terror was entrusted to the 'Extraordinary Commission for Combating Counter-Revolution and Sabtoage', the Cheka, an organization that had no link to the Soviet government, being directly subordinated to the Communist Party and absolved from all pretence of legality. By the end of 1919, Soviet Russia possessed twenty-one registered camps in addition to the regular network of work camps run by the Ministry of Justice. The GULag, the 'State Administration of Camps', was created in 1920. By the end of that year, it had 107 camps to run. From then on, its history was continuous.

Nazi Germany opened its first concentration camp at Dachau, in Bavaria, in March 1933. A year later, the SS took over control of the camps from the SA. Himmler, head of the SS, appointed the first commandant of Dachau, Theodor Eicke, as inspector-general of concentration camps. Eicke closed most of the small SA camps, standardized practice, and formed the SS Death's Head organization to act as camp guards. By 1935 there were five camps, with a total of 3,500 prisoners. This number rose tenfold in late 1938, following the events of Kristallnacht, but it fell again by April 1939 to 21,000. The German historian Ernst Nolte has found himself in hot water for stating that the Nazis benefited from Soviet practice.[50] Nonetheless, it is incontrovertible that the Soviet camps came first, that the German camps came second, and that the Soviet system was much larger than its German counterpart.

Mere names and numbers can be misleading, however. It is more important to define functions and to describe conditions. Here, two comments are required. Firstly, the Soviet and the Nazi German camps were *not* exactly the same. Each of the systems was conditioned by the social, economic, cultural and ideological realities of the countries where they functioned. Secondly, despite the differences, the two systems had much in common. As the Pulitzer Prize-winner Anne Applebaum puts it, 'they were related'; 'They were constructed to incarcerate people not for what they had done, but for who they were'; they 'belong to the same intellectual and historical tradition'.[51] And further:

> The notion that some types of people are superior to other types of people was common enough in Europe at the beginning of the twentieth century. And this, finally, is what links the camps of the Soviet Union and those of Nazi Germany in the most profound sense of all: both regimes legitimized themselves, in part, by establishing categories of 'enemies' or 'sub-humans' whom they persecuted and destroyed on a mass scale.[52]

What is more, herein lies the central paradox of the Second World War in Europe. The two principal combatant states, which fought a series of campaigns of unparalleled ferocity, were both engaged in systems of internal repression of unparalleled inhumanity. The balance sheet between them is hard to establish. Some historians emphasize the commonalities; others emphasize the differences.

Leaving aside a miscellaneous assortment of transit camps, feeder camps, processing stations and interrogation centres, five main types of camp may be distinguished during the Second World War:

- the POW camp designed to hold military prisoners in accordance with the Geneva conventions (see p. 269) and administered by the regular armed forces;
- POW camps not designed to conform with the Geneva conventions;
- the work camp, as provided in the Reich for East-workers, and administered by the State Labour Office;

- the concentration camp, as administered by the Soviet GULag or the Nazi SS;
- the death camp, as introduced by SS for no other purpose than killing people as rapidly as possible.

For the sake of precision, it is very important to separate concentration camps such as Dachau, Belsen or Sachsenhausen from the Nazi death camps such as Treblinka, Bełżec and Sobibór. The former may be defined as penal work camps of the harshest regime, from which, as a rule, there was no release and where inmates met death on a massive scale. The SS defined them as places of 'protective custody', meaning that they kept prisoners in custody in order to protect society. The death camps made no provision for work or for housing. Their facilities were limited to reception areas, temporary accommodation, gas chambers and crematoria. They belong exclusively to the Holocaust (see below).

A typical Nazi concentration camp like Dachau consisted of five departments: Department I was taken up by the commandant's staff, Department II by the Political Office, run by the Gestapo, Department III by the SS officers responsible for discipline and work schedules, Department IV by the camp administration, and Department V by the medical station. The SS Death's Head guards answered from 1940 to the Waffen SS, who put suitable contingents at the commandant's disposal.

The camp complex at Auschwitz – which is the German name for the Polish town of Oświęcim – was neither a typical concentration camp nor a typical death camp. It was a hybrid. For one thing, it consisted of three separate camps. Auschwitz I was a relatively small concentration camp created in 1940 for Polish prisoners. Auschwitz II–Birkenau was much larger, and was capable of housing up to 60,000 prisoners at any one time. Auschwitz III–Monowitz was essentially a work camp attached to the adjacent chemical factory. None of these camps was primarily intended to house Jewish prisoners. The inmates consisted of men and women of many nationalities, the great majority of them innocent of any offence. They were subjected to extremes of brutality and deprivation. Many died from overwork and exhaustion. Some 40,000 were shot at the 'wall of death' for minor disciplinary incidents. And another large group was forced to undergo lethal pseudo-medical experiments. In December 1944, when the winter offensive of the Red Army was awaited, the SS dynamited the main installation, and drove some 60,000 prisoners on a 'march of death' to other camps deeper in the Reich. The present estimate of deaths among prisoners stands at 450,000.[53]

From 1942 to late 1944, however, the gas chambers and the main crematoria which lay outside the main gate at Auschwitz II were used by the SS as a major extermination centre for Jews condemned by the 'Final Solution' (see pp. 359–64). The selection of Jews for extermination was made on 'the ramp', the railway platform outside the entrance gate, whence some 900,000 walked directly to their deaths. Only a small minority of Jewish arrivals – around 20 per cent – were selected for labour. If they were, they then joined the non-Jewish prisoners inside the camp.

A dozen principal SS concentration camps were operating in the years 1934 to 1945. They were, in the sequence of their organization.

1934	Dachau (near Munich)
1936	Sachsenhausen (near Berlin)
1937	Buchenwald (near Weimar)
1938	Mauthausen (near Linz, Austria)
1938	Flossenbürg (Bavaria)
1939	Ravensbrück, for women (north of Berlin)
1939	Neuengamme (near Hamburg)
1940	Auschwitz I (General Government)
1941	Auschwitz II–Birkenau
1941	Stutthof (near Danzig)
1941	Gross Rosen (near Breslau)
1941	Natzweiler (Alsace)
1941	Majdanek (General Government)
1942	Auschwitz III–Monowitz
1943	Bergen-Belsen (near Hanover)

All these camps were run by the SS Death's Head formations, under their chief inspector Theodor Eicke, who was succeeded in 1943 by Richard Glücks. Placements and occasional releases were handled by the Gestapo. The whole system was subject to the SS Chief Security Office in Berlin, and to the Reichsführer-SS, Heinrich Himmler.

The Soviet GULag system exceeded its German counterpart many times over. It operated for more than twice as long. It contained far more camps, scattered over a much vaster area. And its inmates, the zeks, outnumbered their KL fellows by five or ten to one. The whole was supervised by the Camp Directorate of the NKVD, and, from 1939, by the NKVD Chief, Lavrentii Beria.

Mythology holds that the worst Stalinist practices had ended before the war began. This is no more than partly true. The Great Terror was curtailed in 1939, together with the era of random shootings. Yet the decline of one form of terror encouraged the rise or the revival of others. In many ways the GULag staged a revival both in 1939–41 and in 1944, owing to the sheer numbers of new populations that the NKVD processed. 'Death rates doubled in 1941 and quintupled in 1942 over the previous period.' Apart from that, the GULag had been steadily evolving since its foundation in 1917, and specialists in the subject regard the early war years as the point when its organization crystallized for the duration:

> It might be said ... that by the end of the [1930s] the Soviet concentration camps had attained what was to be their permanent form. They had penetrated ... nearly every region of the Soviet Union, all twelve time zones, and most of its republics ... They were now no longer a group of idiosyncratically run work sites, but rather a full-fledged 'camp–industrial complex', with internal rules and habitual practices, special distribution systems and hierarchies. A vast bureaucracy, also with its own particular culture, ruled the GULag's far-flung empire ... The era of trials and experiments was over. The system was now in place. The group of procedures which prisoners called 'the meat grinder' – the methods of arrest, interrogation, transport, food and work – were, at the start of the '40s, set in stone. In essence, these would change very little until Stalin's death.[54]

The most extensive 'encyclopedia' of the GULag identifies five principal periods of its development:

- to 1922 – the chaotic period of the Civil War;
- 1923–29 – decentralization under the Chief Board of Places of Detention (GUMZ);
- 1930–40 – the integration of the Chief Board of Camps (GULag) into the planned economy of the USSR (the cryptonym ULag, later GULag, derived from a decree of 25 April 1930);
- 1940–53 – a period of increased emphasis on productivity, marked initially by the separation of the security apparatus

NKVB and SMERSH from the National Commissariat of
Internal Affairs.[55]

The same guidebook identifies 36 administrative divisions of the GULag,
and 476 principal camps dependent on the central organization. Many of
the camps were dedicated to particular short-term projects, such as the
working of a quarry or the building of a road, and they functioned for
only two or three years. Others were in full operation for decades, and
were kept going by dozens of smaller feeder camps. One of the oldest
centres was located on the Solovietsky Islands in the Bay of Murmansk,
where a special forced-labour camp for up to 70,000 inmates had operated
from 1923 to 1932. The establishment was then moved to the nearby
Karelian ASSR, where the 'Bielbaltlag' toiled until 1941 in a vain effort to
build a viable canal between the White Sea and the Baltic Sea. During the
Second World War, the names of a score of major camps scattered the
length and breadth of the USSR spread fear and trembling. They were
places from which few returned. As one entered, one passed under an
archway adorned with a Russian slogan, like 'Trudom Domoi' – 'Back
home, through work' – or 'Work is a matter of honour and glory'. These
express the exact same cynical sentiments as 'Arbeit Macht Frei'.

The extraordinary precision of the official inmate numbers is misleading, not to say incredible. The key statistics for the GULag were not the
totals at any given date, but the average death rate and the overall through-
put. Official records from the NKVD suggest that the global total never
exceeded 2.5 million at any one time. The information in the table on
p. 332, is not adequate to indicate what was really happening.

Even so, now that the GULag archives are open, many fascinating
details are being gleaned from the records. The Norilstroy camp, for
example, which lay near the mouth of the Yenisei in northern Siberia, was
categorized as an ITL or 'corrective labour camp'. Apart from building a
town in the wilderness, the zeks built a copper–nickel combine, an iron-
ore mine, an electrolite cobalt factory, an aqueduct to bring water from
the river, a port and a shipyard. They also renovated the cabin in the
village of Kureyka where Stalin had once been exiled. Three of the first
four commandants were successively arrested during the Terror. And
nearly 40 per cent of the early intakes were there for 'counter-revolutionary crimes'. The climate, both physical and political, was surreal.[56]

The story of the 'Dalstroy' also deserves to be told, because it was
probably the largest concentration camp in world history, and because it

reached its apogee during the war years. It consisted of hundreds of mining settlements strung out along the Kolyma River in north-east Siberia along the 1,064-km trail that led from Magadan on the Pacific to the port of Ambartchik on the Arctic Ocean. It could only be reached by a small fleet of slave ships – the *Dzurma*, *Soulatvia*, *Dalstroy* and *Decabrist* – each carrying up to 12,000 prisoners on the twelve-day trip from Vladivostok to the Sevost base camp at Magadan. Created in 1932, it worked for the Central Soviet Gold Monopoly, and in 1937–42 it was subjected to the semi-autonomous Administration of the North-East Corrective Labour Force (USVITL). Mortality reached 30 per cent in the first year of imprisonment, and over 90 per cent in the second. The peak years were 1941 and 1942. From one known group of 12,000 Poles sent there in 1940, only 583 (including the future president Ryszard Kaczorowski) were still alive to benefit from the amnesty of 1941. According to Robert Conquest, 3 million lives were lost. Gold production rose to 400–500 tonnes p.a. – roughly 1 kg per human life. After the US vice-president Henry Wallace was sent on a three-day fact-finding mission to Kolyma in August 1944, he returned with the conviction that 'no such camps exist'.[57]

If historians of forced labour can write that 'work was a synonym for extermination', similar judgements can be made about concentration camps. Conditions were inhuman. Food was deliberately kept at starvation levels. Medical care was minimal. Brutal guards kept order through beatings and shootings. Work norms were fixed at a level beyond the ability of exhausted workers. Minor infringements were punished by humiliating rituals or by reduction of rations. The fifty Nazi camps were further plagued by the prevalence of pseudo-medical experiments. Soviet camps were afflicted by extremes of weather that could see the thermometer drop in Vorkuta to −40°C or in Kolyma (near the coldest point on the globe) to −60°C. Nazi camps were enclosed by barbed wire and watchtowers. Many Soviet camps were left open. Zeks were retained by the invisible fence of knowing that the pains of staying might not be so bad as the pains of being eaten by bears, or wolves, or in the summer by midge clouds.

The camps consumed men and women of all nationalities. If one leaves Jewish victims aside for the overlapping category of genocide (see below), the largest cohorts in the Nazi camps would be Poles, Russians and Ukrainians. In the Soviet camps they would be Russians, Ukrainians

Camps of the GULag: a selection[58]

Name of camp	Location	Years of operation	Maximum registered inmates	Work schedule
Dolnoamurski	Amur River, Far East	1939–55	65,056 (1943)	Railway, pipeline construction
Dzhydynlag	Buryat-Mongol ASSR	1941–9	9,693 (1945)	Metallurgy
Ivdyelag	Sverdlovsk, Urals	1937–60	30,203 (1941)	Chemical works
Karlag	Karaganda, Kazakhstan	1939–59	65,673 (1949)	Agriculture
Kargopolski	Archangelsk	1937–60	30,069 (1939)	Timber, paper
Kraslag	Krasnoyarsk, Siberia	1938–60	30,546 (1953)	Timber
Privolzhlag	Saratov	1942–7	7,000 (1942)	Saratov–Stalingrad railway
Norilstroj	Norilsk, N. Siberia	1935–56	68,849 (1952)	Building the town of Norilsk
Yuzhlag	Buryat-Mongol ASSR	1938–45	12,558 (1941)	BAM – railway line
Piechorlag	Pechora, Komi ASSR	1940–50	102,354 (1942)	Kotlas–Vorkuta railway
Severurallag	N. Urals	1938–60	33,757 (1942)	Timber, paper
Sevostlag	Magadan, Far East	1932–52	190,309 (1940)	Servicing Dalstroy camp complex
Sevzheldorlag	Komi ASSR	1938–50	84,893 (1941)	Kotlas–Vorkuta railway
Sryedniebyellag	Amur River, Far East	1939–49	5,741 (1941)	Sryedni–Byelaya railway
Stalingradski	Stalingrad	1942–53	7,183 (1953)	Evacuated to Privolzhlag
Siblag	Novosibirsk	1929–60	70,370 (1942)	Regional workforce
Sazlag	Tashkent	1930–43	34,240 (1939)	Cotton-picking

			Maximum	
		Years of	*registered*	
Name of camp	*Location*	*operation*	*inmates*	*Work schedule*

Camps of the GULag (*cont.*)

Name of camp	Location	Years of operation	Maximum registered inmates	Work schedule
Tagilstroy	Urals	1942–53	43,423 *(1943)*	Steelworks construction
Tyemlag	Mordvin ASSR, Volga	1931–48	22,821 *(1939)*	Local products
Uchtizemlag	Komi ASSR	1938–55	39,087 *(1941)*	Oil and gas production
Unzhlag	Gorkii	1938–60	27,278 *(1941)*	Firewood for Moscow
Usollag	Solikamsk	1938–60	37,111 *(1942)*	Timber
Ustvymlag	Komi ASSR	1937–60	24,256 *(1943)*	Timber
Vyatlag	Kirov oblast	1938–60	28,643 *(1942)*	Timber
Vladlag	Vladivostok	1939–43	56,033 *(1940)*	Fish-processing
Vorkutlag	Vorkuta, Komi ASSR	1938–60	72,940 *(1952)*	Coal-mining
Vostlag	Amur River	1938–40	21,880 *(1940)*	Komsomolsk Railway line

and Poles. But all nationalities were present. There was a Scottish woman who died in Auschwitz (see below), and a number of British and American people perished in the GULag.[59]

Neither the SS nor the NKVD kept accurate records of the numbers of people that they drove to death in their concentration camps. The German figures are surprisingly low – around 450,000 registered deaths, or more probably 'a number exceeding 600,000'.[60] Estimates for the Soviet camps vary enormously, but are clearly much higher. According to Robert Conquest, they averaged 1 million per annum, or a total of 6 million for 1939–45.[61] Solzhenitsyn, a professional mathematician as well as a zek, calculated from his own observations that 1 per cent of the camp inmates perished every day. Applied to the overall GULag population, his sum would work out at 100,000 daily, or 36.5 million annually. He obviously made a mistake somewhere. But it is a good indication of the staggering figures that are discussed. A more recent estimate puts the death rate in the Nazi camps at 40 per cent, compared with 14 per cent (of a much higher number) in the GULag.[62]

Occasionally someone dares to ask, 'Which were worst, the Nazi or the Soviet camps?' There was not much to choose between them. Survivors of one system cannot imagine another system that might compare. In theory the Soviet camp inmates were serving set sentences, which gave them a distant hope of release, whereas the inmates of the Nazi camps were told unambiguously, 'You will work till you drop' or 'The only way out is up the chimney.' In practice, the Soviet sentences usually proved to be a fiction. They were far longer than the average expectation of life, and could be extended or reimposed without redress. A small number of individuals are known to have been officially released from the Nazi camps, usually through outside intervention at a high level. A much larger number of Soviet zeks survived, like Alexander Solzhenitsyn, only to be sent from the camps to places of administrative exile. The main difference lay in the fact that the Nazi camp system was interrupted after only a few years by the collapse of the Reich, while the Soviet system continued to operate throughout the post-war decades. Another difference derived from the climate. The challenge of survival was significantly harsher in the Arctic region or in 'the Pole of Cold' in Siberia, known as 'Stalin's Death Ring', where one faced six or seven months of winter, including two or three months of total darkness, and temperatures which could literally freeze the eyeballs. (The all-time low temperature of $-68°C$, i.e. almost 125° of frost on the Fahrenheit scale, was once recorded at Verkhoyańsk, not far from Kolyma.) Apart from that, the camp experience was much the same: hunger, cold, filth, back-breaking work, sadistic guards, beatings, exposure, debilitation, despair, disease, depression and daily death.

Most people who perished in the concentration camps perished anonymously. But the contrasting fate of two people, both captured in Budapest, is instructive. Jane Haining (1898–1944) was a Christian missionary from Glasgow, working among orphans for the Jewish Mission of the Church of Scotland. When Budapest was occupied by German troops in March 1944, she was ordered to leave. And when she failed to obey she was arrested, transported to Auschwitz and gassed. Raoul Wallenberg (b. 1912) was a Swedish businessman and diplomat, who joined the Swedish legation in Budapest in June 1944. His energies were directed to protecting Jews threatened by the Nazis with deportation, placing them in 'safe houses' or giving them diplomatic passes. He is credited with saving up to 100,000 people. He was last seen in January 1945 during the siege of Budapest, accompanied by a Soviet officer, who was apparently taking him into custody.

Jane Haining's family duly received an official death certificate, which had been issued by the Gestapo in Auschwitz and which falsely cited death from 'cachexia'. Raoul Wallenberg simply disappeared. Soviet sources claimed unconvincingly that he had died in the Lubyanka from a heart attack in 1947. But numerous later sightings of him in the GULag suggested that he could have survived. An international commission, which convened in 2001 to discuss his fate, reached no conclusion.[63]

Contrary to popular opinion, considerable numbers of people had the misfortune to suffer in both German and Soviet camps. At the end of the war, for example, it was normal practice for the NKVD to rearrest East Europeans who had survived incarceration by the SS. Such unfortunates, in the eyes of Soviet officialdom, had been contaminated; most would never be seen again.

Yet one can also find individuals who served time in the GULag first and in a Nazi concentration camp second. Margarete Buber-Neumann (1901–89) was one of them. She was the widow of a German Communist who had fled the Third Reich only to fall victim to the terror in the USSR. She had spent two or three years in the GULag before being caught in 1940 in one of the Nazi–Soviet exchanges of prisoners. She remained for the rest of the war in Ravensbrück.[64]

Buber-Neumann's story came to light in 1949 when she was brought in as a witness to a libel trial in Paris. It was used to verify some of the basic facts contained in a book written by an early Soviet defector, Victor Kravchenko,[65] who had reported on the Ukrainian Famine, on the Great Terror and on the GULag. Thanks to her evidence, Kravchenko successfully sued a French magazine had had called his account 'a pack of lies'. But his damages were minimal. And the case failed to dint the mindless admiration of the Soviet system that still prevailed in many circles. Even at the start of the Cold War, most people did not wish to hear unpalatable truths.

Western commentators fight shy of discussing the concentration camps as an integrated phenomenon. They know that it is a shameful subject, and since the USSR was an Allied power they prefer to avoid invidious comparisons. If they write about the GULag at all, they do so in a closed compartment. The habit is improper. A concentration camp was a concentration camp whoever ran it – friend or foe.

Prisons

All countries maintain prisons to detain criminals. And in the mid-twentieth century death sentences for capital offences were the norm in most European countries. So incarceration and death in prison were not in themselves subjects for outraged comment.

Yet the state of affairs in the totalitarian countries *does* require a word of explanation. For under regimes where concentration camps had assumed the role of parallel detention systems, the function of prisons changed significantly. Prisons were now used mainly either as interrogation centres or as holding stations for persons awaiting trial. In the hands of the Gestapo or the NKVD, they became places of intensive terror. Suspects would be brought in not just for questioning but for extended interrogation over weeks and months, when beatings, torture and inhuman humiliations were routine. Summary trials were often organized on the spot, and summary executions were regularly carried out in prison basements. Transfer to a concentration camp could be seen as an act of (temporary) mercy.

A comparative study of Nazi and Soviet interrogation techniques would be very worthwhile. The Gestapo and the SS had a well-deserved reputation for needless brutality – for ranting and raving, for the pulling of fingernails and the breaking of limbs. The NKVD relied more on persistence and on mental torture. They invariably interrogated their victims in the middle of the night, and aimed to break their resistance through psychological confusion, sleep deprivation, relays of questioners, or incarceration in icy flooded cells. But they, too, had no compunction about murder.[66] See 'Prisoners' below, pp. 410–12.

All the cities of occupied Europe, therefore, were subjected to a similar pattern of totalitarian policing. A security centre would be established, such as the Gestapo HQ on the Prinz Albrecht Strasse in Berlin, or the NKVD's Lubyanka prison in Moscow. From there, a series of departments would run all manner of operations, from political intelligence and action against local crime to state security and informer networks. Each centre would have its cells for special prisoners, its interrogation rooms, and its basements for 'special duties'. Each of the city's jails, like the Moabit or the Butyrka, would then be turned into a subsidiary of the centre, dealing with the constant flow of suspects, interrogees and convicts. Most of the jails' clients would never see a regular court. Most of the individuals

Dominant war leaders

After 1942, the leaders of the Allied Coalition adopted the policy of unconditional surrender, so negotiations between the warring parties never took place.

Above. The 'Big Three' at Yalta, February 1945. Churchill, Roosevelt and Stalin met together on only two occasions.

Below. Hitler reviews his last troops, April 1945.

Mass deportation

was practised by all totalitarian regimes. Tens of millions were forcibly removed, millions perished.

Above. Exiled women and children sent to Kazakhstan from eastern Poland, 1940. The NKVD routinely seized the families of all 'enemies of the people'.

Below. A German peasant family from Bessarabia resettled by the SS, 1942 or 1943.

Prisoners of war

Conditions in the East were incomparably worse than elsewhere.

Above. About 80 per cent of five million Soviet POWs died in German captivity. Most of the survivors were killed by the NKVD on return to the USSR.

Below. German prisoners trudge toward the Siberian camps. Their survival rate prior to release in the 1950s was no better than that of Soviet counterparts.

Concentration camps

were established by both the Soviet and the Nazi regimes.

Above. Vorkuta. A rare view of the NKVD's Vorkutlag, the largest concentration camp in wartime Europe.

Below. KL-Auschwitz I established by the SS in 1940 in German-occupied Poland. The notorious slogan of 'Work Liberates' had its Russian equivalents in the Gulag.

Mass murder

took many forms under numerous practitioners.

Above. The Katyn massacres, 1940. The shooting of *c.* 25,000 Allied officers, mainly Polish reservists, partly came to light in 1943, but was denied as the work of the NKVD until President Gorbachev's admission in 1990.

Below. Nemmersdorf, 1944. East Prussian villagers slaughtered by a Soviet raiding party.

Six million Jews

perished in the Holocaust, which was perpetrated by the Nazi SS in 1941–5. The victims died from shootings, from starvation in the Nazi-built ghettoes, and from gassing in the extermination camps.

Left. Einsatzkommando at work, 1941. Vinnitsa, Ukraine.

Below. The Warsaw Ghetto. Passers-by and Jewish policemen look on death in the street.

Corpses

of innocent Europeans killed by deliberate intent became a common sight.

Above. Dresden, February 1945, a funeral pyre in a city square following the firestorm caused by Allied bombers.

Below. KL-Bergen–Belsen, May 1945. British soldiers, having liberated the camp, prepare mass graves. These pictures transfixed post-war Western opinion.

Yugoslavia shattered

Some groups, including Croats and Bosnian Muslims, supported the Axis Powers, but others, like the Cetniks of Serbia and Tito's Communist partisans, resisted. All fought each other.

Above. A Bosnian division of the Waffen SS, reviewed by the Grand Mufti of Jerusalem.

Below. On the right of the picture, Josif Broz – Tito – backed by the West, the ultimate victor.

judged surplus to requirements could be rapidly disposed of, either by a bullet or by transfer to a camp.

The Paviak prison in Warsaw holds a special place in the roll-call of wartime dishonour. It was located inside the Jewish ghetto, and non-Jewish prisoners – many from the underground resistance – were brought in for their ordeals with the Gestapo through the streets of human misery. Yet the locations which are most symptomatic of Europe's double ordeal are those which passed directly from Nazi to Soviet control. In Vilnius, Minsk, Lublin, Budapest, Prague, Kiev and elsewhere there are prisons which one day were run by Gestapo and the next day by the NKVD. And there were thousands of innocent Europeans who had to face incarceration and 'investigation' by each of the continent's tormentors in turn. The NKVD were notoriously suspicious of persons who had earlier been in contact with the Gestapo, and would invariably 'reprocess' them.

The prominent role of the totalitarian security forces – which had no equivalent in the Western world – is nicely illustrated by the activities of the NKVD's 4th Department (Special Operations) during the Battle of Moscow. In October 1941, fearing an imminent German attack, Stalin ordered the evacuation of the Soviet government from Moscow to Kuibyshev. The 4th Department had to evacuate the government's prisoners as well as its ministers and papers – especially since a further purge of army officers was in progress. As members of the department prepared the trains, they camouflaged the Kremlin with netting, they gave special priority to Lenin's corpse and its embalming team, they mined all key roads and buildings, and they even arranged for an assassination team to go into hiding, in case Hitler dared to hold a victory parade in Moscow. But then, at the last minute, there was no room on the last train for 300 prisoners. So the 300 were shot in Moscow, and other officers due for purging were shot in Kuibyshev.[67]

Sudden events of that sort are sure to have disturbed the statistics. Nonetheless, for what it's worth, the NKVD made a scrupulous annual return of the numbers supposedly detained in its 415 prisons:

1 January 1939	352,508
1 January 1940	186,278
1 January 1941	470,693
1 January 1942	268,532
1 January 1943	237,534

1 January 1944   151,296
1 January 1945   275,510[68]

The fluctuations were considerable. The loss of more than 200,000 in 1941, for example, is connected with the fact that the NKVD abandoned many large prisons to the German invaders and shot their inmates before leaving. When the Germans arrived in places like Lwów or Vinnitsa in Ukraine, they found the prison basements and courtyards overflowing with corpses. German soldiers would then be given the stomach-churning task of removing the corpses for disposal. Photographs taken on those occasions were assumed after the war to be proof of German atrocities. They were not.

Rape

Shame surrounds rape in everday life, and diffidence about the subject can affect historians. In former times it was rarely discussed except in generalities. Yet in war it is omnipresent. Soldiers for the most part are young, sexually segregated males, who carry knives and firearms. They are supposed to use their weapons against the enemy. But, let loose among civilians, they are sorely tempted to exploit their power for other purposes. All armies without exception commit rape. None is eager to admit it.[69]

Discussions of sexual violence are also surrounded by much prejudice and innuendo. It was said, for instance, very outrageously, that black US troops had to be segregated because of their sexual promiscuity and the need for special discipline. (The British War Cabinet took a formal decision *not* to interfere in the segregatory practices of US forces stationed in Britain.) Similarly, it has been said on the basis of little more than hearsay that the relatively orderly record of German troops was due to propaganda condemning interracial or inter-ethnic intercourse. It could equally be due to other factors – such as the Wehrmacht's provision of brothels. One fact, however, is undeniable. The offspring of European women who were violated by non-white rapists were visible, whilst the origins of the offspring of white–white unions could easily be hidden.

The British and the Americans spent a shorter time on the continent than other armies, so they had fewer opportunities to offend. Equally, they did not allow themselves to become involved in generalized hostility towards a subject population, so their troops were less likely to be involved in the grosser forms of sexual hostility. And as victors they were in the best position to suppress scandalous information. Even so, accusations were made. Condoms, then known as 'French letters', were made universally available, not to protect the women but to protect the army from venereal disease, and the Americans, in particular, were charged with using their relative wealth to buy sexual favours. Of a pair of nylon 'pantyhose', it was said that they could be pulled down before they were put on: 'One yank and they're off.' Consensual fraternization – if that's not the wrong word – was probably most in evidence in Italy, but matters appear to have got out of hand in Naples, as in 1944–5 in occupied Germany. There were reports from the Naples district in the summer of 1944 that a Moroccan division from the colonical troops of the Free French had committed over a hundred murders as well 3,000 rapes. In post-war Germany, extreme social deprivation and the loss of 4–5 million German men can only have increased problems. 'Americans', wrote one New York magazine, 'look on the German women as loot, just like cameras and Lugers.' During the final push of the Western allies into Germany in 1945, the US Army's judge-advocate had to deal with 500 rape cases per week. 'The behaviour of our troops', an American intelligence officer regretted, 'was nothing to brag about ... There is a tendency among the naive or the malicious to think that only Russians loot and rape. The warriors of Democracy were no more virtuous than the troops of Communism were reported to be.'[70]

German troops certainly had a greater choice of countries in which to misbehave but they did not behave uniformly badly. In the first instance, the large network of Wehrmacht brothels – some 500 in all – served to give vent to the soldiers' baser instincts whilst attempting to maintain sexual hygiene for both parties. Local, non-German women were forcibly recruited. But, beyond the brothels, there was a great difference in the ways that German troops treated the opposite sex. In general, for instance, the SS was the worst offender, not only because those soldiers on concentration-camp guard duty or anti-partisan activity had the greatest opportunity, but also because their supremacist ideology encouraged such excesses against perceived 'lesser' races. Strangely, in the twisted logic of the Third Reich, such offenders – where they were liable to prosecution at all – were most likely to be accused of *rassenschande*, the crime of race defilement, or the lesser charge of 'undermining military discipline'.

The Wehrmacht too committed numerous sexual crimes – especially on the Eastern Front, where commanders were less scrupulous about enforcing discipline and preserving their own reputation. But, for the ordinary, apolitical Wehrmacht soldier, rape was much more likely to be a simple exercising of power than an expression of any perceived racial superiority. In all, the soldiers of Nazi Germany committed rape on a massive scale, but given the size of the opportunity presented by their occupation of much of the European continent, it might not be considered excessive. As one historian has argued, 'troubling though the situation was, [the incidence of sexual crime] remained both quantitatively and legally within the bounds of what could be expected under conditions of military occupation.'[71]

Without the slightest shadow of doubt, however, it was the record of the Red Army that exceeded all others. As soon as it left Soviet territory and passed into liberation mode, its commanders took it for granted that all Germans and collaborators were to be collectively punished. The punishment for males was to be shot. The punishment for females was to be gang-raped. No mercy was shown to the young or the aged. The nursing staff in hospitals were raped en masse. Nuns in convents were literally lined up and raped. Eight-year-old schoolgirls and eighty-year-old widows were raped – serially pumped and pummelled until the blood flowed and the unresisting body expired. On more than one occasion, on liberating German work camps full of Soviet slave labourers, Soviet troops would rape their own women in exactly the same way.[72] They had been taught to despise such women, who, as the saying went, had 'sold themselves to the Germans'.

The climate of violence which facilitated such outrages was fanned by official calls for revenge as exemplified by the novelist Ilya Ehrenburg's blood-curdling articles in the army newspaper *Krasnaya Zvyezda* ('Red Star'). Ehrenburg did not explicitly urge rape, as Goebbels claimed, but he undoubtedly assisted the unwritten rule which said that anything goes. Lev Kopelev, later a famous writer, was arrested by SMERSH for criticizing Ehrenburg and for spreading 'the bourgeois propaganda of humanism and pity on the enemy'.[73] Political officers saw refusal to inflict revenge as an offence. It was no accident that when the Red Army first crossed on to German territory at Nemmersdorf in East Prussia it was the local women who suffered: raped and then crucified.[74]

The culture of mass rape was encouraged both by the attitudes of the men and by the dispositions of the military authorities. 'Red Army soldiers don't believe in "individual liaisons" with German women,' wrote a Soviet playwright in his war diary. 'Nine, ten, twelve men at a time, they rape them on a collective basis.' They could misbehave with impunity. 'The NKVD . . . did not punish their own soldiers for rape, only if they caught venereal disease from victims, who had usually caught it from a previous rapist.'[75] This echoes practice in the US Army, whose soldiers, after being forbidden to 'fraternize', were fined $65 for attendance at a VD clinic.

Both at the time and after the war, the subject of rape was hidden by a screen of prudery and fear:

> Rape itself, in a typical Stalinist euphemism, was referred to as an 'immoral event'. It is interesting that Russian historians today still produce evasive circumlocutions. 'Negative phenomena in the army of liberation', writes one on the subject of mass rape, 'caused significant damage to the prestige of the Soviet Union and the armed forces and could have a negative influence in future relations with the countries through which our troops were passing.'[76]

One should note that the historian was not, apparently, referring to Germany.

Faced with this onslaught, the women of Soviet-occupied countries followed a variety of strategies. One was to seek an abortion, contrary to the ethos of the Third Reich. On learning of this, in March 1945 Bormann issued a decree ordering the Kripo to interrogate all German refugee women seeking abortions.[77] Another strategy was to seek protection from Soviet officers, by offering to become their concubines. The Red Army had long approved the practice of 'front-line wives', and the arrival of non-Soviet concubines did not encounter strong opposition. The third strategy was suicide. It was not unknown for German families, especially in the eastern provinces, to debate such a course of action collectively.

The crazed culmination of this nightmare was reached in Berlin in the last days of the war. Some 60,000 Soviet soldiers were killed, and 100,000 German women were raped and still more were driven to 'sleeping for food' at a time when four cigarettes meant 'all night'. For many years the facts were not much publicized or believed. But the publication of Antony Beevor's *Berlin: The Downfall 1945* (2002) coincided with the revelation in Germany of the identity of a female author whose candid memoir *A Woman in Berlin* (1959) had once provided a sensation.[78] (Marta Hillers (1911–2001) survived by becoming the 'front wife' of a Soviet major.) It also vindicated the theme of a much earlier American volume, Austin J. App's *Ravishing the Women of Conquered Europe*, which had been much reviled for 'siding with the enemy'. It suggests the overall figure of 2 million German rape victims.[79]

Rape is always a criminal violation. Gang rape is a violation with compound interest. And, perpetrated in Soviet style, it was often accompanied by murder, double murder (if the mother was pregnant) or suicide. Tens if not hundreds of thousands of German women killed themselves to evade the fate of their sisters, or in post-traumatic self-revulsion.

Looting

As everyone knows, the Nazis were keen, untiring looters. The Nazi leaders set up private, loot-based foundations, like Hitler's Sonderauftrag Linz or Alfred Rosenberg's Einsatzstab-Rosenberg (ERR) or Ribbentrop's 'Special Service Battalion'. And the Nazi state assumed that all the possessions of the conquered countries, public and private, were at its disposal. Paintings, sculpture, furniture, libraries and archives were carried off to Germany either following straightforward theft or after artificial auctions at knock-down prices. The operations began in Vienna in 1937, and left a string of empty vaults and plundered museums in Prague, Warsaw, Amsterdam, Paris, Kiev, Rome, Florence and everywhere in between. Warsaw alone reported 13,512 missing works of art. Four palaces outside Leningrad, including Tsarskoe Selo, lost 34,000 items. The Reichsbank acquired the gold reserves of Austria, Czechoslovakia, Danzig, Belgium, the Netherlands, Luxemburg and Italy – a haul worth $621 million at wartime prices.

Nowhere was so systematically looted as Warsaw. In the weeks after the failure of the rising in October 1944, the Germans built a special railway spur into the centre of the empty and evacuated city to facilitate the plunder of the ruins. Heavy machinery was brought in to pull out all the city's electricity cables, and to dig up all the tram tracks. Gangs of slave workers dragged the scrap to loading points where the valuable metals were sorted, cut into neat lengths, and piled high on waiting wagons. German officers supervised companies of soldiers who combed the abandoned shops and houses for movables of value, such as chandeliers, mirrors, oriental rugs or antiques. And only when the stripping was complete was the order given to the *Brandkommandos* to proceed with final demolition. Someday someone might think of presenting a symbolic bill.

It is, however, foolish to imagine that the Germans alone practised looting. The British, admittedly, were not specially adept, and the Americans' want list was mostly directed towards scientific and technical equipment, although, many years after the war, German art treasures would turn up in the USA. A priceless Carolingian Bible, for example, was found in a Texas garage after the death of a former soldier. Yet the Soviet Union was absolutely top of the class. Ordinary Soviet soldiers were obsessed by watches and bicycles, which they had never possessed back home. Soviet officials liked high-quality clothes, cars and jewellery, and trainloads of grand pianos were seen rolling eastward. In 1945 officially authorized Soviet reparation squad or 'trophy brigades' descended like locusts on German towns and factories. Indeed, on their way into Germany through Poland, Czechoslovakia or Hungary, they were not always clear in their minds where Germany began. They did not merely dismantle industrial plant or purloin locomotives and rolling stock – which to a degree was understandable. They ripped out fixed installations – railway tracks, power cables, radiators, light fittings. All the damage was automatically blamed on 'the Fascists'. And much of their spoil was rusted and ruined long before it reached Russia.[80]

In the final phase of the war, Allied bombing obliged German officials to store much of their loot in remote castles or mines, especially in Silesia. As a result, almost all the Nazi treasures salted away in the East fell into Soviet hands – the looters were themselves looted. In western Germany, investigation teams from SHAEF and OSS found valuable hoards at Alt Aussee and Grasleben in Bavaria, and the Reichsbank gold was recovered from a mine at Merkers in Thuringia.[81]

For nearly fifty years, the Western world believed the fiction that 'loot' meant Nazi loot. Much detective work was undertaken to identify items that had found their way on to the international art market, and huge speculation surrounded the fate of spectacular pieces like the 'Amber Room' from the Peterhof Palace.[82] Yet the collapse of the Soviet Union in 1991 revealed the likely whereabouts of much that had been written off as missing. A colossal and secret Trophy Museum, never opened to the public, was found to be housed in a complex of hangars in the Moscow suburbs. It was crammed to the ceilings with goodies that for the most part had never been unpacked, let alone catalogued. The contents of this and other caches started with 'Priam's treasure' from Schliemann's Mycenae collection and went on to include further surprises, such as the archives of the British Expeditionary Force that had been abandoned in

1940 on the Dunkirk beaches.[83] Clearly, the full story of wartime loot remains to be written.

Even so, as knowledge about wartime loot increases, the chances of its return decrease. Despite numerous revelations and legal actions, it remains true that 'possession is nine-tenths of the law'. Post-war owners procrastinate; claims are contested; and some countries, like Russia, refuse to countenance restitution. Most of the disputed cases turn out to be infernally complicated. A collection of Dürer drawings stolen from the Ossolineum Institute in Lemberg, now in western Ukraine, was recovered after the war, but was then sold on by a plausible aristocrat with a dubious claim to ownership. The priceless collection of Beethoven and Mozartian scores that was removed by German officials from the Reichsmusikkammer and Prussian Staatsbibliotek in Berlin and sent in 1943 to occupied Poland for safe keeping was eventually discovered in the vaults of the Jagiellonian Library in Kraków.[84] There had been no looting. Frontiers had moved, conversely, collections from Bresau and Danzig are now stored in Berlin.

All looting is a form of violation, and it is right to remember that looters often resort to physical violence. One will never know how many Europeans were beaten or murdered so that the Nazi collector could get his painting, or the drunken Soviet soldier could get his watch.

Expropriation

Property is a dangerous thing to possess in wartime. It gets bombed. It gets damaged. It gets stolen or sequestered, usually without compensation. And the former owners, if they survive, are left at the end of the war wondering what, if anything, can be done.

Generally speaking, the Nazis respected property rights. They made no general move against landowners or industrialists as a class, and they did not nationalize private companies en masse. Yet there were major exceptions. By 1939 they had 'acquired' the movable possessions of almost all Jews in Germany. And when the Reich moved east, in September 1939, expropriation was practised wholesale. All major Polish landowners (not simply Jewish ones) were robbed of their estates, and all Polish firms and industrial concerns were closed down without compensation. A swarm of risky German businessmen – like Oskar Schindler – was then invited in to receive or manage the sequestered assets. All Polish state property, from city halls to armament factories, automatically became German state property. No such drastic policy was implemented in France, Belgium or the Netherlands. But in 1941, when the Reich moved east again, into the USSR, expropriation on the grandest scale followed. Since all Soviet enterprises were state enterprises in any case, and since Stalin had collectivized the land and the peasants in the previous decade, no more than a stroke of the pen was required for all Soviet state property in the occupied regions to fall under direct German control.

Soviet doctrines on property, therefore, were far more radical than those of the Nazis. In theory at least, private capital was seen as a great social and economic evil. Landowners were oppressors, and businessmen were bloodsuckers. In 1939 Stalin had just completed the biggest property transfer in world history, liquidating the Soviet farming class (whom he derisively called kulaks) and taking over their assets. And under his five-year plans the USSR had just completed the first decade of totally state-controlled economic planning. One could have been forgiven for assuming that he intended to pursue the same policy in every country that he annexed.

In fact Soviet wartime policy was unexpectedly cautious in this regard. In 1939–41 the newly annexed lands were *not* immediately collectivized. Former Baltic, Polish and Romanian state property was sequestered, but many areas were left undisturbed, sealed off behind a watertight economic cordon. In 1944–5, as well, the Soviet authorities did not rush to introduce revolutionary changes. In Poland, for example, the Lublin Committee said nothing about collectivization or nationalization, concentrating instead on moderate agrarian reform, which was very popular. (The committee didn't have to nationalize the economy, because the Nazis had done it for them.) If it wasn't for the fact that the USSR had expropriated half of the entire country, one might have believed the propaganda about moderate, patriotic priorities.

So long as Communism lasted, no one whose assets had been illegally expropriated during or after the war had any hope of redress. But in 1991 the issue could finally be addressed. The Church, which had been dispossessed by the Communist regimes, was able to recover some of its properties. So too were some landowners, who found that in many instances the Communists had not bothered to register their thefts in the land registry, or to change the title deeds.

Yet the wider problem of unscrambling fifty years of proprietorial lawlessness was all but insoluble. In 1999, a man living in Manchester sued the Polish government for $11 million as compensation for the mansion in Wrocław which his family had once owned. It turned out that the mansion had been seized by the Nazis in 1939, when Wrocław – then called Breslau – had been in the Reich. It had been completely destroyed by Soviet tanks in April 1945. And since then it had never existed.[85]

The complications of the situation are well illustrated by a film that was made by the British journalist Robert Fisk, who lives in Lebanon. Fisk's Arab neighbours, Palestinian refugees, had shown him the key of the house that they had once owned in Haifa, before it was taken from them by Israelis. So he visited the Jewish family living in the house and asked them where *they* had come from. The answer was Chrzanów, a small town near Kraków, in Poland, and they showed him a photo of their former Polish home, which they had lost during the war. So he travelled to Poland, and sought out the woman living in the house in Chrzanów. She was a 'repatriant' from Lemberg, now in western Ukraine. It wasn't hard to guess the next link in the chain. The repatriate had been driven out of her home city when it was seized by the USSR. No doubt her house was taken over by Russians who had been brought in by the post-war regime in its campaign to sovietize the city. And where, one wonders, did the Soviet authorities find Russians who wanted to migrate to western Ukraine in 1946? As likely as not they came from eastern Ukraine, which had been terribly damaged by the fighting on the Eastern Front and which had lost many of its inhabitants through forcible deportations . . .[86] Such were the consequences of war, and in practice they were all but irreversible.

Yet expropriation is soaked in misery. Losing one's home involuntarily is traumatic in itself. But loss compounded by violence or death causes multiple trauma. And, as one well knows, there were very few expropriations in 1939–45 that were accompanied by smiles and handshakes.

Resettlement

'Resettlement' is one of the nastiest words in the vocabulary of the Second World War. It sometimes means resettlement. But in its German form of *Umsiedlung* it was a Nazi euphemism for extermination. Jews on their way to the death camps were told that they were being 'resettled'. Treblinka (see p. 362) was fitted with a phoney railway station with fictional timetables posted on the platform to make it look like a junction for journeys further east.

Genuine resettlement was, however, the sequel to expropriation, evacuation, flight or deportation. Sometimes it proved temporary – like that of the Baltic Germans brought into Poland in 1940 only to be moved out a few years later. And sometimes it was permanent. It affected millions.

British people were not involved in European resettlement in 1939–45, either as the organizers or the organized. So it is not an experience that is particularly well known or understood in the UK. But it was one of the many activities which totalitarian regions practised in common. It was part of the Soviet way of life for decades. And the Nazis would have indulged in it much more had they not been defeated.

It is ironic, therefore, that the Germans themselves, whose leaders had shown such enthusiasm for coercive resettlement, became the object of the largest resettlement scheme of all. Nazi propagandists loved to show paintings of medieval German settlers setting out in their ox wagons in the great *Drang nach Osten* to 'civilize' the East. They had a romantic vision, like that of the Boers in Africa, of bold Germanic pioneers braving the wild tribes and the perils of nature to claim their new *Lebensraum*. It's odd that they conceived of Eastern Europe as a sort of *terra nulla* inhabited only by a few aboriginals – like an empty frontierland beyond the Ohio or the Mississippi, waiting to be tilled. But that was the vision, and it was destined almost inevitably to come to grief. It ended after 1945 with the great German *Drang nach Westen*, the great 'Drive to the West'.

It would be wrong, however, to think that German resettlement was merely an act of wartime revenge. It was the culmination of a long-standing Allied policy that had been simmering for decades. Nineteenth-century panslavism had long seen East Prussia as the point of a Germanic spear directed at the heart of Slavdom, and the Prussian Junkers who had taken over supposedly Slavic land along the Baltic coast had long been seen as the bearers of militarism. The German victory at Tannenberg in East Prussia in 1914 was certainly remembered in Russia as a historic setback that needed to be reversed. Shortly after it, the tsarist foreign office published a 'Map of the Future Europe' on which East Prussia had been absorbed by the Russian Empire, and the kingdoms of Poland and Bohemia were to be restored as Russian protectorates.[87] It is hard to believe that Stalin's diplomats were unaware of these precedents. On the other hand, it was Churchill, not Stalin, who made the first move in suggesting a solution of this sort. Churchill too belonged to an Allied generation which saw Prussian militarism as the root of Europe's miseries, and which, during the First World War, had considered various proposals for eradicating it. So he and his advisers were preconditioned to favour the idea that 'friendly Slavs' should replace 'enemy Germans' in one of Europe's most strategically sensitive regions. It is not too much to say, the resettled Germans of the East therefore paid the price not for supporting the Nazis, but for offending against crude and ancient notions of separating 'Germanity' from 'Slavdom'.

Further east, Stalinist planners were moving on from the eradication/ resettlement of undesirable social classes, like the kulaks, to the resettlement of whole national groups. There is evidence, in fact, that campaigns such as the one against the Volga Germans had been prepared years in advance, and that the onset of the 'Great Patriotic War' merely provided the pretext for premeditated action. At all events, a Decree of Banishment was issued on 28 August 1941, and the forced evacuation of the entire population of the Volga German ASR was implemented three days later.

The Volga Germans were descendants of colonists invited to Russia by Catherine the Great at the end of the Seven Years War. They were mainly Lutherans from Hesse, and they built over a hundred farming centres on the virgin steppe in the district of Saratov. By the twentieth century they numbered up to 2 million, and remained quite distinct from Russian society as a whole. This was their principal offence. During the First World War, a law of liquidation was passed, but not enacted.

Bolshevik rule hit the Volga community hard. Lutheran pastors were sent to the GULag. One-third of the population perished in the famine of 1920–21. And land was collectivized in the 1930s. The establishment of an Autonomous German Soviet Republic, with its capital at Engels, was a means of exerting closer control. The Decree of Banishment, therefore, must be seen as the culmination of a long process of intensifying persecution. The charge of collaboration with the Nazis was absurd. Young adult males were drafted into the Soviet Labour Army. young women were dispatched for labour service elsewhere. The rest of the community were packed into cattle wagons that rolled east for four weeks to the Altai mountains on the Chinese frontier of Western Siberia and Kazakhstan. There they were assigned to closed 'stations' in the wilderness, where their only neighbours were native peoples and groups of deported Poles. Their legal banishment was nullified in 1965, but they have never been allowed to return to their original homes. At the end of the twentieth century, many of the survivors were trying to emigrate to Germany.[88]

In 1943–4 after the Wehrmacht had briefly occupied the fringes of the Caucasus, the Soviet regime took the opportunity to inflict similar repressions on a group of Muslim Caucasian peoples, including the Chechens, Ingush, Balkars, Karachays and Kalmyks. Once again the charge of collaboration was outrageous. What it meant was that the natives had not resisted the German invasion with the same fervour with which they had traditionally fought against Russian rule. Fifty thousand Chechens were serving in the Red Army, rendering the nation defenceless. Once again, men, women and children were driven to the cattle wagons, and resettled wholesale in Central Asia. One-quarter of them perished. Grozny, the Chechen capital, was repopulated with Russians. The Soviet authorities built a statue to the tsarist general Yermolov. The inscription read, 'No people under the sun is more vile and deceitful than this one.' The surviving exiles began to trickle back after 1956. Their tragedy and their resentments continue to the present day.[89]

The turn of the Crimean Tatars came in 1944, following the reoccupation of Crimea by Soviet forces. The Tatars, like the Chechens, were Muslims, whose sunny homeland had long been coveted by Russia. They were Turkic speakers, whose khanate had once been a major power in the Black Sea region. The Crimean People's Republic of 1917–18 was crushed by the Bolsheviks, and the first generation of national leaders was destroyed during Stalin's Great Terror. Under German rule (1941–4) a Tatar Legion was formed, but it attracted far fewer men than served in the Red Army. Nonetheless, the axe fell. On 5 May 1944, half a million Tatars were rounded up by the NKVD en masse, and transported to Uzbekistan. Mortality was said to be nearly 50 per cent. No return was permitted until 1967 – by which time the best lands of Crimea had been overtaken by an influx of Russians, and the country had been transferred by Moscow to Ukraine.[90]

The Meskhetians were a small mountain tribe of Shia Muslims who inhabited the mountain ranges on the border of Georgia and Turkey. They had no allies in the power politics of the region. In 1944, 115,000 civilians were removed, to be joined in 1945 by 40,000 redundant Soviet soldiers. Their place of exile has not been specified. But the largest group of post-war refugees has continued to live in Azerbaijan.[91]

Stalin's resettlement programmes were concealed from the outside world at the time, and have never been widely publicized. They do not figure on the conventional balance sheet of the Second World War. Since most Westerners confused the USSR with 'Russia', and assumed that Russia was inhabited by Russians, they had no reason to notice.

Ethnic cleansing

Needless to say, no one talked of 'ethnic cleansing' during the Second World War. (It is a term from the Yugoslav wars of the 1990s.) But the phenomenon, if not the name, was all too widespread. It referred to the practice whereby one nationality or ethnic group terrorized its neighbours and drove them from their homes, so as to create a population that was ethnically homogeneous or 'pure'.

Ethnic cleansing is sometimes described as limited genocide. It certainly provoked scenes of mayhem and slaughter reminiscent of the worst genocides. Yet one must be careful not to miss the point. The Ustashe regime in Croatia, for example, did not aim to exterminate all Serbs. Indeed, its leaders would have said that they harboured no ill feeling against Serbs in general, so long as they lived in Serbia. Their actions were driven by an uncompromising belief in the ultra-nationalistic ideal which holds that each nation possesses the absolute right to preserve its own God-given land for itself and for itself alone. Twentieth-century Europe produced many groups professing such ideals.

Croatia, which before 1918 had formed part of Austria–Hungary, was a multinational country. Its capital, Zagreb (Agrem), was a fine Central European city, reminiscent of Vienna or Budapest. Its dominant national group, the Croats, were an interesting case of an *ethnos* defined mainly by religion. They spoke the same South Slav language as the Serbs – outsiders called it 'Serbo-Croat' – but they wrote it in the Latin as opposed to the Cyrillic alphabet; and, whilst the Serbs were Orthodox Christians, they were Roman Catholics. Whereas the Serbs traditionally looked east for inspiration and support – to Russia – the Croats looked west – to Germany and Italy. In pre-war Yugoslavia they had regarded themselves as an oppressed minority, and they felt that the limited autonomy granted in 1939 was too little and came too late.

After the fall of Yugoslavia in 1941, therefore, the nominally independent state, the Nezavišna Država Hrvatska (NDH), fell quite naturally into the hands of an extreme Fascist group, the Ustashe, who were sponsored by the Nazis. The Ustashe leader, Ante Pavelić (1889–1959), who had spent most of the preceding years in Mussolini's Italy, wasted no time in 'cleansing' his country of all non-Croats. Since the NDH included the provinces of Bosnia and Hercegovina, he was hostile to the Bosnian Muslims, even though the Nazis had declared them to be Aryan. But his main targets were the Serbs, and to a lesser extent the Jews, the Roma and, as political opponents, the Communists. The population of the NDH was only 60 per cent Croat. So there was much work to be done. The programme envisaged that one-third of the 1.9 million Serbs would be killed, one-third would be expelled, and one-third would be forcibly converted to Catholicism. Some 30,000 Roma were also destined for extermination, while 40,000 Jews were to be handed over to Nazi Germany. The methods adopted were unusually barbaric. They started with village-burnings and massacres in the Kraina region, but soon embraced concentration camps. The complex at Jasenovać was not, as sometimes claimed, 'the third largest in Europe', but it was certainly high on the list of infamy. Estimates of its victims start at 56,000 and go up to an impossible 600,000 or 700,000. Its operators, lacking gas chambers, resorted to techniques such as decapitation by handsaw. In all, some 390,000 Serbs perished.[92]

West Ukraine, like Croatia, was another beautiful but unhappy land. It had historically formed part of the kingdom of Poland, though from 1773 to 1918 it had been annexed by Austria and renamed Galicia. Its capital – variously known as Lemberg, L'viv, Lwów, Lvov or Leopolis – was a large, elegant city dating mainly from the baroque and Habsburg periods. The population of the province was ethnically, religiously and linguistically mixed. The majority, who called themselves *Rusini* or Ruthenes, were Ukrainian-speaking Uniates, mainly peasants. The social and political elite were Roman Catholic Poles. And Yiddish-speaking Jews, many of them Hasids, formed a strong contingent in all the towns and cities. Their fate was similar to that of their neighbours in the adjacent province of Volhynia.

In 1939, when Poland fell, and in 1941, when the Germans took over from the Soviets, many West Ukrainians hoped to restore the republic which they had briefly enjoyed after the First World War. But, since neither the Nazis nor the Soviets were interested, they had to forget former aspirations. Yet the more extreme among them, including the underground Ukrainian Insurrectionary Army (UPA), thought like the Croats that they could create an ethnically homogeneous society. The Jews of the region had already been killed by the Nazis. So in 1943–4 the wrath of the UPA fell on the helpless Poles. The German occupiers, who had more urgent business fighting the Red Army, did not intervene. Villages were torched. Roman Catholic priests were axed or crucified. Churches were burned with all their parishioners. Isolated farms were attacked by gangs carrying pitchforks and kitchen knives. Throats were cut. Pregnant women were bayoneted. Children were cut in two. Men were ambushed in the fields, and led away. The perpetrators could not determine the province's future. But at least they could determine that it would be a future without Poles. They killed any number between 200,000 and half a million.[93]

Ironically, the USSR finished the UPA's work for them. The surviving Poles were 'repatriated', as they were from adjacent Byelorussia and Lithuania. They were largely replaced by Russians. In 1991 West Ukraine became part of the independent Republic of Ukraine.

There remains the thorny question of whether the expulsion of Germans from the East in 1944–5 should be counted as a programme of ethnic cleansing. Most commentators would say 'Yes'. Although the expulsions were carried out on the orders of the Allied governments, and may be seen as motivated by international politics, they betrayed strong streaks not only of revenge but of social thought worthy of Ante Pavelić. What is more, in two countries at least, local action preceded the Potsdam Conference. The harshest of the notorious Beneš Decrees were promul-gated in Czechoslovakia in May–June 1945, *before* the Potsdam conference. They did not authorize expulsion directly, but, by changing the legal status of German- or Hungarian-owned land and property, they created con-ditions in which an exodus began spontaneously. In the early summer of 1945, floods of German refugees were streaming from Bohemia and floods of Hungarians from Slovakia. In two instances at least, atrocious excesses were perpetrated by so called 'Revolutionary Guards'. Both the 'death march' from Brno to the Austrian frontier and the bridge at ÚstinadLabem, where many Sudeten German refugees died, are associated in expellee literature with martyrdom.

Flight

War produces refugees like boiling water produces steam. People flee to escape fighting, injury and oppression, or from fear of some looming threat. In 1939–45 Europe saw refugees not in millions, but in tens of millions.

The last *Kindertransport* pulled out of the station in Berlin on 1 September 1939. It was taking a trainload of refugee children, mainly Jewish, to safety. In 1938–9, on the private initiative of a (non-Jewish) English solicitor, over 10,000 such children were saved in this way.[94]

The first wartime refugees fled on the very first day of the war. The Polish government advised the population of the border with Germany to flee eastward. They did so only to clog the roads, obstruct military traffic, and provide easy targets for dive-bombers and strafing Messerschmitts. In 1939 some 300,000 Polish citizens fled to the USSR. In 1939–40 similar numbers, including Jews, fled from the Soviet zone of Poland to the Nazi zone, believing that nothing could be worse than Soviet oppression.

All subsequent campaigns generated similar chaos. In the winter of 1939 Finnish refugees flooded out of Karelia. In 1940 the roads of Belgium and northern France were clogged with refugees trying to move south, and Baltic shipping was overladen with refugees from Estonia, Latvia and Lithuania trying to reach Scandinavia. In 1941 refugees streamed out of Belgrade and Athens. In 1943–4 all parts of Italy were filled with civilians driven from their homes by the fighting on a moving front. In 1944 France and the Low Countries saw refugee columns on the move for a second time.

The British state made its own arrangements. Pre-war officials calculated that sustained bombing raids could kill 2 million people. So on 1 September 1939 the first waves of evacuees began to leave London and other big cities for destinations in Wales, Scotland and the English countryside. In all, 4 million evacuees were cared for. Private schemes were also encouraged. About 2,000 found temporary foster homes in Canada and the USA.[95] Among them were the future Dame Shirley Williams and the future historian Sir Martin Gilbert.

The Germans, also fearing bombs, made arrangements of a different sort. In response to the British bombing of Berlin in 1940, the German government ordered the evacuation of the most vulnerable from the capital. In time, a voluntary scheme of evacuations (the *Kinderlandesverschickung*)

was begun, whereby children of under fourteen years of age from the
urban areas of the north could be housed for a six-month spell in children's
homes and monasteries in the rural south and east of Germany. The
evacuees' experiences, in which many were exposed to petty prejudice
and even outright cruelty, left many preferring to return to their families
in the bomb-threatened cities. In 1943 the evacuations were made compulsory.[96]

In the USSR, little thought was given to the evacuation of special
categories. In 1941 and again in 1942 priority was given to the colossal
operations of moving industry and industrial workers. A million fled or
were moved from Byelorussia ahead of Operation Barbarossa; 400,000
were safely evacuated from Leningrad, and 1.4 million from Moscow. But
no provision was made for the large Jewish population of the western
republics, which was obviously vulnerable. Generally speaking, the spaces
available to receive evacuees and refugees were immense. Unless you
were a production worker, assistance in getting there was minimal.

On the Eastern Front, refugees had special difficulties, because the rear
areas were patrolled so fiercely by security forces. But in the winter of
1944–5, as the Red Army advanced, the (second) great *Ostflucht* broke
loose. No one knows for certain how many millions were involved. But
large sections of the German population from the Baltic, East Prussia,
Pomerania, Galicia and Silesia did not wait. They were often accompanied
by non-Germans who had equal reason to fear the Soviet juggernaut.
Many moved in horse-drawn wagons, looking for all the world like
medieval pioneers. Others trudged in rags among the weary columns of
retreating German soldiers. Tens of thousands, or more, lost their lives
when they tried to walk across the frozen Baltic, or when trapped on the
coastal *haffs*.[97]

The Germans trapped on the Courland Peninsula in Latvia consisted
mainly of military personnel from the former Army Group North. Soviet
attacks were repeatedly repulsed, and a few relief boats were able to sail.
But the majority awaited their inevitable fate: which was to surrender in
May 1945 and to be sent to the Soviet camps.

The most critical situations, however, were shaping up further south.
The city of Königsberg was besieged from January 1945 to 9 April. The
3rd Panzer Army opened up and maintained a corridor to the port of
Pillau (now Baltyjsk), from which successful evacuations took place. But
food rations in the city were running out, and to avoid starvation many
civilians preferred to risk the trek across the frozen lagoon to the Frisches

Haff. Some 2,000 men, women and children were still making the daily journey when the ice began to melt in the spring, and thousands were drowned.

Admiral Dönitz's 'Sea Bridge' operation functioned well, and some 2 million refugees may have been ferried to safety overall. But two maritime disasters – the sinking of the *Wilhelm Gustloff* in January, and of the *General von Steuben* in February 1945 – greatly inhibited the refugees' willingness to take to the water.

The *Wilhelm Gustloff* (named after an assassinated Swiss Nazi) was a cruise liner, not a military vessel. It sailed from Gotenhaven at 12.30 on 30 January, carrying up to 9,000 civilian refugees and 162 wounded soldiers. When darkness fell it was fully illuminated, on the captain's orders. Fear of night-time collision was greater than fear of submarines. The decision was fatal. Soviet sub S-13 out of Hangö in Finland caught sight of the condemned ship around midnight. Three torpedoes were fired at 1,000 metres – the first with the shout 'For the Motherland!' They all struck. The *Gustloff* quickly developed a thirty-degree list, but it hung suspended above its watery grave for over an hour. Despite the presence of an escort and rescue vessels, as many as 8,000 persons drowned. It was the greatest marine disaster of the war. The wreck is marked on charts of the Bay of Gdansk as 'Obstacle No. 73'.[98]

The city of Danzig, where the war had begun, was not besieged until March 1945. It contained a population of around 3 million, swollen by 2.5 million refugees from East Prussia and from eastern Pomerania. And once the Soviet Army had driven to the Baltic coast in the district of Stolp and Köslin (now Koszalin) the escape route to the West was cut off. The sole place of refuge lay on the peninsula of Hela, which continued to hold out after Danzig fell and whence, despite severe losses among German defenders, some 387,000 people were safely evacuated to Schleswig-Holstein and Denmark. Even then, another maritime disaster intervened. In the last days of the war, in May 1945, the MV *Hela*, overloaded with 6,000 passengers, pulled out of Hela. It was never seen again.

In 1945 Europe's refugees were relabelled by UN bureaucrats as 'Displaced Persons'. They were estimated at 30 million. Apart from the dead and the maimed, they formed the biggest group of war victims.

Austerity

Studies of the home front in wartime Britain concentrate on subjects such as food rationing, air raids, civil-defence, war work, directed labour, the evacuation of children, the division of families, and the 'wartime spirit'.[99] With the exception of the Blitz of 1940–41 and of the V-1/V-2 rockets of 1944–5, the list of experiences contains little that might be rated higher than hardship. There was no starvation. There were no atrocities. And there was no foreign occupation. Above all, the level of casualties in Britain was low. Statistically, a British serviceman had a 1 in 23 chance of being wounded or killed. Britain's civilian losses represented 0.1 per cent of the population. Losses in Poland reached at least 18 per cent, and in Byelorussia around 25 per cent.

In these circumstances, it is important to recognize that the British experience was by no means typical and that a comparative perspective is essential to any broad understanding. The point of this is in no way to diminish Britain's war effort, which was admirable, but simply to establish the wider context within which all wartime experiences must be judged. If this is done, some conclusions will have been predictable, others surprising.

On the issue of rationing, for instance, it turns out that British citizens were obliged to endure as harsh a regime as their average German counterparts. (One says 'average German' advisedly, because there were many millions of people in the Reich who were deliberately underfed and whose deprivation helped raise the average welfare of German bellies.) Right to the penultimate stage of the war, the British had to make do on a diet that their American allies would have considered unacceptable but which was comparable to that of their German enemies.

Weekly food rations in Britain for 1 adult (in grams)[100]			
Date	*Bread*	*Meat*	*Fats*
1940	no limit	640	no limit
1941	no limit	500	no limit
1942	no limit	500	no limit
1943	no limit	500	200
1944	no limit	500	200
1945	no limit	500	200

Weekly food rations in Germany for 1 adult (in grams)[101]

Date	Bread	Meat	Fats
Sept 1939	no limit	550	310
1940	2,400	450	280
1941	2,300	400	269
1942	2,125	356	206
1943	2,475	437	215
1944	2,525	362	218
Feb 1945	2,225	156	156
Mar	2,225	148	190
April	900	137	75

In the USSR, food allocations for industrial workers in 1942 were three to four times higher for heavy industrial workers (3,181–4,418 calories per day) than for ordinary employees (1,074–1,176 calories) and dependents (780 calories). Allocations were rarely met. Peasants were allocated nothing, being expected to fend for themselves. The well-fed and well-clothed appearance of the German population is thought to be one of the factors that drove the Red Army to a frenzy in 1944–5. According to one historian, Soviet troops would often single out the 'fatty' Nazi wives to rape first.[102]

Paradoxically, the German diet deteriorated dramatically in the second half of 1945. This was due to an accumulation of deficiencies. But the Allied occupation regimes bore the blame.

Basically, the civilian population of combatant states had to adapt to wartime conditions on three different planes: material, organizational and psychological. The first, material, involved a huge shift in the quantity and nature of goods available, as the economy was redirected from domestic to military priorities. The second, organizational, witnessed massive changes in labour practices, in gender roles, in transport, and, above all, in the relationship between the state and the individual. Clement Attlee's explanation of the Emergency Powers (Extension) Act to the House of Commons in May 1940 is worth quoting. The government, he said, had now taken 'complete control over persons and property, not just some persons of a particular class of the community, but of all persons rich and poor, employer and workman, man or woman, and all property'.[103] Such at least was the theory. It sounds alarmingly totalitarian. No one complained.

Yet it was the third plane, the psychological one, which was the most demanding. Even in Britain the necessary adjustments were considerable. In other countries, where hardship and austerity were accompanied by foreign oppression, physical danger and human losses beyond comprehension, the mental pressures were not only greater, they were well-nigh unbearable.

Disease

Traditional depictions of the Grim Reaper show him carrying his tools: the scythe of death and the flail of famine. Certainly in the First World War the killing fields of the military fronts were accompanied by high death rates from epidemics and hunger. If one adds the victims of 'Spanish flu' in 1918 to the victims of the 'Volga Famine' which followed in the wake of war and revolution in Russia, one reaches a total far in excess of the numbers killed in the trenches.

Of course, the Second World War also took its toll of the sick and starving. The death rate in the ghettos and concentration camps was horrendous. Nonetheless, there were no extensive famines or epidemics either during or immediately after the war. This fact may be surprising. It may partly be due to the greatly reduced number of mouths to feed, and partly, for certain, to the activities of UNRRA. At all events it represents one small patch of sunlight amid the life-threatening storms which engulfed Europe's civilian population.

Genocide

The term 'genocide' was invented in 1943 by a Polish-Jewish lawyer, Rafał Lemkin, who was working for the War Department in the USA. He used it to describe a phenomenon of which the world was only just becoming aware: namely, an attempt to exterminate every single member of one branch of the human race. (The Latin *genus* mean 'species'; *uccidere* is 'to kill'.) At the time, the Hebrew word 'Shoah' was not in general circulation; and the old Greek word 'holocaust' had not acquired its present-day connotation. (In 1938 Chamberlain had used the word 'holocaust' to refer to blood-letting on the scale of the First World War.) The German Nazis, the perpetrators, had no name for what they were doing other than a euphemism: 'the Final Solution of the Jewish Question'.

Of course, there were various precedents, though none exactly apposite. In 1915, during the First World War, the Ottoman government had authorized a campaign of extermination against the Armenians, who were suspected of working with the Ottoman Empire's Russian enemy. Ever since, Armenian organizations have sought to gain international recognition of their people's tragedy, and in recent decades to have it defined as genocide. Hitler was aware of the precedent. In August 1939, having prepared the attack on Poland, he asked rhetorically, 'Who nowadays remembers the Armenians?' On that occasion he was thinking of the people of Poland as a whole.[104]

The Nazis' hostility towards the Jews was never a secret. It provided a prominent theme in Hitler's *Mein Kampf* (1925). It had inspired the Nuremberg Laws of 1935, which in turn caused a series of escalating persecutions in Germany. But until 1941 it had been ugly and brutal but it had not been exterminatory. From mid-1941, however – i.e. from the start of Operation Barbarossa – it assumed the unmistakable characteristics and proportions of genocide. The historian's duty is firstly to explain the context and secondly to present the facts.

The context is that of the Nazi regime in triumphant mood as it launched its forces eastward into what was intended as the definitive conquest of the new *Lebensraum*. In 1939, during the Reich's earlier leap of eastward expansion, the possibilities were still limited. Poland was the country where most Jews lived, and where the core territory of the *Lebensraum* lay. But only half of Poland had been conquered. The other half was still in the grip of the USSR, which the Nazis regarded as the home of 'Jewish Bolshevism'. So, from the Nazis' point of view, any ultimate reckoning with the Jews or the Slavs in 1939–41 was beyond their reach. From the minute that Barbarossa moved off, however, the prospects for the Nazis' plans of 'racial reconstruction' in Eastern Europe improved dramatically. The realm of Hans Frank's General Government was extended. Within a week or two virtually all the lands of the former Pale of Settlement to which, under Tsarist Russian rule, the largest reservoir of Jewish population had once been confined, were under Nazi control.[105] The SS saw its historic chance. The 'Holocaust' was on.

In this respect, the Final Solution must be seen as the culmination of a mounting series of preceding persecutions which had included at least three alternative 'solutions'. The first solution, practised in the Rhineland and elsewhere from 1933, had involved clearances. After each action, particular districts of Germany were declared *Judenrein*, or 'free of Jews'. The second solution had been that of compulsory emigration. Enforced in

Germany, Austria and Bohemia in 1933–9, it had caused the exodus of some 250,000 Jews. The third solution, of ghettoization, as instituted in the German zone of Poland in 1939–41, was occasioned by the outbreak of the war, and was proclaimed as a temporary measure pending resettlement. The Final Solution, therefore, was the fourth of a series.

Hitler's order to authorize the Final Solution has not survived. It probably never existed in documentary form. In the view of the late Alan Bullock, Hitler was concerned to cover his tracks, having incurred considerable criticism in Germany over the preceding euthanasia campaign. But there can be absolutely no doubt that, in a dictatorial and hierarchical system like the Third Reich, the order could only have come from the very top. It would have been given either by telephone or in person to Himmler, Reichsführer of the SS, and via Himmler to all lower organs. Reinhard Heydrich, head of the RSHA, was told about it by Göring in July 1941. But it is likely to have originated some weeks earlier during final preparations for Barbarossa, when the *Einsatzgruppen* were organized.

Equally, it is not known whether the original order referred to Jews only, or to all the categories of human being which the Nazis aimed to exterminate. The Roma people, for example, were also numerous in Eastern Europe and also faced the same genocidal treatment as the Jews. It could be that they, and others, were added as an afterthought. In several respects the implementation of the Holocaust showed signs of improvisation.

The killing of the Jews took three main forms: generalized maltreatment, shooting and gassing. Although the different methods were initiated at different times, they were running simultaneously for much of the time.

The maltreatment of Jews in the Nazi-built ghettos was not designed initially to kill them. It was just part of the scheme to segregate them from the population at large. But within a matter of months the overcrowding, disease, starvation diet and neglect were doing their work, and the 'problem' was beginning to solve itself as tens of thousands died. (To the SS, the ultimate outcome would have seemed similar to that of the treatment of Soviet POWs.)

As policy evolved, however, two trends can be observed. One was to speed up the killing and systematize it. The other was to put the segregated Jews to useful work as they waited their turn to be killed. As a result, some of the ghettos, such as that in Łódź, which was geared to war work, were kept in operation much longer than others. At the same time, some of the younger or healthier Jews, who were fit to work, were assigned to concentration camps as opposed to the dedicated death camps.

Shooting Jews, usually in large groups, was the speciality of the *Einsatzgruppen*. It mainly took place on German-occupied territory which before Operation Barbarossa had been occupied by the USSR, and hence in Lithuania, Byelorussia, eastern Poland and Ukraine. The sites of the largest shootings lay near the largest centres of population – in the Kaiserwald near Riga, at Ponary near Vilnius, in the Ninth Fort at Kaunas, in the Ratomskaya Ravine near Minsk, in the Drobitsky Ravine near Kharkov, and in the beautiful Gorge of Babi Yar near Kiev, where 33,000 men, women and children were killed in three days. In districts occupied by Germany's Romanian allies, like Bessarabia, Romanians often did the shooting. Captive Jews were forced to strip, lined up in rows on the edge of a mass grave, and mown down with machine-gun bullets. Up to a million died in this way.[106]

The work of the *Einsatzgruppen* was observed by other German soldiers, by local police, by passers-by and by German officials. Some of these officials felt that the methods used were intolerable. William Kube, the *Reichskommissar* at Minsk, wrote to Berlin on 27 October 1941 urging that the Führer be informed of the 'beastliness'. The reaction of the SS was to enforce greater secrecy.

At that very time the SS was opening a new 'Race and Resettlement Office' as Department IV of the RSHA. Its director was to be SS-Obersturmbahnführer Adolf Eichmann (1906–62), an ardent thirty-five-year-old Nazi, who would henceforth administer the logistics of the Final Solution.

The technique of killing people by gas was perfected in December 1941 following experiments conducted at Kulmhof (Chełmno), a village not far from Łódź in occupied Poland. The first tests, using mobile gas vans, proved inefficient. The programme therefore turned to stationary gas chambers, using Zyklon B gas, to which the victims would have to be transported. Estimates of the numbers killed at Kulmhof range from 150,000 to 400,000.

By now, Eichmann was getting into his stride. On 24 January 1942, together with Heydrich, he convened a conference at a villa in the elegant Berlin suburb of Wannsee. His purpose was to coordinate the activities of the various German agencies – the state railways, the Foreign Office and the different branches of the SS – whose cooperation was required. No doubt to the raised eyebrows of some present, he produced statistics for the number of Jews to be deported not only from German-occupied Europe but also from neutral countries, like Spain and Eire, and from the UK. In retrospect one can see that he was overstretching himself. But the scale of Nazi ambitions at that time was unmistakable.

Early in 1942, three purpose-built death camps were opened in remote parts of the General Government in an operation code-named 'Reinhard' in Heydrich's honour. These camps, at Sobibór, Bełzec and Treblinka, were not concentration camps, and they had no equivalent in the Soviet GULag. They were purely and simply killing stations, consisting of a railway terminal, a complex of gas chambers, and crematoria. As soon as they had served their purpose, they were ploughed into the earth. Sobibór consumed over 300,000 Jews, mainly from central Poland. Bełzec consumed about 600,000, mainly from the districts of Kraków and Lwów, together with around 1,500 Catholic Poles who had tried to help them. Treblinka consumed at least 700,000, including the inhabitants of the Warsaw Ghetto.[107] It is a source of great confusion that Auschwitz and not Treblinka has emerged as the prime memory site of the Holocaust.

The use of gas vans was not abandoned, however. It was reintroduced at various sites, including Maly Trostenets in Byelorussia, to which up to 250,000 were deported, and Zemun near Belgrade, where many Yugoslav Jews were killed.

In March 1942, under pressure of growing numbers, KL Auschwitz II–Birkenau was pressed into service. Its main section remained as a typical concentration-camp compound, with brick guardhouses, wooden huts, and an electrified barbed-wire fence. But its enlarged gas chambers and crematoria were turned over to the same purposes as those of the death camps. Its facilities were not reserved exclusively for Jews, although Jews came to form the clear majority of its million-plus victims (see p. 328). In 2006 the figure for Jewish deaths as given to tourists was 900,000. The figure of 4 million Jewish victims at Auschwitz, which had circulated during the Cold War, was a Soviet fabrication.[108]

Within a year of the Wannsee Conference a majority of the Jews of Central and Eastern Europe had already been destroyed, and the administrators of the Final Solution were facing two growing problems. One concerned the complexity of transporting Jews from ever more distant locations such as Rhodes, Bordeaux and even northern Norway. The other related to demands on the SS for supplying workers to Germany's shrinking labour pool. As from 1943, therefore, Eichmann's office followed a dual policy. On the one hand it organized a vast transport operation whereby hundreds of trains would be moved systematically round Europe's railway network and would deliver their human cargoes to Auschwitz and elsewhere in orderly sequence. Meanwhile, Jewish prisoners, especially men, who were still capable of work would be kept alive in their ghettos and camps and would be hired out as slave labourers on day release until their turn came in the gas-chamber queue. The Łódz Ghetto, for example, which made uniforms for the Wehrmacht, was kept at work until August 1944, and Auschwitz II–Birkenau was kept working until December 1944, when the arrival of the Red Army was imminent.

In the event, the Final Solution was left unfinished. The Reich collapsed before the SS could complete what they had regarded as their most constructive project. Some 150,000 hidden Jews survived in Poland, 200,000 remained untouched in France, 300,000 in Britain, and perhaps 500,000 in the USSR. What might have happened if the SS had been granted a few more years is worth considering.

News of the Holocaust provoked minimal reaction in the outside world. The alarm raised by the exiled Polish government in 1942 was ignored. Eyewitness reports brought out by couriers like Nowak or Karski fell on deaf ears. Appeals by Zionist organizations in 1944 for the approaches to Auschwitz to be bombed were rejected.[109]

Total Jewish losses from the Holocaust have been calculated many times, and they invariably amount to a figure between 5 and 6 million. That figure, generally rounded up to 6 million, is uncontestable. Nonetheless, historians must be careful not to exaggerate the subtotals. One cannot quote a figure of 4 million for Auschwitz and 2.25 million for Birkenau if one also wants to keep 2 million for the death camps and 1 million for the *Einsatzgruppen*, and still leave room for realistic estimates of the death toll in the ghettos, in the slave-labour gangs and in other concentration camps. The figures have to add up to be credible. In geographical terms, the 6 million total is usually apportioned between 3 million Polish Jews, 2 million from the USSR, and 1 million from other European countries.[110]

The impact of the Holocaust on international relations was felt before the killing stopped. Militant Zionists in Palestine began a war of terror against the mandated British authorities. They thought that the British were too pro-Arab and indifferent to their demands for greatly increased Jewish immigration. In contrast, the Grand Mufti of Jerusalem, Hadj Amin El-Husseini (1897–1974), who thought the British pro-Zionist, found his way to Berlin, where he conducted pro-German propaganda. Such were the origins of the crisis that was to lead to the creation of the state of

Israel, and to unending Arab–Israel conflict. Refugees from the Holocaust would soon render the Zionist cause unstoppable.[111]

Holocaust denial is a peculiar activity undertaken mainly by oddballs and political fanatics, who, like flat-earthers, demand their right to be heard. The well-known American scholar Noam Chomsky has taken a principled stand on the issue. If freedom of speech means freedom of speech, he maintains, then people should be free to speak absurdities like denying the Holocaust or denying the globular shape of the earth. He has a point, but is not popular with the so-called 'Holocaust enforcers', who try to insist not merely that the Holocaust was a reality but also that it was attended by a variety of ancillary realities of a less convincing kind.[112]

Needless to say, the heritage of the Holocaust is burdened with weighty moral and historical problems. The central historical problems revolve round the issue of comparison, which is one of the historian's basic tools and which cannot be discarded when inconvenient. The moral problems are legion. One relates to the danger of relativism, and to the need to apply the same criteria when judging different events. Another relates to moral equivalence, and to the imperative of giving the same infinite value to all human life and suffering. A third is concerned with the ethics of collaboration and hence with the sensitive issues of the Jewish ghetto police, of the *Kapos* and of the *Sonderkommandos* in the death camps. A fourth, which applies to all historians, centres on the duty of compassion. History without compassion is a very empty vessel.

Overall civilian losses

It is often said that one man or woman is a real person, who can be loved and painfully lost, but that the loss of 'a million' or of '10 million' is just an abstraction that leaves one cold. Certainly when discussing the civilian losses of the Second World War one is dealing with very large numbers that are hard to imagine.

The task of estimating the losses of 1939–45 presents many problems. Records were not always kept, and post-war authorities were forced to make improvised calculations. Boundaries had changed, and post-war officials were not always concerned with the fate of pre-war populations. Sometimes politics interfered. Some regimes were interested in minimizing their figures; others in maximizing them. Above all, in the region of Europe where losses were clearly highest, sound information was hardest to find. Official histories of the United Kingdom could state that the total of 'killed or missing, believed killed', came to 60,595. In the Soviet Union, experts drew up estimates to the nearest million or two, and even then were not allowed to publish them. Figures for countries which are now independent but which in 1939–45 were part of the USSR could not be drawn up until the 1990s.

It is important to realize that many of the largest categories overlap. Jewish losses, for example, reached nearly 6 million. Polish losses, based on post-war territorial definitions, were officially put at slightly more than 6 million (6,027,000). This does *not* mean that the joint losses of Jews and Poles come to 12 million. They are actually closer to 9 million, because about half of the Jews were Poles, i.e. Polish citizens, while large numbers of Poles and Polish Jews became Soviet citizens (see Diagrams overleaf).

As the above example shows, the definition of categories by citizenship, by nationality or ethnicity, or by religion is significant. Total losses for the Soviet Union – military and civilian, including Soviet Asia – are now estimated at 27 million. Until recently, most Westerners would have thought of them as 'Russians'. In reality, the old slogan of 'Twenty Million Russian War Dead' is false on all counts. They were 'neither twenty million, nor Russians, nor war dead'. Russians probably constituted a majority of Soviet military losses, although they were never counted as such. In the category of Soviet civilian losses by nationality, Ukrainians and Byelorussians top the list. The so-called 'war dead' included all the people killed by Stalin as well as those killed by the German invasion.[113]

Deportations, expulsions, evacuations and migrations complicate the issue further. Post-war censuses might show that the population of Ukraine was 12 or 15 million people short of natural projections from the 1939 figures. This does *not* mean that 12 or 15 million Ukrainians were killed during the war. A sizeable portion of the missing cohorts is certainly attributable to war deaths. But another portion must be attributed to individuals who were never born owing to the death of their potential parents, and a third portion can be explained by people leaving the country. But, there again, what happened to those who left? The answer is that they could have died or that they could have lived. One knows that the death rate among Ukrainian deportees, evacuees and slave labourers was 'high'. But it is impossible to calculate accurately.

Finally, the distinction between 'war dead' (meaning people killed as a direct result of the war) and 'human losses during the war' is not a trivial one. There were presumably a certain number of people who died

The wartime death-toll in Europe, 1939–45
(main categories)

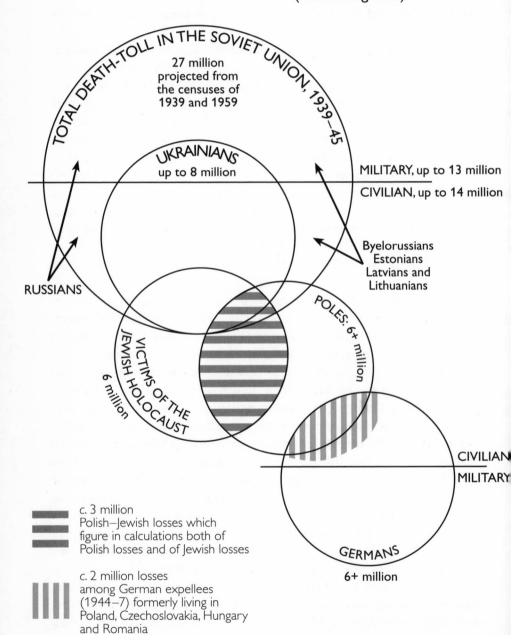

TOTAL DEATH-TOLL IN THE SOVIET UNION, 1939–45

27 million
projected from
the censuses of
1939 and 1959

UKRAINIANS
up to 8 million

MILITARY, up to 13 million

CIVILIAN, up to 14 million

Byelorussians
Estonians
Latvians and
Lithuanians

RUSSIANS

POLES: 6+ million

VICTIMS OF THE
JEWISH HOLOCAUST
6 million

CIVILIAN

MILITARY

c. 3 million
Polish–Jewish losses which
figure in calculations both of
Polish losses and of Jewish losses

c. 2 million losses
among German expellees
(1944–7) formerly living in
Poland, Czechoslovakia, Hungary
and Romania

GERMANS
6+ million

unnatural deaths in 1939–45 as a result of wartime murders and traffic accidents. They were not war dead. By the same token, two of the largest categories of civilian casualties of 1939–45, the victims of the Holocaust and the wartime victims of the GULag, have little direct connection with the war. They were the subject of internal repressions, and strictly speaking should be counted separately.

Nonetheless, despite the problems, attempts to estimate losses *are* made. And they *must* be made if any overall view of the war is to be constructed. Popular sources can easily be found that propose 37 million, as opposed to 25 million, military deaths, and a total of 62 million for the Second World War as a whole. One more circumspect authority quotes figures of 14.201 million military deaths, 24.042 million civilian deaths, and 38.343 total losses, including the USA, China and Japan.[114] If one subtracts figures from North America, the Far East and the British Commonwealth, one ends up with a credible result for 'war-related deaths' in Europe:

Military	9.326 million
Civilian	16.625 million
Total	**25.951 million**

Further breakdowns are usually effected either by country or by cause of death. In the civilian sector, the latter would include 'deaths in concentration camps', 'deaths from bombing' and 'deaths from other war-related causes'. This at least provides a basis for discussion.

Refinements can be made, however, without recourse to drastically new sources. It makes sense, for instance, to subdivide the figures for civilian losses by country into those for countries possessing established records and those for countries using demographic projections. And, in the case of the Soviet Union, there seems to be no point in repeating the numbers offered by the above-mentioned authority in his Table 1 (based on Khrushchev's rhetoric) instead of the updated numbers mentioned in his footnote. In consequence, the working figure for the USSR moves up to 27 million total deaths less 8.668 million military deaths or 18.332 million civilian deaths. And to recapitulate, not forgetting overlaps, the 18 million Soviet civilian losses would have included around 2 million Jews, 1–2 million Poles, 2–3 million Russians, 2–3 million Balts, 3–4 million Byelorussians and 5–8 million Ukrainians. Overall, Europe's civilian losses would appear to have exceeded military losses by a ratio not of 2:1 but of more than 3:1:

Recorded deaths *(Germany Italy, Austria, Finland,*	
UK, France, Benelux, Norway)	2.961 million
Projected deaths *(USSR, Romania, Hungary, Poland,*	
Czechoslovakia, Yugoslavia, Greece, Bulgaria,	
Albania)	25.327 million
Total	**28.288 million**

None of these calculations can be regarded as definitive, not least because many of the constituent estimates are constantly being questioned and reviewed. Even so, they provide the best working guide to overall dimensions.

Twenty-eight million is equivalent to the total population of a medium-sized European country or US state. It is mind-numbingly high, if one thinks in terms of individual lives and human suffering. Yet in demographic terms it represents hardly a minor blip on the screen. Europe's population, including European Russia, had grown by 3 million or more per annum during most decades of the previous century, taking the estimated total from 180 million in 1800 to *c*.500 million in 1939. In this light, a loss of 28 million in 1939–45 would be only slightly more than the loss of six years' natural increase. It is not to be numbered among the continent's biggest catastrophes – like the Black Death, which carried off perhaps a third of the population. After 1945, increase was resumed, bringing the estimated European total up to 728 million by 2000.[115]

Miscellaneous groups in wartime

Aristocrats

The French Revolution had taken place 150 years ago and the Russian Revolution only 25 years earlier. But most European countries had experienced no root-and-branch social revolution, and in 1939–45 the aristocracy was still alive and kicking. The Second World War brought another crop of casualties.

In Britain, for example, the hereditary House of Lords still formed an influential part of government. Churchill, though a lifelong democrat, was a scion of the Marlboroughs. And Churchill's rival for PM in 1940, and later British ambassador in Washington, Lord Halifax, sported a viscount's title. The extraordinary episode of Rudolf Hess, Hitler's deputy, who flew secretly to Britain in May 1941 to arrange peace talks, was based on his mistaken belief that the Duke of Hamilton must be a powerful political figure.

The Nazis, however, were social radicals, opposed as much to privilege as to Communism. (Ribbentrop, a former wine-seller, was a phoney aristocrat, who had added the aristocratic 'von' to his name for effect. In the aristocratic league table, he was many rungs below Mussolini's foreign minister and son-in-law, Galeazzo Ciano, Conte di Cortellazzo.) When the Reich moved east, all the great Polish landowning families were dispossessed. The Nazis believed in blood, but not in 'blue blood'.

Germany's military defeat spelled disaster for the old Prussian nobility. In 1939, the Junker families still held many high positions in the army and still maintained their estates in the eastern provinces. In 1944–5, they were eliminated as a coherent social group. One historian, who studied a large sample of 8,827 such nobles, found that 6,448 were killed during the war. About 500 committed suicide after the war, and a similar number died in Soviet captivity. Several hundred were murdered by slave workers who had been allocated to their estates.[116] What is more, the disaster had been foreseen. Even before the First World War, Chancellor Bethmann-Hollweg had dissuaded his son from planting oak trees on their Prussian estate, because 'the Russians will come before the trees mature'.

In theory, the Soviet regime was fundamentally hostile to aristocrats, of which in the USSR there were none left on public view. Yet in 1944, when the Red Army re-entered Eastern Europe, posing for the time being as a moderate social force, the presence of a 'Red Prince' in their baggage was part of the show. The Lublin Committee of 1944–5 broke up the larger estates in Poland for the benefit of poor peasants, but briefly restored some of the country houses to their owners, so that the post-war Stalinist regime could subsequently dispossess them for a second time.

Watching developments in East Prussia, Countess Marion Dönhoff (1909–2002) did not wait to test the Red Army's benevolence. Her brothers had been killed at the front, and she had been left alone running the family house and estate at Friedrichstein. In January 1945 she mounted her horse, joined the *Ostflucht*, and rode over 950 km to West Germany, stopping only once, at the Bismarcks', to freshen up. The world of her childhood vanished. She turned to journalism, becoming the long-term editor of *Die*

Zeit. 'The highest forms of love,' she reflected, 'are not connected to possessions.'[117]

Assassins

Killing is the normal business of war. So mere assassinations, which in a peacetime context might seem distressing, cease to shock. A commando who knifes a sentry in cold blood becomes a brave man. And a political opponent felled by an ice-axe swung at his skull during the Battle of Britain becomes a forgotten footnote.

Few people care to reflect on the fact that Adolf Hitler was surrounded by would-be assassins, and constantly ran their gauntlet. They varied from ordinary German citizens and soldiers to high-placed members of the Abwehr and the Nazi Party. If one believes his testimony at Nuremberg, they included Albert Speer. They all failed.[118]

Among the numerous conspiracies against Hitler, one of the most curious was the non-event prepared by the Soviet NKVD. Stalin had successfully plotted the murder of all his rivals, from Bukharin to Kamenev, and from Kirov to Trotsky. And if the long arm of the NKVD could reach to Mexico, it could easily reach to Berlin or to Berchtesgaden. So the assassination of Hitler would have been standard Stalinist procedure. What is more, as shown by the case of Colonel von Stauffenberg, who carried a bomb into Hitler's presence on three separate occasions, the Führer's security was rather inefficient. Yet no Soviet plan was attempted. It seems, apparently, that Stalin rated Hitler less useful dead than alive.

Stalin himself took elaborate precautions against assassination. He used doubles, and on his annual visit to his mother in Georgia five identical trains, carrying five identical Stalins, were said to leave Moscow by different routes. And, as far as is known, no assassin came near to success. Stalin did not have to suffer the sort of near-miss which on 20 July 1944, but for the intervention of a solid oak table support, would have torn Hitler to pieces.

The death of General Sikorski in July 1943 is an event which many people still refuse to accept as an accident. It is known that an attempt was made to sabotage his plane earlier, on a trip to Canada. So long as British intelligence files remain closed, rumours and speculative theories will continue to thrive.

Bankers

No war can be fought without money. And the bankers who finance wars have been called the 'unseen militarists'.

The Bank of England in 1939 had already lost many of its former powers to the Treasury. Under its long-serving governor, Sir Montagu Norman (1871–1950), it played a secondary role in negotiating the arrangements whereby Britain's finances were rescued by the USA.

In Nazi Germany, Dr Hjalmar Schacht (1877–1970) was the most prominent banking figure. Three times president of the Reichsbank, he slipped in and out of favour, and ended the war under suspicion in Dachau. He was acquitted by the Nuremberg Tribunal. The banking system of the Reich was saved from isolation by its access to Switzerland, which otherwise would probably have been occupied.[119]

The USSR was officially opposed to capitalism, but it needed banking services like everyone else. The state-owned Gosbank, created in 1929 to service the centrally planned economy, financed the entire Soviet war effort by printing non-convertible roubles. Its chairman throughout the war, General N. A. Bulganin, was to emerge as a leading figure of the post-Stalin era.

By the 1940s, however, no one could have any illusions about the fact that the USA had become the world's principal financial power. Roosevelt's long-term adviser in the field was Marriner Stoddard Eccles (1890–1977), a Mormon from Utah, who had organized the financing of the New Deal via the Banking Act of 1935, and who served for seventeen years as chairman of the Federal Reserve. At the Bretton Woods conference of 1944, Eccles, after whom the 'Fed Building' in Washington, DC, is named, played a strong hand in the founding of the World Bank and the IMF, and in the launch of the Marshall Plan. He is unseen in most accounts of the war.[120]

Bystanders

To those who were trapped in the worst hellholes of the Second World War – such as the Nazi ghettos – it seemed that humanity could be divided into three categories. There were the perpetrators or tormentors, who deliberately inflicted suffering. There were the victims of the perpetrators. And there were the bystanders – who simply stood and watched.[121]

In reality, things were rather more complicated. Totalitarian oppression was a moving machine. It caught different people at different moments. Those who appeared to be bystanding might only have been waiting their turn. And victims, if they survived with hatred in their hearts – as some did – could turn perpetrator. One must shun simplistic categorizations, therefore, especially those that are based on ethnic stereotyping.

Israel Shahak (1933–2001) confessed to having been a bystander. His family lived in a section of the Warsaw Ghetto that was among the last to be cleared. They had a modest reserve of food. So in April 1943 they sat down as usual to a Passover meal, for the last time. Their aim was to live in dignity for as long as possible. They watched their neighbours being driven off. Finally it was their turn. The young Israel, a boy of ten, escaped through the sewers.[122]

Ryszard Kapuscinski (b. 1932) lived in Pińsk, a few hundred kilometres further east, in the Soviet zone. He was seven, and in the first class at school. He remembers how every day another empty place appeared in the classroom. And everyone pretended that nothing was happening. Eventually, when only a handful of children were left, the Soviet security police came for his teacher as well. Young Richard ran out of school, found the line of cattle trucks parked in the station siding, and saw his teacher standing by an open door. He wanted to climb on the train himself.[123]

The most frequent accusations of bystanding are directed at people who watched the Holocaust happen. These charges take little account of the high walls that surrounded the ghettos, the terrible punishments that awaited any would-be helper, and the military force that was used during the clearances. One such clearance – of the ghetto in Kraków – was well portrayed in Steven Spielberg's film *Schindler's List*. What the film did not show was a Nazi 'action' that was in progress at the same time. One day in July 1943 all the men and youths of the Catholic parish of Wola Justowska in Kraków were rounded up by the SS on suspicion of helping the resistance. They were forced to dig a pit, in which they were then buried alive. The womenfolk of the parish were forced at gunpoint to watch. They too were bystanders.

Children

The Second World War was particularly catastrophic for children. Apart from those successfully evacuated (see below), millions perished in bombings, in the deportations, and in the genocide. In one night 5,586 children died at Hamburg; an estimated 1.2 million died in the Holocaust. In 1945 Europe had to cope with 13 million abandoned children. Poland alone was left with a million orphans.

In the totalitarian countries, party ideology (like that of the Jesuits) believed in catching its recruits young. Both the *Hitlerjugend* and the Soviet Pioneers taught that loyalty to the party state was supreme, superseding ties to family, friends or faith. Though the League of German Maidens instilled its members with a more conventional role, it shared with Soviet organizations the public glorification of motherhood. Some 75–80 per cent of youth was forcibly co-opted. But the USSR saw no counterculture groups such as the *Swing-Jugend* or the *Edelweisspiraten*.

In the nature of things, most children are too young to take independent action, and thus remain faceless to history. But the small group of identical twins kept alive in Auschwitz for genetic research left their mark. So too did the urchin ghetto-smugglers and the boy soldiers on all sides. Soviet Pioneers were renowned as partisan scouts; and in the nemesis of 1944–5 their counterparts in the *Hitlerjugend* were brought to the front line.

Anne Frank (1929–45) was the daughter of German Jewish refugees, who lived in hiding in Amsterdam. Betrayed in August 1944, she died in Bergen-Belsen. But her diary, recovered and published after the war, recorded the inner life and intimate thoughts of a youngster who was very much alive, and wanted to live.[124]

Antek 'Rozpylacz' (1932–44), literally 'Tony the Flamethrower', was a twelve-year-old (illegal) anti-Nazi fighter who died on the barricades of the Warsaw Rising. His speciality was crawling out through the rubble under fire to cut the cables of German 'Goliath' robot tanks. Ignoring the reprimands of adult comrades, who in theory accepted no one under eighteen, he attached himself to one of the Home Army battalions, and died, like most of them, in the cause. A monument to the 'Little Insurrectionary' now stands near the Barbican in Warsaw's Old Town.[125] Soviet wartime legends are full of similar cases.

Portrayals of children as victims or as mini-heroes, however, hardly do justice to the complexity of the subject. According to the most reflective observer of events in Germany, the supreme quality which children displayed in extreme circumstances was adaptability. They had no earlier experience with which to compare their trauma, and so gained the habit of treating the exceptional as normal. The result was surprising resilience. Little girls played with their dolls, to protect them from the enemy. In the cellars of Berlin, German boys played at 'Russian soldiers', because the Russians were winning. There was even a game called 'Gas Chamber'. Older children learned to beg, to steal and to smuggle. They were also susceptible to the propaganda of the regime. In 1945 tens of thousands of fourteen-year-olds volunteered for the *Volkssturm*, and met their deaths with eager faces. A young teenager, given a rifle, found himself on a beach in East Prussia herding a group of Jewish women, who were about to be shot. Not surprisingly, at the end of the war, juvenile delinquency was rife.[126]

Children, Jewish children, were the concern of Irena Sendler (b. 1910), who in 1942 was an employee of the Social Welfare Department in Warsaw. In her capacity as a health inspector, she was able to visit the Ghetto, where she wore a Jewish armband and was appalled by the desperate plight of the children. She was a Roman Catholic, and the mother of a small child of her own.

Knowing both of the high infantile death-rate and the imminent prospect of 'resettlement', Irena conceived a plan of smuggling out as many babies as possible. The plan was put into operation with the help of Zegota, the Polish Council for Aid to the Jews. Parents had to be persuaded. Accomplices had to be found to hide the fugitives in carts, ambulances and hearses, or to carry them out in sacks and suitcases. Nuns were recruited to give them shelter and to change their identities and childless couples were sought to act as substitute parents. Records were kept, and hidden in buried jars, so that after the war the children's original names could be recovered. Some 2,500 were saved before the Ghetto was liquidated.

In October, the Gestapo arrested Irena Sendler, and beat her so badly that both her legs were broken. They extracted no information, so sentenced her to death. She was saved by a prison guard who took a bribe before posting her name on a list of executed people.

Irena's story was largely unknown outside Poland until 1999, when a group of school kids from Uniontown, Kansas, wrote a play about her called *Life in a Jar*. The play was performed many times, and eventually the young dramatists were flown out to Warsaw to meet her. 'What I did was not extraordinary,' she told them, 'It was a normal thing to do.'[127]

Probably the largest single evacuation of children during the war took place alongside the withdrawal of the Anders Army from Central Asia to Iran in 1943. Some 40,000 Polish orphans, who had been deported to the USSR with their families two or three years earlier and had lost their parents, were now taken to safety. On arrival in Iran, they were welcomed by the British, who encouraged them to write depositions that are now in the Hoover Archives in California. The majority were taken with the women and elderly to India; some travelled to camps in Tanganyika and Kenya, and at least one shipload was taken to New Zealand.[128]

Sixty years after the war, much interest centred on the boyhood of Joseph Ratzinger (b. 1927), who in 2005 became Pope Benedict XVI. Ratzinger was born to a Bavarian Catholic family at Marktl am Inn, in a very similar *heimat* to that of Adolf Hitler, and tabloid reaction asked 'was he a Nazi?' He wasn't. His father, a police officer who opposed the Nazi regime, lost his job, and the family had to move four times in the 1930s in search of work. At Traunstein, where they eventually settled, the growing boy could not have failed to hear of ugly events. Anti-Semitic violence erupted on Kristallnacht. A local anti-Nazi shot himself to avoid arrest. And a cousin of the family with Down's syndrome was taken away and murdered. In April 1941 the young Joseph was obliged to join the *Hitlerjugend*, and two years later the *Luftwaffenhilfer* as an air-force auxiliary. He helped construct anti-aircraft defences on the Hungarian frontier, underwent basic army training, ran away, and was briefly interned by US forces. Like many Germans, he did not rebel. But neither did he show the least enthusiasm. According to his biographer, he was simply biding his time until he could pursue the path of the priesthood.[129]

It is important to remember that all armies in Europe relied on the conscription of youths who were physically mature but psychologically still maturing. At the age of eighteen, boys were more malleable and more vulnerable than they would become a few years later. In Britain, where the legal age of adulthood stood at twenty-one, they were put into uniform and sent off to kill before they were allowed to vote. American boys were plucked from the streets of New York or from a farm in Kansas, and shipped to a new country. They were still children.[130]

Clergy

With the exception of the USSR, where the Orthodox Church had been tamed and the clergy decimated by the Bolsheviks, Europe in the 1940s was still a predominantly Christian continent. Issues of life and death came to the fore in wartime, and the views of clergy were widely sought. Under Pius XII, the Vatican had condemned both Fascism and Communism, but was notoriously reluctant to risk bold statements or practical action.

In Britain, the Protestant Establishment gave its blessing to the war, although the Archbishop of Canterbury, William Temple, was notably restrained, and his *Christianity and the Social Order* (1942) was a bestseller. George Bell, Bishop of Chichester, represented the openly critical wing of opinion, while Hewlett Johnson, the 'Red Dean' of Canterbury, fatuously believed that Christianity was compatible with Soviet Communism. His views were eccentric, but it is significant that they were tolerated.[131] Owing to the neutrality of Catholic Ireland, some fundamentalist Protestants, especially in Belfast, tried to make out that British Catholics were potentially disloyal.

In the USSR, the German invasion of 1941 saved the Russian Orthodox Church from total extinction. Only a handful of churches were still operating on Soviet territory after two decades of persecution. But Stalin was forced to relent. Church leaders emerged from the catacombs, and in regions occupied by the Germans a remarkable revival took place both of the Orthodox and of the Ukrainian Churches. In 1943 Stalin restored the Orthodox patriarchate of Moscow.

In Germany, the Christian Churches were confused by the rise of pagan Nazism. A pro-Nazi movement of 'German Christians' emerged with 'the swastika on their arms and the Cross in their hearts', and some Christian leaders supported the crusade against 'godless Bolshevism'. But bewilderment, sometimes coupled with active resistance, was the most usual reaction. The Protestant theologian Dietrich Bonhoeffer (1906–45) met Bishop Bell in Stockholm in 1942 in a vain attempt to win British support for the anti-Nazi resistance. He was subsequently arrested by the Gestapo and murdered.[132]

In several countries, Christian clergy were targeted by the totalitarian regimes. In parts of Greece, for instance, Orthodox priests paid the price for supporting the resistance. In occupied Poland, Roman Catholic priests were murdered or deported en masse from the territories annexed to the

Reich, as part of the Nazi campaign of repression against the intelligentsia. They were spared the same treatment in the General Government, where the Catholic Church remained intact under its doughty Cardinal-Prince, Adam Sapieha (1867–1951). But their turn would undoubtedly have come had the German occupation lasted a little longer. The Polish Primate, Cardinal Hlond, was living in exile. In western Ukraine, the Germans permitted the Greek Catholic (Uniate) Church to continue, although it was threatened with persecution and repression each time that the Red Army approached. The Greek Catholic Metropolitan, Andrey Sheptytskyi (1865–1944), proved a tower of strength – one of very few prelates in Europe who dared to stand up against Nazidom in the name of the faith. He saved thousands of Jews, begged the Vatican to intervene, and preached a famous sermon in 1942 on the Fifth Commandment – 'Thou shalt not kill.'[133]

Considerable debate has swirled over the years round Pope Pius XII, and his stance towards Fascism in general and the Holocaust in particular (see p. 376). Yet Pius XII was not alone in attracting suspicion. In December 1944, Mgr Angelo Roncalli, the future Pope John XXIII, was sent to Paris to replace a nuncio who had worked too closely with the Vichy regime. He had strong anti-Nazi credentials, having helped thousands of fugitive Jews during his previous posting in Turkey. He went on to be *il papa buono*, the father of ecumenism, and 'the most popular Pope of modern times'. Examination of his wartime correspondence, however, has somewhat dented the image. It turns out that Roncalli thought that the defeat of 'worked-out French democracy' in 1940 had been well deserved. And his advice to his relatives in Fascist Italy was to work, pray, suffer, obey and keep quiet, keep quiet, keep quiet.'[134]

Collaborators

The concept of collaboration is loaded with negative associations that go far beyond literal definitions. It refers to activities which in military codes are called 'aiding and abetting the enemy', and which for moral reasons are avoided by decent people. It involves a variety of forms of assisting oppressors in their oppression, and by implication contains a strong streak of betrayal, of taking sides against the weak and the oppressed. Vidkun Quisling was a collaborator (see p. 304). So too were all the informers and auxiliaries who helped the Gestapo or the NKVD to find and torment their neighbours.

The phenomenon of collaboration, however, is complicated by three factors. Firstly, it could be a collective as well as an individual activity. There were collaborationist regimes, which put all the resources of a state or nation at the disposal of an oppressor. Secondly, collaboration often overlaps with the category of victimhood. If one enquires into the motives and circumstances of collaboration, one soon discovers that the collaborators were often oppressed themselves in some way, and that they acted as they did to alleviate their own condition, to protect their own families or to save their own skins. People living in free countries rarely appreciate the devilish means whereby totalitarian regimes can force human beings to prey on each other. And, thirdly, if collaboration is to be judged fairly, it must be judged by standards that apply to all. If it was wrong for one person or group to assist in the persecution of others, it is also wrong if in parallel circumstances the persecuted do not refrain from persecuting someone else. Many people who were directly familiar with the horrendous realities of 1939–45 refuse to judge others. But, if condemnation does take place, historians and others can permit themselves the luxury only if they apply the same criteria to all groups for the same sorts of offences.

For example, in all parts of Europe occupation regimes raised local police forces to assist them. Uniformed civilian police are a standard feature of all civilized societies, and generally speaking the recruits were not told beforehand what they might be ordered to do. To begin with they were just doing a job, glad to be fed and paid. As police, they would have been controlling traffic, or hunting for smugglers, or issuing identity cards. Yet the day would surely come when the order was given to stand guard at a prison camp, to pack women and children into cattle trucks, or to shoot a line of prisoners on the edge of a mass grave. To refuse the order meant certain death. To run away spelled death or ruin for one's family. And, from the moral point of view, it made little difference if the order was given by the SS or by the NKVD.

Calel Perechodnik (1916–44) was a local policeman who faced acute dilemmas. He was recruited by the Nazis as a member of the Jewish Police Force that kept order in the ghetto of Otwock, a little town near Warsaw. To begin with he did nothing extraordinary. But in 1942, when deportations to the death camps began, he obeyed orders to herd, to beat and to kill his own people. Torn by remorse, he managed to escape the ghetto and survived long enough to write a memoir, which was discovered after his death. It is called *Am I a Murderer?*[135]

Salomon Morel (b. 1919) came from those same parts, and survived the war. But in 1944 he joined the Communist security service, and for several months served as commandant of a prison camp, which used the facilities of the former Stalag VIIIB at Lamsdorf in Silesia. During his tenure, it is alleged that 1,500 prisoners died of maltreatment. The indictment took fifty years to arrive. When it did, Morel fled to Israel, where he was in no danger of extradition.[136]

Communists

As members of one of the two premier radical movements of the twentieth century, Communists saw themselves, and were often seen by others, as leaders in 'the struggle against Fascism'. Directed from 'the centre' in Moscow, especially up to 1943 by Comintern, they operated in virtually all European countries, including those where the Communist Party was illegal. They had been very strong in Germany, but were all but crushed out of existence there after the Nazis' rise to power. They were secretive, manipulative, violent and ruthless, and were highly effective in resistance organizations, especially in France, Italy, Greece and Yugoslavia. From 1935, when the USSR was admitted to the League of Nations, they had pursued the strategy of 'popular fronts', whereby they sought to work inside the democracies alongside other 'progressive forces'. For this reason, though essentially hostile to Western democracy, they never roused the same fears as Fascism did – except in those countries where they were known by their deeds.

In the first phase of the war, however, the Communist parties of Europe were in total disarray. Schooled for years in the struggle against capitalism and Fascism, their leadership was totally disoriented by Stalin's partnership with Hitler. 'To stand aside from this conflict,' wrote Harry Pollitt, the British party secretary, on 2 September 1939, 'would be a betrayal of everything our forebears have fought to achieve.'[137] For this he was reprimanded by Moscow, and demoted.

Yet in the last phase of the war Communism was riding high – higher, in fact, than at any point before or since. The victories of the Red Army had lent great prestige not only to the USSR but to Communist theory and practice, especially on issues such as social welfare and state direction of industry. In actual fact, Communism in the 1940s meant Stalinism and

Soviet power and nothing much else: the Comintern was abolished; and the welfare of human beings, like economics, was among the weakest features of its armoury.

Most of the Communist leaders from continental Europe passed the war in Soviet exile; they stayed in the International Hotel in Moscow. They were members of a worldwide political sect that, at the time, had global ambitions. It was widely feared that they would foment social unrest when they returned home. But they only resorted to violence in conjunction with the NKVD in Eastern Europe. Elsewhere, in the absence of the Red Army, they resorted under Stalin's orders to the tactics of the popular front.

Maurice Thorez (1900–1964) returned to France in 1944, and, at the head of the PCF, commanded the strongest grouping in French politics. He joined the government of General de Gaulle as vice-premier, but never progressed further. Palmiro Togliatti (1893–1964) followed a similar course. Exiled from Fascist Italy since the 1920s, he returned in 1944 and was supported by the largest block of Communist voters in Europe. Through the *svolta di Salerno*, he abandoned revolutionary politics, and was able to enter the first post-war coalition.[138]

The East European Communists had a harder time. Their activities were closely directed by Soviet advisers, and the peasant societies of the East were staunchly opposed to Communism on both economic and religious grounds. Violence ensued. In Poland, Bolesław Bierut (1892–1956) was virtually unknown. Participating in underground resistance from 1943, he surfaced with the Lublin Committee, pretending to be a neutral, non-party figure. He did not show his true colours until 1948. In Czechoslovakia, Klement Gottwald (1896–1953) returned in 1945, and acted in public like the Communist leaders of Western Europe, serving as vice-premier in the Beneš government. After the Communist coup of February 1948, however, he turned both on his democrat partners and on his rival, Rudolf Slánský, who was liquidated by show trial. In contrast, Mátyás Rákosi (1892–1972), who had once been an officer of the Comintern, returned to his native Hungary as general secretary of the Communist Party, and remained in power until the Budapest Rising in 1956. Walter Ulbricht (1893–1973), a Saxon, was a founder member of the Communist Party of Germany (KPD). He was a member of the Reichstag in 1928–33, and an exile from 1933 to 1945 first in Prague, then in Moscow. 'Nobody,' he said in 1961, 'intends to build a wall.'

In Romania, a duel developed between the 'Muscovite faction' led by

Ana Pauker (Rabinsohn, 1893–1960) and the so-called 'prison faction' led by Gheorghe Gheorghiu Dej (1901–65), who spent the war in one of Marshal Antonescu's jails. The Muscovites held the upper hand until 1952. Among the Bulgaria comrades, the dominant figure was Georgi Dimitrov (1882–1949), who, as Comintern secretary general, was the senior East European comrade in wartime Moscow. Before the war, Dimitrov had figured in the Reichstag-fire trial. After the war he showed great enthusiasm for a Balkan Socialist Federation, which was not to Stalin's liking. He was recalled to Moscow, and died suddenly, possibly from irradiation or poisoning.[139]

Without doubt, the most delicate issue in the history of the Communism movement centres on the fact that a disproportionate percentage of its supporters were Jewish or rather, as Isaac Deutscher put it, 'non-Jewish Jews'. Lenin himself was Jewish (according to traditional Jewish rules), and the same can be said of an absolute majority of the original Bolshevik leadership. The Nazis exploited the fact to the full, talking habitually of 'Jewish Bolshevism.' As if Jewishness and Communism were interchangeable. They completely ignored some other indisputable facts, including the incompatibility of Judaism and Communism and the overwhelming majority of Jews in general who strongly opposed Communist ideology. Stalin, who had killed all the surviving Bolshevik leaders and who was planning a Jewish purge when he died, is often judged to have been an anti-Semite. Nonetheless, the various Communist parties that began to take over Eastern Europe in 1944–5 still contained strong Jewish contingents, especially in the security services, and their oppressions inevitably caused old tensions to resurface. As a result, the Jewish issue did not disappear when the Nazis were defeated.

In short, the paths followed by the Communist movement varied from country to country. Tito in Yugoslavia was exceptional in that he succeeded in forming a post-war regime in large measure through his own efforts.[140]

Criminals

Crime is a constant in human society. But crime rates go up and down according to prevailing conditions. They certainly went up in 1939–45, owing to the violence, the deprivations and the disorder which war promoted.

In the totalitarian countries, two factors were significant. One lay in the concept of 'political crime' – which could be taken to mean opposition to anything which the regime decreed. The other lay in the extreme severity with which even minor offences could be punished. In police states, the hard-pressed police could react with impunity against 'politicals' and civilian criminals alike. In Nazi Germany and the USSR, social order appeared to reign for the simple reason that the criminal classes could be eliminated with no questions asked.

In Italy, the war came as a lifesaver to the Mafia, which had been under attack for two decades by the Fascist regime. The arrival of foreign armies not only removed official controls but also offered lucrative opportunities. It is said that the US Army brought in gang leaders from the US to re-establish links with the Sicilian godfathers.

Even in Britain, which had prided itself on its orderly pre-war society, the stresses of war brought a marked increase in crime, not least in London. Looting occurred as soon as the bombs of the Blitz began to fall. Bombed houses were raided. Valuables disappeared. Carpets and lead pipes were ripped out. In the first prosecutions, in November 1940, it was members of the ARP and of the AFS who faced the charges. The blackout created ideal conditions for burglars, pickpockets and rapists. Offences proliferated as the rate of police successes dropped.

Fraudulent claims provided another problem. People who had lost their home were entitled to a £500 advance on post-war compensation up to £20,000. People who took in evacuees or service personnel were entitled to payment of 10s. 6d. per week. The National Assistance Office was swamped with claimants, and found it easier to pay than to verify.

A British MP called black-marketeering 'treason of the worst kind'. But, with food, fuel and clothes rationing in force, illegal trade of all sorts flourished. In Glasgow, many people died from drinking home-brewed 'hooch'.

Murders in England and Wales increased by 22 per cent. The increase was partly due to the ready supply of firearms, and partly to opportunism. Bombed-out ruins provided good cover for murderers, who sought to disguise their prey as Blitz victims.

The arrival of the Americans in 1943 inevitably impacted on civilian life. American luxury goods – like cigarettes and nylons – boosted the black market, whilst no few rape cases ended in death sentences. An exception was made in the case of a black US soldier who was badly beaten by the police at Combe Down, Dorset, before being found guilty of rape. He was reprieved. Another GI, Karl Halten, caused a sensation in 1944 when he went on a rampage of theft and killing with his Welsh stripper girlfriend. He was executed.[141]

In the Third Reich and the Soviet Union, however, the basic problems derived from the fact that criminals – i.e. people who showed no respect for the rights, dignity, lives or property of others – had taken control of the state. In a very real sense, the war on the Eastern Front can be described as a fight to the death between gangsters.

Culture lords

Totalitarianism aims to embrace culture, and to subject it, like everything else, to the control of the dictatorial state. And war only intensifies its ambition.

In the Third Reich, therefore, a *Reichskulturkammer* was established in 1933, under the close supervision of Goebbels's propaganda ministry. It consisted of seven chambers, controlling literature, cinema, music, theatre, the arts, the press and broadcasting, each with its own 'little *Führer*', such as the theatrical boss Robert Ley, founder of the 'Strength through Joy' movement, or the painter Adolf Ziegler. It claimed a monopoly, and demanded certificates of political and racial correctness from all its members. It caused the pre-war exodus of some 5,000 artists and intellectuals, and enforced Nazi standards of aesthetics and artistic priorities on those who remained.

The Soviet Union exercised control through the cultural department of the Party, and the bureaucrats of the dependent state ministries. Even so, the pattern was different from that in Germany. Whereas the Nazis constantly tightened their grip, the Soviets, having created a fearsome culture machine in the 1930s, somewhat relaxed it in 1941–5, then had to reassert it afterwards. Figures such as Alexander Fadeev, the literary chief, or Ilya Ehrenburg, were genuinely popular. Most striking, however, is the remarkable similarity with the Nazis' cultural ethos: the glorification of war, the gigantism of so-called Realism, and the appeal to nationalistic history.

In Britain, though war censorship, paper rationing and the Ministry of Information had their effect, there was no state-run culture machine. Instead, there was a widespread realization that the nation's very existence was at stake, and that culture constituted an essential element of national identity. One might say that this attitude was rather un-English, but the times were exceptional and the results were spectacular. Kenneth Clark, the art critic and director of the National Gallery, presided over a War Artists' Committee, while the economist John Maynard Keynes ran a Committee for the Encouragement of Music and the Arts. The prestige of the BBC was never higher.[142]

Diplomats

Despite first appearances, wartime foreign relations were not conducted exclusively by armies. All parties to the conflict conducted diplomatic relations with their allies or partners, and with representatives of conquered or occupied countries. There are long stories to be told both about the Axis and about Allied diplomacy.

Axis diplomacy was one-sided in nature and limited in time. Hitler always guarded a soft spot for Mussolini – who 'showed that everything was possible'. But the Wilhelmstrasse lost patience with Count Ciano early on, and the whole affair ended badly in 1943. He produced a telling maxim. 'Victory has a hundred fathers,' he said in 1942, 'defeat is an orphan.' The Axis link with Japan, which seemed to be prospering in its early stages, was not cultivated after 1941 and was allowed to wither.

Nonetheless, diplomatic relations were maintained among members of the Axis block. And the German ambassadors in Budapest, Helsinki, Bucharest, Sofia and Tokyo, as in Moscow to 1941 and Rome to 1943, were powerful figures. In Romania, for instance, ambassador Manfred von Killinger played a critical role during the royal coup of 1944.

Allied diplomacy was more complicated, not least through the gulf of political views that separated the participants. In the first phase it was dominated by the triangle of Britain–France–Poland. From 1941 to 1945 it shifted to the new triangle of the 'Big Three': Britain–USA–USSR. In practice this meant the complicated relationships between the war leaders, Churchill, Roosevelt and Stalin: between their foreign ministers, Anthony Eden (1897–1977), Cordell Hull (1871–1955) and Vyacheslav Molotov (1890–1956); and between the professional diplomats in London, Washington and Moscow (see Table opposite).

Diplomats were very active in London, where representatives of all the exiled governments were in constant session. The big topic for them was the future of Europe, and it was in London – in the hands of Paul-

	UK	USA	USSR
Ambassador			
in London		Joseph P. Kennedy *1938–40*	Ivan Maisky *1932–43*
		John G. Winant *1941–6*	Fyodor Gusev *1943–6*
in Moscow	Stafford Cripps *1940–2*	Laurence Steinhardt *1939–Nov. 1941*	
	Archibald Clark Kerr *Mar. 1942–6*	William H. Standley *Feb. 1942–Sept. 1943*	
		Averell Harriman *Oct. 1943–Jan. 1946*	
in Washington	Marquess of Lothian *1939–40*		Maxim Litvinov *1941–3*
	Lord Halifax *1940–6*		Andrei Gromyko *1943–6*

Wartime ambassadors of the 'Big Three'

Henri Spaak, Jean Monnet, Salvador de Madariaga and Józef Retinger – that the foundations of the post-war European Movement were laid.[143]

Diplomacy also continued in the neutral capitals, where Axis and Allied representatives rubbed shoulders. Stockholm, Berne and Ankara all provided the setting for important exchanges, especially in the scramble for realignments in the final phase of the war.

None of the wartime diplomats was more remarkable than Vyacheslav Molotov, Stalin's voice in foreign affairs throughout the war. A fanatical Bolshevik of long standing, known for his blood-curdling denunciations of the victims of Stalin's purges, he was undiplomatic in the extreme: rude, grumpy and often uncommunicative. He was the exact opposite of the emollient Maxim Litvinov, whom he replaced in May 1939 in expectation of the Nazi–Soviet Pact. Yet he was obviously very competent; he survived all the crises and changes of tack; and his hard-nosed style, by disconcerting his fellow diplomats, kept them all at the required distance. Molotov more than anyone was the engineer of the Western Allies' inability to penetrate the Soviet puzzle.[144]

Dispossessed

Wartime Europe was full of the dispossessed. They came as individuals, as families, as communities, and as entire nations. Very often they were people who were lucky not to have lost their lives. They were survivors of war, bombing, deportations, ethnic cleansing and genocide.

The question of restitution arose before the war ended, and in some countries of Western Europe various compensation schemes were instituted. But in the broad zone where Nazi occupation had been followed by Soviet occupation the defence of property rights was not on the official agenda. The Soviets were the most active dispossessors of all, and the Soviet-style post-war regimes – like the Nazi order before them – saw property-owners as fair prey.

Apart from that, chains of dispossession, repossession and redistribution often rendered property claims all but incalculable. A hypothetical case may help to illustrate the complexities. The owner of a substantial freehold plot with house and surrounding land was driven out by the Nazis and his property was seized. He and/or his descendants were the object of a clear act of injustice, and they feel that they are owed restitution. But the house was turned into a hospital, and the land was divided up between German settlers from the Baltic States. In 1944–5, the Red Army arrived. The German hospital was turned into a state orphanage; the German settlers fled; the land was given to 'repatriants' from the East, who had also been dispossessed; and the whole district ceased to be part of the Reich. How can justice be possibly achieved for all?

The state and private property chains involved tens of millions. Most people had little choice but to write off their pre-war assets and to start a new life in a new place, frequently in a new country. Such was the case of Dr Horst Koehler, sometime managing director of the IMF, and the ninth federal president of Germany, born in 1943 to resettled peasant parents at Skierbieszów in the General Government. Relocated to Germany at the end of the war, he lost all trace of his family's origins.[145]

Entertainers

In former times, soldiers had to entertain themselves. But in the era of mass conscript armies, entertainment for the troops was organized on high. The British and the Americans were particularly strong in this branch of warfare. ENSA, Britain's Entertainments National Service Association, recruited popular singers and performers, who were formally under military orders. And the US United Services Organization did the same on a grander scale. Thanks to radio broadcasting, their activities forged a strong link between the civilian and military worlds.

In Britain, Gracie Fields, the 'Lancashire nightingale', vied for popularity with Vera Lynn, the 'forces' sweetheart', singing 'There'll be Bluebirds over the White Cliffs of Dover' and 'We'll Meet Again'. Wartime factories adopted the American fashion for 'Music While You Work', while danceband leaders like Henry Hall and Victor Sylvester were better known than most generals.

Without doubt, however, the most remarkable career was made by Marlene Dietrich (1901–92), a German immigrant to the USA, who helped universalize the haunting German song of 'Lili Marlene', the war's top number. British troops serving in North Africa had picked up the song in 1941 from a German radio station in Yugoslavia, and translated it. Its theme of human longing and separation appealed to all. It was banned by the German authorities after the fall of Stalingrad.[146]

Glenn Miller (1904–44) was a USAAF bandleader who brought 'swing' to Europe. American influences on popular music had been strong since jazz and Tin Pan Alley in the 1920s. But the arrival of millions of US troops, with their gramophones, their dance halls, and their uninhibited manners, sparked a cultural revolution, especially in Western Europe. Major Miller, who started as a freelance trombonist in Iowa, had reached the top of the pre-war US rankings with his soothing saxophone sound, and especially with the inimitable melody 'In the Mood' (1940). He shunned improvisation, preferring carefully crafted, orchestrated numbers. On 14 December 1944, following a concert at an airbase near Oxford, he climbed into his plane for a continental tour, rose into the night sky, and disappeared without trace.[147]

By the 1940s, jazz had become a worldwide sensation. Over the preceding decades it had spread from New Orleans to New York, and then round the whole world. It was the favourite listening of millions. In wartime Europe, British jazz-lovers were the most fortunate. American jazz bands flew in with US forces. In Germany, the Nazi authorities disliked 'nigger music'. But they permitted it when they found that soldiers were listening to foreign stations. Only in the USSR was a public ban on 'decadent' jazz rigorously enforced.

Adi Rosner was the best-known jazz trumpeter in pre-war Warsaw. He possessed a photograph of Louis Armstrong signed with the words 'To the white Louis Armstrong from the black Adi Rosner'. When he fled with his wife to the USSR in 1939, he found himself lionized. Their contracted series of public concerts was curtailed, but for the private parties and closed concerts of the Communist elite he was the hottest guest in the country. He performed, for example, in Leningrad during the siege without any outsider hearing of it. He performed to sumptuous gatherings in all the major Soviet cities. On one occasion in Moscow he was commanded to play in the middle of the night in an empty, blacked-out theatre to an audience of one. His wife caught sight of a shadowy, moustachioed figure sitting at the back of a darkened box. At every stage they were showered with expensive presents, in a life of 'champagne and mink coats'. But early in 1945, on hearing that the Red Army was nearing Berlin, they applied to go home. They were denounced as 'worshippers of Western culture' and immediately cast into the GULag. Their offence, presumably, was ingratitude. Rosner did not survive.[148]

Exiles

An exile is a refugee with somewhere to stay, usually in a foreign country. Europe was full of them. London, as the only Allied capital to remain unoccupied, was swarming with Dutch, Belgians, Free French, Poles, Czechs, Yugoslavs and many others. Lisbon, too, had more than its share. And Buenos Aires was a favourite destination for Germans and Italians who had left their home country but who were not welcome in Europe.

The life of a wartime exile was characterized less by an empty stomach than by a troubled mind: by the inability to fit in, by the loss of familiar surroundings, by worries over an uncertain future. George Mikes, a Hungarian and author of How to be an Alien (1946), described the condition perfectly. An exile, he wrote, is 'someone who has lost everything except his accent'. 'The British,' he noted observantly, 'do not have sex: they have hot-water bottles.'[149]

Westerners tend to think of exiles as citizens of Allied countries. But there were exiles from the Reich as well. Herbert Ernst Frahm (1913–92) was a young German socialist, the son of an unmarried Lübeck shopgirl, and a lifelong pigeon fancier. In 1931 the left wing of the Social Democratic Party of Germany (SPD), to which he belonged, was expelled from the party, and subsequently, as a member of the Socialist Workers Party, he went abroad, working as a correspondent in Spain and Norway. His activities led the Gestapo to revoke his German citizenship. As a result, he survived the war in neutral Sweden. Returning to Germany in 1946, 'Willi Brandt' kept his wartime pseudonym, rising to be mayor of Berlin and in 1969–74 federal chancellor. Many of his political beliefs, expressed in his *Ostpolitik* and in the Brandt Commission, which aimed to reconcile the rich and poor of the world, reflected his humble origins.[150]

Eye Witness

Thousands upon thousands, if not millions of memoirs and eye-witness accounts of the Second World War have been written. They come in dozens of languages, from people of all ages and nationalities, and from all ends of Europe. Each is partial; each relies on a memory that is more or less fallible. The choice is vast.

Yet where better to begin than in the country where the war began, at the place where the two greatest armies of the continent first met? Brześć on the Bug (once Brest Litowsk and now Brest in Belarus) lay on the river which in 1939 divided the Nazi from the Soviet zones. It was one of the largest cities where Jews held an absolute majority: the home of Menahem Begin.

Nathalie Hartmann (b. 1919 as Natalie Kisovska) was just twenty years old when war came. Her parents, who had married in Kiev during the First World War, had just divorced. Her Polish father was the local Fiat car dealer. Her Russian mother had gone off to Warsaw for a more exciting life. Nathalie herself was a student, and had come home to Brest for the vacation:

> Some scrupulous historian . . . may remember the exact date of the first German bombardment of Brest. I am not sure whether it was on 6 or 7 September. In our apartment on the second floor of the house, my university friend and I had just started our early lunch

with red beetroot soup. With the first spoonful, something unheard-
of happened. Through a shrill howling of alarm sirens, we heard a
terrible crash. Our whole building shook. All the windowpanes fell
down with the clatter of broken glass. The table with our meal was
lifted and the beetroot soup splashed our light blouses. I looked at
Krystyna . . . supposing she was soaked in blood. She had the same
reaction looking at me. We both exploded in hysterical laughter . . .

Then I thought of our young neighbour. She lived in the same
square in a nice one-family house in the midde of a garden full of
flowers. I grasped Krystyna's hand . . . Bursting into the small garden,
we saw only the rich crimson dahlias in full bloom, but the house
itself had disappeared, disappeared completely. Before us was simply
the huge crater, full or rubble and sand; and beside it, an undamaged
car with a Warsaw registration stood in the half-smashed garage . . .

In [early] September, the Brest Command of the Polish Army
took all our cars . . . paying for them in cash. After the Polish Army's
withdrawal, a lot of other cars were left on the roads. Father and his
boy brought [them] in for repairs; . . . and one day they brought in
two huge military cauldrons . . . The Germans, coming to Brest some
days later, took all his eight cars, without any recompense. Only the
two cauldrons and a small Fiat 500 were left, which gave us the
ability to buy some foodstuffs from the local villages . . . With
potatoes, onions and salt bacon procured in this way, we started to
cook soup for the refugees . . .

. . .

At the end of September, Brest on Bug was handed by the
Germans to the Russians. The new rulers started immediately to put
Brest's residents in jail, . . . my father among them . . . We had not
seen the official transfer ceremony, but all the residents were asked
to attend the celebration parade.

Before us, marching in close array, first came the ranks of
disciplined Germans: well dressed and armed, in clean uniforms and
shining boots, with modern weapons and rucksacks of good quality,
all leather and brass.

After them appeared the horde of Soviet comrades: dirty,
unwashed, in uniforms of low quality and overcoats all torn to
shreds. It was the same with the primitive boots, dirty and smelling
of the tar used for cleaning them . . . They were bearing guns of a

much older and heavier type, not on leather slings but on cotton
strings . . . I could not believe my eyes.

. . .

Our contact with the soldiers of both armies was likewise
different. The Germans used to come every morning to our backyard,
asking politely for some warm water to shave . . . The Russians
required only drinking water, and they asked to show them our
hands. This was some kind of a political check-up, to find if we
belonged to the working class or to the detestable bourgeoise, the
hated enemies . . . One resolute young soldier, at the sight of my
comparatively clean hands, despite much potato-peeling, asked me:
'Hey, you, bourgeois, have you never worked with your hands?'

'I am a student,' I replied.

'And how come you speak Russian so well?'

'My mother was Russian.'

'Your mother was Russian? And where is she now, this Russian
mother?

'She is dead.' It was a lie . . .

For the first time I realized it. We were living on the frontline
between the West and the East . . .

. . .

During October and November 1939 [the Russians] took [my
father] in five times, releasing him for a few days, then imprisoning
him anew. When he was arrested for the sixth time, we expected
him to be back in a couple of days. But he did not return. He
remained in Soviet prisons for a couple of years. It was his good
fortune not to be shot . . . Father came from a land-owning family.
Merely for that he could have been sent to Siberia, if not sentenced
to death. [But] the eager comrades wanted to prepare his accusation
for a much greater crime, which was complete rubbish. During the
search of our Brest apartment, the security men found a leather-
bound album with photographs of our 1938 holiday in Italy . . . The
comrades in Minsk tried to accuse Father of being an Italian-German
spy. They simply could not believe that a private person . . . could
spend holidays in Italy. In their opinion only a well-paid spy could
afford such a luxury . . .

. . .

In December 1939, when Father was in jail, Staszek and I decided to get married. Staszek and two of his friends managed to escape [Soviet captivity] by jumping from the open window of their wagon in the night. [His other friends] were sent to the Kozielsk and Starobielsk camps, and were shot at Katyn in 1940, all of them. (We learned about that many years later.) Staying in Brest was dangerous. The Soviet police had started deportation to Siberia of arrested people's families. Father's business, Auto-Polsie, was sealed . . . and our apartment was requistioned for a Soviet police officer . . .

We began our preparations to leave for Warsaw, where my husband's family lived . . . The frontier on the Bug was much more rigorously guarded [than earlier] We were advised to go to Malkinia, a small city to the north-west of Brest, and to pass the frontier with a local guide. We left in an overcrowded train in the late afternoon. It was already dark when we arrived at the tiny station. With the footpath hardly visible under the snow, we reached a small forester's cottage where we waited in the barn till late into the night. At a signal from our guide, we forced our way silently, stealthily through the forest in deep snow, walking in Indian file with rucksacks and bundles. From afar, we could see our aim – the lights of Malkinia railway station belonging to the Germans.

The recollection of that starless, frosty night, of crawling under barbed wire and listening intently to the barking of the Soviet patrol's dogs returned long afterwards in my dreams. Ten years later, I still used to leap from my bed at night, waking the whole house with my screams . . .[151]

In other words, ten years later Nathalie was still alive and so were her parents. They were among the fortunates. Her mother got married again, to a fellow Russian exile, and went to live in Tunis. Her father had escaped Soviet captivity, being in transit between two prisons when Operation Barbarossa struck. He later married a Jewish girl, Barbara, who had worked for him in his business and who had turned to him for help when she fled the Ghetto. They brought up Barbara's niece as their own daughter. Natalia missed the Warsaw Rising by two weeks, when she took her own asthmatic child to the mountains in the summer of 1944. She parted company with her husband, but followed a fascinating road through life via West Africa, Switzerland and eventually Australia, which she reached exactly fifty years after leaving Brest.

Families

The united family is the first casualty of total war. Young men are conscripted. Young women are left to cope with loneliness and young children. Separation and bereavement are everyday occurrences. Fathers face the shellfire. Mothers, sons and daughters face the bombs or the refugee train or the telegram.

In 1939–45, since civilian casualties were so high, the burden of wartime stresses fell less on soldiers than on soldiers' families. The worst experiences, one might think, were those of parents and children killed together by an enemy bomb, or pushed together into a cattle truck bound for Siberia or for 'resettlement'. Not necessarily so. War fosters psychological alienation. The sharpest pangs could be suffered by those who waited in vain for survivors who chose not to return, or who returned home to find that there was no welcome.

The British royal family, though hardly typical, was a model of familial solidarity. The King, George VI, was a reluctant monarch following his brother's abdication. The Queen, the former Elizabeth Bowes-Lyon, had expected to be no more than a duchess and resented the impositions placed on her shy and stuttering husband. The two princesses, Elizabeth and Margaret Rose, were teenagers. The former spent most of the war years mooning over a handsome naval lieutenant. But as 'Us Four' they stuck together marvellously, as the next generation of royals could not. When Buckingham Palace was bombed, they refused to move house. 'If we moved,' the Queen said, 'we could not look the East End in the face.'[152]

In Germany, the establishment of the Nazi regime played havoc with some families, and created splendid opportunities for others. For instance, in 1930, the twenty-nine-year-old Magda Quandt, newly divorced, was footloose and fancy free. She had been born in Berlin in humble circumstances as the illegitimate child of a serving girl and was brought up mainly in Brussels, where her mother, and her mother's Jewish partner, Max Friedlander, had worked in the hotel trade. But having attended a prestigious finishing school in Goslar, thanks to a generous subsidy from her father, she married a prosperous businessman, Günther Quandt: not, however, before changing her maiden name by legal deed from Friedlander to Rietschel. Her marriage to Quandt lasted eight years, produced a son called Harald, made her financially independent and was terminated due to her long-time affair with Chaim Arosorov, an ardent Zionist.

Ever the opportunist, Magda then joined the Nazi Party, and in 1931 was married to the Gauleiter of Berlin, Dr Joseph Goebbels. Adolf Hitler acted as a witness at the wedding, which, according to rumour, had been arranged at Hitler's request. Harald then accompanied them under the crossed swords of the SA honour guard.

From then on, until her death in the *Führerbunker*, Magda's family and relations prospered mightily. Her husband was Propaganda Minister. Her former husband gained lucrative contracts, using slave labour in his factories. Her six children lived a life of privilege. Since Hitler was unmarried, Magda herself was talked of as 'the unofficial first lady of the Reich'. Harald joined the Luftwaffe as a pilot, and in 1945 was a POW in Italy. He was the only one of Magda's offspring to survive.

After the war, together with his half-brother, Harald and Herbert Quandt revived their father's fortunes. They and their descendants became multi-billionaires, with controlling interestes in VARTA batteries, IWKA machine industries and BMW cars.[153]

Fascists

As members of one of the two premier radical movements of the twentieth century, Fascists saw themselves as leaders in the international struggle against Bolshevism. There was no 'Fascist International'. But Fascists, and admirers of Fascists, operated in virtually every European country, and they fed on each other's success. Led initially by Mussolini in Italy, they took over Germany in 1933 and Spain in 1936–9. And they united all who thought that Red revolution in the Soviet style presented the greatest menace to world peace and prosperity. Like the Communists, they were fundamentally opposed to Western democracy. But, unlike the Communists, they did not succeed in persuading the democracies to think well of them. In Britain, for example, Sir Oswald Mosley (1896–1980), leader of the British Union of Fascists, was interned in May 1940, together with thirty-three associates. Even though the USSR was Germany's partner at the time, the Defence Regulations (ISB), under which he was detained, did not apply to Communists.[154]

In the first phase of the war, in Hitler's heyday, Fascists floated to the surface in many German-occupied countries, and joined the 'crusade against Bolshevism'. In France, in Belgium – among both Flemings and Walloons – in the Netherlands, in Norway, in Slovakia, Croatia, Hungary,

Romania and the Baltic States, pro-Nazi groupings made an appearance. But they rarely assumed a commanding presence.

After 1943, however, the Fascists' star waned. Mosley was released as harmless. Mussolini collapsed. The Nazis retreated into the redoubt of the Reich. And no one admitted to having admired them. In the battle of the totalitarians, the Fascists were totally defeated.

Konstantin Vladimirovich Radzaevsky (1907–46) was the *Vozhd* or *Duce* of the Russian Fascist Union. His organization, which had twenty-six worldwide branches, was banned in the USSR and operated out of Harbin in Japanese-ruled Manchukuo. His stormtroopers wore black uniforms with swastika armbands. He surrendered to the Red Army in 1945, and was shot in the Lubyanka in 1946.[155]

Heroines

It is simply not true that men show physical courage and women show moral courage. What is true is that the front lines of 1939–45 were largely a man's world, and that the call to heroism was largely heard by women beyond the din of battle. Danger, however, was not confined to battlefields.

Pearl Witherington (b. 1914), the daughter of a British military family, lived in Paris and until June 1940 worked as a cipher clerk at the British Embassy. She stayed on after the fall of France, organizing an escape line for MI9 based in Marseilles. A period of training with SOE's F Section followed in England. But early in 1943 she was parachuted into the Indre department, where she took the code name of 'Pauline' and acted as assistant to the controller of the underground 'Stationer' network, Maurice Southgate. After Southgate's arrest, however, she took command of a new network of 1,500 agents, called 'Wrestler', which was organized in conjunction with a local man, Henri Cornioley, and which played an active role in sabotage operations before D-Day. Pearl was never caught. She married Cornioley at the end of the war, and refused a British medal. Originally recommended for the MC, she was told by officials that the honour was reserved for men and that she would be given the MBE for civil distinction. She sent it back, explaining that 'I have done nothing civil'.[156]

Sophie Scholl (1923–44) was a biology student at the University of Munich. Although brought up in a decidedly non-Nazi family, she had joined the girls' section of the Hitler Youth, and had completed war service in a labour brigade. In the summer of 1944 her father was serving a prison sentence, having been overheard criticizing Hitler. The injustice done to him may have been the reason why she joined the secret anti-Nazi 'White Rose' organization. She had distributed only six pamphlets before she was arrested, interrogated and guillotined.[157]

Soviet heroines were extremely numerous, the spirit of self-sacrifice being heavily cultivated among Soviet women. Like the Third Reich, the USSR also propagated the idea of Heroic Motherhood, as if human reproduction was to be included in the same category as Stakhanovite work schedules or front-line combat. Totalitarian regimes certainly believed that a woman's body belonged as much to the state as to the private marriage partners. As from 1944, the Soviet Medal of Motherhood (First Class) was awarded to women who had borne and raised six children. Sceptics might suggest that the practice was not entirely irrelevant to the squandering of human life by the Stalinist regime.

Maternal instincts, in fact, cannot be fairly hijacked by politics. They could be found inside the USSR, outside the USSR, and among the victims of the USSR. Zofia Litewska, then aged thirty-three, found herself with her four children in an Arctic lumber camp 3,000 km from her home on the banks of the River Niemen. Her only offence was to have been a foreign schoolteacher, and therefore educated and an 'enemy of the people'. She chopped wood for nearly two years during the Nazi–Soviet Pact, and then was released – with no money, no food, no means of transport, and five mouths to feed. In the company of others, she and her children floated on an improvised raft to the White Sea coast, then set off walking towards the sun. They were saved by a young Russian soldier, whom they met in the middle of a forest. On hearing their story, he handed them his wallet, saying that he was going to get killed and wouldn't be needing it. On reaching the railhead, they could then buy a ticket to the south. Working on collective farms between stages, they worked their way to the Caspian Sea, and then to Iran and India, and in due course to a new life in Oxford.[158]

Historians

Extreme events inspire people to record them, and trained historians are better placed than most to do it. Conflict equally drives historians to think more carefully about issues of analysis and causation, and hence to advance their subject.

Much of our detailed knowledge of the Holocaust can be traced to dedicated witnesses who recorded what they saw. Among their records are the *Chronicle of the Lodz Ghetto*[159] and the remarkable medical studies from the Warsaw Ghetto, which monitored the degeneration of the researchers' own dying bodies. These accounts were buried, and found after the war.

Elsewhere in the Reich, historians benefited from unusual opportunities. Pieter Gehl (1887–1966), a respected Dutch historian, was incarcerated in Buchenwald, where he composed his epoch-making study of *Napoleon: For and Against*. He was suspect for having taught at London University before the war, and was arrested as a hostage against the safety of Germans interned in the Dutch East Indies. His classic study of Napoleon, which demonstrated that there are as many valid interpretations of a historical event or personality as there are historians to attempt it, was deeply subversive to the totalitarian point of view. Gehl saw history as an endless, and endlessly inconclusive, exercise.[160] Hugh Trevor-Roper (1914–2003) used his experiences as a British intelligence officer to write the first coherent account of the *Last Days of the Reich*. He was not sharp enough, however, when asked to confirm the forged *Hitler's Diaries* as genuine.[161]

In the case of the Soviet Union, a significant discrepancy arose between the huge influence of Marxist-Leninist theory on Western historians and the tiny trickle of credible information about Soviet realities. A whole generation of British, French and American historians, deeply affected by the war, began publishing before it was over. (See Chapter Six.) But sober studies about Stalin and Stalin's policies had to wait for decades. One small window into the Stalinist world was opened by the Smolensk party archives that were captured by the Wehrmacht in 1941.[162]

The Nazis took history very seriously, and in the short time given them they sought to document the correctness of their racial theories with respect to all branches of human development. The SS *Ahnenerbe* Institute, founded by Himmler in 1935, was the powerhouse of these activities. Many of its scholars – Grunlagen, Wüst, Altheim, Böhmers, Beger, Jahnkun, Schäfer, Kiss, Kersten, Huth, Hirt, Schweizer, Paulsen and others – melted into post-war obscurity. Its director, Hermann Wirth, was hanged in August 1947 in the courtyard of Landsberg jail, where Hitler had penned *Mein Kampf* twenty-odd years before.[163]

Arguably the greatest wartime loss to history was that of Professor Marc Bloch (1886–1944) – medievalist, co-founder of the journal *Annales*, and one of the greatest influences on modern historiography. Bloch was himself the son of a history professor from Lyons, but he was no academic nerd. He was twice decorated for bravery in battle – once as an infantryman in the First World War, and then in 1940, when he had rejoined the army at the age of fifty-four and was evacuated from Dunkirk.

Bloch's ordeal began, however, when he returned to his home at Fougres in the Creuse, and was required to register under the terms of Vichy's *Statut des Juifs*. He had always insisted that he was not a French Jew, but 'a Frenchman of Jewish descent', an *Israélite*; and, despite receiving a dispensation personally signed by Pétain, he found the whole episode deeply distasteful. Recruitment into the Resistance followed, and a double life under the pseudonym of 'Narbonne', which led in due course to denunciation by a neighbour, arrest, torture, and death in a field from the guns of the Gestapo.[164]

Interpreters

None of the war leaders was an accomplished linguist. So all needed interpreters. The interpreters' view of the Second World War, therefore, was gained at the very top tables.

Paul Schmidt (1899–1970) had intepreted for Hitler and Chamberlain at the Munich Conferences. On the morning of 3 September 1939 he was asked to be present at the German Foreign Ministry on the Wilhelmstrasse after Ribbentrop refused to accept the British ultimatum from Ambassador Henderson. Schmidt was told to receive the ultimatum in his place:

> On that Sunday, I overslept and had to take a taxi to the Foreign Office. I could just see Henderson entering the building as I drove across the Wilhelmsplatz. I used a side entrance, and stood in Ribbentrop's office ready to receive Henderson punctually at 9 o'clock . . . He remained solemnly in the middle of the room . . . 'If His Majesty's Government has not received satisfactory assurances of the cessation of all aggressive action against Poland . . . by 11 o'clock British Summer Time . . . a state of war will exist between Great Britain and Germany' . . . I then took the ultimatum to the Chancellery. Most of the Cabinet and the leading Party men were collected in the room

next to Hitler's office . . . When I entered, Hitler was sitting at the
desk and Ribbentrop stood by the window . . . I stopped some distance from Hitler's desk, and translated the ultimatum. When I finished, there was complete silence. Hitler sat immobile, gazing before
him. He was not at a loss, as was afterwards stated, nor did he rage
as others alleged. He sat completely silent and unmoving. After an
interval which seemed like an age, he turned to Ribbentrop. 'What
now?' Hitler asked with a savage look.'[165]

Vladimir Nikolaevich Pavlov was a polyglot interpreter who worked
in German and English for both Stalin and Molotov. He attended the
signing of the Nazi–Soviet Pact and the conferences of Teheran, Yalta and
Potsdam. On one or two occasions, he may have been replaced by Dr
Valenty Berezhkov (b. 1916), who later defected to the USA and brazenly
exaggerated his own importance. Pavlov's strongest language was German.
His English was shaky, but improved. At Yalta, Churchill decorated him
with the CBE.[166]

Roosevelt's favourite Russian interpreter was Charles 'Chip' Bohlen
(1904–73), a professional foreign service staffer, who had mixed with
White Russian exiles in pre-war Prague and who, unlike many in the
Roosevelt circle, was above reasonable suspicion as a possible Communist
sympathizer. (Roosevelt's ambassador to the USSR, William Bullitt, was
married to the widow of the author John Reed, who had been a paid-up
Soviet agent.) Bohlen worked at Teheran, Yalta and Potsdam. He was to
be sent to Moscow as US ambassador by President Eisenhower in 1953,
but not without a vehement challenge from Senator McCarthy.[167]

Churchill's first Russian interpreter, Dunlop, worked for the British
embassy in Moscow, but died. He was followed by two military officers,
Arthur Birse and Hugh Lunghi. (Despite claims to the contrary, he was
not replaced by Ed Stevens, an American correspondent in Moscow who
was a notorious Stalinish apologist.) Arthur Birse had the priceless advantage of being brought up in tsarist Russia. According to Pavlov's memoirs,
'he had a magnificent command of the Russian language'.[168] There were
moments when the slant placed by an interpreter on a key phrase or
sentence could change the course of world history. In October 1944, for
instance, when Churchill told Stalin that the Curzon Line would be the
basis for discussion, one wonders how the phrase was translated. Stalin
certainly seems to have gained the impression that there would be *no*
further discussion about the Soviet Union's Western frontier.

Pavel Sudoplatov was a high-ranking spymaster of the NKVD's Special Operations directorate. One of the many anecdotes in his memoirs claims that he organized the assassination of Trotsky. Another describes how he used an interpreter to disarm the US ambassador, Averell Harriman, on the eve of the Yalta Conference. It must have been January 1945. The Soviets were desperate to discover what US tactics would be. So, posing under a false name as an official of the Foreign Ministry, Sudoplatov invited Harriman for dinner at the Aragvi, the best Georgian restaurant in town. For the purposes of interpretation he was accompanied by Prince Janusz Radziwiłł, a colourful Polish aristocrat, who had been in the clutches of the NKVD since his capture in 1939 but who in pre-war days, among other things, had hosted Herman Göring's hunting trips to Poland. In the smoothest possible way, Harriman was alternately threatened and tempted. He was told to keep a tighter rein on his socially adventurous daughter, because 'Moscow is full of hooligans'. And he was told how his friends in New York could have great opportunities for post-war investment in Russia. And the conversations were taped for subsequent analysis.[169]

Some day a scholar will write an exhaustive study of the many mistranslations which enlivened wartime diplomacy. Some of them were serious. Others were comical. In the Kremlin in August 1939, for example, when the unutterably pompous British envoy, Admiral Sir Reginald Aylmer Ranfurly Plunkett-Ernle-Erle-Drax, was spelling out the endless list of his names and titles, he mentioned that he was a knight of the Order of the Bath. The Soviet interpreter relayed it as 'the Order of the Bath-tub'. '*Vanna?* [bath-tub]' retorted Marshal Voroshilov. The admiral was unperturbed. 'In the reign of our early kings,' he explained, 'our knights used to ride round Europe on horseback, slaying dragons and rescuing damsels in distress. They returned home travel-stained and grimy . . . and the king would sometimes offer them a luxury – a bath in the royal bathroom.'[170] The admiral's mission failed.

Hugh Lunghi was just twenty-three when he was fished from his artillery regiment and sent as an assistant interpreter to Yalta and later to Potsdam. He was an English public schoolboy with a Russian mother, and was to be the first British officer to see the inside of Hitler's bunker. His observations on the contrasts between 'The Big Three' are inimitable:

The three great leaders spoke in very different styles. Stalin was very economical with his words, very precise. He seemed to know exactly what he was talking about, in absolute command of his facts. But very quiet. It was very difficult [to follow] because of this mumbling and modest way of speaking. President Roosevelt, on the other hand, was rather inclined to ramble, and would go on, I think, longer than his interpreter would have liked him to. Churchill's language was the language of an orator. He prepared what he said very carefully. But very often, as we used to say – that is, the interpreters – you could almost see the right phrase rumbling round his brain and slowly coming down to his tongue, to his mouth. And then he'd come out with this wonderful phrase, which would keep you spellbound for a moment . . .

We used to say that an interpreter was like a concert artist – and his object was to get over the meaning, the tone of the score . . . You were performing . . . You can't just be a translating machine.[171]

Journalists

In the age of film cameras and the international telegraph, journalists and war correspondents could influence public opinion strongly and quickly. In Germany and the Soviet Union they were essentially propagandists, writing to order for the authorities. They included no such strong figures as those who independently influenced British and American perceptions of the war.

Ed Murrow (1908–65) was the CBS radio correspondent in London during the Blitz. His reports, dramatized by real sound effects, were a significant factor in boosting Roosevelt's policy of 'everything short of war', and in undermining isolationism.[172] At the time, he was consciously going against the grain of American public opinion.

Alexander Werth was a BBC and *Sunday Times* correspondent on the Eastern Front in 1941–5. His experiences with Soviet censorship and his unrivalled proximity to the Red Army combined to form a sober view of Soviet realities that was not shared at home. His description of the Nazi concentration camp at Majdanek, which he filed in July 1944, was suppressed as incredible.[173]

Soviet correspondents had fewer opportunities to publish what they saw, but they made notes. Vasily Grossman covered the Eastern Front for the Red Army newspaper *Krasnaya Zvyezda*. In 1943 he filed a piece saying that '100,000 Jews have vanished'. This too went unpublished, as

did many of his revelations about the treatment of Soviet soldiers and
the cruel fate of civilians. His notebooks had to wait sixty years for
publication.[174]

Lovers

War is driven by hate, by anger, by domination – by everything that love
is not. Yet love could be met at every turn: love snatched for a moment,
love awakened, love triumphant; filial love, maternal love, paternal love,
the love of lifelong lovers . . .

Soldiers dying was commonplace: a Canadian soldier who witnessed one instance was only unusual in writing down in detail what he
saw:

> This was in Holland. There was a lot of snow on the ground. We
> were on patrol, and we ambushed this bunch of Jerries. Eight of
> them . . . coming round the edge of the forest . . . So we're standing
> there, and I'm thinking we'll have to take these prisoners back . . .
> And then this lieutenant, he just turned to the guy with the Bren and
> said, 'Shoot them.' . . . One of our guys who understood German
> [told us what the officer] had said just before he was shot down. It
> was 'Mother'.[175]

Somewhere in Germany a mother would grieve without ever learning the
facts.

The commandant of Auschwitz, Rudolf Höss, also recorded human
conduct at close quarters. He was impressed by the way that Jewish
mothers heading for the gas chambers shielded their children, and helped
them undress, or even laughed and joked with them. He closely watched
the men of the *Sonderkommando* who were on hand to load the corpses
into the crematoria. On one occasion he saw a man hesitate as he dragged
out the body of his own wife, and he wondered whence such people
'derived the strength to carry on'. After all, he too had to suppress his
feelings: 'I was no longer happy at Auschwitz once the mass exterminations
had begun . . . My family, for sure, were well provided for. The children
could live a free and untrammelled life . . . Every Sunday, I had to walk
them all across the fields and visit the stables . . . Our two horses and the
foal were especially beloved.'[176]

One of Höss's clients who survived Auschwitz attributed his strength to the will to see his wife again. His memoir is called *The Survival of Love*.[177]

Maria was seventeen years old when she was taken at gunpoint from her family's farm in Leśniów and sent as a slave labourer to a factory at Seesen near Hanover. In the spring of 1945 she was liberated by the Americans, and for the following months worked as an interpreter in a Red Cross Hospital.

> There was a young Englishman from Sunderland who used to deliver medication. I got to know him. He asked me if I wanted to go home, but I didn't know if home was still there. He said that he would take me to England . . . I had to have a lot of papers which was almost impossible so his Captain said, 'Why don't you get married? It is easier, he is a good chap.'
>
> We had known each other for about a year and I was fond of him and I knew he loved me. At that point of time I found difficulty in loving anyone.
>
> We got married. The Army paid for the wedding – a white dress, flowers, everything. There were two vicars, one Catholic and one Church of England. After the wedding, Ted, my husband, returned to England but I had to stay in the camp . . . Eventually, I was put on a Royal Navy ship . . . At Sunderland Station, I was met by my husband's mother, and we got on very well. Ted was a glass-blower . . . and we got a council house. I was cared for in England by a Jewish doctor. The Red Cross found my family, but they moved to another farm. Ten years later I went to Poland with my two daughters. Ted was a very kind and loving man, and I grew to love him very much.[178]

In Britain, the arrival of a million GIs and more gave rise to 'the greatest sexual free-for-all in living memory'.[179] On the one hand, there was a marked rise in prostitution, especially in London. On the other hand, there was a strong incentive for young British women to break the traditional taboos, and to seek their fortune. One-third of British babies born during the war were illegitimate. Their mothers came from every social class. And 50,000 radiant GI brides sailed across the ocean.

Music lovers

War does not stop music. Music continues to be performed, to be composed, and to be listened to. But the nature of its links with war can be complicated, varying from the close, as with marches or soldiers' songs, to the remote and escapist. Composers can be excited or inspired by the climate of wartime, or be repelled by it.

Wartime Britain, which did not experience the extremes of deprivation, was not specially conducive to creativity. But it is interesting that some of the emblematic uses of music, such as the BBC's choice of the opening notes of Beethoven's Fifth Symphony for its overseas call sign, or Dame Myra Hess playing Bach at the National Gallery concerts in London, deliberately involved German music. Benjamin Britten worked during the war years on his opera *Peter Grimes*. He also wrote a piece, *The Ballad of Little Musgrave and Lady Barnard*, for a POW music festival at Oflag VIIB in 1944.

Nazi Germany stifled musical appreciation. Mendelssohn and Mahler were banned for their Jewishness, and modern music like that of Hindemith for its 'decadence'. Wagner was unlucky to be declared the Führer's favourite composer, and time was wasted on questions such as whether Lehár was permissible or not. The highlight of the week for many Germans was the Sunday radio request programme *Wunschkonzert*, which linked soldiers at the front with friends and families at home.

Germany's foremost conductor, Wilhelm Furtwängler (1886–1954), soon ran into trouble with the Nazi regime, but, despite many offers he refused to emigrate, and he stayed on until 1944 as director both of the Berlin Philharmonic and the Leipzig Gewandhaus. His concerts were regularly attended by Hitler and other Nazi prominents, and his presence in Germany was extensively exploited by Nazi propaganda. Even so, he felt obliged to flee to Switzerland during the witch-hunt sparked by the Bomb Plot, and after the war he was forced to submit to a denazification trial.

The bitter criticism which was directed at Furtwängler for more than twenty years emanated largely from émigré circles that resented his independent stance. Yet none of the charges of collaboration and of culpable indifference to being manipulated carried much substance. Unlike Herbert von Karajan, he never joined the Nazi Party, and he obstinately refused to deliver the obligatory Nazi salute – even when faced by the Führer in person. He resigned several positions, such as that of director of the German state opera, when he felt that his musical integrity was threatened. And he constantly sought to protect friends and colleagues, including Jews, who faced persecution. All the charges against him at his trial were rejected. 'Beethoven's message of love and freedom,' he said in 1943, 'has never been needed more urgently than today.' And again, 'Wherever Wagner and Beethoven are played, human beings are free.'[180]

Paradoxically, the Nazis insisted that their concentration camps should operate to musical accompaniment. Camp brass bands and camp orchestras were a standard feature. Excellent musicians were available. As one inmate recalled, 'They murdered to the best music.'

Even in the USSR, and even in the war zone, music rallied to people's needs. Shostakovich's Seventh Symphony was written inside the siege of Leningrad, and, as a sign of solidarity with the Soviet people, was performed in London on 22 June 1942. Prokofiev was also active, producing, among other things, the opera *War and Peace*, staged in 1946. A strange pseudo-religious oratorio style emerged, and Dmitri Kabalevsky's super-patriotic repertoire caught the mood of the day. The great fund of Russian folklore was drawn upon to produce thousands of front-line song-and-dance concerts in the fashion made famous after the war by the Red Army Choir.

Despite the onset of mechanization, most Second World War soldiers still spent much of their time 'foot-slogging', and their marching tunes rang in the ears not only of the marchers but also of the local population of the countries through which they passed. The infantry of the Wehrmacht in particular, which was not highly motorized, must have totted up a record number of melodic man-miles. Many of the favourite marches, like 'Tipperary' or the wonderful American Sousa collection, were of First World War vintage, or older. But a new crop appeared in 1939–45. The British had their irresistible 'Colonel Bogey', often sung to obscene words concerning the Nazi leaders' manliness, and the Americans their 'Dogface Soldier'. The Soviet style combined pathos, patriotism and pomposity. But no single item was so redolent of the times as the Germans' 'Horst Wessel Song', the Nazi Party anthem. Written by a storm trooper, who was killed in a pre-war brawl with Communists and who became a Nazi martyr, the words were dark and grossly political. Indeed, they were to become

unrepeatedly offensive to a later generation. Yet they were attached to a
tune of great seductive power but unknown origin – probably religious-
revivalist. The song conjures up both the joy of the collective and the
mesmerizing fascination of Hitlerism for impressionable youngsters who
were told they belonged to the 'Master Race':

Die Fahne hoch, die Reihen fest geschlossen	*The banner's high: the ranks are firmly closed*
S.A. marschiert mit ruhig festem Schritt	*The SA march: with strong and silent step*
Kam'raden die Rotfront und Reaktion erschossen	*The comrades shot by 'Red Front' and Reaction*
Marschier'n im Geist in unsern Reihen mit.[181]	*March in our ranks, still with us in spirit.*

The band and the bass drum added impetus to every bar, especially
when combined with the short emphatic sound of *Schritt* and *mit* at the
end of the second and fourth lines. The four silent beats which had to be
counted in the singers' heads at the close of the tune carried them
effortlessly on to the next stanza. And thus for mile after mile. Nothing
could be more redolent of the quasi-religious Nazi ethos, where the doubts
and failings of the individual were swept away and where the supreme
virtue was conformity – i.e. marching in step.

Occupiers

Occupying a foreign country without prior consent is a hostile act.
However, it is invariably undertaken by armies which say that they are
bringing freedom to those whose land they occupy. Amazing though it

may seem, when they started the war in 1939, the troops of Nazi Germany marched into Poland singing about 'Europe's freedom'. It is a sobering thought. Occupying forces are always saving the occupied from someone or something.

Europe in 1939–45 saw many occupations. And every occupation brought about a different symbiosis between the occupiers and the occupied. The uneasy modus vivendi between the Germans and the Belgians or the Dutch, for example, bore little resemblance to the unbridled hostility between the Germans and the Poles, the Yugoslavs and the Greeks. The conduct of the Soviets in 1939–41 was not the same as their deportment in 1944–5. And when it came to the occupation of a defeated Germany, each occupation zone – British, French, American and Soviet – had its own specific climate, and its own specific difficulties.

The soldiers of the occupying power, however, form only a small part of the problem. They may use a heavy hand to begin with, but as often as not they move on or settle down in their barracks. It is the policemen, the administrators and the mealy-mouthed politicians of the subsequent occupation regimes that cause the resentment. Claiming to do good, or at least to restore order, behind the barrel of a gun does not inspire confidence.

Many towns and cities of Eastern and Central Europe were subjected to multiple occupations. For instance, the city of Plsen (Pilsen) in Bohemia, the home of lager beer, was occupied by Nazi Germany from 1939 to April 1945, by the US Army in 1945–6, and by the Soviets from 1946. The city of Vilnius (Wilno), which was in Poland before the war, was occupied by Soviet forces in September 1939, by the Lithuanian Republic in 1939–40, by the USSR in 1940–41, and by the German Ostland regime in 1941–4; it ended up under Soviet rule, for the third time, in July 1944. There is great scope for a study of comparative occupation policies.[182]

Peasants

In the 1940s, about half of Europeans were still small farmers, crofters, peasants – families living off the land from subsistence agriculture. Apart from in Ireland, there were not many such families left in the British Isles. But they were still numerous in the poorer parts of France and Italy and in some regions of Germany. In East Central Europe, before industrialization, they formed the overwhelming majority of the population. In the

USSR, where they had been collectivized and effectively enserfed since 1929, they were still in the process of being destroyed, and the smiling, tractor-driven, modern agriculture of the propaganda posters often remained a fiction. Honest descriptions of life on the Stalinist *kolkhoz*, where sullen resistance, drunkenness and primitive methods prevailed, do not make pretty reading. As often as not, therefore, under the soldier's uniform a peasant lurked.

From the viewpoint of war planners, the good news was that peasants produced food and sons. Both in Britain and in Germany, city-dwellers were urged to revert to peasant habits and to grow their own vegetables on allotments. In much of occupied Europe, military requisitioners scoured the countryside looking for livestock and grain stores. And in the occupied republics of the USSR, despite their denunciations of Bolshevism, the Nazis made no move to free the peasants. Their purposes were well enough served by Slavs toiling as food-producing serfs.

Stanisław Mikołajczyk (1901–66), who succeeded General Sikorski as prime minister of Poland's exiled government in 1943, was leader of the country's Peasant Party (PSL), and in other circumstances he could have expected to return home and to mobilize the country's most numerous social class. He was a successor of the famous Wincenty Witos, the prime minister who had worn a peasant smock in Cabinet, and who in the summer of 1920, at the height of the Bolshevik War, had gone home to help with the harvest. In 1944, when Mikołajczyk heard that the Communists were proposing agrarian reform, not collectivization, he agreed to return and to form a coalition government. In Western eyes he was the only reasonable Polish politician. Yet, as Churchill later admitted, he was lucky to escape with his life.[183] After democratic socialists, peasants were regarded by the victorious Communists as the most dangerous enemy.

Poets

All the textbooks say that the poetry of the First World War was superior to that of the second. The assessment could be correct, though it may be somewhat Anglocentric. For in the darker regions of wartime Europe poetry was valued beyond price.

Anna Akhmatova (Anna Gorenko, 1889–1966) is generally regarded as the greatest Russian woman poet of all time. To put it mildly, she was no supporter of Stalin's regime. She led a shambolic life, filled with personal tragedies. Her first husband was shot by the Bolsheviks as a counter-revolutionary. Her third husband died in the GULag. And her son, who also spent years in the camps, was psychologically scarred. From 1925 to Stalin's death, in 1953, her poems were unpublishable, and in 1945 Stalin's cultural chief, Andrey Zhdanov, denounced her as 'half nun, half whore'. Even so, in the depth of Russia's distress, she was flown out of Leningrad by official plane, and on one solitary occasion, in 1942, a poem of hers appeared on the front page of *Pravda*. By the standards of the day, it was politically incorrect. It said nothing about the party, or the 'Great Stalin', or the evils of Fascism. But it exuded defiance:

МУЖЕСТВО

Мы знаем, что́ ныне лежит на весах
И что́ совершается ныне.
Час мужества пробил на наших часах.
И мужество нас не покинет.
Не страшно поц пулями мергвыми лечь,
Не горько остаться без крова, –
И мы сохраним тебя, русская речь,
Ведикое русское слово.
Свобоцным и чистым тебя пронесем,
И внукам цацим, и от плека спасем
Навеки!

Courage

We know what now hangs in the balance.
We understand what is happening.
Our clock is striking the hour of courage.
And courage will never desert us.
We do not fear to be shot dead,
Nor feel bitter at losing our homes.
But we will defend our Russian speech;
And guard you, great Russian tongue.
Free and untarnished, we will carry you through
And save you from bondage, for our children, Forever.

Anna Akhmatova said that she was 'appointed by God to sing of this suffering'.[184]

Politicians

If politics is the art of the possible, it had little chance to be fully practised during the Second World War in Europe except in the domestic sphere. The two largest states were totalitarian dictatorships, where there were administrators and officials but no politicians. The nearest thing to political activity in the NSDAP or in the Soviet Communist Party had been reduced to a game for survival. In Germany, in the Night of the Long Knives in 1934, Hitler killed almost a hundred of his own party comrades in a move to show who was boss. Not to be outdone, in the Terror and the purges in the USSR Stalin killed some 500,000 loyal Communists.

So wartime politics was largely confined to Britain and to the neutral states. In Britain, once party politics was suspended and the War Cabinet was supported by a coalition, it was principally concerned with drawing up plans for post-war reforms. Here the Labour Party was paramount. So too was Sir William Beveridge, an Oxford don, whose report on the creation of a welfare state, and a national health service, published in December 1942, started the debate of the decade. The Education Act of 1944 introduced secondary education for all.

The leader of the Labour Party, Clement Attlee (1883–1967), served as Churchill's deputy. A prim, unassuming man, Attlee's old-fashioned appearance belied his progressive views and his strong sense of discipline. (He had once been a schoolmaster.) He acted energetically against the infiltration of the Labour Party by Communists, and he kept the warring wings of the labour movement in line with a wonderfully dry wit. 'A period of silence from you,' he once told the garrulous Harold Laski, 'would be most welcome.' Together with his colleagues Ernest Bevin and Herbert Morrison, who served with him in the War Cabinet, he was an excellent foil to Churchill's brilliance and unpredictability. In July 1945 he won the general election hands down.[185]

Prisoners

Europe's jails worked overtime in wartime. POWs were the responsibility of the military (see p. 269ff.). But a crime wave connected to the black market, and a torrent of 'politicals', kept the civilian prison services busy as well.

In September 1939 the Luftwaffe bombed the jail in Lwów in eastern Poland, and many prisoners escaped. Among them were a group of Communists, including 'Wiesław' Gomułka, who had been jailed for subversive activities, thereby missing the purges which hit their comrades in the USSR. After escaping, Gomułka had to choose between fleeing to the Nazi zone or to the Soviet zone. He chose the former, and survived to lead the post-war Polish Communist Party.[186]

Britain's 'hottest' prisoner was Rudolf Hess. Churchill refused to talk to him, and had him incarcerated first in mental hospitals and then in the Tower of London. Condemned to life imprisonment at Nuremberg, he remained in Spandau jail until his death in 1987.

Among the Gestapo's many involuntary guests, the defendants of the Verona Trials of January 1944 were perhaps the most prominent. They consisted of all the Italian leaders, including Ciano, who had voted to remove Mussolini the previous year. All but one were hanged.

The Lubyanka jail at the NKVD's headquarters in Moscow was Europe's largest and busiest prison. Almost all Beria's important prisoners were held there for investigation under torture. The most bizarre era of Soviet prison policy, however, arrived in 1945, when wartime resistance leaders and Nazi criminals were both classed as 'anti-Soviet' and often shared the same fate. *Conversations with an Executioner*, written by a Home Army officer placed in the same cell as SS-Oberführer Jürgen Stroop, the destroyer of the Warsaw Ghetto, provides one of the most revealing insights into the war.[187]

Interrogations in the Lubyanka hovered in that brittle sphere that was both comic and deadly. The experience has been described many times, but never better than by Leopold Trepper, a lifelong Communist and Soviet agent. The irony was that he went to the Lubyanka of his own accord, to seek help in saving his former comrades in the Red Orchestra spy ring:

'Why did you let that gang of traitors talk you into working in a foreign country?'

'Excuse me, how should I address you?'

'General.' This was General Abakumov who ran SMERSH, a special section of the Ministry of Security created in 1943: the name meant, literally, 'death to spies'.

'Comrade General,' I went on, 'I did not work for a gang. I ran a military intelligence network for the Red Army high command, and I'm proud of it.'

Changing the subject, he asked 'Why did you ask to see someone in the ministry?' . . .

The farce started all over again. They came [to the cell] and took me to the examining officer . . .

'Keep your hands on the table!'

The officer picked up a piece of paper. This was an interrogation.

'Last name? First name?'

'Trepper, Leopold.'

'Nationality?'

'Jewish.'

'If you're Jewish, why is your name Leopold?'

'Too bad you can't ask my father: he's dead.'

'Citizenship?'

'Polish.'

'Social background?'

'What do you mean?'

'Was your father a labourer?'

'No.'

He said aloud as he wrote, 'Background: *petite bourgeoisie*.'

'Profession?'

'Journalist.'

'Political party?'

'Member of the Communist Party since 1925.'

He wrote still talking aloud, 'He says that he has been a member of the Communist Party since 1925.'

The interrogation was over.

Every night at ten o'clock they came and got me for interrogation, which lasted after that first one until 5.30 in the morning. After a week without sleep I wondered how long I could hold out. Remembering my hunger strike in Palestine, I observed that a 'sleep strike' was even more difficult . . . For the moment, I was standing up under the interrogations [which] were more like sessions designed to wear me out. Every night the same game started all over again.

'Tell me about your crimes against the Soviet Union.' . . .

'I have committed no crimes against the Soviet Union.'[188]

The Righteous

Righteousness is not the preserve of any particular ethnic or national group. And no one can fairly arrogate the right of designating its distribution among the human population at large. But it happens to be the term adopted by Israel's Yad Vashem Institute in Jerusalem to characterize the noble individuals who saved Jews during the Holocaust.

As from 1963, Yad Vashem, whose charter obliges it to perpetuate the memory of six million Jewish victims of the Holocaust, has also sought to honour 'the Righteous Among Nations who risked their lives to save Jews'. It operates by strict criteria, demanding full documentation, an examination of the rescuers' motives, and evidence from the rescued. The people who are honoured by Yad Vashem receive a specially minted medal, a certificate of honour, and the privilege of seeing their name being added to the Wall of Honour in the Garden of the Righteous. (Until the Garden became overcrowded, they also had a tree planted in their name.)

In the forty-two years from 1964 to 2005, 20,757 persons have been so recognized. They incude a number of diplomats, such as Feng-Shah Ho, the Chinese Consul at Vienna in 1938–40, and Sellahatin Ulkume, the Turkish Consul-General on German-occupied Rhodes in 1944, who issued passes and passports to Jewish fugitives. They include a large contingent of priests, nuns and religious ministers – such as the French Protestant Pastor André Trocme of Chambon-sur-Lignon in the Haute-Loire, who saved 5,000 – and a still larger company of ordinary men and women from the German-occupied countries, who acted from basic human compassion. Martha Sharp, an American Unitarian from Boston, Mass., was active in Prague in 1939 following the German invasion. Frank Foley (1895–1958) was a British Intelligence Officer working at the Embassy in Berlin in 1938–39. He has been credited with saving 10,000. He was reported as saying that he 'wanted to show how little the "Christians" then in power in Germany had to do with Christianity'.

Yad Vashem also issues a list of 'Righteous Persons by Country'. The list stretches from Estonia to Albania, from Portugal to Russia. But it is interesting that it is topped by the only country where the Nazis introduced an automatice death penalty for giving aid to Jews:

Yad Vashem: righteous persons by country[189]			
Poland	5,941	Hungary	671
Netherlands	4,726	Slovakia	460
France	2,646	Lithuania	630
Ukraine	2,139	Belarus	564
Belgium	1,414	Germany	427

It would be wrong, however, to forget righteous Jews. In early October 1939, Jerzy Zubrzycki had just been captured by the Wehrmacht, and was marching with a column of POWs through a small town in Poland. Passing an empty side-alley, he darted away and dashed up the alley with two German soldiers in hot pursuit. Rounding a corner, he threw himself into a small shop. The Jewish shopkeeper understood immediately. Without a word, he pointed to the stairs leading to a first-floor room and prepared to confront the soldiers. No, he had not seen a prisoner. No, he had not served any customers. No, there was no one upstairs except his wife. Zubrzycki escaped detection. He fled to France and then to England, and after the war became a distinguished professor of sociology in Canberra, 'the father of multicultural Australia'. But for the Jewish shopkeeper, he would have been a corpse.[190]

Saints

People of all races and all religions turn out good, bad and indifferent. The Second World War produced an ugly crop of criminals, a lot of people who aimed first and foremost to stay alive and to protect their families, and a few individuals of self-sacrificing saintly disposition. These saints could come from any of the oppressed communities. The Catholics were not exceptional, except for the fact that they give their saints and martyrs official status.

Father Maximilian Kolbe (1894–1941) a Franciscan friar and mission-ary, had been active in pre-war journalism. He was in Japan for most of the 1930s, and accusations against him of xenophobia and anti-Semitism have been disproved. He and all his companions were sent to Auschwitz, where he died a slow horrible death from starvation on the parade ground, having volunteered to take the place of a married man in the punishment bunker.[191]

Sister Edith Stein (1891–1942) was a highly intellectual Jewish girl from Breslau who converted to Catholicism and who became a philosopher and a Carmelite nun. From 1938, she lived in a convent in Echt in the Netherlands, whence she regularly visited her family in Breslau and attended synagogue with them. She and all other Catholics of Jewish origin were rounded up when the Dutch bishops protested publicly about Nazi treatment of Jews. She was last seen in the doorway of a cattle truck in a siding in her native Breslau, asking a railwayman for water for her companions. She, too, died in Auschwitz.[192]

A somewhat mean controversy developed after the war as to whether people like Edith Stein were killed because of their Catholicism or their

Jewishness. The answer is that the Nazis cared little about religion and much about 'race'. With the Stalinists it was the other way round.

Nonetheless, the number of Catholics who were martyred by the Nazis for their faith was considerable, and in 1999 Pope John Paul II added 108 names to the ranks of the 'Blessed' for having died in 1939–45 *in odium fidei*. They included 3 bishops, 52 secular priests, 26 members of religious orders, and a score of monks, nuns and seminarians. Professor Dr Antoni Nowowiejski (1858–1941) had been bishop of Płock. Marianna Biernacka (1888–1943), a mother of six children, chose death as a German hostage in place of her pregnant daughter. And Anicet Koplinski (1875–1941), despite his Polish name, was a German friar who was killed, like St Maximilian Kolbe and St Edith Stein, in Auschwitz (camp no.: 30,376).[193]

The Greek Catholic Church of Western Ukraine was similarly persecuted. It was sorely pressed by the Soviet occupation of 1939–41, tolerated by the German occupation of 1941–44, then savagely suppressed after 1944 by the return of the Soviets. Its martyrs include Father Joachim Senkivskyi (1896–1941), who was boiled alived in a Soviet prison, Father Zynovii Kovalyk (1903–1941), who expired during a mock crucifixion, Father Emilian Kovch (1884–1944), who died in KL-Majdanek for helping Jews, Sister Tarsykiia Matskiv (1919–44), who was shot by the Red Army at the door of her convent, Father Romen Lysko (1914–49?), who was walled up by the NKVD alive, Archpastor Nykyta Budka (1877–1949), who had worked as a priest in Canada, and who, arrested in April 1945, died in Central Asian exile, and Bishop Gregory Lakota (1883–1950), who was sentenced to ten years' hard labour in Vorkuta.[194] Most martyrs, of course, are nameless.

Scientists

Science had made its debut as a major branch of warfare in the First World War, and by 1939 governments were much more conscious than previously of its importance. Government projects both for research and development of equipment and for operational research became an integral part of the military landscape.

In Britain, Sir Henry Tizard's Scientific Survey of Air Defence, which started work in 1934 and which produced radar, is generally credited with giving the edge to the RAF in the Battle of Britain. And Tizard's chief rival, Frederick Lindemann (1886–1957), an Alsatian, who as Lord Cher-well became Churchill's chief scientific adviser, was one of the most influential persons in the country.

The totalitarian regimes, though professing love for science, proved inefficient in practising it. It did not help that the Nazis declared Einstein's Theory of Relativity invalid because he was Jewish, or that Stalin cast the USSR's leading radar scientist into the GULag. The USA was the chief beneficiary. Enrico Fermi (1901–54), who in 1942 demonstrated by the controlled release of nuclear energy that an atomic bomb was possible, had fled Mussolini's Italy.

The USSR made little independent progress on atomic weapons. Its chief atomic scientist, Igor Kurchatov (1903–1960), was working on mines and tank armour until 1943, when a copy of Britain's Maud Report alerted the Kremlin to progress elsewhere. Andrey Sakharov (b. 1921) did not reach the top echelon of research until 1945, and was largely responsible for post-war development of the hydrogen bomb.

A sobering aspect of the story relates to scientific advances that were *not* used. Germany's G. Schraeder had invented the deadly nerve gases Tabun and Sarin. And Britain possessed anthrax, and the capacity for bacteriological warfare. Neither was applied, presumably through fears of retaliation. This fact underlines the importance of the new field of scientific intelligence.

Werner von Braun (1912–77) owed his career to a curious oversight in the Treaty of Versailles, which did not include rockets in its list of prohibited weapons. An engineering graduate, he started work in the German Army Ordnance Department in pre-Nazi times, and for years won little support. He was given a nominal rank in the SS, but later claimed to have been inactive. His break came in 1943, when Hitler ordered the development programme which turned Braun's A-4 into the V-2 rocket. In 1944 he survived arrest in a Gestapo cell in Stettin on suspicion of 'defeatism'. In March 1945, he led a group of 500 engineers who success-fully stole a train, crossed Germany, and surrendered to the Americans. His post-war success in the USA took him to be director of the NASA Space Flight Center.[195]

Spies

Most spies are pretty mundane, but some seem too dramatic to be true. Such was Dusko Popov (1912–81), a raffish Yugoslav businessman, who worked both for the Abwehr and, as a double agent, for MI6. Code-named 'Tricycle', he was sent to the USA, where he was ignored by the FBI, and in 1944 he played a significant role for Britain's 'XX-Committee', which used double agents as part of the deception campaign connected with the Normandy landings.[196]

Walthère Dewé (d. 1944) was unusual in running a spy ring in Belgium in both world wars. He was an engineer from Liège with a wide circle of friends and colleagues who were willing to cooperate. His first organization, code-named 'La Dame Blanche', possessed over a thousand members in 1915–18, and concentrated on train-watching. Every week, a 300-page report was sent to General Haig's HQ, where all German troop movements to the rear of the British sector would be analysed. His second organization, code-named 'Clarence', started up at the outbreak of war in 1939, and was even bigger than the first. It worked closely with SOE, through which it was supplied with radios and full-time coordinators. It came to a sudden end on 14 January 1944 in Brussels, where the German Security Police tried to seize Dewé. He made a run for it, but was gunned down on the avenue de la Couronne. His two daughters were sent to Ravensbrück. A memorial tablet 'Au Fervent Patriote Liégeois, Héros de Deux Guerres' now marks the place of his death.[197]

Leopold Trepper (1904–82) ran the famous 'Red Orchestra' network in Belgium and France between 1938 and 1942: and lived to write about it. Born in Nowy Targ and educated in Vienna, he belonged to the elite generation of Polish-Jewish Communists. Expelled from Poland in 1924, and from Palestine in 1929, he went to the USSR and was recruited as a professional officer of the Soviet GRU. His discoveries included advance warning of Operation Barbarossa and plans for the Tiger-VI tank. His capture by the Gestapo in a dentist's chair was no less extraordinary than his escape in 1943 or his time with the French Resistance. His reward was ten years in the Lubyanka on suspicion of treason. Trepper returned to Poland in 1955, and then to Israel, where he wrote *The Great Game* (1975). None of his experiences shook his faith in the worldwide mission of Communism.[198]

Harold Philby (1912–88), known as 'Kim', was born in India, the son of a British administrator who converted to Islam and who went to live in Saudi Arabia. As a student of history at Trinity College, Cambridge, he was influenced by young Marxist dons like Maurice Dobb, was attracted to left-wing socialism, and in the early 1930s volunteered (without being asked) to become a Soviet agent. Indifferent or oblivious to the true nature of Stalin's regime, he was initiated into the service of the OGPU in 1934 in Vienna.

The course and consequences of Philby's career during the Spanish Civil War were instructive. His true allegiance was concealed by the fact that he worked as a *Times* correspondent with General Franco's forces, and he was personally decorated with a medal by Franco himself. Delaying his return until 1940, he reached England among the refugees from the Dunkirk beaches, with the reputation of being a right-wing adventurer. His recruitment by MI6 followed without a hitch.

During the Second World War, Philby served as a professional intelligence officer, specializing in anti-Soviet counter-espionage. In 1941–4, he ran the Iberian Section V of MI6, and he was present at Gibraltar during the crash that killed General Sikorski. In 1944–5 – hard to believe – he headed Section X, which was set up to counter the penetration of British institutions by Soviet agents. From Moscow's standpoint he was ideally placed.

Philby's star did not wane until 1950–51, when he worked at the British Embassy in Washington and came under suspicion as the 'third man', who had tipped off Burgess and Maclean. Exiled to Beirut, he sent articles to the *Observer* and *Economist*, but was denounced by an Israeli woman who claimed that his opinions were pro-Arab and therefore pro-Soviet. After one official interview, he fled to Moscow in January 1963, and never returned.[199]

During the Second World War, however, neither Philby nor any other member of the ring which would later be known as 'the Cambridge Five' was exposed. A similar situation prevailed in the USA. As is now known for certain, a core of professional Soviet controllers were in place from 1942, if not earlier, and they succeeded in creating an extensive network of spies, agents and couriers in all the main institutions of the US government. The Manhattan Project was one of the centres of their attention, but by no means the only one. The entourage and administration of President Roosevelt was deeply penetrated at the highest level. Alger Hiss at the State Department, Harry Dexter White at the US Treasury, Maurice Halpern, head of project research at the OSS, Judith

Coplon at the FBI and William Perle in jet-engine development. The high-flying economists Laughlin Currie and Gregory Silvermaster formed the tip of a huge unseen iceberg of espionage that was serviced by members and sympathizers of the American Communist Party. A person critical to post-war developments was Elizabeth Terrill Bentley (1905–63), who throughout the war was involved in an intimate liaison with Jakub Golos, the chief Soviet intelligence officer in the USA.

As early as 1943, British and American intelligence chiefs launched a joint programme, later code-named 'Venona', which aimed to crack the secrecy surrounding the Soviet embassies in London and Washington and to penetrate the encrypted radio traffic. No significant progress was made until 1946. What is more, the intelligence chiefs kept the knowledge to themselves, failing to inform either President Truman or Prime Minister Attlee. As a result the Venona evidence was not made available either to prosecutors at the various post-war spy trials or to the House Un-American Activities Committee (HUAC) of the McCarthy era. The vast majority of the 349 spies named in 1995, when the Venona files were declassified, had never even been investigated.[200]

Julius Rosenberg (1918–53) and his wife, Ethel Greenglass Rosenberg (1915–53), were the two small fry who did *not* escape. They participated in the chain of activists who were filching atomic secrets from Los Alamos during the war and passing them on to Soviet officers. (Many decades later, information from the Moscow archives was to indicate that Rosenberg met Soviet contacts on fifty occasions.) Nonetheless, they were not yet under serious suspicion when Julius was fired in 1945 from his job with the US Army Signal Corps for undeclared membership of the Communist Party. But the net began to close on them through the deposition of Elizabeth Bentley and the confessions of Harry Gold and David Greenglass, Ethel's brother. Their trial on charges of conspiracy took place in 1950 in parallel to that of Klaus Fuchs, a far more important figure, in Britain. The HUAC had already started its investigations, and, amid misplaced protests about an anti-Semitic witch-hunt, the 'Hollywood Ten' had already been imprisoned for refusing to name their political associates. The Rosenbergs also refused to cooperate with the authorities, and their predicament deteriorated. In the end, after three years of legal wrangling, they were refused the indulgent treatment extended to Gold and Greenglass, and on 19 June 1953 they were executed in the electric chair.[201] Jean-Paul Sartre called it 'legal murder'.

Survivors

In a sense, anyone who stayed alive through the Second World War was a survivor. But to deserve the label one needed to have passed through an ordeal of mortal danger – indeed, to have survived an event which the majority did not survive. Hence there were survivors of Stalingrad, there were survivors of the Holocaust, there were survivors of air crashes, and there were survivors of the darkest camps and dungeons. And there were a few, amazingly, who survived all manner of perils.

Dr Józef Garliński (1913–2005) was one of those rare multiple survivors. Born in Kiev in tsarist Russia, he moved to Poland as a boy and was educated in Warsaw and Kalisz. In 1939, as a young cavalry officer, he married an Irishwoman, Eileen, before surviving front-line service – and escaping imprisonment with the help of a friendly Bavarian. As a director of underground intelligence, he was responsible in Warsaw for monitoring the inroads of the Gestapo, and in due course he found himself under observation. Garliński's arrest and subsequent dispatch to Auschwitz were the work of a former classmate, an informer, who had been kept alive by the Gestapo for exactly such purposes and who was personally forgiven by Garliński when traced after the war to Israel. In Auschwitz, (camp no.: 121, 421) Garliński's ordeals included demotion to the penal brigades, service attending executions at the Wall of Death, and secret work in the camp resistance network. His war ended with release from KL-Neuengamme and reunion with Eileen, who had survived the Warsaw Rising: 'the happiest day of my life'. Sixty dedicated years followed as a devoted family man and historian. Having gained a PhD at the London School of Economics, aged fifty-nine, Garliński authored many valuable works, including *Fighting Auschwitz* (1975), *Poland in the Second World War* (1985) and *Hitler's Last Weapons* (1978).[202]

Survivors of the Holocaust are a special category who deserve the greatest celebration and respect. They include well-known figures such as Elie Wiesel and Primo Levi, and masses of people of no special prominence. In the interests of 'Never again', they are rightly encouraged to tell their stories, to publish their memoirs, and to inform the younger generation. However, some of the activities undertaken in their name can fall short of the best practice. Professor Norman Finkelstein in particular, whose parents were genuine survivors, has bitterly denounced organizations which purport to be helping survivors but in fact may be acting from motives of financial gain or political interest.[203] As with other aspects of the Second World War, the task of distinguishing the facts from the scams can be tricky. But one thing is certain: every false or ungenerous claim can only prolong the continuing problem of Holcaust denial.

Trade unions

With some delay, the growth of trade unions proceeded in parallel with industrialization. As industrialists organized their factories and enterprises, their labour force increasingly organized the unions in defence of pay and conditions. The Second World War coincided with the peak of this process.

In Britain, the Trades Union Congress had long been subdued by unemployment and Conservative governments, but the war revived its fortunes. There was a major problem in the coal mines, where a shortage of workers combined with dinosaur private employers. But the Minister of Labour, Ernest Bevin (1881–1951), the leading unionist of the day, solved the blockade by sending one in ten conscripts down the mines as 'Bevin Boys'. Essentially, the unions postponed all disputes for the length of the war, in the expectation of post-war rewards – which they duly received.

Bevin had previously been leader of Britain's largest union, the Transport and General Workers' Union. A sometime socialist firebrand, he was made a Cabinet minister by Churchill before he was an MP, and pulled it off brilliantly. He ended the war as a highly successful foreign secretary, completely out of the mould, and Britain's representative at the Potsdam Conference.[204]

In Germany, the Nazi regime quickly overcame unemployment, and removed the causes of worker discontent. Labour organization soon became the transmission belt for party instructions, not least because obstreperous workers could easily be transferred to the army or to a concentration camp. German unions were most concerned to preserve the skilled trades for themselves, and to protect them from the tide of foreign workers and slave labourers.

The Soviet trade unions were totally impotent. They were the outcome of a power struggle in the early days of the Soviet Union when the 'Workers' Opposition was crushed and the Bolsheviks imposed centralized, dictatorial control of labour. They were run by the Communist Party, which also controlled the state employers. So bargaining was unknown, and everyone followed the state plan. Hence the official friendship which grew up during the war between British and American labour leaders and their alleged Soviet counterparts was based on a basic misunderstanding.

Traitors

The definition of treason in wartime is simple: it pertains to any act that betrays the interests of one's own country or that helps the enemy. In all countries in 1939–45 the penalty for treason was death.

Views of what might be meant by 'helping the enemy' differed widely, however. Everyone agreed that serving in the enemy's armed forces was treasonable. General Vlasov's fate – he was shot – was therefore not disputed (see above). The British authorities also included the broadcasting of hostile propaganda under this heading. Defence lawyers for William Joyce (1906–46), who as 'Lord Haw-Haw' had worked for Radio Berlin during the war, did not dispute his hostility to Britain, but he contested the claim that he was British. Born in New York and raised in Ireland, Joyce had been a prominent member of Mosley's British Union of Fascists, and as a US citizen had acquired a British passport under false pretences. He was convicted and hanged.[205]

Both in the Third Reich and in the Soviet Union, any act or word against the ruling regime could be construed in the courts as treasonable. But Soviet practice went further. It included the assumed offences of failing to be killed, and, for any Soviet citizen who had been abroad, of failing to join the partisans. The fact that there were no partisans in most parts of occupied Europe was immaterial.

John Amery (1910–45) was the son of a prominent British Conservative politician, who had carefully concealed his family's origins. His father, Leo Amery, had written the text of the Balfour Declaration, and in May 1940, as a Conservative MP, he had quoted the words of Oliver Cromwell, 'In the name of God, go', that brought down Chamberlain's government. John's brother, Julian Amery, served as an SOE officer in Albania. But John was the black sheep of the family. Despite his unlikely connections, he, like Joyce, was a Fascist. After he had fought against the republicans in Spain, he lived in France and went to Germany in 1942. He met Hitler, and was involved in recruitment for the Legion of St George – the prospective British branch of the Waffen SS. He was hanged in Wandsworth jail in December 1945, having pleaded guilty to treason.[206]

Victims

It is a truism to say that war produces victims. But each war brings its own crop, and its own special varieties. In 1939–45, apart from the perennial war widows, refugees and what the French with brutal honesty call the *mutilés de guerre*, 'the mutilated', there were new categories: victims of mass bombing, victims of expulsions and deportations, and, above all, victims of the Holocaust.

Yet victimhood remains a disturbing concept. It has legal as well as moral implications. And it is easily attached in the popular mind to whole communities, individual members of which may or may not have been victimized. In the post-war world it has generated none too seemly campaigns. For recognition of victim status brings both public sympathy, expressed in history books and memorials, and the opportunity for material compensation.

Sixty years after the end of the war, controversy still swirls round its victims. And ideas of collective guilt and of collective victimization provide the main source of trouble. For example, the German nation, usually called 'the Germans', has long been placed into the category of aggressor, and the widespread attribution of collective crime is strengthened by titles such as 'Hitler's Willing Executioners'. The apologists of the Soviet state have likewise insisted on the USSR being classed as a 'victim of aggression', and hence on the automatic dismissal of criminal charges directed at Soviet agencies. To this way of thinking, aggressors cannot claim to be victims, and victims cannot also be accused of aggression.

Historians, however, are required to be more discriminating. They can only be guided by facts, not by generalizations, and they must make their judgements accordingly. Aggressors are particular people who authorize or implement aggressions. Murderers are people who authorize or perpetrate murder. And victims are people who have been victimized by specific acts or policies. In this light, it is perfectly possible for some members of the same group or nation to be categorized as 'aggressors' or 'murderers' or 'warmongers' and others to be categorized as 'victims'. By the same token, it can be perfectly proper for a state to be labelled an aggressor in relation to one set of events and as the victim of aggression in relation to other events. This is the position of the German nation, which on the one hand brought the Nazis to power democratically and on the other suffered great injustice from the mass bombings and expulsions. Where, one wonders, is the problem? Similar principles apply to individuals. There is no absolute reason why a particular man or woman might not be the victim of one crime and the perpetrator of another crime. The Second World War was certainly an era of international banditry. And it is not too difficult to define what banditry involves. In which case it should not be too difficult to understand the implications of a scenario in which one bandit attacks another.

Another problem surrounds the evaluation of victims, who are frequently equated with heroes or martyrs. This, too, is a questionable practice. The essence of victimization is to be the object of other people's bad conduct. Victims do not *do*: they are done to. As such, they deserve pity and comfort. But they cannot be automatically ascribed virtue, which they may or may not possess.

Even so, innocence is a quality that appertains to all victims – not absolute innocence, but innocence of the offence to which the victim is subjected. And no one is more innocent than children. Here lies the deepest 'pity of war'. The conflict of 1939–45 destroyed not thousands but millions of children: innocents systematically starved; innocents incinerated by firestorm attack; innocents packed into cattle wagons; innocents gassed in the death camps. The story must be told and retold. For, as time passes, historical reality is harder and harder to believe.

War leaders

None of the most prominent European war leaders of 1939–45 was a professional soldier. All were politicians who rose to the top of their country's government. Adolf Hitler, a founder member of the Nazi Party, became chancellor of Germany by democratic means before taking dictatorial powers and declaring himself *Führer* of the German nation. In the First World War he had served bravely as an NCO in a Bavarian regiment in the trenches of the Western Front. He took over as *Feldherr*, or commander in the field, as well as commander-in-chief in December 1941.[207] Joseph Stalin was an old Bolshevik, and served as General Secretary of the Soviet Communist Party, the highest executive position in the land, from 1922 to 1953. He twice had experience of front-line command – as a political director during the Siege of Tsaritsyn in 1918 and on the South-West Front against Poland in 1920. During the war, he briefly served as prime minister for purposes of coordination, and as from June to July 1941 he acted both as supreme commander and as chairman of the Defence Council.[208] Winston Churchill had more military experience than either of them. He started his career as a junior cavalry officer, and had ridden into battle on horseback at Omdurman; later he was First Lord of the Admiralty in 1911–15 and again in 1939–40. Churchill succeeded Chamberlain as prime minister in May 1940 and remained in post until July 1945. He chaired the War Cabinet, and numerous lesser committees, but unlike Roosevelt was never commander-in-chief.[209]

Hitler, Stalin and Churchill had all tasted the bitter pill of defeat. Hitler, gassed in the trenches, was obsessed with the 'Stab in the Back' of 1918. Stalin's career, which saw three periods of exile as a convict in Siberia, almost came to end through his seemingly treacherous role in the Red Army's defeat in Poland. And Churchill's authorship of the disastrous Gallipoli expedition of 1915–16 has always tarred his reputation as a gifted amateur strategist. His 'years in the wilderness' in the 1930s similarly blighted his reputation as a gifted politician.

The performances of these war leaders, however, followed very different paths. Churchill started on the brink of catastrophe, master-minded Britain's recovery, then gradually settled into the role of Roose-velt's understudy. Hitler started brilliantly, gambled on a quick victory, then failed to adapt to the demands of a worsening scenario and charged headlong to annihilation. Stalin, in contrast, started as Hitler's partner, survived a calamity of indescribable proportions in 1941, then steadily found his feet. The victory of 1945 in Europe was above all his. *Da, privyet pobyeda!* Its consequences were not uniformly benign.

Women

'This war, more than any war in history,' announced the US ambassador in London, John G. Winant, 'is a woman's war.' A slight exaggeration one might say. Men still had a part in it. But since women formed roughly half the general population, and since the stress was hitting civilians and combatants alike, the involvement of women – already considerable in the First World War – was increasing yet again.

Whereas Germany tried to solve its labour shortage by importing for-eigners, both the UK and the USSR coped by mobilizing women. The frontier between 'men's work' and 'women's work' was pushed back. Women worked not only in the factories and on the land, and in the auxiliary services, but also, being better educated than previously, in administration, business and the professions. In the USSR, 80 per cent of wartime collective farmworkers were female, while a million young women joined the armed forces. Britain's SOE sent female agents into action.

The separation of millions of soldiers from their homes promoted both sexual liberation and promiscuity. Reactions occurred. The Vatican objected to women wearing trousers, and members of Britain's ATS were unfairly labelled 'officers' groundsheets'. The phenomenon of 'war brides' appeared alongside the more familiar one of war widows.

Karolina Lanckorońska (1898–2002) was an Austrian princess, born in Vienna, who chose to revert to her family's Polish origins and to follow an academic career. She never married. Between the wars she had been professor of art history in Lwów, and after 1939 she lived through both the Soviet and the German occupations of Poland. The Germans appointed her to run a welfare organization in the General Government, then arrested her after belatedly realizing that she was not on their side. Prisons and concentration camps followed. In Sachsenhausen, the princess-professor was subjected to medical experiments, but somehow managed to organize assistance and educational activities for her fellow prisoners. She lived to be over a hundred.[210]

This short list of wartime experiences runs from 'Aristocrats' to 'Women'. But it could easily have run from 'Angels' to 'Zouaves', or from 'Youth' to the 'Aged'. What is important is to have an idea of the variety of experience, of the geographical range, and of the extraordinary cohabitation of humanity with inhumanity.

CHAPTER SIX

PORTRAYALS

The Second World War in
Pictures, Literature and History

DEPICTIONS OF HISTORICAL EVENTS are usually divided into the contemporary and the retrospective: that is, between those which were produced at the time, and those which were produced afterwards. The former would include diaries, newsreels, press reports, battlefield poems and photographs. The latter might take in memoirs, feature films, historical novels and analytical history. All these categories, and more, are abundantly represented in relation to the Second World War; and all must be taken into account when one inquires into how the conflict has been recorded and remembered by posterity. Of course, the distinction between the contemporary and the retrospective does not always hold good. Archives remain closed for decades. Eye-witness accounts may be unpublished for years. Nonetheless, one has a useful starting point for discussion.

Historians might be expected to stress the importance of history-writing. And, yes, if done well, clear narratives, hard evidence and coherent interpretations can be produced. Yet history in itself is clearly insufficient. It can account for only part of the record. For one thing, it operates by a process of constant statement and revision, as new sources and new authors appear: and, though authoritative positions can be established, it is by its nature inconclusive. For another, it is slow: its practitioners are forever beating their heads against myths and misunderstandings created by swifter media. And, thirdly, it does *not* command a mass audience. The best of history books, like Antony Beevor's *Stalingrad* or Max Hastings's *Armageddon*, will be read by tens of thousands, or even hundreds of thousands. The worst of Hollywood films, like *U-571* or *Saving Private Ryan*, which overflow with dubious historical assumptions, will be seen by millions.

It would be wrong to assume, however, that the contemporary is necessarily superior to later reconstructions. Every witness's viewpoint is partial. And the whole can only be approached through the widest examination of varied sources. The soldier writing up his diary in his foxhole might present an authentic account of one sector of the front. But he cannot possibly know what is happening in the enemy camp, let alone in other theatres of the war. By the same token, Churchill writing his *The Second World War* in post-war Britain can only speculate about what had been in the heads of Hitler or Stalin at any particular wartime moment. One is not helped by the fact that neither Hitler nor Stalin – the central dramatis personae – left nothing resembling a memoir.

Nor should one despise the role of fiction in establishing the full panorama of historical fact. There are some branches of fiction, whether on paper or on screen, which are purely fictional. But there are others which use fictional instruments to explore historical reality with subtlety and accuracy. There are realms of human experience which cannot be accessed by direct methods or documentary records, but which well presented in fictional form nonetheless make a vital contribution to understanding the past. The Second World War may not yet have inspired such masterworks as *Le Rouge et le Noir* or *The Leopard* – which was written almost a century after the historical setting which it describes. But it would be hard to argue that a novel such as Nicholas Monsarrat's *The Cruel Sea* (1951) or a film like *Mrs Miniver* (1942) does not provide a valid point of entry into a knowledge of events that really happened.

Lastly, it is impossible to overestimate the impact of post-war events on our understanding of the wartime years that preceded them. The Cold War descended before any outline consensus had been established concerning the conflict of 1939–45, and for nearly fifty years it acted as a vast dark barrier against all attempts to illuminate numerous crucial but controversial aspects. Throughout those decades, the largest combatant power of the Second World War continued to be ruled by a totalitarian regime which actively suppressed all forms of free inquiry and which used history as a weapon of state propaganda. As a result, some of the largest chapters of the war in Europe escaped both critical examination and impartial exposition. Huge blank spots remained, and the implications of the 'war in the East' were largely left to fester in a separate, closed, compartment. Western commentators, meanwhile, were free to pursue Western-oriented concerns and private interests, to aggrandize the role of the Western Powers without challenge, and to erect a one-sided construct that will only be modified slowly (if at all). The USSR collapsed before its spurious historical contentions could be rectified. The sixteen years since the end of the Cold War are too short a period in which to counteract the ravages of sixty years of historiographical apartheid, or to construct an integrated and consensual synthesis.

Film

Before the arrival of TV, cinema had no rival as a mass medium for entertainment and information. And all governments were aware of its potential for wartime propaganda. Weekly newsreels as introduced by Charles Pathé were an established institution. By the 1940s, the era of silent films had passed: soundtracks were the norm, and colour film was being introduced. Goebbels had seen Sergei Eisenstein's *The Battleship Potemkin* (1925), and was impressed. It was enough, he said, to make every viewer a Bolshevik.

All the combatant countries of 1939–45 produced documentary films under conditions of strict censorship. Britain's Ministry of Information, for instance, came up with titles like *London Can Take It* (1940), about the Blitz, or *Desert Victory* (1943), about El Alamein.[1] Goebbels's ministry produced similar items on the Polish campaign and the fall of France. The US government sponsored war documentaries while still neutral. *Churchill's Island* (1941), by admiring Britain's stand, justified Roosevelt's policy of 'all but war'.[2] From 1942 the series 'Why We Fight' was intended to give the American public confidence in the war effort, whilst *Prelude to War* (1942) tried to address criticisms about America's long hesitation. *Moscow Strikes Back* (1942) was a rare example of detailed interest in the Eastern Front, and the start of America's wartime love affair with the USSR.[3] At a later stage, *The True Glory* (1945) documented the liberation of (Western) Europe. In the Soviet Union, the propaganda machine was dedicated in 1939–41 to masking Soviet involvement in the war. But as from *Defence of Moscow* (1942) the genre of documentary began to merge with that of military epic.

All the combatant armies employed film crews at the front line. Many of the resultant films were not intended for public screening, but made valuable records, which still exist. Extraordinary footage was shot in August 1944 both by the Polish Home Army in the Warsaw Rising and by the French Resistance in the Paris Rising. Max Douy's production *Libération* from insurgent Paris has become a classic. It was made by a team of fifteen cameramen placed at strategic locations, while relays of cyclists raced round the back streets to the Gaumont Studios.

Air reconnaissance also produced quantities of invaluable records, sometimes unintentionally. It turned out, for example, that both the RAF and the USAAF had filmed the concentration camp at Auschwitz without knowing it. In the summer of 1944 their reconnaissance flights were directed not at the camp but at the nearby synthetic fuel plant. It was many years before someone realized that, by forgetting to switch off their cameras, the pilots had captured perfect images of selection at the ramp, of lines of people walking to the gas chambers, and of smoke rising from the crematoria.[4]

The subject matter of wartime feature films cannot easily be summarized. But certain themes recur. One is the recourse to history, and the appeal to patriotic pride through depiction of the victorious ordeals of previous wars. A second is the home front, and the attempt to sympathize with the problems of non-combatants. A third is ideological: that is, the choice of topics designed to illustrate the correctness of the ruling party's programme. In this last respect the British and Americans could be no more restrained, and considerably less subtle, than their German or Soviet counterparts (see Table opposite).

Many of these films ran into trouble with the authorities. *Alexander Nevsky*, for example, which was completed before the war, could not be screened in 1939–41, because its anti-German message clashed with the imperatives of the Nazi–Soviet Pact. It tells the tale of a thirteenth-century Russian prince who stemmed the advance of the Teutonic knights. The culminating scenes of the 'Battle on the Ice', in which iron-clad German warriors sink beneath the freezing floes, is a classic of cinematography. In Britain, the screening of *Love on the Dole* was also postponed, presumably because its depiction of social hardships during the Depression was thought unpatriotic. Nonetheless, it marked the onset of films with a social conscience that distinguished British cinema after the war. Eisenstein's *Ivan the Terrible*, which tackled the theme of tyranny, was always sailing close to the wind under the watchful eye of Stalin's censors, and the director did not live to see its premiere. Ozerov's *Liberation*, which was another five-part colossus, fell foul of the Establishment through implied criticisms of the Soviet High Command in 1941, and it was not shown in full for twenty years.[5]

The availability of real soldiers in large numbers provided one of the characteristics of the wartime epics. Bondarchuk was to have whole divisions of Red Army recruits at his disposal during the making of *War and Peace*, while Veit Harlan used no fewer than 187,000 extras for the battle scenes of *Kolberg*.

However, the production of war films could only develop after 1945, and for many years it was only the victorious Allies who could engage in

Western approaches

The Western Allies made three major landings on the continent: in Sicily in 1943, in Normandy in June 1944, and on the French Riviera.

Left. Monte Cassino, stormed at the third attempt. Allied armies crawled through Italy facing effective German delaying tactics.

Below. D-Day, 6 June 1944. British soldiers come ashore on Sword Beach.

Catastrophes in the East, 1944

Despite sensational Soviet advances, the Eastern Front produced many surprises.

Above. The Warsaw Rising, unaided, persisted for sixty-three days instead of five or six. The daily death toll was similar to that of D-Day, every day for nine weeks.

Below. Courland Pocket, where thirty-one German divisions of Army Group North were stranded, undefeated.

The final winter, 1944–5

Allied forces struggled to advance in Western Europe, while the Red Army rapidly overran all the countries of Eastern Europe.

Left. The Netherlands are liberated after six months' delay due to the setback at Arnhem.

Below. Lublin: a Communist Manifesto, not mentioning Communism, announces the takeover by a Soviet-run committee.

Flight and surrender

Europe in the last months of the war was painfully chaotic.

Above. Ostflucht. Not waiting to be expelled, a flood of Germans from East Prussia and other eastern provinces took to the road.

Below. The Cossack Brigade, which had fought under German command, surrendered to the British in Austria, then resisted forcible repatriation to the USSR.

Nemesis in Berlin

Owing to troop shortages and the continuing war against Japan, the US command invited the Red Army to capture Berlin single-handed.

Above. Soviet tanks surge past the Brandenburg Gate after two weeks of savage fighting.

Left. The 'Hammer and Sickle' flies over the Reichstag in Khaldei's famous picture.

The pride and the pity

Above. Stalin takes the salute atop Lenin's Mausoleum in Red Square; his victorious legions cast captured German standards at his feet.

Left. The Berghof, April 1945. An American GI pauses for reflection in front of the empty ruins of Hitler's home. The Nazis' 'last stand' in a non-existent Alpine redoubt never took place.

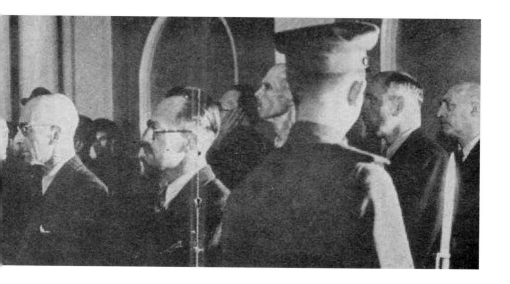

Shame and retribution

The justice of the victors cannot escape criticism.

Above. Moscow Trial, June 1945. Sixteen leaders of Poland's democratic underground, all survivors of the Warsaw Rising, were kidnapped by the NKVD and accused of 'illegal activities'.

Below. Nuremberg Tribunal, 1946. Germans, and Germans alone, had to answer for their crimes. One of the chief prosecutors was Andrei Vyshinskiy, star of Stalin's show trials in the 1930s.

Fragmented memory

Monuments and memorials to the Second World War rarely pay respect to all the tragedies of 1939–45.

Above. Berlin's Holocaust Memorial, 2005. Eisenman's concrete steles.

Left. The Soviet War Memorial in Vienna, 1955. The Soviet authorities ordered memorials to be erected in all towns and cities liberated by the Red Army.

Films of the Second World War

History	Home Front	Ideology
Carl Friedrich's *Heart of a Queen* (Germany, 1940): an anti-English musical about Mary, Queen of Scots.	*London Can Take It* (1940): official British film on the Blitz.	Fritz Hippler's *The Wandering Jew* (1940): a racist caricature.
Sergei Eistenstein's *Alexander Nevsky* (1938) and *Ivan the Terrible* (3 parts, 1943–6), Russian classics.	John Baxter's *Love on the Dole* (1941): film version of a novel of the Depression.	Veit Harlan's *Jud Süss* (1940): a high-budget, historical story on the career of Suss Oppenheimer.
Billy Wilder's *Five Graves to Cairo* (1943) war and romance in the Western desert	Alberto Cavalcanti's *Went the Day Well?* (1942): an English village is occupied by disguised German paratroopers.	Stuart Legg's *Churchill's Island* (1941): Anglo-American solidarity – using German documentary footage.
Henry V (1944): Shakespeare's historical drama, starring and directed by Laurence Olivier.	William Wyler's *Mrs Miniver* (1942): a British middle-class family dodge bombs and stand together in hard times.	Michael Curtiz's *Mission to Moscow* (1943): making the Soviet Union respectable through the story of ambassador Joseph Davies.
Josef von Baky's *Münchhausen* (1943): pure escapism in the adventures of Baron Munchhausen.	Michael Powell's *A Canterbury Tale* (1944): Allied solidarity – a Land Girl, a GI and a British soldier are thrown together in wartime England.	Yuri Ozerov's *Liberation* (1971): a Soviet version of Stalin's war aims.
Jean Duvivier's *Heart of a Nation* (1943): an anti-German chronicle of Paris from the time of the Franco-Prussian war. Suppressed by Vichy censorship.	Humphrey Jennings's *A Diary for Timothy* (1945): a fanfare for the common man and for a war baby.	Garson Kanin's *The True Glory* (1945): an American version of the war's finale. US Army, *Here is Germany* (1945): explaining Germany's good and bad traditions in good dialetical fashion.
Veit Harlan's *Kolberg* (1945): reconstruction of a Prussian military epic at the siege of Kolberg in 1806.	Donald Taylor's *Battle for Music* (1943): the wartime ordeals of the London Philharmonic.	
	Mark Donskoi's *Raduga* (1944): a pregnant partisan returns to her native village.	

it. With very few exceptions, therefore, the war-film genre was devoted to celebrations of the Allied cause, and hence to the assumed superiority both of Allied arms and of Allied war aims. Not surprisingly, the bravado factor was high, and the level of intelligent criticism was low. No one made popular post-war films about the successes of the Wehrmacht, or about episodes such as the Hamburg raid or the Warsaw Rising, which might have brought the Allied cause into disrepute. Indeed, as time went on and Hollywood got into its stride, the tendency towards patriotic exaggeration moved almost imperceptibly into the realm of downright falsification (see Table on p. 436).

Films that bucked the Hollywood trend were few and far between. An early one was *The Cruel Sea* (1953). Based on the novel by Nicholas Monsarrat, it painted naval warfare in a less than flattering light. *Die Brücke* (*The Bridge*, 1959), a German production, aimed to portray the futility of war. It showed German soldiers in a different light: not as blond beasts barking orders, but as ill-armed teenagers sent out to be killed by American tanks. Sam Peckinpah's *Cross of Iron* (1977) went further. With James Coburn starring as the hard-bitten Corporal Steiner, it humanized the Wehrmacht. It follows the ordeals of a battalion on the Eastern Front which is struggling not only against the overwhelming firepower of the Red Army, but also against the arrogance and inflexibility of an old-fashioned captain, played by Maximilian Schell, who is intent on winning his Iron Cross at all costs.[6]

Nonetheless, Western films about the Eastern Front remained relatively rare, and the average cinema-goer in Britain or America would never have realized the scale of the Soviet victory. On the contrary, the great majority of films were devoted to four or five standard topics: the air war, the Battle of the Atlantic, the North African campaign, the commando raids and the prisoner-of-war camps. And the Red Army did not figure in any of them. When the central subject of continental warfare made its appearance, in films like *The Longest Day* or *Battle of the Bulge*, it was confined exclusively to fighting in Western Europe. No major film has ever been made about the most decisive battle of the war, at Kursk – perhaps because there were no Americans involved.

After some delay, television came into its own in the 1960s. Unlike the cinema, it was able to exploit the timescale of multi-part series, which gave a broader panorama of wartime action, and it drew heavily on original documentary material. But it offered little in terms of fresh interpretation. Its heyday also coincided with a sustained wave of interest in the Jewish Holocaust, which had been passed over in the early post-war decades. In Britain, ITV's twenty-six-part series *The World at War* (1974) presented a more global perspective than any previous production. It was still predominantly Western in outlook, being directed to a Western market. But, while skating over the moral and political complications of the Soviet alliance, it paid due attention to the Soviet military achievement. Martin Chomsky's eight-part *Holocaust* series (1978) also had a great impact. It can be criticized for its narrow historical context, but it rendered a valuable service – not least in Germany, where the horrors of the Final Solution were brought home to a mass audience for the first time. In the USA, HBO's ten-part series *Band of Brothers* (2001) was a major success. It followed a company of American soldiers from the 101st Airborne Division as they 'liberated Europe', from D-Day to Berlin. In Poland, a very similar but earlier concept entitled *Czterej Pancerni i Pies* ('Four Tankmen and a Dog', 1966–70), which crossed *Band of Brothers* with *Lassie,* had followed the adventures of another company of Allied heroes as they approached Berlin from the opposite direction. Despite the obligatory eulogies to the Red Army, the twenty-one episodes were immensely popular. The BBC's *Auschwitz: The Nazis and the 'Final Solution'* (six parts, 2005) had the virtue of putting the Holocaust into one of its political settings, namely, the priorities of Allied war policy.

Given the persistence of the Cold War, it may not be surprising that Western film-making about the Second World War unfolded in a different context from that which prevailed in the Soviet Bloc. Yet it is surprising, as well as thought-provoking, to realize that the productions of the highest quality undoubtedly did not appear in the West. For all its money and its lack of formal censorship, Hollywood simply could not compete in terms of human sensitivity and political sophistication. The 'golden years' arrived during the brief interval of the so-called thaw following the death of Stalin in 1953. The flagship production, which won the Palme d'Or at Cannes, was Mikhail Kalatozov's *The Cranes are Flying* (1957). It explores the gamut of emotions experienced by a couple of lovers, Veronica and Boris, who meet on the streets of Moscow, and who are then cruelly separated by the war. It was soon followed by another masterpiece, Greigori Chukhrai's *Ballad of a Soldier* (1959), which has been called 'social realism with a human face'. The soldier, Alyosha, who inevitably dies, is observed both amid the slaughterhouse of the battlefront and in the tender embrace of a refugee girl. The public exposition of wartime sexuality was a significant milestone for puritanical Soviet audiences. In those same years the Polish director Andrzej Wajda pushed the limits of censorship with two stunning

A select list of post-war war films

Date	Title	Director	Subject matter
1951	The Desert Fox	Henry Hathaway	Rommel, 1941–3
1952	Angels One Five	George More O'Ferrall	Britain's air war
1953	The Cruel Sea	Charles Frend	Atlantic convoys (based on Nicholas Monsarrat's novel)
1953	The Desert Rats	Robert Wise	Endurance and valour at Tobruk, 1941
1954	The Dambusters	Michael Anderson	RAF precision bombing
1955	The Cockleshell Heroes	José Ferrer	Operation Frankton: commando raid
1955	The Colditz Story	Guy Hamilton	Allied officers' escape club
1956	Reach for the Sky	Lewis Gilbert	Douglas Bader: RAF Fighter Command
1957	Kanał	Andrzej Wajda	The Warsaw Rising, 1944
1958	Dunkirk	Leslie Norman	Operation Dynamo, 1940
1958	Orzel	Leonard Buczkowski	Submarine saga
1960	Sink the Bismarck	Lewis Gilbert	The Royal Navy hunts a German battleship
1961	The Dirty Dozen	Robert Aldrich	(Fictional) commando raid
1961	Generation	Andrzej Wajda	Resistance in Poland
1961	Guns of Navarone	J. Lee Thompson	Crete, 1941 (based on the novel by Alistair MacLean)
1962	The Longest Day	Ken Annakin et al.	D-Day landings
1963	The Great Escape	John Sturges	Stalag VIIIA at Sagan, 1944
1965	Battle of the Bulge	Ken Annakin	The Ardennes, 1944–5
1968	Where Eagles Dare	Brian Hutton	Bavarian rescue (based on Alistair MacLean's novel)
1968	Sullivan's Marauders	Armando Crispino	Italo-American raiders in the North African desert
1969	Army of Shadows	Jean-Pierre Melville	French Resistance (fiction)
1969	Battle of Britain	Guy Hamilton	1940 dogfights (based on The Narrow Margin)

A select list of post-war war films (*cont.*)

Date	Title	Director	Subject matter
1970	*Patton*	Franklin Schaffner	The story of General Patton
1974	*The Execution of Eddie Slovik*	Lamont Johnson	US deserter
1977	*A Bridge Too Far*	Richard Attenborough	Operation Market Garden, Arnhem, 1944
1977	*Cross of Iron*	Sam Peckinpah	Germans on the Eastern Front
1981	*The Boat*	Wolfgang Peterson	German submarine epic
1985	*Come and See*	Elem Kimov	Partisans in Byelorussia
1990	*Korczak*	Andrzej Wajda	Hero of the Warsaw Ghetto
1990	*Winter War*	Pekka Parikka	Finland, 1939–40
1993	*Schindler's List*	Steven Spielberg	The Jewish ghetto in Nazi-run Kraków
1993	*Stalingrad*	Joseph Vilsmaier	German ordeal
1998	*Saving Private Ryan*	Steven Spielberg	US Army in Normandy
1998	*When Trumpets Fade*	John Irvin	American–German combat, 1944
2000	*U-571*	Jonathan Mostow	Falsified story of submarine warfare
2001	*Captain Corelli's Mandolin*	John Madden	Italian occupation of Cephalonia
2001	*Enemy at the Gates*	Jean-Jacques Annaud	Sniper duel at Stalingrad
2002	*The Pianist*	Roman Polanski	Warsaw, 1943–4: the story of a survivor
2002	*Ambush*	Olli Saarenen	Winter war (based on a novel by Antti Tuuri)
2003	*The Fallen*	Ari Taub	Soldiers' fate in Italy
2003	*Letters from the Dead*	Ari Taub	Italian partisans
2004	*Downfall*	Oliver Hirschbiegel	Final agony of the Third Reich

films on the war and its aftermath. *Kanal* ('Sewer', 1957) must be one of
the most harrowing films ever made. Apart from portraying the heroism
of the Warsaw Rising, which the Communist authorities unreservedly
condemned, it contained scenes hinting at Soviet betrayal. *Ashes and
Diamonds* (1958), based on a novel by Jerzy Andrzejewski, is predicated on
the unspoken fact that wartime society had been predominantly both anti-
Communist and anti-Fascist. Wajda's daring on this score may be compared to Chukhrai's stance in *Clear Skies* (1961), which relates the story of
a Soviet pilot who survives both a crash in combat and German imprisonment, only to be arrested by the NKVD on false accusations of espionage.
Most Western audiences, untrained in reading between the lines, would
probably miss the references.[7]

In the period following the fall of Communism, little was done to
bridge the gulf between Western and non-Western perceptions of the war.
Though half a century had passed since the war's end, the intellectual
framework and the dominant images differed widely. Hollywood's priorities of America First and the Holocaust remained unchanged, as exemplified in Steven Spielberg's films *Schindler's List* (1993) and *Saving Private
Ryan* (1998). Both films were moving, brilliant works; but both were very
weak on historical context. Russia's priorities changed, in that Stalin and
the Soviet system were no longer above criticism. But the great victory in
the Great Patriotic War remained sacred. For the time being at least, no
Russian film-maker had anything new to add. Western attempts to
approach the Eastern Front, as in *Enemy at the Gates* (2001), which features
a duel of snipers at Stalingrad, had touches of Western priorities dressed
up in Eastern clothing, although it was unusual in placing the principal
protagonists on the Soviet side of the front. And the controversy that
broke out in 2005 over the film *Downfall*, which was accused of 'humaniz-
ing' Adolf Hitler, shows how deeply entrenched are conventional preferences for a mindless black-and-white scenario (in colour).[8] David Denby
expressed reservations in the *New Yorker*: 'By emphasizing the painfulness
of Hitler's defeat, [Ganz] has . . . made the dictator into a plausible human
being.' Ian Kershaw replied in the *Guardian*: 'I found it hard to imagine
that anyone [other than the usual neo-Nazi fringe] could possibly find
Hitler a sympathetic figure during his last bizarre days. . . . Hitler, after all,
was a human being, even if an especially obnoxious, destestable specimen.'

In the last resort, cinema is never going to produce a complete or
definitive account of the Second World War. It is good at reliving episodes,
at dramatizing small-scale actions, and at interpreting the dilemmas and

quirks of particular personalities. But it seems to lose its power in proportion to the size of the subject. One battle, one campaign, one general can be dealt with convincingly. But 'The Longest Day' is the longest span that the cinematic medium can cope with. And there were 2,076 such days between 1 September 1939 and 9 May 1945. So far, at least, no director has found a satisfactory way of embracing both the Eastern Front and the Western Front on one screen. Yet the relationship between them provides the key to how the war was won and lost.

Photography

Most people who know a little about the Second World War will have heard of Robert Capa (1913–54), or at least will have seen his work. He was the photographer who swam ashore with American troops at Omaha Beach armed with two 50-mm Contax II cameras and whose pictures of D-Day were printed shortly afterwards in *Life* magazine. Born in Hungary as Andrei Friedmann, he became a legend of the American media when he was killed in Vietnam in 1954.[9] Capa was a good technician, and a brave professional, but one has to ask why his name is so much better known than that of other photographers. After all, the Red Army alone lost nearly three hundred front-line photographers killed in action. The only answer can be publicity – and relentless Western publicity, pursued to the greater glory of Western interests, is one reason why the war as a whole is so partially understood.

All sides in the war went into action well supplied with cameras and photographers; and none better than the Germans. (An undamaged Leica was one of the most prized trophies of Allied soldiers.) Front-line photography had important military uses, including reconnaissance training and battle analysis. So, alongside the commercial journalists dressed up in uniform, like Capa, were professional, camera-toting soldiers, whose work has to be sought in military archives. The Germans in particular were famous for pedantically photographing everything they did – not excepting their atrocities, about which in the prevalent atmosphere of the day they had little sense of shame. The *Militärarchiv* in Koblenz is a copious source of such material.

The rear areas inevitably attracted the attention of war photographers. Harrowing pictures of burning buildings, of frightened refugees or of mangled corpses were all part of the reality that had to be captured. One of the deservedly celebrated images of the Eastern Front came through the lens of Dmitri Baltermants (1912–90) and shows a group of mourning peasant women trying to identify the dead left on a battlefield. It was taken in 1942 near Kerch, in Crimea, and was later named *Grief '41*. Baltermants, born in Warsaw, photographed numerous scenes and action shots which, like *Grief '41*, were not released until after the war.[10]

Baltermants's picture, however, was not spontaneous, it was staged. Like so many other aspects of Soviet life, it had to be orchestrated, recommended by a *politruk*, and approved by the NKVD before release to the press and final authorization by the censor. Any number of similar examples can be found, but each would usually have arisen from real incidents which had already happened and which were painstakingly reconstructed. The T-34 tank would be parked at exactly the right angle, with its cannon glinting in the sun. Smiling tankmen would be jumping down from the hatch. In the centre, the captain in his black-leather headgear would be extravagantly embraced by the liberated farmer, while the farmer's family, carefully lined up to one side, were told to bow stiffly in deference to Soviet power. The resultant image was perfect in its clarity, in its contrast of light and shade, in its unity of composition. But was it authentic?

Other techniques were preferred on the Western Front. Capa snapped 108 frames on his first day in Normandy. All but eleven were ruined by a laboratory technician who was rushing to develop them in super-quick time before flight across the Atlantic. In New York, the editors of *Life* chose eight out of the eleven, and apologized for their being 'slightly out of focus'. Readers were led to believe that Capa's hand had been shaking, or that his camera was rocked by explosions. They knew nothing about the technician's miscalculation of the temperature of the developer fluid. But the effect was convincing.

The Allies were rightly concerned to capture images of their enemy's misdeeds. British pictures of Belsen and Soviet pictures of Auschwitz form the basis of an essential record. An important problem arises, however, when it is realized that no one could take parallel pictures of the GULag. Nazi crimes were publicized for all to see. Pictorial proof of Soviet crimes is very hard to find; and some people assume that what wasn't photographed didn't happen. Such pictures as do exist portray hard work, but not corpses. Independent photographers were not let into a terrible place like Vorkuta until the 1990s.[11] So one can only imagine. Solzhenitsyn and others have described the Soviet practice of stacking the frozen corpses of dead prisoners head to foot and foot to head, 'like salted herrings in a barrel'. The stack would grow ever larger through the winter, until disposal was possible in the spring. Given the right angle of pale sunlight on the snowblown heads and feet, what chilling, world-famous images might have been captured. But they weren't. At least, as far as we know they weren't.

During the Second World War, commercial journalism was in its infancy. But *Picture Post* in London and *Life* magazine in the USA were already in business, and they influenced the way that the war was viewed. Their photographers accompanied the troops on all fronts. Bill Brandt (1904–83), who had chronicled pre-war London life, became known as the 'photographer of the Blitz'. He was author of *The Camera in London* (1948). His colleague Bert Hardy (1913–95) worked for *Picture Post*. He was posted to Dieppe in 1942, but was replaced at the last moment, and his replacement was killed. He then joined a British Army photographic unit, advancing from Normandy to the Rhine. Apart from Capa, the American contingent included Carl Mydans (b. 1907) and George Rodger (1908–95), both of whom worked for *Life*. The former served in Italy, especially at Monte Cassino, and on the D-Day beaches before being sent to the Far East, where his shot of General MacArthur wading ashore on his return to the Philippines became famous. Rodger, who was English in origin, served on all sectors from North Africa to Berlin. He was the first Allied photographer to enter Belsen.[12]

War photography brought women correspondents into the fighting zones. Margaret Bourke-White (1904–71) is often said to be the pioneer. She was a left-wing activist, who campaigned against American poverty and racism and who made several visits to the USSR. Together with her husband, Erskine Caldwell, she was the only Western correspondent to witness Operation Barbarossa from the Soviet side. Their experiences were reflected in a book, *All Out on the Road to Smolensk* (1942).[13]

Captain Elizabeth Lee Miller (1907–77), US Army, had the distinction both of appearing on the cover of *Vogue* magazine and of contributing to it as a photographer. Her book *Grim Glory* (1940) recorded her work during the London Blitz. In 1944–5 she accompanied US troops across Western Europe, capturing the momentous pictures of their junction with Soviet forces on the Elbe. Together with Bourke-White, she recorded the liberation of Buchenwald, before making a special study of other Nazi concentration camps.[14]

The organization of the *Kriegsberichter*, or war correspondents, in Germany was much more centralized. All of them, whether journalists, photographers or artists, worked directly or indirectly for Goebbels's propaganda ministry, and most contributed either to the weekly cinematic *Wochenschau* or to various state-controlled newspapers and magazines. Their problem was to produce fresh and interesting images when both the defeats of the Wehrmacht and the dirty work of the SS were off limits. The environment became more and more stifling. So it should cause no surprise that the photographers of the Polish Home Army, like Sylwester 'Kris' Braun and Eugeniusz Lokajski, inspired by the brief weeks of freedom during the Warsaw Rising, produced work of a superior order.[15]

Yet it stands to reason that the largest collection of war photos accumulated on the Eastern Front, where the largest amount of fighting occurred. The Soviet Union could boast some superb practitioners, even if they were obliged to use Leica-derivatives. Among them, apart from Baltermants, were Robert Diament (1907–87), Max Alpert (1899–1980), and Yevgeni Khaldei (1917–97). Diament was attached to the Northern Fleet in Murmansk, and his portrait of the grinning, splay-toothed *Sailor Pashkóv* (1944) is a classic.

In the 1930s Alpert had specialized in the social dramas of industrialization and the five-year plans. His cultivation of images of heroic shock-workers prepared him well for the requirement for heroic front-line Soviet soldiers. Khaldei, who was the youngest of the troika, preferred reflective pictures of warriors resting or enjoying themselves behind the front. He lived long enough to complete commissions for portraits of Stalin, Gorbachev and Yeltsin. He was the official Soviet photographer at the Nuremberg Tribunal.[16]

The political authorities of all combatant countries demanded symbolic photographs that carried unmistakable messages. In the days of German success, Wehrmacht photographers specialized in pictures of marching, singing infantry columns; of panzers cruising across the endless steppe; and of a haughty Führer with outstretched arm reviewing his victorious legions. They captured the moment when German troops gleefully tore down the first Polish frontier post or stormed across the bridge on the Bug at Brest on to Soviet-held territory. German pilots snapped the spires of the Kremlin from the air, and German climbers were framed at the summit of Mount Elbrus, the highest peak in Europe.

Thereafter, though the shutters never ceased to click, the best photo opportunities fell increasingly to the Allies. In the Pacific, the supreme image was produced when US marines planted 'Old Glory' atop the island of Iwo Jima. In Europe, the supreme image was captured by Khaldei, as Red Army soldiers planted an enormous 'Hammer and Stickle' atop the Reichstag in Berlin. Like all famous pictures, this last one has a story attached. At the first take, Khaldei noticed that the left arm of the soldier holding the bottom of the flagpole was covered by a long line of looted watches. So he had to call for a second take.[17] Which only goes to show that the apparent veracity of photographs must always be open to question. In one way or another, the camera always lies.

War artists

Winston Churchill took his paints and easel to Casablanca, and found a few hours to capture some relaxing Moroccan landscapes. Some of the professionals followed his example. When not painting death and destruction, both John Piper (1903–92) and Graham Sutherland (1903–1980) turned to the English landscape for consolation.

War art stretched from cartoons and propaganda posters at one end of the scale to avant-garde oils and watercolours at the other. Many artists could turn their hand to all the genres; and many, like Paul Nash (1889–1946) in Britain and Kurt Arnold (1883–1953) in Germany, were active in both world wars.

In an age of films and photographs, representational art made little sense even for purposes of historical record. Britain's best-known war painting is probably Paul Nash's allegory with a German title: *Totes Meer* ('Dead sea', 1941). On close examination, the jagged surface of the lake is made up of aeroplane parts. The artist had visited a scrap dump near Cowley, in Oxfordshire, which was full of German wrecks from the Battle of Britain.[18]

Portraiture, however, is eternal. Feliks Topolski (1907–89), settled in Britain before the war, and developed a highly individual style. From 1939 he was an official war artist, and he chronicled the fighting on all continents. Indeed, he produced portraits of all the leading figures of Britain's wartime generation, from Churchill to H. G. Wells and G. B. Shaw. His depiction of the opening ceremony of the United Nations Organization in 1945 triggered a glittering post-war career.[19]

The war poster is a vast subject in itself. Each country had its own style, although German and Soviet heroics exuded similar flavours. The home front provided the main target audience, especially women who were mobilized for work. In this regard, Soviet posters were reminiscent of American ones. In Britain, a gentler tone prevailed. Both H. M. Bateman (1887–1970) and Cyril Bird (1887–1963) had been employees of *Punch*, and they preserved their wry humour. Bird's *Careless Talk Costs Lives* is inimitable.[20]

In Germany, where dissident artists could expect a visit from storm-troopers, many of the prominent names of the 1920s, like George Grosz, emigrated or stopped work. Kurt Arnold was an exception. He had belonged to the pacifist movement, and, as a contributor to *Simplissimus*, in 1932 drew a famous portrait of Hitler that made his subject look plain silly. Thereafter he fell into line, kept his job, and lost his reputation.

In the USSR, controls were equally tight. Under Stalin, the experimental and revolutionary art which had caused a furore throughout Europe in the 1920s had been suppressed. Socialist Realism was obligatory. Towering, muscular workers and defiant, square-jawed soldiers were ubiquitous. Alexei Kokorekin's poster *All for the Front* set the standard. So called Socialist Realism of course was not realistic. It was unadulterated political idealism.

And then there was Kilroy, whose face appeared on walls and washrooms from Berlin to Tokyo. Legend has it that James Kilroy was a ship inspector in the Boston dockyards who chalked his name on the hulls of unfinished vessels to warn the welders of his presence. Whatever the truth, the stylized face with the caption 'Kilroy was here' became the most ubiquitous visual image of the Second World War. Legend also has it that an executive lavatory was provided at Potsdam for the use of the 'Big Three'. When Stalin emerged from the facility, he asked his aides, 'Kto etot Kilroi' – 'Who's this Kilroy?'[21]

Cartoons

Cartooning, which is a branch of pictorial satire, aims to provoke thought through funny, striking and paradoxical images, often accompanied by a lapidary text or quotation. It was practised actively during the Second World War, and was capable of exposing the essence of a complicated situation at a glance. David Low's *Rendezvous*, for example, which appeared in the *Evening Standard* on 20 September 1939, perfectly explains the Nazi–Soviet Pact and hence the complicated international set-up which made the outbreak of war possible.

Low (1891–1963), a New Zealander who came to Britain after the First World War, was more than Britain's premier cartoonist. He rose during the war to become one of the unofficial arbiters of good political taste. This was because he combined several of the contradictory streams of wartime opinion. A leftist radical, who had invented the stereotypical figure of 'Colonel Blimp', he persuaded Lord Beaverbrook to give him a free hand on the *Evening Standard*, where his merciless satirizing of appeasement drew protests from the German Embassy. In 1939 he became an ardent Churchillian. *All Behind You, Winston* appeared on 14 May 1940. Yet he was closely associated with the social concerns that swept Churchill from power in 1945. And, like Beaverbrook, he was pro-Soviet to a fault[22].

The best loved of US wartime cartoonists was probably Bill Maulden (1921–2003), who worked for the army newspaper *Stars and Stripes*. He invented a couple of eternally grousing GIs, Willie and Joe, who didn't upset Eisenhower but who drew the ire of General Patton. Maulden was hauled before Patton in March 1945, and was asked in no uncertain terms why he persisted in drawing 'anti-officer cartoons'. He told Patton that the men had genuine grievances.

Neither the Third Reich nor the Soviet Union was famed for a subtle sense of humour. And the preferred cartoon styles in both countries were similar – crude, nasty and hate-laden. Adversaries were there to be humiliated. The favourite Nazi stereotype was that of the hook-nosed Jew loaded with moneybags. The Nazis also liked sketches of Churchill smoking a booby-trapped cigar, and of Roosevelt trying to pocket the globe. In the USSR the fat and greedy capitalist with his bowler hat and gold watch chain had long provided the butt of ridicule. But in 1939–45

Soviet cartoonists had to lay off their earlier lampoons of the Fascists, and after 1941 of British and American capitalists. They soon found new targets. One was Hitler with a bayonet stuck into his backside. Another was Göring presented as a rapidly deflating balloon. The standard repertoire, which was laid out in the magazine *Krokodil*, was most frequently signed 'Kukryniksy': the composite pen name of Kuprianov, Krylov and Nikolai Sokolov.

The cartoons of the Allied camp shared much in terms of negative targets. They all fired at the Nazi enemy. But they had little positive in common. The Anglo-Americans could promote 'Uncle Joe', but they could not draw benign pictures of Communism. And the Soviets could not smile on Western democracy. The essential emptiness of the Grand Coalition did not bode well for the future.[23]

Literary fiction

In 1939, Europe's literary Establishment was extremely large and varied. And the range of human experience for writers to digest in 1939–45 was almost limitless. So it may seem odd that few of the major established figures cared to participate in the digesting. The reasons for this are no doubt complex. For one thing, the pre-war generation of writers were still trying to cope with the events of 1914–18. For another, many of them – Wells, Shaw, Forster, etc. – were already too old to be directly involved. And, for another, many of the rest – W. H. Auden, Thomas Mann, Berthold Brecht – had left Europe for American exile. In the Soviet Union, many of the best writers had either been repressed and killed, like Isaac Babel, or permanently silenced, like Akhmatova and Pasternak. P. G. Wodehouse (1881–1975), one of the most prolific and widely read authors of his day, was captured at Le Touquet in 1940 by Germans and interned. As a result, the literature of the Second World War was left to a large extent to a younger generation, who experienced the war in their youth and who picked up their pens and their typewriters afterwards.

Nonetheless, crucial distinctions need to be made between wartime writing, writing about the war and war-inspired writing. There were figures like William Faulkner (1897–1962) in distant Mississippi, Eugene

O'Neill (1888–1953), the New York dramatist, or even T. S. Eliot (1888–1965), whose *Four Quartets* appeared in 1943, for whom the war was almost incidental to their main concerns. There were authors like Alexander Solzhenitsyn (b. 1918), a veteran Red Army artillery captain, and Heinrich Böll (1917–85), a battle-hardened *Obergefreiter* of the Wehrmacht, who brought their wartime experiences more directly onto the pages of their books. And there was a further group, including Jean-Paul Sartre (1905–80), who had been a POW in Germany, and William Golding (1911–93), who had commanded a Royal Navy rocket ship, who were propelled by the ordeals of war to examine the complexities of human nature and human society.

Yet Second World War literature did not end with the people who lived through the war. It was still going strong at the start of the twenty-first century, when it had branched out into many streams and substreams, and when it thrived in the minds of the children and the grandchildren of the wartime generation.

The conventional view that the Second World War produced few war poets is largely based on Anglo-American perceptions. But even the English had their soldier bards. Keith Douglas (1920–44), who died in Normandy, had earlier served in North Africa. He was an interesting mixture of tankman and literary student. His *Alamein to Zem-Zem* has moments of brilliance. His 'Actors Waiting in the Wings' was started as he waited to be embarked on the eve of D-Day:

> Actors waiting in the wings of Europe
> we already watch the lights on the stage
> and listen to the colossal overture begin.
> For us entering at the height of the din
> it will be hard to hear our thoughts, hard to gauge
> how much our conduct was due to fear or fury.
>
> Everyone, I suppose, will use these minutes
> to look back, to hear music and to recall
> what we were doing and saying that year
> during our last few months as people, near
> the sucking mouth of the day that swallowed us all
> into the stomach of war . . .[24]

The poet was killed by a mortar round three days later, before his poem was finished.

Solzhenitsyn tried his hand at a Russian epic in *Prussian Knights*: and Krzystof Kamil Baczyński (1921–44), who died on the fourth day of the Warsaw Rising, was a major talent cut short before his prime. He had eerie premonitions both of his own end and of the destruction of Warsaw, and searing visions of the intimate co-habitation of beauty, love and death:

Bryła ciemna, gdzie dymy bure	*[It was] a dark clod where the dense smoke*
poczerniałe twarze pokoleń	*had blackened the faces of generations.*
nie dotknięte miłości chmury	*And clouds of love, untouched*
przeorane cierpienia role	*Had ploughed the fields of suffering.*
Jakie szczęscie, że nie można tego dożyć,	*Oh hero! What luck one can't live to see it!*
kiedy pomnik ci wystawią, bohaterze,	*They'll erect a monument to your memory,*
i morderca na nagrobkach kwiaty złoży.[25]	*And a murderer will lay flowers on your grave.*

In Britain, Eliot's *Four Quartets* contained occasional references to the Blitz. But their main emphasis was on religion and tradition – through which, perhaps accidentally, they conveyed a much needed message of stability and continuity. Dylan Thomas (1914–53) made his debut with a collection called *Deaths and Entrances* (1946). But the British author to reach a wartime apogee, in addition to worldwide fame, was George Orwell (Eric Blair, 1903–50).

Orwell, an Old Etonian socialist, was concerned as much with social deprivation as with international politics. His memoir *Homage to Catalonia* (1938) had recorded his disillusionment with the Communist-backed republican cause in Spain. And from 1939 on he became progressively appalled by the betrayal of socialism by the USSR. Unlike his left-wing colleagues, he was well ahead of his time in seeing the totalitarian similarities between the Nazi enemy and the Soviet ally. As an editor of the socialist *Tribune*, he pulled no punches over Soviet misconduct during the Warsaw Rising. By then he was writing his political satire on totalitarianism *Animal Farm* (1945), which was to become the prime classic of the genre, and which was to be followed after the war by *Nineteen Eighty-four* (1949). 'All animals are equal, but some animals are more equal than others' says it all.[26]

British post-war fiction carried strong overtones of the recent conflict. All the leading names – Graham Greene (1904–90), Evelyn Waugh (1903–66), Lawrence Durrell (1912–90) and E. M. Forster (1879–1970) – returned to writing after wartime breaks, and all but Forster took up war-related themes. Greene's *The End of the Affair* (1951) centred on notoriously fragile wartime romances. Waugh, who had served in the Mediterranean, in the Royal Marines, wrote the semi-satirical *Sword of Honour* trilogy

(1952–61) about the adventures of Captain Guy Crouchback. And Durrell in the four volumes of his *Alexandria Quartet* (1957–60) conducted 'an investigation of modern love' in the seedy setting of late imperial Egypt.

The dark horse in the stable, however, was undoubtedly William Golding (1911–93), late Lieutenant RN, whose *Lord of the Flies* (1954) struck a powerful note. At one level Golding was putting his acid pen to retelling the age-old tale of men stranded on a desert island. But at another level he was propounding his conviction about the inner savagery of human nature. His conviction that savagery lay close beneath the surface of civilization had obviously been nourished by the author's wartime observations.[27]

Among the writers who sought to make realistic fiction more real than history, one of the first and one of the best was Nicholas Monsarrat (1910–79), like Golding, a former naval officer. His *The Cruel Sea* follows HMS *Compass Rose* and HMS *Saltash* on convoy-protection runs across the North Atlantic, where danger lurks under every wave. It begins, 'This is the story – the long and true story – of one ocean, two ships, and about a hundred and fifty men . . .'[28] It was soon made into a superb film, starring Jack Hawkins and Donald Sinden.

A special place must also be reserved for Norman Lewis (1908–2003), who served in the British Intelligence Corps in Italy 1943–45 and who once described himself as 'an invisible observer'. Certainly his prowess as a post-war writer owed much to the skills developed as a wartime sleuth. Graham Greene called him 'unsurpassed', and some critics have used the term 'the writer's writer'. Although Lewis's range was wide, and his geographical range was worldwide, several of his books drew directly on his experiences during the Italian campaingn. One of these was *The Honoured Society* (1964) about the Mafia. Another was *Naples '44* (1978).[29]

In France the war spawned on the one hand existentialism and on the other a lot of *marxisant* posturing. All the leading names were affected. Albert Camus (1913–60), who was born in Algeria, produced *L'Etranger* (1942) during the war, and *La Peste* (1947) and *L'Homme revolté* (1951) soon afterwards. He was deeply obsessed with the absurdity of the human condition, and was perhaps less overtly political because of it. Sartre, in contrast, saw no contradiction between being a card-carrying Communist and philosophizing about freedom. His output defies easy summary. His companion Simone de Beauvoir (1908–86) was one of the pioneer sirens of feminism.[30]

In the USA, the war fronts had been far away; and ex-servicemen authors were a relatively rare breed. Norman Mailer's *The Naked and the*

Dead (1948) brought the horrors of war home, though it reflected the author's service in the Pacific, not in Europe. Joseph Heller's *Catch-22* (1961) is set on the island of Pianosa, off Italy, which he had seen as a USAAF bombardier, and Kurt Vonnegut's *Slaughterhouse-Five* (1969) reflects the author's presence as a POW during the Dresden raid. Twenty or twenty-five years was clearly not too long for wartime experiences to be mentally processed and to bubble to the surface.

In Germany, the trauma of defeat ran deep. The nation had been tossed from a time when 'defeatism' had been a punishable offence to a time when negative thoughts alone were permissible about the late Nazi era. Unlike the British or the Americans, the Germans had been in the thick of it. And, unlike the Russians, they had nothing to show for their sacrifices. Hence the most urgent psychological exercise in the post-war years was *Vergangenheitsbewältigung* – 'coming to terms with the past'. Bernhard Schlink's novel *Der Vorleser* (*The Reader*, 1995) is often mentioned in this context. It tells the story of a young student who has a brief romance with an older woman, but who later discovers that she had been a concentration-camp guard. However, two names stand out over several decades. One, born in the West, lived in East Germany. The other, born in the East, lives in West Berlin.

The oeuvre of Heinrich Böll (1917–85) covers forty years and many subjects. But as an ex-soldier, many times wounded, he could write with conviction about men who served their country and did their duty. What is more, his war novels, such as *A Soldier's Legacy* (1948), *The Train Was on Time* (1949) and *Absent without Leave* (1964) reached an eager public. One of his last novels, *Silent Angel* (1992), deals with the bombing of Dresden. He sold millions of books in the USSR alone.

Günter Grass (b. 1927), a Danziger who lost his homeland, is acutely sensitive to social as well as political oppression, and his novels are a complicated mixture of humour, experimentation and biting comment. He has often been tagged with the epithet of 'Rabelaisian'. He made his name with *Die Blechtrommel* (*The Tin Drum*, 1959), featuring a boy who stopped growing in protest against the Nazi regime. More recently he has turned to the problems of the German expellees, of whom he is one, and to the realization that Germans could be victims of the war as well as its initiators. *Im Krebsgang* (*Crabwalk*, 2002) deals with the sinking of the refugee ship *Wilhelm Gustloff*, in 1945 (see p. 355).[31] The Nobel Prize for Literature was awarded to him in 1999. But his standing in Germany as a peace activist and high moral authority was somewhat dinted by his very belated confession after more than sixty years that in 1944–5 he had briefly served in the Waffen SS Frundsberg Division.

German reactions to the war, and to defeat, were conditioned both by the division of the country into two rival states and by the strange reluctance to view the victorious Soviet Union realistically. Denazification was pursued with varying degrees of success both in the Federal Republic and in the Democratic Republic, but it was never accompanied by a willingness to judge Soviet-style Communism by the same standards. Perhaps because denunciations of Bolshevism had once been standard Nazi fare, it now became politically correct to turn a blind eye on Soviet crimes and to concentrate on self-flagellation. As a result, the fashion for guilt was encouraged, even among youngsters who were unborn in the *Hitlerzeit*, and rose-coloured radicals gained prominence among the arbiters of literary and intellectual taste. A former policeman of the Stalinist security service, Marcel Reich-Ranicki (b. 1920), could become an influential literary critic.[32] Professor Jürgen Habermas (b. 1929), a neo-Marxist sociologist and philosopher, is famed both for his impenetrable prose and for a propensity for disputation. The *Historikerstreit* (see pp. 469–70) was largely his doing.

Meanwhile, in the Soviet Union, a second ice age had descended. Far from initiating a period of relaxation and reform after the war, the triumphant Stalin retightened the screws, relaunched the witch-hunts, and dashed all hopes of fundamental change. A very limited 'thaw' took place after Khrushchev's 'secret speech' of 1956. But, in essence, 200 million Soviet citizens and a string of captive nations were held in a mental and physical straitjacket for half a century.

In such a climate, the scope for writing honestly about the Second World War was minimal. Triumphalism was obligatory. Criticism of the Great Stalin, or of the Soviet High Command, was forbidden. The activities of Soviet agencies in occupied countries, either in 1939–41 or in 1944–5, were removed from the intellectual map.

Nonetheless, the war was too big a subject to be avoided; and a number of brave souls took up the challenge. Not for the first time, Ilya Ehrenburg (1891–1967) showed the way. Best described as a political escapologist, Ehrenburg had defied the laws of Stalinist gravity many times, even though he was an old Bolshevik, an associate of the late Nikolai Bukharin, and a regular foreign traveller. He had already published one war novel, *Padeniye Parizha* (*The Fall of Paris*, 1941) during the war, and followed it after the war with *Burya* (*The Storm*, 1948) and *Ottepel* (*The Thaw*, 1954). The former, while relating a typical Soviet war saga, contained hints about taboo subjects such as the Holocaust, the Nazi–Soviet Pact and foreign marriages. The latter gave its name to a whole period of Soviet history. Ehrenburg may have been 'a real heretic', as the ideological Chief Zamyatin called him. But he was indispensable. He had become very popular during the war for his blood-curdling (not to say racist) calls to kill Germans, and he made similar noises about the Americans during the early Cold War. Molotov once said, 'Ehrenberg is worth several divisions.'[33]

Ehrenburg's younger protégé, Vasily Semenovich Grossman (in reality Iosif Salomonovich Grossman, 1905–64), did not enjoy the same good luck. A war correspondent of the Red Army paper *Krasnaya Zvyezda*, he published a number of orthodox volumes, like *The People Immortal* (1942) and *Stalingrad* (1943), and he even got away with a first-hand Holocaust piece, *Treblinskii Ad* (*The Hell of Treblinka*, 1944). But he increasingly ran up against the official buffers. His considered work on Stalingrad, *Za Pravoye Delo* (*In the Right Cause*, 1954) was published only in mutilated form, after eight years' delay. And his masterwork, *Zhizn i Sudba* (*Life and Fate*, 1960) was suppressed for twenty years. Had he lived he would have been pleasantly surprised, because the chief Soviet ideologist, Mikhail Suslov, had once told him it would not be published for 250 years.[34]

Grossman, like Ehrenburg, was Jewish, and they long collected materials for a Black Book about the fate of Soviet Jews. The problem was: they knew about the Nazi Holocaust, and they wanted to make comparisons. But to the Soviet mind the very idea of Soviet criminality, let alone of comparisons with Nazi criminality, was anathema.

It is in this context that the long poem by Yevgeni Yevtushenko (b. 1933) entitled *Babi Yar*, which appeared in 1958, must be regarded as an act of great courage:

> No monument stands at Babi Yar, I fear:
> Just a steep cliff, like a primitive headstone . . .

Yevtushenko's main thrust, however, was not to publicize the massacre of 1941 (see p. 361), but rather to bemoan the refusal of the Soviet authorities to permit discussion of Jewish history in general. 'I am Dreyfus,' he said. He talked of the tsarist pogroms:

> I see myself as a boy in Belostok,
> And blood spills on the floor
>
> I am hated like a Jew
> And that's why I call myself a Russian.[35]

The literary pugilist packing the heaviest punch, however, was undoubtedly Alexander Solzhenitsyn. A wartime veteran, and a profoundly patriotic Russian, he was outraged by his lost years in the GULag, and he was determined to show the world the reality of Soviet repressions – which had not stopped during the war, as many Westerners thought, and which were still continuing. His first choice of medium was fiction. His novella *One Day in the Life of Ivan Denisovich* (1962), which was only a start, caused a sensation. *Cancer Ward* (1968) and *The First Circle* (1969) continued the theme of human reactions to extreme predicaments. For this he was expelled from the Union of Soviet Writers. But these were mere puffs of steam preceding the volcanic eruption to come when he was abruptly deported from the USSR.[36]

By this time, Second World War fiction was growing into a major industry. Not thousands but tens of thousands of books were being written on almost every aspect and every phase of the war. This extraordinary output had far surpassed the ability of any one person to read more than a fraction, and it clearly included the good, the bad, the indifferent and the indescribable. Yet it attests to the power of the Second World War in the popular imagination: that is, to the continuing impact of the most memorable of past events on present consciousness. It can be broken down by genre and subgenre, and it can be catalogued according to author, date, country of origin, theatre of action, or type of warfare. Different subjects came to the fore at different times. Wartime spy thrillers, for example, emerged late, after John Le Carré (b. 1931), Graham Greene and others had blazed the trail in Cold War settings. Alan Furst (b. 1941) has an enviable touch and a feel for the exotic side of Eastern Europe. Alternative history, or 'Allohistory', in contrast, seems to have grown out of science fiction. In the hands of writers like Len Deighton and Robert Harris, its main preoccupation has been 'What if Operation Sealion had succeeded?'

For the historian, however, the main interest lies in the progressive shifts of focus. In the early post-war years the emphasis lay on the actions of the victorious Allies – hence on the naval war, the air war or the Western Desert. Many of the novels and memoirs of that era were turned into films. Germans were also writing in German for a German market, Russians in Russian . . . Poles in Polish, and Finns in Finnish. But there was little cross-fertilization. In the 1970s and 80s the Holocaust became a major concern, after long neglect. As in the field of history, its fictional treatment was characterized by deep compassion for the Jewish tragedy and much liberty-taking with the setting. Especially in the USA, authors like William Styron (b. 1925) and Leon Uris (b. 1924) reached near-obligatory status in schools and colleges, where semi-documentary films like Claude Lanzmann's *Shoah* (1986) were designed to promote the desired effect.

Nonetheless, slowly but surely, the Eastern Front rightly imposed itself as a dominant topic – first in narratives of unadulterated 'blood and guts', then in widespread translations of German and Russian authors, and eventually, after the collapse of the USSR, in works that laid bare the moral bankruptcy of Stalinism. The clash of two titanic tyrannies that lay at the heart of the Second World War could finally take centre stage. The sheer scale of the suffering demanded no less.

For half a century, one dimension had been missing from these descriptions of the Eastern Front. The stories of hellish combat, as per Sven Hassel, were not false. But they were not combined with any attempt to convey the nature of the régimes whose future hung in the balance. German soldiers were sent to fight in the East, where they ran into Russians who were defending their 'Motherland' with raw, desperate and animal courage. And that was that. The patterns of similarity and contrast, and the social and political mechanisms underpinning the war effort of the two monsters, remained beyond the Western imagination.

At last, it would seem, the gap may be closing. Thirty years after Solzhenitsyn's revelations, a young American author, since deceased, invented a plot to combine the Eastern Front with the GULag. It did no harm that the novelist was also a historian. Russ Schneider's posthumous *Siege* (2001) follows the ordeals of three fictional German soldiers in the real setting of the Battle of Velikie Luki of 1942. But it starts and finishes not at the battlefront, but in Europe's largest concentration camp:

> Vorkuta lay just before the Ural Mountains. It lay not in remotest Siberia, but at the gates of Siberia . . . It was all unspeakable . . . The Gulag is everywhere, and everywhere is Russia. There are rivers of death, and long stretches of railroad track laid yard by yard on the bones of men . . .[37]

The starting point was chosen to introduce the gruesome realities of a Soviet penal battalion, whose men are taken from Vorkuta and lined up in chains to face the Wehrmacht. The end point should perhaps not be given away, but it is not too difficult to guess the fate of captured Germans. When novelists contrive to link the largest theatre of military action with the largest organs of civilian repression, they are penetrating the most crucial areas of the Second World War in Europe.

The Second World War in Europe – selected fiction, by theme

Outbreak

Ilya Ehrenburg, *The Fall of Paris* *(1942)*
Alan Furst, *The Polish Officer* *(1944)*
Jean-Paul Sartre, *La Mort dans l'âme* ('*Iron in the Soul*') *(1949)*
Antti Tuuri, *The Winter War* *(1984)*

Battle of Britain and the Blitz

Graham Greene, *The Ministry of Fear* *(1943)*
Elizabeth Bowen, *Heat of the Day* *(1949)*
Alan Pearce, *Dunkirk Spirit* *(2006)*
Sarah Walters, *The Night Watch* *(2006)*

War at sea

Nicholas Monsarrat, *The Cruel Sea* *(1951)*
Alistair MacLean, *HMS Ulysses* *(1955)*
Lothar Buchheim, *Das Boot* *(1971)*
Günter Grass, *Crabwalk* *(2002)*

Air war

Neville Shute, *Pastoral* *(1944)*
Gert Ledig, *Payback* *(1956)*
Kurt Vonnegut, *Slaughterhouse-Five* *(1969)*
Len Deighton, *Bomber* *(1970)*
Heinrich Böll, *The Silent Angel* *(1992)*

Holocaust

Elie Wiesel, *Night* *(1958)*
Leon Uris, *Mila 18* *(1961)*
Jerzy Kosiński, *The Painted Bird* *(1965)*
Anatoli Kuznetsov, *Babi Yar* *(1969)*
Saul Bellow, *Mr Sammler's Planet* *(1970)*
William Styron, *Sophie's Choice* *(1979)*
Primo Levi, *If Not Now, When?* *(1982)*
Martin Amis, *Time's Arrow* *(1991)*

The Second World War in Europe – selected fiction, by theme (*cont.*)

Eastern Front

Heinrich Böll, *A Soldier's Legacy (1948)*
Vaino Linna, *The Unknown Solder (1954)*
Willi Heinrich, *Cross of Iron (1955)*
Gert Ledig, *Die Stalinorgel (1955)*
Guy Sayer, *Forgotten Soldier (1971)*
Sven Hassel, *Blitzfreeze (1976)*
Leo Kessler, *Forced March (1976)*
Theodore Plevier, *Stalingrad (1984)*
Russ Schneider, *Demyansk (1995)*
Russ Schneider, *Siege (2001)*
David Robbins, *Last Citadel (2003)*
Debra Dean, *Madonnas of Leningrad (2005)*

Italy and the Western Front

Joseph Heller, *Catch-22 (1961)*
Louis de Bernières, *Captain Corelli's Mandolin (1994)*
Alan Furst, *Red Gold (1999)*
Eugenio Corti, *The Red Horse (2000)*
Mary Doria Russell, *Thread of Grace (2005)*

Espionage

Ken Follett, *Eye of the Needle (1978)*
Alan Furst, *Dark Star (1991)*
Robert Harris, *Enigma (1995)*
Ken Follett, *Jackdaws (2001)*
Philip Kerr, *Hitler's Peace (2005)*

Allohistory

Philip K. Dick, *Man in the High Castle (1962)*
Len Deighton, *SS-GB (1978)*
Joe Poyer, *Vengeance 10 (1980)*
John Hackett, *Third World War (1985)*
Robert Harris, *Fatherland (1992)*
Peter Tsouras, *Disaster at D-Day (1994)*
Douglas Nile, *Fox on the Rhine (2000)*
David Downing, *The Moscow Option (2001)*

The historical record

The Second World War lasted six years. Yet sixty years has not been enough to collect, sift, catalogue and make accessible the mountains of papers, pictures and assorted artefacts that the war left behind. The operation is vast, incomplete and, to a degree, heartbreaking. Many of the records, in their files and storages boxes, will never be looked at again, and, as fragments without context, many throw no light whatsoever on the war as a whole. Records may be an invaluable first step in the complicated process of preserving and explaining the past for posterity. But there are several further steps to be taken.

Many wartime events were veiled in secrecy, and they often stayed veiled for decades. In the case of the Katyn massacres, for example, which are a key episode for gauging the moral standing of the combatants, the world was kept waiting for exactly fifty years. The 25,000 murdered officers had disappeared in 1940; and it was 1990 before President Gorbachev admitted the NKVD's guilt for the crime. Indeed, it was 1992 before President Yeltsin released a written order for their murder, signed by Stalin on 5 March 1940. Throughout the intervening decades, any enquiries or speculation about the massacres were met with howls of outrage, claiming anti-Sovietism, falsification of history, and calumny of the Allied cause.[38]

All governments on the victorious side were eager to publish selections of documents which justified their wartime policies. The British and Americans received a bonus by capturing the archives of the German Foreign Ministry, which enabled them to publish a selection of German documents at an early date. The evidence submitted to the Nuremberg Tribunal also found its way into print without much delay.[39] In due course, the British, US, French, Polish, Soviet and Yugoslav governments issued their documentary series.[40]

These official publications obviously form an important body of evidential material. But one shouldn't imagine that they are in any way complete or completely reliable. They are, in their nature, selective; and the criteria for selection could vary from the mild and practical to the shamelessly distorting. They inevitably leave a number of skeletons, large or small, in the farther reaches of the historical cupboard.

For instance, one might have thought that the publication in 1946 of the secret protocols of the Nazi–Soviet Pact, based on the most authoritative documents of Ribbentrop's Foreign Ministry, would have decided the matter once and for all. Not a bit of it. The Soviet government, whose own archives were not open for inspection, simply declared the 'alleged protocols' to be a provocative falsification, and pretended for forty years that its own conduct in 1939 had been above reproach. Documentary collections of the Soviet Academy either omitted the pact of 23 August 1939 *in toto* or else printed the main text of the pact and omitted the secret protocols.

Of course, paper documents, still less government documents, do not form the sole historical record. Collections of wartime newspapers are a valuable source of information about public opinion and social history, especially in countries like Britain and the USA, where press censorship did not eradicate conflicting points of view. *The Times*, which was still Britain's broadsheet of record in 1939–45, maintained a distinctive voice, especially in foreign affairs, where its foreign editor, E. H. Carr, was as much an appeaser of Stalin as he had once been of Hitler.[41] Sound archives are equally valuable, and in more spheres than wartime radio. Oral history, too, makes a sterling contribution. During the war, and immediately after it, people's reminiscences could be preserved only by written transcript. But since the arrival of convenient recording machines, in the 1950s, large numbers of veterans and eye-witnesses have been persuaded to talk on tape or disc. And a living voice links listeners to the past more directly than the written word does. In Britain, the Second World War Experience Centre, based in Leeds, specializes in this kind of material, and publishes its own journal.[42] In the USA, several major projects have been launched. One of them, entitled 'The Good War', consists largely of interviews with Americans engaged in various aspects of the home front.[43]

Archives have enjoyed a long period of reverence among historians which they don't always deserve. In some quarters they are thought to be repositories of truth, whose revelations are limited only by the indolence and prejudice of historians. In reality, like all human institutions, they have their strengths and a long list of inbuilt drawbacks. Their files and catalogues are not faultless; they are subject to bureaucratic control, sometimes infuriatingly restrictive; and they produce their fruits very slowly. In the case of Britain's Public Record Office (now ridiculously renamed the National Archives as if they were an imitation of the National

Archives of the USA), papers relating to the First World War had not begun to be released before the deluge of papers from the Second World War arrived for processing: the fifty-year rule for access was only changed to a thirty-year rule in 1969; and sixty years after the end of the war many categories of documents, including the crucial archives of the intelligence services, remain firmly closed. An annual windfall of moderately interesting papers is allowed to dribble into the public domain to keep the waiting historians happy. In Britain, the guardians of archivism still rule. They inevitably create the impression of hiding something.

Thanks to the Freedom of Information Act (1966), US government archives are considerably more user-friendly. So, too, are the archives of countries whose post-war regimes have collapsed. In 2005 the Polish government announced its intention of releasing the files of the Communist-run security services going back to 1944. This initiative promises to throw much light on the murky events in Poland during the last months of the war.

The biggest problems, however, relate to the biggest wartime combatant country. The USSR may have collapsed, but a brief free-for-all among ex-Soviet collections in Moscow under President Yeltsin was barely started before it was stopped. Under President Putin, Russian archival policy has been more restrictive; and in some of the other ex-Soviet republics it is non-existent. In the 1990s, historians made their first independent examinations of wartime files from the NKVD and the Soviet Foreign Office. Yet huge lacunae remain, especially in respect to the Soviet Ministry of Defence and the Trophy Archive (see p. 343). Adolf Hitler died in April 1945. His skull was not located (in a shoebox) in the NKVD archive until 1992,[44] and the full file held on Hitler by the NKVD was not released until 2002.[45] The first archive-based guide to the Soviet concentration camp system was not published until 1998.[46] In the meantime the world had grown accustomed to the idea that the Nazis alone ran concentration camps during the war.

Westerners, however, who often boast about their open society, have little reason for complacency. The basic facts of the Ultra secret – i.e. the deciphering of the German Enigma system – were known in 1945 to at least 20,000 people. All of them had signed the Official Secrets Act, and every single one of them kept their mouth shut for at least thirty years. The silence was broken by a Frenchman, Michel Garder, who was writing on wartime French intelligence, and Garder's mistakes led to a flurry of

supposedly corrective publications, among them one by F. W. Winter-
botham, which only compounded the errors. An account described as
'reasonably accurate' was produced by R. Lewin in 1978, but the authoritative, official account had to wait yet another decade.[47]

All of which shows how very, very slowly the historical record is
established. Historians who do not move until the documentary foundations are in place are eternally trying to catch up with the statements and
misstatements of others. In the meantime, all forms of invention and
myth-making are free to run riot. Archives and records are so much dead
wood until a historian comes along to bring them to life in a coherent
narrative. Yet the appearance of the life-giving historian is no guarantee of
ultimate success. Historians are fallible like everyone else. They contain
their share of charlatans, conformists and incompetents. A bad historian is
even more dangerous than dead documentary wood.

The Internet

The Internet is widely thought to be just a new and accelerated form of
communication. If one wishes to know the holdings of the Oxford libraries
on the Second World War, one no longer needs to visit the catalogue
room of the Bodleian Library and thumb through the massive indexes.
One simply enters OLIS into one's computer, followed by 'Second World
War' and 'Subject Search', and a task that might previously have taken
days or weeks is completed in seconds. If one cannot visit the Kursk
Museum in person, one looks up the museum's English-language website
and examines the museum's contents.

Yet increasingly the Net is much more than a rapid means of
technological access to existing collections. It is becoming more and more
a historical resource in itself, carrying documents, articles, collectables,
pictures, discussions and 'blogsites' which may or may not exist elsewhere.
There is, for example, an excellent website, www.warsawuprising.com,
which is run out of southern California of all places, and which contains
items which no book or museum possesses. There is equally a very
indifferent website, www.secondworldwar.com, that is obviously run by
interested amateurs, and there is Wikipedia, the self-regulating Internet

encyclopedia, to which anyone can contribute. Professional historians tend to distrust such websites. The Web they say, is dangerous. It is full of dubious statements and manifest errors. So, too, one might add, is every other source of historical information.[48]

History-writing

The task whereby a coherent historical narrative is constructed from the jumbled events of the past is very complicated, and requires collaborative effort from numerous participants. It starts with the marshalling of sources – documents, pictures, memories and statistics – and it can move into the stages of compilation, analysis and synthesis only when the groundwork has been completed. The final overview, which is produced by the interplay of contending judgements and by a process of constant revision of previous findings, can never be definitive.

It is often said that history is written by the victors; and in the case of the Second World War the historians of Britain, the USA and the USSR certainly enjoyed a head start. Yet the historiographical triumph of the victors is at best short-lived, and frequently illusory. For it tends to lack one of the essential qualities of good history-writing, namely self-criticism. After 1945, another major problem arose. The victorious Allies were divided. They disagreed fundamentally not only about current politics, but also about interpretations of the past. The result was a long-lasting divergence of opinions concerning wartime history that had little chance of discussion, let alone of resolution, for over forty years.

In this regard, one must register a note of warning: all governments, and all types of regime, have habitually legitimized their existence by specious interpretations of history. The USA, for instance, which emerged from the Second World War as the principal world power, naturally held up its war effort against Nazi Germany and imperial Japan as a justification for its continuing stand in defence of freedom and democracy. In American eyes, the war rapidly became a necessary prelude to the present, a convenient platform for the ongoing promotion of the struggle between 'Good' and 'Evil'.

Parallel attitudes developed in the USSR, where the hard-won victory over Nazi Germany was used both as an argument to prove the superiority of the so-called 'socialist system' and as a political weapon to be wielded against all the system's adversaries. Since in the meantime the USA had become Adversary No. 1, 'Uncle Sam' joined Adolf Hitler in the gallery of rogues who opposed the Soviet 'Good'. In Soviet eyes, no less than in American eyes, the Second World War was a necessary prelude to the present. But it was used in an exactly opposite sense. To the Soviet way of thinking, it was scandalous that Americans should claim equal credit for a victory in which American and Soviet sacrifices had been anything but equal. These opposing world views remained irreconcilable so long as the Cold War lasted.

Other countries faced dilemmas deriving from similar miscontructions. In Britain, considerable ingenuity was needed to explain how the war had been won but the Empire had been lost. In Yugoslavia, the triumphant Titoists had to claim that they alone had fought the Fascists, and that the defeated Chetniks were collaborators. In Poland, the imported Communist regime had to thank the Soviet Union for a victory which was marked by 6 million Polish dead and the loss of half the country.

Historians must also do battle with a phenomenon that the French academician Pierre Nora has called *lieux de mémoire*, that is, historical sites and events which appeal to the collective memory so powerfully that they exclude or minimize all others.[49] In the USA, Pearl Harbor and Omaha Beach have become exactly such focuses. In Britain, the 'miracle of Dunkirk' plays the same role. In Jewish history it is Auschwitz. In the Soviet story it is Leningrad and Stalingrad. These near-sacred subjects actively obstruct the broader vision and discriminating approach that are so badly needed. Indeed, in a fragmented post-war world, it was simply not possible for disparate memory spots to coalesce into a single agreed picture. What is more, they often led to serious misunderstandings. In 1945, for instance, a terse communiqué from Moscow announced that 4 million people had perished in Auschwitz. The figure was totally unrealistic, but stood for nearly fifty years. And official censorship in the Soviet Bloc concealed the fact that the majority of the victims of Auschwitz were Jews. By the same token, no one in the West seemed to realize that Auschwitz had consumed several hundred thousand Catholic Poles and Soviet POWs, and the erroneous statistic of '4 million Jewish victims' in that one camp was often repeated.[50]

In the Western world, Winston Churchill's *The Second World War*, which began to appear in 1948, set out a self-justifying scenario in such authoritative tones that it could hardly be contested. The thesis was simple. Hitler was the source of the trouble. The struggle was just. The 'appeasers' were misguided. The Anglo-American partnership provided the winning combination. The 'turning of the tide' took place when Britain survived. The Soviet Union was acknowledged as an accessory to victory, but no mention was made either of the scale of the Soviet contribution or of Stalin's crimes. The liberation of Europe started from Normandy. Freedom and democracy had triumphed.[51]

In the Soviet Bloc, meanwhile, a rather different scenario was being propounded. The USSR was a peace-loving country. It had nothing to do with the events of 1939–40, when the capitalist powers decided to fight each other. The 'Great Patriotic War' started in June 1941, when Nazi Germany attacked the USSR gratuitously – and the Eastern Front was the only theatre of military action that really counted. Despite the treacherous promises of Churchill and Roosevelt, the Western Powers steered clear of the hard fighting until the outcome was already settled. Neither the air war nor the Battle of the Atlantic nor the Western assistance to the USSR deserved prominence. The liberation of Europe flowed from the guns of the Red Army. Freedom and democracy (Soviet-style) had triumphed.[52]

The Soviet version wobbled a little after Stalin's death. Up to 1953 Stalin was presented as an all-seeing military genius. After 1953 the official line suggested that the war had been won without him, or even despite him. But after Khrushchev's demise in 1964 he was gradually rehabilitated, not least through the authorized publication of many of his marshals' memoirs.[53]

Nonetheless, the two scenarios of the war, Western and Eastern, were well established within the first post-war decade. And nothing much could be done thereafter to change them. Western historians ignored the Soviet position, partly because some aspects of it, such as the denial of the Nazi–Soviet Pact, were ridiculous; partly because they were unable to verify it by independent research; and partly, one supposes, because they recoiled at giving the Red Army the lion's share of the credit. Soviet historians, locked in their closed cage, stuck to their guns, issuing regular denunciations of the 'falsifications of bourgeois history'. Both sides moved on to researching the details long before a broad framework had received general acceptance.

Churchill was the only top-line player to publish memoirs or diaries.

In the second or third line, Queen Wilhelmina, General de Gaulle, Count Ciano, Albert Speer, Joseph Goebbels and Marshals Zhukov, Chuikov and Rokossovsky had been within reach of the top tables, and furnished records of varying quality. Personal accounts of the Holocaust, like the diary of Anne Frank, far outnumbered narratives emanating from the GULag. Among the Nazis, the works of two condemned criminals, Hans Frank and Rudolf Höss, confirmed the worst. But in terms of political revelations the most shocking testimony probably came from a leading Yugoslav Communist, Milovan Djilas, who felt free to spill the beans once Tito had split from Stalin. The kindly 'Uncle Joe' of Western myth was losing his shine. Stalin, it seems, was a squat, ape-like figure with yellow eyes and overlong arms. Still worse, he had created a regime which was run not by the workers, but by a brutal, dictatorial 'New Class' of party yes-men.[54] Over the years, an impressive library of memoirs was assembled, covering numerous episodes and countries. But their disparate nature did not encourage generalizations.

The 'Hitler industry' started early, and has had a long run. The Oxford historian Alan Bullock was given privileged access to captured German archives; and his pioneering *Hitler: A Study in Tyranny* was already in print by 1951. At the time, five years before the 'thaw', Stalin was still alive, and no one had yet conceived a study of Stalinist tyranny. Since then, countless works on Hitler and Hitler's Reich have appeared, culminating in the works of Fest, Lukacs, Burleigh, Evans and Kershaw.[55] Yet the interesting thing is that several of Hitler's biographers have also been drawn to Stalin. The epic duel of the two men during the Second World War is a central theme, without which much could be misunderstood about both of them. Bullock, who had emerged from the pre-war anti-Fascist camp, could not quite bring himself to draw direct comparisons. But thirty years after his big success he bravely published *Hitler and Stalin: Parallel Lives* (1991).[56] More recently, Richard Overy has take the bull more firmly by the horns. No one has suggested that the two tyrants and their regimes were identical. But they were both foul tyrants. And it is pointless to argue – as it was the fashion to do for decades – that Stalin was somehow less of a tyrant because he had fought the tyrant Hitler.[57]

Official histories were also prepared, though some governments gave up before their series were complete. Multi-authored and/or multi-volumed works turned out to be killingly dull, and therefore unreadable except for reference. Rear Admiral Samuel Morison wrote a fifteen-volume work on US naval operations (1947–62), and a Cambridge don, Sir James Butler (1889–1975), oversaw a series that would eventually run to nearly a hundred volumes. He himself contributed to six volumes on *Grand Strategy* (1956–76), which was accompanied by four volumes on *The War at Sea* by Stephen Roskill, by two on *The Strategic Air Offensive*, by Charles Webster and Noble Frankland, five on *Foreign Policy* by Llewellyn Woodward, and six volumes on *Intelligence* by Harry Hinsley. It was a stroke of great compassion that the editors hit on the idea of an abridged volume summarizing the findings of each sub-series. The British *Medical History* of the Second World War reached twenty-five volumes, and the 'UK Civil Series' twenty-eight volumes. What on earth could they find to write about? One is tempted to conclude that countries spilled ink in inverse proportion to their wartime importance. The Soviet Academy of Sciences, which could presumably have planned a thousand volumes, satisfied itself with six on *Istoriya Velikoy Otechestvennoy Voiny Sovetskogo Soyuza* (Moscow, 1960–65). Official historiography at least gave favoured access to materials from which ordinary mortals were barred. And some of the best products were also the shortest ones. Margaret Gowing on *The British War Economy* (1949) and Michael Howard on *Strategic Deception* (1992) deserve mention.[58]

For obvious reasons, German historians did not rush after the war to study the Nazi period, and it is fair to say that the subject was put on ice for many years. The strongest post-war voice, that of Professor Gerhard Ritter (1888–1967) came from the national conservative corner, and denied all connections between the Nazis and their predecessors. As expressed in *Europa und die deutsche Frage* (1948), Hitler and the Nazis were to be seen as a criminal clique, who had only been able to seize power through the chaos generated by the Weimar Republic. Ritter, who had links with the Bomb Plot, had been imprisoned in 1944–5, and no one could call him a Nazi sympathizer. Nonetheless, by painting Hitler as an aberration, he was widely seen to have evaded some vital questions.[59] The same cannot be said of Fritz Fischer (1908–99), whose *Griff nach der Weltmacht* (1961) created a storm. Though the book dealt with the First World War, not the Second, and in particular with the policy of Chancellor Bethmann-Hollweg, it argued that Germany had been following a *Sonderweg* or 'special path' ever since the Empire. What is more, by stressing Germany's responsibility for the outbreak of war of 1914, it suggested that Germans had to bear the guilt of two world wars, not just one. In the eyes of his critics, Fischer was as unpatriotic as he was unfair, and opinion in West

Germany began to crystallize. Right-wing commentators condemned the *Sonderweg*, and left-wingers praised it.[60] There was no consensus. In East Germany, all comment remained tied to official Soviet interpretation.

In the 1960s the dam of reticence broke on two important subjects particularly relevant to the Second World War. Neither was completely unknown, but neither had been extensively explored. One was the Jewish Holocaust. The other was Stalin's criminal record.

Exactly why the Holocaust burst on the scene in the 1960s as it did is not quite clear, but the timing was in some way connected with the passing of the traumatic post-war silence in Israel itself, and the appearance there of a militant, right-wing brand of Zionism. The Israeli victory in the Six Day War of 1967 may have acted as a stimulus. The receptivity of the Western audience was also a factor. In the middle of the Cold War, both Americans and West Europeans were more than content to publicize an event which confirmed the irrational evil of Nazism but which did not draw attention to the wartime sufferings of the people of the Soviet Bloc. It was not long before historians were being pressed to sign up to the contention that the Holocaust was unique.

Within a short period, the principal historians of the Holocaust – Dawidowicz, Hilberg, Bauer, Gilbert and others – had built up an unchallengeable body of evidence and argument. They put the main thesis about the Nazi genocide of around 6 million Jews, mainly in German-occupied Poland, beyond dispute. At the same time, they opened the gate to a stream of sub-theses, spins and political statements which invited quarrels and threatened to bring the topic into disrepute. Attempts to enforce a Holocaust orthodoxy, if necessary by legal action, conflict with the principle of intellectual freedom and have not been very successful. Holocaust denial seems to be a sort of sick exercise in contrariness.[61]

The subject of Stalin's crimes burst on to the scene as a direct result of Khrushchev's not-so-secret speech in February 1956, the subsequent 'thaw' in Soviet culture, and the vicious suppression of the Hungarian Rising. Thanks to Budapest, the Communist parties of the free world lost half their members overnight, and the widespread Soviet-admiration societies, which had been in business ever since the Battle of Stalingrad, fell strangely silent. Most informed people in the West now realized that the wartime eulogies of 'our great Soviet ally' had been misconceived. The realization was strengthened by the writings of Solzhenitsyn, by the historical sleuthing of Robert Conquest, and by the next round of Soviet oppression in Czechoslovakia.

Yet the psychological and intellectual barriers to the full absorption of the information were formidable. Many Westerners were willing to register the growing evidence against Stalin, but not to internalize it to the point of feeling disgust or outrage. They would accept it as ammunition for arguments over current politics, but not as a reason to modify their gut feelings about 1939–45. The publicity was too weak. Solzhenitsyn could be dismissed as a crackpot or an agent of the CIA. There were no newsreels of Vorkuta or Kolyma. There were no blockbusting TV series. Diehard GULag deniers continued to talk of thousands, not millions, of deaths. They put it all down to politics. So, until the 1990s, works criticizing the USSR were dubbed 'controversial' or 'anti-Soviet', and hence not exactly trustworthy. The only volumes to win general acclaim stuck closely to military topics, and (exactly as the Soviet authorities would have wished) kept political comment to a minimum. The works of Professor John Erickson, *The Road to Stalingrad* (1975) and *The Road to Berlin* (1983), fitted neatly into that category.[62]

In that same era, the historical profession took a number of new turnings. Firstly, traditional political, diplomatic and military history fell out of fashion, and gave ground to social, economic, gender and cultural studies. Secondly, under pressure from the philosophical trends of deconstructionism and postmodernism, historians lost confidence in their ability to undertake impartial analysis or to write coherent narrative. Thirdly, faced with torrents of unmanageable data, historians sought refuge in ultra-specialization. In the field of Second World War studies, none of these trends worked in favour of building a new consensus. Fragmentation proceeded apace.

In military history, a new approach was pioneered by John Keegan's famous *The Face of Battle* (1976). In the past, historians had put themselves in the mental armchairs of the generals, poring over maps and worrying over issues of strategy and command. Keegan, in contrast, put himself alongside the troopers in their trenches or foxholes, dealing with chaos, slaughter and incoming fire. This was history at 'the sharp end', and a very valuable corrective it was. It provoked an interest in tactics, and in small-scale actions. C. B. MacDonald's *Company Commander* (1961) and Stephen Ambrose's *Pegasus Bridge* (1984) and *Band of Brothers* (1992) were also conceived in that vein. The last named followed the fortunes of E Company, 506th Regiment, 101st Airborne Division, from Normandy to Berchtesgaden.

Ambrose (1936–2002) was particularly influential. The biographer of

Eisenhower, he accompanied his interest in the qualities of the American GI with an ideological stance holding that democracies raise the best soldiers. His *Band of Brothers* was made into a TV series. His *D-Day* (1994) was behind Spielberg's film *Saving Private Ryan*, and his *Citizen Soldiers* (1997) was based on oral testimony. He represents a form of Americocentrism that most non-Americans would instinctively reject.[63]

History progresses through controversy. And three long-standing confrontations relating to the Second World War consumed much time and space. One of them was fired by A. J. P. Taylor's study *The Origins of the Second World War* (1963). Taylor (1906–90), the tearaway kid of the profession and, at the time, an active member of the Campaign for Nuclear Disarmament, was no respecter of conventions. He had already caused offence by suggesting that appeasement had been the product of 'all that was best in European politics'. He campaigned very publicly against the '50-year rule' in British archives. And he now floated a thesis holding that Adolf Hitler in the 1930s had not been working to a planned timetable of aggression. Instead, he proposed that Hitler was a chancer, a bluffer, a gambler and an opportunist, who deliberately exaggerated the figures of German rearmament and who (like Taylor himself) loved nothing more than stirring up trouble to see what trouble might bring. The outburst was immediate. By the 1960s the demonization of Hitler was well advanced, and the idea that the Führer had not been following the devilish plan he had laid out in *Mein Kampf* was taken by many as an affront. What is more, historians of a Marxist persuasion saw the thesis as a gauntlet thrown down against their most fundamental beliefs. If one believes in the primacy of 'socio-economic forces', one simply cannot accept that a major conflict could be started by accident or by the miscalculations of a political gambler. The Oxford-based journal *Past and Present* virtually lived off this dispute for the next decade.[64]

The second long-running controversy arose from the concept of a European Civil War. Many historians, including Taylor, had noticed that the origins of the Second World War were intimately connected to the consequences of the First. And it was only one step further to maintain that the two wars were but successive stages in one and the same chain of conflict. In this case the causes of the war could not be attributed to the ambitions of a Kaiser or a Führer, but rather to the deep-seated rivalries of Europe's national states. In *The Last European War* (1976) John Lukacs argued that Europeans had now been cured of nationalism and that henceforth the rivalries of the global superpowers would take over. Ten

years later, in *The European Civil War* (1986), the German historian Ernst
Nolte (b. 1923) brought ideology into the equation. The First World War
had spawned the Bolshevik Revolution, he maintained, and Fascism should
be seen as a 'counter-revolution' against Communism. Most pointedly,
since Fascism followed Communism chronologically, he argued that some
of the Nazis' political techniques and practices had been copied from those
of the Soviet Union. Needless to say, such propositions were thought
anathema by leftists who believe that Fascism was an original and
unparalleled evil.[65] At one point Nolte was 'disinvited' from giving a
lecture at Oxford University, then re-invited by a committee headed by Sir
Isaiah Berlin.

In a sense, therefore, Nolte was adding his voice to a still older debate
about totalitarianism. The notion that Communism and Fascism had much
in common, not least in their aspirations of total control, went back to the
interwar era. But when revived by a German-American thinker, Hannah
Arendt (1906–75), in *Origins of Totalitarianism* (1951), it caused a storm.
Arendt was Jewish, and her espousal of the totalitarian idea – albeit with
reservations – was seen by some as a betrayal. It raised uncomfortable
issues such as the uniqueness of the Holocaust and the role of Jewish
Communists. She poured more oil on to the fire with her study *Eichmann
in Jerusalem* (1963). She called her comments on Eichmann's trial, 'A report
on the banality of evil'.[66] The quarrels rumbled on until the 1990s, when
the Soviet Union collapsed and its last principled defenders finally packed
their bags.

In the years before the fall of the Berlin Wall, the quarrels in Germany
were particularly acidic. They were graced with a special name – the
Historikerstreit or 'Historians' Row'.[67] At the time that he published *The
European Civil War*, Ernst Nolte wrote an explanatory article, entitled 'The
Past Which Will Not Pass On', in which he described Fascism as a
'defensive reaction' to Communism. The word 'defensive' was a red rag
to the red bulls. It was bad enough for Nolte to have suggested earlier
that Fascism was a reaction to Communism. But to state that Communism
had been the aggressor and Fascism the defender was too much to bear.
What is more, in that same year Andreas Hilgrüber published a book
provocatively entitled *Zweierlei Untergang*, or 'Double Ruin' (1986). The
subject was the expulsion of Germans from the east in 1945–7. But the
clear implication was that Germany had been victimized twice over – once
by the military defeat, and again by the expulsions. The explosion was
immediate. Habermas and other left-wingers went into action with a flurry

of articles and of letter-writing. They claimed that the uniqueness of the Holocaust was under attack. They disliked comparisons, particularly between the tragedy of Jews and the misfortunes of Germans. And they vehemently objected to the idea that the Holocaust could in any way be seen as a reaction to the misdeeds of the Stalinists.

In the 1990s, many of the earlier arguments became redundant. Once Russian voices were added to long-standing condemnations of the Soviet system, most of its erstwhile defenders were deflated. The publication in 1997 of *The Black Book* of *Communism*, which was compiled by a team of disillusioned French Communists and East Europeans, proved conclusive. Henceforth, Soviet crimes were on the agenda alongside Nazi crimes. As a reviewer in the *New York Times* put it, 'The myth of the well-intentioned founders – the good czar Lenin betrayed by his evil heirs – has been laid to rest for good. No one will any longer be able to claim ignorance or uncertainty about the criminal nature of Communism, and those who had begun to forget will be forced to remember anew.'[68] It also turned out that the millions of Europeans who had been forced to live under both Fascism and Communism had few qualms about the totalitarian concept being applied to both systems.

As information multiplied, and the list of specializations grew, the number of scholars engaged in the study of the Second World War increased, and a need was felt for an organization to bring them all together. The outcome was the founding in the 1960s of an International Committee for the History of the Second World War (CIHDGM), which operates out of the Institute of Contemporary History (IHTP) in Paris. The committee, presided over by Prof. Gerhard Hirschfeld, edits a bulletin on its activities, operates a website at www.ihtp.cnrs.fr/cih2gm/cih2gm.html, and organizes congresses, the most recent being 'Sydney 2005'.[69]

In the dozen years or so since the collapse of the USSR, however, the main advances have been made in Soviet history. Not all the studies live up to their claim to be 'based on unrestricted access to the Russian archives', but it is nonetheless true that historians have been seeing things that were never seen before. From Dmitri Volkogonov (1928–1995), Robert Service (b. 1947) and Simon Sebag-Montefiore (b. 1965) have come new and ever more unflattering portraits of Stalin. From Antony Beevor (b. 1946) and others we have had new studies of the Red Army, not sparing the ugly side. From Anne Applebaum (b. 1964) came a sober, damning and Pulitzer-winning study of the GULag, which puts all doubters and deniers out of business. The workings of the NKVD can now be documented. And through the devoted work of the Memorial organization the victims of Soviet Communism can now be granted the same dignity and recognition as the victims of Nazism have long enjoyed. All these building blocks fill major holes in established knowledge.[70]

One may equally observe in the USA that the patriotic vision of the war associated with Ambrose and Spielberg has produced its own antidote. As the United States emerged after the Cold War as the world's sole superpower, a huge temptation arose to explain present success in terms of a similarly unbounded victory that was presumed to have happened in 1945. American power was unrivalled in the 1990s, therefore American power must have been unrivalled in the 1940s. This romantic assumption underlay Tom Brockaw's popular book *The Greatest Generation* (1998), which told a story about the GIs who won the war and who as veterans went on to build America's greatness in the post-war era. The chief critic of this romantic stance is Paul Fussell (b. 1924), a veteran himself and a professor of literature, who was wounded in France in 1945. Fussell's criticism is based not only on his experience of wartime horrors, but also on his awareness of the way that perceptions of past wars can vary and evolve. His study of 1914–18 – *The Great War and Modern Germany* (1975) – has a universal message. Human memory is fallible, and is open to manipulation. 'The Allied part of the war of 1939–45,' he wrote in one of his later works, 'has been sanitized and romanticized beyond recognition by the sentimental, the loony patriotic, the ignorant and the bloodthirsty.'[71]

The task of composing an accurate and concise framework history of the Second Word War would appear therefore to be growing more feasible. Several people in the English-speaking world have tried in the past, including A. J. P. Taylor, John Ray, and R. A. C. Parker.[72] Gerhard Weinberg, an American of German origin, produced a massive tome in 1994 combining an American perspective with Germanic thoroughness.[73] But the most praised of these volumes is *Total War*, written by Peter Calvocoressi, Guy Wint and John Pritchard. First published in 1972, it has run through four editions, and in its latest transformation is entitled *The Penguin History of the Second World War*. Each of the editions has involved considerable rewriting, and the most recent edition reveals after thirty years that Calvocoressi was a member of the Ultra project. Even so, the perspective remains decidedly Anglo-American, not to say Churchillian.

The section devoted to the period of the Nazi–Soviet Pact is still headed 'Hitler's Wars'. In the section on the defeat of the Reich, 'The Victory of the USSR' occupies just one chapter out of twenty-five. Such emphases do not adequately reflect historical realities.[74] If this is the best that historians can do, they must keep on playing the spider and 'try, try and try again'.

Museums and monuments

When the Second World War broke out, Europe was awash with museums that were still arranging their collections and exhibitions from the previous war. The premier museum of its type was the Kriegsmuseum-Zeughaus, which was housed in Berlin's elegant Arsenal and which had been founded after the Franco-Prussian War to celebrate the glories of the Prussian Army. It remained in business until October 1945, when it was closed down by order of the city's Allied commandants. It was replaced in 1950 by the Museum of German History.

In Britain, the Imperial War Museum, which had been founded in 1917 and was dedicated to all three armed services, received an order already in 1939 to extend its collection to the conflict that was just beginning. Unlike its German counterpart, it was *not* disbanded. As a result, the imperialism and militarism of former times, though toned down, was preserved. In the post-war period the museum was extended to three new sites – at Duxford, Cambridgeshire, for aircraft; at IWM North, in Manchester; and at the Cabinet War Rooms in Whitehall – and a dedicated Holocaust Exhibition was opened in June 2000.[75]

As these examples suggest, access to historical memory via museums is uneven, and is organized into national compartments. Moreover, it has been controlled by post-war politics. The victorious Allies were able to close down centres of German militarism and nationalism, while leaving their own militarist displays intact. The Soviet Union was able to close down all independent monuments to the war in Eastern Europe, while making tributes to its own victories compulsory.

In the USA, there is no war museum of similar size or standing that bears comparison to the US Holocaust Memorial Museum that was opened in Washington, DC, in 1993. For reasons that are more connected with post-war politics than with the USA's war effort, Americans have chosen to make the Jewish tragedy the focal point of their remembrance. It was not until 2000 that the US D-Day Museum in New Orleans was designated the National Museum of World War Two. This choice needs little explanation. Operation Overlord, which began on D-Day, was the biggest set-piece battle in which US troops were involved. Yet, once again, the museum does not encourage a view of the war as a whole. Few visitors are likely to come away with the knowledge that D-Day does not figure among the top ten battles of the war.[76]

In Britain, the Imperial War Museum has been supplemented by a number of newer centres. One of the more enterprising is the Second World War Experience Centre, in Leeds. It aims to 'collect, preserve, exhibit and encourage access to the surviving material evidence and associated information of the men and women who participated in the war in whatever capacity'. The emphasis is on the ordeals and recollections of individuals, and of specific military units and associations. And a refreshing feature lies in the intention of documenting the Axis as well as the Allied experience. For those who can't easily reach Leeds, the centre runs a useful website at www.war-experience.org. In some respects, however, it follows conventional tracks. Whenever the Soviet Union is at issue, for example, the centre calls it 'Russia'. And in the centre's 'Timeline' or chronological list of 'the main events of World War Two', all but one of the main battles of the war are omitted.[77]

In the museums of continental Europe, the German occupations are well displayed, but the Soviet occupations have emerged only recently as suitable subject for remembrance. In Amsterdam, for instance, the Verzets-museum, or Resistance Museum, has been functioning for decades.[78] In Warsaw, the Muzeum Powstania celebrating the rising of 1944 could not be organized until the sixtieth anniversary in 2004. It was blocked by the post-war Communist regime, and not supported by post-Communist governments.[79] There is a Communist museum in Vilnius, and a 'Socland' ('Commie-land') theme park is planned in Poland. The Baltic States and Ukraine offer the likeliest sites for future developments of that sort. The State Museum of Auschwitz–Birkenau near Katowice has become a major tourist attraction. (Tourists are now free to travel to Vorkuta in northern Russia. If they do, there is nothing much to see, other than private crosses left in the wilderness by relatives of former inmates.)

Military museums are more numerous then one might think. Those in Western Europe are on the beaten track, but those in Eastern Europe are gradually becoming better known. A modest display at Westerplatte in Gdańsk marks the opening salvo of the war. The fort of Eben-Emael in the Belgian Ardennes has been preserved to recall the German break-through of May 1940. And the fortress of Brest-Litovsk, which since 1991 is in the state of Belarus, has preserved its grandiose Soviet-era expositions. It was the scene of fierce action both in September 1939 and in June 1941. (Visitors should not yet expect to find traces of the Nazi–Soviet victory parade.) Further east, now under Russian sponsorship, all the main battles of the German–Soviet campaign have their monuments and museums. In present-day Volgograd, the museum devoted to the Battle of Stalingrad nestles beneath the towering statue of *Motherland Calling*. One wonders how much the locals care about the recent change in the 'Motherland's' identity. At all events, it is worth comparing the text of the museum's website with the texts of Antony Beevor. In Normandy, under British and American sponsorship, a clutch of museums, monuments and cemeteries – at Pointe du Hoc, Ste-Mère-Eglise, Colville, Omaha Beach and Avranches – commemorate the D-Day landings.[80] The Lüneberger Heath is now a wartime reserve.

Museums devoted to one or other of the armed services are common. The US Air Force Museum, containing much about the Second World War, is situated at Dayton, Ohio. The museum of Britain's Royal Marines is in Portsmouth, close to a D-Day museum. In Germany a U-boat museum operates at Bremerhaven, and a *Panzermuseum*, which would have warmed Guderian's heart, at Münster.

Museums frequently go hand in hand with monuments. They complement each other. In Britain, however, the memorials to the second war are markedly inferior to those of the first. A Memorial Gate has been erected in London to the dead of the Empire and the Commonwealth; and the new cube-shaped memorial to women who served in 1939–45, stands in Whitehall, near the Cenotaph. Most controversialy, a huge memorial to 'animals who died in all conflicts' has recently appeared in the central reservation of Park Lane. Many people might find the anthropomorphism offensive, a tribute to 'Disneyfication'. Yet many in pre-war days found the nearby Royal Artillery monument offensive; and it is now accepted as a great work of art. Only time will tell whether or not 'War memorials are the great blessing of the English . . . their finest cultural creation.'[81] In Washington the Holocaust Museum (see p. 473) and the World War Two Memorial stand virtually side by side.

As befits the realities of the war, however, Soviet war memorials are the largest and the most ostentatious. In Vienna, for example, a huge construction towers above the Schwarzenbergplatz. The inscription reads 'In honour of the soldiers of the Soviet Army who died liberating Austria from Fascism'. In accordance with the treaty of 1955, which returned Vienna to the Austrian government, the memorial has to be maintained by the city in perpetuity.

Berlin displays a similar monument near the Tiergarten. In the days of the Cold War, it found itself in the British Zone: and Soviet honour guards had to be given the right of passage from East Berlin. For the benefit of the Allied troops, the Russian inscription was translated into a sort of English:

ETERNAL GLORY

TO HEROES

WHO FELL IN THE

STRUGGLE AGAINST

THE GERMAN

FASCIST INVADERS

FOR THE FREEDOM

AND INDEPENDENCE

OF THE SOVIET UNION.[82]

The National War Memorial of Belarus stands at a place called Khatin. It was built in Soviet times on the site of a village destroyed by the Germans in reprisal for partisan activity. The Byelorussian SSR, as it was known during the war, was the country that suffered the highest percentage of human loss in 1939–45, and it is entirely fitting that a colossal memorial should recall a colossal tragedy. Yet nothing on the site explains why this particular site was chosen. Hundreds of Belarussian villages suffered the same fate, but were not chosen for fame. The clue lies in the name. To the uninformed, Khatyn can be very easily mistaken for Katyn – which is not far away and whose memory was supposed to be forgotten.[83]

Nowadays tourists can even visit the site of the Second World War's most decisive battle. The Kursk Regional Tourist Office advertises six

Tours round the battlefields on the Kursk Salient[84]		
	Location	Price per person in roubles
Memorial complex 'The Kursk Bulge'	Kursk	50
Memorial complex 'To the Soldiers Killed during the Great Patriotic War in 1941–45'	Kursk	50
The Historical Museum of the Kursk Battle	Kursk	50
The Historical Museum of War 'The Headquarters of the Central Front'	Svoboda	170
Memorial complex 'To the Heroes of the Battles in the Northern Face of the Kursk Bulge'	Ponyri	250
Memorial complex 'The Great Tank Battle on the Kursk Bulge'	Prohorovka	300

tours. The Soviet authorities opted for deliberate mystification. (See Table above.)

After 1945, no authority existed that was capable of forming an overall view of the Second World War, or of organizing a comprehensive exhibition of the conflict. In consequence, every interested country or local council was left to its own devices to sponsor whatever museums or monuments were thought suitable. The net result is a disparate scattering of memorials large and small which often display strong national bias, but which nonetheless reflect the partial, local and fragmented character of European memory. In sixty years, neither the Council of Europe, whose membership spanned both sides of the Iron Curtain during the Cold War, nor the European Union, whose roots lay in the West, managed to address the issue. And Europe's memory about the events of 1939–45 remains fragmented – distressingly fragmented.

Inconclusions

IT IS SAID THAT THE ACTOR Michael Caine sent his children back to Britain after they were taught in a US school that 'World War Two' began in 1941. The anecdote may or may not be accurate. But the problem is real enough. Every former combatant country has its own version of the war, and every single one puts its own role into the forefront. And the fixation with 1941, which obstructs any understanding of how the conflict started, is not just an American weakness. Notwithstanding the passing of sixty years, no one has succeeded in establishing a universally accepted framework within which all the constituent parts of the war can be reconciled. Indeed, one suspects that several powerful interests have little desire to find one. It is by no means certain that children in Britain learn about the war in a fuller or more rounded fashion than children in other countries.

The fixation with 1941 derives from the coincidence of four major events: the German attack on the USSR, Pearl Harbor, Hitler's declaration of war against the USA, and the onset of the Holocaust. As a result, Russian, American and Jewish perspectives all point to 1941 as the starting line. Any number of books, chapters and memorials have been dedicated to 'The Great Fatherland War, 1941–45', to 'World War Two, 1941–45' and to 'The Holocaust, 1941–45'. And they imply that events before 1941 were somehow just a minor foretaste or a prelude to the main performance. It is a simple fact that, in terms of popular publicity, the voices drawing attention to 1941 are louder than the assorted squeaks from Germans, Poles, Britons, Finns, Danes, Norwegians, Dutch, Belgians, French, Balts, Serbs, Greeks, Albanians and others who try to protest 'What about the rest of us?'

Chronology, however, is but one of half a dozen basic problems that have never been properly resolved. Patriotism, politics, perspective, language, outcome, proportions and criminality all deserve an airing.

Patriotism, meaning love of one's country and pride in its achievements, is a very natural emotion; and it can frequently be observed in the work of historians. In the case of Second World War history, it is all but ubiquitous in accounts written by historians from nations who count themselves among the victors and who have been taught for the last two or three generations to take pride in 'their' victories. In principle there is nothing to complain of – particularly when historians are skilled enough to distinguish impartial facts from patriotic comment.

Yet the subject is a tricky one. Stories of human conflict in which lives were lost and pain inflicted can easily arouse fiercer feelings of 'my country right or wrong', and patriotism can easily merge into chauvinism and xenophobia. It is an absolute rule among chauvinists and xenophobes that they imagine themselves to be nothing more than staunch patriots. Then, if one examines what they do and say, one finds that they hold other nations in contempt and deny them due acknowledgement. True patriotism, in fact, needs to be strong enough to take cognizance not only of one's compatriots' achievements but also of their failings and follies. For some nations the act of contrition is more painful than for others. But no nation is faultless – even those that have every right to regard themselves as victims – and the process of 'coming to terms' is a long one.

Furthermore, one cannot pretend that historiography is unaffected. Generally speaking, historians are more willing to accept evidence of criminal behaviour if the criminals themselves, or the criminals' successors, have made a clean breast of the crime. In this regard the Germans have been readier than either the Japanese or the Russians to acknowledge and expiate the crimes committed in their name; and for that reason, the Nazi record has very few defenders left. Stalin's record is more problematic – partly through continuing concealment, and partly through the continuing Russian posture of denial. Unlike the Germans, the Russians were among the victors, and many of them take rapid offence at suggestions that the Soviet record was less than spotless. A historian who dares to use the Moscow archives to document the scale of Red Army raping can still be berated by the Russian ambassador for his temerity.

History is always liable to political manipulation. But the Second World War, which in large measure created the present-day world, presents special temptations. For fifty years the two superpowers that emerged in 1945 pursued their separate visions of the war as an integral part of their rivalry. Then, in the 1990s, after the USA was left as the sole superpower, a new, and more Americocentric view of the Second World War appeared. Stephen Ambrose became the historian of the hour, and *Saving Private Ryan* and *Schindler's List* became the war films of the decade.

There can be little doubt that the Ambrose–Spielberg axis, combining a specific historical stance with the preferences and commercial power of Hollywood, chimed perfectly with the rise of the 'neoconservatives' and the declaration of 'a new American century'. Nor was it coincidental that President George W. Bush kept a bust of Winston Churchill on his desk and a copy of Ambrose's *D-Day* by his bedside. When planning the invasion of Iraq in 2003, it was only to be expected that the chief of the Pentagon would liken his president to Winston Churchill and Saddam Hussein to Hitler. (In reality, Saddam and his Baa'th Party were closer to Stalin.) It all formed part of the same package. A very superficial and Americanocentric view of history was a necessary adjunct to the reigning Americanocentric view of world affairs.

All one can say is that someday, somehow, the present fact of American supremacy will be challenged, and with it the American interpretation of history. All the prospective challengers have their own take on the Second World War. The Chinese, for example, remember the war years as a period of immense suffering inflicted by imperial Japan and as a necessary prelude to the victory of the Chinese Revolution. In a Sinocentric world one could expect the importance of Europe and of Europe's suffering to be downgraded; the victories of Russians and Americans would be pushed to the margins; the Japanese militarists, not the Nazis, would represent the prime force of Evil; the 'memory spot' par excellence might be the city of Nanking; and the screen epic of the mid-twenty-first century (if screens still exist) might show some unknown Chinese private being rescued on some as yet unremembered beach.

A historical narrative would be very dull if it did not reveal its author's sympathies. But it can proceed to the stage of personal opinions only after facts and analysis have been carefully distinguished and presented. As all novelists know, every narrative can be presented from a variety of perspectives. Narrators describe the action from standpoints of their own choosing. Historians are well advised to observe this phenomenon carefully, for when it comes to relating their subject, as opposed to verifying the facts, they too must choose their vantage points. Indeed, in order to understand all sides of a complex and evolving military conflict, they must be prepared to handle multiple perspectives. They don't have to justify Nazi or Soviet actions, for instance, but they do need to grasp the workings of the mindsets involved. And they can't afford to be selective in what they attempt to explain and what they might otherwise like to attribute to the unspecified forces of darkness. The operation is not easy.

The minute that historians provide explanations for detestable events they
will be charged with excusing them. Such are the built-in risks of the trade.

Language and terminology constitute a sphere in which many British
and American histories lack precision. Spades should be called spades, but
very often they are not. 'War criminal', for instance, doesn't refer to all
war criminals. And the term 'concentration camp' doesn't quite mean
'concentration camp'. It refers not to all concentration camps, but only to
those organized by the enemy. Concentration camps organized by others
are usually called something else. Similarly, 'collaborator' doesn't refer to
all collaborators, i.e. to all who assisted oppressive occupying powers
against their own people. In practice it applies only to those who assisted
the occupying forces of Nazi Germany. In other words, the prevailing
language is biased, because the underlying thought processes are biased.
The Western obsession with Hitler leads to many distortions. A term like
'Hitler's War', if used as a synonym for the Second World War, is
manifestly dubious. But it is widely used by unthinking Westerners, as
well as by Communists, who want to heap all the blame onto one man.
And it is also used by the few oddball admirers of Hitler, who take
pleasure in placing the Fuhrer in the limelight.[1]

The point may be illustrated by the case already cited where the campaigns of 1939–41 are equated with 'Hitler's Wars'. The implications are
not difficult to divine. The first campaign of the war, in September 1939,
was conducted against Poland jointly by Nazi Germany and the USSR. Yet
it is widely called 'the German invasion of Poland'. The second aggression
of the war, in November 1939, was launched against Finland solely by the
USSR. Yet, if not ignored completely, it is often labelled by euphemisms
such as 'the Soviet dispute with Finland' or as a 'move to strengthen the
defences of Leningrad'. Only the third campaign, against Denmark and
Norway, was a straightforward case of German aggression. The fourth
campaign, against France – via Belgium and the Netherlands – had been
prompted by the Western Powers' declaration of war against Germany, and
it was accompanied by Stalin's annexation of the three Baltic States. To put
all of this into the category of 'Hitler's War' or 'Hitler's Wars' surely
represents an inadmissible oversimplification.

Descriptions of the outcome of the war are beset by further impreci-
sions. Almost universally, Western historians talk of 'victory' and 'liberation'. They then proceed to explain how the fruits of victory were
squandered or circumscribed by the onset of the Cold War. It might be
better if they had refrained from talking about 'victory' in such absolute

terms in the first place. For the outcome can only be gauged by reference to previous hopes, aims and expectations, and it is here that several qualifiers need to be introduced. From 1943, the Allied coalition had pursued the unconditional surrender of Germany as the one war aim on which all the Allied powers could agree. And in this aim they certainly succeeded. Yet, in the course of their single-minded pursuit, various other Allied aims and obligations were abandoned. It had been assumed, for example, that the victorious Allies would reintroduce freedom and democracy to Europe, at least within the limits of the pre-war frontiers. With regard to the original *casus belli*, it was generally expected that the independence of Poland would be restored. And, with specific reference to US policy, it was expected that the sovereignty of the Baltic States would be respected. To resolve all other outstanding issues – of which there were many – it was widely announced that a post-war peace conference would be convened, as in 1919. In practice, none of these things happened. And they had no chance of happening, because the war had come to an end without the clear-cut victory of one party or of one agreed programme. To be precise, the war in Europe had ended not just with the defeat of the Third Reich, but also with a military stand-off between the co-victors and with the reimposition of a totalitarian tyranny in the Soviet half of Europe. This outcome was well understood in private by the political leaders. But it did not coincide with their gushing public statements. Historians should be able to distinguish the reality from the rhetoric.

Unlike the Great War of 1914–18, the Second World War has never generated a critical consensus of sufficent weight to discredit the overblown claims of the victors. In consequence, numerous untenable myths and legends have continued to flourish. In the case of 1914–18, for instance, politicians had talked about 'the war to end all wars'. Yet very soon, and by 1939 at the latest, no such hyperbole could be supported, and public opinion in most countries settled down to the gloomy theme of 'futility'. War literature played its part. Millions were judged to have died for no good reason. All sides bore their share of responsibility. When the Russian Revolution was closely followed by the Russian Civil War and by the rise of Fascism, all but the most myopic could see that military conflict had spawned as many problems as it had solved.

The Second World War, however, was thought different. To begin with, the initial war aims of the participants were distinctly fuzzy, and soon disappeared from view. Germany had originally expected only a limited war. The Western Powers had wanted to curb German expansion. The Soviet Union had wanted both the Nazis and the 'Western capitalists' to exhaust themselves. All these underlying calculations proved to be gravely mistaken. As a result, everyone's war aims changed focus as the conflict progressed. In Germany, the Nazis saw their historic opportunity, and decided to go for broke, launching their bid for total supremacy in June 1941. From the viewpoint of the Grand Coalition, the project moved up several gears to aim at the unconditional surrender of the Third Reich and its complete dismantlement. Indeed, the enemy proved so obnoxious that all previous anxieties about the propriety of the war evaporated. Nothing rings truer than the words of a British soldier who in April 1945 had just helped liberate Belsen. 'This,' he discovered, 'is what we've been fighting for.' In other words, whatever the earlier doubts and soul-searching, he was finally convinced of the justice of the cause.

Many Britons and Americans were convinced in the same fashion. They all felt that war had been imposed on them, and that they had taken to arms reluctantly. There was none of the wild enthusiasm of their fathers' generation. Yet when they learned of the extreme inhumanity of their enemy, and heard the details spelled out at Nuremberg, they ran out of objections. Evil had been defeated. The 'Good' had triumphed. Hence, freedom, justice and democracy must have prevailed.

The Soviet authorities were able to impose a parallel version of events, which equally left little room for doubt. The Soviet Union, innocent of all offence, had been brutally attacked by the Fascist beast. Despite the ill-willed passivity of the Western Powers, the Red Army had fought with unsurpassed heroism to repel the invaders and to liberate half of Europe. Once again the word was that Evil had been defeated. 'Good', as defined by Soviet propaganda, had triumphed. And freedom, justice and democracy, Soviet-style, had prevailed.

In other words, it is not difficult to see that powerful myths have arisen that override all accurate records or recollections of what actually happened in 1939–45. The victorious countries hang on to these myths, endlessly repeating the simplified storylines that serve both as parables of Right and Wrong and as guides to political action. If politicians fear the rise of adversaries like Colonel Nasser or Saddam Hussein, they quickly denounce them as 'a new Hitler' or equate them with 'Fascists'. If they or their allies have to face a missile attack, great or small, they readily liken it to Nazi V-1s and V-2s, and justify their own disproportionate retaliations in terms of the Strategic Bombing Offensive. They feel no threat in their own possession of nuclear weapons, whilst denouncing the threat of 'illegal weapons' by others. For they have convinced themselves that they, the self-styled 'international community', like the united nations of old, is fighting the good fight with a pure heart, a just cause and a big stick.

As time passes, uncritical attitudes appear to multiply as later generations lose all sight of wartime complexities. Nonetheless, in judging the Second World War in Europe, historians need to pay special attention to two core issues, that prick the predominant complacency. One of the issues is proportionality. The other is criminality. The former is rarely explored by Western apologists. The latter has been carefully avoided by Soviet apologists. Together they provide the keys to what really happened.

The problem of proportionality is easy to define, and less easy to resolve. In history-writing, it revolves around the requirement that the largest space and the greatest emphasis be given to the biggest and the most decisive events; or, inversely, that events of lesser import be allotted less space and less emphasis. Everyone would agree, one assumes, that an outline history of the Second World War which devoted the greater part of its comment to Luxembourg would be distinctly odd. This is not because Luxembourg's wartime story is uninteresting or irrelevant, but because Luxembourg's fate, like that of everywhere else in Europe, was decided by battles fought and by decisions taken elsewhere.

How then should the historian decide where the emphasis should lie? One way, if the aim were simply to flatter the British or the American market, would be to put the emphasis on British and American affairs. It is the sort of approach which dismisses the Battle of Kursk in five lines, whilst spending fifty pages on the D-Day landings. Another way would be to start by drawing up a checklist of the main battles, the decisive campaigns and the key policies of the war, and then to allot the space and emphasis accordingly.

As things stand, this approach is rather rare. For, in reality, the Soviet war effort was so overwhelming that impartial historians of the future are unlikely to rate the British and American contribution to the European theatre as much more than a sound supporting role. The proportions were *not* 'fifty–fifty', as many imply when talking of the final onslaught on Nazi Germany from East and West. Sooner or later people will have to adjust to the fact that the Soviet role was enormous and the Western role was respectable but modest.

Western commentators who accept the fact of Soviet predominance in the land war sometimes try to counterbalance it by stressing Western predominance in the air and at sea. This argument would carry greater weight if the air offensive had achieved more decisive results, and if Germany had been more vulnerable to naval operations. As it was, the Reich held out successfully against bombardment and blockade. And it was only finished off by the land assault to which the Red Army made by far the most effective contribution.

Other commentators seek to argue that the Red Army's success was dependent on Western aid and that the Western Allies were better equipped than the USSR to have defeated the Reich on their own. The Red Army could not have won single-handed, they say, whereas the Western armies, if necessary, could have done so:

> It is not . . . true to say . . . [one historian protests] that the Soviet Union won the war. Without her allies, the Soviet Union would have faced the full force of German airpower, and would have been short of munitions and weapons – in 1943 Lend-Lease provision to the USSR was equivalent to one-fifth of total Soviet production. The Soviet Union could not have held out without Western help. The Western Allies, by contrast, could have won the war without the Soviet Union. The cost of doing so would have been terribly high, but sooner or later bombing would have ground Germany down and America would eventually have mobilised a vast army . . . If all else failed, America would presumably have settled matters by dropping an atom bomb on Berlin.[2]

Such a scenario is inevitably speculative. But it contains so many false assumptions that it fails to convince. One hardly knows where to start. The critical years for the Soviet Union did not start in 1943 when Lend-Lease was coming on full stream, but in 1941–2, when Western aid was still marginal. At that juncture, the Red Army *did* face the brunt of German airpower; it did not run short of weapons or munitions, which of necessity were mainly home-produced; and in spite of everything, it *did* hold out. What is more, much of the early Lend-Lease aid was unusable. British tanks were not what the Red Army needed, and British Army greatcoats (like German greatcoats) were totally unsuited to the Russian winter. The Soviets had already gained the upper hand on their own account before Western aid began to reach them in quantity.

One must also give credit to the Red Army for achievements beyond the mustering of numerical advantage. In fact, since the population of the

Reich stood in 1941 at 81 million against the USSR's 197 million, the overall Soviet advantage of 2.43:1 fell short of the usual requirements for sustained offensive warfare. The Red Army barely survived the German onslaught, but nonetheless took the initiative from mid-1943 onwards. Even in the war's final phase, when the Germans could assign a maximum of 70–75 per cent of their forces to the East, the Soviet advantage was only raised to perhaps 3.2:1. Hence, if the superior quality of German forces was as marked as often assumed, one would have expected the Wehrmacht to hold its ground more effectively, especially as the front was narrowing. Yet the Red Army proved unstoppable. Contrary to predictions, it had gained superiority not only in numbers, but also in generalship, in tactics, in military production and in key areas of technology. Western aid may have been something more than the icing on the cake, but it was *not* the decisive factor.

As for the notion that the Western Allies could have won without the Soviet Union, it totally ignores the realities. If the Red Army had been knocked out, the Germans would not have stood idly by as the USA built up its strength and prepared to drop an atomic bomb on them. The German armed forces would have been immediately turned in their entirety on Great Britain; the outcome of the Battle of the Atlantic could have been reversed; the Western Allies would probably have lost the base for their bombing offensive; the 'vast' American army (which didn't exist) would have had no safe landing-place; and a European counterpart of *Enola Gay* would have had nowhere to take off.

The key reason why the Western input was significantly smaller than generally supposed centres on timing, and in particular on the lateness of American engagement. The Allied cause had been brought to the brink of collapse in the summer of 1940, and it had no hope of recovery in the West until the USA was fully engaged. Yet American involvement took time to organize. It did not begin until January 1942, and it could not reach peak efficiency instantaneously. Hence, in the months when the Americans were still girding their loins, the Soviets were already racing towards a position of near-total dominance. One need look no further than the second week of July 1943. At that point in the war the very first US soldiers to set foot in continental Europe were being deposited on a distant beach in southern Sicily. At the same time, on the Eastern Front, the Red Army was breaking the Wehrmacht's back to such an extent that the German war machine would never regain its offensive capacity.

What is more, the American military build-up was far from complete by the time that the war in Europe ended. One forgets that the starting point had been extraordinarily low. In 1939 the establishment of the US Army was smaller than that of Poland. Thereafter, no one could seriously doubt that US military capacity would catch up rapidly. American industry, science trade and finance were providing the US government with resources that no other combatant country could match. Yet the timescale was crucial. Despite titanic progress, the USA did not surge into an unassailable lead. In the last months of European fighting before May 1945, the USA did not possess either an atomic weapon or superiority in conventional arms. It had not yet moved into the nuclear league, where from July 1945 to 1949 it would be the sole player, and it possessed barely a hundred battle-ready divisions, compared with German and Soviet troop levels that were two or three times higher. As Generals Marshall and Eisenhower were only too well aware, they could not possibly have risked a serious confrontation with the Red Army. And they could not possibly have won in Europe single-handedly. Indeed, with the Japanese war still moving slowly, they desperately needed Soviet assistance both in Europe and in the Far East.

People forget. They are influenced by later developments. They tend to imagine that the USA was all-powerful from the start. And they are easily led to believe that the failure to challenge Stalin earlier or more energetically must be put down to purely personal or political factors. Such was not the case. American forces had not gained parity with the USSR by May 1945; and their actions were duly constrained. As things were, it was the Soviet Union, not the USA, which fought the final phase of the war as the strongest power in Europe. It was the Red Army which scored the most crushing victories over Nazi Germany, culminating in the Battle for Berlin. And it was Soviet Communism, not liberal democracy, that made the most striking advances.

Evaluations of criminality are equally central to any account of the Second World War. For criminality was unusually prevalent, even if the full extent of criminal conduct did not become apparent until long afterwards. In this regard one can say that it is only relatively recently that historians have been empowered to make an informed assessment of the overall picture. It is only since the collapse of the Soviet Union that the long list of conjectures and estimates about the crimes of the Stalinist era have been extensively documented. And it is only in the last decade or so that the

Soviet record could be properly compared to the better-known Nazi record. Winston Churchill, for example, writing in the late 1940s, simply did not possess the hard information which later became available. 'History will be kind to me,' he said, 'because I intend to write it.'

Even so, the main obstacle to an impartial exposé of wartime criminality does not lie exclusively in the poor flow rate of information. It has a psychological dimension. It has been compounded by the reluctance of Western historians to stain the reputation of the Allied coalition. The psychological term for such reluctance is 'denial'. And, consciously or subconsciously, many Westerners continue to deny that the hard facts of massive Soviet criminality requires them to modify their overall assessment of the war.

The widespread characterization of the conflict as 'the Good War', therefore, is particularly dubious. 'Good' does not seem to be quite the right adjective when one bears in mind the unprecedented killing and suffering of innocents that took place on all sides. To some extent it reflects the notion of 'a noble crusade' (though one which was only partly successful), as well as the theological concept of a 'just war' (which requires one to identify the just and the unjust). And it would seem to be inspired by a peculiarly parochial Anglo-Saxon perspective which has been strengthened in recent decades and which in some respects does not match historical reality. It is used, in fact, as the necessary complement to the ultimate evil of the Holocaust. And yet, as is often pointed out, the Western Allies did not go to war to rescue the Jews, and, when the first reports of the Final Solution leaked out, the Western response was little short of lamentable. Certainly in American eyes the principal action was thought for much of the war to be unfolding in the Pacific, not in Europe. Wartime attitudes are mirrored by the fact that the USA interned its Japanese-American but not its German-American citizens. And when firm news of the Holocaust finally arrived in 1944, few, even among American Jews, were prepared to believe it.[3]

All in all, therefore, the storyline about the forces of democracy 'fighting the good fight' and 'winning the war' must be viewed with a strong dose of scepticism. Stalin may have been nearer the mark. 'England provided the time,' he said, 'America provided the money, and Russia provided the blood.'[4] England, meaning the British Empire, passed much of the war in a state of convalescence. But Churchill's defiance in 1940–41 preserved the springboard for subsequent Allied resurgence. America, meaning the USA, entered the war too late to take the leading part in Europe. Its role as 'the arsenal of democracy' was no less significant than the contribution of its armed forces. Russia, meaning the Soviet Union, was called on to make incomparable sacrifices, and it deserves the largest laurels for the defeat of Nazi Germany. Even so – and this is the central paradox – Stalin, the chief victor, was also a mass murderer and a bloody tyrant in his own right. He had nothing in common with the normal concept of 'the Good' or of 'the Good War'.

Moreover, from the purely soldierly point of view, caution must be expressed concerning the notion that the free citizens of democratic states supply the best fighting material. In 1939–45, the lion's share of the fighting was undertaken by the forces of two totalitarian states; and the soldiers who came out on top belonged to the slave-driven cohorts of a ruthless dictatorship. When the armies of democracy clashed with the Nazi legions in Italy or Western Europe, the former did not perform particularly well. It is arguable that technology and air power, rather than top-class soldiery enabled the British and the American to compete on roughly equal terms.

Equally, it is not possible to sustain the usual comparison between the inhuman war of the trenches in 1914–18 and the relatively bearable war of 1939–45. This comparison provides one more example of Westerners generalizing from their own limited experiences. Taken as a whole, the realities were somewhat different. On the Eastern Front, where the largest slice of military action took place, existential conditions were relentlessly inhuman both for Germans and for Soviets. The physical pains were only compounded by the draconian measures which both sides took against their own men to keep them fighting. In the Western sphere, where area bombing formed the principal means of attacking Germany, the so-called 'collateral damage', i.e. the incineration and maiming of innocent civilians, occurred on such a scale that no one can fairly contend that Western methods of warfare were anything other than ugly.

In this regard a word needs to be said about the weasel phrase of 'collateral damage'. In all official statements, spokesmen of the British or American bomber commands always regretted civilian losses, whilst maintaining that the aim was to hit military and industrial targets. This reasoning, however, does not withstand examination. Vast bombing fleets of 1000 aircraft or more were in their very nature incapable of confining their targets to particular factories, railway junctions or military installations. They were sent to obliterate whole cities, in which it was perfectly well known in advance that the great majority of inhabitants were innocent civilians. The civilian deaths, therefore, were in no sense accidental or collateral. They were one of the integral and calculated consequences of misguided operations, which continue to stain the reputation of their authors.

Lastly, despite frequent protestations to the contrary, one is saddened to affirm that scholarship and comment about wartime events do not operate in a completely free environment. In many Western countries the law has been mobilized to shore up an official view of history. In Britain, for instance, war crimes are not regarded as war crimes if they were not perpetuated by Germans or by German associates. In France, according to the Fabius-Gayssot Law of 1990, anyone who denies the Holocaust or minimizes it can face severe penalties, including imprisonment. Half a dozen other European countries, from Austria to Poland, have followed suit. In a period when the right to freedom of speech was being loudly proclaimed in Europe, when Muslims were staging protests against offensive cartoons of their Prophet, an attention-seeking historian from Britain was being imprisoned in Austria for expressing the wrong shade of opinion.[5] This atmosphere is not healthy. Historical knowledge does not need artificial protection. The Holocaust is an incontestable fact. Yet the paths to a fuller understanding are obstructed. The truth about the past can only be established and strengthened by the clash of wisdom and absurdity. If absurdity is banned by the law, wisdom too is diminished.

A clear view of the war in Europe inevitably has repercussions on assessments of the war in the Pacific, and indeed on global conclusions about the outcome of the Second World War as a whole. The twin features of Soviet triumph and of limited Western success in Europe set the scene for the key decision of early 1945, when the Soviet Union was pressed to participate in the Far East. So long as the Pacific War was confined to naval fighting and 'island-hopping', US forces coped almost single-handedly. But as soon as the prospect loomed of large-scale land warfare, both against the Kwantung Army in China and against the garrison of the main Japanese islands, the Americans were forced to seek a major partner. Their dilemma was solved partly by the entry of the Red Army.

When asked in the 1950s about the effects of the French Revolution, the Chinese foreign minister Chou En-lai is reported to have replied, 'It's too early to say.' His words are generally taken as a famous bon mot of no great seriousness. Yet they should make one think. The time span between

Chou En-lai's education in France in the 1920s and Robespierre's reign of terror in the 1790s was exactly 130 years. Hence, since the sixty-fifth anniversary of 1939 has already passed, the world has waited for over half the same span of time without establishing a firm framework vision of the Second World War. Current affairs appear to move at breakneck speed, whilst history moves at a snail's pace. If one were to be asked, therefore, what stage historians have reached on their road to a final judgement, one would be tempted to echo Churchill's words after the Battle of El Alamein. 'It is not even the beginning of the end,' he said. 'But it is, perhaps, the end of the beginning.'[6]

Hence, despite the arrival of the twenty-first century, many thinking people are still trying to grapple with the aftermath of the Second World War. A leading British cardiologist with a flair for poetry expressed the problem perfectly:

> My patient lay in the hospital bed
> Unshaven, smelling of urine,
> And bitten by lice,
> Of no fixed abode,
> Living on the street,
> And unemployed,
> Without family or friends.
> In his Slavic accent
> He declared
> 'I fought at Monte Cassino.'
> And my junior doctors in their ignorance
> Remained unmoved by man or by history.
> And I turned to them
> With my hand on the shoulder
> Of my patient,
> To address them on the greatness
> Of the Second Polish Corps
> And the infinite value
> Of all human beings.[7]

Notes

Introduction   *pp. 1–8*

• **1.** Gerhard Weinberg, *A World at Arms* (Cambridge, 1994). • **2.** Ian Dear et al. (eds.), *The Oxford Companion to the Second World War* (Oxford, 1995; New York, 1996). • **3.** A. W. Purdue, *The Second World War*, European History in Perspective (Basingstoke, 1999), back cover.

One – Interpretation   *pp. 9–72*

• **1.** Alan Bullock, *Hitler: A Study in Tyranny*, (London, 1952); A. J. P. Taylor, *The Origins of the Second World War* (London, 1961). • **2.** Antony Beevor, *Stalingrad* (London, 1998); *Berlin: The Downfall* (London, 2002). • **3.** Janusz Zawodny, *Death in the Forest: The Story of the Katyn Forest Massacre*; (Notre Dame, 1962), Louis MacGibbon, *The Katyn Cover-up*, foreword by Airey Neave (London, 1972); Owen O'Malley, *Katyn: despatches of Sir Owen O'Malley* (Chicago, 1973); A. Moszyński (ed.), *Lista Katyńska: jeńcy obozów Kozielsk, Ostashkov, Starobielsk*, (London, 1977). Prior to 1989, the Katyn list, containing the names of all the missing officers, was rigorously banned throughout the Soviet Block. • **4.** See P. M. H. Bell, *John Bull and the Bear: British Public Opinion, Foreign Policy and the Soviet Union, 1941–45* (London, 1990); also *Katyn: British reaction to the Katyn massacres, 1943–2003*, FCO History Notes (London, 2003). • **5.** Norman Davies, 'The Allied Scheme of History' in *Europe: A History* (Oxford, 1996), p. 40. • **6.** Norman Davies, 'Selectivity in History . . .', *New York Review of Books*, April 1996, republished in *Europe East and West: Collected Essays* (London, 2006), pp. 240–8. • **7.** B. Slavinsky, *The Japanese-Soviet neutrality pack, 1941–45* (London, 2004). • **8.** After H. C. Hillman, *The Comparative Strength of the Great Powers* (London, 1939). • **9.** John Ellis, *The World War Two Databook* (London, 1993), pp. 227–8. • **10.** Ibid., Section 5 (London, 1993). • **11.** This conclusion is confirmed by a calculation of German War Effort in 'aggregated months', which from a total of 9032 allots 7146 or 79.1 per cent to the Eastern Front, 637 to Western Europe, 393 to Italy, 91 to North Africa and 665 to 'others'. Ellis, op. cit., p. 229. • **12.** Ibid., pp. 253–4, table 51. • **13.** Numerous sources: almost all of them estimates. No precise figures are available for deaths or casualties on the Eastern Front. • **14.** A prize-winning English-language film, *Orzel*, directed by Leonard Buczkowski, was produced in 1958 about the submarine's escape. See A. Suchcitz, *Poland's Contribution to the Allied Victory in the Second World War* (London, 1995). • **15.** Data collated from http://www.naval-history.net/WW2CampaignsAtlanticDev.htm. • **16.** J. Rohwer, *War at Sea, 1939–45* (London, 2001); S. W. Roskill, *The War at Sea, 1939–45* (Imperial War Museum, London, 1994–). • **17.** Ellis, op. cit., pp. 231–44. • **18.** T. D. Biddle, *Rhetoric and Reality in Air Warfare: the evolution of British and American ideas about strategic bombing, 1914–45* (Princeton, 2002). • **19.** D. Hölsken, *Die V-Waffen: Enstehung, Propaganda, Kriegeinsatz* (Stuttgart, 1984). • **20.** Alan Milward, *War, Economy and Society, 1939–45* (Harmondsworth, 1987). • **21.** Mark Harrison (ed.), *The Economics of World War II* (Cambridge, 1998), p. 10. • **22.** Michael Lynch, *Nazi Germany* (London, 2004), p. 81. • **23.** Ellis, op. cit., pp. 277–8, tables 87, 88 and 92. • **24.** Harrison, op. cit., p. 10. • **25.** Ellis, op. cit., pp. 277–8, tables 87 and 92. • **26.** Ibid., pp. 277–80, tables 87, 92 and 95. • **27.** See George C. Herring, *Aid to Russia 1941–1946: Strategy, Diplomacy, the Origins of the Cold War* (New York, 1973). • **28.** B. Gunston, *Rockets and Missiles* (London, 1979). • **29.** Richard Rhodes, *The Making of the Atomic Bomb* (London, 1986); *Dark Sun, the making of the hydrogen bomb* (London, 1995). • **30.** M. Smith, *Station X: the Codebreakers of Bletchley Park* (London, 1998); *Marian Rejewski, 1905–1980: Living with the Enigma Secret*, intro. Z. Brzeziński (Bydgoszcz, 2005). • **31.** S. Korboński, *The Polish Underground State: a guide to the underground, 1939–45* (Boulder, Colo., 1978). • **32.** F. W. D. Deakin, *The Embattled Mountain* (London, 1971); M. Djilas, *Wartime* (London, 1977). • **33.** M. D. Brown, *Dealing with Democrats: The British Foreign Office and Czechoslovak emigrés, 1939–45* (Frankfurt, 2006). • **34.** Himmler, 1944, quoted in Norman Davies, *Rising '44* (London, 2003), p. 249. • **35.** Martin Gilbert, *The Holocaust, the Jewish Tragedy* (London, 1987); Paul Johnson, *The Holocaust* (London, 1996). • **36.** See Orlando Figes, *A People's Tragedy: The Russian Revolution, 1891–1924* (London, 1996). • **37.** Leszek Kołakowski, *Main currents of Marxism: its rise, growth and dissolution* (Oxford, 1978); Angus Walker, *Marx: his theory and its context* (London, 1989). • **38.** Piotr Wandycz, *The Price of Freedom: a history of East Central Europe* (London, 1992). • **39.** Sidney and Beatrice Webb, *Soviet Communism: A New Civilisation* (London, 1933); *The Truth about Soviet Russia* (London, 1944). • **40.** S. J. Taylor, *Stalin's apologist: Walter Duranty, the New York Times' Man in Moscow* (Oxford, 1990). • **41.** Robert Conquest, *The Great Terror: Stalin's Purge of the thirties* (New York, 1969); *The Great Terror: A Reassessment* (London, 1992). • **42.** <www.brainyquote.com>. • **43.** Churchill, ibid. • **44.** Ronald H. Spector, *Eagle against the Sun: the American War with Japan* (London, 2001). • **45.** Georg Schild, *Bretton Woods and Dumbarton Oaks: American post-war planning in the summer* *of 1944* (Basingstoke, 1945). • **46.** Davies, *Rising '44*, pp. 629–35. • **47.** Lynn Davis, *The Cold War Begins* (Princeton, 1974); Vojtech Mastny, *Russia's Road to the Cold War, 1941–45* (New York, 1979). • **48.** *The Black Book of Communism: crimes, terror, repression* (Harvard, 1999). • **49.** Simon Heffer, in *Country Life* (2003). • **50.** Roy Hattersley, review of *Stalin: Court of the Red Tsar* by Simon Sebag-Montefiore (*Observer*, 20 July 2003). • **51.** Joram Sheftel, *Show Trial: the conspiracy to convict John Demjanjuk as 'Ivan the Terrible'* (London, 1995). • **52.** Robert Conquest, *Kolyma: the arctic death camps* (Oxford, 1979); Edward Buca, *Workuta* (London, 1976). • **53.** Henry Probert, *Bomber Harris, his life and times* (London, 2003). • **54.** Nicholas Tolstoy, *The Monster and the Massacres* (London, 1986); *Victims of Yalta* (London, 1977). • **55.** Alfred De Zayas, *The German Expellees: victims in war and peace* (Basingstoke, 1993).

Two – Warfare   *pp. 73–130*

• **1.** Nicholas Bethell, *The War Hitler Won, September 1939* (London, 1972). • **2.** Purdue, op. cit., p. 43. • **3.** See Jan Tomasz Gross, *Revolution from Abroad: the Soviet Conquest of Poland's western Ukraine and western Byelorussia* (Princeton, 1988); Keith Sword (ed.), *The Soviet takeover of the Polish eastern provinces, 1939–41* (Basingstoke, 1991). • **4.** Davies, *Rising '44*, op. cit., pp. 83–5. • **5.** Purdue, op. cit., p. 46. • **6.** Hugh Trevor-Roper (ed.), *Hitler's War Directives, 1939–45* (London, 1964), pp. 93–8. • **7.** Anthony Upton, *Finland, 1939–40* (London, 1974); C. V. Dyke, *The Soviet Invasion of Finland, 1939–40* (London, 1997); W. R. Trotter, *The Winter War* (London, 2002); A. F. Chew, *The White Death* (Michigan, 1971); J. Langdon-Davies, *Finland: the first total war* (London, 1940). • **8.** J. Adams, *The Doomed Expedition: the Campaign in Norway, 1940* (London, 1989). • **9.** E. Turner, *The Phoney War* (London, 1961). • **10.** A. J. P. Taylor, *The Second World War: an Illustrated History* (London, 1975). • **11.** Alistair Horne, *To Lose a Battle, France, 1940* (London, 1969); Basil Karslake, *The Last Act* (London, 1979); L. Mysyrowicz, *Autopsie d'une defaite* (Lausanne, 1973); J. Blatt (ed.), *The French Defeat of 1940: re-assessments* (Oxford, 1998). • **12.** L. Fenby, *The Sinking of the 'Lancastria'* (New York, 2005). See also www.lancastria-association.org. • **13.** A. Marder, *From the Dardanelles to Oran* (Oxford, 1974). • **14.** See Brian Crozier, *Franco: A Biographical History* (London, 1967). • **15.** Georg Rauch, *The Baltic States, 1917–40* (London, 1995); M. Ilmjärv, *Silent Submission* (Stockholm, 2004); O. Mertelsman, *The Sovietisation of the Baltic States, 1940–56* (Tartu, 2003). • **16.** 'In the middle of June, after a series of ultimata, the Red Army occupied all three Baltic States, ending the independence of their peoples, and arranging for their formal incorporation into the Soviet Union as Soviet Socialist Republics', Gerhard Weinberg, *A World at Arms* (Cambridge, 1994),

p. 135. • **17.** Quoted by John Ray, *An Illustrated History of the Second World War* (London, 1999), p. 65. • **18.** Len Deighton, *Battle of Britain* (London, 1980); R. Hough and D. Richards, *The Battle of Britain: A Jubilee History* (London, 1990). • **19.** From Adam Zamoyski, *The Forgotten Few: The Polish Airforce during the Second World War* (London, 1995). • **20.** C. Fitzgibbon, *The Blitz*, drawings by Henry Moore (London, 1970); A. Price, *Blitz on Britain* (Shepperton, 1977). • **21.** J. P. Lash, *Roosevelt and Churchill, 1939–41: the partnership that saved the West* (London, 1976). • **22.** Stephen Fischer-Galatz, *Twentieth Century Romania* (Boulder, Col., 1970); Dennis Deletant, *Hitler's forgotten ally: Ion Antonescu and his regime, 1940–44* (Basingstoke, 2006). • **23.** Trevor-Roper, op. cit., pp. 93–8. • **24.** David Murphy, *What Stalin Knew: the enigma of Barbarossa* (Yale, 2005) • **25.** Ibid., p. 25. • **26.** Ray, op. cit., p. 135. • **27.** Stevan K. Pavlowitsch, *The Improbable Survivor: Yugoslavia 1918–88* (London, 1988); C. M. Woodhouse, *The Struggle for Greece* (London, 1979). • **28.** C. Macdonald, *The Lost Battle: Crete 1941* (London, 1993). • **29.** See Philip Guedalla, *The Middle East, 1940–42: a study in airpower* (London, 1944); also Y. Lapidot, 'David Raz'iel', in <www.JewishvirtualLibrary.org/source/biography>. • **30.** Weinberg, *A World at Arms*, op. cit., p. 4. • **31.** Taylor, op. cit., p. 97. • **32.** Victor Suvorov (pseudonym), *Icebreaker: who started the Second World War?* (London, 1990): see also Gabriel Gorodetsky, *Grand Delusion: Stalin and the German invasion of Russia* (New Haven, 1999); David Glantz, *Barbarossa: Hitler's invasion of Russia* (Stroud, 2001); J. Keegan, *Barbarossa* (London, 1971); Alan Clark, *Barbarossa: the Russian-German conflict, 1941–45* (London, 2000); Ernst Topitsch, *Stalin's War: a radical new theory of the origins of the Second World War*, (London, 1987); B. V. Sokdov, 'World War II revisited: Did Stalin intend to attack Hitler?' in *Journal of Slavie Military Studies*, 11 (1998) Nr 2, pp. 113–41. • **33.** The information regarding Stalin's order to the Red Army to advance on all three fronts, as issued at 13.00 hours on 22 June, derives from Marshal Zhukov, who was interviewed in 1965–6. See William Spahr, *Zhukov: the Rise and Fall of a Great Captain* (New York, 1995), pp. 58–62. • **34.** C. Johnson, *An Instance of Treason* (Stanford, 1990). • **35.** Ministry of Defence (Navy), *The U-Boat War in the Atlantic, 1939–45* (London, 1989). • **36.** B. Villa, *Unauthorized Action: Mountbatten and the Dieppe Raid* (Oxford, 1990). • **37.** C. Messenger, *'Bomber' Harris and the strategic bombing offensive* (London, 1984); J. Fyfe, *The Great Ingratitude* (Wigtown, 1993); H. Probert, *Bomber Harris: his life and times* (London, 2003). • **38.** P. Foster, (ed.), *Bell of Chichester* (Chichester, 2004); G. Bell, *Christianity and the World Order* (London, 1940). • **39.** S. Bungay, *Alamein* (London, 2003); N. Barr, *The Pendulum of War: the three battles of Alamein* (London, 2005). • **40.** Beevor, *Stalingrad*, op. cit., pp. 166–77. • **41.** Ibid, passim. (Illustrations) • **42.** N. Gelb, *Desperate Venture: the story of Operation Torch* (London, 1992); C. Whiting, *Disaster at Kasserine* (Barnsley, 2003). • **43.** Nik Cornish, *Kursk: History's*

Greatest Tank Battle (Rochester, 2002); D. Glantz, *The Battle of Kursk* (London, 1999); J. Piekalkiewicz, *Operation Citadel; Kursk and Orel* (Novato, Ca, 1987); C. Zetterling, A. Franlsson, *Kursk 1943: a statistical analysis* (London, 2003). • **44.** R. Lamb, *War in Italy, 1943–5: a brutal story* (London, 1995). • **45.** H. Salisbury, *The 900 Days: The Siege of Leningrad* (New York, 1969). • **46.** Davies, *Rising '44*, op. cit., p. 316. • **47.** The document was first published in Moscow in 1997. • **48.** Max Hastings, *Armageddon: the Battle for Germany 1944–45* (London, 2004). • **49.** Davies, *Rising '44*, op. cit., p. 165. • **50.** Krisztian Unguary, *The Siege of Budapest: 100 Days in World War II* (Yale, 2005). • **51.** Davies, *Rising '44*, op. cit., p. 235. • **52.** C. Ryan, *A Bridge Too Far* (London, 1974); R. J. Kershaw, *'It never snows in September . . .'* (New York, 1994); P. Harclerode, *Arnhem: a tragedy of errors* (London, 1994). • **53.** C. Macdonald, *The Battle of the Bulge* (London, 1984). • **54.** Norman Davies and Roger Moorhouse, *Microcosm: History of a European City* (London, 2000). • **55.** F. Taylor, *Dresden: Tuesday, 13 February 1945* (London, 2004); D. Irving, *Apocalypse, 1945: the destruction of Dresden* (London, 1995). • **56.** Beevor, *Berlin*, op. cit.

Three – Politics   *pp. 131–203*

• **1.** Ernst Nolte, *Der europäische Bürgerkrieg, 1917–1945: Nationalsozialismus und Bolschewismus* (Berlin, 1987). • **2.** Norman Davies, *White Eagle, Red Star: The Polish–Soviet War, 1919–20* (London, 1972; New York, 1973). • **3.** Simon Sebag-Montefiore, *Stalin: The Court of the Red Tsar* (London, 2003), p. 268. • **4.** Hugh Trevor-Roper (ed.), *Hitler's War Directives, 1939–45* (London, 1964), pp. 37–40. • **5.** Sebag-Montefiore, *Stalin*, op. cit., pp. 268–9. • **6.** The text of this speech did not surface until 1994. See T. Bushuyev, 'Proklinaya – proprobuite ponyat', *Novy Mir* (Moscow), nr 12, 1994, pp. 230–7. • **7.** Sebag-Montefiore, *Stalin*, op. cit., pp. 273–4. • **8.** Alvin Cox, *Nomonhan: Japan against Russia, 1939* (Stanford, 1985); John Colvin, *Nomonhan* (London, 1999). • **9.** Sebag-Montefiore, *Stalin*, op. cit., pp. 275–6. • **10.** R. J. Sonntag, J. S. Beddie (eds.), *Nazi–Soviet Relations 1939–41: Documents* (Washington, 1948), p. 78. • **11.** Quoted by Sebag-Montefiore, *Stalin*, op. cit., p. 276; notes pp. 620–21. • **12.** A. P. Dobson, *US Wartime Aid to Britain* (New York, 1986). • **13.** Trevor-Roper, op. cit., pp. 93–8. • **14.** Purdue, op. cit., p. 65. • **15.** Murphy, *What Stalin Knew*, op. cit. (New Haven, Conn., 2005), Chapters 18 and 21, 'The Renewal of the Purges' and 'A Summer of Torture'. • **16.** Ibid., Chapter 19, 'Secret Letters'. • **17.** Ibid. • **18.** Sebag-Montefiore, *Stalin*, op. cit., p. 314. • **19.** Ibid., p. 317. • **20.** T. A. Wilson, *The First Summit: Roosevelt and Churchill at Placentia Bay, 1941* (Lawrence, Ka., 1991); E. Borgwardt, *A New Deal for the World* (Cambridge, Mass., 2005). • **21.** Keith Sword, *Deportation and*

Exile: Poles in the Soviet Union, 1939–48 (Basingstoke, 1994); Władysław Anders, *An Army in Exile: the story of the Polish Second Corps* (London, 1949). • **22.** Milward, *War, Economy and Society*, op. cit., p. 25, quoted by Richard Vinen, *A History of Fragments* (London, 2000). • **23.** See R. Dallek, *Franklin D. Roosevelt and American Foreign Policy* (New York, 1979). • **24.** Weinberg, *A World at Arms*, op. cit., p. 300. • **25.** See L. Dawidowicz, *The War against the Jews, 1933–45* (London, 1975), Appendix. • **26.** Daniel Goldhagen, *Hitler's Willing Executioners: ordinary Germans and the Holocaust* (London, 1996). • **27.** On the constituent divisions of the Waffen SS, see Norman Davies, *Europe: A History*, (Oxford, 1996), Appendix III, pp. 1326–7. • **28.** B. Rigg, *Hitler's Jewish Soldiers: the untold story of Nazi racial laws and men of Jewish descent in the German military* (Lawrence, Kan., 2002). • **29.** See Andrew Rothstein, *History of the USSR* (Harmondsworth, 1950). • **30.** Sebag-Montefiore, *Stalin*, op. cit., pp. 327–33. • **31.** One meets rumours, not evidence. • **32.** Conquest, *The Great Terror*, op. cit. • **33.** Soviet military production, 1941–5 *Oxford Companion* . . ., op. cit., p. 1216, after M. Harrison, *Soviet Planning in Peace and War* (Cambridge, 1985), p. 118. • **34.** Soviet military build-up, 1942–3, ibid., p. 1217, after Harrison, op. cit., p. 264. • **35.** See R. Lamb, *War in Italy*, op. cit. • **36.** J. Garliński, *Poland during the Second World War* (Basingstoke, 1985). • **37.** Allen Paul, *Katyn: the Untold Story of Stalin's Polish Massacre* (New York, 1991); Vladimir Abarinov, *The Murderers of Katyn* (translated from Russian) (New York, 1993). • **38.** T. Jan and I. Gross (eds.), *War Through Children's Eyes* (Stanford, 1981). • **39.** G. Botjer, *A Short History of Nationalist China, 1919–49* (New York, 1979). • **40.** Davies, *Rising '44*, op. cit., p. 45, 61–3. • **41.** Ibid., pp. 65–6. • **42.** Evan Luard, *A History of the United Nations*, 2 vols (London, 1982–9). • **43.** See J. Lacouture, *Charles de Gaulle*, vol. 1: *The Rebel, to 1944* (London, 1991). • **44.** Davies, *Rising '44*, op. cit., 'Interim Report', pp. 619–37. • **45.** See Indro Montanelli, *L'Italia della guerra civile, 1943–6* (Milan, 1983). • **46.** See Davies, *Europe*, op. cit., p. 1037. • **47.** Davies, *Rising '44*, op. cit., pp. 441–2. • **48.** Z. C. Szkopiak, (ed.), *The Yalta Agreements: Documents Prior to During and After the Crimea Conference* (London, 1986); K. Kersten, *Yalta W perspektywie polskiej* (London, 1989). • **49.** *Stalin: Court of the Red Tsar*, op. cit., passim. • **50.** Jan Karski, *The Great Powers and Poland: from Versailles to Yalta* (London, 1985). • **51.** Harry Hopkins, quoted by A. J. P. Taylor, *Second World War*, op. cit., p. 218. • **52.** F. C. Pogue, *George C. Marshall: Statesman, 1945–59* (New York, 1987); Joseph McCarthy, *America's Retreat from Victory: the Story of George Catlett Marshall* (New York, 1954). • **53.** SS-M, p. 431. • **54.** N. Tolstoy, *Victims of Yalta* (London, 1979), *The Minister and the Massacres* (London, 1986). • **55.** Peter Calvocoressi, *The Oxford Companion to the Second World War*, op. cit., p. 264. • **56.** Z. Stypułkowski, *Invitation to Moscow* (New York, 1962). • **57.** SS-M, pp. 443–5. • **58.** Ann and John Tusa, *The Nuremberg Trial* (London, 1988).

• **59.** Quoted in Davies, *Europe*, p. 1066. • **60.** Winston Churchill, 'Iron Curtain Speech', 5 March 1946, Modern History Sourcebook, <www.fordham.edu/halsall/mod>. • **61.** J. Gimbel, *The Origins of the Marshall Plan* (Stanford, 1976); M. J. Hogan, *The Marshall Plan* (Cambridge, 1987). • **62.** George Kennan, 'The Sources of Soviet Conduct, by X' <www.historyguide.org/europe/kennan.htlm>. • **63.** Ann and John Tusa, *The Berlin Blockade* (London, 1988); *The Berlin Airlift* (Staplehurst, 1998).

Four – Soldiers *pp. 205–281*

• **1.** B. Rigg, *Hitler's Jewish Soldiers: the untold story of Nazi racial laws and men of Jewish descent in the German military* (Lawrence, Kan., 2002). • **2.** Norman Davies, *Europe: a History* (Oxford, 1996), pp. 1017–8. • **3.** Catherine Andreyev, *Vlasov and the Russian liberation movement* (Cambridge, 1987); George Fischer, *Soviet opposition to Stalin* (Harvard, 1970). • **4.** See Geoffrey Hosking, *Russia: people and empire* (London, 1997); *Homo sovieticus or homo sapiens?* (London, 1987). • **5.** O. Subtelny, *Ukraine: a history* (Toronto, 1988). • **6.** Ariel Sharon, Independence Day speech, 9 May 2005, <www.mfa.gov.il/MFA> • **7.** *Oxford Companion*, op. cit., 'United Kingdom, Armed Forces', pp. 1144–53. • **8.** *Oxford Companion*, op. cit. • **9.** Heinz-Dietrich Loeuwe, in *Oxford Companion*, op. cit., p. 1235. • **10.** Ibid., p. 1232. • **11.** Ibid., p. 1235, after Harrison, *Soviet Planning*, op. cit. • **12.** David Gardner, 'The Last of the Hitlers', *Sunday Times*, 18 Oct 1998. • **13.** C. B. Clare, *Women at War* (London, 1993). • **14.** Slapton Sands (Exercise 'Tiger'), 28 April 1944. C. MacDonald, 'Slapton Sands: the cover-up that never was', *Army*, No. 6 (June 1988), pp. 64–7. • **15.** See W. J. K. Davies, *The German Army Handbook, 1939–45* (London, 1973). • **16.** Loeuwe, *Oxford Companion . . .*, op. cit., p. 1234. • **17.** The wreck has discovered on 12 July 2006 off the Polish port of Keba, <http://wiadomości.gazeta.pl/53600,3505105.html>. • **18.** R. Moorhouse, *Killing Hitler* (London, 2006), Chapter 7, 'Honour Redeemed'. • **19.** See 'Generals' below, p. 239ff. • **20.** W. B. Huie, *The Execution of Private Slovik* (Yardley, PA 1954); also the films, *The Victors* (1963), and *The Execution of Private Slovik* (1974). • **21.** Desmond Young, *Rommel: the Desert Fox* (London, 1989). • **22.** Omer Bartov, *Hitler's Army: Soldiers, Nazis and War in the Third Reich* (New York, 1992); *The Eastern Front: German Troops and the Barbarization of Warfare* (London, 2001). • **23.** Davies, *Rising '44*, op. cit., op. cit. • **24.** See *Oxford Companion*, p. 873. • **25.** Ibid., p. 1226. • **26.** Beevor, *Stalingrad*, op. cit.; Sebag-Montefiore, *Stalin*, op. cit., passim. • **27.** Witold Sagaillo, quoted in Davies, *Rising '44*, pp. 222–3. • **28.** Catherine Merridale, *Ivan's War: Life and Death the Red Army, 1939–45* (London, 2005): reviewed by Anne Applebaum, 'The Real Patriotic War', *New York Review of Books*

(6 April 2006). • **29.** *Vernichtungskrieg, Verbrechen der Wehrmacht, 1941 bis 1945* (Hamburg, 1996). • **30.** Christian de la Mazière, *Le Rêveur Casqué* (Paris, 1972). • **31.** David Saul, *Mutiny at Salerno* (London, 1995). • **32.** Zenon Andrzejewski, 'Rozkaz: Zamknąć Most', Pomocnik Historyczny; *Polityka* (Warsaw), 22 July 2006. • **33.** On the NKVD in war, see Beevor, op. cit., Merridale op. cit. • **34.** Leonard Mosley, *Marshall, Organizer of Victory* (London, 1982); Carlo D'Este, *Eisenhower: a Soldier's Life* (London, 2003). • **35.** Carlo D'Este, *A Genius for War: a Life of General George S. Patton* (London, 1995). • **36.** Heinz Guderian, *Panzer Leader* (London, 2000); see also J. Strawson, *Hitler as a Military Commander* (London, 1970). • **37.** R. T. Paget, *Manstein: his campaigns and his trial* (London, 1951); see also Corelli Barnett (ed.), *Hitler's Generals* (London, 1989). • **38.** S. Mitcham, *Hitler's Field Marshals and their Battles* (London, 1988). • **39.** Walter Goerlitz, *Model: strategie der Defensive* (1982). • **40.** H. Salisbury (ed.), *Marshal Zhukov's Greatest Battles* (London, 1969); *The Memoirs of Marshal Zhukov* (London, 1971); D. Glantz, *Khukov's greatest defeat* (Lawrence, Ka, 1999). • **41.** See Adam Zamoyski, *The Forgotten Few: the Polish Airforce in the Second World War* (London, 1995). • **42.** R. Overy, *Russia's War* (London, 1997), p. 147, quoted by Vinen, *History in Fragments*, op. cit. • **43.** I. Hogg, in *Oxford Companion*, op. cit., p. 57. • **44.** William Jackson, ibid., p. 337. • **45.** C. MacDonald, *By Air to Battle* (London, 1970). • **46.** M. R. D. Foot, *SOE: an outline history* (London, 1990). • **47.** R. H. Smith, *OSS: The Secret History of America's First Central Intelligence Agency* (Berkeley, 1972). • **48.** Michael Howard, *Strategic Deception in the Second World War* (London, 1992); T. Harris, *Garbo: the spy who saved D-Day* (Kew, 2004). • **49.** L. Paine, *The Abwehr: German Military Intelligence in World War Two* (London, 1984); R. Bassett, *Hitler's Spy Chief: the Wilhelm Canaris Mystery* (London, 2005). • **50.** David Murphy, *What Stalin Knew* (New Haven, 2005). • **51.** F. W. Deakin and G. R. Storry, *The Case of Richard Sorge* (London, 1966). • **52.** F. E. Noel-Baker, *The Spy Web: a study of communist espionage* (London, 1954); R. Seth, *Forty Years of Soviet Spying* (London, 1965); Philip Knightley, *Philby: the Life and Views of the K.G.B. Masterspy* (London, 2003); K. Philby, *My Silent War* (London, 1968). • **53.** M. Bridge and J. Pegg (eds.), *Call to Arms: a history of military communications* (London, 2001). • **54.** Beevor, *Stalingrad*, op. cit., p. 173. • **55.** *Oxford Companion*, op. cit., p. 1235. • **56.** See M. Harrison, op. cit., 'Medical Sciences', op. cit., pp. 727–8. • **57.** Antony Beevor, *Stalingrad*, passim. • **58.** R. Kapuscíński, in Davies, *Rising '44*, op. cit., p. 395. • **59.** Patrick Dalzel-Job, *From Arctic Snow to Dust of Normandy* (Stroud, 1991). • **60.** C. Whiting, *American Hero: the Life and Death of Audie Murphy* (York, 2000). • **61.** Norman Davies and Roger Moorhouse, *Microcosm: History of a European City* (London, 2000). • **62.** H. Sakaida, *Heroes of the Soviet Union, 1941–45* (Moscow, 2005). • **63.** P. Brickhill, *Reach for the Sky* (London, 1954); L. Lucas, *Flying Colours* (London, 1981). • **64.** Hans-Ulrich

Rudel, *Stuka Pilot* (Maidstone, 1973). • **65.** M. Devyataev, *Polyot k solntsu* (Moscow, 1972). • **66.** Max Hastings, *Armageddon* (London, 2004). • **67.** Source not verified. • **68.** J. D. Clarke, *Gallantry Medals and Decorations of the World* (Sparkford, 1993). • **69.** See note 62 above. • **70.** M. D. R. Foot and J. M. Langley, *MI9* (Boston, 1950). • **71.** A. Scotland, *The London Cage* (Maidstone, 1973). • **72.** 'Russia displays "Hitler Skull Fragment"', *BBC News*, 26 April 2000. The Exhibition, in the Federal Archives in Moscow was called 'The Agony of the Third Reich.' • **73.** See Mitcham, op. cit. • **74.** C. Andreyev, *Vlasov and the Russian Liberation Movement* (Cambridge, 1987). • **75.** C. Davis, *Von Kleist: From Hussar to Panzer General* (Houston, 1979), p. 26. • **76.** Slavomir Rawicz, *The Long Walk* (London, 1956). • **77.** Paul Routledge, *Public servant, secret agent: the elusive life and violent death of Airey Neave* (London, 2003). • **78.** Lambholm Italian Chapel, Orkney. • **79.** K. Burt, *The One That Got Away* (London, 1956). • **80.** Sebag-Montefiore, *Stalin*, op. cit. • **81.** A. Maslov, *Captured Soviet Generals: the fate of Soviet generals captured by the Germans, 1941–45* (London, 2001). • **82.** <www.generals.dk/general/von_Seydlitz_Kurbach>. • **83.** M. Leeds, *The Vonnegut Encyclopedia* (London, 1995). • **84.** M. R. D. Foot, *Six Faces of Courage* (London, 1978). • **85.** James Bacque, *Other losses: an investigation into the mass deaths of German prisoners . . . after World War II* (London, 1989). • **86.** J. M. Winter, in *Oxford Companion*, op. cit., p. 289. • **87.** Ibid.: J. M. Winter, under 'Demography of War', quotes 10 million Soviet military deaths (p. 289), Earle Siemke, under 'German–Soviet War', quotes 13.6 million (p. 434), and Hans-Dietrich Loeuwe, under 'USSR', quotes 8.668 million (p. 1232). • **88.** Statistics collated from different entries in the *Oxford Companion*, op. cit. • **89.** Shepton Mallet Prison was also used to store some of Britain's national treasures, including a copy of the Domesday Book. • **90.** See Sven Hassel, *Monte Cassino* (London, 2003); D. Hapgood, *Monte Cassino: the Most Controversial Battle of World War II* (Cambridge, Mass. 2002). • **91.** P. Kann, *Leningrad: a guide* (Moscow, 1990). • **92.** Murphy, *What Stalin Knew*, op. cit., pp. 201–6, 210–17, 230–31. • **93.** P. Thompson, A. Delgado, *Maxwell: a portrait of power* (London, 1988); M. Maloney and W. Hall, *Flash! Splash! Crash! All at Sea with Cap'n Bob* (London, 1996); G. Thomas, *The Assassination of Robert Maxwell: Israel's Superspy* (London, 2002). • **94.** Spike Milligan, *Adolf Hitler: My Part In His Downfall* (London, 1971).

Five – Civilians

pp. 283–426

• **1.** Roy Foster, *Modern Ireland, 1600–1972* (London, 1988). • **2.** D. G. Kirby, *Finland in the Twentieth Century* (London, 1979). • **3.** Madeleine Bunting, *The Model Occupation: the Channel Islands under German Rule, 1940–45* (London, 2004); G.

Forty, *Channel Islands at War: a German Perspective* (Shepperton, 1999). • **4.** D. McGray, *Coventry at War* (Stroud, 1997). • **5.** See Wolfgang Schreyer, *Eyes on the Sky* (c.1981). • **6.** A. N. Frankland, 'Strategic Air Offensives' in *Oxford Companion*, op. cit., pp. 1066–76. • **7.** Byelorussia (Belarus) and Ukraine, independent since 1991, formed part of the USSR in 1939–45, and no separate wartime statistics for them were issued until recently. • **8.** H. Lottman, *The People's Anger: justice and revenge in post-Liberation France*, (London, 1986); H. R. Kedward, N. Wood, eds., *The Liberation of France: image and event* (Oxford, 1995). • **9.** H. Salisbury, *The 900 Days: the Siege of Leningrad* (New York, 1969). • **10.** Davies and Moorhouse, *Microcosm*, op. cit. • **11.** P. M. Hayes, *Quisling: the career and political ideas of Vidkun Quisling* (Newton Abbot, 1971); O. Hoidal, *Quisling: a study in treason* (Oxford, 1989). • **12.** Robert Gildea, *Marianne in Chains* (London, 2003); Ian Ousby, *Occupation: the ordeal of France, 1940–44* (London, 1999); P. Davies, *France and the Second World War* (London, 2001). • **13.** C. Kozłowski, *Namiestnik Stalina* (Warsaw, 1993); T. Żenczykowski, *Polska lubelska* (Paris, 1987). • **14.** W. Warmbrunn, *The Dutch under German Occupation, 1940–45* (Stanford, 1963). • **15.** Martin Conway, *Collaboration in Belgium: Leon Degrelle and the Rexist Movement 1940–44* (Yale, 1993). • **16.** T. Snyder, *Sketches From a Secret War* (Yale, 2005). • **17.** J. T. Gross, *Polish Society under German Occupation: the Generalgouvernement 1939–44* (Princeton, 1979); R. Lukas, *The Forgotten Holocaust: Poles under German occupation* (Lexington, Ky, 1996). • **18.** H. W. Koch, *In the name of the Volk: political justice in Hitler's Germany* (London, 1989). • **19.** W. E. Butler, *Soviet Law* (London, 1983). • **20.** See N. Lewis, *Exercise Tiger* (New York, 1990). • **21.** R. Wapiński, *Dzieje Gydni* (Gdańsk, 1980). • **22.** See Norman Davies, *God's Playground* (Oxford, 1985, 2005), p. 448; M. Hope, *Polish Deportees in the Soviet Union* (London, 1998). • **23.** E. Krepp, *Mass Deportations from the Soviet-occupied Baltic States* (Stockholm, 1981); T. Sobierajski, *Red Snow* (London, 1996); Olars Stepens, *The 14 June 1941 Deportations in Latvia* (Riga, 2001). • **24.** A. de Zayas, *Nemesis at Potsdam: the Anglo-Americans and the expulsion of the Germans* (London, 1979). • **25.** See Eugenia Huntingdon, *The Unsettled Account* (London, 1986); Keith Sword, *Deportation and Exile* (Basingstoke, 1994); D. Teczarowska, *Deportation into the Unknown* (Braunton, 1985). • **26.** As shown by documents released on 1 Jan 2006, Churchill advocated in the War Cabinet as early as 1942 summary execution of captured Nazi leaders. • **27.** A memorial tablet marks the event beside the parish church. • **28.** I. Komentetsky, *The Tragedy of Vinnytsia* (Toronto, 1989). • **29.** Joe Haines, *Maxwell* (London, 1988). See: 'Revealed: Maxwell under investigation for war crimes', *Independent*, 10 March 2006. • **30.** Ibid. • **31.** E. Stehlik, *Lidice: the story of a Czech village* (Prague, 2004). • **32.** Y. Gutman, *The Jews of Warsaw, 1939–43: ghetto, underground revolt* (Bloomington, Ind., 1982). • **33.** I. A. Mikuš, *Slovakia: a political history* (Milwaukee, 1963). • **34.** R. Mackness,

Oradour: massacre and aftermath (London, 1994). • **35.** Davies, *Rising '44*, p. 252ff. • **36.** B. Fisch, *Nemmersdorf: Oktober 1944* (Berlin, 1997). • **37.** J. Olsen, *Silence on Monte Sole* (New York, 2002). • **38.** L. Kosmodemanskaya, *The Story of Zoya and Shura* (Moscow, 1953). • **39.** Phyllis Auty, *Tito: a biography* (London, 1970). • **40.** C. M. Woodhouse, *The Struggle for Greece, 1941–9* (London, 1976). • **41.** S. Korboński, *Warsaw in Chains* (London, 1959); R. Staar, *Poland 1944–62: Sovietisation of a captive people* (Baton Rouge, 1962). • **42.** W. Seifler and Fritz Todt, *Baumeister des Dritten Reiches* (Munich, 1986). • **43.** *Oxford Companion*, op. cit., p. 384. • **44.** Ulrich Herbert, in ibid., table p. 384. • **45.** Ibid., p. 585. • **46.** G. Lilienthal, *Der 'Lebensborn e.V'* (Stuttgart, 1993); C. Henry and M. Hillel, *Children of the SS* (London, 1976). • **47.** J. Wnuk, *Losy dzieci polskich w okresie okupacji hitlerowskiej* (Warsaw, 1980). • **48.** J. Kotek, P. Rigoulet, *Le Siècle des Camps* (Paris, 2001), quoted by Anne Applebaum in *Gulag: a history of the Soviet camps* (London, 2003). • **49.** Applebaum, op. cit., p. 32. • **50.** Ernst Nolte, *Die Europäische Bürgerkrieg, 1914–45* (Berlin, 1987). • **51.** Applebaum, op. cit., pp. 18, 19, 24. • **52.** Ibid., p. 20. • **53.** See F. Piper, *Auschwitz: central issues in the history of the camp 1940–45* (Oświęcim, 2000); *Auschwitz: how many perished . . . ?* (Kraków, 1992). The official name of the camp, now a state museum, is 'The former Nazi German concentration camp of Auschwitz-Birkenau'. • **54.** Applebaum, op. cit., p. 124. • **55.** N. Ochotin and A. Roginski (eds.), *Sistiema ispravitielno-trudovych lageriei v SSSR, 1923–60, Spravochnik* (Moscow, 1998), pp. 57–9. • **56.** *Spravochnik*, nr. 333, pp. 411–12. • **57.** Ibid., pp. 103–6. • **58.** After *Spravochnik*. • **59.** See <www.dumfries-and-galloway.co.uk/people/haining.htm>. The website mentions nine other Scots who perished in Nazi camps. • **60.** *Oxford Companion*, op. cit., p. 262. • **61.** Robert Conquest, *Kolyma: The Arctic Death Camps* (New York, 1978); J. O. Pohl, *The Stalinist Penal System: A Statistical History* (Jefferson, NC 1997). • **62.** Sebag-Montefiore, from his review of R. Overy, *The Dictators*. • **63.** D. Smith, *Lost Hero: Raoul Wahenberg's Quest* (London, 2001). • **64.** Margarete Buber-Neumann, *Under Two Dictators* (London, 1949): *Als Gefangene bei Stalin und Hitler* (Stuttgart, 1958). • **65.** V. Kravchenko, *I Chose Freedom* (London, 1945). • **66.** See Menahem Begin, *White Nights: the story of a prisoner in Russia* (Jerusalem, 1977). • **67.** V. S. Kristoforov, *The Lubyanka in the Days of the Battle of Moscow* (Moscow, 2002). • **68.** Ochotin and Roginski, op. cit., p. 555. • **69.** Joanna Bourke, *An Intimate History of Killing* (Oxford, 1993). • **70.** Ibid. • **71.** Omer Bartov, *Hitler's Army* (Oxford, 1992), p. 69. • **72.** Davies, Moorhouse, *Microcosm*, op. cit. • **73.** Beevor, *Berlin*, p. 28. • **74.** Ibid. • **75.** Ibid., pp. 28, 107. • **76.** Ibid., p. 107. • **77.** Ibid., pp. 157–8. • **78.** Anon., *A Woman in Berlin: eight weeks in the conquered city: a diary* (New York, 2000), reviewed by Ursula Hegi, *Washington Post*, 4 September 2005; also 'Row over naming of rape author', *Observer*, 5 October 2003. • **79.** Austin J. App, *Ravishing* the *Women of Conquered Europe* (New York, 1946). • **80.** See Norman Naimark, *The Russians in Germany, 1945–9* (Cambridge Mass, 1995). • **81.** Rumours persist of unrecovered treasures, such as 'The Weissensee Gold', supposedly hidden by SS-Chief Odilo Globocnik. See <www.istrianet.org/istria/history/ww2/globocnik-gold.htm>. • **82.** C. Caryl, 'Mysteries of History: Not forever Amber, Treasure hunters seek a golden room', *US News and World Report*, 24 July 2000. • **83.** State Special Trophy Archive, Moscow. • **84.** A. Patalas, *Catalogue of early music prints from the former Prussian Staatsbibliotek in Berlin* (Cracow, 1999). • **85.** Davies and Moorhouse, op. cit. • **86.** Source not verified. • **87.** K. Rosen-Zawadzki, 'Karta Buduszczej Jewropy', *Studia z dziejów ZSRR i Środkowej Europy* (Wrocław, 1972), pp. viii, 141–5. • **88.** E. Frankel, *The Soviet Germans, Past and Present* (London, 1986). • **89.** R. Conquest, *The Nation Killers: the Soviet deportation of nationalities* (London, 1970). • **90.** Ibid. • **91.** Ibid. • **92.** L. Boban, 'Jasenovac and the manipulations of history', *East European Politics and Societies*, 5 (1990), pp. 580–93. • **93.** M. Terles, *Ethnic Cleansing of Poles in Volhynia and Eastern Galicia* (Toronto, 1993); R. Torzecki, *Polacy i Ukraińcy . . .* (Warsaw, 1993); W. Poliszczuk, *Gorzka prawda . . .* (Warsaw, 1995). • **94.** Edith Milton, *The Tiger in the Attic: memories of the kindertransport and of growing up English* (Chicago, 2005). • **95.** B. Johnson (ed.), *The Evacuees* (London, 1968). • **96.** See Nicholas Stargardt, *Witnesses of War* (London, 2005). • **97.** Gitta Sereny, *The German Trauma* (London, 2001); Ursula Hoffman-Lange, *East Germany: what happened to the Silesians in 1945* (Lewes, 2000). • **98.** C. Dobson, *The Cruellest Night . . . the Sinking of the Wilhelm Gustloff* (London, 1979). • **99.** Juliet Gardiner, *Wartime Britain 1939–1945* (London, 2005). • **100.** Beevor, *Berlin*, op. cit., pp. 168–9. • **101.** Michael Lynch, *Wartime Germany* (London, 2004), p. 79. • **102.** Beevor, *Berlin*, op. cit., passim. • **103.** Mary Davis, 'The Labour Movement and World War Two' TUC History Online, <www.unionhistory. info/timeline/1939–45.php>. • **104.** From the notes of Admiral Canaris, quoted by L. P. Lochner, *What About Germany?* (New York, 1942). • **105.** Herman Rosenthal, 'Pale of Settlement', <www.JewishEncyclopedia.com>. • **106.** P. Dempsey, *The Einsatzgruppen and the Destruction of European Jewry* (Measham, 2003). • **107.** Y. Arad, *Belzec, Sobibor, Treblinka: the Operation Reinhard Death Camps* (Bloomington, Ind., 1987); W. Chrostowski, *Extermination Camp Treblinka* (London, 2004). • **108.** F. Piper, *Auschwitz; how many perished, Jews, Poles, Gypsies* (Kraków, 1992). • **109.** See M. Gilbert, *Auschwitz and the Allies* (London, 1991); D. Wyman, *The Abandonment of the Jews: America and the Holocaust, 1941–45* (New York, 1985). • **110.** See Lucy Dawidowicz, *The War Against the Jews, 1933–45* (New York, 1990), Appendix. • **111.** Martin Gilbert, *Israel: a history* (London, 1999). • **112.** Deborah Lipstadt, *Denying the Holocaust: the growing assault on truth and memory* (Oxford, 1993); also R. Evans, *Telling Lies about Hitler . . . the David Irving*

Trial (London, 1999). • **113.** Norman Davies, 'Neither Twenty Million, nor Russians, nor War dead', *Independent*, 29 December 1987. • **114.** J. M. Winter, in *Oxford Companion . . .*, op. cit., p. 290. • **115.** F. Rothenbacher, *The European Population, 1850–1945* (Basingstoke, 2002). • **116.** Naimark, *The Russians in Germany*, op. cit., pp. 142–3. • **117.** Marian Dönhoff, *Before the Storm: Memoirs of my Youth in Old Prussia* (London, 1993). • **118.** Moorhouse, *Killing Hitler*, op. cit. • **119.** E. N. Peterson, *Hjalmar Schacht: For and Against Hitler* (Boston, 1954). • **120.** S. Hyman and S. Marriner, *Eccles: private entrepreneur and public servant* (Stanford, 1976). • **121.** Y. Bauer, *The Holocaust in Historical Perspective* (London, 1978); Victoria Barnett, *Bystanders: conscience and complicity during the Holocaust* (London, 1999). • **122.** I. Shahak, 'The Life of Death: an exchange', *New York Review of Books*, 29 January 1987, pp. 45–50. • **123.** R. Kapuściński, *Imperium* (London, 1998). • **124.** Anne Frank, *The Diary of Anne Frank* (London, 1989). • **125.** Antek Rozpylacz, see Davies, *Rising '44*, p. 601. • **126.** Nicholas Stargardt, *Witnesses of War: children's lives under the Nazis* (London, 2005); also R. Lukas, *Did the Children Cry?* (New York, 1994). • **127.** <www.irenasandler.org>. Irene Tomaszewski and Tecia Werbowski *Żegota, The Rescue of Jews in Wartime Poland* (Montreal, 1994). • **128.** Keith Sword, *Deportation and Exile: Poles in the Soviet Union, 1939–48* (Basingstoke, 1994). • **129.** J. Allen, *Pope Benedict XVI: a biography* (London, 2005). • **130.** P. Fussell, *The Boys' Crusade: the American infantry in Northwestern Europe, 1944–5* (London, 2003). • **131.** W. M. Temple, *Christianity and the Social Order* (London, 1942); E. Robertson, *Unshakable Friend: George Bell and the German Churches* (London, 1995); R. Hughes, *The Red Dean: the life and riddle of Dr Hewlett Johnson* (Worthing, 1987). • **132.** E. Robertson, *The Shame and the Sacrifice: the life and preaching of Dietrich Bonhoffer* (London, 1987). • **133.** Hansjakob Stehle, 'Sheptytskyi and the German regime', Shimon Redlich, 'Sheptytskyi and the Jews', in R. Magosci (ed.), *Morality and Reality: the Life and Times of Andrei Sheptytskyi* (Edmonton, 1995), pp. 125–62. • **134.** John Hooper, 'Between good and evil', *Guardian*, 6 January 2005. • **135.** Calel Perechodnik, *Am I a Murderer? Testament of a Jewish Ghetto Policeman* (Oxford, 1996). • **136.** Instytut Pamięci Narodowej, 'Przegląd Mediów', 30/4/2004. <www.ipn.gov.pl/wp_przegląd_300404.html>. • **137.** Harry Pollitt, *How to win the war* (London, 1939). • **138.** P. Robrieux, *Maurice Thorez* (Paris, 1975); G. Seniga, *Togliatti i Stalin* (Milan, 1978). • **139.** Richard Crampton, *A Concise History of Bulgaria* (Cambridge, 2005). • **140.** M. Djilas, *Wartime: with Tito and the partisans* (London, 1980); *Tito: the story from inside* (London, 1981). • **141.** Edward Smithies, *Crime in Wartime* London, 1982); Donald Thomas, *An Underworld at War* (London, 2003); Steve Jones, *When the Lights Went Out: Crime in Wartime London* (London, 1995). • **142.** M. Secreste, *Kenneth Clark: a biography* (London, 1984). • **143.** F. J. Fransen, *The supranational politics of Jean Monnet* (Westport, 2001); Paul-Henri Spaak, *The Continuing Battle:*

memoirs 1936–66 (London, 1971); Jan Pomian, *Joseph Retinger: Life of an eminence grise* (London, 1975). • **144.** D. Watson, *Molotov: a biography* (Basingstoke, 2005). • **145.** Horst Koehler, b. 1943, 'Biographical Information', <www.imf.org/external>. • **146.** Lili Marlene, see Norman Davies, *Europe*, op. cit., pp. 912–13. • **147.** G. Butcher, *Glenn Miller and his orchestra* (London, 1974). • **148.** Ruth Turków-Kamińska, *Mink Coats and Barbed Wire*, intro. Harrison Salisbury (London, 1979). • **149.** George Mikes, *How to be an Alien* (London, 1946). • **150.** Willi Brandt, *In Exile . . . 1933–47* (London, 1971). • **151.** Nathalie Hartmann, *The Girl from Polesie* (London, 2005), pp. 84–100 (extracts). • **152.** Denis Judd, *King George VI* (London, 1982). • **153.** J. Von Rudiger, *Die Quandts* (Berlin, 2002). • **154.** E. Nolte, *Three Faces of Fascism* (London, 1965). • **155.** J. J. Stephan, *The Russian Fascists: tragedy and farce in exile* (London, 1982). • **156.** H. Letocq, *Pauline* (Paris, 1997). • **157.** F. J. Muller, *The White Rose: the resistance by students against Hitler* (Munich, 1991). • **158.** Zofia Litewska, *A Memoir* (Oxford, 1995). • **159.** L. Dobroszycki, ed., *Chronicle of the Lodz Ghetto* (Yale, 1984). • **160.** Pieter Gehl, *Napoleon: For and Against* (London, 1949). • **161.** H. R. Trevor-Roper, *The Last Days of Hitler* (London, 1947); *Hitler's Table Talk* (London, 1973). • **162.** Fainsod Merle, *How Russia is ruled: Smolensk under Soviet Rule* (Harvard, 1953). • **163.** Heather Pringle, *The Master Plan* (New York, 2006). • **164.** Carole Fink, *Marc Bloch: A Life in History* (Cambridge, 1989). • **165.** Paul Schmidt, *Hitler's Interpreter* (London, 1951). • **166.** With thanks to Hugh Lunghi. See V. Berezhkov, *At Stalin's Side* (Secaucus, NJ, 1996). • **167.** Charles Bohlen, *Witness to History* (London, 1973). • **168.** With thanks to Hugh Lunghi. From E. Stevens, *Russia is no Riddle* (London, 1945). • **169.** See Pavel Sudoplatov, *Special Tasks: Memoirs of an Unwanted Witness* (London, 1973). • **170.** Sebag-Montefiore, *Stalin*, op. cit., p 274. • **171.** <www.bbc.co.uk/worldservice/people/features/mycentury/wk44.shtml>, broadcast 1 November 1999. • **172.** Stanley Cloud and Lynne Olson, *The Murrow Boys* (New York, 1996). • **173.** A. Werth, *Russia at War, 1941–45* (New York, 1965). • **174.** Vasily Grossman, *With the Red Army in Poland and Byelorussia* (London, 1945); A. Beevor (ed.), *A Writer at War . . .* (London 2005). • **175.** Barry Broadfoot, *Six War Years, 1939–45* (Toronto, 1974), quoted in P. Fussell, (ed.), *The Bloody Game: An anthology of Modern War* (London, 1991), pp. 448ff. • **176.** R. Hoess, *Commandant of Auschwitz* (London, 1959), pp. 505ff. • **177.** Jożef Garliński, *The Survival of Love* (Oxford, 1991). • **178.** *WW2 People's War: An Archive of Memories*, BBC, 2003–2006, 'Maria's Story'. • **179.** Christopher Hudson, 'Sex, please – we're British', *Sunday Times* Magazine, 11 December 2005. • **180.** Sara Shirakawa, *The Devil's Music Master* (Oxford, 1992). • **181.** George Broderick, *Die Fahne Hoch! history and development of the Horst-Wessel-lied* (Ramsey IOM, 1995). • **182.** Z. S. Brzozowski, *Wilno, 1910–45* (Paris, 1987). • **183.** Stanisław Mikołajczyk, *The Rape of Poland* (New York, 1948). • **184.** Elaine Feinstein, *Anna of all the Russias*

(London, 2005). • **185.** Kenneth Harris, *Attlee* (London, 1995). • **186.** N. Bethell, *Gomułka, his Poland and his Communism* (London, 1969). • **187.** Kazimierz Moczarski, *Conversations with an Executioner* (New Jersey, 1991). • **188.** Leopold Trepper, *The Great Game: The Story of the Red Orchestra* (London, 1975), pp. 342–6. • **189.** As of 1 Jan 2006. 'Righteous Among Nations per country & ethnic origin,' <www1.yadvashem. org/righteous/righteous-table.html>. • **190.** As related by Prof. J. Zubrzycki. • **191.** P. Treece, *A Man for Others: saint of Auschwitz* (San Francisco, 1982). See also *St Louis Jewish Light* (30.6.1982). • **192.** H. Graef, *The Scholar and the Cross* (London, 1955). • **193.** '108 Martyrs of World War Two', <www.catholic_forum.com/SAINTS/martyr08.htm>. • **194.** O. Turij, *Church of the Martyrs* (L'viv, 2004). • **195.** R. Spangenburg, *Wernher von Braun, space visionary and rocket engineer* (New York, 1995). • **196.** Dusko Popov, *Spy? Counterspy* (London, 1974). • **197.** 'Walthère Dewé, a giant in Resistance' <www.freebelgians.net>. • **198.** Trepper, *The Great Game*, op. cit. • **199.** H. R. Trevor-Roper, *The Philby Affair* (London, 1968); Kim Philby, *My Silent War* (London, 1989). • **200.** N. West, *Venona: the greatest secret of the Cold War* (London, 2000). • **201.** M. Garber and R. Walkowitz, *Secret agents: the Rosenberg Case . . .* (New York, 1995). • **202.** Obituary, *Daily Telegraph* (London), 1 December 2005. • **203.** Norman Finkelstein, *The Holocaust Industry, reflections on the exploitation of Jewish suffering* (London, 2000). • **204.** A. Bullock, *The Life and Times of Ernest Bevin*, 2 vols (London, 1960–85). • **205.** J. A. Cole, *Lord Haw-Haw* (London, 1987); F. Selwyn, *Hitler's Englishmen* (London, 1987). • **206.** D. Faber, *Speaking for England* (London, 2005); Rebecca West, *The Meaning of Treason* (London, 1965). • **207.** Ian Kershaw, *The Hitler 'myth' and reality* (Oxford, 1987); *Hitler: nemesis, 1936–45* (London, 2000); Joachim Fest, *Hitler* (London, 1995). • **208.** D. Volkoganov, *Stalin: triumph and tragedy* (London, 1991); R. Service, *Stalin: a biography* (London, 2004). • **209.** Elizabeth Barker, *Churchill and Eden at War* (London, 1978); J. Charmley, *Churchill: the end of glory* (Dunton Green, 1993); Andrew Roberts, *Churchill: embattled hero* (London, 1996); Martin Gilbert, *Finest Hour: Churchill, 1939–41* and *In search of Churchill: a historian's journey* (London, 1994). • **210.** Karolina Lanckorońska, *Memoirs* (London, 2006).

Six – Portrayals   *pp. 429–477*

• **1.** *London Can Take It* (1940), director Humphrey Jennings; *Desert Victory* (1943), director Roy Boulting. <www.britmovie.co.uk/genres/documentary>. • **2.** *Churchill's Island* (1941), director John Grierson. <www.classicmovies.com/cm/film_detail>. • **3.** *Moscow Strikes Back* (1942), narrator Edward G. Robinson: based on footage from the Moscow Central Newsreel Service. <http://moviesZ. nytimes.com>. • **4.** Norman Davies, *Europe*, op. cit., pp. 1026–7. • **5.** *Osvobozhdzenie*

(Liberation) (1967–71), directed by Yuri Ozerov, 5 parts. <www.imdb.com>. • **6.** *Cross of Iron* (1977), directed by Sam Peckinpah, starring James Coburn. <www.ihffilm.com>. • **7.** A. Wajda, *Double Vision: my life in film* (London, 1990); B. Michalek, *The Cinema of Andrzej Wajda* (London, 1973). • **8.** *Der Untergang* (*Downfall*), directed by Oliver Hirschbiegel and based on the biography by Joachim Fest. Kershaw: 'The Human Hitler', *Guardian* 17 September 2004. • **9.** Alex Kershaw, *Blood and Champagne: the life and times of Robert Capa* (London, 2002). • **10.** <www.mdf.ru/english/search/>. • **11.** Tomasz Kiźny, *GULAG: Life and Death inside the Soviet concentration camps*, (Richmond Hill, 2004). (Photograph album.) • **12.** M. E. Harris, 'Carl Mydans: a life goes to war,' *Camera and Darkroom* (Beverley Hills, CA), vol 16, nr 6, 1994; 'George Rodger', <www.magnumphotos.com/photographers.htm>. • **13.** S. Callahan, *Margaret Bourke-White: photographer* (London, 1998). • **14.** Antony Penrose (ed.), *Lee Miller's War* (London, 2005). • **15.** Lokajski's photos are available on the website of Warsaw's Muzeum Powstania. 'Kolekcja zdjęć Eugeniusza Lokajskiego', <www.1944.pl/indeks>; E. Kamińska, M. Kamiński, *The Warsaw Uprising in the photographs of Sylwester 'Kris' Braun*, (Warsaw, 2004). • **16.** See S. Morozov, *Soviet photography: the new photo journalism* (London, 1984). • **17.** A. and A. Nakhimovsky (eds.), *Witness to History: the photographs of Yevgeny Khaldei* (New York, 1997). • **18.** Margot Eates (ed.), *Paul Nash's paintings: drawings and illustrations* (London, 1948). • **19.** F. Topolski, *Russia in War* (London, 1941), *Britain in Peace and War* (London, 1942), *Three Continents* (London, 1946), *Auschwitz* (by Ronald Duncan) (Bideford, 1978). • **20.** J. Darracott, *Second World War Posters* (London, 1972). • **21.** <www.kilroywashere.org>. • **22.** David Low, *Low: the twentieth century's greatest cartoonist* (London, 2002). • **23.** Peter Tory, *Giles at War* (London, 1994). • **24.** D. Graham, *Keith Douglas: a biography* (Oxford, 1974); Keith Douglas, *Complete Poems* (Oxford, 1978). • **25.** Baczyński, Krzystof Kamil, 'Warsaw', *Śpiew z pożogi*, (Warsaw, 1947). • **26.** P. Lewis, *George Orwell: the Road to 1984* (London, 1981). • **27.** Craig Raine, *William Golding* (London, 1988). • **28.** Nicholas Monsarrat, *The Cruel Sea* (London, 1951), p. 1. • **29.** 'Norman Lewis', Obituary, *Guardian*, 23 July 2003. • **30.** W. McBride (ed.), *Sartre's French contemporaries and enduring influences* (London, 1987). • **31.** Julian Preece, *The Life and Work of Günter Grass* (Basingstoke, 2001); Günter Grass, *Crabwalk* (London, 2004). • **32.** Marcel Reich-Ranicki, *The Author of himself* (London, 2002). • **33.** A. Goldberg (ed.), *Ilya Ehrenburg: writing, politics and the art of survival* (London, 1984). • **34.** A. Beevor (ed.), *A Writer at War* (London, 2005). • **35.** Yevgeni Yevtushenko, *Poems – English and Russian* (G. Reavy (ed.), London, 1969). • **36.** A. Solzhenitsyn, *The Gulag Archipelago, 1918–56: an experiment into literary investigation*, trans. T. Whitney and H. Willetts (London, 1985). • **37.** <http://russschneider.net>. • **38.** See Chapter One, note 3: Chapter Three, note 37. • **39.** HMSO, *The trial of major German war* *criminals: proceedings* . . . (London, 1946–51). • **40.** The National Archives, *Federal Records of World War II*, 2 vols, Vol 1 *Civilian Agencies*, Vol 2 *Military Agencies*, Washington DC. • **41.** C. Jones, *E. H. Carr and International Relations: a duty to lie* (Cambridge, 1998); J. Haslam, *The Vices of Integrity: E. H. Carr, 1892–1982* (London, 1999); M. Cox (ed.), *E. H. Carr: a critical appraisal* (Basingstoke, 2000). • **42.** See <www.war-experience.org>. • **43.** Studs Terkel, *'The Good War': an oral history of World War Two* (London, 1984). • **44.** Ada Petrova and P. Watson, *The Death of Hitler: the final words from Russia's secret archives* (London, 1995). • **45.** *Das Buch Hitler* (from GARF archive, Moscow: 462a/5/30) (Bergisch Gladbach, 2003). • **46.** See Chapter Five, n. *55.* • **47.** Ronald Lewin, *Ultra Goes to War* (London, 1978); F. Hinsley, *British Intelligence in the Second World War* (London, 1993); *Codebreakers: the inside story of Bletchley Park* (Oxford, 1993). • **48.** J. Naughton, *A brief history of the future: the origins of the internet* (London, 2000). • **49.** Pierre Nora, *Les lieux de mémoire* (Paris, 1992), trans as *Realms of Memory* (New York, 1998). • **50.** In Hilberg's view, non-Jewish deaths at Auschwitz reached 300,000. According to Piper, a minimalist 'evidenced deaths' included 95,000 Jews, 64,000 Poles, 19,000 Roma, and 12,000 Soviet POWs. 'Non-evidenced deaths', especially of Jews and Soviet POWs, were far higher. Piper, op. cit. (Polish edition) 91–3. • **51.** Winston S. Churchill, *The Second World War*, 6 vols (London, 1948–53). • **52.** Soviet Academy of Sciences, *Istoriya Vtoroi Mirovoi Voiny* (Moscow, 1956). • **53.** See Chapter Four, n. 40. • **54.** Milovan Djilas, *Conversations with Stalin* (London, 1962) and *The New Class* (1955). Both these works had to be smuggled out of prison to reach the West. • **55.** Alan Bullock, *Hitler: A Study in Tyranny* (London, 1952). • **56.** Alan Bullock, *Hitler and Stalin: Parallel Lives* (London, 1991). • **57.** Richard Overy, *The Dictators: Hitler's Germany and Stalin's Russia* (London, 2004). • **58.** Published by the HMSO under the generic title, *History of the Second World War.* • **59.** Gerhard Ritter, *The German problem: basic questions of German political life, past and present*, (Columbus, Ohio, 1965): *The sword and the scepter: the problem of militarism in Germany* (Princeton, 1988). • **60.** Fritz Fischer, *War of Illusions: German policies from 1911 to 1914* (London 1975). • **61.** P. Rassinier, *The Holocaust Story and the lies of Ulysses* (Costa Mesa, Calif., 1978): A. Baron, *Holocaust Denial: new Nazi lie or new inquisition?* (London, 1994); D. Felderer, *Anne Frank's Diary: a hoax* (Torrance, Calif., 1979); R. Eaglestone, *Postmodernism and Holocaust Denial* (Cambridge, 2001); R. A. Kahn, *Holocaust Denial and the Law* (Basingstoke, 2004). • **62.** John Erickson, *The Road to Stalingrad* (London, 1975); *The Road to Berlin* (London, 1983); *Main Front: Soviet leaders look back on World War II* (London, 1987). • **63.** Stephen E. Ambrose, *Eisenhower: soldier and president* (London, 1984); *Pegasus Bridge* (London, 1985); *Eisenhower and Berlin: the decision to halt at the Elbe* (New York, 1967); *D-Day: the climactic battle of World War II* (New York, 1994); *Citizen Soldiers* (New York, 1998). • **64.** Gordon Martel (ed.),

The Origins of the Second World War Reconsidered: A. J. P. Taylor and the Historians (London, 1999). • **65.** Ernst Nolte, *Der Europäische Bürgerkrieg, 1917–1945: National-sozialismus und Bolschewismus* (Berlin, 1987). • **66.** Hannah Arendt, *The Burden of our Time* (London, 1951) published in the USA as *The Origins of Totalitarianism: Eichmann in Jerusalem: a report on the banality of evil* (London, 1963); Robert Fine, *Political investigations: Hegel, Marx, Arendt* (London, 2001). • **67.** *Forever in the shadow of Hitler? Original documents of the Historikerstreit* (Atlantic Highlands, NH., 1993). • **68.** Tony Judt, review of *The Black Book of Communism, New York Times*, 22 December 1997. • **69.** Comité International d'histoire de la Deuxième Guerre Mondiale; Institut d'histoire du temps présent Paris) <www.ihtp.cnrs.fr/cih2gm.html>. • **70.** 'Who and what is Memorial', <www.memo.ru/eng/about/whowe.htm>. • **71.** P. Fussell, *Wartime and Behavior* (New York, 1989); *The Boys' Crusade*, op. cit. • **72.** A. J. P. Taylor, *The Second World War*, John Ray, *The Second World War: A Narrative History* (London, 1999), R. A. C. Parker, *The Second World War: A Short History* (Oxford, 2001). • **73.** Gerhard Weinberg, *A World At Arms: a global history of World War II* (Cambridge, 1994). • **74.** P. Calvocoressi et al., *Total War: causes and courses of the Second World War* (London, 1972); 2nd edition (London, 1989); 3rd edition, *The Penguin History of the Second World War* (London, 2002). • **75.** *The Imperial War Museum* (London, 1996): <www.iwm.org.uk>. • **76.** The National World War II Museum, New Orleans: <www.ddaymuseum.org>. • **77.** World War Two Experience Centre, Leeds: <www.war-experience.org>. • **78.** <www.verzetsmuseum.org/home.html>. • **79.** Museum of the Warsaw Rising. <www.1944.pl>. • **80.** *Maj & Mrs Holts Battlefield Guide to the D-Day Landing Beaches* (Sandwich, 2005). • **81.** A. A. Gill, 'The British say it with war memorials', *Sunday Times*, 13 November 2005. • **82.** <www.glasssteelandstone.com/DE/BerlinSovietMemorial.html>. • **83.** <www.belarusguide.com/travel1/khatyn.html>. • **84.** Kursk Regional Tourist Office, www.kursk.netclub.ru2005.

Inconclusions   *pp. 477–490*

• **1.** David Irving, *Hitler's War* (London, 1977). • **2.** Richard Vinen, 'The Second World War in Europe', in *A History in Fragments* (London, 2000), p. 236. • **3.** Geoffrey Best, *War and Law Since 1945* (Oxford, 1994). • **4.** Geoffrey Wheatcroft, 'How Good was the Good War?', *Boston Globe*, 8 May 2005. • **5.** 'British historian David Irving has been found guilty in Vienna of denying the Holocaust of European Jewry and sentenced to three years in prison', *BBC News*, 20 February 2006. • **6.** Winston Churchill, speech at the Mansion House, 10 November 1942. • **7.** John Martin, 'The Second Polish Corps', in *The Origins of Loneliness: Poems and Short Stories in Five Moods* (London, 2004), p. 64.

Further Reading

So many books have been written about the Second World War that no one can hope to read more than a fraction. As of September 2006, the online bookshop Amazon.com was showing 54,673 titles, from which to choose. If the aim is to find more detailed information on particular aspects or episodes, the task is easy. The copious endnotes of the present volume provide, I hope, a practical first step towards that goal. If the aim is to enquire more deeply into the reigning intellectual assumptions, conflicting perspectives and structural distortions, one needs to adopt a more methodical strategy from the outset.

Firstly, an overview of the Second World War as a whole must be obtained. This can be done either by examining some of the compact accounts such as those of John Keegan, *The Second World War* (London, 1997), John Ray, *The Second World War: A Narrative History* (London, 1999), or R. A. C. Parker, *The Second World War: A Short History*, (Oxford, 2001) or by dipping into the weightier volume, *A World at Arms* (Cambridge, 1994) by Gerhard Weinberg. The war in the Pacific did not impinge directly on the war in Europe, but it is an essential subject for understanding the constraints placed on American military performance in Europe and hence on the Western alliance as a whole.

Secondly, it is important to know something of the official Soviet version of the war. This topic is not easily accessible to non-Russian readers, but it is the source of numerous misconceptions. It rightly puts the German–Soviet conflict in centre stage. At the same time, it caricatures the causes of the war and the events of 1939–41, and it carefully avoids any hints about the criminal nature of Stalin's regime. In this way, it suppresses the key elements in any proper understanding of the political and moral dilemmas of the Grand Coalition. Fortunately, *The Great Soviet Encyclopedia* was translated into English in 1970, and provides a valid point of entry. Articles on 'The Great Patriotic War', on 'Finland' and the Baltic republics present a good introduction, as do any of the more overtly ideological articles on 'Capitalism', 'Fascism' or 'the USA'. Failing that, it is instructive to read some of the pro-Soviet military accounts, such as those of the late John Erickson, in *The Road to Stalingrad* (London, 1975) and *The Road to Berlin* (London, 1983). They reflect the Soviet position indirectly in that they stress the colossal and victorious war effort of the USSR whilst turning a blind eye to the manifest failings of the Soviet political system.

Thirdly, responsible searchers after historical reality need to ensure a reasonable balance of information between each of the three great forces that were present in the war in Europe: the Axis Powers, the Soviet Union, and the Western Allies. As often as not, British and American readers will have some familiarity with both the Third Reich and with the wartime policies of their own countries. If not, they need to catch up by reading one of the many studies of Hitlerism, such as those by Ian Kershaw (*Hitler, 1889–1936: Hubris* (London); *Hitler, 1936–1945: Nemesis* (London, 2000), Richard Evans (*The Coming of the Third Reich* (London, 2003); *The Third Reich in Power* (London, 2005) or Michael Burleigh (*The Third Reich: A New History* (London, 2000), as well as something on the governments of Churchill and Roosevelt. In all probability, however, and without even noticing it, most people will have absorbed the prevailing view of the Second World War as a simple, two-sided contest between the Nazis and the doughty champions of Freedom and Justice. In this case, they can find the necessary antidotes by exploring into the copious literature now readily available. A good start could be made by taking a comparative approach to the two dominant warleaders, Hitler and Stalin. This can be done either through Richard Overy's excellent *The Dictators: Hitler's Germany and Stalin's Russia* (London, 2004) or, if the Nazi phenomenon has already been grasped, by studying one of latest generation of studies of Stalin and Stalinism. Simon Sebag-Montefiore's *Stalin: the Court of the Red Tsar* (2003) will open many eyes. After that, one should come to grips with some of the institutional deformities of the Soviet system. This can be approached through Anne Applebaum's superb *Gulag* (2003) together with Robert Conquest's *The Great Terror: a re-assessment* (1992). Finally, the path will be open to read up with greater awareness on the extraordinary story of the Red Army, its inimitable aims and methods, and its crushing victory in Europe. To this end, the two volumes by Antony Beevor, *Stalingrad* (1998) and *Berlin: the downfall* (2004) are an indispensable pleasure. So, too, is a more recent volume *Ivan's War* (2005) by Catherine Merridale, which appeared too late for my own researches.

Only then, when one has gained a sense both of the grandeur and of the horrors of the Eastern Front, is it permissible to return to the well-trodden territory of the Western Desert, the Italian Campaign, Battle of the Atlantic, the Strategic Air Offensive or the D-Day Landings. Most readers, I am sure, will feel that their perspective has shifted, and that sober but critical assessments of the Western war effort, such as Max Hasting's *Armaggedon, 1944–5* (2005), carry greater conviction. Only then, will people be ready to decide whether the 'inconclusions' of the present volume are tending in the right direction or not.

Index